COMMERCIAL ARBITRATION IN GERMANY

COMMERCIAL ARBITRATION IN GERMANY

Richard Kreindler
Reinmar Wolff
Markus S. Rieder

OXFORD
UNIVERSITY PRESS

OXFORD
UNIVERSITY PRESS

Great Clarendon Street, Oxford, OX2 6DP,
United Kingdom

Oxford University Press is a department of the University of Oxford.
It furthers the University's objective of excellence in research, scholarship,
and education by publishing worldwide. Oxford is a registered trade mark of
Oxford University Press in the UK and in certain other countries

First Edition published in 2016
Impression: 1

Published in the United States of America by Oxford University Press
198 Madison Avenue, New York, NY 10016, United States of America

British Library Cataloguing in Publication Data
Data available

Library of Congress Control Number: 2015952333

ISBN 978–0–19–967681–1

Printed and bound by
CPI Group (UK) Ltd, Croydon, CR0 4YY

FOREWORD

That it was one of the hazards of the job of the President of the ICC International Court of Arbitration to be asked to "say a few words"—often without any prior warning—at arbitration-related functions and conferences was a lesson quickly learned. That experience did not make it any less a pleasure to accept Richard Kreindler's invitation to provide these few words by way of a preface to his, Markus Reder's, and Reinmar Wolff's, *Commercial Arbitration in Germany.*

The three authors of this book have made their mark as scholars, commentators, and practitioners of commercial arbitration, both in their "home" jurisdiction of Germany and internationally. They have combined that expertise and practical experience to considerable effect in this new textbook with the result that each of the principal features and stages of the arbitral process (the arbitration agreement, the constitution of the tribunal, the arbitration proceedings, interim relief, and the award) is set in the context of a masterly review of current German arbitration law and practice.

But there is nothing "parochial" about this book; it will be a unique reference point for anyone faced with, or considering, domestic or international arbitral proceedings in Germany or involving German counterparts. The authors have the breadth of expertise and experience to be able to describe and explain the extent to which current arbitration law and practice in Germany follow, or depart from, what have become accepted as international norms.

It is for that reason alone that the introductory chapter merits close attention by German and non-German arbitration users and practitioners alike: it deals with a number of features of domestic German court practice and procedure, which inevitably inform the approach taken by many German lawyers and parties, who find themselves involved in commercial arbitration proceedings.

For German lawyers and their clients, it is important to understand that to the non-German practitioner or user, certain of these features may seem to be out of kilter with what might be thought to be the international norm. The former need to be aware of the fact that differences of approach are likely to be encountered, particularly in international proceedings in which parties and lawyers from a variety of legal traditions are likely to be involved, and that it may well be necessary to reach at least a procedural accommodation. The latter need to respect the fact that from a German perspective, such procedural points are unexceptional and that it will be necessary to anticipate, and address, any issues to which the expectation that these essentially domestic practices will form part of the process might give rise.

While it will be said with every justification that German practitioners and arbitrators are not unique in having a natural tendency to draw on the practice and procedures of their home jurisdiction, one of the achievements of this book is precisely to identify and elucidate features peculiar to German legal practice (which include such matters as the prominent place of written submissions, an antipathy to disclosure anywhere approaching the US or English discovery model, and the proactive role of the judge, not least, so far as the structuring of proceedings in light of the development of issues of fact ("*Relationstechnik*") and the facilitation of a settlement or the proffering of an evaluation of the facts are concerned). It does so in clear terms and sets them just as effectively in a comparative, international context—for example, by reference to the IBA Rules on the Taking of Evidence in International Arbitration (helpfully included among the documents in the Annex).

It is no easy task to maintain a balance between theory and practicality, which results in a book such as this having the potential to become an indispensable, respected, and trusted source. The authors are to be congratulated for having produced just such a commentary on German arbitration, grounded in practical experience gained at the highest level and thorough academic analysis.

John Beechey
London, December 2015

PREFACE

Arbitration in Germany continues to grow as the country builds on its reputation as a suitable venue for international arbitration. Even where the place of arbitration is outside Germany, German arbitration law plays an increasingly important role for the recognition and enforcement of arbitral awards. This particular significance is highlighted by Germany's strong export-oriented economy and is reflected by the fact that German parties are the second most frequently encountered nationality worldwide among parties in arbitrations under the International Chamber of Commerce Rules.

The present work seeks to address the growing interest in arbitration with a German nexus, in particular among practitioners and academics who do not have facility with the German language. It navigates along the lifecycle of an arbitration, commencing with the arbitration agreement, continuing with the arbitral tribunal, the arbitral proceedings, and interim relief, and concluding with the arbitral award including its recognition and enforcement. At any one of these stages, the work has been drafted with the goal of providing practitioners and academics alike with a detailed commentary on and analysis of German arbitration law and practice.

Chapters 1 to 4 have been authored by Markus S. Rieder and Richard Kreindler, Chapters 5 and 6 by Reinmar Wolff. All authors have contributed to all chapters with insights and recommendations.

The publication of this work would not have been possible without the assistance of several colleagues. Representative for all those who have contributed to the accomplishment of this work, we express our gratitude to Johannes Schmidt in Frankfurt, to Masud Ulfat and Miriam Kerzan in Marburg, as well as to Bettina Müller and Natela Dzvelaia in Munich. Last but not least, we are indebted to Jamie Berezin of Oxford University Press, who has provided important support leading up to publication.

As this work intends to be a source of guidance and support to the reader, the authors welcome observations, comments, and constructive criticisms.

Frankfurt, Marburg, and Munich, December 2015

Richard Kreindler
Reinmar Wolff
Markus S. Rieder

CONTENTS

DETAILED TABLE OF CONTENTS

6. The Arbitral Award

Reinmar Wolff

TABLE OF CASES AND AWARDS

EUROPEAN COURT OF JUSTICE

Court	Date	File No	Source	Para
ECJ	March 23, 1982	C-102/81	NJW 1982, 1207 – *Nordsee*	2.58
ECJ	November 17, 1998	C-391/95	EuZW 1999, 413 – *Van Uden Maritime*	5.19
ECJ	June 1, 1999	C-126/97	EuZW 1999, 565 – *Eco Swiss*	2.58, 6.322
ECJ	November 5, 2002	C-208/00	NJW 2002, 3614 – *Überseering* = ECR 2002 I-09919	2.64
ECJ	September 30, 2003	C-167/01	NJW 2003, 3331 – *Inspire Art* = ECR 2003 I-10155	2.64
ECJ	January 27, 2005	C-125/04	EuZW 2005, 319 – *Denuit and Cordenier*	2.58
ECJ	October 6, 2009	C-40/08	EuZW 2009, 852 – *Asturcom Telecomunicaciones* = ECR 2009 I-09579	2.86

GERMAN CONSTITUTIONAL COURT

Court	Date	File No	Source	Para
BVerfG	February 8, 1967	2 BvR 235/64	BVerfGE 21, 139 = NJW 1967, 1123	1.31
BVerfG	July 19, 1972	2 BvR 872/71	BVerfGE 34, 1	6.152
BVerfG	February 8, 1994	1 BvR 765, 766/89	BVerfGE 89, 381 = NJW 1994, 1053	6.234
BVerfG	May 11, 1994	1 BvR 744/94	NVwZ-RR 1995, 323	4.22
BVerfG	December 7, 1994	1 BvR 1279/94	NJW 1995, 649	2.193
BVerfG	April 30, 2003	1 PBvU 1/02	BVerfG 107, 395 = NJW 2003, 1924	6.208

GERMAN CIVIL COURTS

Court	Date	File No	Source	Para
RG	June 17, 1889	VI 93/89	RGZ 23, 432	6.97, 6.191
RG	June 29, 1896	VI 89/96	JW 1896, 434 (no 14)	6.97
RG	December 8, 1897	I 272/97	RGZ 40, 401	6.198
RG	November 29, 1899	I 312/99	RGZ 45, 382	3.26
RG	February 1, 1901	VII 328/00	RGZ 47, 424	4.12

Court	Date	File No	Source	Para
RG	April 19, 1904	VII 558/03	RGZ 57, 331	6.232
RG	November 4, 1910	III 636/09	RGZ 74, 321	4.186
RG	December 2, 1911	V 266/11	RGZ 78, 28	6.94
RG	January 4, 1912	B 6/11 IV	JW 1912, 305	4.175
RG	March 2, 1920	VII 367/19	JW 1920, 703	6.220
RG	June 4, 1920	VII 3/20	RGZ 99, 129	6.259
RG	June 29, 1923	VII 28/23	LZ 17 (1923), 649	6.97
RG	November 22, 1927	VI 341/27	RGZ 119, 29	6.209
RG	March 30, 1928	104/27 (VII) VI	JW 1928, 1496	4.12
RG	June 2, 1931	VII 529/30	RGZ 133, 16	2.134
RG	April 26, 1932	VII 336/31	JW 1932, 2877 (no 25)	6.103
RG	February 1, 1935	IV 272/34	JW 1935, 2050	6.146
RG	October 11, 1935	VII 74/35	RGZ 149, 45	6.220
RG	January 3, 1939	VII 121/38	RGZ 159, 92	6.218
RG	February 16, 1939	IV 201/38	RGZ 159, 254	2.112
BGH	October 10, 1951	II ZR 99/51	BGHZ 3, 215 = NJW 1952, 27	6.217, 6.229
BGH	September 24, 1952	II ZR 305/51	BGHZ 7, 187 = NJW 1952, 1369	2.25
BGH	November 29, 1952	II ZR 23/52	LM s 1025 ZPO prior version no 5 = ZZP 66 (1953), 152	3.163, 3.169, 3.181
BGH	May 27, 1953	II ZR 147/52	BB 1953, 811	6.232
BGH	April 1, 1954	IV ZR 177/53	BGHZ 13, 71 = NJW 1954, 880	6.163
BGH	October 6, 1954	II ZR 149/53	BGHZ 15, 12	3.189
BGH	February 9, 1955	IV ZR 173/54	NJW 1955, 709	3.168
BGH	March 10, 1955	II ZR 193/53	BGHZ 17, 7	3.115
BGH	January 23, 1957	V ZR 132/55	BGHZ 23, 138 = NJW 1957, 592	6.8, 6.9, 6.12
BGH	January 30, 1957	V ZR 80/55	BGHZ 23, 198 = NJW 1957, 589	2.145, 2.156, 2.157, 4.31
BGH	February 28, 1957	VII ZR 204/56	BGHZ 24, 15 = NJW 1957, 791	2.130
BGH	May 22, 1957	V ZR 236/56	ZZP 71 (1958), 427	6.13
BGH	March 5, 1958	IV ZR 307/57	BGHZ 26, 391 = NJW 1958, 826	6.163
BGH	April 11, 1958	VIII ZR 190/57	NJW 1958, 950	6.114
BGH	April 28, 1958	III ZR 43/56	BGHZ 27, 163 = NJW 1958, 1186	6.209
BGH	May 12, 1958	VII ZR 436/56	BGHZ 27, 249 = NJW 1958, 1538	6.190, 6.227, 6.232, 6.322
BGH	April 23, 1959	VII ZR 2/58	BGHZ 30, 89 = NJW 1959, 1438	6.97, 6.190, 6.232
BGH	October 8, 1959	VII ZR 87/58	BGHZ 31, 43 = NJW 1959, 2213	4.22, 4.26, 6.211, 6.229
BGH	July 11, 1960	II ZR 260/59	BGHZ 33, 105 = NJW 1960, 1997	5.47
BGH	November 30, 1961	VII ZR 12/61	ZZP 75 (1962), 119	6.262

Court	Date	File No	Source	Para
BGH	January 31, 1963	II ZR 117/62	BGHZ 39, 60 = NJW 1963, 637	6.28
BGH	July 11, 1963	VII ZR 120/62	BGHZ 40, 65 = NJW 1963, 1971	6.94
BGH	November 28, 1963	VII ZR 112/62	BGHZ 40, 320 = NJW 1964, 591	2.114, 2.115, 2.128
BGH	December 12, 1963	VII ZR 23/62	NJW 1964, 593	3.84, 4.150
BGH	February 27, 1964	VII ZR 134/62	KTS 1964, 172	6.190, 6.232
BGH	November 19, 1964	VII ZR 8/63	BGHZ 42, 313 = NJW 1965, 298	3.161, 3.189, 4.183, 4.188
BGH	November 24, 1964	VI ZR 187/63	NJW 1965, 300	2.133
BGH	December 6, 1965	VII ZR 149/63	NJW 1966, 549	4.26
BGH	May 20, 1966	KZR 10/64	GRUR 1966, 576	6.232
BGH	June 2, 1966	VII ZR 292/64	BGHZ 45, 282 = NJW 1966, 1960	2.85
BGH	October 25, 1966	KZR 7/65	BGHZ 46, 365 = NJW 1967, 1178	6.190, 6.232, 6.322
BGH	October 18, 1967	VIII ZR 145/66	BGHZ 48, 327 = NJW 1968, 354	6.320
BGH	February 29, 1968	VII ZR 102/65	BGHZ 49, 384 = NJW 1968, 1233	2.12
BGH	May 20, 1968	VII ZR 80/67	NJW 1968, 1928	2.140
BGH	February 27, 1969	KZR 3/68	NJW 1969, 978	6.232, 6.322
BGH	June 26, 1969	VII ZR 32/67	BGHZ 52, 184 = NJW 1969, 2093	6.313
BGH	October 20, 1969	II ZR 162/68	BGHZ 53, 11 = NJW 1970, 324	6.94
BGH	February 27, 1970	VII ZR 68/68	BGHZ 53, 315	2.160
BGH	May 25, 1970	VII ZR 157/68	KTS 1971, 37	2.25
BGH	November 5, 1970	VII ZR 31/69	BGHZ 54, 392 = NJW 1971, 139	1.42, 6.319
BGH	December 10, 1970	II ZR 148/69	WM 1971, 308	2.128
BGH	January 7, 1971	VII ZR 160/69	BGHZ 55, 162 = NJW 1971, 986	6.291, 6.318
BGH	May 31, 1972	II ZR 113/70	NJW 1972, 2180	6.190, 6.231, 6.232, 6.322
BGH	May 14, 1973	II ZR 144/71	BB 1973, 957	2.20
BGH	July 3, 1975	III ZR 78/73	BGHZ 65, 59 = NJW 1976, 109	1.31
BGH	November 25, 1976	III ZR 112/74	WM 1977, 319	6.73
BGH	May 5, 1977	III ZR 177/74	BGHZ 68, 356 = NJW 1977, 1397	2.122, 2.123
BGH	May 16, 1977	VII ZR 311/75	WM 1977, 948	4.24
BGH	September 22, 1977	III ZR 144/76	NJW 1978, 212	2.88
BGH	March 2, 1978	III ZR 99/76	BGHZ 71, 162 = NJW 1978, 1585	2.122
BGH	March 9, 1978	III ZR 78/76	BGHZ 71, 131 = NJW 1978, 1744	6.318

(Contined)

Court	Date	File No	Source	Para
BGH	October 5, 1979	III ZR 148/79	VersR 1982, 92	6.177
BGH	October 11, 1979	III ZR 184/78	NJW 1980, 1049	2.85
BGH	October 11, 1979	III ZR 25/77	NJW 1980, 1284	6.171, 6.262
BGH	December 5, 1979	VIII ZR 155/78	DB 1980, 967	3.196
BGH	December 3, 1980	VIII ZR 300/79	NJW 1981, 1549	2.109
BGH	February 12, 1981	IVa ZR 103/80	NJW 1981, 2295	2.108
BGH	April 9, 1981	IVa ZB 6/80	BGHZ 80, 246 = NJW 1981, 1736	2.106
BGH	October 8, 1981	III ZR 42/80	NJW 1982, 1224	6.298, 6.302
BGH	October 8, 1981	III ZR 190/79	NJW 1982, 437	3.197
BGH	November 11, 1982	III ZR 77/81	BGHZ 85, 288 = NJW 1983, 867	1.43, 4.22, 6.171, 6.262
BGH	December 2, 1982	III ZR 85/81	NJW 1983, 1267 = XV Y.B. Com. Arb. 662 (1990)	2.87
BGH	January 25, 1983	X ZR 47/82	BB 1984, 561	2.55
BGH	April 13, 1983	VIII ZR 320/80	NJW 1984, 128	6.117
BGH	October 25, 1983	KZR 27/82	BGHZ 88, 314 = NJW 1984, 1355	2.41, 6.232
BGH	October 27, 1983	IX ZR 68/83	BGHZ 88, 364 = NJW 1984, 312	6.29
BGH	March 27, 1984	IX ZR 24/83	NJW 1984, 2765	6.295
BGH	May 10, 1984	III ZR 206/82	NJW 1984, 2763	6.313
BGH	March 7, 1985	III ZR 169/83	BGHZ 94, 92 = NJW 1985, 1903	3.20, 3.184, 3.186
BGH	July 11, 1985	III ZR 33/84	NJW 1986, 2765	2.156
BGH	September 26, 1985	III ZR 16/84	BGHZ 96, 40 = NJW 1986, 1436	1.43, 6.97, 6.135, 6.221, 6.222
BGH	December 5, 1985	III ZR 180/84	WM 1986, 688	2.197
BGH	April 10, 1986	VII ZR 286/85	NJW 1986, 2508	6.115
BGH	May 5, 1986	III ZR 233/84	BGHZ 98, 32 = NJW 1986, 3077	3.161, 3.162, 3.171, 3.187, 6.8
BGH	May 5, 1986	III ZR 235/84	NJW 1986, 3079	6.215
BGH	May 15, 1986	III ZR 192/84	BGHZ 98, 70 = NJW 1986, 3027	1.41, 6.319
BGH	October 10, 1986	V ZR 247/85	NJW 1987, 1069	2.69
BGH	December 3, 1986	IVb ZR 80/85	BGHZ 99, 143 = NJW 1987, 651	2.12, 6.121
BGH	March 26, 1987	II ZR 87/86	NJW-RR 1988, 572	6.313
BGH	April 2, 1987	III ZR 76/86	NJW-RR 1987, 1194	2.69, 6.198
BGH	June 1, 1987	II ZR 128/86	BGHZ 101, 113	4.41
BGH	November 12, 1987	III ZR 29/87	BGHZ 102, 199 = NJW 1988, 1215	2.133, 2.140
BGH	February 25, 1988	III ZR 272/85	NJW-RR 1988, 957	6.163
BGH	March 17, 1988	IX ZR 43/87	NJW 1988, 2880	2.71
BGH	April 14, 1988	III ZR 12/87	NJW 1988, 3090 = XV Y.B. Com. Arb. 452 (1990)	2.163

Court	Date	File No	Source	Para
BGH	June 7, 1988	IX ZR 278/87	NJW 1988, 3268	5.113
BGH	December 21, 1988	VIII ZR 277/87	NJW 1989, 2133	6.112
BGH	June 14, 1989	IVa ZR 180/88	NJW-RR 1989, 1048	5.14
BGH	December 7, 1989	VII ZR 343/88	NJW-RR 1990, 340	2.71
BGH	January 18, 1990	III ZR 269/88	BGHZ 110, 104 = NJW 1990, 2199 = XVII Y.B. Com. Arb. 504 (1992)	3.174, 4.25, 6.319
BGH	July 3, 1990	XI ZR 302/89	BGHZ 112, 54 = NJW 1991, 30	6.163
BGH	July 12, 1990	III ZR 174/89	NJW 1990, 3210	4.26, 6.231
BGH	January 14, 1991	II ZR 190/89	NJW 1991, 1052	4.62
BGH	October 10, 1991	III ZR 141/90	BGHZ 115, 324 = NJW 1992, 575 = XIX Y.B. Com. Arb. 201 (1994)	2.41, 2.100, 3.21
BGH	December 19, 1991	IX ZR 96/91	BGHZ 117, 1 = NJW 1992, 1172	6.116
BGH	May 14, 1992	III ZR 169/90	NJW 1992, 2299	6.209
BGH	June 4, 1992	IX ZR 149/91	BGHZ 118, 312 = NJW 1992, 3096	2.193, 6.322
BGH	September 23, 1992	I ZR 224/90	NJW 1993, 333	6.116
BGH	October 15, 1992	IX ZR 231/91	NJW 1993, 1270	6.322
BGH	November 20, 1992	V ZR 279/91	BGHZ 120, 261 = NJW 1993, 593	5.113
BGH	March 4, 1993	IX ZB 55/92	BGHZ 122, 16 = NJW 1993, 1801	6.322
BGH	July 7, 1993	VIII ZR 103/92	BGHZ 123, 137 = NJW 1993, 2684	6.115
BGH	September 29, 1993	III ZR 213/82	WM 1983, 1207	6.190
BGH	December 10, 1993	V ZR 168/92	NJW 1994, 735	4.95
BGH	March 30, 1994	VIII ZR 132/92	BGHZ 125, 351 = NJW 1994, 2769	6.117
BGH	May 19, 1994	III ZR 130/93	NJW 1994, 2155	4.33, 6.220
BGH	September 26, 1994	II ZR 236/93	NJW 1995, 260	4.41
BGH	November 11, 1994	V ZR 46/93	NJW 1995, 967	6.115
BGH	December 7, 1994	VII ZR 153/93	NJW 1995, 665	4.45
BGH	July 14, 1995	V ZR 171/94	NJW 1995, 2993	6.112
BGH	December 19, 1995	III ZR 194/94	NJW-RR 1996, 508	6.121
BGH	March 29, 1996	II ZR 124/95	BGHZ 132, 278 = NJW 1996, 1753	1.78, 2.50, 2.54, 2.59
BGH	May 2, 1996	III ZR 50/95	NJW 1996, 1960	2.69
BGH	June 14, 1996	V ZR 85/95	NJW 1996, 2503	2.69
BGH	July 11, 1996	III ZR 133/95	NJW 1996, 3151	6.116
BGH	July 12, 1996	V ZR 202/95	NJW 1996, 2792	2.110
BGH	December 5, 1996	IX ZR 67/96	NJW 1997, 743	6.117
BGH	January 15, 1997	VIII ZR 303/96	NJW 1997, 1241	4.96

(*Contined*)

Court	Date	File No	Source	Para
BGH	April 10, 1997	VII ZR 266/96	NJW-RR 1997, 1157	4.96
BGH	October 2, 1997	III ZR 2/96	NJW 1998, 371	2.69, 2.124
BGH	October 30, 1997	VII ZR 321/95	NJW-RR 1998, 234	6.65
BGH	November 13, 1997	IX ZR 289/96	NJW 1998, 450	3.194
BGH	January 12, 1998	II ZR 82/93	BGHZ 137, 378	4.41
BGH	April 1, 1998	XII ZR 278/96	NJW 1998, 1857	2.72, 2.91
BGH	April 21, 1998	XI ZR 377/97	BGHZ 138, 331 = NJW 1998, 2358	6.316
BGH	September 24, 1998	III ZR 133/97	NJW 1999, 282	2.100
BGH	February 9, 1999	VI ZR 9/98	NJW 1999, 1257	6.163
BGH	March 4, 1999	III ZR 72/98	BGHZ 141, 90 = NJW 1999, 2370	3.110, 6.215
BGH	May 3, 1999	II ZR 119/98	GmbHR 1999, 714	4.41
BGH	May 6, 1999	VII ZR 132/97	NJW 1999, 2266	4.232
BGH	May 6, 1999	III ZR 265/98	NJW 1999, 3126	6.116
BGH	May 18, 1999	X ZR 158/97	NJW 1999, 2887	4.153
BGH	July 15, 1999	III ZB 21/98	BGHZ 142, 204 = NJW 1999, 2974	6.187, 6.271, 6.282
BGH	November 4, 1999	VII ZB 19/99	NJW 2000, 960	5.51
BGH	March 20, 2000	II ZR 250/99	NJW 2000, 1958	6.116
BGH	April 3, 2000	II ZR 194/98	NJW 2000, 2099	2.109
BGH	May 3, 2000	XII ZR 42/98	NJW 2000, 2346	2.72
BGH	August 17, 2000	III ZB 43/99	NJW 2000, 3650	6.329
BGH	September 11, 2000	II ZR 34/99	NJW 2001, 144	2.106
BGH	September 14, 2000	III ZR 33/00	NJW 2000, 3720	2.158
BGH	September 21, 2000	I ZR 135/98	BGHZ 145, 170	4.153
BGH	September 26, 2000	VI ZR 279/99	NJW 2001, 157	6.116
BGH	November 2, 2000	III ZB 55/99	BGHZ 145, 376 = NJW 2001, 373	6.163, 6.180, 6.230, 6.273, 6.302, 6.321
BGH	February 1, 2001	III ZR 332/99	NJW-RR 2001, 1059 = XXIX Y.B. Com. Arb. 700 (2001)	6.319, 6.329
BGH	February 8, 2001	III ZR 268/00	DStR 2001, 1129	2.24
BGH	February 22, 2001	III ZB 71/99	NJW 2001, 1730 = XXIX Y.B. Com. Arb. 724 (2004)	6.329
BGH	July 31, 2001	XI ZR 217/01	NJW 2001, 3616	6.117
BGH	October 4, 2001	III ZR 281/00	NZG 2002, 83	2.114, 2.128
BGH	October 23, 2001	XI ZR 63/01	NJW 2002, 368	2.83, 2.85
BGH	June 6, 2002	III ZB 44/01	BGHZ 151, 79 = SchiedsVZ 2003, 39	6.56, 6.87, 6.187, 6.193
BGH	July 5, 2002	V ZR 143/01	NJW 2002, 3164	2.110
BGH	August 1, 2002	III ZB 66/01	NJW-RR 2002, 1462	2.124, 2.169
BGH	March 27, 2003	III ZB 83/02	SchiedsVZ 2003, 133	6.199
BGH	June 26, 2003	I ZR 269/00	NJW 2003, 3058	6.112
BGH	September 25, 2003	III ZB 68/02	SchiedsVZ 2003, 281 = XXIX Y.B. Com. Arb. 767 (2004)	6.298, 6.330, 6.336

Court	Date	File No	Source	Para
BGH	December 16, 2003	XI ZR 474/02	BGHZ 157, 224 = NJW 2004, 1456	6.117
BGH	December 18, 2003	I ZB 18/03	NJW-RR 2004, 856	6.81
BGH	January 15, 2004	IX ZR 152/00	ZIP 2004, 843	2.108
BGH	March 3, 2004	IV ZB 43/03	NJW 2004, 1805	6.112
BGH	May 17, 2004	II ZR 261/01	NJW 2004, 2449	3.194
BGH	May 27, 2004	III ZB 53/03	BGHZ 159, 207 = SchiedsVZ 2004, 205	2.40, 6.171
BGH	July 19, 2004	II ZR 65/03	BGHZ 160, 127 = NJW 2004, 2898	2.48, 2.49, 2.130
BGH	October 6, 2004	IV ZR 287/03	NJW-RR 2005, 506	4.96
BGH	January 13, 2005	III ZR 265/03	BGHZ 162, 9 = SchiedsVZ 2005, 95	2.103, 2.123, 4.104, 6.190
BGH	February 10, 2005	VII ZR 184/04	NJW 2005, 1356	2.71
BGH	February 24, 2005	III ZB 36/04	NJW 2005, 1273	2.82
BGH	April 18, 2005	II ZR 151/03	NZG 2005, 551	4.41
BGH	May 9, 2005	II ZR 29/03	AG 2005, 613	4.41
BGH	May 18, 2005	VIII ZR 368/03	NJW 2005, 2395	4.62
BGH	June 29, 2005	VIII ZR 299/04	NJW 2005, 2991	6.163
BGH	June 29, 2005	III ZB 65/04	SchiedsVZ 2005, 259	6.199
BGH	September 13, 2005	VI ZR 137/04	BGHZ 164, 87 = NJW 2006, 154	6.163
BGH	September 21, 2005	III ZB 18/05	SchiedsVZ 2005, 306	6.311
BGH	December 13, 2005	XI ZR 82/05	NJW 2006, 762	2.86
BGH	December 14, 2005	XII ZR 241/03	NJW-RR 2006, 338	2.109
BGH	January 12, 2006	III ZR 214/05	BGHZ 165, 376 = NJW 2006, 779	2.138
BGH	February 23, 2006	III ZB 50/05	BGHZ 166, 278 = SchiedsVZ 2006, 161 = XXXII Y.B. Com. Arb. 328 (2007)	6.236, 6.298, 6.336
BGH	March 30, 2006	III ZB 78/05	SchiedsVZ 2006, 278	6.254
BGH	April 4, 2006	X ZR 122/05	NJW 2006, 2472	4.186
BGH	June 29, 2006	III ZB 36/06	NJW-RR 2006, 1502	4.41
BGH	January 18, 2007	III ZB 35/06	NJW-RR 2007, 1008 = XXXIII Y.B. Com. Arb. 506 (2008)	6.87, 6.302
BGH	January 23, 2007	VI ZB 61/06	NJW-RR 2007, 784	6.66
BGH	January 25, 2007	VII ZR 105/06	WM 2007, 698	2.91, 2.119
BGH	March 1, 2007	III ZB 7/06	SchiedsVZ 2007, 160 = XXXIII Y.B. Com. Arb. 234 (2008)	2.42
BGH	March 1, 2007	III ZR 164/06	SchiedsVZ 2007, 163	2.102, 2.103
BGH	March 8, 2007	III ZB 21/06	NJW-RR 2007, 1366	6.270
BGH	July 18, 2007	VIII ZR 227/06	NJW-RR 2007, 1697	2.111
BGH	November 8, 2007	III ZB 95/06	SchiedsVZ 2008, 40	6.277, 6.278
BGH	January 17, 2008	III ZR 320/06	SchiedsVZ 2008, 94	6.242

(Contined)

Court	Date	File No	Source	Para
BGH	January 17, 2008	III ZB 11/07	SchiedsVZ 2008, 148	6.277
BGH	January 18, 2008	V ZR 174/06	NJW 2008, 1659	2.106
BGH	March 14, 2008	V ZR 13/07	NJW-RR 2008, 1397	6.115
BGH	April 17, 2008	III ZB 97/06	SchiedsVZ 2008, 196	6.198
BGH	May 21, 2008	III ZB 14/07	SchiedsVZ 2008, 195 = XXXIII Y.B. Com. Arb. 510 (2008)	6.301
BGH	October 29, 2008	XII ZB 75/08	NZM 2009, 51	4.96
BGH	October 30, 2008	III ZB 17/08	SchiedsVZ 2009, 66	2.86, 6.226, 6.231, 6.316
BGH	January 15, 2009	III ZB 83/07	SchiedsVZ 2009, 126	6.211
BGH	January 29, 2009	III ZB 88/07	BGHZ 179, 304 = SchiedsVZ 2009, 176	6.66, 6.177, 6.227, 6.228, 6.232, 6.285, 6.316
BGH	February 5, 2009	IX ZB 89/06	SchiedsVZ 2009, 174	5.40
BGH	April 6, 2009	II ZR 255/08	BGHZ 180, 221 = SchiedsVZ 2009, 233	1.78, 2.63
BGH	April 17, 2009	VII ZR 164/07	NJW 2009, 2199	4.153
BGH	April 30, 2009	III ZB 5/09	NJW-RR 2010, 425	3.25
BGH	April 30, 2009	III ZB 91/07	SchiedsVZ 2009, 287	6.198
BGH	July 2, 2009	IX ZR 152/06	SchiedsVZ 2009, 285 = XXXV Y.B. Com. Arb. 374 (2010)	6.295
BGH	September 2, 2009	XII ZB 50/06	BGHZ 182, 204 = NJW 2010, 153	6.229, 6.320
BGH	March 10, 2010	IV ZR 264/08	NJW-RR 2010, 1378	4.62
BGH	June 8, 2010	XI ZR 349/08	SchiedsVZ 2011, 46 = XXXVII Y.B. Com. Arb. 216 (2012)	2.7, 2.77
BGH	July 29, 2010	III ZB 48/09	SchiedsVZ 2010, 275 = XXXVI Y.B. Com. Arb. 277 (2011)	6.278, 6.327
BGH	September 30, 2010	III ZB 69/09	BGHZ 187, 126 = SchiedsVZ 2010, 332 = XXXVI Y.B. Com. Arb. 282 (2011)	6.311, 6.312
BGH	September 30, 2010	III ZB 57/10	SchiedsVZ 2010, 330 = XXXVI Y.B. Com. Arb. 279 (2011)	6.276, 6.278, 6.327
BGH	October 28, 2010	VII ZR 172/09	NJW 2011, 594	5.62
BGH	December 16, 2010	III ZB 100/09	BGHZ 188, 1 = SchiedsVZ 2011, 105	6.324
BGH	January 25, 2011	XI ZR 350/08	SchiedsVZ 2011, 157 = XXXVII Y.B. Com. Arb. 223 (2012)	2.6
BGH	February 24, 2011	VII ZB 108/08	NJW-RR 2011, 931	5.62
BGH	March 1, 2011	XI ZR 48/10	BGHZ 188, 373 = NJW 2011, 2515	5.21
BGH	June 7, 2011	II ZR 186/08	NJW-RR 2011, 1059	1.94
BGH	July 14, 2011	III ZB 70/10	SchiedsVZ 2011, 284	2.165

Court	Date	File No	Source	Para
BGH	July 21, 2011	IX ZR 148/10	BeckRS 2011, 21743	4.45
BGH	September 29, 2011	IX ZR 170/10	NJW-RR 2012, 294	3.197
BGH	November 30, 2011	III ZB 19/11	SchiedsVZ 2012, 41	6.290, 6.318, 6.331
BGH	March 28, 2012	III ZB 63/10	BGHZ 193, 38 = SchiedsVZ 2012, 154	3.180, 3.186, 6.52, 6.59, 6.60, 6.72, 6.73
BGH	July 12, 2012	VII ZR 134/11	NJW-RR 2012, 1107	4.96
BGH	July 19, 2012	III ZB 66/11	SchiedsVZ 2012, 281	3.34
BGH	October 2, 2012	III ZB 8/11	Unreported	4.16
BGH	January 30, 2013	III ZB 40/12	SchiedsVZ 2013, 110 = XXXVIII Y.B. Com. Arb. 384 (2013)	6.251
BGH	April 23, 2013	III ZB 59/12	SchiedsVZ 2013, 229 = XXXIII Y.B. Com. Arb. 510 (2008)	6.335
BGH	April 25, 2013	IX ZR 49/12	NZI 2013, 934	2.130
BGH	July 4, 2013	III ZR 52/12	NJW-RR 2014, 492	1.94
BGH	November 27, 2013	III ZB 59/13	NZG 2014, 110	4.41
BGH	December 18, 2013	III ZB 92/12	SchiedsVZ 2014, 31	6.52, 6.276, 6.277, 6.278
BGH	January 28, 2014	III ZB 40/13	SchiedsVZ 2014, 98	6.226, 6.231
BGH	May 8, 2014	III ZR 371/12	SchiedsVZ 2014, 151	2.124
BGH	July 24, 2014	III ZB 83/13	NZG 2014, 1155	2.88, 2.90, 4.104
BGH	December 11, 2014	I ZB 23/14	NJW-RR 2015, 1087	6.216, 6.218
BGH	April 16, 2015	I ZB 3/14	NJW 2015, 3234	2.62, 6.105, 6.212, 6.229
BayObLG	February 24, 1984	3Z 197/83	BayObLGZ 1984, 45 = BB 1984, 746	6.114, 6.124, 6.256
BayObLG	February 24, 1999	4Z Sch 14/98	NJW-RR 2000, 360	6.214, 6.216
BayObLG	December 15, 1999	4Z Sch 23/99	BB 2000, Beil. 12, p 16	6.165, 6.228
BayObLG	February 28, 2000	4Z SchH 13/99	BB 2000, Beil. 8, p 15	2.119
BayObLG	April 20, 2000	4Z Sch 2/00	NJW-RR 2001, 1363	6.277
BayObLG	June 20, 2000	4Z SchH 12/99	BayObLGZ 2000, 187	3.22
BayObLG	August 11, 2000	4Z SchH 5/00	BB 2000, Beil. 12, p 10	6.329
BayObLG	October 25, 2001	4Z SchH 6/01	BayObLGZ 2001, 311	2.49
BayObLG	November 19, 2001	4Z Sch 15/01	NJW-RR 2002, 933	3.26
BayObLG	January 16, 2002	4Z SchH 9/01	BayObLGZ 2002, 17 = NJW-RR 2002, 933	3.26
BayObLG	November 22, 2002	4Z SchH 13/02	SchiedsVZ 2003, 142 = XXIX Y.B. Com. Arb. 754 (2004)	6.300, 6.302, 6.313, 6.329
BayObLG	July 10, 2003	4Z Sch 12/03	BB 2003, Beil. 8, p 26	6.262
BayObLG	November 13, 2003	4Z SchH 08/03	SchiedsVZ 2004, 45	2.128
BayObLG	August 25, 2004	4Z Sch 13/04	SchiedsVZ 2004, 319	6.230

(*Contined*)

Court	Date	File No	Source	Para
KG	March 1, 1913		OLGRspr. 27 (1913), 196	6.7
KG	December 21, 1925	7 U 9531/25	JW 1926, 2219	6.220
KG	November 8, 1927	22 U 10292/27	JW 1928, 735	6.13
KG	March 22, 1928	22 W 183/27	JW 1929, 143	6.263
KG	February 5, 1976	16 U 1275/75	NJW 1976, 1357	6.177
KG	October 15, 1999	28 Sch 17/99	BB 2000, Beil. 8, p 13	2.113, 2.119
KG	May 6, 2002	23 Sch 01/02	SchiedsVZ 2003, 185	3.13, 3.83, 3.84
KG	August 11, 2004	23 Sch 11/03	SchiedsVZ 2005, 100	2.130
KG	August 18, 2006	20 Sch 7/04	SchiedsVZ 2007, 108	6.304, 6.305
KG	December 17, 2007	20 Sch 05/07	SchiedsVZ 2009, 179	6.191
KG	April 21, 2008	20 SchH 4/07	NJW 2008, 2719	4.79
KG	December 7, 2009	20 SchH 1/09	BeckRS 2011, 07078	3.124
KG	July 7, 2010	20 SchH 2/10	SchiedsVZ 2010, 225	3.120, 3.129, 3.132
KG	August 12, 2010	20 Sch 2/10	SchiedsVZ 2011, 110	6.59, 6.60, 6.91, 6.155, 6.210
KG	January 20, 2011	20 Sch 9/09	SchiedsVZ 2011, 285	6.311
KG	April 28, 2011	23 U 33/11	NJW 2011, 2978	2.17, 2.20, 2.119
KG	April 23, 2012	20 SchH 3/09	NZI 2012, 759	2.130
KG	June 4, 2012	20 Sch 10/11	SchiedsVZ 2013, 112 = XXXVIII Y.B. Com. Arb. 384 (2013)	6.230, 6.322, 6.323
KG	September 3, 2012	20 SchH 2/12	SchiedsVZ 2012, 337	2.113, 2.119
OLG Brandenburg	March 5, 2008	4 U 132/07	BB 2008, 901	4.45
OLG Brandenburg	February 16, 2011	13 U 11/10	BauR 2011, 1533	5.9
OLG Brandenburg	July 24, 2015	11 Sch 2/13	SchiedsVZ 2016, 43	6.322, 6.327, 6.329
OLG Braunschweig	May 12, 2005	8 Sc 1/04	SchiedsVZ 2005, 262	6.223, 6.231
OLG Bremen	December 14, 1956	1 U 369/55	NJW 1957, 1035	6.114
OLG Bremen	October 25, 1971	1 W 74/71 (c)	NJW 1972, 454	3.26
OLG Bremen	September 30, 1999	(2) Sch 4/99	BB 2000, Beil. 12, p 18	6.220
OLG Bremen	November 10, 2005	2 Sch 02/05	Unreported, available at http://www.disarb.org (last visited December 1, 2015)	6.228
OLG Bremen	June 28, 2006	2 Sch 2/06	SchiedsVZ 2007, 51	2.41
OLG Bremen	October 30, 2008	2 Sch 2/08	OLGR Bremen 2009, 155 = NJOZ 2009, 1188	2.99
OLG Celle	February 19, 2004	8 Sch 09/03	OLGR Celle 2004, 396; also available at http://www.disarb.org (last visited December 1, 2015)	4.9, 6.210, 6.211

Court	Date	File No	Source	Para
OLG Celle	October 6, 2005	8 Sch 06/05	Unreported, available at http://www.disarb.org (last visited December 1, 2015)	6.301
OLG Celle	December 4, 2008	8 Sch 13/07	IPRspr. 2008, no 207, 658	2.99
OLG Dresden	May 10, 1938	12 W 19/38	JW 1938, 2154	3.121
OLG Dresden	April 20, 1999	11 Sch 02/99	Unreported, available at http://www.disarb.org (last visited December 1, 2015)	6.285
OLG Dresden	May 8, 2001	11 Sch 1/99	BB 2001, Beil. 7, p 22	6.123, 6.255
OLG Dresden	October 28, 2003	11 Sch 9/03	SchiedsVZ 2004, 44	6.73
OLG Dresden	January 27, 2005	11 SchH 02/04	SchiedsVZ 2005, 159	3.113, 3.119, 3.137
OLG Dresden	April 24, 2005	11 Sch 1/05	SchiedsVZ 2005, 210	6.226, 6.231, 6.277
OLG Dresden	March 15, 2006	11 Sch 19/05	SchiedsVZ 2006, 166	6.208
OLG Dresden	January 31, 2007	11 Sch 18/05	SchiedsVZ 2007, 327 = XXXIII Y.B. Com. Arb. 510 (2008)	6.335
OLG Dresden	December 7, 2007	11 Sch 8/07	IPRspr. 2007, no 222, 631 = XXXIII Y.B. Com. Arb. 549 (2008)	2.99
OLG Dresden	July 16, 2008	11 SchH 03/08	SchiedsVZ 2009, 69	3.25
OLG Dresden	February 24, 2009	11 Sch 01/09	Unreported, available at http://www.disarb.org (last visited December 1, 2015)	6.267
OLG Düsseldorf	October 27, 1975	6 U 2/75	BB 1976, 251	6.13, 614
OLG Düsseldorf	February 13, 1978	6 U 184/77	WM 1978, 359	5.47
OLG Düsseldorf	January 19, 2005	I-26 Sch 5/03	SchiedsVZ 2005, 214	6.277
OLG Düsseldorf	August 14, 2007	I-4 Sch 2/06	SchiedsVZ 2008, 156	6.106, 6.178
OLG Düsseldorf	February 7, 2008	I-20 W 152/07, 20 W 152/07	SchiedsVZ 2008, 258	5.21
OLG Düsseldorf	July 8, 2008	I-4 Sch 4/08	BeckRS 2008, 20508	3.149
OLG Düsseldorf	December 9, 2009	6 W 45/09	ZIP 2010, 28	2.15
OLG Frankfurt	December 21, 1983	21 U 2/83	NJW 1984, 2768	6.165
OLG Frankfurt	June 29, 1989	6 U (Kart.) 115/88	RIW 1989, 911	6.336
OLG Frankfurt	May 18, 2000	13 W 29/00	NJW-RR 2000, 1117	5.11
OLG Frankfurt	April 5, 2001	24 Sch 1/01	NJW-RR 2001, 1078	2.38, 5.85, 5.101
OLG Frankfurt	April 18, 2001	13 U 66/01	IPRspr. 2001, no 205, 440	6.229
OLG Frankfurt	September 6, 2001	3 Sch 02/00	Unreported, available at http://www.disarb.org (last visited December 1, 2015)	6.171
OLG Frankfurt	September 25, 2002	17 Sch 3/01	IHR 2003, 93	6.221, 6.228

(*Contined*)

Court	Date	File No	Source	Para
OLG Frankfurt	June 26, 2003	1 Sch 01/02	Unreported, available at http://www.disarb.org (last visited December 1, 2015)	6.263
OLG Frankfurt	May 17, 2004	2 Sch 2/03	SchiedsVZ 2005, 311	6.152
OLG Frankfurt	September 8, 2005	26 Sch 06/05	Unreported, available at http://www.disarb.org (last visited December 1, 2015)	6.226
OLG Frankfurt	April 27, 2006	26 SchH 1/06	SchiedsVZ 2006, 329	3.100, 3.122
OLG Frankfurt	October 24, 2006	26 Sch 6/06	SchiedsVZ 2007, 217	2.119
OLG Frankfurt	May 10, 2007	26 Sch 20/06	SchiedsVZ 2007, 278	6.89, 6.90
OLG Frankfurt	October 4, 2007	26 Sch 8/07	NJW-RR 2008, 801	3.121
OLG Frankfurt	November 2, 2007	26 SchH 3/07	NJW-RR 2008, 590	6.127, 6.243
OLG Frankfurt	January 10, 2008	26 Sch 21/07	NJW 2008, 1325	3.120, 3.132
OLG Frankfurt	April 10, 2008	26 Sch 42/07	FamRZ 2008, 1978	6.208
OLG Frankfurt	October 16, 2008	26 Sch 13/08	IPRspr. 2008, no 203, 646 = XXXIV Y.B. Com. Arb. 527 (2009)	4.152, 6.329
OLG Frankfurt	May 12, 2009	14 Sch 4/09	NJW-RR 2010, 788	2.17
OLG Frankfurt	October 29, 2009	26 Sch 12/09	SchiedsVZ 2010, 52	3.124, 3.143, 6.215, 6.217
OLG Frankfurt	November 23, 2009	26 Sch 12/09	SchiedsVZ 2010, 227	6.283
OLG Frankfurt	March 30, 2010	26 SchH 15/09	Unreported, available at http://www.disarb.org (last visited December 1, 2015)	6.267
OLG Frankfurt	September 9, 2010	26 SchH 4/10	NZG 2011, 629	2.61
OLG Frankfurt	October 14, 2010	26 Sch 6/10, 26 Sch 22/10	Unreported, available at http://www.disarb.org (last visited December 1, 2015)	6.183
OLG Frankfurt	October 28, 2010	26 SchH 3/09	IPRspr. 2009, no 276, 709	3.21
OLG Frankfurt	February 17, 2011	26 Sch 13/10	SchiedsVZ 2013, 49	4.16, 6.208, 6.209, 6.210, 6.213, 6.223, 6.226, 6.228, 6.229, 6.231
OLG Frankfurt	June 13, 2013	26 SchH 6/13	SpuRt 2013, 206	5.5, 5.15
OLG Frankfurt	June 21, 2013	26 SchH 3/13	Unreported, available at http://www.disarb.org (last visited December 1, 2015)	6.267
OLG Frankfurt	July 11, 2013	26 SchH 8/12	SchiedsVZ 2013, 294	3.36
OLG Frankfurt	January 6, 2014	26 Sch 2/13	SchiedsVZ 2014, 206	6.322, 6.329
OLG Frankfurt	April 11, 2014	26 Sch 13/13	SchiedsVZ 2014, 154	6.226, 6.228, 6.277
OLG Hamburg	September 21, 1901		OLGRspr. 5 (1902), 205	3.121
OLG Hamburg	June 3, 1918	Bs. Z. I. 42/ 1918	JW 1918, 572	3.121

Court	Date	File No	Source	Para
OLG Hamburg	March 11, 1953	2 U 487/52	NJW 1953, 1309	6.232
OLG Hamburg	March 28, 1958	5 W 20/58	NJW 1958, 1046	6.263
OLG Hamburg	May 14, 1964	3 U 22/64	MDR 1965, 54	6.73
OLG Hamburg	August 2, 1968	14 U 84/68	MDR 1968, 1018	6.208
OLG Hamburg	December 14, 1982	9 U 22/82	VersR 1983, 787	3.84
OLG Hamburg	February 17, 1989	1 U 86/87	RIW 1989, 574 = XV Y.B. Com. Arb. 455 (1990)	2.132
OLG Hamburg	May 6, 1996	6 W 32/96	NJW 1997, 749 = RIW 1996, 857	5.19
OLG Hamburg	September 4, 1998	14 U 111/98	NJW-RR 2000, 806	6.87
OLG Hamburg	May 14, 1999	1 Sch 02/99	Unreported, available at http://www.disarb.org (last visited December 1, 2015)	6.228
OLG Hamburg	June 8, 2001	11 Sch 1/01	Unreported, available at http://www.disarb.org (last visited December 1, 2015)	6.210
OLG Hamburg	November 8, 2001	6 Sch 04/01	Unreported, available at http://www.disarb.org (last visited December 1, 2015)	6.208
OLG Hamburg	August 27, 2002	6 Sch 04/02	Unreported, available at http://www.disarb.org (last visited December 1, 2015)	6.332
OLG Hamburg	January 24, 2003	11 Sch 06/01	SchiedsVZ 2003, 284	2.119, 6.183, 6.333
OLG Hamburg	January 29, 2004	11 W 93/03	SchiedsVZ 2004, 266	2.70
OLG Hamburg	July 12, 2005	9 SchH 1/05	SchiedsVZ 2006, 55	3.119, 3.140
OLG Hamburg	March 15, 2012	6 Sch 13/11	Unreported	2.26
OLG Hamm	September 10, 1981	6 U 151/81	BauR 1982, 285	5.46
OLG Hamm	May 11, 1993	26 U 76/93	MDR 1994, 307	5.55
OLG Hamm	June 20, 2001	8 Sch 2/00	NJW-RR 2001, 1362	6.277
OLG Hamm	September 27, 2005	29 Sch 1/05	SchiedsVZ 2006, 106	6.329
OLG Hamm	March 28, 2006	21 U 134/04	OLGR Hamm 2006, 527	2.80, 2.85
OLG Hamm	July 18, 2007	8 Sch 2/07	AG 2007, 910 = MDR 2007, 1438	2.20, 2.84, 2.85, 2.119
OLG Hamm	July 13, 2012	I-25 Sch 3/11	SchiedsVZ 2013, 182	6.236, 6.323
OLG Hamm	July 9, 2013	21 U 16/13	SchiedsVZ 2014, 38	2.183
OLG Jena	November 24, 1999	4 Sch 3/99	BB 2000, Beil. 12, p 22	5.93, 5.111
OLG Jena	January 13, 2011	1 Sch 1/08	IPRspr. 2011, no 293, 781 = XXXVII Y.B. Com. Arb. 220 (2012)	2.99
OLG Karlsruhe	March 8, 1994	3 U 45/93	NJW-RR 1994, 1084	3.197
OLG Karlsruhe	May 7, 1996	2 UF 59/96	NJW-RR 1997, 450	5.28
OLG Karlsruhe	March 18, 1999	19 U 59/98	BB 2000, 635	4.232

(*Contined*)

Court	Date	File No	Source	Para
OLG Karlsruhe	March 27, 2006	9 Sch 2/05	SchiedsVZ 2006, 335 = XXXII Y.B. Com. Arb. 342 (2007)	4.130
OLG Karlsruhe	July 14, 2006	10 Sch 1/06	BeckRS 2006, 19851	3.132
OLG Karlsruhe	January 4, 2012	9 Sch 2/09	SchiedsVZ 2012, 101 = XXXVIII Y.B. Com. Arb. 379 (2013)	6.61, 6.100, 6.208, 6.316, 6.325
OLG Karlsruhe	March 27, 2013	8 Sch 2/12	SchiedsVZ 2015, 145	6.307, 6.329, 6.331, 6.332
OLG Kiel	May 18, 1927	4 U 60/27	JW 1927, 1656	3.201
OLG Koblenz	June 24, 1954	5 U 476/53	KTS 1957, 94	3.178
OLG Koblenz	July 15, 1998	5 W 464/98	MDR 1999, 502	5.9
OLG Koblenz	October 22, 2001	2 SchH 1/01	BeckRS 2001, 30213028	3.26, 3.27
OLG Koblenz	July 28, 2005	2 Sch 4/05	SchiedsVZ 2005, 260	6.199, 6.277, 6.331
OLG Koblenz	October 23, 2009	2 Sch 9/09	r+s 2010, 84	6.261
OLG Köln	September 22, 1950	I ZS 137/49	MDR 1951, 28	2.25
OLG Köln	July 3, 1952	6 U 43/52	NJW 1952, 1420	6.232
OLG Köln	March 18, 1969	2 W 5/69	KTS 1970, 52	6.263
OLG Köln	December 2, 1970	2 U 37/70	KTS 1971, 222	6.214
OLG Köln	June 10, 1976	1 U 192/74	ZZP 91 (1978), 318	6.336
OLG Köln	December 16, 1992	16 W 43/92	RIW 1993, 499 = XXI Y.B. Com. Arb. 535 (1996)	4.149
OLG Köln	March 31, 1995	19 U 197/94	NJW-RR 1995, 1463	4.45
OLG Köln	October 6, 2000	9 Sch 23/00	Unreported, available at http://www.disarb.org (last visited December 1, 2015)	6.217
OLG Köln	April 12, 2002	6 U 142/01	IPRspr. 2002, no 209, 540	5.11, 5.19, 5.59
OLG Köln	April 11, 2003	9 SchH 27/02	Unreported	3.147
OLG Köln	January 15, 2004	9 Sch 17/03	SchiedsVZ 2004, 269	6.87
OLG Köln	March 23, 2004	9 Sch 1/03	SchiedsVZ 2005, 163	6.228, 6.277
OLG Köln	March 30, 2004	9 Sch 02/04	Unreported, available at http://www.disarb.org (last visited December 1, 2015)	6.263
OLG Köln	July 5, 2005	9 U 190/04	MDR 2006, 201	2.16, 2.20, 2.21
OLG Köln	October 26, 2005	9 Sch 12/04	IPRspr. 2005, no 189, 521	2.119
OLG Köln	November 17, 2006	16 W 27/08	NJW-RR 2009, 1074	6.163
OLG Köln	March 20, 2008	18 U 98/07	Unreported	2.54
OLG Köln	June 28, 2011	19 Sch 11/10	SchiedsVZ 2012, 161	6.187, 6.208, 6.209, 6.221, 6.228, 6.244, 6.286

Court	Date	File No	Source	Para
OLG Köln	December 23, 2011	19 Sch 27/10	Unreported, available at http://www.disarb.org (last visited December 1, 2015)	6.228
OLG Köln	February 26, 2014	19 Sch 12/13	SchiedsVZ 2014, 203	6.323
OLG Köln	August 7, 2015	I-1 U 76/14, 1 U 76/14	SchiedsVZ 2015, 295	6.163, 6.164
OLG München	January 19, 1940	5 U 945/39	HRR 1940, no 627	6.220
OLG München	February 25, 1971	12 W 570/71	BB 1971, 886	3.93
OLG München	June 26, 1992	23 U 2229/92	NJW 1994, 527	4.45
OLG München	April 5, 1995	15 U 4943/94	NJW-RR 1996, 239	2.106
OLG München	May 30, 1996	21 W 1564/96	NJW-RR 1996, 926	5.50
OLG München	October 8, 1998	15 W 2631/98	CR 1999, 368	4.45
OLG München	October 26, 2000	U (K) 3208/00	NJW-RR 2001, 711 = SpuRt 2001, 64	5.11
OLG München	June 22, 2005	34 Sch 10/05	SchiedsVZ 2005, 308	6.191, 6.222
OLG München	July 26, 2005	31 Wx 50/05	GmbHR 2005, 1568	6.21, 6.45
OLG München	November 28, 2005	34 Sch 19/05	SchiedsVZ 2006, 111	6.320
OLG München	February 6, 2006	34 SchH 10/05	NJOZ 2006, 1194	3.142
OLG München	February 22, 2006	34 Sch 2/06	SchiedsVZ 2006, 165	6.278
OLG München	April 26, 2006	34 SchH 4/06	MDR 2006, 1308	3.26
OLG München	May 17, 2006	7 U 1781/08	WM 2006, 1556	2.57
OLG München	August 7, 2006	34 SchH 9/05	SchiedsVZ 2006, 286	3.140
OLG München	December 20, 2006	34 Sch 16/06	Unreported, available at http://www.disarb.org (last visited December 1, 2015) and at BeckRS 2007, 00913	3.110, 6.97, 6.215
OLG München	January 10, 2007	34 SchH 7/06	BeckRS 2007, 00709	3.140
OLG München	October 23, 2006	34 SchH 8/06	BeckRS 2006, 27806	3.146
OLG München	February 21, 2007	34 Sch 1/07	NZBau 2007, 311	6.40
OLG München	May 23, 2007	34 SchH 01/07	Unreported	2.20
OLG München	January 3, 2008	34 SchH 3/07	SchiedsVZ 2008, 102	3.125, 3.141, 3.142
OLG München	February 1, 2008	34 Sch 18/07	SchiedsVZ 2008, 151	6.277
OLG München	April 10, 2008	34 SchH 5/07	BeckRS 2008, 10261	3.126
OLG München	May 7, 2008	34 Sch 26/07	Unreported, available at http://www.disarb.org (last visited December 1, 2015)	6.224
OLG München	October 17, 2008	34 SchH 11/08	SchiedsVZ 2008, 307	2.177, 6.174
OLG München	January 28, 2009	34 Sch 22/08	SchiedsVZ 2009, 127	6.254, 6.265
OLG München	February 27, 2009	34 Sch 19/08	IPRspr. 2009, no 273, 703 = XXXV Y.B. Com. Arb. 365 (2010)	6.329
OLG München	May 11, 2009	34 Sch 23/08	SchiedsVZ 2009, 343 = XXXV Y.B. Com. Arb. 367 (2010)	6.305

(Contined)

Court	Date	File No	Source	Para
OLG München	June 18, 2009	34 SchH 3/09	NJOZ 2009, 4781	3.24
OLG München	June 22, 2009	34 Sch 26/08	SchiedsVZ 2010, 169 = XXXV Y.B. Com. Arb. 371 (2010)	6.209, 6.301, 6.329, 6.331
OLG München	October 12, 2009	34 Sch 20/08	SchiedsVZ 2009, 340 = XXXV Y.B. Com. Arb. 383 (2010)	2.69, 6.311
OLG München	October 29, 2009	34 Sch 15/09	Unreported, available at http://www.disarb.org (last visited December 1, 2015)	6.175
OLG München	November 12, 2009	34 Sch 17/09	Unreported, available at http://www.disarb.org (last visited December 1, 2015)	6.270
OLG München	November 23, 2009	34 Sch 13/09	SchiedsVZ 2010, 50 = XXXVI Y.B. Com. Arb. 273 (2011)	6.329
OLG München	January 5, 2010	34 Sch 7/07	Unreported, available at http://www.disarb.org (last visited December 1, 2015)	6.267
OLG München	January 29, 2010	34 SchH 11/09	SchiedsVZ 2010, 168	3.22
OLG München	February 3, 2010	34 Sch 24/09	SchiedsVZ 2010, 336	6.174, 6.329
OLG München	April 1, 2010	34 Sch 19/09	BeckRS 2010, 08692	6.174
OLG München	October 14, 2010	34 SchH 7/10	NJOZ 2011, 413	3.26, 3.167
OLG München	December 17, 2010	34 SchH 6/10	SchiedsVZ 2011, 107	3.149
OLG München	March 2, 2011	34 Sch 6/11	SchiedsVZ 2011, 167	6.101, 6.223, 6.226, 6.282
OLG München	March 14, 2011	34 Sch 8/10	SchiedsVZ 2011, 159	6.97, 6.208, 6.210, 6.222
OLG München	April 12, 2011	34 Sch 28/10	SchiedsVZ 2011, 230	4.25, 6.208, 6.209, 6.210
OLG München	July 11, 2011	34 Sch 15/10	SchiedsVZ 2011, 337	6.329
OLG München	November 14, 2011	34 Sch 10/11	SchiedsVZ 2012, 43 = XXXVII Y.B. Com. Arb. 231 (2012)	6.208, 6.210, 6.329
OLG München	December 16, 2011	34 Sch 30/11	Unreported, available at http://www.disarb.org (last visited December 1, 2015)	6.189
OLG München	January 23, 2012	34 Sch 33/11 (2), 34 Sch 33/11	SchiedsVZ 2012, 107	6.232
OLG München	February 29, 2012	34 SchH 6/11	SchiedsVZ 2012, 96	2.157, 6.175
OLG München	April 11, 2012	34 Sch 21/11	SchiedsVZ 2012, 156 = XXXIX Y.B. Com. Arb. 389 (2014)	6.66, 6.208, 6.209, 6.282, 6.329, 6.331
OLG München	June 12, 2012	34 Sch 7/10	SchiedsVZ 2012, 217	6.91, 6.106
OLG München	June 21, 2012	34 Sch 4/12	SchiedsVZ 2012, 287	6.73, 6.282, 6.329
OLG München	July 23, 2012	34 Sch 19/11	SchiedsVZ 2012, 282	4.35, 6.80

Court	Date	File No	Source	Para
OLG München	July 30, 2012	34 Sch 18/10	SchiedsVZ 2012, 339 = XXXIX Y.B. Com. Arb. 394 (2014)	6.264, 6.308, 6.314, 6.329
OLG München	November 19, 2012	34 Sch 7/11	SchiedsVZ 2013, 62	6.323, 6.331
OLG München	February 25, 2013	34 Sch 12/12	SchiedsVZ 2013, 230	6.94, 6.101
OLG München	March 27, 2013	34 Sch 27/10	SchiedsVZ 2013, 179	6.278, 6.327, 6.329
OLG München	September 10, 2013	34 SchH 10/13	RNotZ 2013, 639	2.88
OLG München	June 24, 2014	34 Sch 1/14, 34 Sch 1/2014	SchiedsVZ 2015, 205	6.266, 6.267
OLG München	January 12, 2015	34 Sch 17/13	IBRRS 2015, 0349	6.304
OLG München	January 15, 2015	U 1110/14 Kart	SchiedsVZ 2015, 40	6.322
OLG München	March 27, 2015	34 Sch 5/15	BeckRS 2015, 09565	6.263
OLG München	May 19, 2015	34 Sch 24/14	BeckRS 2015, 12786	6.276, 6.277, 6.278
OLG Naumburg	December 19, 2001	10 SchH 3/01	SchiedsVZ 2003, 134	3.119, 3.121, 3.132, 3.141
OLG Naumburg	February 21, 2002	10 Sch 8/01	NJW-RR 2003, 71	6.209
OLG Naumburg	May 19, 2003	10 SchH 01/03	SchiedsVZ 2003, 235	3.23, 3.26
OLG Naumburg	June 26, 2003	10 Sch 4/01	JurBüro 2003, 389	6.198
OLG Naumburg	May 21, 2004	10 Sch 06/03	Unreported, available at http://www.disarb.org (last visited December 1, 2015)	6.183
OLG Naumburg	June 8, 2010	10 Sch 2/10	SchiedsVZ 2010, 277	6.251, 6.254, 6.265
OLG Naumburg	March 4, 2011	10 Sch 4/10	SchiedsVZ 2011, 228	6.115, 6.208
OLG Neustadt	February 16, 1955	2 W 18/55	NJW 1955, 635	3.36
OLG Nürnberg	November 26, 1965	6 U 73/64	KTS 1966, 111	6.293
OLG Nürnberg	November 30, 2004	12 U 2881/04	SchiedsVZ 2005, 50	5.21
OLG Rostock	October 28, 1999	1 Sch 3/99	BB 2000, Beil. 8, p 20	6.329
OLG Rostock	November 22, 2001	1 Sch 3/2000, 1 Sch 3/00	IPRax 2002, 401	6.330
OLG Saarbrücken	May 17, 1990	7 W 7/90	BauR 1993, 348	5.46
OLG Saarbrücken	July 2, 1997	1 U 847/96	WM 1998, 833	6.116
OLG Saarbrücken	October 29, 2002	1 Sch 2/02	SchiedsVZ 2003, 92	6.18, 6.216
OLG Saarbrücken	February 27, 2007	4 Sch 1/07	SchiedsVZ 2007, 323	5.78, 5.98, 5.101, 5.102, 5.103, 5.105
OLG Saarbrücken	May 30, 2011	4 Sch 3/10	SchiedsVZ 2012, 47	6.209, 6.230, 6.322
OLG Schleswig	March 30, 2000	16 SchH 5/99	RIW 2000, 706	6.310
OLG Schleswig	July 15, 2003	16 Sch 1/03	SchiedsVZ 2003, 237 = XXX Y.B. Com. Arb. 524 (2005)	6.329, 6.330
OLG Schleswig	February 15, 2009	16 Sch 1/09	SchiedsVZ 2010, 276	6.226, 6.327, 6.329
OLG Stuttgart	October 21, 1927	563/27	JW 1928, 1322	3.119

(*Contined*)

Court	Date	File No	Source	Para
OLG Stuttgart	October 4, 2000	1 Sch 13/99	OLGR Stuttgart 2001, 50	2.79
OLG Stuttgart	December 20, 2001	1 Sch 13/01	BeckRS 2001, 30229524	6.146, 6.147
OLG Stuttgart	June 4, 2002	1 Sch 22/01	NJW-RR 2003, 1438 = BB 2002, Beil. 7, p 44	6.66, 6.101, 6.148, 6.268
OLG Stuttgart	July 16, 2002	1 Sch 8/02	SchiedsVZ 2003, 84	3.84, 3.111, 4.212, 6.230
OLG Stuttgart	October 13, 2008	1 Sch 02/08	SchiedsVZ 2009, 67	6.267
OLG Stuttgart	July 30, 2010	1 Sch 3/10	SchiedsVZ 2011, 49	6.187, 6.208
OLG Stuttgart	December 20, 2011	10 U 141/11	MDR 2012, 212	5.47
OLG Stuttgart	November 5, 2013	1 Sch 2/11	SchiedsVZ 2014, 307	6.254
LG Arnsberg	August 7, 2006	2 O 83/06	Unreported, available at http://www.disarb.org (last visited December 1, 2015)	3.178
LG Berlin	February 6, 2006	5 O 39/06	CaS 2006, 73	5.11
LG Berlin	June 8, 2011	94 OH 2/10	BeckRS 2012, 09512	5.9
LG Braunschweig	August 4, 2015	9 O 1494/15, 9 O 1494/15 (176)	SchiedsVZ 2015, 292	5.5
LG Dortmund	May 29, 2007	23 S 5/07	NJW-RR 2008, 441	2.103
LG Frankfurt	November 15, 2013	2-23 O 55/13	Unreported	2.126
LG Hamburg	July 27, 1990	70 O 56/89	RIW 1991, 419	6.189
LG Köln	January 15, 2013	29 O 159/12	NJW-RR 2013, 1273	3.163, 3.197, 3.199
LG Mönchen-gladbach	July 14, 2006	2 O 134/05	SchiedsVZ 2007, 104	3.178
LG München I	February 29, 2000	7 O 3106/00	IPRspr. 2000, no 182a, 396	5.11

GERMAN LABOR COURTS

Court	Date	File No	Source	Para
BAG	November 13, 2007	9 AZR 134/07	IPRspr. 2007, no 50, 166	2.56
BAG	May 19, 2010	5 AZR 253/09	NJW 2010, 2827	2.84
LAG Berlin-Brandenburg	February 16, 2011	4 Sa 2132/10	BB 2011, 2298	4.117
LAG Köln	July 11, 2001	8 TaBV 4/01	NZA-RR 2002, 270	3.136
LAG Köln	May 24, 2007	10 Sa 593/06	Unreported	2.56

GERMAN ADMINISTRATIVE COURTS

Court	Date	File No	Source	Para
VG Berlin	February 11, 2010	4 K 403.09	SchiedsVZ 2010, 107	3.137

ARBITRAL TRIBUNALS

Arbitral Tribunal	Date	File No	Source	Para
Schiedsgericht der IHK Kassel	December 15, 2004	01/04	SchiedsVZ 2006, 167	2.40
Court of Arbitration of the Hamburg Chamber of Commerce	May 5, 2009		SchiedsVZ 2010, 173	4.36

LIST OF ABBREVIATIONS

AAA	American Arbitration Association
ADR	Alternative Dispute Resolution
AG	*Amtsgericht* (German Local Court)/*Aktiengesellschaft* (Stock Corporation)
AGB	*Allgemeine Geschäftsbedingungen* (General Terms and Conditions)
AktG	*Aktiengesetz* (German Stock Corporation Act)
alt	alternative
Am. Rev. Int'l Arb.	The American Review of International Arbitration (journal)
Anh	*Anhang* (Appendix)
AnwBl	*Anwaltsblatt* (journal)
Arb. Int'l	Arbitration International (journal)
ArbGG	*Arbeitsgerichtsgesetz* (German Labor Court Act)
art/arts	article/articles
ASA Bull.	Bulletin of the Swiss Arbitration Association
BAG	*Bundesarbeitsgericht* (German Federal Labor Court)
BauR	*Baurecht* (journal)
BayObLG	*Bayerisches Oberstes Landesgericht* (Former Highest Regional Court of Bavaria)
BayObLGZ	*Sammlung der Entscheidungen des Bayerischen Obersten Landesgerichts in Zivilsachen* (Decisions of the Former Highest Regional Court of Bavaria in Civil Matters)
BB	*Betriebs-Berater* (journal)
BBG	*Bundesbeamtengesetz* (German Federal Public Officials Act)
BeckOGK	*Beck'scher Online-Großkommentar* (commentary)
BeckOK	*Beck'scher Online-Kommentar* (commentary)
BeckRS	*Beck-Rechtsprechung* (journal)
Beil.	*Beilage* (Supplement)
BGB	*Bürgerliches Gesetzbuch* (German Civil Code)
BGBl	*Bundesgesetzblatt* (Federal Law Gazette)
BGH	*Bundesgerichtshof* (German Federal Supreme Court)
BGHZ	*Entscheidungen des Bundesgerichtshofes in Zivilsachen* (Decisions of the German Federal Supreme Court in Civil Matters)
BNotO	*Bundesnotarordnung* (Federal Notary Code)
BRAGO	*Bundesrechtsanwaltsgebührenordnung* (Former German Federal Code on Attorneys' Fees)
BT-Drucks	*Bundestags-Drucksache* (Official Publication of the Bundestag)

BVerfG	*Bundesverfassungsgericht* (German Federal Constitutional Court)
BVerfGE	*Entscheidungen des Bundesverfassungsgerichts* (Decisions of the German Federal Constitutional Court)
CAS	Court of Arbitration for Sport
cf	*confer*
ch/chs	chapter/chapters
CISG	United Nations Convention on Contracts for the International Sale of Goods (April 11, 1980)
cl/cls	clause/clauses
DAJV	*Deutsch-Amerikanische Juristen-Vereinigung*
DAV	*Deutscher Anwaltverein* (German Bar Association)
DB	*Der Betrieb* (journal)
DIS	*Deutsche Institution für Schiedsgerichtsbarkeit* (German Institution of Arbitration)
DIS-Mat.	*DIS-Materialien*
DNotZ	*Deutsche Notar-Zeitschrift* (journal)
DÖV	*Die öffentliche Verwaltung* (journal)
DRB	*Deutscher Richterbund* (German Association of Judges)
DRiG	*Deutsches Richtergesetz* (German Judiciary Act)
DS	*Der Sachverständige* (journal)
DStR	*Deutsches Steuerrecht* (journal)
DZWIR	*Deutsche Zeitschrift für Wirtschafts- und Insolvenzrecht* (journal)
EC	European Community or European Communities
ECJ	European Court of Justice
ECR	European Court Reports
ed/eds	editor/editors
edn	edition
EEA	European Economic Area
EGBGB	*Einführungsgesetz zum Bürgerlichen Gesetzbuch* (Introductory Act to the German Civil Code)
EGZPO	*Gesetz, betreffend die Einführung der Zivilprozeßordnung* (Introductory Act to the German Code of Civil Procedure)
et seq.	*et sequens/sequentes*
etc	et cetera
EU	European Union
European Convention	The European Convention of 21 April 1961 on International Commercial Arbitration
EuZW	*Zeitschrift für Europäisches Wirtschaftsrecht* (journal)
EWiR	*Entscheidungen zum Wirtschaftsrecht* (journal)
FamFG	*Gesetz über das Verfahren in Familiensachen und in den Angelegenheiten der freiwilligen Gerichtsbarkeit* (German Act on Proceedings in Family Matters and in Matters of Non-contentious Jurisdiction)

FamRZ	*Zeitschrift für das gesamte Familienrecht* (journal)
fn(s)	footnote(s)
GbR	*Gesellschaft bürgerlichen Rechts* (Civil Law Partnership)
GDV	*Gesamtverband der Deutschen Versicherungswirtschaft* (German Insurance Association)
GG	*Grundgesetz* (German Constitution, "Basic Law")
GKG	*Gerichtskostengesetz* (German Court Costs Act)
GMAA	German Maritime Arbitration Association
GmbH	*Gesellschaft mit beschränkter Haftung* (Limited Liability Company)
GmbHG	*Gesetz betreffend die Gesellschaften mit beschränkter Haftung* (German Limited Liability Companies Act)
GmbHR	*GmbH-Rundschau* (journal)
Großkomm AktG	*Aktiengesetz Großkommentar*
GRUR	*Gewerblicher Rechtsschutz und Urheberrecht* (journal)
GVG	*Gerichtsverfassungsgesetz* (German Courts Constitution Act)
GWB	*Gesetz gegen Wettbewerbsbeschränkungen* (German Act Against Restraints of Competition)
HGB	*Handelsgesetzbuch* (German Commercial Code)
HRR	*Höchstrichterliche Rechtsprechung* (reporter)
IBA	International Bar Association
IBA Rules	IBA Rules on the Taking of Evidence in International Arbitration
IBR	Immobilien & Baurecht (journal)
IBRRS	*IBR-Rechtsprechung* (reporter)
ICC	International Chamber of Commerce
ICC Rules	Arbitration Rules of the International Chamber of Commerce, 2012 edition
ICCA	International Council for Commercial Arbitration
ICSID	International Centre for Settlement of Investment Disputes
IDR	Journal of International Dispute Resolution
ie	*id est*
IHK	*Industrie- und Handelskammer* (Chamber of Industry and Commerce)
IHR	*Internationales Handelsrecht* (journal)
InsO	*Insolvenzordnung* (German Insolvency Statute)
IPRax	*Praxis des internationalen Privat- und Verfahrensrechts* (journal)
IPRspr.	*Die deutsche Rechtsprechung auf dem Gebiete des internationalen Privatrechts* (reporter)
JR	*Juristische Rundschau* (journal)
JurBüro	*Das juristische Büro* (journal)

JuS	*Juristische Schulung* (journal)
JW	Juristische Wochenschrift (journal)
JZ	*Juristenzeitung* (journal)
KapMuG	*Gesetz über Musterverfahren in kapitalmarktrechtlichen Streitigkeiten* (German Capital Markets Model Case Act)
KG	*Kammergericht* (Berlin Higher Regional Court)/ *Kommanditgesellschaft* (Limited Commercial Partnership)
KTS	*Zeitschrift für Insolvenzrecht—Konkurs, Treuhand, Sanierung* (journal)
LCIA	London Court of International Arbitration
LCIA Rules	Arbitration Rules of the London Court of International Arbitration
LG	*Landgericht* (German Regional Court)
LM	*Das Nachschlagewerk des Bundesgerichtshofs in Zivilsachen, Lindenmaier and Möhring* (eds) (reporter)
LMK	*Kommentierte BGH-Rechtsprechung Lindenmaier-Möhring*
LZ	*Leipziger Zeitschrift* (journal)
M&A	Mergers & Acquisitions
MAC	Material Adverse Change
MDR	*Monatsschrift für Deutsches Recht* (journal)
MediationsG	*Mediationsgesetz* (German Mediation Act)
Model Law	UNCITRAL Model Law on International Commercial Arbitration, 1985 (with amendments as adopted in 2006)
MünchKommAktG	*Münchener Kommentar zum Aktiengesetz*
MünchKommBGB	*Münchener Kommentar zum Bürgerlichen Gesetzbuch*
MünchKommGmbHG	*Münchener Kommentar zum Gesetz betreffend die Gesellschaften mit beschränkter Haftung (GmbHG)*
MünchKommHGB	*Münchener Kommentar zum Handelsgesetzbuch*
MünchKommZPO	*Münchener Kommentar zur Zivilprozessordnung*
NJW	*Neue Juristische Wochenschrift* (journal)
NJW-RR	*NJW-Rechtsprechungs-Report Zivilrecht* (reporter)
no/nos	number/numbers
NVwZ	*Neue Zeitschrift für Verwaltungsrecht* (journal)
NVwZ-RR	*Neue Zeitschrift für Verwaltungsrecht Rechtsprechungs-Report* (reporter)
NYC	New York Convention
NZBau	*Neue Zeitschrift für Baurecht* (journal)
NZG	*Neue Zeitschrift für Gesellschaftsrecht* (journal)
oHG	*Offene Handelsgesellschaft* (General Commercial Partnership)
OLG	*Oberlandesgericht* (German Higher Regional Court)
OLGR	*OLG-Report* (journal)
OLGRspr.	*Die Rechtsprechung der Oberlandesgerichte auf dem Gebiete des Zivilrechts* (reporter)

p/pp	page/pages
para/paras	paragraph/paragraphs
PatG	*Patentgesetz* (German Patent Act)
ref	reference(s)
Rev arb	*Revue de l'arbitrage* (journal)
RG	*Reichsgericht* (Supreme Court of the German Reich until 1945)
RGBl	*Reichsgesetzblatt* (Imperial Law Gazette)
RGZ	*Entscheidungen des Reichsgerichts in Zivilsachen* (Decisions of the Supreme Court of the German Reich in Civil Matters)
RIW	*Recht der Internationalen Wirtschaft* (journal)
r+s	*Recht und Schaden* (journal)
RVG	*Gesetz über die Vergütung der Rechtsanwältinnen und Rechtsanwälte* (German Law on the Remuneration of Attorneys)
s/ss	section/sections
SchiedsVZ	*Zeitschrift für Schiedsverfahren* (German Arbitration Journal)
SL Bau	*Streitlösungsordnung für das Bauwesen* (Regulation of Dispute Resolution for Construction)
SOBau	*Schlichtungs- und Schiedsordnung für Baustreitigkeiten* (Conciliation and Arbitration Rules for Construction Disputes)
SpuRt	*Zeitschrift für Sport und Recht* (journal)
SRCoLD	DIS Supplementary Rules for Corporate Law Disputes 2009
StGB	*Strafgesetzbuch* (German Criminal Code)
StPO	*Strafprozeßordnung* (German Code of Criminal Procedure)
suppl	supplement
TDM	Transnational Dispute Management (journal)
TFEU	Treaty on the Functioning of the European Union
UINL	International Union of Notaries
UK	United Kingdom
UmwG	*Umwandlungsgesetz* (German Transformation Act)
UNCITRAL	United Nations Commission on International Trade Law
US	United States
USC	United States Code
UWG	*Gesetz gegen den unlauteren Wettbewerb* (German Act Against Unfair Competition)
v.	*versus*
VersR	*Versicherungsrecht* (journal)
Vol	Volume
VwGO	*Verwaltungsgerichtsordnung* (German Code of Administrative Court Procedure)

WpHG	*Gesetz über den Wertpapierhandel* (German Securities Trading Act)
WM	*Wertpapier-Mitteilungen, Zeitschrift für Wirtschafts- und Bankrecht* (journal)
Y.B. Com. Arb.	Yearbook of Commercial Arbitration (journal)
ZD	*Zeitschrift für Datenschutz* (journal)
ZfRV	*Zeitschrift für Rechtsvergleichung* (journal)
ZGR	*Zeitschrift für Unternehmens- und Gesellschaftsrecht* (journal)
ZIP	*Zeitschrift für Wirtschaftsrecht* (journal)
ZPO	*Zivilprozessordnung* (German Code of Civil Procedure)
ZVertriebsR	*Zeitschrift für Vertriebsrecht* (journal)
ZZP	*Zeitschrift für Zivilprozess* (journal)
ZZPInt	*Zeitschrift für Zivilprozess International* (journal)

1

INTRODUCTION

Markus S. Rieder/Richard Kreindler

In this introductory chapter, after a brief overview (paras 1.2 *et seq.*), we explore commercial arbitration in Germany against the background of German state court litigation (paras 1.9 *et seq.*), before we address key features of the German arbitration law (paras 1.30 *et seq.*). In a next step, we look at potential advantages and disadvantages of arbitration compared to German state court litigation (paras 1.47 *et seq.*). In this chapter, we also address special types of arbitration (paras 1.77 *et seq.*) and means of alternative dispute resolution (paras 1.84 *et seq.*). **1.1**

A. Overview

Before addressing more deeply the substance of commercial arbitration in Germany, it is worth recalling the notion of arbitration (para 1.3), including the meaning of "commercial" arbitration (paras 1.4 *et seq.*). In this overview, we also provide a brief history of arbitration in Germany (para 1.6) and certain key statistics (paras 1.7 *et seq.*). **1.2**

I. The Notion of Arbitration

Arbitration is the final and **binding resolution** of a dispute by a **neutral decision-maker** appointed pursuant to an **agreement of the parties** and to the **exclusion** **1.3**

of the state courts.[1] This definition contains the following elements: Arbitration relates to the resolution of a specific dispute between the parties, s 1029 para 1 ZPO. Furthermore, arbitration is generally conditioned on an agreement of the parties, s 1029 para 1 ZPO.[2] The agreement to submit to arbitration constitutes an exclusion of the jurisdiction of the ordinary courts, s 1032 para 1 ZPO. Arbitration is intended to result in a binding resolution of the dispute by way of a decision (award) which has the same effects as a final court judgment, s 1055 ZPO. The decision is final and subject to only limited scrutiny on largely procedural grounds which are not meant to entail a *de novo* review of the substance of the underlying decision, s 1059 ZPO.

II. Commercial Arbitration

1.4 "Commercial" arbitration refers to arbitration related to civil law disputes between the parties, including merchants or similar persons, as opposed to public law arbitration and public international law (especially investment treaty-based) arbitration on the one hand and consumer arbitration on the other hand.[3]

1.5 The parties to a commercial arbitration may be individuals, legal entities and states, state-owned entities, and sub-entities of a state with separate legal personality (districts, municipalities, etc). Since the legal regime is the same for commercial and consumer arbitration (apart from the form requirements for arbitration agreements), these two forms of arbitration usually do not need to be distinguished.

III. A Brief History of Arbitration in Germany

1.6 The earliest forms of arbitration go back centuries and thus can be found in every era.[4] Indeed, the state court system also has its roots in ad hoc tribunals based on consent.[5] Present-day arbitration in Germany has its roots in the **1879 version of the ZPO,**[6] which—as far as arbitration is concerned—for more than one hundred years remained substantially unchanged.[7] In 1997, the Tenth Book of the ZPO underwent fundamental change in order to adapt it to the **UNCITRAL Model**

---

[1] Lachmann, paras 1–8; Kreindler/Schäfer/Wolff, para 5; Lionnet/Lionnet, p 48; Geimer, in: Zöller (ed), Vor s 1025 para 1; Gaillard/Savage, paras 12 *et seq.*

[2] With the exception of certain instances of extra-contractual arbitration, eg by way of will (s 1066 ZPO).

[3] Kreindler/Schäfer/Wolff, paras 23 *et seq.*; Lachmann, paras 1, 13 *et seq.*; Lionnet/Lionnet, pp 43 *et seq.*; Gaillard/Savage, paras 58 *et seq.*

[4] Münch, in: MünchKommZPO, s 1025 paras 97 *et seq.* For a more in-depth discussion of the history of arbitration in Germany, see Krause, *Die geschichtliche Entwicklung des Schiedsgerichtswesens in Deutschland*, Berlin 1930. Internationally see Born, pp 6 *et seq.*; Blackaby/Partasides/Redfern/Hunter, paras 1.13 *et seq.*

[5] Böckstiegel/Kröll/Nacimiento, in: *Arbitration in Germany*, p 4 para 1.

[6] RGBl 1877, 83.

[7] Böckstiegel/Kröll/Nacimiento, in: *Arbitration in Germany*, p 4 para 2.

Law on International Commercial Arbitration of 1985.[8] Since then, only minor amendments have been made. The intention in revising the former law was to **strengthen the attractiveness** of Germany as a locale for international arbitration, to place arbitration tribunals on a statutory footing equivalent to state courts, and to strengthen the cooperation between tribunals and courts.[9]

IV. Selected Statistics

It is difficult to provide reliable statistics on German arbitration. There are no credible overall numbers on arbitration. For instance, there are **no reliable statistics** on the number of ad hoc arbitral proceedings in Germany. Estimates in the range of 1,000 ad hoc proceedings per annum are not uncommon.[10] With regard to institutional arbitral proceedings, the German Institution of Arbitration (DIS) publishes certain statistics on an annual basis. Since 2007, the total number of new proceedings filed with the DIS was between approximately 100 and 180 per annum.[11] By comparison, the total number of new proceedings filed with the ICC since 2007 was in a range between approximately 600 and 800 new cases per annum, with a significant portion of the parties coming from Germany.[12] **1.7**

Overall, these statistics, within their limitations, provide two indications: on the one hand, arbitration is still somewhat uncommon compared with the overall number of state court proceedings;[13] on the other hand, arbitration is clearly on the rise in Germany. **1.8**

B. Commercial Arbitration in Germany against the Background of German State Court Litigation

While clearly distinct from litigation in German state courts, the way in which arbitration in Germany is approached and practiced, particularly by German parties and counsel, can be considerably influenced by particular concepts and notions embedded in or otherwise inspired by German litigation. By extension, it behoves parties and counsel from outside of Germany to be sufficiently familiar with the structure of the German legal and court system (paras 1.11 *et seq.*) and **1.9**

---

[8] BGBl 1997 I p 3224; Schütze, para 22 with further references.

[9] BT-Drucks 13/5274, p 1; Gottwald/Adolphsen, DStR 1998, 1017; Kreindler/Mahlich, NJW 1998, 563.

[10] Wilske, in: *Arbitration in Germany*, pp 727, 730 para 3; Hanefeld, in: Weigand (ed), 2nd edn, para 7.09.

[11] Statistics on an annual basis available at www.disarb.org (last visited December 1, 2015).

[12] Pörnbacher/Baur, BB 2011, 2627; statistics available at www.iccwbo.org (last visited December 1, 2015).

[13] In 2012, the German local courts (AG) dealt with more than 1.1 million commercial cases, the regional courts (LG) more than 350,000 (as court of first instance); statistics available at www.destatis.de (last visited December 1, 2015).

certain relevant German legal traditions and practices which frequently play a role, directly or indirectly, in German state court litigation (paras 1.13 *et seq.*).

1.10 Inasmuch as many arbitration practitioners in Germany have grown up with these court-inspired traditions, German parties and counsel often tend, consciously or for that matter unconsciously, to import them into their approach to arbitration procedure and substance, indeed even if German substantive law does not apply. This tendency is encountered particularly in disputes where one or more current or retired state court judges are appointed as arbitrators, who may approach the arbitration wholly or partly in a manner similar to a court proceeding. Foreign parties and counsel should be prepared for and be able to recognize such tendencies, which we now briefly describe in this section.

I. Overview of the German Legal and Court System

1.11 The German legal system is divided into **federal and state law**. Most aspects of German commercial law are regulated by federal laws, such as the laws of contracts, property and torts, the laws of commercial transactions, corporate law, and the law of civil procedure. In addition, there are municipal ordinances. Overlaying these laws is the **German Basic Law**, or Constitution (GG). Furthermore, **European law** constitutes part of German law, fitting into different layers in the legal hierarchy (partly on a par with or even superseding the German Basic Law, partly "between" the German Constitution and German federal law).

1.12 The German court system is an integrated **state/federal system**. The courts of first instance in civil matters are state courts called **local courts** (AG), which are intended for smaller claims (eg monetary claims up to €5,000), and **regional courts** (LG) for all other claims. Likewise, the German **higher regional courts** (OLG) are state courts. A further appeal based solely on legal grounds is available to the **German Federal Supreme Court** (BGH). To the extent German arbitration law provides for the jurisdiction of state courts with respect to matters of arbitration, the OLG designated in the arbitration agreement or, in the absence of such designation, the OLG in the district within which the seat of the arbitration is located has jurisdiction (s 1062 ZPO). For example, such OLG has jurisdiction over the appointment or challenge of an arbitrator, the termination of mandate of an arbitrator, the declaration whether arbitral proceedings are permissible, and the setting aside of arbitral awards (s 1062 para 1 ZPO).

II. Relevant German Legal Traditions and Practices

1.13 Obviously, Germany, like any other country, has a host of legal traditions, and their enumeration would be beyond the scope both of this work and of what is relevant to our readers. In the context of commercial arbitration in Germany, the traditions and practices most relevant to practitioners from outside Germany include the following: the concept of codified law (para 1.14); the lack of binding precedent (no stare decisis, paras 1.15 *et seq.*); the strong emphasis on written pleadings in German state court litigation and the primacy of a corresponding concept called "*Relationstechnik*" (paras 1.17 *et seq.*); the strong disinclination toward pre-trial discovery and extensive document disclosure (paras 1.24 *et seq.*); and the traditionally proactive role of state court judges in conducting and deciding state court disputes and in attempting to settle them amicably (paras 1.27 *et seq.*).

1. Codified Law

German law is largely codified in comprehensive federal acts of law, such as the German Civil Code (BGB), the German Commercial Code (HGB), the German Penal Code (StGB), the German Code of Civil Procedure (ZPO), and the German Code of Criminal Procedure (StPO). These codes date from the nineteenth century and are considered to be exemplary exercises in legal craftsmanship. They often exhibit a **high level of abstraction**, such as in particular the German Civil Code and the German Commercial Code. It is a fundamental belief that in principle the answer to any legal issue can be found by reference to the codified law, either by interpreting the codified law or by extending it via analogy and other means of legal methodology to the concrete situation. As might be expected, this school of thought is also consistently reflected in the weight accorded to the codified law in written pleadings in arbitration authored by German practitioners. **1.14**

2. No Binding Precedent, No Stare Decisis

The German legal system does not adhere to the concept of binding precedent of decisions. Rather, in principle each German court, irrespective of its rung in the court hierarchy, is at liberty to decide a case as it considers correct under the law. Indeed, lower courts are not bound by prior decisions of higher courts in another case. At the same time, a precedent does have a certain **factually persuasive force** in Germany. At a minimum, lower court judges are not particularly interested in the overturning or reversal of their decisions by a higher court on the grounds that the lower court judges failed or refused to apply an interpretation of the law which that higher court is known to have applied or endorsed. **1.15**

Transposed from the state court context to arbitration, this generally means that an arbitral tribunal with its seat in Germany (and indeed elsewhere) is not bound to apply any German civil court precedent, and that this perception is even further entrenched in German arbitral practice than in most common law seats of arbitration. At the same time, many leading German arbitrators consider it to be self-evident that parties to the arbitration should be entitled to expect that the arbitral tribunal will strongly consider and indeed heed the precedent of the BGH. **1.16**

3. Emphasis on Written Pleadings and the "Relationstechnik"

Civil proceedings in German state courts rely heavily on written pleadings, especially when compared to many common law jurisdictions. The basic idea in German civil proceedings is that the case should be thoroughly pleaded and "fully **1.17** developed" in writing, without the use of significant pre-trial discovery, and that oral hearings are reserved for a **judge-driven** discussion of contentious issues and for the taking of witness evidence, with the role and length of such evidence-taking often quite modest by common law standards. By contrast, there is no requirement that a document must be introduced in the hearing in order to form part of the formal record or the like, and indeed particularly the formalism of US trials pursuant to the US Federal Rules of Evidence or comparable US state codes is largely unknown in German court practice.

1.18 As "unformalistic" as German oral court proceedings can be, the written proceedings in German court practice follow a **particularized pleading standard** which tends to be more stringent and even demanding than in many common law jurisdictions. Thus, US-style "notice pleading" with little to no **"substantiation" requirements** is insufficient in a German court pleading, and indeed a failure to adequately "substantiate" a claim, the basis for liability and the quantification of damages can lead to dismissal on the merits, even after the initial pleading, on the basis of lack of substantiation.[14]

1.19 Particularized pleading means, among other things, that each factual assertion is to be pleaded with sufficient specificity as to "who did what and when and why," to the extent reasonably possible for the party bearing the burden of substantiation. Here, again the presumption is that the party already "knows" its case at the beginning and will not be able to rely on discovery later on to fill in or optimize major factual or evidentiary gaps. Regarding factual assertions that could be denied or contested by the opposing side, it is customary and necessary to include, even in the initial pleading, **specific offers of evidence** on an assertion-by-assertion basis, most frequently in the form of a specific document that is meant to prove the assertion or an available fact witness who needs to be "offered" by furnishing his or her name and summonable address.

1.20 The foregoing can and does demand a certain **"front-loading"** of preparation of the claimant's case factually, legally, and ultimately tactically in a manner not frequently encountered in common law-influenced "notice pleading." By extension, a commensurately "front-loaded" statement of complaint may be seen as putting a procedural and tactical onus on the respondent party to file a statement of defense, with or without counterclaim, containing a corresponding degree of substantiation.

1.21 In a typical German court proceeding based on detailed written pleadings, it is the task of the state court judge to **structure the adjudication** by ensuring the submission of comprehensive statements regarding all relevant facts and the proper applications, or "prayers," for relief. In particular, the German judge is tasked with structuring the factual allegations of both parties by testing their relevance for the

[14] Schellhammer, paras 366 *et seq.*

outcome of the case. Where an alleged fact is uncontested, it is to be taken as true (s 138 para 3 ZPO). Where it is contested, the question is whether the party bearing the burden of proof has made sufficiently "substantiated" allegations and additionally has offered one or more elements of admissible evidence. This structuring exercise is called ***"Relationstechnik,"*** which is considered to be an important technique in achieving **judicial economy**.[15]

Only to the extent these requirements have been fulfilled will, as a next step, the judge proceed to consider and assess such evidence. Consequently, in German court proceedings, it is not possible for a party unilaterally to "put on" witnesses at a hearing unless the judge has been convinced that the prospective testimony is susceptible of being sufficiently related to already substantiated allegations of a party and, additionally, that such testimony is therefore relevant for the outcome of the case. **1.22**

German arbitration practitioners often use an approach to arbitral proceedings that is heavily influenced by the above concepts of state court litigation. It is readily imaginable how this approach can lead to potential **"disconnects"** in an international arbitration, particularly involving one German and one common law party or counsel. **1.23**

4. No Pre-trial Discovery and Only Limited Document Disclosure

The notion of pre-trial discovery, particularly in the US sense of potentially extensive fact-finding efforts prior to trial (including, eg, oral depositions, written interrogatories and requests for admission, and especially requests for production of documents), is alien to German state court proceedings in civil matters. Instead, the German paradigm, also to be found in many other jurisdictions, is that a party is expected to access and assemble any and all information and documentation which it requires **before bringing a lawsuit**, and to assume that it will be confined to that universe of information in order to present and substantiate its case. At the same time, German law provides for only **limited legal means** to access and assemble such information and documentation, and notably that which may not already be in the party's possession, custody, or control. **1.24**

Relatively recently, this paradigm foreclosing pre-trial discovery has been somewhat altered, and effectively softened, by the amendment of a provision of the ZPO **(s 142 ZPO)** which now allows the state court to order disclosure of specific documents that, as effectively implemented, the court deems to be relevant to the case and material to its outcome.[16] In current practice, German courts still differ significantly in applying this provision, and in any event, this provision still does not allow document production requests which are deemed to have as their purpose **1.25**

15 Trappe, SchiedsVZ 2013, 167, 168 *et seq.*; Pantle/Kreissl, paras 308 *et seq.*, 659 *et seq.*
16 Prütting, AnwBl 2008, 153; Kuhn/Löhr, JR 2011, 369.

or focus the "mere" ascertainment, or "discovery," of potentially relevant evidence (**no "fishing expeditions"**).[17]

1.26 Many domestic arbitration practitioners in Germany, whether as counsel or also as arbitrator, directly or indirectly subscribe to and seek to implement this type of restrictive approach to discovery and, in particular, document disclosure in the arbitration context.[18] Not surprisingly, such efforts often give rise to misunderstandings and for that matter friction between parties or between a party and the arbitral tribunal, all the more so where a US- or UK-inspired procedural background is at play.[19]

5. Active Role of Judges in Conducting the Proceedings

1.27 Traditionally, German state court judges in civil matters play a much more active role in conducting and indeed steering the proceedings, and notably the **taking of evidence**, than judges generally in most common law-influenced jurisdictions. The German judge is expected and obliged to **actively structure the case** (cf para 1.21), to prepare for and steer the oral hearings, and to conduct (and not just to "supervise") the questioning of witnesses and experts (s 139 ZPO). Generally, German judges disfavor and look with a jaundiced eye on the utility of aggressive and tactically structured cross-examination of adverse witnesses by counsel.

1.28 As a matter of law, at all stages of the proceedings, German judges are also meant, of their own accord, to take any and all appropriate steps toward resolving the dispute by **amicable settlement** (s 278 para 1 ZPO). To that end, German judges may even make **unsolicited assessments** of the strengths and weaknesses of the merits of the claims and propound unsolicited settlement proposals to the parties with greater or lesser degrees of commercial specificity.[20]

1.29 In view of the foregoing, when serving as arbitrators, active or retired German state court judges may well exhibit a similarly proactive or even activist approach to the conduct of the arbitration. Likewise, many arbitration practitioners in Germany may tend to adopt a similarly active style in their role as arbitrators or, for that matter, expect such active style from the arbitrators—which may again be a matter of serious disconnect with parties, counsel, and arbitrators with a common law background.

---

[17] Stadler, in: Musielak/Voit (eds), s 142 para 3; Greger, in: Zöller (ed), s 142 para 2.

[18] Trappe, SchiedsVZ 2013, 167, 168.

[19] As we will explore in more detail in paras 4.115 *et seq.*, the IBA Rules on the Taking of Evidence in International Arbitration (2010), and in particular art 4 respecting requests for production of documents, are considered by many practitioners to offer a satisfactory compromise between approaches. They can thus serve as a tool of choice to bridge gaps in understanding or approach respecting the permissible extent of taking of evidence in international arbitrations.

[20] Cf s 278 para 6 ZPO which provides, in part, that a settlement may be achieved by the court making a settlement proposal and the parties accepting such proposal by means of a written submission to the court.

C. Key Features of the German Arbitration Law

The German legal background to arbitration is shaped by its constitutional and statutory legal basis (paras 1.31 *et seq.*). The statutory basis in the Tenth Book of the ZPO, while overwhelmingly rooted in the UNCITRAL Model Law, has a number of features and particularities which are worth exploring, including in contrast to other Model Law jurisdictions (paras 1.34 *et seq.*). At the same time, as in those venues and others, the most important general legal principles applicable to arbitration in Germany are party autonomy, neutrality, equal treatment, the right to be heard, and procedural efficiency (paras 1.39 *et seq.*). **1.30**

I. The Constitutional and Statutory Legal Basis under German Law

The German Constitution, the "Basic Law" (GG) does not contain any express provisions on arbitration. German courts have recognized that the German Constitution nevertheless **clearly allows for arbitration** as long as the fundamental principles of neutrality, equal treatment, and the right to be heard are upheld.[21] Thus, there is no doubt that arbitration as such, with its effect of ousting the jurisdiction of the otherwise competent state courts, is a constitutional means of dispute resolution leading to a binding result. **1.31**

The German arbitration law, which in its current version entered into force on January 1, 1998, is contained in the **Tenth Book of the ZPO**, entitled "Arbitral Proceedings." Pursuant to the legislative materials, arbitration is considered to be **principally equivalent** to state court litigation.[22] The Tenth Book follows closely the 1985 UNCITRAL Model Law and contains ten sub-chapters addressing general provisions on arbitral proceedings seated in Germany, the arbitration agreement, the constitution of the arbitral tribunal, the jurisdiction of the arbitral tribunal, the conduct of arbitral proceedings, the making of the award and termination of proceedings, recourse against the award, the recognition and enforcement of awards, state court proceedings related to arbitration, and extra-contractual arbitral tribunals. **1.32**

Many if indeed not most provisions of the Tenth Book, consistent with the overall concept of the Model Law, are subject to **derogation** by more specific or otherwise different party agreement. A certain few of the provisions, however, are **mandatory** (s 1042 para 3 ZPO), which we will address in the later chapters of this book.[23] **1.33**

---

21 BVerfGE 21, 139, 145 *et seq.* = NJW 1967, 1123; BGHZ 65, 59, 61 = NJW 1976, 109.

22 BT-Drucks 13/5274, p 34.

23 For instance in ss 1025 para 1, 1029–1031, 1042 para 2, 1046 para 1, 1047 paras 2 and 3, 1048 para 4 cl 1, 1049 para 3 and 1066 ZPO; cf Saenger, in: Saenger (ed), s 1042 para 14.

II. Noteworthy Features of the German Arbitration Law

1.34 Notwithstanding its quite strict adherence to the wording and spirit of the Model Law, the German arbitration law does contain certain noteworthy deviations in reflection of German arbitration and indeed litigation practice.[24]

1.35 *First*, the German arbitration law foresees a **relatively strong potential role of state courts** in assisting the arbitral tribunal and supervising the arbitral proceedings. For instance, s 1032 para 2 ZPO allows each party to petition the competent state court for a determination that the arbitral proceedings based on a particular arbitration agreement are admissible or inadmissible (for more detail, see para 2.142).

1.36 *Second*, unlike certain other national arbitration statutes such as those of France and Switzerland, as a general matter the German arbitration law makes **no distinction** between so-called **domestic and international** commercial arbitration;[25] nor does the law distinguish between commercial and non-commercial matters. However, the German law does contain separate provisions which distinguish between the enforcement of domestic arbitral awards on the one hand (s 1060 ZPO) and the recognition and enforcement of foreign arbitral awards (s 1061 ZPO) on the other (for more detail, see para 6.246).

1.37 *Third*, as regards form requirements, German arbitration law is in some respects **more flexible than the 1985 Model Law**. For instance, pursuant to s 1031 para 2 ZPO the form requirement of s 1031 para 1 ZPO can be met even if the arbitration agreement is contained in a document transmitted "in one direction" by one party to another party, or by a third party to both parties. Primarily, this applies to so-called commercial letters of confirmation.[26]

1.38 *Fourth*, German law stipulates a greater **number of exceptions to the territoriality principle** than does the Model Law. Pursuant to s 1025 para 2 ZPO, certain provisions apply even if the place of arbitration is outside of Germany. In addition, s 1025 para 3 ZPO fills a gap in legal protection and determines that as long as the seat of arbitration has not yet been determined, the German courts shall be competent to exercise the court tasks designated in ss 1034, 1035, 1037, and 1038 ZPO, provided the respondent or the claimant has its registered seat or habitual place of residence in Germany.[27]

III. Overview of Applicable General Legal Principles

1.39 Like most legal systems, German law foresees a basic set of general legal principles applicable to all commercial arbitration proceedings seated in Germany, namely

---

[24] See also Schumacher, BB 1998, 6, 8 *et seq.*

[25] Hanefeld, in: Weigand (ed), 2nd edn, para 7.03.

[26] Hanefeld, in: Weigand (ed), 2nd edn, para 7.12. For details see below para 2.25.

[27] Böckstiegel/Kröll/Nacimiento, in: *Arbitration in Germany*, p 8 para 14; Geimer, in: Zöller (ed), s 1025 para 18; Voit, in: Musielak/Voit (eds), s 1025 para 6.

party autonomy (para 1.40), neutrality (paras 1.41 *et seq.*), equal treatment and the right to be heard (paras 1.43 *et seq.*), and procedural efficiency (paras 1.45 *et seq.*).

1. *Party Autonomy*

Party autonomy is one of the **most important and fundamental principles** of commercial arbitration, including in Germany, s 1042 para 4 ZPO.[28] It is limited only by mandatory law and ordre public considerations.[29] The ability of the parties to shape the rules for the conduct of a commercial dispute is one of the key advantages of arbitration over state court litigation (paras 1.55 *et seq.*). **1.40**

2. *Neutrality*

As a matter of constitutional law (see above para 1.31), commercial arbitration in Germany is also governed by the principle of neutrality (impartiality and independence).[30] Neutrality is a key requirement both for the constitution of the arbitral tribunal (paras 3.112 *et seq.*) and the conduct of the arbitral proceedings (paras 4.207 *et seq.*). There is a **public interest,** not merely an interest of the parties, in following the principle of neutrality.[31] **1.41**

In keeping with this principle, s **1034 para 2 ZPO** provides for a procedure to rectify the composition of an arbitral tribunal that results from an arbitration agreement which allows one party to outweigh the other to its disadvantage in constituting the arbitral tribunal (paras 3.35 *et seq.*). Also, the principle of neutrality prohibits the appointment of the entire arbitral tribunal by only one party.[32] Arbitrators who are not impartial are subject to challenge and removal pursuant to the procedure set forth in s 1037 ZPO (paras 3.134 *et seq.*). **1.42**

3. *Equal Treatment and the Right to be Heard*

Equal treatment and the right to be heard is the third basic principle of commercial arbitration in Germany, ss 1042 para 1, 1047 para 3, 1059 para 2 ZPO.[33] Equal treatment (paras 4.19 *et seq.*) is relevant, eg, regarding the **allotment of time** for written and oral submissions and examination of witnesses. At the same time, it is not simply an arithmetic exercise of granting equal time, and it is to be seen in the overall context of the considerable procedural discretion bestowed on the arbitral tribunal, including in deciding whether, how and to what extent to admit requests **1.43**

---

[28] Böckstiegel/Kröll/Nacimiento, in: *Arbitration in Germany*, p 31 paras 86 *et seq.*; Geimer, in: Zöller (ed), Vor s 1025 para 3, s 1042 para 22; Lachmann, paras 213, 1376–1379; Lionnet/Lionnet, p 42.

[29] Böckstiegel/Kröll/Nacimiento, in: *Arbitration in Germany*, p 17 para 38 with further references; Geimer, in: Zöller (ed), s 1042 para 1; Münch, in: MünchKommZPO, s 1042 paras 6 *et seq.*

[30] Böckstiegel/Kröll/Nacimiento, in: *Arbitration in Germany*, p 29 paras 74 *et seq.*; Geimer, in: Zöller (ed), s 1036 para 1; Kreindler/Schäfer/Wolff, para 523; Lionnet/Lionnet, p 244; Münch, in: MünchKommZPO, s 1036 paras 1 *et seq.*

[31] BGHZ 98, 70, 72 = NJW 1998, 3027.

[32] BGHZ 54, 392, 396 *et seq.* = NJW 1971, 139.

[33] BGHZ 85, 288 = NJW 1983, 867; BGHZ 96, 40 = NJW 1986, 1436, 1438.

for taking of evidence. Indeed depending upon the particular facts and circumstances, equal treatment can still be upheld, including in the German concept, if all parties are treated equally but not to the satisfaction of any one of them.

1.44 The right to be heard (paras 4.22 *et seq.*) can be violated in a number of different ways, one frequently problematic area being undisclosed ***ex parte* communications** between a party and an arbitrator.[34] In German court practice, the prohibition on *ex parte* communications is often not viewed as strictly as often experienced in Anglo-American practice. Thus, some German arbitration practitioners tend to attempt or conduct *ex parte* communications with the arbitrator appointed by their party, or even with the presiding arbitrator, although not necessarily for illicit purposes. At the same time, this is a practice that can only be discouraged.

4. Procedural Efficiency

1.45 Efficiency of the arbitral proceedings is a fundamental goal of commercial arbitration in Germany, although not per se a mandate.[35] Indeed there is frequently a potential **tension** between resolving a dispute **expeditiously** and deciding it **correctly**. Express statutory implementations of the efficiency principle can be found in:

- ss 1032 para 3, 1037 para 3 cl 2, 1040 para 3 cl 3 ZPO, allowing the arbitral proceedings to progress notwithstanding the pendency of a decision of the state court regarding the permissibility of arbitration or the challenge of an arbitrator;
- ss 1027, 1031 para 6, 1040 para 2 ZPO, providing for waiver of rights in the event of a failure to timely object;
- ss 1046, 1048 ZPO, regulating the consequences of the failure or refusal of a party to meet deadlines or to appear; and
- s 1039 ZPO, providing for a vacancy on the arbitral tribunal to be filled by an alternate candidate, rather than declaring that the arbitral mandate and the validity of the arbitration agreement cease to exist (which was the solution under the previous Tenth Book).

1.46 Apart from and beyond these specific statutory implementations of the efficiency principle, efficiency is a key consideration in arbitration practice today in Germany, especially when considered as an alternative to state court litigation with an expectation of greater speed. A perception has arisen at many German companies, probably not unlike companies elsewhere, that arbitration is becoming **increasingly institutionalized and complex**, that proceedings are too long, that arbitrators are not necessarily sufficiently prepared and, above all, that the taking of evidence and especially document disclosure ("discovery") have found undue acceptance and created unnecessary burdens not previously known in German practice.[36]

---

[34] Böckstiegel/Kröll/Nacimiento, in: *Arbitration in Germany*, pp 14 *et seq.*, paras 31, 34, 39.

[35] Lachmann, paras 214-227; Markert/Wilske, SchiedsVZ 2010, 62; Münch, in: MünchKommZPO, Vorbem ss 1025 *et seq.* paras 73 *et seq.*; Semler, SchiedsVZ 2009, 149.

[36] Reul, in: *Alternative Streitbeilegung*, pp 25 *et seq.*

D. Potential Advantages and Disadvantages of Arbitration in Germany

When faced with the choice between state court litigation and arbitration in Germany, parties have a number of potential advantages and disadvantages of arbitration in Germany which it behoves them to weigh (paras 1.48 *et seq.* and 1.60 *et seq.*).[37] Furthermore, the parties must consider certain potential advantages of arbitration in the international context (paras 1.69 *et seq.*). **1.47**

I. Potential Advantages over German State Courts

The potential advantages—perceived or real—of arbitration are many, and indeed there may be different views about whether a certain feature is actually an advantage or a drawback. We focus on four such features: the parties' influence on the selection of the decision-maker (paras 1.49 *et seq.*), confidentiality (paras 1.51 *et seq.*), the availability of tailor-made proceedings (paras 1.55 *et seq.*), and the potential speed of arbitral proceedings (paras 1.57 *et seq.*). **1.48**

1. Influence on Choice of Decision-makers

One of the most important advantages of arbitration over state court litigation in most legal systems—and Germany is no different in this context—is the ability of the parties to influence and indeed control the selection of the persons who will decide their disputes. The parties control the number of decision-makers. They can take into account **skills, experience, availability, and resources** of a particular candidate. Also, they can seek to choose a person with a reputation of being particularly "neutral," or someone with a reputation for greater proactivism in the role of party arbitrator. **1.49**

This is to be contrasted with the determination of the decision-makers in **state court litigation**, namely the judges, who in Germany are determined and assigned to cases pursuant to a **predetermined allocation scheme** which is meant to implement the right to a judge predetermined by law, but often does not take into account the suitability of a specific judge for a specific case. **1.50**

[37] Of course, there is also a choice to be made between arbitration seated in Germany or elsewhere. This choice can be discussed thoroughly only in comparison to one or more specific other jurisdictions. Certain general positive factors weighing in favor of Germany as the seat for arbitration may have become apparent already from the discussion in this chapter, such as the fact that Germany closely follows the Model Law. By contrast, whether certain other typical German features—such as the focus on written pleadings, an informal approach to the taking of evidence, or the general reluctance towards document disclosure—are an advantage or a disadvantage is a question that requires a case-by-case analysis. What may be a clear advantage in the eyes of one party may be a strong disincentive to choose Germany in the eyes of another party.

2. *Confidentiality*

1.51 When asked, most business people, and for that matter even experienced attorneys, would voice an expectation that arbitral proceedings are by their very nature confidential. As a matter of express statutory law or case law, this is in fact not correct in many if not most legal systems. Nor is it even correct as a matter of implied statutory law or case law in most legal systems, with few notable exceptions. Germany is not one of those exceptions.[38]

1.52 Accordingly, the **Tenth Book of the ZPO remains silent** on the question of confidentiality obligations of the parties.[39] This applies to any and all aspects of the arbitration, including the fact of its existence, its participants, its content, and its outcome. Nor does German case law endorse an implied confidentiality obligation as arising out of the agreement to arbitrate in principle.

1.53 Thus, where parties wish the existence, conduct, contents, and outcome of their arbitral proceedings with a German seat to be and remain confidential, they **must expressly so provide**, either by making reference to rules of arbitration which themselves foresee confidentiality or, for example, in a non-institutional, or ad hoc arbitration, stipulating confidentiality in the agreement to arbitrate. Examples of such rules of arbitration expressly providing for confidentiality to the one or other extent are first and foremost the **DIS Rules** (s 43.1), the Swiss Rules (art 44 para 1), and the World Intellectual Property Organization Rules (arts 73–76). Notably, the ICC Rules of Arbitration including in their most recent form enacted in 2012 do not expressly or for that matter impliedly provide for the confidentiality of proceedings.[40]

1.54 The foregoing is to be distinguished from the confidentiality obligation which is generally considered both in German and international practice to apply to **arbitrators** themselves. This obligation, in the German context, is seen to derive either from the applicable arbitration rules or at least as an implied covenant of the **arbitrator agreement.**[41] In addition, counsel to a party is typically subject to professional confidentiality obligations, independent of the context of representation in

[38] Especially in the UK, courts consider an implied obligation not to disclose any evidence given by a witness or any documents prepared for and used in an arbitration, cf Blackaby/Partasides/Redfern/Hunter, paras 2.165 *et seq.*

[39] Lachmann, paras 147–151.

[40] However, art 22.3 ICC Rules provides that "[u]pon the request of any party, the arbitral tribunal may make orders concerning the confidentiality of the arbitration proceedings or of any other matters in connection with the arbitration and may take measures for protecting trade secrets and confidential information."

[41] Lachmann, paras 145, 4293–4295. This concept of the arbitrator agreement, or a "contract" between and among the arbitrators and the parties, is a construct that has found strong acceptance in Germany, different from some other jurisdictions. However, it is also recognized in the international context, see Gaillard/Savage, paras 1103 *et seq.* and Born, pp 1975 *et seq.* with further references. We explore the arbitrator agreement more thoroughly in paras 3.159 *et seq.*

the arbitration. However, these obligations extend solely towards the party being represented and not toward the opposing party or third persons.

3. Tailor-made Proceedings

Arbitration allows the parties to agree on, or in the absence of agreement to advocate for acceptance by the arbitral tribunal, procedural rules, and other aspects of the proceedings that are tailor-made to their agreed or respective needs. Such needs may relate to **deadlines, content, and sequence** of written and oral proceedings including the taking of evidence, issues of **language** and translation, **locale** of hearings and site visits, and rights of attendance of parties and non-parties, etc. The largely rigid, written pleading-driven approach of the ZPO provisions governing state court proceedings may not be seen as suitable for all types of disputes, especially where foreign parties are involved but even in certain German–German arbitration disputes in which the parties intentionally seek an alternative to state court proceedings. **1.55**

In particular, the parties to an arbitration will wish to obtain a clear understanding of the **timeplan** for a dispute and indeed to contribute to its conception, a routine possibility in arbitration which is almost never to be found in German state court litigation. Depending on the circumstances and their respective assessment of the dispute, the parties to the arbitration may also consider the almost complete lack of **document disclosure** in a typical state court litigation pursuant to the ZPO to be inadequate to the needs of the case and to be ill-fitting to the arbitrators whom they have chosen to consider the evidence. To the extent these types of considerations are important to a party, the selection of the members of the arbitral tribunal is key. **1.56**

4. Speed?

While speed is often rightly invoked as a potential and important advantage of arbitration as compared with state court litigation,[42] especially in international disputes, a word of caution is certainly in order, also in the German context. To begin with, speed is not necessarily a virtue per se. The desire for speed may collide naturally with the **necessity to arrive at a correct decision**. Also, in the German context the expectation that an arbitration proceeding will truly be speedier and thereby perhaps also more cost-efficient than a German civil litigation is already ambitious, in the sense that German court proceedings are generally more efficient and streamlined than litigation in numerous other countries.[43] **1.57**

The reasons why arbitration, whether domestic or international, carries the promise of being more expeditious in Germany include that it is **not subject to a general right of appeal** but only subject to setting aside proceedings based on a very limited **1.58**

[42] Trappe, SchiedsVZ 2013, 167 *et seq.*; Schmidt-Diemnitz, DB 1999, 369, 370.
[43] See Zimmermann, in: MünchKommZPO, s 198 GVG para 27. Statistics regarding German courts are available at www.destatis.de (last visited December 1, 2015).

number of grave defects of the arbitral proceedings, that jurisdiction for setting aside proceedings lies with specialized and dedicated court chambers having a certain familiarity with arbitration issues, and that a certain degree of harmonization of vacatur decisions by such courts across Germany has developed which promotes the predictability and certainty of enforceability standards.

1.59 The other side of the coin, also in German arbitration, is of course that precisely due to the flexibility of the mechanism and the possible tension between party autonomy and arbitrator discretion, the speed and efficiency of arbitration can dramatically vary from case to case while many state court proceedings can be highly speedy and efficient.[44] Among the factors accounting for slowness and inefficiency partly particular to German arbitration are the **polarization of German and non-German counsel** in their competing approaches to procedure, disagreements or misapprehensions as to efficient use of disclosure techniques including by analogy to the IBA Rules (paras 4.115 *et seq.*), and disruptions caused by intermittent but unsuccessful efforts at **mediation and conciliation** by the arbitral tribunal. The authors' general experience is that the **emerging "mixture"** of civil law and common law techniques in German-seated international arbitration, and in particular the arbitral tribunal's customary effort not to abdicate complete control of the duration and scope of evidence-taking and especially oral hearings, leads to an above-average efficiency and speed not often matched in many other jurisdictions.

II. Potential Disadvantages and Recent Criticisms

1.60 As is common knowledge today, arbitration has certain potential downsides compared to state court litigation, depending upon the case, the parties and the arbitrators. Some of these potential downsides have been amplified by recent more or less fundamental criticisms of arbitration in Germany. The most important issues in this context are cost and efficiency (paras 1.61 *et seq.*), settlement pressure (paras 1.65 *et seq.*), and the fact that it is often more difficult to include third parties in arbitral proceedings than in state court litigation (para 1.68).

1. Cost and Efficiency

1.61 While for many years there was a mantra that arbitration is invariably destined to be less costly and more efficient than state court litigation, at least as far as Germany is concerned there has recently been somewhat of a **backlash in opinion**. Commentators have noted that arbitration internationally and in Germany has become too institutionalized, too "balkanized," too "Americanized," and thereby also too expensive and inefficient.[45] Document disclosure or even US-style discovery including depositions and broad requests for production of even electronically

---

44 Trappe, SchiedsVZ 2013, 167 *et seq.*

45 Lachmann, paras 163, 4666–4733; Schütze, para 33; Blackaby/Partasides/Redfern/Hunter, paras 1.123 *et seq.*

stored information is perceived by some as the main driver for an undue increase in cost and duration.[46]

These criticisms are noteworthy, not least because they contain a measure of truth, but also because at least as far as German arbitration practice is concerned, there is still a relatively widespread reluctance of arbitral tribunals, and even counsel themselves in the interest of their clients, to embark on far-flung discovery processes. **1.62**

It is very difficult to provide meaningful abstract cost comparisons between state court litigation and different forms of ad hoc and institutional arbitration. The costs of state court proceedings depend heavily on the **number of appeals** contemplated in the calculation, the amount in dispute,[47] and on whether a party has agreed with its own counsel on statutory fees or alternative **fee arrangements** (eg time-based billing). Likewise, as regards arbitration, the fee scales of different arbitral institutions differ. In addition, to the extent a party has agreed with its counsel on time-based billing, the overall costs will depend on how efficient and speedy the tribunal and the parties conduct the proceedings. Other factors driving costs are **party expert reports, document disclosure**, and related document review, and the preparation of sometimes many and lengthy **written witness statements**. **1.63**

Against this background, detailed calculations and comparisons may be done—and have been done[48]—but should, in our view, be used with a high degree of caution. They cannot replace a **thorough analysis** of the pros and cons of arbitration in each individual case. On a very generalized note, one could say that arbitration tends to be particularly efficient as compared to state court litigation when the stakes are high, either financially or strategically or both. At a minimum, where the amount in dispute is well in the seven-digit range, costs should generally not be a factor that weighs against arbitration. For arbitration with a German nexus, cost-conscious parties should seriously consider the DIS, even if they come from another jurisdiction and may thus be culturally reluctant to agree on a "German" institution. **1.64**

2. *Settlement Pressure*

Another recent and persistent criticism, particularly among Anglo-American observers, is the perception that arbitration in Germany almost inevitably leads to a tribunal-driven or even effectively coerced settlement on commercial terms, rather than to an award on the merits.[49] Indeed, arbitrators with a German law background have tended for many years to take a proactive approach to conducting the proceedings and to taking "appropriate steps" toward encouraging, cajoling, **1.65**

[46] Reul, in: Alternative Streitbeilegung, pp 25, 40 *et seq*.

[47] In German state court litigation, court costs and generally also lawyer's fees are calculated upon the amount in dispute.

[48] Lachmann, paras 163, 4666–4733.

[49] Böckstiegel/Kröll/Nacimiento, in: *Arbitration in Germany*, pp 20 paras 45 *et seq*.

or inducing settlement, much like German state court judges are both allowed and indeed obligated to do (above para 1.28).

1.66 In fact, the German arbitration law—unlike the ZPO provisions governing state court proceedings (s 278 ZPO)—does **not contain any express mandate** on the part of the arbitrators to actively pursue settlement of the dispute. Section 1053 ZPO merely provides for the resolution of the dispute by way of settlement, including by way of an award on agreed terms, "if the parties settle the dispute." Thus, it is clear that the German arbitration law itself does not expressly authorize, let alone encourage, an arbitrator with a German seat to take such steps. At the same time, it is notable that the **DIS Rules,** which not coincidentally also entered into force on January 1, 1998, expressly provide, in s 32.1, that arbitral tribunals "should," "[a]t every stage of the proceedings," "seek to encourage an amicable settlement of the dispute or of individual issues in dispute."

1.67 The net result in the authors' experience is that in the last decade or so the tendency of arbitrators in German arbitrations to seek even, somewhat insistently, to settle the arbitration has slowly but surely declined, but that both parties and arbitrators consider it to be a legitimate option which in many if not most disputes will be addressed sooner or later, at the latest upon the conclusion of the oral witness examination. At the same time, of course there are parties and disputes that do not lend themselves as easily to settlement as others.

3. Inclusion of Third Parties

1.68 In some cases, the consequences of a dispute commercially affect a non-party to the dispute. As a typical example, the main contractor will try to recover damages paid to the customer from its subcontractor. Instruments such as third-party notice (*Streitverkündung*) that are known in German state court proceedings are not instantly available in arbitration. This gap, however, can be filled by way of separate agreement (see para 4.212).

III. Special Potential Advantages in the International Context

1.69 In addition to the general potential advantages of arbitration over state court litigation explained above, among the most important further advantages in an international context, also with a German seat, are intercultural acceptance, including an appropriate language for the arbitral proceedings (paras 1.70 *et seq.*), the potential to tailor the taking of evidence and particularly document disclosure (para 1.75), and the ability to recognize and enforce an arbitral award abroad pursuant to the New York Convention (para 1.76).

1. Intercultural Acceptance and Appropriate Language

1.70 Arbitration may be especially appropriate for parties from different countries, with **different languages and different social and legal backgrounds.** Typically, in cross-border commercial transactions, the parties are reluctant if not also mistrustful of the prospect of entrusting disputes to the local court system, usually in a foreign language and under foreign procedural rules, of the other party. Such reluctance and mistrust, apart from the element of foreign language, may be unfounded in many cases and with respect to many—if not most—developed legal systems. Nevertheless, the appetite to use one's own dispute as a guinea pig to test this hypothesis is usually slim to non-existent. In such situations, arbitration is often the dispute resolution mechanism of choice, allowing for agreement on a neutral forum, the means of constitution of the tribunal, the choice of the language of the proceedings, and opportunities as described above for tailoring the procedure and its rules to the parties' wishes.[50]

A particular phenomenon of relevance here in arbitrations with a German seat is what can be called "**mixing and matching.**" Particularly in high-stakes cross-border transactions such as mergers or acquisitions and notably those in which multinational law firms are involved, there is often the tendency, in the interest of "compromise," to draft the contract documents more or less in line with one particular legal tradition but to agree to a governing law from a wholly different legal tradition. **1.71**

By way of example, in connection with a complex commercial or M&A transaction international counsel might agree on a somewhat sparely drafted contract document, more in the tradition of German codified law, but for the sake of compromise agree to New York or English law as the governing law. Or in reverse, for that same transaction those same counsel might agree on a highly elaborate and voluminously crafted contract document, more in the tradition of common law contract drafting, but for the sake of compromise agree to Swiss law as the governing law. To add realistic complexity to the compromise, the parties may have included in the draft, in the spirit of "for the avoidance of doubt," specific technical terms, eg, related to representations and warranties or limitations of liability, rooted in the legal philosophy in which the contract was drafted but not rooted and perhaps not even known in the agreed governing law. **1.72**

To be sure, **party autonomy** by and large allows for such mixing and matching, which usually does not affect or threaten mandatory norms. At the same time, such mixing and matching, which is not infrequently encountered in contracts providing for a German seat, poses **challenges for the interpretation of the rights and duties** during the contract and during any later arbitration. **1.73**

On the level of the composition of the arbitral tribunal, the foregoing trends, seen increasingly in international arbitration with a German seat, are potentially highly significant to the selection of a suitable arbitrator, which is arguably the single most important advantage and task of an arbitration. For this reason too, it is crucial that **1.74**

---

[50] Choice of language, seat, and applicable substantive law will be addressed in detail in paras 2.170 *et seq.*, when we discuss the arbitration agreement.

such mixing and matching between and among language, contract drafting, and agreed governing law be undertaken with considerable care. And where counsel have "inherited" a contract which already exhibits such diversity, the choice of appropriately qualified arbitrators will be all the more important.

2. *Tailoring of Taking of Evidence*

1.75 In the same vein, agreeing to arbitration may allow the parties to bridge the different approaches to taking of evidence and particularly document disclosure between and among legal traditions, and most notably between Anglo-American and continental European legal systems. Whereas Anglo-American practitioners often take as their point of departure what they are used to, eg, in US state court proceedings, German practitioners often take the very same approach based on Germany's state court tradition of very limited document disclosure, if any (above paras 1.24 *et seq.*). The perceived dilemma can possibly be overcome by agreeing on the application of, or at least seeking inspiration from, the **2010 IBA Rules on the Taking of Evidence in International Arbitration.** Thus, especially from the viewpoint of a European party and its counsel, the choice of arbitration may avoid having to deal with a lawsuit in US courts.

3. *Enforcement of Awards Abroad Under the New York Convention*

1.76 One of the most **manifest legal advantages** of arbitration over state court litigation in an international context is the much easier enforcement of arbitral awards in jurisdictions where the defeated party has assets. Parties seeking to enforce local state court judgments in other countries often face considerable legal, administrative, and practical difficulties, sometimes rendering enforcement even illusory. By contrast, arbitral awards are generally much easier to enforce due to their recognition by foreign states as a result of the New York Convention on the Recognition and Enforcement of Foreign Arbitral Awards of 1958.[51] By now, **more than 150 countries** have become parties to the convention.

E. Special Types of Arbitrations

1.77 This section provides an overview of selected special types of arbitration available in Germany: corporate law disputes (including now also challenges against shareholder resolutions, paras 1.78 *et seq.*), sports arbitration (para 1.80), labor law arbitration (para 1.81), administrative law arbitration (para 1.82), and public international law arbitration (in particular investment arbitration, para 1.83).

[51] Lachmann, para 183; Blackaby/Partasides/Redfern/Hunter, para 1.101—we will discuss enforcement of arbitral awards in detail in Chapter 6.

I. Corporate Law Disputes, Including Challenge of Shareholder Resolutions

Corporate law disputes have long been an established realm for arbitration. Subjects such as exiting shareholders and the valuation of their shareholdings benefit significantly from the typical advantages of arbitration, for instance specialized and knowledgeable decision-makers and confidentiality. For a long time, there was one notable carve-out where German courts were very reluctant to allow arbitration and as a consequence, corporate practice did not embark upon arbitration—disputes on the validity of shareholder resolutions.[52] However, in a recent ruling the BGH clarified its position, expressly allowing for arbitration also on these topics, as long as certain conditions are met in order to ensure **due process for all shareholders** affected by a declaration of invalidity of a resolution.[53] Specifically, (1) all shareholders must have **approved** the arbitration agreement, (2) the arbitration agreement must provide for the **information** of all shareholders once arbitration is initiated and allow them to participate in the proceedings, (3) the arbitration agreement must provide all shareholders with an opportunity to **participate** in the selection of arbitrators, and (4) the arbitration agreement must ensure that all disputes related to the same shareholder resolution are dealt with by the **same arbitral tribunal.** **1.78**

The **DIS** has developed specific rules for the conduct of such disputes which implement the German Federal Supreme Court's requirements and which should be seriously considered when parties wish to agree on arbitration regarding disputes related to the validity of shareholder resolutions.[54] **1.79**

II. Sports Arbitration

Arbitration is well-suited for resolving certain sports disputes.[55] The swift handling of disputes arising during the **Olympics** may be the best known example. However, arbitration is widely used in the field of sports, not only in the context of major sporting events but also by small clubs. The most important sport arbitration institution is the **Court of Arbitration for Sport** (CAS), with its headquarters in Lausanne and founded in 1984. In Germany, the **DIS** offers sports arbitration based on its **sports arbitration rules of 2008** which may be considered for various types of sports-related disputes, such as sponsoring agreements, licenses, violations of anti-doping provisions, and challenges of anti-doping sanctions.[56] **1.80**

---

52 BGHZ 132, 278 = NJW 1996, 1753—*Schiedsfähigkeit I;* Wolff, in: *Münchener Handbuch des Gesellschaftsrechts*, Vol 3, § 40 para 116 with further references.

53 BGHZ 180, 221 = SchiedsVZ 2009, 233—*Schiedsfähigkeit II.*

54 DIS Supplementary Rules for Corporate Law Disputes 2009 (SRCoLD), available at www.disarb.org (last visited December 1, 2015).

55 Lachmann, paras 39 *et seq.*

56 For details see www.dis-sportschiedsgericht.de (last visited December 1, 2015).

III. Labor Law Arbitration

1.81 Labor law arbitration is regulated by law in ss 101–110 of the German Labor Court Act (ArbGG).[57] Only disputes involving **collective agreements** or the existence of collective agreements can be the subject of labor law arbitration (s 101 para 3 ArbGG). The arbitration clause has to be part of the collective agreement (s 101 para 2 ArbGG). The practical significance of labor law arbitration continues to be fairly limited.

IV. Administrative Law Arbitration

1.82 Arbitration in the realm of administrative law is still somewhat of a myth in Germany. On the one hand, German administrative law expressly permits arbitration of administrative law disputes (**s 173 VwGO**), eg, between the government and a company taking a public law concession. However, thus far, arbitration has not been used much in this area, and there is only a limited range of legal literature on the topic.[58] On the other hand, probably the largest arbitration ever held with a seat in Germany is an administrative law arbitration dealing with the delayed start of a large infrastructure and software project, ie a new toll system for heavy trucks on German Autobahns (Toll Collect).

V. Public International Law Arbitration, Especially Investment Arbitration

1.83 Arbitration also exists in the public international law context, in particular in the context of **investment protection treaties**. However, since this is a topic that is not specific to Germany, we refrain from exploring it further here and refer our readers to specialized literature.[59] Suffice it to say that a number of qualified German arbitration practitioners work in this field, both as counsel and as arbitrators.

F. Alternative Dispute Resolution Mechanisms in Germany

1.84 Besides arbitration, a number of other mechanisms are available in Germany to seek resolution of disputes outside the state court system. After a brief look into the background and history of ADR in Germany (para 1.85), we will explore mediation (paras 1.86 *et seq.*), expert determination (paras 1.93 *et seq.*), and (briefly) adjudication and dispute boards (para 1.96) as the most important ADR mechanisms

57 For more details see Hohmann, in Hohmann (ed), s 101 paras 1 *et seq.*

58 Schill, DÖV 2010, 1013 with some further references; Schlosser, in: *Festschrift Bülow*, pp 189 *et seq.*; from an international perspective Gaillard/Savage, paras 70 *et seq.*

59 Reed/Paulsson/Blackaby, *Guide to ICSID Arbitration*, 2nd edn, 2010; Schreuer, *The ICSID Convention: A Commentary*, 2001; Böckstiegel, SchiedsVZ 2012, 113.

in Germany outside arbitration.[60] This section also addresses combinations of various dispute resolution mechanisms (paras 1.97 *et seq.*).

I. Background and History

Germany has a long tradition of resolving disputes outside the state court system. For instance, wage disputes between workers' unions and employers or employer organizations have been resolved by **conciliation** (*Schlichtung*) for decades. In addition, the ZPO in its **s 278 para 1** encourages state court judges to consider settlement at all stages of the proceedings and since July 2012 enables specific state court judges to make use of all types of ADR mechanisms including mediation (s 278 para 5 cl 2 ZPO). In recent years, the German legislator has added additional features to the ZPO attempting to achieve more amicable solutions of legal disputes.[61] Most recently, extra-judicial conciliation has become a hot-button political topic for large infrastructure projects, such as the new Stuttgart train station (*Stuttgart 21*). **1.85**

II. Mediation

In 2012, Germany enacted the **Mediation Act**, a federal law which contains a definition of the notion of mediation and sets forth a **framework** of basic principles and procedures for mediation in Germany (paras 1.87 *et seq.*). We will also explore briefly mediation under the rules of both the DIS and the ICC (para 1.91) before offering our perspectives on the pros and cons of mediation in Germany (para 1.92). **1.86**

1. German Mediation Act

After an intense debate in the legal community, the German Mediation Act (MediationsG) came into force on July 26, 2012,[62] **implementing the European Mediation Directive 2008/52/EC** into German law. The most contested issue in the political debate was the **role of state court judges in mediation**, ultimately resulting in a political compromise that now provides for mediation as well as two further types of non-contentious dispute resolution mechanisms involving German state courts. The German Mediation Act applies to domestic and cross-border mediation. **1.87**

Section 1 para 1 German Mediation Act **defines mediation** as a confidential and structured proceeding in which the parties, voluntarily and on their own **1.88**

---

60 Given our focus on arbitration, we will keep our analysis of ADR fairly short; for a more detailed analysis, we refer our readers to specialized literature available on the topic, eg Böckstiegel (ed), *Schiedsgerichtsbarkeit*, 2007; Eidenmüller (ed), *Alternative Streitbeilegung*, 2011; Greger/Stubbe, *Schiedsgutachten*, 2007; Seybold, *Mediation und gerichtliches Verfahren*, 2009; Weiler/Schlickum, *Praxisbuch: Mediation*, 2012.

61 See, eg, the conciliation proceedings (*Güteverfahren*) provided for in s 278 ZPO.

62 BGBl 2012 I p 1577.

responsibility, seek an amicable settlement of their dispute with the assistance of a mediator. The parties choose the mediator as a neutral person (s 2 para 1 MediationsG). The mediator does not have the power to render a binding decision; rather, the parties are free to discontinue the mediation proceedings at any time (s 2 para 5 MediationsG). An agreement reached in mediation can be rendered enforceable via notarization by a German notary public or a German court or by means of a lawyers' settlement deed.[63]

1.89 Under the German Mediation Act, the mediator must **adequately inform the parties** and ensure that the parties are aware of the principles and the course of the mediation (s 2 para 2 MediationsG). The mediator is equally committed to all parties. The mediator may make **proposals for a solution** if the parties so request. The German Mediation Act imposes **strict confidentiality obligations** upon mediators, allowing them to refuse to testify in civil court proceedings. Mediation tolls the statute of limitations (s 203 cl 1 BGB).

1.90 In addition to standard out-of-court mediation, the German Mediation Act provides for **in-trial mediation** upon proposal of the court and mediation in judicial conciliation proceedings. Regarding in-trial mediation, s 278a ZPO empowers the trial court to propose mediation or another form of ADR without subjecting the acting judges to any challenge on the basis of lack of neutrality. If the mediation is successful, the court proceedings are terminated. As regards **mediation by judicial conciliation**, s 278 para 5 ZPO provides for a procedure whereby the parties to a dispute pending in state court can seek the guidance of a judge (who may not be presiding over their dispute) and who acts as a judicial conciliator. Whilst not authorized to render a binding decision, a judicial conciliator may make use of the established methods of ADR, including mediation.

2. *Institutional Mediation Rules*

1.91 Most arbitral institutions also provide rules for institutional mediation, such as the **DIS Mediation Rules**[64] and the **ICC Mediation Rules**.[65] As with the choice between ad hoc and institutional arbitration, the choice between ad hoc and institutional mediation is something that needs to be considered in each individual case. In our experience, institutional mediation may be particularly appropriate in a commercial context where a dispute has already seriously arisen and where there has been a certain breakdown of communication between the parties. Where the parties have difficulty in agreeing on anything, it usually helps to have a set of predetermined rules that allows for the swift and efficient start and conduct of mediation proceedings (as well as a shift to arbitration or litigation, should mediation prove fruitless).

---

[63] Sections 794 para 1 no 5, 796a ZPO.
[64] Available at www.disarb.org (last visited December 1, 2015).
[65] Available at www.iccwbo.org (last visited December 1, 2015).

3. *Pros and Cons of Mediation*

Mediation has been greeted with a certain level of enthusiasm in Germany. Its main advantages appear to be **cost-efficiency, confidentiality**, the potential for "out of the box" and **"face-saving" solutions** as well as the chance to preserve a longstanding **relationship.**[66] At the same time, it should not be overlooked that one size does not fit all, and there may be a number of disputes where mediation is either not fit for purpose from the start, or at least unlikely to succeed. A party may need to seek a **principled decision** on a certain topic, and may not be willing to compromise on what it regards its sound and solid legal or factual position. Also, in **high-stakes corporate or commercial cases**, decision-makers may need more than merely a mediated solution in order to discharge their own management obligations under applicable corporate laws and corporate governance rules (business judgment rule).[67] In fact, commercial mediation has up to now not appeared to have taken root as firmly as its protagonists had hoped for. **1.92**

III. Expert Determination

Expert determination is another widely agreed mechanism for ADR outside arbitration. It is commonly used in corporate by-laws, **M&A, construction, infrastructure, and real estate** agreements. A statutory basis for expert determination may be found in ss 317 *et seq.* BGB. Expert determination means that an expert renders a **binding decision on certain elements of the parties' legal or factual relationship**. Unlike an arbitral award, an expert determination is generally subject to review by state courts based on a **fairness standard** (s 319 para 1 BGB), unless the parties agree to exclude such review. **1.93**

M&A agreements typically contain expert determination provisions regarding **purchase price elements**, in particular where the parties choose a closing account mechanism for determining the purchase price.[68] It is important to align the expert determination clauses with the general dispute resolution mechanism for the M&A agreement, which in a German M&A context is often arbitration. In particular, to the extent the parties wish to allow for a judicial fairness review of the expert's determination (s 319 para 1 BGB) and they have provided for arbitration as a general dispute resolution mechanism, they are well advised to make sure that such fairness review should be done by the arbitral tribunal, not by a state court. As long as the parties have not followed the expert determination mechanism for the purchase price, arbitration on the purchase price claim would usually be premature.[69] **1.94**

---

66 Seybold, pp 33 *et seq.*
67 Section 93 paras 1 and 2 AktG.
68 Rieder, in: Schütze/Weipert/Rieder (eds), pp 351 *et seq.*
69 BGH NJW-RR 2014, 492, 493 para 28; NJW-RR 2011, 1059, 1060; Rieder, in: Schütze/Weipert/Rieder (eds), p 351.

1.95 The advantages of expert determination may include **lower costs and shorter proceedings** due to very limited legal or factual issues to be discussed and examined by experts as opposed to full scale arbitration proceedings covering all facts and legal aspects of a dispute.[70] However, the decision by an expert would regularly **not constitute an enforceable title**, but be regarded as a contractual agreement by the parties based on the specification by a third party (s 317 BGB).[71] An expert determination may be preferable where the parties are to resolve the dispute while other parts of their business relationship are ongoing and where the dispute is narrowed to a certain limited issue on which an expert may have more specific knowledge than lawyers who usually would form an arbitral tribunal.[72]

IV. Adjudication and Dispute Boards

1.96 In **construction and infrastructure projects**, it has become good practice to establish dispute boards entitled to take preliminary decisions on evolving disputes, such as to allow the project to go forward at least with an interim solution (as opposed to a potential roadblock derailing the entire project).[73] These mechanisms are explored in specialized literature, and we do not see significant peculiarities in the German practice that would warrant a more detailed discussion here. Suffice it to say that parties to large projects are well advised to agree on such types of panels.

V. Combination of Various Dispute Resolution Mechanisms

1.97 A party seeking to enforce its rights can contemplate a combination of various dispute resolution mechanisms if so agreed upon in the contract. The combinations that we explore in this section are arbitration and expert determination (para 1.98), arbitration and litigation (paras 1.99 *et seq.*), as well as arbitration and mediation (paras 1.102 *et seq.*).

1. *Combination of Arbitration and Expert Determination*

1.98 As already set forth above in para 1.94, **M&A agreements** in Germany typically contain a combination of expert determination for purchase price elements and an arbitration clause for other disputes. A similar combination can often be found in **construction and infrastructure project agreements**. As pointed out above, in each case, the different mechanisms need to be aligned thoroughly. It can be costly and cumbersome to litigate or arbitrate conflicting dispute resolution mechanisms. Often, once a dispute has arisen, the parties may no longer be able to agree which

---

70 Kasolowski/Schnabl, SchiedsVZ 2012, 84, 86; Sessler, in: Böckstiegel/Berger/Bredow (eds), pp 97, 108; Borris, in: *Liber Amicorum Boeckstiegel*, pp 75, 80.

71 Kasolowski/Schnabl, SchiedsVZ 2012, 84, 86 *et seq.*; Sessler, in: Böckstiegel/Berger/Bredow (eds), pp 97, 108; Borris, in: *Liber Amicorum Böckstiegel*, pp 75, 78, 87.

72 Sessler, in: Böckstiegel/Berger/Bredow (eds), pp 97, 108 *et seq.*

73 Lachmann, paras 86 *et seq.*

of the conflicting mechanisms to use. Typically, one party will see an advantage in one mechanism, and the other in exactly the other one.

2. Combination of Arbitration and Litigation

Combining litigation and arbitration is usually not something that the parties consider during the drafting stages of a commercial agreement. When turning to the negotiation of the desired dispute resolution mechanism, they mostly have either arbitration or litigation on their minds, but not both at the same time. This is usually commercially sensible since multiple fora multiply costs and efforts. **1.99**

The picture may change once a dispute has arisen. A party may bring arbitral proceedings, and at the same time contemplate starting litigation on certain aspects of the dispute. As far as **interim relief** is concerned, this is a common and accepted course of action that is even expressly provided for by law (s 1041 para 1 ZPO, paras 5.71 *et seq.*). **Parallel litigation on the merits** may be instituted against certain persons or entities that are not bound by the arbitration agreement, but contributed to the wrongdoing that the claimant seeks recourse for (eg tort law claims based on misrepresentation and fraud against individuals). Nevertheless, litigating the same substantive issues at the same time in front of multiple fora entails risks and downsides that need to be seriously considered, in particular as far as the costs and the risk of conflicting decisions or even undesired obiter dicta are concerned. **1.100**

In certain cases, an interesting combination of arbitration and litigation may be the launch of proceedings in the US under **28 USC s 1782** in order to **obtain discovery against a US respondent**. US courts are split on whether s 1782 proceedings can be used to support arbitral proceedings.[74] In circuits where US courts permit this vehicle, it is an option that may be seriously considered. **1.101**

3. Med/Arb and Arb/Med

Mediation and arbitration are frequently combined in resolving a dispute. Dispute resolution clauses often provide for mandatory mediation before arbitration may be commenced. **1.102**

Conversely, mediation is often considered **during arbitral proceedings**. The arbitral tribunal may have developed and shared with the parties what it considers its preliminary views on the issues raised by the parties' dispute, and based on these views, the parties may wish to explore options to resolve their dispute amicably without the need to proceed all the way to an arbitral award. Under today's prevailing view—certainly in Germany—a member of the arbitral tribunal is not precluded per se from acting as a mediator, and more importantly, is not precluded **1.103**

74 For a detailed discussion see Wilske, DAJV Newsletter 2011, 114, 117 with further references.

per se from continuing to act as an arbitrator should mediation fail.[75] This holds true at least as long as the mediator refrains from entering into bilateral discussions with only one of the parties. It is of course best practice that the tribunal and the parties enter into an **express stipulation** to this effect before a member of the arbitral tribunal takes on the role of the mediator.[76]

[75] Pitkowitz/Richter, SchiedsVZ 2009, 225; Horvath, SchiedsVZ 2005, 292, 296; crit. Lachmann, para 90.
[76] Pitkowitz/Richter, SchiedsVZ 2009, 225, 230.

2

THE ARBITRATION AGREEMENT

Markus S. Rieder/Richard Kreindler

A. Overview

In this chapter, we explore the arbitration agreement from a variety of perspectives. Section B deals with the required content and the validity of an arbitration agreement. In Section C we look at its scope, effects, and issues of termination. Finally, Section D deals with typical additional contents of arbitration agreements, in particular as regards the place of arbitration, the language of the proceedings, the selection of the applicable substantive law, and the selection of ad hoc or institutional arbitration. **2.1**

Despite the length of this chapter, it should be noted at the outset that arbitration agreements in Germany are typically **short** and crisp. The arbitration clause recommended by the DIS is a good example: **2.2**

> All disputes arising in connection with this contract or its validity shall be finally settled in accordance with the Arbitration Rules of the German Institution of Arbitration (DIS) without recourse to the ordinary courts of law. [...] The place of arbitration is... The number of arbitrators is... The language of the arbitral proceedings is... The applicable substantive law is...[1]

[1] Available at http://www.disarb.org, DIS Model Arbitration Agreement (last visited December 1, 2015).

B. Required Content and Validity of the Arbitration Agreement

2.3 An arbitration agreement is first and foremost an agreement between the parties under the law of contracts (below paras 2.11 *et seq.*) that needs to have a certain minimum content in order to qualify as an arbitration agreement (below paras 2.32 *et seq.*). As an agreement, it is subject to grounds for invalidity (below paras 2.44 *et seq.*) and, once found valid, subject to interpretation (below paras 2.105 *et seq.*). We end this section with examples of what should be "dos and don'ts" in drafting arbitration agreements with a German nexus (below paras 2.117 *et seq.*). Before addressing these points in turn, a word on the applicable law is in order (below paras 2.4 *et seq.*).

I. Law Applicable to the Arbitration Agreement

2.4 Naturally, the analysis below focuses on German law and thus assumes that German law applies to these issues. However, in an international context, one first needs to establish the law applicable to the determination of the content and the validity of an **arbitration agreement** (*Schiedsvereinbarungsstatut*). The law applicable to arbitration agreements needs to be distinguished from the law governing the **arbitral proceedings** (*Schiedsverfahrensstatut—lex arbitri*) and the law governing the **substance** of the parties' agreement.[2]

2.5 Frequently, arbitration agreements do not contain a stipulation of the law applicable specifically to the arbitration agreement itself (as opposed to frequent choice-of-law clauses applying to the underlying transaction).[3] This applies in particular to arbitration clauses contained in the main agreement of the parties.

2.6 Depending on the forum in which a dispute on the law applicable to the arbitration agreement arises, **different methods** for determining the applicable law may need to be considered. For state-court litigation the Rome I Regulation[4] provides a particular choice-of-law regime for contractual relations under German law. However, according to the express derogation in Art 1 para 2 lit e Rome I Regulation this regime does not apply to arbitration agreements. Section 1059 para 2 no 1 lit a ZPO may be used as a point of departure for the analysis, providing for **party choice**, and, as a default option, for the application of German law, ie the law of the **seat of the arbitration**. However, in the absence of an express agreement by the parties,

[2] Münch, in: MünchKommZPO, s 1029 para 29; Voit, in: Musielak/Voit (eds), s 1029 para 28; Geimer, in: Zöller (ed), s 1029 para 119; Gaillard/Savage, paras 412 *et seq.*; Blackaby/Partasides/Redfern/Hunter, paras 3.09 *et seq.*

[3] Münch, in: MünchKommZPO, s 1029 para 35.

[4] Regulation (EC) No 593/2008 of the European Parliament and of the Council of 17 June 2008 on the law applicable to contractual obligations ("Rome I Regulation").

German law need not necessarily be the only remaining alternative. Instead, the most prominent options are to look at the law applicable to the **substantive law agreement** under which the dispute arises or the law of the seat of arbitration.[5] Each situation requires a careful **case-by-case analysis.**

2.7 Importantly, because arbitration clauses are to be treated separately from the main agreement (s 1040 para 1 cl 2 ZPO), the law applicable to the main agreement need not necessarily apply to an **arbitration clause.**[6] Nevertheless, applying the same law as to the main contract may often reflect the intentions of the parties since commercial parties will not necessarily even be aware of the separability principle. In such a case, the main contract's choice of law clause may give rise to an implied agreement on the law governing the arbitration agreement.[7]

2.8 Conversely, where the parties chose to enter into a **separate arbitration agreement** without express reference to an unambiguous choice-of-law agreement, the application of the *lex loci arbitri* will often be preferable. This is in line with the provisions of s 1059 para 2 no 1 lit a ZPO and Art V para 1 lit a of the New York Covention (NYC) which create a special choice-of-law regime:[8] in the absence of an indication regarding the applicable law, the request to the state court to set aside an award based on the contention that the arbitration agreement is invalid is to be determined under the law of the country where the award was made.[9]

2.9 The situation may be less clear where the parties have chosen German substantive law, but a foreign place of arbitration. In such a case, unless there is some indication that the parties wanted German law to govern the arbitration clause, it may be preferable to use the law of the **place of arbitration as the default.**[10] As we explain below (para 2.177), the definition of a place of arbitration contains the choice to submit a dispute to the mandatory procedural rules at this place. Given that the arbitration agreement is a substantive-law agreement on procedural-law relations (below para 2.12), it seems reasonable to assume that the parties wanted to subject its content to the selected procedural rules. Another difficult situation may arise where the **place of arbitration has not yet been determined** (cf s 1025 para 2 alt 2 ZPO). In this scenario, the most appropriate test is to look for the **closest connection**, which may be the seat or residence of the parties, the place of the arbitral institution chosen by the parties or, as a default, the law governing the main agreement.[11]

---

5 Geimer, in: Zöller (ed), s 1029 para 107; Voit, in: Musielak/Voit (eds), s 1029 para 28. For the determination of applicable law under former Arts 27 *et seq.* EGBGB, see BGH SchiedsVZ 2011, 157, 159 = XXXVII Y.B. Com. Arb. 223, 225 (2012); Lachmann, paras 269 *et seq.*

6 Geimer, in: Zöller (ed), s 1029 para 112; Münch, in: MünchKommZPO, s 1029 para 35; Voit, in: Musielak/Voit (eds), s 1029 para 28.

7 BGH SchiedsVZ 2011, 46, 49 = XXXVII Y.B. Com. Arb. 216, 219 (2012); Geimer, in: Zöller (ed), s 1025 para 10; Trittmann/Hanefeld, in: *Arbitration in Germany*, s 1029 para 11.

8 König, SchiedsVZ 2012, 129, 130; Mankowski, RIW 2011, 30, 33.

9 For further cases see http://newyorkconvention1958.org (last visited December 1, 2015).

10 Münch, in: MünchKommZPO, s 1029 para 37; Lachmann, paras 268 *et seq.*

11 Münch, in: MünchKommZPO, s 1029 paras 37 *et seq.*; Voit, in: Musielak/Voit (eds), s 1029 para 28.

2.10 Where the determination of the applicable law leads (in all likelihood) to a legal system outside Germany, **Art II NYC** applies and there is no room for the requirements under the ZPO, as far as the NYC contains autonomous provisions of law, ie in particular with regard to form. Pursuant to Art II para 1 NYC, each Member State shall recognize a written agreement in which the parties submit their differences in respect of a defined legal relationship to arbitration. Pursuant to Art II para 2 NYC, it is sufficient that the agreement be signed by both parties or that it be contained in written correspondence. In other words, where and to the extent German law is not applicable, courts must recognize an agreement once it meets this standard and need not deal with the requirements of the specific legal system.

II. Agreement of the Parties

2.11 For purposes of the analysis that follows, we will assume that German law applies to the arbitration agreement at hand. As a first step, the legal nature of an arbitration agreement needs to be established; under today's prevailing view in Germany, it is a substantive-law agreement on procedural-law relations (below paras 2.12 *et seq.*). Thus, it needs to satisfy the general requirements under German civil law to form a contract (below paras 2.18 *et seq.*). In addition, an arbitration agreement can be formed by trade usage (below paras 2.24 *et seq.*). The amendment of arbitration agreements follows rules similar to their original formation (below paras 2.29 *et seq.*).

1. *Legal Nature of the Arbitration Agreement: Substantive-law Agreement on Procedural-law Relations*

2.12 For several decades, German scholars have debated as to the legal nature of arbitration agreements. The two main schools of thought were (1) to qualify arbitration agreements as substantive-law agreements, and (2) to view them as procedural agreements.[12] German courts have adopted a compromise view, qualifying arbitration agreements as **substantive-law agreements on procedural-law relations.**[13] This formula captures well what an arbitration agreement is about. Its effects relate primarily to procedural issues. It provides that a legal dispute between the parties shall be decided by an arbitral tribunal to the exclusion of the ordinary courts. It regulates how arbitral proceedings shall be conducted, either as a result of an express agreement of the parties or by reference to a default set of rules, such as the rules of an arbitral institution or the rules of the *lex arbitri.*

2.13 Nevertheless, an arbitration agreement also has **substantive-law elements.** Specifically, it triggers ancillary obligations of the parties, including the duty to act

---

[12] Münch, in: MünchKommZPO, s 1029 para 12 with further references.

[13] BGHZ 99, 143, 147 = NJW 1987, 651, 652; BGHZ 49, 384, 386 = NJW 1968, 1233; Münch, in: MünchKommZPO, s 1029 para 12; Lachmann, para 266; Hartmann, in: Baumbach/Lauterbach/Albers/Hartmann (eds), s 1029 para 10; Voit, in: Musielak/Voit (eds), s 1029 para 3.

in a way that **furthers the proceedings and their conclusion** by way of an arbitral award or otherwise (for details see below para 2.148).[14] In addition, the qualification as a substantive-law agreement has the advantage of offering a ready-made set of rules governing issues such as **formation, validity, interpretation, and termination of agreements**, which in Germany can be found in the BGB. The proponents of a pure procedural-law qualification would need to look for an applicable set of rules, possibly defaulting to the provisions of the BGB at least by way of analogy—a methodological complication that seems unnecessary.

German law recognizes **two types** of arbitration agreements (*Schiedsvereinbarung*): (i) an arbitration agreement in the form of a **separate agreement** (*Schiedsabrede*), and (ii) an **arbitration clause** contained in a main contract (*Schiedsklausel*) (s 1029 para 2 ZPO). In a commercial context, arbitration clauses are much more common than separate arbitration agreements. The latter may be used when a dispute arises and the parties then agree to submit it to arbitration. **2.14**

This is fairly rare in German practice. Once a dispute has arisen, very often only one side will find arbitration advantageous, while the other may think it has tactical advantages by having the dispute decided by a state court. Nevertheless, **separate arbitration agreements** are sometimes concluded on an ad hoc basis, for instance where both parties are intent on having confidentiality. This may occur in cases that involve wrongdoing which could trigger claims by third parties if it became visible in open (state) court. German state courts often notify the public prosecutor when they spot serious **criminal behavior** in connection with a civil law dispute in front of them. Thus, for instance, where possible corruption is at issue, not only may the perpetrator be intent upon confidentiality, but also the corporation on whose behalf it occurred, because otherwise—as a matter of German administrative offences law—it might be subject to painful sanctions such as disgorgement of profits. Similarly, **management liability** cases may lend themselves to arbitration, because quite often the wrongdoing alleged against a manager may also be the basis for contract or tort claims of a third party against the corporation. For example, in the context of the recent global financial crisis there have been numerous cases of allegedly faulty risk management, which may trigger management liability as well as contract claims based on improper disclosure (*Informationshaftung*).[15] **2.15**

The arbitration agreement itself needs to be distinguished from agreements of the parties on the **conduct of arbitral proceedings** and other **procedural issues**,[16] even though the general standards outlined above for concluding agreements also apply to **2.16**

---

[14] Münch, in: MünchKommZPO, s 1029 paras 13, 117.

[15] For a prominent example, see OLG Düsseldorf, ZIP 2010, 28—*IKB Deutsche Industriebank AG*. In this case, contractual counterparties of a bank sought damages on the theory that the bank should have disclosed to them that the bank's risk management procedures were improper. At the same time, minority shareholders attempted to enforce management's liability based on a similar theory.

[16] OLG Köln, MDR 2006, 201.

agreements regarding the conduct of arbitration proceedings.[17] Such procedural agreements are clearly permissible pursuant to **s 1042 para 3 ZPO**. They are separate and different from the arbitration agreement. Thus, for instance, the form requirements set forth in s 1031 ZPO do not apply to procedural agreements (paras 2.70 *et seq.*).

2.17 The distinction is clear beyond doubt where the parties conclude such agreement on procedural issues separately, which in most cases happens only after conclusion of the arbitration agreement or in close connection with the actual arbitration. Where the document containing the arbitration agreement also contains provisions on the conduct of the arbitral proceedings, the distinction becomes less clear. This distinction is relevant primarily where the alleged nullity of a procedural clause may affect the arbitration agreement as a whole. In line with the **general preference to uphold the validity of arbitration agreements**,[18] invalid parts relating to the conduct and the procedure of the arbitration should be interpreted in case of doubt as not being material to the parties' fundamental choice to submit their dispute to arbitration (cf s 139 BGB).[19]

2. *General Requirements for a Party Agreement*

2.18 Given the substantive-law nature of arbitration agreements governed by German law, the general provisions for formation and validity of (substantive-law) agreements under German civil law apply (ss 104 *et seq.* BGB). Under general German civil law, in order to form an agreement an **offer and a corresponding acceptance** are required, ss 145 *et seq.* BGB.[20] Offer and acceptance need to correspond with respect to their substance—a **meeting of the minds** is required to conclude an arbitration agreement, ie a legally binding agreement to submit disputes regarding a certain legal relationship to an arbitral tribunal which shall render a final and binding decision (s 1029 para 1 ZPO).

2.19 As with any other contract, an arbitration agreement can be formed by a full-fledged offer that the other side accepts. Likewise, it is possible for the parties to negotiate and then write down the arbitration agreement together. An offer needs to be accepted within the stipulated **time frame**, or, in the absence of such stipulation, within a reasonable time; otherwise, it expires and thus becomes ineffective (s 148 BGB). **Changes to the offer** by the other party are considered a rejection of the offer, combined with a new **counter-offer** (s 150 para 2 BGB).

2.20 A contract is not formed unless and until the parties have **agreed on all essential aspects** of their agreement (s 154 para 1 BGB), which for an arbitration agreement

[17] Geimer, in: Zöller (ed), s 1029 para 11; Münch, in: MünchKommZPO, s 1031 para 5; Voit, in: Musielak/Voit (eds), s 1031 para 2; opposing view: eg, Lachmann, para 265.

[18] Geimer, in: Zöller (ed), s 1029 para 1; see also below para 2.109.

[19] OLG Frankfurt, NJW-RR 2010, 788 *et seq.*; KG NJW 2011, 2978; Geimer, in: Zöller (ed), s 1029 para 11; Voit, in: Musielak/Voit (eds), s 1031 para 15.

[20] Münch, in: MünchKommZPO, s 1031 para 17; Lachmann, para 319; Jauernig, in: Jauernig (ed), s 145 paras 1 *et seq.*; s 147 paras 1 *et seq.*

are set forth in s 1029 para 1 ZPO (below para 2.32). Failure to agree on non-essential (immaterial) aspects does not prevent the finding of an agreement (s 155 BGB). Therefore, if the parties abstained from agreeing on the minimum contents required to form an arbitration agreement, then they did not form a valid arbitration agreement at all. Questions regarding the formation of the agreement arise especially where the parties **refer to a "separate agreement"** in their main agreement which was actually never concluded. Some German courts have found such a clause sufficient to serve as a binding arbitration agreement where it contained the essential elements of s 1029 ZPO.[21] Missing parts were substituted by supplementary interpretation or by the Tenth Book of the ZPO. Conversely, where not even this minimum content was present, the parties' election of arbitration remained disregarded.[22] Only in specific circumstances do the courts find in such a clause at least a pre-contractual arrangement manifesting an intention to enter into a separate arbitration agreement (*Schiedsvorvertrag*).[23]

Such circumstances were found in a slightly different case where the court held that the parties did not enter into an arbitration agreement but the clause contained in negotiation minutes clearly expressed their intention to conclude an arbitration agreement.[24] While it is obvious that each situation needs to be decided on its specific facts, as a general matter, and in line with general principles of German contract law, we believe that where the parties state that they intend to do something later, this expression of their will should be taken seriously. This seemingly restrictive approach has nothing to do with the question whether Germany is an "arbitration friendly" jurisdiction. The threshold question is always whether there is arbitration in the first place. And as long as the parties have not agreed in a binding manner to arbitration, there is none. Imposing arbitration instead of state-court litigation even though at least one party has not (yet) entered into a final and binding agreement to arbitration would not appear to be a sign of "arbitration friendliness," but rather a sign of disrespect to party autonomy. **2.21**

As an alternative, the arbitration agreement can be concluded by referring to an arbitration clause recommended by an **arbitral institution** or contained in **general terms and conditions (AGB)**. In the case of AGB used vis-à-vis consumers, formation of an arbitration agreement is subject to the further requirements for inclusion and validity of AGB contained in s 305 paras 2 and 3 BGB.[25] By contrast, as far as **2.22**

---

21 KG NJW 2011, 2978; OLG München, May 23, 2007, 34 SchH 1/07 (unreported); opposing view: OLG Hamm, AG 2007, 910.

22 OLG Köln, MDR 2006, 201.

23 BGH BB 1973, 957.

24 OLG Köln, MDR 2006, 201; Lachmann, para 320; opposing view: Kröll, SchiedsVZ 2006, 203, 204.

25 Hartmann, in: Baumbach/Lauterbach/Albers/Hartmann (eds), s 1031 para 7; Geimer, in Zöller (ed), s 1031 para 9; Münch, in: MünchKommZPO, s 1031 para 37; Lachmann, para 348.

commercial parties are concerned, it is sufficient to satisfy the general requirements for contract formation outlined above (s 310 para 1 cl 1 BGB).[26]

2.23 In case of **conflicting AGB**, the general principles governing such situations apply. This means that the AGB apply only to the extent they are congruent; the conflicting parts do not apply at all, no matter who had the first or the last say in the negotiations.[27] Whether and to what extent a congruent part remains needs to be analyzed on a case-by-case basis. The mere fact that both parties somehow wished to have arbitration will not be sufficient if the differences between their clauses are too great.[28] For instance, where one party's AGB provide for DIS arbitration seated in Germany and the other party's AGB stipulate AAA[29] arbitration seated in the US, it will be hard to see a common ground for excluding the jurisdiction of the state courts.

3. Arbitration Agreement by Trade Usage

2.24 Because general principles of contract formation apply to arbitration agreements, an arbitration agreement can be formed by trade usage (s 346 HGB). The most relevant trade usage in the context of arbitration agreements with a German nexus are the principles of **commercial confirmation letters** (*kaufmännisches Bestätigungsschreiben*). Under this doctrine, a contract is deemed to be concluded according to the content of a confirmation letter from one side summarizing prior contract negotiations between the parties if the other side, a merchant, does not object without undue delay after receipt of this letter. This applies even where the contents of the confirmation letter are somewhat different from the prior discussions of the parties which they purport to summarize, unless the difference is so significant that the party sending the letter could not reasonably expect that the other side would accept it without further discussion.[30]

2.25 Under German law, this concept can easily be applied to arbitration clauses contained in commercial confirmation letters, even where the prior discussions of the parties did not address arbitration. This is implied by **s 1031 para 2 ZPO** which stipulates that the written form required by s 1031 para 1 ZPO may also be complied with by acceptance via trade usage, and trade usage includes silence upon receipt of a commercial confirmation letter.[31] However, it is important to note that s 1031 para 2 ZPO is only a clarification with respect to form. The **substantive prerequisites of the commercial confirmation letter doctrine** still need to be

---

26 Basedow, in: MünchKommBGB, s 305 para 93.

27 Basedow, in: MünchKommBGB, s 305 paras 103 *et seq.* with further references.

28 Similarly Münch, in: MünchKommZPO, s 1031 para 41.

29 American Arbitration Association.

30 BGH DStR 2001, 1129; NJW 1994, 1288; Canaris, s 23 para 8.

31 BGH KTS 1971, 37; BT-Drucks 13/5274, p 26; Geimer, in: Zöller (ed), s 1031 paras 8, 29; Hartmann, in: Baumbach/Lauterbach/Albers/Hartmann (eds), s 1031 para 6; cf also BGHZ 7, 187, 189 *et seq.* = NJW 1952, 1369 *et seq.*

fulfilled. The analysis therefore turns on the issue of whether a specific arbitration clause, if added without prior discussion, would still fall within the parameters of what the other side needs to expect in the context of a commercial confirmation letter or not. As far as arbitration as such is concerned, it is certainly not unusual in the context of international trade; in some instances, it may even be the norm. In a purely domestic context, the business practices may be different. Nevertheless, arbitration is, as a matter of German law, **principally equivalent** to state-court litigation, and merchants must be expected to be familiar with it. Thus, in our view, adding an arbitration clause as such generally falls within the parameters of the commercial confirmation letter doctrine and any different assessment requires exceptional circumstances.[32]

The analysis does not end at this point, though. In a next step, the **specific contents of the clause** need to be looked at. The contents may be so **unusual** that the sender of the letter could not reasonably expect the recipient to accept it without further discussion. For instance, an arbitration agreement stipulating that the arbitral tribunal shall **decide *ex aequo et bono*** (s 1051 para 3 ZPO) would seem to be too unusual, unless there are reasons in the specific case to assume otherwise. It is notable that in the context of commercial confirmation letters German courts tend to give little weight to the separability principle pursuant to s 1040 para 1 cl 2 ZPO. The Higher Regional Court of Hamburg, for instance, held that there was no valid arbitration agreement in such a letter reasoning that the price contained in the letter was completely unexpected, even though the price is clearly an issue relating to the main agreement of the parties and not the arbitration clause.[33] This approach appears reasonable with a view to the characteristics of trade usage because it would be inappropriately time consuming to abstract and reject single provisions of one overall confirmation letter.[34] **2.26**

In contrast to the rules governing commercial confirmation letters, it will generally not be sufficient to include an arbitration clause in an **invoice** even if it was issued in the close context of negotiations regarding its contents. In this case, the unilateral declaration regarding arbitration would be considered as a mere offer to conclude an arbitration agreement.[35] Unless there is acceptance of the offer, no agreement is concluded under general German standards of contract formation. **Mere silence** on the part of the invoice recipient, or **payment** of the invoice without objection, is not sufficient to be qualified as acceptance, whether under general principles of contract law or under the principles of commercial confirmation letters.[36] However, **2.27**

[32] BGH NJW 1952, 1359; OLG Köln, MDR 1951, 28; Münch, in: MünchKommZPO, s 1031 para 36.

[33] OLG Hamburg, March 15, 2012, 6 Sch 13/11 (unreported).

[34] Kröll, SchiedsVZ 2013, 185, 186.

[35] Geimer, in: Zöller (ed), s 1031 para 7.

[36] Lachmann, para 349; Hopt, in: Baumbach/Hopt (eds), s 346 para 35; Münch, in: MünchKommZPO, s 1031 para 27; Hartmann, in: Baumbach/Lauterbach/Albers/Hartmann (eds), s 1031 para 4.

the invoice recipient is free to accept the offer to conclude an arbitration agreement by express or implied declaration.

2.28 More generally, **trade usage** can be the basis for an arbitration agreement where there is a commercial conduct that typically includes the conclusion of arbitration agreements,[37] even though "real life" examples seem to be rare. One example would be an industry where nearly all conflicts are solved by arbitration, in particular if such an industry formed specialized arbitration bodies or institutions.[38]

4. Amendment of Arbitration Agreements

2.29 Amendments to arbitration agreements follow the **general principles for amendment of contracts.** Unless one party has a unilateral right to amend the contents of the arbitration agreement, an agreement of the parties will be required. The formation of such an amendment agreement again follows the general principles of contract formation outlined above, ie offer and corresponding acceptance. Here, too, trade usage—in particular the principles of commercial confirmation letters—apply. In addition, the form requirements set forth in s 1031 ZPO need to be observed as far as the parties intend to change any of the essential elements contained in s 1029 ZPO, in particular where the parties intend to broaden the personal or subject matter scope of the arbitration agreement (see below para 2.72).[39]

2.30 Complementary amendments can become necessary or desirable while the parties contemplate starting arbitration or even while an arbitration is already pending. For instance, the parties may find that the **number of arbitrators** or the **seat** of the arbitration no longer fits the purpose of the potential or present arbitration case. Similarly, the arbitral institution may have amended its **rules**, and the parties may agree that the amended rules have features that are not acceptable to them. Conversely, the parties may have agreed to the rules of an **institution** as of a certain date, and in the meantime amendments may have been put into place that both parties actually find more suitable. This may happen in particular with M&A[40] agreements where certain German practitioners still believe that for purposes of satisfying form requirements it is safer to refer to a static set of rules as of a certain date. Even though this view may seem overly cautious under German law (see below para 2.90), the practice still occurs. In case the institution has since amended its rules, parties should seriously consider using the new rules for a new dispute. Most of the time, institutional reform is a balanced exercise that tends to benefit all parties of a dispute. In addition, arbitrators may have become used to the new rules, and may find it awkward or even difficult to apply the former ones.

---

[37] Lachmann, paras 322 *et seq.*; Schütze, in: Wieczorek/Schütze (eds), s 1027 para 22.

[38] Berger, DZWIR 1993, 466 *et seq.*

[39] Lachmann, para 588; Münch, in: MünchKommZPO, s 1031 para 14; Hartmann, in: Baumbach/Lauterbach/Albers/Hartmann (eds), s 1031 para 11.

[40] Mergers & Acquisitions.

Finally, the parties may have conducted an arbitration under the arbitration agreement and may agree that for **future additional disputes**, they would like to optimize the arbitration agreement, for instance by introducing mandatory ADR/mediation or a dispute resolution board before arbitration. Such an amendment to the original arbitration agreement is not subject to the form requirements of s 1031 ZPO. **2.31**

III. Minimum Content

In order to qualify as an arbitration agreement, pursuant to s 1029 para 1 ZPO, an agreement must relate to a dispute within a defined legal relationship (below paras 2.33 *et seq.*) and must provide for arbitration—as opposed to other mechanisms—for binding conflict resolution (below paras 2.39 *et seq.*). It is easy to satisfy these minimum requirements, as the **model clause suggested by the DIS** demonstrates (see above para 2.2). The same applies to the **ICC model clause**: **2.32**

> All disputes arising out of or in connection with the present contract shall be finally settled under the Rules of Arbitration of the International Chamber of Commerce by one or more arbitrators appointed in accordance with the said Rules.[41]

1. Dispute Related to a Defined Legal Relationship

Pursuant to s 1029 para 1 ZPO, the arbitration agreement must relate to a dispute regarding a defined legal relationship. Dispute means a **legal controversy**, as opposed to a controversy merely on facts or theoretical questions of law.[42] The German law thereby tracks the terminology of the Model Law.[43] The ZPO uses the term "legal relationship" also in other contexts, such as s 256 ZPO, which addresses requests for declaratory judgments and which also must relate to such a defined legal relationship. A defined legal relationship in this regard can be understood broadly as a **specific legal relation of one person to another person or of a person to a right or an object**, such as legal claims and rights as well as contracts.[44] Unlike the dispute, the relationship need not necessarily exist between the parties to the arbitration agreement.[45] Thus, for instance, **third parties** may invoke rights out of a contract. **2.33**

The term "legal relationship" is **broader than the term "subject of the dispute"** (*Streitgegenstand*) within the meaning of s 253 ZPO. In order to bring a claim before a German state court, the plaintiff in its statement of claim must specify such "subject of the dispute" (s 253 para 2 ZPO) with regard to a certain set of facts and **2.34**

---

41 Available at http://www.iccwbo.org (last visited December 1, 2015).

42 Münch, in: MünchKommZPO, s 1029 para 83; Schwab/Walter, ch 3 para 4; internationally see Blackaby/Partasides/Redfern/Hunter, paras 1.59 *et seq.*

43 Regarding the Model Law see Blackaby/Partasides/Redfern/Hunter, para 2.22.

44 Münch, in: MünchKommZPO, s 1029 para 69; see also Greger, in: Zöller (ed), s 256 para 4; Foerste, in: Musielak/Voit (eds), s 256 para 2.

45 Münch, in MünchKommZPO, s 1029 para 70.

a resulting claim. By contrast, an arbitration agreement can take an entire legal relationship away from the jurisdiction of the state courts without the need for the parties to define the individual disputed subjects.

2.35 On the other hand, the relationship must at least be a defined legal one. It is not sufficient to state that all disputes arising between two persons or all disputes arising from a certain commercial or business relationship shall be subject to arbitration.[46] The parties may instead agree that they want to choose arbitration for any and all present or future disputes arising out of or in connection with a certain contract. It is not even required that the legal relationship already be validly formed at the time when the arbitration agreement is concluded.[47] It is well established that an arbitration agreement contained in a **framework agreement** is also valid for services and other subsequent actions based on the framework agreement.[48]

2.36 Notably, s 1029 ZPO does not require the parties to submit any and all disputes arising out of a legal relationship to arbitration, but allows **limiting the submission** according to the parties' needs. For instance, in **M&A agreements** governed by German law, it is not uncommon to refer disputes regarding closing accounts (for purposes of purchase price adjustments) to expert determination, and to refer all other disputes to arbitration.[49] Another example may be that the parties subject disputes from a certain legal relationship to arbitration only to the extent they exceed certain **thresholds**, eg in terms of amounts in dispute.[50] This option should be **used with caution**, since the amount in dispute may well vary over the lifecycle of a dispute (including counterclaims). Speaking more broadly, parties should generally be cautious in narrowing down the scope of arbitration agreements or carving out certain disputes. If they choose to do so, they should carefully consider the **interface** between arbitration and whatever other dispute resolution mechanism exists for disputes not covered by the arbitration agreement. If they fail to do so, they risk finding themselves in **unnecessary and costly** disputes as to which dispute resolution mechanism should apply.

2.37 The parties may also choose to subject only a **separable part of a dispute** to arbitration. For instance, the arbitration agreement may refer only to liability, but not quantum, or vice versa. However, parties must again be cautious regarding separability. For instance, it would not be possible to separate defenses (eg statute of limitations) from the claim as such.[51]

---

46 Voit, in: Musielak/Voit (eds), s 1029 para 16; Münch, in: MünchKommZPO, s 1029 para 74.
47 Münch, in: MünchKommZPO, s 1029 para 74; Voit, in: Musielak/Voit (eds), s 1029 para 16.
48 DIS Interim Award, SchiedsVZ 2005, 166, 168; Münch, in: MünchKommZPO, s 1029 para 74.
49 Rieder, in: Schütze/Weipert/Rieder (eds), p 351 para 12; Kasolowski/Schnabl, SchiedsVZ 2012, 84.
50 Münch, in: MünchKommZPO, s 1029 para 86; Geimer, in: Zöller (ed), s 1029 para 38; Voit, in: Musielak/Voit (eds), s 1029 para 22.
51 Münch, in: MünchKommZPO, s 1029 para 86; Geimer, in: Zöller (ed), s 1029 para 38; Voit, in: Musielak/Voit (eds), s 1029 para 22.

As far as the Tenth Book of the ZPO is concerned, the legal relationship must be **civil** in nature (s 13 GVG, art 3 EGZPO).[52] An arbitral tribunal under the Tenth Book of the ZPO may replace a state court only within the limits of the state court's own jurisdiction pursuant to the ZPO.[53] State courts acting under the ZPO have jurisdiction only over civil matters (art 3 EGZPO). Thus, for instance, **criminal matters** may not be brought before an arbitral tribunal. The same applies to matters that are referred to the jurisdiction of the German **social courts** and the German **tax courts**.[54] Regarding disputes related to **administrative law** (s 40 para 1 VwGO), **s 173 VwGO** contains a special provision allowing for arbitration and referring to the provisions of the Tenth Book of the ZPO, which shall apply *mutatis mutandis*, unless the principal differences between administrative law and civil law proceedings require otherwise (para 1.82). **Insolvency proceedings** follow their own rules under the German Insolvency Statute (InsO). Thus, an arbitral tribunal cannot conduct insolvency proceedings. However, individual disputes in connection with an insolvency may—to some extent—be referred to arbitration insofar as the choice of arbitration does not infringe the genuine rights of the insolvency administrator (*Insolvenzverwalter*; for details see below para 2.130).[55] **2.38**

2. Dispute Resolution by an Arbitral Tribunal

Arbitration is the final and binding resolution of a dispute between the parties to the exclusion of the ordinary courts. Thus, the parties must be found to have intended the agreed mechanism to result in a **decision**, as opposed to mere recommendations or other forms of support in resolving a dispute, as may be provided by other means of alternative dispute resolution, such as, eg, mediation, conciliation (*Schlichtung*), or expert determination (see above paras 1.84 *et seq.*). **2.39**

The parties must further intend the decision to be **final and binding**, to the exclusion of the ordinary courts. This is not the case where an agreement refers disputes to particular **association courts** (*Verbandsgerichte*) which can be found mainly in the areas of sports and labor law. Those institutions are mere executive bodies for decisions on specific issues like penalties or expulsion. As these decisions are as such not enforceable and subject to judicial review by the state courts, association courts are not recognized as arbitral tribunals—even where the parties erroneously use this term.[56] On the other hand, the parties need not expressly use the words **2.40**

[52] OLG Frankfurt, NJW-RR 2001, 1078, 1079; Schwab/Walter, ch 3 para 2; Münch, in: MünchKommZPO, s 1029 para 77.

[53] Münch, in: MünchKommZPO, s 1029 para 76; Zimmermann, in: MünchKommZPO, s 13 GVG para 3.

[54] Münch, in: MünchKommZPO, s 1029 para 79.

[55] Münch, in: MünchKommZPO, s 1029 para 81; opposing view: Saenger, in: Saenger (ed), s 1030 para 9; Voit, in: Musielak/Voit (eds), s 1029 para 5, according to whom insolvency proceedings are arbitrable.

[56] BGHZ 159, 207, 210 *et seq.* = SchiedsVZ 2004, 205, 207 *et seq.*; Münch, in: MünchKommZPO, s 1066 para 21; Schwab/Walter, ch 32 para 17.

"exclusion of the ordinary courts" if such effect is clear from their intentions.[57] However, where the parties **merely expressly exclude the jurisdiction of the ordinary courts**, they need not necessarily have agreed to arbitration if they fail to say so. It is well possible that the parties intended to completely exclude the enforceability of a claim (*pactum de non petendo*).[58]

2.41 The parties may agree that arbitration is only an option next to state-court litigation, and that the party commencing the dispute may elect between litigation and arbitration.[59] The parties may even agree—at least outside the scope of AGB—that only one party may be entitled to make the election.[60] Likewise, the parties may agree that there is a choice between two different arbitration mechanisms, eg two different arbitral institutions. It is not possible, however, that the parties agree to litigate the same legal dispute in parallel in front of both a state court and an arbitral tribunal, or before two arbitral tribunals.[61]

2.42 Under the precedent of the German Federal Supreme Court (BGH), a dispute resolution mechanism can still be qualified as an arbitration agreement, even where the parties have provided that an arbitral award is **subject to judicial review.**[62] Under this doctrine, the parties can therefore set forth in the arbitration agreement that the arbitral award can be subject to judicial review or to appeal levels of jurisdiction.[63] The above decision of the BGH is contrary to the pre-existing prevailing view in German legal doctrine, and it has been met with considerable criticism, which we share.[64] Section 1029 ZPO requires a "decision" by an arbitral tribunal, and s 1055 ZPO accords such "decision" the same effects as a final and binding judgment of a state court. For purposes of legal clarity, a dispute resolution mechanism that does not result in such a decision, but is subject to court review beyond the limits of the set aside grounds set forth in s 1059 para 2 ZPO should not qualify as "arbitration," but is to be regarded as another form of alternative dispute resolution more akin to conciliation (*Schlichtung*).[65]

---

57 Schiedsgericht der IHK Kassel, SchiedsVZ 2006, 167; Münch, in: MünchKommZPO, s 1029 para 90.

58 Münch, in: MünchKommZPO, s 1029 para 93.

59 BGHZ 88, 314, 317 = NJW 1984, 1355.

60 BGHZ 115, 324, 325 = NJW 1992, 575 = XIX Y.B. Com. Arb. 201 (1994); OLG Bremen, SchiedsVZ 2007, 51, 52; Münch, in: MünchKommZPO, s 1029 para 96; Saenger, in: Saenger (ed), s 1029 para 12; Voit, in: Musielak/Voit (eds), s 1029 para 21; Geimer, in: Zöller (ed), s 1029 para 35.

61 Münch, in: MünchKommZPO, s 1029 paras 97 *et seq.*; Saenger, in: Saenger (ed), s 1029 para 12; Voit, in: Musielak/Voit (eds), s 1029 para 22.

62 BGH SchiedsVZ 2007, 160, 162 = XXXIII Y.B. Com. Arb. 234 (2008); Lachmann, para 2167; Schlosser, in: Stein/Jonas (eds), s 1029 paras 30 *et seq.;* same view from an international perspective Gaillard/Savage, para 489.

63 Lachmann, para 2167; Schlosser, in: Stein/Jonas (eds), s 1029 para 31.

64 See Münch, in: MünchKommZPO, s 1029 para 90 with further references; Geimer, in: Zöller (ed), s 1029 para 6*; Reichold,* in: Thomas/Putzo (eds), s 1029 para 3; Wolff, ZZP 120 (2007), 371.

65 Münch, in: MünchKommZPO, s 1029 para 92; Schwab/Walter, ch 3 paras 5 *et seq.*

Finally, it goes almost without saying that the parties **need not designate a certain arbitral institution**, but may rely instead on the rules for ad hoc arbitration provided for as default by the Tenth Book of the ZPO. We will explore more deeply the choice between institutional and ad hoc arbitration in paras 2.198 *et seq.* **2.43**

IV. Validity

When looking at the validity of an arbitration agreement, as a first step, we need to look at the separability principle (below paras 2.45 *et seq.*). In other words, the fact that there may be grounds for invalidity of the remainder of the parties' agreement containing an arbitration clause does not necessarily render the arbitration clause invalid. An arbitration agreement can be invalid for lack of objective or subjective arbitrability (below paras 2.48 *et seq.* and paras 2.64 *et seq.*). In addition, depending on the parties to the agreement, certain form requirements apply (below paras 2.67 *et seq.*). It goes almost without saying that further general grounds for invalidity applying to all agreements may be relevant to arbitration agreements as well, in particular lack of proper representation (below paras 2.91 *et seq.*). Finally, the German law on AGB provides for further invalidity grounds related to arbitration clauses contained in such AGB (below paras 2.95 *et seq.*). **2.44**

1. *The Separability Principle*

Pursuant to s 1040 para 1 cl 2 ZPO, in line with international standards,[66] an arbitration clause is to be treated separately from the remainder of the agreement in which it is contained. Thus, grounds for invalidating the remainder of the agreement do not necessarily render an arbitration agreement invalid. This **overrides** the general principle of German contract law as expressed in **s 139 BGB**. Pursuant to s 139 BGB, in case of doubt, where one provision of an agreement is invalid, the entire agreement is deemed invalid unless it can be established that the parties would have concluded the agreement even without the invalid provision. The separability principle helps concentrate a legal dispute before an arbitral tribunal, without "front-loading" the jurisdiction phase of an arbitration with a discussion of grounds for invalidity, which in most cases are substantive issues (eg, error, fraud, duress, violations of statutory prohibitions etc). **2.45**

Thus, the contents of the overall agreement may be in **violation of the law or against good morals** (ss 134, 138 BGB), and the arbitration clause can still be valid. For example, an agreement may be induced by **corruption** and therefore be invalid. A dispute regarding claims for performance or compensation under the agreement would still need to be brought before the competent arbitral tribunal under the arbitration clause of the agreement, and it will be upon the tribunal to decide whether the remainder of the agreement is indeed invalid or not. In general, **2.46**

66 See Born, pp 349 *et seq.*; Gaillard/Savage, paras 389 *et seq.*; Blackaby/Partasides/Redfern/Hunter, paras 2.89 *et seq.*

a finding of invalidity will not do away with the arbitration clause and thus the very basis of the tribunal's jurisdiction.[67] Likewise, the overall agreement containing an arbitration clause may well be invalid for failure to follow the proper **form** (eg notarization pursuant to s 128 BGB). This, in our view, would not render the arbitration clause invalid, as long as the arbitration clause satisfies the specific form requirements of s 1031 ZPO.

2.47 As a result of the separability principle, an arbitration agreement can be considered invalid only if the defect at issue **specifically applies to or is inherent to the arbitration agreement itself**. In the corruption context mentioned above, one scenario could be that the parties concluded the arbitration agreement specifically for the purpose of effecting a corrupt payment or to enable some other form of money laundering.[68] Similarly, defects such as deception and duress may apply to the arbitration agreement itself.[69] These examples may be rare; nonetheless, they exist in practice.

2. Objective Arbitrability

2.48 a) **General Principles** Objective arbitrability of a dispute means that a certain subject matter of a dispute can be submitted to arbitration because the law has not reserved the dispute to the ordinary courts. Under German law, a **broad concept** of objective arbitrability applies, which is enshrined in s 1030 ZPO. The German legislator considers arbitration to be **principally equivalent** to state-court litigation.[70] Based on a liberal concept of freedom of contract (*Vertragsfreiheit*) and private autonomy (*Privatautonomie*), the parties are free to derogate the competence of state courts in favor of "private justice," unless the law contains a specific exception in order to protect certain public or private interests.[71] As a rule of thumb, in case of doubt, a dispute is arbitrable.[72] The German rules on objective arbitrability are mandatory for arbitrations seated in Germany and may not be derogated by party agreement.[73]

2.49 Thus, as a general matter, **all disputes on claims involving economic interests** (*vermögensrechtliche Ansprüche*) are objectively arbitrable without limitation (s 1030 para 1 cl 1 ZPO). Economic means that the dispute arises from or relates to a right

---

[67] Lachmann, para 536; Rieder/Schoenemann, NJW 2011, 1169, 1172 *et seq.*; Schlosser, in: Stein/Jonas (eds), s 1040 para 7.

[68] Kreindler, p 251; Lachmann, paras 537 *et seq.*; Münch, in: MünchKommZPO, s 1059 para 47; Eilmansberger, SchiedsVZ 2006, 5, 7 *et seq.*; others have expressed the view that even in such scenarios, the arbitration agreement should be considered valid, but the arbitrators should notify public prosecutors if there is a suspicion of violations of international *ordre public*; see v Schlabrendorff, in: *Festschrift Schlosser*, pp 851 *et seq.*

[69] Lachmann, paras 540 *et seq.*; Voit, in: Musielak/Voit (eds), s 1029 para 11; Schlosser, in: *Festschrift Böckstiegel*, pp 697 *et seq.*

[70] BT-Drucks 13/5274, p 34 ("*die Schiedsgerichtsbarkeit als eine der staatlichen Gerichtsbarkeit im Prinzip gleichwertige Rechtsschutzmöglichkeit*"); see also BGHZ 160, 127, 133 *et seq.* = NJW 2004, 2898, 2899; Münch, in: MünchKommZPO, s 1030 para 1.

[71] Münch, in: MünchKommZPO, s 1030 para 2.

[72] Münch, in: MünchKommZPO, s 1030 para 10 ("*in dubio pro Schiedsfähigkeit*").

[73] Münch, in: MünchKommZPO, s 1030 para 22; Geimer, in: Zöller (ed), s 1030 para 24.

with a **quantifiable financial value**. This includes all disputes on payment claims, but also claims for declaratory judgment regarding economic interests[74] and non-waivable economic interests. The latter already follows from the wording of s 1030 para 1 cl 1 ZPO, which includes all economic interests regardless of their capability of settlement. Accordingly, the BGH classified the non-waivable claim of a limited liability company (GmbH) against its shareholders for their capital contributions (s 19 para 2 cl 1 GmbHG) as arbitrable.[75] Damage claims are generally considered to be monetary claims.[76] IP-related disputes are generally arbitrable, with the exception of patent annulment claims (see below para 2.55).

Disputes on **non-economic interests** are arbitrable under German law to the extent the parties can **dispose of a dispute by way of settlement** (s 1030 para 1 cl 2 ZPO). Thus, disputes on matters of personal status, eg the divorce of a marriage, are not arbitrable, whereas monetary claims resulting from a divorce (support payments and the like) are, at least in principle, arbitrable.[77] Other examples of non-economic interests, which are arbitrable, are violations of personality rights[78] or disputes about exclusions from associations.[79] **2.50**

Where an arbitration agreement relates to disputes which are not covered by s 1030 ZPO, the agreement is null and void as far as this dispute is concerned.[80] Apart from that, objective arbitrability of a dispute is subject to **review by state courts** in several respects. First, prior to the formation of the arbitral tribunal, a party can apply to the German state courts in order to **determine the admissibility or inadmissibility of arbitral proceedings** (s 1032 para 2 ZPO, for details see below paras 2.142 *et seq.*). In that context, the requesting party can point to the lack of arbitrability of a dispute. Second, where an arbitral tribunal renders a preliminary ruling affirming its jurisdiction, each party can file an action with the state courts challenging such **preliminary ruling** (s 1040 para 3 cl 2 ZPO) by arguing lack of arbitrability. Third, lack of arbitrability is a ground for **set aside** pursuant to s 1059 para 2 no 2 lit a ZPO (see below para 2.64). Fourth, it is a recognized objection against **enforcement** of an arbitral award (s 1060 para 2 ZPO). **2.51**

Where an arbitration agreement relates to **both arbitrable disputes and non-arbitrable disputes**, the agreement is without effect as far as non-arbitrable disputes are concerned. The **remainder of the agreement** is generally valid and **2.52**

[74] Geimer, in: Zöller (ed), s 1030 para 1; Münch, in: MünchKommZPO, s 1030 para 13; Saenger, in: Saenger (ed), s 1030 para 2.

[75] BGHZ 160, 127, 133 = NJW 2004, 2898, 2899.

[76] BayObLGZ 2001, 311, 313; Münch, in: MünchKommZPO, s 1030 para 13.

[77] BGH NJW 1996, 1753, 1754; Lachmann, para 285; Geimer, in: Zöller (ed), s 1030 para 6; Münch, in: MünchKommZPO, s 1030 para 14; Voit, in: Musielak/Voit (eds), s 1030 para 6; Hartmann, in: Baumbach/Lauterbach/Albers/Hartmann (eds), s 1030 para 7.

[78] Münch, in: MünchKommZPO, s 1030 para 20.

[79] Voit, in: Musielak/Voit (eds), s 1030 para 6; Münch, in: MünchKommZPO, s 1030 para 20.

[80] Trittmann/Hanefeld, in: *Arbitration in Germany*, s 1030 para 7; Münch, in: MünchKommZPO, s 1030 para 16.

binding. Some authors derive this result from the structure of s 1030 ZPO and the fact that lack of arbitrability is the exception, and arbitrability is the rule.[81] In our view, the **general provisions of German contract law** need to be applied, given that an arbitration agreement is a substantive-law agreement (see above para 2.12). Thus, in principle, s 139 BGB applies. This means that the question is first one of contract interpretation. In other words, would the parties have refrained from concluding an arbitration agreement at all, had they considered the lack of arbitrability, or would they have restricted the arbitration agreement to the arbitrable disputes? In case of remaining doubts, s 139 ZPO provides for the invalidity of the entire agreement. In most cases, however, it should be possible to find that the parties would still have elected arbitration for those disputes that are arbitrable.[82] For instance, where an arbitration clause covers all sorts of corporate disputes between a shareholder and a corporation, but it does not follow the stringent requirements of the German courts for disputes relating to the validity of shareholder resolutions (see para 1.78), it is reasonable to assume that in most cases the parties—had they been aware of the defect of their arbitration agreement—would still have subjected the remaining types of corporate disputes to arbitration. On the other hand, where the main subject of an arbitration agreement is not arbitrable (eg divorce, see above para 2.50), it is probably against the will of the parties to uphold the arbitration agreement for ancillary monetary disputes as this would lead to a costly split of fora.

2.53 **b) Exceptions** In addition to the broad concept of objective arbitrability, German law contains very few specific exclusions. For instance, arbitration is not permissible for certain disputes regarding residential leases (s 1030 para 2 ZPO).[83] The exclusion applies to disputes regarding the **"existence" of the residential lease**. This means, in particular, termination and eviction disputes, whereas, for instance, disputes regarding lease payments are arbitrable.[84] The purpose of this exclusion is to protect tenants and to guarantee their access to the state courts. Where a lease agreement nevertheless contains such an arbitration clause, it is invalid, whereas the remainder of the lease agreement is valid and binding (s 1040 para 1 cl 2 ZPO, in derogation of s 139 BGB).[85] The exception to arbitrability contained in s 1030 para 2 ZPO is a narrow one, and it **does not lend itself to any extensions** regarding other private or consumer-related disputes.[86] In fact, the

[81] Eg Münch, in: MünchKommZPO, s 1030 para 16.

[82] Similarly Born, pp 914 *et seq.*

[83] For further specific exclusions pursuant to s 1030 para 2 ZPO in the areas of employment and certain IP disputes see Lachmann, paras 301 *et seq.*

[84] Geimer, in: Zöller (ed), s 1030 para 21; Münch, in: MünchKommZPO, s 1030 paras 27 *et seq.*; Voit, in: Musielak/Voit (eds), s 1030 para 5; Reichold, in: Thomas/Putzo (eds), s 1030 para 4.

[85] Münch, in: MünchKommZPO, s 1030 para 25; Reichold, in: Thomas/Putzo (eds), s 1030 para 7.

[86] Münch, in: MünchKommZPO, s 1030 para 15; Geimer, in: Zöller (ed), s 1030 para 22.

exception is itself questionable from a political and public policy point of view, but from a legal perspective it has to be accepted as is stands right now.

2.54 Furthermore, there are limited exceptions to arbitrability contained in **provisions outside the ZPO** (s 1030 para 3 ZPO). The mere fact that German law provides for the exclusive jurisdiction of certain courts for certain types of disputes does not mean that such disputes are not arbitrable.[87] Rather, exclusive jurisdiction is a means to allocate jurisdiction among state courts, provided state courts are competent to decide on a dispute in the first place. Where the parties have deprived the state courts of such competence by way of an arbitration agreement, the provisions on exclusive jurisdiction are no longer relevant.

2.55 Two clear and practically important examples of non-arbitrability are patent validity disputes and individual employment disputes.[88] The prevailing opinion in German practice continues to be that **German patent courts** have exclusive jurisdiction for declaring patents invalid (ss 65, 81 PatG).[89] As a patent in Germany is granted by an administrative deed, it cannot be subject to party disposition and requires declaration of invalidity with effect *erga omnes*.[90] Nevertheless, arbitral tribunals may deal with patent issues. They may even consider a patent invalid as a threshold issue, if such a determination is necessary to come to a decision on the claim brought by one of the parties (eg a damage claim).[91]

2.56 Regarding labor law disputes, German law provides for arbitration mainly with regard to disputes between the parties of collective bargaining agreements (*Tarifvertragsparteien*).[92] By contrast, **individual disputes between an employer and the employee**, eg regarding the termination of an employment agreement or the payment of wages, are **considered non-arbitrable by the German labor courts.**[93] The reason is that the strict procedural rules in labor court proceedings are meant to ensure a high level of security and consistency in case law which typically concerns the sensitive area of fundamental rights of employees.[94]

---

87 BGHZ 132, 278, 281 = NJW 1996, 1753, 1754; OLG Köln, March 20, 2008, 18 U 98/07 (unreported); Münch, in: MünchKommZPO, s 1030 para 32; Saenger, in: Saenger (ed), s 1030 para 3.

88 Further examples with less practical relevance exist in the areas of cross-border banking disputes (s 53 para 3 KWG) and arbitration agreements of guardians and similar persons unless approved by the competent court (ss 1822 no 12, 1908i para 1, 1915 para 1 in combination with ss 1828–1830 BGB); see Münch, in: MünchKommZPO, s 1030 para 33.

89 BGH BB 1984, 561, 562; Hartmann, in: Baumbach/Lauterbach/Albers/Hartmann (eds), s 1030 para 12; Münch, in: MünchKommZPO, s 1030 para 33; Voit, in: Musielak/Voit (eds), s 1030 para 3; Lachmann, para 313; opposing view: Geimer, in: Zöller (ed), s 1030 para 15 with further references. The same applies to complaints aiming at the withdrawal of a patent and the granting of compulsory licenses (*Zwangslizenz*).

90 BT-Drucks 13/5274, p 35; Voit, in: Musielak/Voit (eds), s 1030 para 3; Münch, in: MünchKommZPO, s 1030 para 33; opposing view: Geimer, in: Zöller (ed), s 1030 para 14.

91 Lachmann, para 311; Rogge/Grabinski, in: Benkhard (ed), s 143 para 13.

92 Sections 102 *et seq.* German Labor Court Act (ArbGG).

93 BAG IPRspr. 2007, no 50, 166, 176; LAG Köln, May 24, 2007, 10 Sa 593/06 (unreported); Münch, in: MünchKommZPO, s 1030 para 33.

94 Germelmann, in: Germelmann/Matthes/Prütting (eds), s 4 para 1.

2.57 Another example occasionally mentioned in the present context can be found in the decision of the Munich Higher Regional Court (OLG München), which has held that compensation claims of a commercial agent pursuant to s 89b HGB cannot be subjected to dispute resolution by an arbitral tribunal seated outside the EU.[95] It is highly doubtful whether the decision is correct. In any event, it does not deal with arbitrability as such, but the potential consequences of the binding nature of s 89b HGB, and cannot be generalized beyond the narrow scope of its underlying facts.

2.58 c) **Arbitrability of Antitrust Disputes** A number of other disputes that may be doubtful in other jurisdictions are clearly **arbitrable** under German law. For example, generally, **anti-trust related disputes** are arbitrable, both relating to a party seeking damages in arbitral proceedings (offensive) and to a party invoking anti-trust infringements as a defense (Art 101 para 2 TFEU).[96] In arbitration proceedings, the latter will usually play a bigger role. The arbitral tribunal has to apply the mandatory anti-trust rules *ex officio*.[97] Offensive anti-trust cases, where a third party is seeking to enforce claims for compensation or injunctive relief based on anti-trust violations are also increasingly of importance, however this would require that the parties conclude an arbitration agreement before the dispute.[98] Regardless of an offensive or defensive matter, if mandatory anti-trust law is violated by an arbitral award it may be set aside pursuant to s 1059 para 2 no 2 lit b ZPO and not be declared enforceable pursuant to s 1060 para 2 ZPO.[99] Set aside of an award can be sought only within the applicable three-month time limit, also with regard to alleged violations of anti-trust laws.[100] Nevertheless, arbitral awards based on violations of anti-trust laws are not binding upon third parties or the European Commission invoking anti-trust violations.[101] Unlike state courts, arbitral tribunals are generally not allowed to present anti-trust related questions (or for that matter, any other issues regarding the interpretation of EU law) to the ECJ pursuant to Art 267 TFEU.[102]

---

[95] OLG München, WM 2006, 1556; Lachmann, para 317.

[96] K Schmidt, BB 2006, 1397, 1398; Bumiller, in: Wiedemann (ed), s 61 para 14; Eilmansberger, SchiedsVZ 2006, 5, 6; Meessen, in: Loewenheim/Meessen/Riesenkampff (eds), Einführung para 118; K Schmidt, in: Immenga/Mestmäcker, VO 1/2003 Anh 3, para 67.

[97] Eilmansberger, SchiedsVZ 2006, 5, 10; K Schmidt, BB 2006, 1397, 1399; K Schmidt, in: Immenga/Mestmäcker (eds), VO 1/2003 Anh 3, para 69; Meessen, in: Loewenheim/Meessen/Riesenkampff (eds), Einführung, paras 128, 143.

[98] K Schmidt, BB 2006, 1397, 1399; K Schmidt, in: Immenga/Mestmäcker (eds), VO 1/2003 Anh 3, para 67.

[99] ECJ EuZW 1999, 565—*Eco Swiss*.

[100] ECJ EuZW 1999, 565—*Eco Swiss*.

[101] K Schmidt, in: Immenga/Mestmäcker, VO 1/2003 Anh 3, para 70; K Schmidt, BB 2006, 1397, 1399 *et seq.*; Eilmansberger, SchiedsVZ 2006, 5, 14; Meessen, in: Loewenheim/Meessen/Riesenkampff (eds), Einführung, para 143.

[102] ECJ NJW 1982, 1207—*Nordsee*; ECJ EuZW 2005, 319—*Denuit and Cordenier*; Meessen, in: Loewenheim/Meessen/Riesenkampff (eds), Einführung, para 147; Dauses, in: Dauses (ed), P.II para 119; K Schmidt, BB 2006, 1397, 1401. An exception exists for arbitral tribunals established by laws of a EU Member State, see ECJ BB 2014, 723.

d) **Arbitrability of Corporate Law Disputes** In principle, under German law, corporate law disputes are arbitrable. Arbitration is of course a recognized and frequently used means of dispute resolution regarding corporate matters, eg regarding rights and obligations of shareholders among themselves and towards the company, disputes arising from the acquisition or disposal of shares and issues related to non-compete agreements. However, special rules apply regarding certain types of disputes, especially those between a shareholder and a corporation relating to the **validity of shareholder resolutions** (*Beschlussmängelstreitigkeiten*). For a long time, German courts were reluctant to accept that disputes regarding the validity of shareholder resolutions of a corporation are arbitrable.[103] The main concerns were to ensure that like a state court decision, arbitral awards declaring shareholder resolutions null and void are binding not only upon the parties, but all shareholders, and hence to ensure that all shareholders have a fair opportunity to participate in such arbitral proceedings which may affect their rights. **2.59**

As the German legislator decided not to address the issue in the course of the reform of the German arbitration law in 1998, but to continue to leave the issue to the courts to develop adequate solutions, the **German Federal Supreme Court (BGH) in April 2009** took up the issue and developed a set of rules addressing disputes related to the validity of shareholder resolutions (***Schiedsfähigkeit II***, see above para 1.78). The DIS provides rules on such types of arbitration which the parties can choose in order to ensure that their arbitration agreement conforms with these types of requirements.[104] **2.60**

Thus, where a company and its shareholders wish to subject disputes regarding the validity of shareholder resolutions to arbitration today, they have a convenient and safe set of rules to choose from. **Historic arbitration agreements** that pre-date the above-mentioned leading case of the BGH are usually problematic. German courts have applied the requirements of the BGH in a **strict** fashion. If the arbitration agreement does not reflect all of the above criteria, even if the arbitration agreement has been inserted in the company by-laws many years before the pertaining decisions of the BGH, the arbitration agreement is regarded as **null and void.**[105] **2.61**

If the parties nevertheless agree that the pertaining dispute should be resolved by way of arbitration, they ought to **conclude a new arbitration agreement** implementing the above criteria. It is in all likelihood not enough that one party starts arbitration on the basis of the existing but void arbitration agreement and the other party does not object. The voidness will usually result from the fact that the rights of third parties, ie the other shareholders, are not sufficiently respected. As long as they are not brought "on board," the clear rules specified by the BGH do not allow the assumption of a (new) valid arbitration agreement as a consequence of **2.62**

[103] BGHZ 132, 278 = NJW 1996, 1753—*Schiedsfähigkeit I.*
[104] DIS SRCoLD 2009, available at http://www.disarb.org (last visited December 1, 2015).
[105] OLG Frankfurt, NZG 2011, 629.

preclusion (s 1040 para 2 ZPO).[106] By contrast, a different situation arises where the opposing party is not the company but other shareholders. As the legal effect of a claim under s 256 ZPO affects only the involved parties, the other shareholders need not be protected and an implied arbitration agreement or the application of s 1040 para 2 ZPO have to be considered.[107]

2.63 In light of the right to be heard and the fair trial doctrine as well as the tribunal's own interest in producing an award that is enforceable and not subject to set aside (ss 1059, 1060 ZPO), the arbitral tribunal may need to **make the parties aware of the issue** at the appropriate time if the parties apparently fail to see the issue.[108] It may of course be that the respondent (usually the company) then takes a tactical approach and refuses to cooperate in the conclusion of a valid arbitration agreement. From a corporate law perspective, it could be argued that the company and the shareholders are obliged, as a result of their corporate duties of loyalty, to participate in **good faith** in the **"repair"** of an invalid arbitration agreement.[109] Whether such a duty exists in general was expressly left open by the BGH; pursuant to the BGH, it does **not exist with respect to an already pending case.**[110] As a consequence, where a party wants to rely on corporate duties of loyalty to repair an invalid agreement, this has to be done before any dispute arises. However, it may be possible to uphold an arbitration agreement for certain types of disputes. For instance, the arbitration agreement may be invalid only with respect to disputes regarding the validity of shareholder resolutions, but it may be valid and binding regarding all other arbitrable disputes (cf s 139 BGB).

3. Subjective Arbitrability

2.64 Subjective arbitrability means the power of a party to a dispute to enter into an arbitration agreement. Section 1059 para 2 no 1 lit a ZPO provides that lack of subjective arbitrability is a ground for set aside. The Tenth Book of the ZPO does not expressly address the prerequisites for subjective arbitrability in the way it addresses objective arbitrability in s 1030 ZPO. In general, subjective arbitrability is equal to the **power to enter into a binding agreement** (*Geschäftsfähigkeit*). For full-aged German citizens and corporations domiciled in Germany, subjective arbitrability is not an issue. For foreign corporations, it is somewhat unclear whether the statutory seat (*Satzungssitz*) or the seat of the headquarters (*Verwaltungssitz*) should be looked at;[111] in any event, in most cases, subjective arbitrability is not an issue either, as long as corporations established under private law are concerned.

---

[106] Witte/Hafner, DStR 2009, 2052, 2057.

[107] BGH NJW 2015, 3234.

[108] Münch, in: MünchKommZPO, s 1040 para 5.

[109] See, eg Borris, SchiedsVZ 2009, 299, 310; Habersack, JZ 2009, 797, 798; Witte/Hafner, DStR 2009, 2052, 2056.

[110] BGH SchiedsVZ 2009, 233, 237.

[111] At least for corporations within the EU, the case law of the European Court probably points in the direction of the statutory seat; ECJ NJW 2002, 3614—*Überseering* = ECR 2002 I-09919; NJW 2003, 3331—*Inspire Art* = ECR 2003 I-10155; Lachmann, paras 289 *et seq.*

Subjective arbitrability can be more of an issue when **sovereigns or corporations established by or owned by sovereigns** are involved. Historically, such types of parties have often raised the defense of lack of (subjective) arbitrability, contending that under the applicable law they do not have the power to conclude arbitration agreements. More and more authors—both internationally and in Germany—consider such defense to be unavailing. Sovereign entities making such argument usually violate the fundamental **prohibition against contradictory behavior** when raising this objection in the arbitral proceedings, despite having entered into an arbitration agreement with the other side without any reservation as to its own laws governing its legal capacity and relations.[112] **2.65**

German law recognizes only very few **specific statutory limitations** on subjective arbitrability, confined to exceptional and rare scenarios, such as disputes on certain types of securities transactions (s 37h WpHG).[113] **2.66**

4. Form

a) **General Principles** German law distinguishes form requirements for arbitration agreements among **commercial parties** on the one hand and arbitration agreements involving at least one party who is a **consumer** on the other hand (s 1031 ZPO; for the precise legal distinction between commercial parties and consumers see below paras 2.81 *et seq.*). The **general writing requirement** contained in s 1031 para 1 ZPO follows the approach taken by art 7 para 2 Model Law 1985 which is mirrored in art 7 (in its Option 1) para 2 Model Law 2006. German law contains modifications **favoring** the conclusion of arbitration agreements among **commercial parties** (incorporation by trade usage and by reference, s 1031 paras 2 and 3 ZPO) as well as **restrictions** concerning arbitration agreements with **consumers** which require separate documentation (s 1031 para 5 ZPO). Apart from conventional agreements, German law also recognizes arbitration clauses contained in unilateral deeds, such as wills or corporate charters, and subjects them to the same rules that apply to arbitration agreements (s 1066 ZPO). Objection as to the lack of form needs to be **raised prior to entering into argument on the merits**; otherwise, form defects will be deemed cured, both with regard to commercial parties and consumers (**s 1031 para 6 ZPO**). **2.67**

Section 1031 ZPO is **mandatory** for arbitration seated in Germany (s 1025 ZPO); the parties cannot contract out of s 1031 ZPO except by agreeing on arbitration with a seat outside Germany.[114] Interestingly, under German law it is "easier" to exclude the jurisdiction of the state courts entirely and to submit a dispute to arbitration **2.68**

[112] Böckstiegel, in: *Festschrift Sandrock*, pp 95, 101; Lachmann, para 290 with further references; Craig/Park/Paulsson, pp 45 *et seq.*; Geimer, in: Zöller (ed), s 1029 para 19.

[113] See Lachmann, paras 293 *et seq.* for further examples.

[114] Münch, in: MünchKommZPO, s 1031 para 20; Geimer, in: Zöller (ed), s 1031 para 1.

than it is to pre-agree on the jurisdiction of a certain state court. Pursuant to s 38 ZPO, consumers generally cannot validly pre-agree to the jurisdiction of a certain state court (eg a certain venue), whereas they can fairly easily conclude an arbitration agreement with any seat within Germany, provided that they do so in a separately signed document or within the framework of a notarized agreement (s 1031 para 5 ZPO).[115] This is an inconsistency in the German law which the German legislator should resolve soon by allowing consumer choice also for state-court jurisdiction within the same form limits that s 1031 para 5 ZPO imposes for arbitration agreements.

2.69 Section 1031 ZPO contains genuine form requirements. The party relying on the validity of an agreement bears the **burden of proof** that applicable form requirements are observed.[116] Under German law, failure to observe the requisite form makes an agreement **null and void** (s 125 BGB).[117] In limited and exceptional circumstances, it can be against **good faith** and fair dealing (*Treu und Glauben*, s 242 BGB) to invoke the lack of form. Generally, German courts have held that this can be the case where insisting on the form requirement would lead to a result that is **absolutely incompatible with the requirements of justice.**[118] In the context of arbitration agreements, such a case can arise where a party has first successfully challenged the jurisdiction of the state courts by invoking and relying on a certain arbitration agreement, and in subsequent arbitral proceedings brought on the basis of this arbitration agreement the same party now invokes the lack of form.[119]

2.70 Technically, only the arbitration agreement as such needs to follow the form requirements of s 1031 ZPO. By contrast, according to the prevailing view in German literature, **agreements on the conduct of arbitral proceedings** are not subject to s 1031 ZPO.[120] Where the arbitration agreement as such follows the proper form, procedural agreements can be concluded in any form and should be enforced accordingly. Conversely, where the arbitration agreement as such does not follow the proper form, procedural agreements—even if validly concluded—may be useless anyway, unless the form defect of the arbitration agreement is cured by failure to object (s 1031 para 6 ZPO, paras 2.87 *et seq.*).

2.71 It is less clear whether the **typical additional content of arbitration clauses,** such as regarding the seat of arbitration, the number of arbitrators, the language

[115] Münch, in: MünchKommZPO, s 1031 para 4.

[116] OLG München, SchiedsVZ 2009, 340, 341; Münch, in: MünchKommZPO, s 1031 para 10.

[117] Similarly Prütting, in: Gehrlein/Prütting, ZPO, s 1031 para 10; pursuant to other authors, invalidity already results from s 1031 ZPO as such, see eg Münch, in: MünchKommZPO, s 1031 para 10.

[118] BGH NJW 1996, 1960, 1961; NJW 1996, 2503, 2504; NJW 1987, 1069, 1070; Einsele, in: MünchKommBGB, s 125 para 57.

[119] BGH NJW-RR 1987, 1194, 1195; NJW 1998, 371; Voit, in: Musielak/Voit (eds), s 1031 para 16; opposing view: Münch, in: MünchKommZPO, s 1031, para 11.

[120] OLG Hamburg, SchiedsVZ 2004, 266, 268; Geimer, in: Zöller (ed), s 1031 para 15; Münch, in: MünchKommZPO, s 1031 para 5; opposing view: Lachmann, para 343.

of the proceedings and the applicable law, needs to be agreed in the form of s 1031 ZPO.[121] In our view, as a starting point, **only the statutory essentials** contained in s 1029 ZPO are subject to the form requirement of s 1031 ZPO, ie the agreement to submit disputes resulting from a defined legal relationship to the final and binding decision by an arbitral tribunal to the exclusion of the state courts. Whether additional content of an arbitration agreement is subject to form requirements is, in the first step, not a question of s 1031 ZPO. Given that an arbitration agreement is a substantive-law agreement, the provisions and principles of German substantive law apply. Where an agreement contains provisions that require a certain form as well as other provisions that are not subject to form requirements, German courts require that **all those provisions follow the form requirement that form part of the agreement.**[122] Thus, in most cases, the above-mentioned typical additional content will be a necessary part of the arbitration agreement from the parties' perspective and thus need to follow the form requirements of s 1031 ZPO. For instance, an oral agreement on the place of arbitration or the language of the proceedings will not be binding. It is then a **question of interpretation what happens to the remainder** of the arbitration agreement that follows the proper form. Pursuant to general principles of German law and precedent, in case of doubt, the entire agreement—ie the entire arbitration agreement—should be found invalid (s 139 BGB).[123] In the scenario discussed here, however, in our view in **most cases the parties would still probably want arbitration** to occur, even if their agreement on seat or language is found to be invalid for lack of proper form.

Further, the form requirements of s 1031 ZPO need to be observed in respect of certain **amendments** to the arbitration agreement.[124] Given the objective limitation of s 1031 ZPO for the formation of the agreement itself, not every amendment falls within the scope of this rule. Rather, it applies **only where the statutory essentials contained in s 1029 ZPO are affected**, meaning the "basic agreement to submit disputes resulting from a defined legal relationship to final and binding decision by an arbitral tribunal to the exclusion of the state courts." Thus, for instance, it is possible to merely change the **seat** of the arbitration or the **language** of the proceedings by way of an amendment agreement without observing special form requirements. The same applies—even though it is an *actus contrarius* to the formation—for the **termination** of an arbitration agreement.[125] Even where s 1031 ZPO is triggered by an amendment, there is no need to repeat the entire arbitration agreement. The **authorization (power of attorney)** to conclude an arbitration **2.72**

[121] Against this view Münch, in: MünchKommZPO, s 1031 para 13; Saenger, in: Saenger (ed), s 1031 para 2; Voit, in: Musielak/Voit (eds), s 1031 para 2; Geimer, in: Zöller (ed), s 1031 para 15.

[122] BGH NJW 2005, 1356; NJW-RR 1990, 340 *et seq.*; NJW 1988, 2880; Einsele, in: MünchKommBGB, s 125 para 32.

[123] Einsele, in: MünchKommBGB, s 125 para 41 with further references.

[124] Lachmann, para 588; Münch, in: MünchKommZPO, s 1031 para 14; Hartmann, in: Baumbach/Lauterbach/Albers/Hartmann (eds), s 1031 para 11.

[125] Münch, in: MünchKommZPO, s 1031 para 14.

agreement does not need to follow s 1031 ZPO either, unless the authorization is irrevocable (cf s 167 para 2 BGB).[126] In case of an **assignment** of rights, an arbitration agreement regarding disputes in connection with such rights automatically transfers to the assignee (s 401 BGB).[127] The form requirements of s 1031 ZPO do not apply. Thus, the assignment can be without form or in a "lesser" form than the one provided for in s 1031 ZPO.[128]

2.73 **b) Arbitration Among Commercial Parties** For arbitration agreements among commercial parties—ie commercial corporations, commercial partnerships, and entrepreneurs (ss 13, 14 BGB)—German law requires an agreement in writing or an exchange of letters, telefaxes, telegrams, or other form of data transmission that enables **proof of an arbitration agreement** (s 1031 para 1 ZPO). The purpose of the form requirement is to enable proof of an arbitration agreement and to provide legal certainty as to the exclusion of state court jurisdiction.[129] The form requirement is a specificity of the ZPO, and it differs from the general requirements contained in German substantive law for agreements that must be "in writing" (s 126 BGB).

2.74 An arbitration agreement among commercial parties **need not be contained in one document**; s 1031 para 1 ZPO expressly allows the exchange of documents which in combination constitute the arbitration agreement. Consequently, the parties, in an agreement observing the requirements of s 1031 para 1 ZPO, can **incorporate by reference** a document containing an arbitration clause (s 1031 para 3 ZPO). This is used mainly for **general terms and conditions (AGB)** as commercial parties are exempted from the requirement of s 305 para 2 BGB. Also, traditional original signatures are not required, because means such as telefax suffice. Finally, not even copies of signatures are necessary; instead, any means of electronic communication is sufficient, as long as it clearly allows proof of an agreement. Thus, this includes a mere **exchange of emails.**[130]

2.75 It is sufficient that the declaration of one party follows the form stipulated by s 1031 para 1 ZPO, as long as the acceptance by the other party can be deemed to exist pursuant to trade usage, such as **silence upon a commercial confirmation letter** (s 1031 para 2 ZPO).[131] It is worth emphasizing that s 1031 para 2 ZPO addresses

---

126 Münch, in: MünchKommZPO, s 1031 para 17; Geimer, in: Zöller (ed), s 1031 para 26; generally BGH NJW 1998, 1857, 1858; Schramm, in: MünchKommBGB, s 167 para 19.

127 German courts classify arbitration agreements as ancillary rights, which leads to a direct application of s 401 BGB instead of an application *mutatis mutandis*, eg BGH NJW 2000, 2346.

128 Geimer, in: Zöller (ed), s 1031, para 17; Voit, in: Musielak/Voit (eds), s 1031 para 3; Münch, in: MünchKommZPO, s 1031 para 18.

129 Münch, in: MünchKommZPO, s 1031 para 8; Geimer, in: Zöller (ed), s 1031 para 5; Schwab/Walter, ch 5 para 4.

130 Geimer, in: Zöller (ed), s 1031 para 7; Münch, in: MünchKommZPO, s 1031 para 31; Lachmann, para 346.

131 Hartmann, in: Baumbach/Lauterbach/Albers/Hartmann (eds), s 1031 para 6; Geimer, in: Zöller (ed), s 1031 para 8; Münch, in: MünchKommZPO, s 1031 para 35; Lachmann, para 347.

only the question of proper form. In addition, formation of an agreement by silence upon receipt of a commercial confirmation letter can be found only where the prerequisites of that doctrine are satisfied, ie, as discussed above, the parties are merchants (or comparable persons), and the arbitration agreement as such as well as its specific contents are not too "far off" the prior oral understanding of the parties (paras 2.24 *et seq.*).[132]

c) **Arbitration Involving Consumers** For arbitration agreements involving consumers, German law contains **special form requirements** in order to protect consumers from **premature or inadvertent** submission to arbitration, thereby excluding the jurisdiction of state courts.[133] Specifically, unless the parties use the notarized form, s 1030 para 5 ZPO requires (i) a **separate "document"** containing only the arbitration agreement and other stipulations on the arbitral procedure and (ii) **the parties' signature.** This provision is without parallel in the Model Law, since the latter applies only to commercial arbitration (art 1 para 1 Model Law). As the heightened form requirements under s 1031 para 5 ZPO are the exception, the party relying thereon bears the burden of proof that a consumer is involved.[134] **2.76**

Under the prevailing view, the separate document requirement does **not necessitate a separate piece of paper.** The arbitration agreement can be contained on the same piece of paper as the remainder of the parties' agreement if it is **clearly separated** therefrom and **signed separately.**[135] However, mere arbitration clauses (s 1029 para 2 alt 1 ZPO, as opposed to separate arbitration agreements within the meaning of s 1029 para 2 alt 2 ZPO) with consumers are not possible, unless notarized.[136] The signature requirement refers to the **traditional handwritten signature** and means that the parties need to generate an original which contains the **original signatures of all parties**; an exchange of letters, an exchange of telefaxes or emails is insufficient.[137] Instead of a traditional signature, a digital signature pursuant to the German Signature Act may be used (s 126a BGB), which is, however, still rare, in particular in the consumer context. Given that para 5 does not require a personal signature, legal representation is possible by way of a separate power of attorney, which in turn is not subject to any form requirements (s 167 para 2 BGB). **2.77**

[132] Münch, in: MünchKommZPO, s 1031 para 36; Voit, in: Musielak/Voit (eds), s 1031 para 5; Schwab/Walter, ch 5 para 4.

[133] Münch, in: MünchKommZPO, s 1031 para 7; Saenger, in: Saenger (ed), s 1031 para 9.

[134] Münch, in: MünchKommZPO, s 1031 para 45.

[135] Hartmann, in: Baumbach/Lauterbach/Albers/Hartmann (eds), s 1031 para 9; Münch, in: MünchKommZPO, s 1031 para 25; Lachmann, para 353.

[136] Münch, in: MünchKommZPO, s 1031 para 59. Instructive BGH SchiedsVZ 2011, 46 and 157 (consumers entering into standard-form service agreements with US-based brokerage house respecting the execution of forward contracts and option transactions; arbitration agreement held invalid for lack of proper form) = XXXVII Y.B. Com. Arb. 216 (2012).

[137] Münch, in: MünchKommZPO, s 1031 paras 27 *et seq.*; Lachmann, para 352; Geimer, in: Zöller (ed), s 1031 para 36; Voit, in: Musielak/Voit (eds), s 1031 para 10.

2.78 The separation requirement does not apply where the parties choose to have their agreement **notarized** (s 1031 para 5 ZPO), because in this case the notary is obliged to **advise the parties** of the significance of submitting to arbitration. Pursuant to the prevailing view, s 1031 para 5 ZPO applies only to notarization by German notaries, as **foreign notaries** are not necessarily obliged to provide the same type of advice as German notaries.[138] However, deeds notarized by Latin Notaries enjoy the benefit of dual presumption of legality and accuracy of content. Given that they meet the standards of the UINL,[139] they should be recognized in all UINL Member States and have the same authenticity as in their country of origin.

2.79 For the same reason, some commentators doubt whether an arbitration clause involving a consumer may be contained in an **award on agreed terms.**[140] In our view, a **court-approved settlement** should fulfil the requirements of s 1031 para 5 ZPO[141] because a German court should generally provide the consumer with the same type of explanation and advice that can be expected from a German notary.[142] That being said, the same should again apply in case of an arbitral award instead of a state court judgment. While it is true that the role of arbitrators can be less proactive compared to state court judges, it is the clear decision of the German legislator to recognize arbitration as a means of dispute resolution which is **in principle equivalent to state-court litigation.**[143] Given that even the arbitral award is on par with a state court decision (s 1055 ZPO), this should apply *a fortiori* for a tribunal-approved settlement.

2.80 Failure to follow the form prescribed by s 1031 para 5 ZPO makes the arbitration agreement null and void (s 125 BGB). **Voidness may be invoked by all parties**, including a party that is not a consumer.[144]

2.81 **d) The Distinction Between Commercial Parties and Consumers** The distinction between commercial parties and consumers pursuant to **ss 13, 14 BGB** is not always entirely clear, and this uncertainty may thus also be relevant when it comes to arbitration agreements. The German Civil Code provides the following definitions:

> S 13: A consumer means every natural person who enters into a legal transaction for a purpose that is outside his trade, business or profession.
>
> S 14: (1) An entrepreneur means a natural or legal person or a partnership with legal personality who or which, when entering into a legal transaction, acts in exercise of his or its trade, business or profession.

---

[138] BT-Drucks 13/5274, p 37; Lachmann, para 354; Goette, DStR 1996, 709 *et seq.*

[139] http://www.uinl.org/146/fundamental-principles-of-the-latin-type-notarial-system (last visited December 1, 2015).

[140] Lachmann, para 356; Schwab/Walter, ch 23 para 14; opposing view: OLG Stuttgart, OLGR Stuttgart 2001, 50.

[141] Schütze, para 224; Lachmann, para 357.

[142] Schütze, para 224; Schwab/Walter, ch 5 para 19; Hausmann, in: Reithmann/Martiny (eds), para 8.352.

[143] BT-Drucks 13/5274, p 1.

[144] OLG Hamm, OLGR Hamm 2006, 527; Voit, in: Musielak/Voit (eds), s 1031 para 16; Lachmann, para 361.

(2) A partnership with legal personality is a partnership that has the capacity to acquire rights and to incur liabilities.

For instance, someone who enters into a purchase or a loan agreement in order to be able to **start his or her business** technically may do so while still being a consumer and not an entrepreneur yet. However, German courts have held that transactions for the purpose of starting one's business as an entrepreneur qualify as entrepreneurial transactions, not consumer transactions.[145] Thus, to the extent such transactions contain arbitration agreements, the less stringent form requirements for commercial transactions set forth above apply (s 1031 paras 1–4 ZPO). **2.82**

By contrast, a person acting for purposes of **administering his or her private assets** is a consumer.[146] Accordingly, in the context of an M&A transaction, a seller holding a minority stake in the target may very well be a consumer for purposes of German law. In order for an arbitration clause typically contained in M&A agreements concluded in Germany to be valid and binding upon such a seller, the form requirements of s 1031 para 5 ZPO need to be observed. **2.83**

Similarly, German courts have considered the **managing directors** of a limited liability company (GmbH) and stock corporation (AG) to be consumers for purposes of concluding their services agreements with the corporation, thus triggering the form requirements of s 1031 para 5 ZPO.[147] This case law may seem odd to a foreign observer. In some instances, it is also subject to legal doubt. For example, qualifying managing directors of German stock corporations as "consumers" for purposes of their services agreements conflicts with their corporate law position as independent managers of the stock corporation under s 76 para 1 AktG.[148] **2.84**

As also set forth above in paras 2.73 *et seq.*, **commercial partnerships** are entrepreneurs; thus, it suffices that they follow one of the form alternatives contained in s 1031 paras 1–4 ZPO. A private partnership that is not engaged in commercial activity, such as a partnership for purposes of administering one's own assets, may not qualify as an entrepreneur but rather be regarded as a "consumer," thereby triggering the form requirement of s 1031 para 5 ZPO.[149] Similarly, private persons joining a partnership may act as consumers to the extent their participation **2.85**

145 BGH NJW 2005, 1273; Münch, in: MünchKommZPO, s 1031 para 49; Hartmann, in: Baumbach/Lauterbach/Albers/Hartmann (eds), s 1031 para 8; Geimer, in: Zöller (ed), s 1031 para 34.

146 BGH NJW 2002, 368, 369; Saenger, in: Erman, s 13 para 14; K Schmidt, JuS 2006, 1, 3.

147 BAG NJW 2010, 2827 (GmbH); OLG Hamm, AG 2007, 910 (AG, arbitration clause in services agreement of managing director); Bauer/Arnold/Kramer, AG 2014, 677, 678.

148 "*Der Vorstand hat unter eigener Verantwortung die Gesellschaft zu leiten.*"—"The management board shall bear responsibility for directing the corporation." Crit. therefore Mülbert, in: *Festschrift Hadding*, pp 582 *et seq.*; Herresthal, ZIP 2014, 345, 348.

149 BGH NJW 2002, 368; OLG Hamm, OLGR Hamm 2006, 527; Lachmann, para 336; Münch, in: MünchKommZPO, s 1031 para 49; Voit, in: Musielak/Voit (eds), s 1031 para 8.

is a matter of administering their own assets.[150] Where a private person joins a commercial partnership as a general partner, the traditional view was that such person would act as an entrepreneur.[151] A newer view in literature advocates the application of s 1031 para 5 ZPO.[152] Thus, for practical purposes, where a consumer is a member of a commercial or private partnership, the safest option is to always follow the requirements of s 1031 para 5 ZPO.

2.86 The ECJ has decided that under Directive 93/13/EEC a national court is obliged to assess whether an arbitration clause in a contract with a consumer is non-binding for the consumer even in the absence of any consumer action against the clause or the final award as the national court can proceed *ex officio*.[153] Even if there is only a limited basis for a judge to review the award in the absence of a consumer action,[154] the ECJ ruling poses a substantial risk to arbitration agreements with consumers. To compound that uncertainty, the BGH tends to take a more generous view, not necessarily qualifying the European regulations on consumer protection as part of the *ordre public*.[155]

2.87 e) **Cure by Failure to Object** Form defects will be cured where a party fails to properly object during the arbitral proceedings (**s 1031 para 6 ZPO**; cf art 4 Model Law). Section 1031 para 6 ZPO applies only to form requirements, but not to other defects. With regard to other defects, s 1027 ZPO may apply. An objection pursuant to s 1031 para 6 ZPO needs to **refer specifically to the lack of proper form** and needs to be stated **before the first argument on the merits**, which can be in a party's first written submission, or, if it occurs earlier, in a pre-trial conference with the Arbitral Tribunal, to the extent it addresses merits issues (which may be rare).[156] Failure to object cures the deficient form of an arbitration agreement with **retroactive** effect.[157] It applies only for purposes of the arbitral proceedings in which the failure occurs. It does not apply to further proceedings brought or to be brought under the same arbitration agreement.[158]

---

150 Lachmann, para 337 with further ref.; Voit, in: Musielak/Voit (eds), s 1031 para 9; Geimer, in: Zöller (ed), s 1031 para 34.

151 See, eg, BGHZ 45, 282, 284 *et seq.* = NJW 1966, 1960, 1961; BGH NJW 1980, 1049.

152 Lachmann, para 339; Voit, in: Musielak/Voit (eds), s 1031 para 9; OLG Hamm, MDR 2007, 1438; Geimer, in: Zöller (ed), s 1031 para 34; Münch, in: MünchKommZPO, s 1031 para 49.

153 ECJ EuZW 2009, 852—*Asturcom Telecomunicaciones* = ECR 2009 I-0957.

154 Hilbig, SchiedsVZ 2010, 74, 80.

155 BGH SchiedsVZ 2009, 66, 67; NJW 2006, 762, 763; Graf von Westphalen, ZIP 2013, 2184, 2189; Münch, in: MünchKommZPO, s 1059 para 48; Hilbig, SchiedsVZ 2010, 74 *et seq.*

156 BGH NJW 1983, 1267, 1269 = XV Y.B. Com. Arb. 662 (1990); Hartmann, in: Baumbach/Lauterbach/Albers/Hartmann (eds), s 1031 para 14; Geimer, in: Zöller (ed), s 1031 para 43; Münch, in: MünchKommZPO, s 1031 para 65; Lachmann, para 368.

157 Münch, in: MünchKommZPO, s 1031 para 68.

158 Münch, in: MünchKommZPO, s 1031 para 69; Voit, in: Musielak/Voit (eds), s 1031 para 14; Lachmann, para 371; similar Hartmann, in: Baumbach/Lauterbach/Albers/Hartmann (eds), s 1031 para 14.

f) No Notarization Requirement Under the clearly prevailing view, arbitration agreements never require notarization. Even where an arbitration agreement is concluded in connection with a main contract that requires notarization—such as, eg, real estate transactions (s 311b BGB) or transactions involving the transfer of shares in privately held corporations (s 15 GmbHG)—such arbitration agreement is **valid and binding as long as it satisfies the form requirements** of s 1031 ZPO.[159] This follows from the clear wording of s 1031 ZPO as *lex specialis* as well as from the explicit **separability principle** in s 1040 para 1 cl 2 ZPO. Taken together, both rules show that the arbitration agreement is an independent contract. **2.88**

In practice, there has been considerable uncertainty surrounding this issue. Specifically, there were doubts as to what requirements apply where the arbitration agreement is contained in a deed notarizing the main transaction and **referring to the arbitration rules of an arbitral institution.** Some practitioners expressed the view that in such case, the full set of arbitration rules of said institution need to be read aloud by the notary in order for the arbitration agreement to be concluded in proper form. Besides being cumbersome, this approach has the further disadvantage that only the rules in place at the time of the notarization can be agreed. Later amendments would need to be excluded, and in fact this is often agreed in German notarized documents. As a result, a frequent approach encountered in practice was that the arbitration agreement was contained in a separate, non-notarized document that follows the requirements of s 1031 ZPO, and the notarial deed would merely contain a reference to the effect that "the parties have concluded an arbitration agreement by way of separate document" or the like.[160] The separate arbitration agreement could then contain a reference to the rules of an arbitral institution, which is generally to be understood as a reference to the version in force at the time arbitral proceedings commence (see, eg, s 1.3 DIS Rules). **2.89**

Based on **recent case law of the BGH**[161] confirming our view that arbitration agreements never require notarial form, these complicated approaches are no longer necessary. **2.90**

5. Further General Grounds for Invalidity

As substantive-law agreements, arbitration agreements can be invalid based on further general grounds for invalidity. Most notably, an arbitration agreement can be invalid for lack of **proper representation**. As stated above (para 2.77), an **2.91**

[159] BGH NZG 2014, 1155, 1157; NJW 1978, 212, 213; Hartmann, in: Baumbach/Lauterbach/Albers/Hartmann (eds), s 1031 para 10; Münch, in: MünchKommZPO, s 1031 para 26; Lachmann, para 362; Broichmann/Matthäus, SchiedsVZ 2008, 274; opposing view: OLG München, RNotZ 2013, 639, 643; Kindler, NZG 2014, 961; Geimer, in: Zöller (ed), s 1031 para 48.

[160] Lachmann, para 365; Voit, in: Musielak/Voit (eds), s 1031 para 6; Schlosser, in: Stein/Jonas (eds), s 1031 para 13; Münch, in: MünchKommZPO, s 1031 paras 37 *et seq.*

[161] BGH NZG 2014, 1155, 1157.

arbitration agreement can be concluded by a representative acting under power of attorney.[162] Under general principles of German law, the power of attorney—unless it is irrevocable—generally need **not follow the same form** as is required for the arbitration agreement (s 167 para 2 BGB).[163] A general power of representation under German commercial law (*Prokura*) pursuant to s 48 HGB is sufficient authority to conclude an arbitration agreement.[164] Section 49 para 1 HGB expressly states that such a general power of representation empowers its holder to perform "all kinds of judicial and extrajudicial dealings associated with the business." By contrast, this is not the case with the more limited form of a commercial power of attorney by virtue of s 54 HGB (*Handlungsvollmacht*).[165] Whether this type of power of attorney is sufficient to conclude an arbitration agreement depends on the typical range and the business practices in the specific industry.

2.92 A lawyer's power of attorney to represent a client in litigation pursuant to ss 80 *et seq.* ZPO (*Prozessvollmacht*) is limited to state-court litigation under the ZPO and generally does not authorize the conclusion of an arbitration agreement.[166]

2.93 Finally, arbitration agreements are subject to the invalidity grounds of **illegality and immorality** (ss 134, 138 BGB). Arbitration as such is generally neither illegal nor immoral; on the contrary, the German legislator views arbitration in principle to be equivalent to state-court litigation.[167] Thus, the illegality or immorality of an arbitration agreement may only **result from its specific, extraordinary contents.** Special provisions of the Tenth Book of the ZPO protecting an oppressed party take precedence over the application of ss 134, 138 BGB. For instance, where there is an improper imbalance of the parties regarding the composition of the arbitral tribunal, s 1034 para 2 ZPO allows the discriminated party to apply to the state court to appoint the arbitrator(s) differently. In such a situation, the provisions of the Tenth Book of the ZPO serve as *leges speciales* and there is no reason and in fact no room to resort to ss 134, 138 BGB.[168]

2.94 In sum, cases where arbitration agreements are to be considered in violation of ss 134, 138 BGB should be rare. An important example is the decision of the BGH where the court held arbitration agreements to be null and void if they do not meet

---

[162] Lachmann, para 344; Geimer, in: Zöller (ed), s 1031 para 6; Hartmann, in: Baumbach/Lauterbach/Albers/Hartmann (eds), s 1031 para 4.

[163] Münch, in: MünchKommZPO, s 1031 para 17; Voit, in: Musielak/Voit (eds), s 1031 para 2; Geimer, in: Zöller (ed), s 1031 para 13; generally BGH NJW 1998, 1857, 1858; Schramm, in: MünchKommBGB, s 167 para 19.

[164] BGH WM 2007, 698 *et seq.*; Lachmann, para 275.

[165] Krebs, in: MünchKommHGB, s 54 para 1.

[166] Geimer, in: Zöller (ed), s 1029 para 20; Münch, in: MünchKommZPO, s 1029 para 9; Voit, in: Musielak/Voit (eds), s 1029 para 6; Lachmann, para 276.

[167] BT-Drucks 13/5274, p 34 (*"eine der staatlichen Gerichtsbarkeit im Prinzip gleichwertige Rechtsschutzmöglichkeit"*).

[168] Lachmann/Lachmann, BB 2000, 1633, 1639; Hanefeld/Wittinghofer, SchiedsVZ 2005, 217, 224.

the whole set of rules which it has developed for disputes related to the validity of shareholder resolutions (***Schiedsfähigkeit II***; see para 1.78). Another instance may be arbitration agreements that are concluded specifically to **cover up illegal activity**, such as corruption or money laundering. Similarly, an arbitration agreement designed to adjudicate the distribution of the proceeds of illegal activity should be considered illegal and therefore null and void. Whilst it is true that the jurisdiction phase of such proceedings requires a "front loading" with substantive issues that may be cumbersome and difficult to establish, such "front loading" seems inevitable to protect public interests of very high importance.

6. Grounds for Invalidity in Case of General Terms and Conditions (AGB)

Where an arbitration agreement is contained in AGB, the provisions contained in **ss 305 *et seq.* BGB** need to be observed; in case of violations, an arbitration agreement may not be concluded or may be invalid. **2.95**

a) **Commercial Arbitration** In a commercial context, ie with respect to a transaction between commercial corporations, commercial partnerships, or entrepreneurs (ss 13, 14 BGB), the use of AGB as such generally does not make a difference with respect to the validity of arbitration agreements. Arbitration clauses in AGB can be validly **agreed by reference to the AGB** (s 1031 para 3 ZPO). In a commercial context, arbitration clauses are common practice and as such should not be considered to fall under the **"surprise" provision of s 305c BGB.**[169] Standard arbitration clauses in commercial agreements likewise withstand the **general fairness scrutiny** provided for in s 307 BGB. As we have stated several times, in Germany, arbitration is considered **principally equivalent** to state-court litigation;[170] thus, the provisions of the ZPO governing state-court litigation may not be regarded as the guideposts for the fairness analysis. **2.96**

However, arbitration clauses may be invalid because of "surprise" under s 305c BGB or due to unfairness pursuant to s 307 BGB if they contain **unusual** provisions or provisions that are **unduly burdensome** to one party. The application of these provisions requires a careful case-by-case analysis. Thus, generic statements need to be met with caution. Nevertheless, submitting to arbitration on the basis of **equity and fairness** (s 1051 para 3 ZPO) is probably a "surprise clause" in most cases.[171] Some commentators have expressed the view that even in a commercial context, the **Swiss Rules** contain a surprise clause to the extent that they provide for unlimited jurisdiction of the arbitral tribunal to decide on claims introduced by way of **set-off**, which goes beyond what most other arbitration rules provide for.[172] **2.97**

---

[169] Lachmann, para 429; Hanefeld/Wittinghofer, SchiedsVZ 2005, 217, 222; Mäsch, in: *Festschrift Schlosser*, pp 529, 534; Schlosser, in: Stein/Jonas (eds), s 1029 para 49.

[170] BT-Drucks 13/5274, p 34.

[171] Ebbing, p 216; with concerns Lachmann, para 430.

[172] Lachmann, para 431; Kreindler/Schäfer/Wolff, para 187.

2.98 Even if they are not "surprising," individual contents of an arbitration clause may be invalid under the fairness analysis to be performed pursuant to s 307 BGB because they unduly burden the other party or jeopardize the purpose of the (arbitration) agreement. Two real-life examples where these issues have become relevant are the following:

2.99 First, German courts have dealt with **arbitrary or discriminatory choices for the place of arbitration** and considered such choices null and void in an AGB context. In the underlying cases, a large Netherlands-based franchisor for a US sandwich chain had obliged its German franchisees to subject themselves to arbitration in the US, which the German courts considered inappropriate in the specific circumstances of these cases.[173] This does not, of course, mean that a US place of arbitration is now impossible to stipulate in AGB with German counterparties. What made the "sandwich" cases special was the fact that the franchisor was a large corporation located outside Germany, whereas the German franchisees were typically small businesses to whom the inconvenience and cost of bringing an arbitration in the US would seem so prohibitive that they may feel genuinely deterred from enforcing their rights, and the franchisor may have counted on exactly that effect when drafting the AGB. If that is the case, arbitration is indeed no longer equivalent to state-court arbitration. By contrast, it is still permissible, for instance, for a US-based supplier of goods to agree with its German (commercial) customer to arbitration in the US if a dispute arises out of the delivery of the goods.

2.100 Second, German courts have dealt with AGB clauses that give the drafter of the AGB the **unilateral choice between arbitration and state-court litigation**. According to the BGH, the decisive criterion in this case is whether the right of choice is limited to the role as plaintiff or is unrestricted.[174] In the first alternative, the clause will generally be considered valid as there may be due cause for this right such as questions of confidentiality or the complexity of the claim. By contrast, the court would see unreasonable discrimination if the drafter were allowed to choose arbitration even in the role of the defendant. In this alternative, the AGB clause would enable him to sabotage the other party's claim after it was brought before a state court. Under normal circumstances, German courts do not recognize a legitimate interest for such a unilateral right.

2.101 **b) Consumer Arbitration** Where consumers are involved, a different analysis is required. Given the form requirements of s 1031 para 5 ZPO, it is **more difficult** to conclude an arbitration agreement by mere reference to AGB.[175] The

---

[173] OLG Dresden, IPRspr. 2007, no 222, 631 *et seq.* = XXXIII Y.B. Com. Arb. 549 (2008); OLG Celle, IPRspr. 2008, no 207, 658 *et seq.;* OLG Bremen, OLGR Bremen 2009, 155, 156 *et seq.* (= NJOZ 2009, 1188, 1190 *et seq.*); OLG Jena, IPRspr. 2011, no 293, 781 *et seq.* = XXXVII Y.B. Com. Arb. 220 (2012); Münch, in: MünchKommZPO, s 1029 para 24.

[174] BGH NJW 1992, 575, 576; NJW 1999, 282; Schwab/Walter, ch 3 para 24.

[175] As the very existence of s 1031 para 5 ZPO shows, arbitration agreements with consumers are not impermissible per se; Lachmann, para 548; Geimer, in: Zöller (ed), s 1031 para 34.

consumer will need to **sign the arbitration clause separately**, unless the main contract is notarized (s 1031 para 5 cl 3 ZPO). Where the consumer signs separately, the arbitration clause should not be considered a "surprise" pursuant to s 305c BGB. By contrast, where an arbitration clause in AGB is incorporated by reference through a notarial deed, the prohibition on "surprise clauses" in s 305c BGB may invalidate the arbitration clause, unless the notary has advised the consumer thereon, because in a consumer context arbitration clauses are still much more unusual than in an (international) commercial context. The same applies, of course, where the arbitration clause itself contains unusual provisions.

Once an arbitration clause is properly included in a consumer agreement and it is not invalid for "surprise" reasons, the clause needs to be subjected to the **fairness analysis** pursuant to ss 307 *et seq.* BGB. Again, as a matter of express intent of the drafters of the German arbitration law, arbitration needs to be considered **principally equivalent** to state-court litigation; thus, there is no need for a special justification in order to include an arbitration clause in a consumer agreement.[176] **2.102**

Clauses requiring additional scrutiny or caution include the following:[177] **2.103**

- Arbitral tribunals **unfamiliar with German law**, especially consumer protection laws, may under narrow circumstances be held impermissible by German courts. Thus, on a case-by-case basis to be valid the clause may need to provide for at least a chairman who is a German-trained lawyer.[178]
- **Nominations** of a sole arbitrator by the drafter of the AGB do not render the arbitration clause invalid; however, the special provisions of s 1034 para 2 ZPO apply (consumer may ask state court to replace arbitrator).[179]
- Stipulations of a minimum **amount in dispute** that is wholly disproportionate to the actual amount in dispute are invalid.[180]
- **Language** requirements different from the language of the consumer or the transaction require special justification; absent such justification, they are considered invalid.[181]
- Decisions ***ex aequo et bono*** or pursuant to *lex mercatoria* are likely unacceptable in AGB with consumers.[182]

[176] BT-Drucks 13/5274, p 34; Lachmann, para 549; BGH SchiedsVZ 2005, 95, 98 with comment Huber/Bach, p 99; BGH SchiedsVZ 2007, 163, 164 *et seq.*; Hanefeld/Wittinghofer, SchiedsVZ 2005, 217, 222; Herresthal, ZIP 2014, 345, 352; Bauer/Arnold/Kramer, AG 2014, 677, 679; opposing view Graf von Westphalen, ZIP 2013, 2184 (regarding directors of German corporations).

[177] For further detail see Hanefeld/Wittinghofer, SchiedsVZ 2005, 217; Lachmann, paras 546 *et seq.*

[178] BGH SchiedsVZ 2005, 95, 98; Lachmann, para 555.

[179] BGH SchiedsVZ 2007, 163, 164; Lachmann, para 562; Schlosser, in: Stein/Jonas (eds), s 1034 paras 5, 12; Voit, in: Musielak/Voit (eds), s 1034 para 3; Münch, in: MünchKommZPO, s 1034 para 10.

[180] LG Dortmund, NJW-RR 2008, 441.

[181] Hanefeld/Wittinghofer, SchiedsVZ 2005, 217, 227; Lachmann, para 566.

[182] Hanefeld/Wittinghofer, SchiedsVZ 2005, 217, 226; Lachmann, paras 569 *et seq.*

2.104 As shown above, it is not always entirely clear whether a party is a consumer or not (see paras 2.81 *et seq.*). The idiosyncrasies of German law regarding AGB and the consumer/non-consumer distinction may seem inappropriate from an international commercial point of view. Thus, there is considerable debate in Germany whether it is possible and desirable to limit the consequences of the approaches taken by German courts as outlined above.[183] It is entirely debatable to "opt out" of the AGB principles by agreeing to arbitration and excluding the application of ss 305 *et seq.* BGB in the context of commercial agreements.[184] It must be clear, however, that it is very likely **not possible** by way of an arbitration agreement to **opt out of the consumer/non-consumer distinction**. An arbitral tribunal which were to accept such an "opt out" would render an award which likely would be subject to challenge and set aside based on s 1059 para 2 no 2 lit b ZPO (*ordre public*).

V. Interpretation of Arbitration Agreements

2.105 When interpreting arbitration agreements, again the applicable law needs to be determined first (see above para 2.4). Assuming the application of German law, the general rules of contract interpretation apply. This is a direct consequence of the fact that arbitration agreements are substantive-law agreements.

2.106 Notably, the bottom line for contract interpretation in German law is **not to adhere to the literal wording**, but to determine the **true joint intentions** of the parties (s 133 BGB). In addition, pursuant to s 157 BGB, agreements are to be interpreted based on good faith and taking into account common usage. Nevertheless, the **wording** of an agreement is still the **starting point** of the analysis.[185] **Technical legal terms** are generally interpreted pursuant to their technical meaning. Otherwise, a term is to be interpreted based on its meaning in ordinary, everyday language.[186] For instance, where an agreement talks of an arbitral tribunal, it will likely mean just that, and not mediation, expert determination or some other form of (alternative) dispute resolution. What is notable, though, is the fact that the German terms for arbitration (*Schiedsverfahren*) and expert determination (*Schiedsgutachten*) are so similar that it may be easy for laymen to confuse them. Should both parties have actually used the wrong term but meant the same (other) thing, their joint true intentions will govern (*falsa demonstratio non nocet*).[187]

---

[183] For an instructive approach regarding directors of German corporations see Herresthal, ZIP 2014, 345 *et seq.*

[184] Pfeiffer, NJW 2012, 1169.

[185] BGH NJW 2001, 144 *et seq.*; Ellenberger, in: Palandt (ed), s 133 para 14.

[186] BGHZ 80, 246, 249 *et seq.* = NJW 1981, 1736, 1737; OLG München, NJW-RR 1996, 239; Busche, in: MünchKommBGB, s 133 para 57.

[187] BGH NJW 2008, 1659; Jauernig, in: Jauernig (ed), s 133 para 9; Busche, in: MünchKommBGB, s 133 para 14; Ellenberger, in: Palandt (ed), s 133 para 8.

Where the wording was drafted by experienced counsel, it will be accorded greater weight.[188] However, outside the context of AGB, German law does **not follow** a general rule of **interpretation against the drafter** (*contra stipulatorem*).[189] **2.107**

In addition to the wording, and as a next step in the analysis, German rules of contract interpretation require consideration of the **dealings of the parties** prior to and possibly after the conclusion of the agreement, in particular the negotiation history.[190] In case of arbitration agreements, the various versions leading up to the final agreement may be looked at. The fact that the parties expressly negotiated and bargained for a certain wording should be accorded considerable weight. **2.108**

Most importantly, the **mutual interests of the parties and the purposes of the agreement** need to be taken into account.[191] Under German rules of contract interpretation, the court or the arbitral tribunal has considerable leeway to give effect to what it considers the **"true intentions of the parties."** A court or an arbitral tribunal should be careful, however, not to replace the contents of an agreement with its own views of what is just and fair. Also as a general rule, agreements are to be interpreted in a way such that they make practical sense and are valid.[192] **2.109**

Where form requirements apply, such as the writing requirement in s 1031 ZPO, circumstances outside the written document can be taken into account, but they need to be **indicated in some way in the document** (*Andeutungstheorie*).[193] A written document will be presumed **true and complete**, and whoever challenges that bears the burden of proof.[194] **2.110**

Additional rules apply again for arbitration clauses contained in AGB (see paras 2.95 *et seq.*). Specifically, in case of doubt, AGB are interpreted against the drafter.[195] **2.111**

Where an agreement contains a gap and the above-mentioned means of interpretation do not allow for a resolution of the issue, the principles of **supplementary interpretation** may apply (*ergänzende Vertragsauslegung*).[196] In such a scenario, supplementary interpretation would require to determine **what reasonable parties would have agreed** had they contemplated and negotiated on what they have left open. The application of these principles requires a showing that without intervention by the court, the commercial goals pursued by the parties in their agreement **2.112**

188 Singer, in: Staudinger (ed), s 133 para 46.
189 Jauernig, in: Jauernig (ed), s 133 para 11.
190 BGH NJW 1981, 2295 *et seq.*; ZIP 2004, 843; Ellenberger, in: Palandt (ed), s 133 para 16.
191 BGH NJW 1981, 1549 *et seq.*; NJW 2000, 2099 *et seq.*; Ellenberger, in: Palandt (ed), s 133 para 18.
192 BGH NJW-RR 2006, 338 *et seq.*; Ellenberger, in: Palandt (ed), s 133 para 18; Münch, in: MünchKommZPO, s 1029 para 105 (specifically regarding arbitration agremeents).
193 BGH NJW 1996, 2792 *et seq.*; Ellenberger, in: Palandt (ed), s 133 para 19; Münch, in: MünchKommZPO, s 1029 para 106.
194 BGH NJW 2002, 3164 *et seq.*; Einsele, in: MünchKommBGB, s 125 para 39.
195 BGH NJW-RR 2007, 1697 *et seq.*; Ellenberger, in: Palandt (ed), s 133 para 26a.
196 Münch, in: MünchKommZPO, s 1029 para 105.

could not be achieved in a way respecting the interests of both parties,[197] and is thus fairly rare in the context of arbitration agreements. To begin with, where an arbitration agreement is missing, it can generally not be "invented" by way of supplementary interpretation.[198] Furthermore, the provisions of the applicable arbitration law, in our case the Tenth Book of the ZPO, generally contain provisions that allow many gaps to be filled, including by way of using the discretion of the arbitral tribunal (s 1042 para 4 ZPO).

2.113 An example could be a case where the parties have clearly agreed that they do not want ad hoc arbitration, but **failed to properly designate an arbitral institution**. In such a case, the Higher Regional Court of Berlin has held that the nomination of the non-existing "German Central Chamber of Commerce" as arbitral institution has to be interpreted as nomination of the DIS. Given that the parties undoubtedly wanted to solve their disputes by way of arbitration and an arbitral institution with a seat in Germany, the court drew the conclusion that only the DIS corresponds to their intention.[199] There may well be cases where such determination is not possible, which means that the gap cannot be closed even by supplementary interpretation.

2.114 Against the backdrop of all these general principles of contract interpretation, it is widely accepted in Germany that arbitration agreements should be **interpreted broadly as far as their subject matter is concerned.**[200] This is correct, because in most cases this is presumably in line with the intentions of the parties and the purposes of an arbitration agreement. Unless the parties specify otherwise, they can be assumed to have intended an encompassing application of an arbitration clause, because the alternative would be to split different disputes among them in connection with one agreement and litigate or arbitrate them in front of different decision-making bodies. Since such disputes are often somehow interrelated, addressing them before different fora is usually not what reasonable parties want in terms of procedural efficiency and cost economy. For instance, disputes regarding compensation claims resulting from an agreement should not be separated from disputes regarding non-performance or defective performance, because the latter may be a reason for the delayed or withheld payment. Similarly, concurring claims based on torts, unjust enrichment or pre-contractual claims should in most cases not be separated from contractual claims, as they may all be based on the same set of core facts. By contrast, tort claims against individuals acting for one party to a contract

---

[197] Ellenberger, in: Palandt (ed), s 157 para 3 with further references.

[198] Münch, in: MünchKommZPO, s 1029 para 105; see also RGZ 159, 254, 256 (regarding agreement on venue).

[199] KG BB 2000, Beil. 8, pp 13, 14 *et seq.*; KG SchiedsVZ 2012, 337. It should be noted that the court appears to have qualified the case as one of ordinary, not supplementary interpretation.

[200] BGHZ 40, 320, 325 = NJW 1964, 591, 592; BGH NZG 2002, 83; Hartmann, in: Baumbach/Lauterbach/Albers/Hartmann (eds), s 1029 para 12; Geimer, in: Zöller (ed), s 1029 para 78; Münch, in: MünchKommZPO, s 1029 para 46; Voit, in: Musielak/Voit (eds), s 1029 para 23; Lachmann, para 472.

in connection with the performance of that contract are usually not encompassed by an arbitration agreement, because these individuals are usually not party to the arbitration agreement (which is, however, foremost not a matter of interpretation but personal scope of the arbitration agreement).[201]

In the same vein, German courts generally consider a **settlement** regarding a dispute arising out of the main contract to be governed by the same arbitration clause as long as the settlement can be considered to be related to the original transaction (as opposed to the settlement being a completely new transaction itself).[202] **2.115**

A practical example may be a case where the parties, along with the settlement of their dispute, agree on a number of additional issues or topics that were not among the items before the arbitral tribunal. In particular where the parties are successful in agreeing on "win-win solutions," this may be the case. A settlement of the dispute may thus be embedded in a much larger transaction. The parties may, for instance, agree on the conclusion of a new supply relationship regarding different or additional products, or they may agree on the transfer of certain unrelated assets. Later on, a new dispute may arise with respect to an issue that is related to elements of this larger transaction, but unrelated to the original dispute and its settlement. Without a clear provision in the settlement agreement, it may be highly uncertain whether the arbitration clause in the original contract giving rise to the first dispute still applies. Thus, the parties are well advised to contemplate express dispute resolution mechanisms where they conclude settlement agreements that go beyond a resolution of the issues that were subject to arbitration. **2.116**

VI. Drafting Considerations, Pathological Clauses, And "Less is More!"

In many cases, parties are well served by concise arbitration agreements, such as the model clauses recommended by leading arbitral institutions (see above paras 2.2 and 2.32 for the model clauses recommended by the DIS and the ICC).[203] This is in line with the **traditional German drafting style** for agreements in general. It tends to be in contrast to the drafting styles of certain other jurisdictions, most notably the US, where—along with lengthy contracts in general—detailed arbitration clauses can often be found. Nevertheless, for purposes of an arbitration to be seated in Germany, less is probably more. Where the parties choose institutional arbitration, the rules of the institution and the practices established thereunder will generally provide a much more suitable and predictable framework for arbitral proceedings than seemingly tailor-made, but often faulty party agreements. **2.117**

---

[201] Voit, in: Musielak/Voit (eds), s 1029 para 9; Münch, in: MünchKommZPO, s 1029 paras 44, 106 with further ref.

[202] So-called *umschaffender Vergleich*—BGHZ 40, 320, 325 = NJW 1964, 591, 592; Münch, in: MünchKommZPO, s 1029 para 48; Voit, in: Musielak/Voit (eds), s 1029 para 23; Lachmann, para 486; Busse, SchiedsVZ 2010, 57, 61.

[203] Similarly Lachmann, para 391 outside the international arena.

Likewise, where the parties elect ad hoc arbitration under the Tenth Book of the ZPO, the statutory provisions provide for a framework that should be suitable and satisfactory in most cases.[204]

2.118 German law allows for considerable flexibility in shaping arbitration clauses. For instance, the parties would be free to agree on a combination of state court and arbitral jurisdiction. It is conceivable to limit the jurisdiction of an arbitral tribunal to amounts in dispute exceeding a certain threshold and to submit smaller claims to a state court.[205] Whilst in theory this may sound like a good idea in order to achieve time and cost efficiencies, in practice this often proves different, eg where an initially small claim is increased during the course of the proceedings or substantial counterclaims are raised. All in all, in most cases keeping it short and simple will serve the parties better.

2.119 Mistakes in drafting arbitration agreements occur more frequently than necessary, not least because often the lawyers drafting an arbitration clause are transactional practitioners who are unfamiliar with the field of arbitration.[206] Listed below are some frequent drafting mistakes that should be easy to avoid:

- Designation of a **non-existent arbitral institution**: an easy check on the internet can avoid this mistake and costly follow-on litigation on the validity of the arbitration agreement, notwithstanding that German courts tend to be generous in finding a way to uphold the validity of the arbitration agreement.[207]
- Reference to **non-existent rules of arbitration**: Same remedy.
- Reference to a separate arbitration agreement that is, however, **never concluded**: German courts are split over whether this constitutes an arbitration agreement or not.[208]
- Agreement on arbitration and a **choice of forum for the ordinary courts** in the same contract: German courts have interpreted such a situation as actually

204 Nevertheless, there can be cases which require a more detailed or customized agreement or at least a reference to additional rules of an institution like the DIS Supplementary Rules on Corporate Law Disputes. To distinguish those cases the parties are well advised to consult an experienced counsel.

205 Lachmann, paras 406 *et seq.* with further references.

206 This seems to be a universal phenomenon that is not limited to Germany; see Craig/Park/Paulsson, § 9.01 (pp 127 *et seq.*); Lachmann, para 380.

207 See OLG Frankfurt, SchiedsVZ 2007, 217 (designation of "ICC Brussels" to mean "ICC Paris, hearings to occur in Brussels"); KG BB 2000, Beil. 8, p 13 and SchiedsVZ 2012, 337 ("German Chamber of Commerce" in both cases found to mean DIS); OLG Hamburg, SchiedsVZ 2003, 284 ("arbitration Hamburg" interpreted as referring to the Court of Arbitration of the German Coffee Association); OLG Köln, IPRspr. 2005, no 189, 521 ("International commercial court of arbitration at the chamber of industry and commerce of the city of Moscow" interpreted as referring to the Court of Arbitration of the Chamber of Industry and Commerce of the Russian Federation). By contrast BayObLG BB 2000, Beil. 12, p 15 ("arbitration by the chamber of craftsmen" (*Handwerkskammer*) found invalid as there were two chambers, but none of them had a court of arbitration) = XXX Y.B. Com. Arb. 509-523 (2005). With the same tendency from an international perspective Gaillard/Savage, para 485.

208 See, on the one hand OLG Hamm, AG 2007, 910 (no arbitration agreement) and on the other hand KG NJW 2011, 2978 (arbitration agreement found).

meaning arbitration. Only to the extent there is jurisdiction for ordinary courts, or the parties do not object to a lawsuit brought in an ordinary court, would the choice of forum clause apply.[209]

- Inserting multiple, **conflicting arbitration clauses** into the same agreement: although this may sound unlikely, this mistake sometimes occurs, in particular where the parties append certain general terms or conditions containing an arbitration clause to an agreement, and the main body of an agreement contains a different arbitration clause. Obviously, litigating which clause applies is unnecessarily costly and time consuming.

C. Scope, Effects, and Termination of the Arbitration Agreement

We start with the personal and subject matter scope of the arbitration agreement (below paras 2.121 *et seq.*) before we turn to the effects of the arbitration agreement (below paras 2.135 *et seq.*) and its termination (below paras 2.156 *et seq.*). **2.120**

I. Personal Scope

The personal scope of the arbitration agreement certainly extends to its parties, and in certain limited circumstances, it may also extend to third parties. The situations in which the potential inclusion of third parties into an arbitration agreement are discussed most often in German-related arbitration are: (1) successors and assignees; (2) matters of joint liability; (3) agreements for the benefit of third parties; (4) corporate law matters; and (5) insolvency administrators. **2.121**

1. Successors and Assignees

Universal successors (*Gesamtrechtsnachfolger*) of a party to an arbitration agreement are **generally bound** by such arbitration agreement. An important example are **statutory mergers** and other forms of corporate restructurings by means of the **German Transformation Act (UmwG)**; the same applies to the **heirs** of a party.[210] **2.122**

Pursuant to the prevailing view in Germany, **assignees**, too, are usually bound by arbitration agreements governing the assigned claims, unless there is clear evidence that the parties intended otherwise (see s 401 BGB).[211] Since the agreement to **2.123**

---

209 BGH WM 2007, 698 *et seq.*

210 BGHZ 68, 356, 359 = NJW 1977, 1397, 1398 *et seq.*; Hartmann, in: Baumbach/Lauterbach/Albers/Hartmann (eds), s 1029 para 24; Geimer, in: Zöller (ed), s 1029 para 63; Münch, in: MünchKommZPO, s 1029 para 45; Voit, in: Musielak/Voit (eds), s 1029 para 8; Lachmann, para 514; internationally see Born, pp 1463 *et seq.*; Gaillard/Savage, para 715.

211 BGHZ 68, 356, 359 = NJW 1977, 1397, 1398 *et seq.*; BGHZ 71, 162, 164 *et seq.* = NJW 1978, 1585, 1586; Hartmann, in: Baumbach/Lauterbach/Albers/Hartmann (eds), s 1029 para 24;

arbitrate forms part of the content of the assigned right, the arbitration agreement is "transferred" to the assignee irrespective of whether the assignment follows the form requirements of s 1031 ZPO.[212]

2.124 As a consequence, a person **acquiring shares in a corporation** or a partnership is bound to an arbitration agreement contained in the by-laws or the partnership agreement with regard to disputes between the corporation or partnership on the one hand and the new shareholder on the other.[213] The same applies to disputes between the current shareholders and the new shareholder.[214] By contrast, **disputes between the former and the new shareholder** arising out of the transfer of the shares are not governed by an arbitration agreement contained in the by-laws or the partnership agreement, unless the former and the new shareholder agree otherwise.

2. Joint Liability

2.125 The scope of the arbitration agreement needs to be determined independently of the underlying claims. Thus, an arbitration agreement generally binds only those parties who conclude the agreement.[215] An arbitration agreement which was concluded between a joint debtor and the creditor does **not generally bind other joint debtors** who are not contracting parties or legal successors even though their rights and obligations may depend on the outcome of the arbitral proceedings.[216]

3. Agreement for the Benefit of Third Parties

2.126 An arbitration agreement may also extend to disputes with a third party who benefits from the main contract as true third-party beneficiary (*Vertrag zugunsten Dritter*, s 328 BGB) to the extent that its rights which are conferred as third party beneficiary are concerned. This requires, however, that the arbitration agreement has been **formed before or at the time** when the third party beneficiary acquired its right. The introduction of an arbitration agreement by later amendment cannot alter the rights already vested to the third party. The third party may bring claims under the arbitration agreement, and it cannot resort to the state courts. The reason is that the third-party right was granted with the arbitration agreement

Geimer, in: Zöller (ed), s 1029 para 68; Münch, in: MünchKommZPO, s 1029 para 47; Lachmann, para 521; Gaillard/Savage, paras 712 *et seq.;* opposing view: Schlosser, in: Stein/Jonas (eds), s 1029 para 87a.

[212] BGH SchiedsVZ 2005, 95; Hartmann, in: Baumbach/Lauterbach/Albers/Hartmann (eds), s 1029 para 24; Geimer, in: Zöller (ed), s 1029 para 68; Lachmann, para 526.

[213] BGH NJW 1998, 371; SchiedsVZ 2014, 151, 153 para 22; Altmeppen, in: Roth/Altmeppen (eds), s 15 para 19.

[214] BGH NJW-RR 2002, 1462, 1463; Voit, in: Musielak/Voit (eds), s 1029 para 8; Lachmann, para 522; opposing view: Schwab/Walter, ch 7 para 32.

[215] Lachmann, para 501; Schwab/Walter, ch 7 para 22.

[216] Schwab/Walter, ch 7 para 25; Kreindler/Schäfer/Wolff, para 172; Schlosser, in: Stein/Jonas (eds), s 1029 para 72.

as its inherent characteristic.[217] By contrast, **counterclaims against the third party will typically not be covered** by the arbitration agreement, as this would be tantamount to an agreement to the detriment of a third party (*Vertrag zulasten Dritter*), which is not possible under German contract law.

4. *Corporate Law Matters*

An arbitration agreement can extend to a third party as a matter of corporate law. Various scenarios need to be distinguished. **2.127**

With respect to **general partnerships as respondents**,[218] it is well established in German practice that a claimant may bring arbitration not only against the partnership, but **also against its general partners**, even if the general partners are not parties to the arbitration agreement.[219] General partners are generally personally liable for the obligations of the partnership pursuant to or, depending on the form of the general partnership, in analogy to **s 128 HGB**. By contrast, these principles do **not apply** to the shareholders of a **corporation** such as a German stock corporation (AG) or a limited liability company (GmbH).[220] **2.128**

Also, the fact that two companies belong to the same **group of companies** (*Konzern*) does as such **not suffice** to extend an arbitration agreement entered into by one company to the other.[221] In other words, German arbitration law does not recognize a general "group of companies doctrine" as it is sometimes advocated in other jurisdictions or under certain rules of arbitration.[222] The only exception is a situation where under substantive corporate law, the **corporate veil of an entity may be "pierced,"** and its parent company is liable for the obligations of such entity. In this case, the parent company is subject to an arbitration agreement that the entity has **2.129**

[217] LG Frankfurt, November 15, 2013, 2-23 O 55/13 (unreported); Jagmann, in: Staudinger (ed), s 328 paras 25, 260; Münch, in: MünchKommZPO, s 1029 para 54; Gottwald, in: MünchKommBGB, s 328 paras 28, 250; Schwab/Walter, ch 7 para 22; Geimer, in: Zöller (ed), s 1031 para 18; Kleinschmidt, SchiedsVZ 2006, 142. Internationally see Born, pp 1455 *et seq.*

[218] Eg, civil law partnership (GbR), general commercial partnership (oHG), limited commercial partnership (KG).

[219] BGH WM 1971, 308, 208; BayObLG SchiedsVZ 2004, 45, 46; BGHZ 40, 320, 325 = NJW 1964, 591, 592; BGH NZG 2002, 83; Hartmann, in: Baumbach/Lauterbach/Albers/Hartmann (eds), s 1029 para 25; Geimer, in: Zöller (ed), s 1029 para 71; Voit, in: Musielak/Voit (eds), s 1029 para 8; Lachmann, para 504. Pursuant to the prevailing view, this does not apply to the limited partners (*Kommanditisten*) of a KG.

[220] Lachmann, para 506; Sessler, BB 1998, Beil. 9, p 21; Schwab/Walter, ch 7 para 35.

[221] Lachmann, para 510; Voit, in: Musielak/Voit (eds), s 1029 para 8; Müller/Keilmann, SchiedsVZ 2007, 113, 118; Busse, SchiedsVZ 2005, 118, 120.

[222] This doctrine goes back to a French ICC tribunal decision (*Dow Chemical*) and was later implemented in France and certain French-based jurisdictions like in Egypt or Lebanon; see Wilske/Shore/Ahrens, 17 Am. Rev. Int'l Arb. 73, 75 *et seq.*, 85, fn. 46 (2006); Gaillard/Savage, paras 500 *et seq.*; Born, pp 1444 *et seq.* There is an ongoing discussion whether this doctrine has even become an international "ICC practice," cf Müller/Keilmann, SchiedsVZ 2007, 113, 118; Busse, SchiedsVZ 2005, 118, 120; Craig/Park/Paulsson, pp 75 *et seq.*; Sandrock, in: Böckstiegel/Berger/Bredow, pp 93 *et seq.*

entered into because the arbitration agreement is a characteristic of the obligations pursuant to which the "piercing" applies.[223]

5. *Insolvency Matters*

2.130 Insolvency administrators (*Insolvenzverwalter*) acting pursuant to the German Insolvency Statute (InsO) are **generally bound** by arbitration agreements concluded by the debtor **prior** to the institution of insolvency proceedings.[224] Likewise, the administrator is bound to **arbitrator selections** made by the debtor prior to the insolvency proceedings.[225] By contrast, disputes regarding **contestation claims** under ss 129 *et seq.* InsO cannot be subjected to arbitration agreements by the debtor. The reason is that the claims of the insolvency estate result from a successful contestation, and not from the contested agreement which may contain the arbitration clause.[226] Similarly, the state courts have jurisdiction over a dispute between the insolvency administrator and the counter-party to a contract concluded by the debtor on whether the insolvency administrator has properly exercised its rights under s 103 InsO (**rejection of executory contracts**), notwithstanding an arbitration clause in the contract rejected by the insolvency administrator. Again, German courts consider this to be a **dispute on the specific rights of the insolvency administrator** under the InsO, and not a dispute arising out of or in connection with the rejected contract.[227] By contrast, s 166 para 2 InsO was held to provide only for the insolvency administrator's right to collect the assigned amount but does not affect the underlying claim, which remains subject to an arbitration agreement.[228]

II. Subject-matter Scope

2.131 The subject-matter scope of an arbitration agreement is first an issue of general contract interpretation (see above paras 2.105 *et seq.*). Typical situations requiring special attention are pre-contractual claims (below para 2.132), claims based on enrichment and tort claims (below para 2.133), as well as set-off and counterclaim situations (below para 2.134).

1. *Pre-contractual Claims*

2.132 Whether pre-contractual claims (such as under *culpa in contrahendo* principles pursuant to s 311 BGB) are covered by an arbitration agreement, is a matter of the

[223] Geimer, in: Zöller (ed), s 1029 para 72; Gross, SchiedsVZ 2006, 194; Müller/Keilmann, SchiedsVZ 2007, 113, 114; internationally see Born, pp 1431 *et seq.*

[224] BGHZ 160, 127, 131 et seq. = NJW 2004, 2898, 2899; Hartmann, in: Baumbach/Lauterbach/Albers/Hartmann (eds), s 1029 para 26; Geimer, in: Zöller (ed), s 1029 para 65; Münch, in: MünchKommZPO, s 1029 para 50; Voit, in: Musielak/Voit (eds), s 1029 para 8; Schlosser, in: Stein/Jonas (eds), s 1029 para 86; Lachmann, para 516.

[225] Lachmann, para 519; for further explanations see also KG SchiedsVZ 2005, 100, 102.

[226] BGHZ 24, 15, 19 = NJW 1957, 791; Geimer, in: Zöller (ed), s 1029 para 65; Voit, in: Musielak/Voit (eds), s 1029 para 8; Schlosser, in: Stein/Jonas (eds), s 1029 para 86; Lachmann, para 520.

[227] KG NZI 2012 759, 760; Kuhli, SchiedsVZ 2012, 321; Heydn, SchiedsVZ 2010, 182, 187; Geimer, in: Zöller (ed), s 1029 para 65.

[228] BGH NZI 2013, 934, 935.

content and thus possibly the **interpretation** of the arbitration agreement. As a rule of thumb, the formula "all disputes arising **out of** this agreement" is considered not to include pre-contractual claims or at least to pass the burden of proof to the opposing party.[229] By contrast, the broader term "all disputes arising **out of** ***or in connection with*** this agreement" would generally cover pre-contractual claims.[230]

2. *Enrichment and Tort Claims*

An arbitration agreement on disputes arising out of or in connection with a commercial contract usually extends to claims for unjust enrichment (ss 812 *et seq.* BGB) **related to such contract**, eg as a result of its invalidity.[231] Likewise, it typically covers tort claims to the extent tort claims result from the **same facts** that give rise to breach of contract.[232] **2.133**

3. *Set-off and Counterclaims*

Where the respondent raises counterclaims or declares set-off with respect to claims that are governed by the same arbitration agreement, no problems arise. Where the counterclaims or claims subject to set-off are governed by **no or another arbitration agreement**, the **arbitral tribunal generally lacks jurisdiction** unless the claimant does not properly object.[233] Upon proper objection, the arbitral tribunal will have to dismiss such counterclaims for lack of jurisdiction. The claims introduced by way of set-off need to be disregarded by the arbitral tribunal.[234] By way of exception, the general view is that claims that are **undisputed or** have been established by **final and binding judgment or award** may be introduced by way of set-off into an arbitration.[235] As a further exception, there is a strong view that set-off with claims resulting from an agreement that is **commercially closely connected** to the **2.134**

[229] Elsing, in: *Festschrift Graf von Westphalen*, pp 121 *et seq.*; Lachmann, SchiedsVZ 2003, 28, 29.

[230] OLG Hamburg, RIW 1989, 574 = XV Y.B. Com. Arb. 455 (1990); Schlosser, in: Stein/Jonas (eds), s 1029 para 27; Voit, in: Musielak/Voit (eds), s 1029 para 16; Lachmann, para 465.

[231] Voit, in: Musielak/Voit (eds), s 1029 para 23; Lachmann, para 478; Trittmann/Hanefeld, in: *Arbitration in Germany*, s 1029 para 31; Gaillard/Savage, para 524.

[232] BGHZ 102, 199, 200 *et seq.* = NJW 1988, 1215; BGH NJW 1965, 300; Hartmann, in: Baumbach/Lauterbach/Albers/Hartmann (eds), s 1029 para 21; Geimer, in: Zöller (ed), s 1029 para 80; Münch, in: MünchKommZPO, s 1029 para 48; Voit, in: Musielak/Voit (eds), s 1029 para 23; Lachmann, para 480; Gaillard/Savage, para 524.

[233] Sachs/Lörcher, in: *Arbitration in Germany*, s 1046 para 14; Lachmann, para 497. Note that art 21.5 Swiss Rules stipulates the opposite; this is, however, an exceptional rule by international standards; Lachmann, para 499.

[234] Geimer, in: Zöller (ed), s 1029 para 85; Voit, in: Musielak/Voit (eds), s 1029 para 24; Lachmann, para 498. There is a strong view that in such a case, the arbitral tribunal should only issue a provisional award: RGZ 133, 16, 19; Schlosser, in: Stein/Jonas (eds), s 1029 para 60; opposing view: Hartmann, in: Baumbach/Lauterbach/Albers/Hartmann (eds), s 1029 para 22; Schwab/Walter, ch 3 para 12.

[235] Geimer, in: Zöller (ed), s 1029 para 86; Lachmann, para 498 Voit, in: Musielak/Voit (eds), s 1029 para 24.

agreement giving rise to the main claim is to be accepted by the arbitral tribunal.[236] For example, such a connection can be found between a purchase agreement and a loan agreement which is entered into to finance the purchase.

III. Effects

2.135 An arbitration agreement gives rise to a jurisdiction defense against state court proceedings (below paras 2.136 *et seq.*) and triggers cooperation and good faith obligations between the parties (below paras 2.145 *et seq.*). Whether or not an arbitration agreement creates a confidentiality obligation, and on whom, is a question which we address below in paras 2.150 *et seq.*

1. Jurisdictional Objection in State Court Proceedings

2.136 a) **General Principles** Where the parties have concluded an arbitration agreement, the state courts lack jurisdiction to the extent the dispute is covered by the scope of the arbitration agreement (s 1032 para 1 ZPO).[237] The **defendant needs to raise this defense** (which for ease of reference we refer to as the jurisdiction defense)[238] in time, ie **prior to the oral hearing on the merits**, otherwise the defense will be considered waived.[239]

2.137 The jurisdiction defense may also be raised by a party to the arbitration agreement who received **third-party notice** (***Streitverkündung***) in a state court proceeding.[240] There is some disagreement regarding this view,[241] but it is supported by the better arguments. Where the parties conclude an arbitration agreement, they intend to resolve certain disputes solely before an arbitral tribunal. In our view, it should therefore be clear that the arbitration agreement needs to prevail where both the person giving and the person receiving the third-party notice are bound by the arbitration agreement. By contrast, the arbitration agreement does not give rise to a jurisdiction defense against third-party notice where the person giving the notice is not a party to the arbitration agreement. Such person has the procedural right to give third-party notice as a matter of law under s 72 ZPO. Others cannot limit such right by way of an arbitration agreement to which the person is not a party; agreements for the detriment of third parties are not recognized under German law.

---

[236] Schlosser, in: Stein/Jonas (eds), s 1029 para 60; Geimer, in: Zöller (ed), s 1029 para 87.

[237] Hartmann, in: Baumbach/Lauterbach/Albers/Hartmann (eds), s 1029 para 20; from an international perspective Gaillard/Savage, paras 662 *et seq.*

[238] One could also say arbitration agreement defense (*Einrede der Schiedsvereinbarung*) or arbitration defense (*Schiedseinrede*).

[239] Lachmann, para 434.

[240] Lachmann, para 437; Schwab/Walter, ch 7 para 23; Schlosser, in: Stein/Jonas (eds), s 1032 para 46; Elsing, SchiedsVZ 2004, 88.

[241] Bartels, BB 2001, Beil. 7, p 20.

An arbitration agreement also **bars accelerated documentary proceedings** (ss 592 *et seq.* ZPO) before the German state courts[242] as well as so-called **debt collection procedures** (ss 688 *et seq.* ZPO).[243] Likewise, the jurisdiction defense may be raised against the set-off with a claim that is subject to an arbitration agreement (see above para 2.134).[244] **2.138**

By contrast, the jurisdiction defense does not apply to **temporary freeze and injunction proceedings** (ss 916 *et seq.*, 935 *et seq.* ZPO) before state courts; German law expressly provides that an arbitration agreement does not limit the power of state courts to issue these types of preliminary measures (s 1033 ZPO). In parallel, the arbitral tribunal may take such measures (s 1041 ZPO; for details on interim relief by state courts and arbitral tribunals see below Chapter 5, including the availability of independent evidence proceedings under ss 485 *et seq.* ZPO). **2.139**

The **jurisdiction defense must be raised**; a state court will not dismiss an action covered by an arbitration agreement *ex officio.* Pursuant to s 1032 para 1 ZPO, the defense must be raised **prior to the oral hearing on the merits** before the state court. Where the defendant raises the jurisdiction defense on time, the state court is bound to dismiss the action as inadmissible,[245] unless the state court finds the arbitration agreement to be null and void, inoperative, or incapable of being performed (s 1032 para 1 ZPO; see para 2.158). Unlike art 8 para 1 Model Law, German civil procedure law does not provide the state court with the option to refer the case to arbitration. In exceptional cases, the jurisdiction defense may be **contrary to good faith** and therefore irrelevant. This applies, for instance, where the party raising the defense has first argued during arbitral proceedings that the arbitration agreement is invalid or unenforceable.[246] Another example is where the defense is raised although it is clear that the party has **insufficient financial resources** for an arbitration proceeding.[247] **2.140**

To the extent there is a dispute as to whether the arbitration agreement invoked by the defendant applies to the present dispute, the state court may decide thereon in advance by way of an **interim judgment** (*Zwischenurteil*, s 280 para 2 cl 1 ZPO), which is subject to immediate appeal.[248] The state court **may continue the** **2.141**

242 BGHZ 165, 376 = NJW 2006, 779; Lachmann, para 495; Münch, in: MünchKommZPO, s 1032 para 11. By contrast, as reiterated by the BGH in this decision, an arbitration agreement does not bar an accelerated bill of exchange proceeding (s 605a ZPO).

243 The defense needs to be raised in the course of an objection according to s 694 ZPO. Cf Münch, in: MünchKommZPO, s 1033 para 10; Geimer, in: Zöller (ed), s 1032 para 11a; opposing view: Schlosser, in: Stein/Jonas (eds), s 1032 para 12.

244 Voit, in: Musielak/Voit (eds), s 1032 para 6; Münch, in: MünchKommZPO, s 1032 para 14 with further references.

245 Münch, in: MünchKommZPO, s 1029 para 116.

246 BGH NJW 1968, 1928, 1929; Lachmann, para 435; Münch, in: MünchKommZPO, s 1032 para 9.

247 BGH NJW 1988, 1215.

248 Münch, in: MünchKommZPO, s 1032 para 21.

proceedings on the merits while the appeal is pending (s 280 para 2 cl 2 ZPO). How a state court approaches such a dispute will depend on the specifics of the individual situation. As a general matter, in order to give effect to arbitration agreements and in view of the requirements of procedural economy, a **state court should be reluctant** to conduct proceedings on the merits as long as there is no final and binding decision as to whether an arbitration agreement applies. Obviously, where a party invokes an arbitration agreement frivolously and its position is clearly unfounded, the state court may find it more appropriate to continue the proceedings in order to enforce the plaintiff's right to a speedy decision. In contrast, where the application of an arbitration agreement is subject to doubt, but the state court is of the view that it does not apply, the court should not continue with proceedings and a decision on the merits as long as the party invoking the arbitration agreement can appeal and is appealing this issue.

2.142 **b) State Court Action on Admissibility of Arbitral Proceedings** German law allows a petition to the competent state court to determine whether certain arbitral proceedings are admissible or inadmissible (s **1032 para 2 ZPO**). Such petition must be made **prior to the constitution of the arbitral tribunal**; once the tribunal is constituted, it also has jurisdiction over the admissibility or inadmissibility of arbitral proceedings (s 1040 para 1 ZPO).[249]

2.143 The process provided for in s 1032 para 2 ZPO is a **German particularity** without a parallel in the Model Law (cf art 8 Model Law). Each party may make a petition pursuant to s 1032 para 2 ZPO. Thus, the (later) claimant of the arbitration may request the state court to declare that certain (contemplated) arbitral proceedings are or would be admissible or inadmissible with regard to a certain arbitration agreement; likewise, the (later) respondent may request a declaration that they would be admissible or inadmissible.[250] These proceedings are unusual in that they allow the determination of a **fairly abstract question of law**. The idea behind s 1032 para 2 ZPO is to provide for a mechanism that allows the issue to be determined early on with **legal certainty**.[251] Parties should note, however, that a petition pursuant to s 1032 para 2 ZPO does **not suspend the statute of limitations** regarding the claim to be brought either in arbitration or before the state courts.[252]

2.144 The competent court is—as is normally the case for matters arising out of the Tenth Book of the ZPO—the **higher regional court** (OLG) of the district in which the place of arbitration is located (s 1062 para 1 no 2 ZPO). Its decision is subject to limited legal review by the BGH pursuant to s 1062 para 1 cl 1 ZPO.

---

[249] Münch, in: MünchKommZPO, s 1032 para 27.
[250] Münch, in: MünchKommZPO, s 1032 paras 23 *et seq.*
[251] BT-Drucks 13/5274, p 38.
[252] Voit, in: Musielak/Voit (eds), s 1032 para 13; Münch, in: MünchKommZPO, s 1032 para 29.

2. *Cooperation and Good Faith Obligations of the Parties*

As a substantive-law contract, the arbitration agreement generates **substantive law obligations** among the parties both to further the proceedings and to refrain from hindering the proceedings.[253] Most notably, from a practical point of view, the arbitration agreement obliges the parties to **pay** their share of the arbitrators' fees, including advance payments requested by the arbitral tribunal.[254] This obligation arises as an implied obligation based on general principles of German law (for details see below para 3.177). **2.145**

The arbitration agreement also creates an **implied obligation** on the parties to refrain from unduly influencing the arbitral tribunal or witnesses and experts, such as by threat, corruption, and the like. Grave violations of this obligation trigger the other party's right to extraordinarily terminate the arbitration agreement for cause if it is unacceptable to continue the proceedings under the given circumstances.[255] **2.146**

The arbitration agreement creates further obligations, such as the duty to **plead truthfully** and generally to **cooperate** in the conduct of the proceedings.[256] These obligations are not enforceable by state court action and their violation usually does not give rise to a right to terminate the arbitration agreement.[257] Instead, they may be sanctioned only by the arbitral tribunal pursuant to the rules applicable to the arbitral proceedings (Tenth Book of the ZPO and/or institutional rules). **2.147**

In addition, to the extent the parties agree on certain **rules of arbitration of an arbitral institution**, the arbitration agreement creates the obligation to obey such rules. Again, however, sanctions for violation of this duty are governed primarily by the agreed arbitration rules.[258] **2.148**

Finally, the arbitration agreement may be viewed to create an **obligation to cooperate in the constitution of the arbitral tribunal.**[259] However, the other party cannot force a party, for instance, to nominate an arbitrator. Instead, in such case, the arbitrator will be determined in accordance with the default rules of the Tenth Book of the ZPO or of the arbitral institution (for details see paras 3.19 *et seq.*). **2.149**

---

253 BGHZ 23, 198, 200 = NJW 1957, 589, 590; Hartmann, in: Baumbach/Lauterbach/Albers/Hartmann (eds), s 1029 para 19; Schlosser, in: Stein/Jonas (eds), s 1029 para 54; Lachmann, paras 441 *et seq.* Some prefer to qualify these obligations not as obligations under substantive law, but as procedural burdens, eg Schwab/Walter, ch 7 para 20. Internationally see Born, pp 1254 *et seq.*

254 Hartmann, in: Baumbach/Lauterbach/Albers/Hartmann (eds), s 1029 para 19; Schlosser, in: Stein/Jonas (eds), s 1029 para 54; Lachmann, para 447.

255 Lachmann, paras 460, 621; Schlosser, in: Stein/Jonas (eds), s 1029 para 100.

256 Schütze, para 156; Lachmann, paras 455 *et seq.*

257 Lachmann, para 457; Schlosser, in: Stein/Jonas (eds), s 1029 para 100; Voit, in: Musielak/Voit (eds), s 1029 para 27.

258 Lachmann, para 458.

259 Münch, in: MünchKommZPO, s 1029 para 117 with further references.

3. *Confidentiality*

2.150 In general, under German law, an arbitration agreement does **not per se trigger confidentiality obligations** of the parties;[260] there is no provision to this effect in the Tenth Book of the ZPO. This is contrary to the widely held belief among persons not familiar with German arbitration law that arbitration is somehow "confidential." It is true that the **arbitrators** are obliged to keep the proceedings and the contents confidential (see below para 3.187). However, in the absence of a contractual confidentiality undertaking or confidentiality provisions in rules of arbitration agreed by the parties, this does not necessarily apply to the *parties and other persons* participating in the proceedings, such as witnesses and experts.

2.151 Notably, the **DIS Rules** do contain a confidentiality provision in their s 43 which reads as follows:

> 43.1: The parties, the arbitrators and the persons at the DIS Secretariat involved in the administration of the arbitral proceedings shall maintain confidentiality towards all persons regarding the conduct of arbitral proceedings, and in particular regarding the parties involved, the witnesses, the experts and other evidentiary materials. Persons acting on behalf of any person involved in the arbitral proceedings shall be obligated to maintain confidentiality.
>
> 43.2: The DIS may publish information on arbitral proceedings in compilations of statistical data, provided such information excludes identification of the persons involved.[261]

2.152 Concerning the ICC, **art 6 ICC Rules** contains provisions on confidentiality only regarding the **ICC Court** as follows:

> Article 6: Confidentiality
>
> The work of the Court is of a confidential nature which must be respected by everyone who participates in that work in whatever capacity. The Court lays down the rules regarding the persons who can attend the meetings of the Court and its Committees and who are entitled to have access to materials related to the work of the Court and its Secretariat.

IV. Termination

2.153 The most important grounds for terminating an arbitration agreement in German arbitration practice are termination by agreement of the parties (below paras 2.154 *et seq.*) and unilateral termination by one party (below paras 2.156 *et seq.*). Other, general grounds for termination are fairly rare (below paras 2.162 *et seq.*).

1. *Termination by Agreement*

2.154 An arbitration agreement, as any agreement, is binding as long as it is not terminated. As an agreement, it can be terminated by **consent of all parties.**[262] For such

260 Lionnet/Lionnet, p 458; Lachmann, para 461.
261 Available at http://www.disarb.org (last visited December 1, 2015).
262 Schlosser, in: Stein/Jonas (eds), s 1029 para 95; Lachmann, para 609.

consensual termination, the parties need not observe the form requirements of s 1031 ZPO.[263] As with any agreement, termination can be **express or implied**. However, in the absence of an express termination, there need to be **clear circumstances** before an implied termination of the arbitration agreement can be found. It will generally not be sufficient that both parties **fail to further pending arbitral proceedings** for an extended period of time.[264] Likewise, a **settlement** outside the arbitral proceedings does not necessarily terminate the arbitration agreement. Instead, the arbitration agreement may still apply to disputes resulting from the settlement (see above para 2.115).[265] An implied termination may be found where the parties agree on a **novation of their main contract** and now provide for the jurisdiction of the state courts without expressly terminating the prior arbitration clause.

By contrast, mere **silence** will generally not be capable of terminating an arbitration agreement, because under German civil law, silence—in the absence of extraordinary circumstances—**normally has no legal significance**.[266] A recognized exception is silence upon **receipt of a commercial confirmation letter** (see above paras 2.24 *et seq*.). Thus, a commercial confirmation letter could be used to terminate an arbitration agreement, and where the other side fails to object within a reasonable period, such termination would be effected by way of silence, unless the termination of the arbitration agreement would need to be qualified as so unusual that the recipient of the confirmation letter did not need to anticipate such contents, which is necessarily a question of a case-by-case analysis. **2.155**

2. *Unilateral Termination*

As a substantive-law agreement with continuing obligations, an arbitration agreement may be subject to termination by one party **for cause** (*Kündigung aus wichtigem Grund*, s 314 BGB).[267] Thus, there must be an important reason for termination which makes it **unacceptable** (*unzumutbar*) for a party to continue to be bound; termination must be declared within an appropriate time frame once cause has arisen (s 314 para 3 BGB). Examples treated by the German courts are failure to nominate an arbitrator, failure to pay advances on costs, delays of the proceedings, and obstruction tactics.[268] **2.156**

---

263 Hartmann, in: Baumbach/Lauterbach/Albers/Hartmann (eds), s 1029 para 27; Münch, in: MünchKommZPO, s 1029 para 120; Voit, in: Musielak/Voit (eds), s 1031 para 2; Schlosser, in: Stein/Jonas (eds), s 1029 para 95; Lachmann, para 610.

264 Münch, in: MünchKommZPO, s 1029 para 120.

265 Münch, in: MünchKommZPO, s 1029 para 120.

266 Ellenberger, in: Palandt (ed), Einf v s 116 para 7.

267 Hartmann, in: Baumbach/Lauterbach/Albers/Hartmann (eds), s 1029 para 27; Münch, in: MünchKommZPO, s 1029 para 127; Lachmann, para 617.

268 BGHZ 23, 198, 202 = NJW 1957, 589, 590; BGH NJW 1986, 2765, 2766; Lachmann, para 620; Schwab/Walter, ch 8 para 11; Geimer, in: Zöller (ed), s 1029 paras 97 *et seq*.

2.157 It should be noted, however, that each case needs to be analyzed carefully on its facts. Termination for cause under s 314 BGB is a **remedy of last resort** (*ultima ratio*). Thus, as a general matter, any **remedies existing within the arbitral process** need to be exhausted first or their exhaustion must be found to be unacceptable for the party seeking termination.[269] For instance, in most cases, there will be a process for **appointing an arbitrator** where one party does not cooperate. Likewise, failure to **plead truthfully** can and needs to be sanctioned by the arbitral tribunal and does not give rise to a right of termination.[270] An arbitral tribunal has ample means to address **delay tactics** of a party. While this may sound unsatisfactory for a party trying to proceed in good faith against a rogue counterparty, care needs to be applied regarding termination for cause in order not to allow a party acting in bad faith to abuse the termination right in order to obstruct or sabotage the arbitral process.[271]

2.158 At the other end of the spectrum, a clear case justifying termination for cause would be **bribery** of or **threats against the arbitrators** by the other side.[272] Also, **war and political unrest** may prevent the constitution of the arbitral tribunal and the conduct of proceedings, in which case termination may be proper.[273] Furthermore, an accepted scenario is the **failure to pay the advance on costs**, including cases where the **claimant is unable to pay**.[274] The BGH has considered such a situation to render the arbitration agreement "inoperative" under s 1032 para 1 ZPO and therefore barred the jurisdiction defense *ipso iure* even without explicit termination by a party.[275] Where a party is not sure whether the arbitration agreement is inoperative *ipso iure*, as a matter of precaution, it certainly makes sense to declare termination of the arbitration agreement for cause. In any event, it would seem preferable to leave the proper course of action to party choice, which is the more flexible and thus more appropriate solution compared to an objective finding of inoperability. After all, one party may well decide to pay the other side's share of the advance on costs and proceed with the arbitration. Where the claimant is unable to pay its share and the claimant does not formally declare termination of the arbitration agreement but simply commences state-court litigation, the commencement of such litigation may be viewed as **implied termination** of the arbitration agreement.[276]

---

[269] Münch, in: MünchKommZPO, s 1029 para 129 with further examples.

[270] BGHZ 23, 198, 201 = NJW 1957, 589, 590; Lachmann, paras 623 *et seq.*

[271] OLG München, SchiedsVZ 2012, 96, 99, 100; Münch, in: MünchKommZPO, s 1029 para 128; Geimer, in: Zöller (ed), s 1029 para 97.

[272] Lachmann, para 621.

[273] Münch, in: MünchKommZPO, s 1029 para 131.

[274] Münch, in: MünchKommZPO, s 1029 para 131; Voit, in: Musielak/Voit (eds), s 1029 para 12; Reichold, in: Thomas/Putzo (eds), s 1029 para 17; Hartmann, in: Baumbach/Lauterbach/Albers/Hartmann (eds), s 1029 para 29.

[275] BGH NJW 2000, 3720, 3721.

[276] Similarly Münch, in: MünchKommZPO, s 1029 para 133.

In German legal doctrine, there are different views as to whether—in addition to or instead of termination pursuant to s 314 BGB—there may be a **right to withdraw pursuant to s 323 BGB**. In particular, some authors argue that a right to withdraw may exist where the arbitral proceedings have not yet commenced and the other party is in default with its obligations under the arbitration agreement.[277] We are skeptical of this view. An arbitration agreement is not necessarily a synallagmatic agreement in the sense of s 323 BGB (*gegenseitiger Vertrag*), like for instance a purchase agreement, where one party promises to deliver a certain good against payment of a certain price.[278] With regard to an arbitration agreement, it would strike us as odd to say that one party is obliged to appoint an arbitrator in order to "obtain" the appointment of the second arbitrator from the other party. Also, from a practical point of view, it would be highly undesirable to have collateral disputes among the parties in the early stages of the main dispute as to whether one party (i) has defaulted on certain obligations resulting from the arbitration agreement, and (ii) whether such obligations were synallagmatic ones justifying the application of s 323 BGB. Instead, the cautious application of s 314 BGB as described above seems to us to be the more persuasive approach. **2.159**

The **termination of the main contract** containing an arbitration clause does **not necessarily** terminate the arbitration agreement (separability principle, s 1040 para 1 cl 2 ZPO).[279] Thus, where a party terminates the main contract, the arbitration clause would generally govern any dispute on the effectiveness of the termination and its consequences. By way of exception, the parties can of course agree not only to terminate the main contract, but also the arbitration agreement. The party invoking such exceptional situation bears the burden of proof.[280] **2.160**

In rare situations, an arbitration agreement may be voidable by one party on the basis of **error, deception, or duress**. The error, deception, or duress must be **specifically related to the arbitration agreement and its conclusion**. Error, deception, or duress regarding the conclusion of the main contract will not necessarily suffice due to the **separability principle** (s 1040 para 1 cl 2 ZPO).[281] **2.161**

3. Other Grounds for Termination

The parties may agree on **conditions** and **time limits** in an arbitration agreement.[282] In most cases, this is **not advisable**. Conditions subsequent and time limits leading to the termination of the arbitration agreement may seem to put welcome pressure on the arbitrators to conduct the proceedings swiftly. However, such strategy may **2.162**

---

277 Hartmann, in: Baumbach/Lauterbach/Albers/Hartmann (eds), s 1029 para 27.

278 Münch, in: MünchKommZPO, s 1029 para 125.

279 BGHZ 53, 315, 318 *et seq.*; Lachmann, para 466; Voit, in: Musielak/Voit (eds), s 1040 para 4; Hartmann, in: Baumbach/Lauterbach/Albers/Hartmann (eds), s 1040 para 2.

280 Lachmann, para 468.

281 Lachmann, paras 613 *et seq.*

282 Lachmann, paras 410 *et seq.*

easily backfire where the other party applies delay tactics or the case for whatever reason becomes much more complex and complicated than originally anticipated. Having the arbitration agreement terminate in such a scenario would seem highly unsatisfactory, because the parties would then be left with the choice of restarting the entire process before the state courts.

2.163 This analysis is in line with the rules of arbitral institutions which tend to avoid the consequence of *ipso jure* invalidity. For instance, the BGH denied an obligatory termination in a case where the arbitrator missed the six-month deadline for the award under the ICC Rules because such an extraordinary result would have required an explicit party agreement.[283] Also, disputes may arise as to whether a condition has in fact happened or a deadline has in fact expired. This may trigger unnecessary and costly litigation parallel to the arbitral proceedings. In addition, it may give a disgruntled party leeway to attempt a challenge against an award that has turned out not to be what a party had hoped for.

2.164 The **termination of arbitral proceedings** does not necessarily terminate the arbitration agreement, unless the arbitration agreement was concluded for this specific dispute only.[284] With regard to arbitration clauses contained in a main contract, this will usually not be the case. Where the arbitration agreement applied only to a specific dispute, termination of the arbitral proceedings, eg by rendering the award, is sufficient for termination of the arbitration agreement. A declaration of enforcement is not necessary, nor is it necessary to wait until the time period for set aside requests has expired. In case there are successful set aside proceedings, s 1059 para 5 ZPO provides that in case of doubt, the arbitration agreement shall be revived with respect to the matter in dispute.[285]

2.165 In rare situations, an arbitration agreement may terminate because it has become **inoperable** (s 1032 para 1 ZPO). This may be the case where the parties have agreed on a **specific person** as arbitrator and such person cannot serve or where the arbitral institution selected by the parties ceases to exist without successor.[286] Prior to finding inoperability, all means of contract interpretation, including **supplementary interpretation** (*ergänzende Vertragsauslegung*), need to be exhausted.[287]

2.166 The **termination of the office of one of the arbitrators** does not terminate the arbitration agreement (unlike under the prior German arbitration law, s 1033 no 1 prior version ZPO). Instead, the arbitrator is to be replaced pursuant to the provisions contained in s 1039 ZPO (see below paras 3.155 *et seq.*). The replacement occurs in accordance with the same provisions that applied to the appointment of

283 BGH NJW 1988, 3090, 3091 = XV Y.B. Com. Arb. 452 (1990).
284 Lachmann, para 627.
285 Münch, in: MünchKommZPO, s 1029 para 121.
286 Lachmann, paras 606, 607.
287 BGH SchiedsVZ 2011, 284, 285.

the original arbitrator (s 1039 para 1 cl 2 ZPO), unless the parties agree otherwise (s 1039 para 2 ZPO).

The **opening of insolvency proceedings** on the part of one of the parties does not terminate the arbitration agreement. Neither s 115 InsO nor s 113 InsO applies. Section 115 InsO applies only to agreements constituting a mandate (*Auftrag*), and the arbitration agreement as such is not a mandate, but an agreement *sui generis* on certain procedural-law relations (see above para 2.12). Likewise, as already stated above (para 2.162), an arbitration agreement is not a synallagmatic agreement in the sense of s 323 BGB and therefore also not in the sense of s 111 InsO. As a consequence, the insolvency administrator (*Insolvenzverwalter*) has no right to choose whether or not to continue an arbitration agreement, but is generally bound to do so. **2.167**

Exceptions exist where the arbitration agreement purports to cover matters that are the **exclusive prerogative of the insolvency administrator**; regarding these matters, the parties cannot bind him or her (no agreement for the detriment of third parties); for more details see above para 2.130. This is, however, not a matter of termination, but a matter of the proper personal scope of the arbitration agreement. **2.168**

Where a **shareholder leaves a company**, an arbitration agreement in the by-laws of the company will generally continue to govern disputes between the company and its former shareholder, to the extent such disputes arise out of the shareholder relationship (see above para 2.124).[288] **2.169**

D. Typical Additional Content of the Arbitration Agreement

While generally with respect to the drafting of the arbitration agreement less is indeed more (paras 2.117 *et seq.*), we do recommend to include certain further content in any arbitration agreement, specifically the place of arbitration (below paras 2.174 *et seq.*), the language of the proceedings (below paras 2.178 *et seq.*), the applicable substantive law (below paras 2.183 *et seq.*), and the choice of an arbitral institution, or, alternatively, ad hoc arbitration (below paras 2.194 *et seq.*). Finally, the number of arbitrators should be indicated, an issue which we explore in more detail in paras 3.2 *et seq.* below. **2.170**

Not much text is needed; an example—following the recommendation of the DIS—could be: **2.171**

> All disputes arising in connection with this contract or its validity shall be finally settled in accordance with the Arbitration Rules of the German Institution of Arbitration (DIS) without recourse to the ordinary courts of law. The place of arbitration is Munich, Germany. The number of arbitrators is three. The language

---

[288] BGH NJW-RR 2002, 1462, 1463; Lachmann, para 469; Voit, in: Musielak/Voit (eds), s 1029 para 8; Geimer, in: Zöller (ed), s 1029 para 74.

of the arbitral proceedings is English. The applicable substantive law is German law (excluding the United Nations Convention on the International Sale of Goods—CISG).

2.172 By contrast, absent specific circumstances, we would be reluctant to recommend much additional content for an arbitration agreement that provides for arbitration seated in Germany. For instance, it is neither necessary nor even useful to provide for rights and obligations of the arbitrators. Instead, the arbitrator agreement is the right place for such provisions.[289] Also, the parties cannot—and should not purport to—derogate mandatory principles of the German arbitration law, such as equal treatment and the right to be heard, and the mandatory provisions of the Tenth Book of the ZPO (see above paras 1.31 *et seq.*).[290]

2.173 Finally, it is **not necessary to make reference to the Tenth Book of the ZPO**, because it applies in any event as long as the seat is in Germany.

I. Place of Arbitration

2.174 Drafters of arbitration agreements in commercial transactions often fail to understand the significance of the place of arbitration. More often than not, practitioners not familiar with the field of arbitration mistake the place of arbitration as the venue for hearings. The legal significance of the place of arbitration is different, though. By selecting the place of arbitration, the parties submit to the **arbitration law of that place** (*lex arbitri*), in Germany, for instance, the provisions of the Tenth Book of the ZPO (s 1025 para 1 ZPO). Ordinarily, the arbitration law at the place of arbitration governs such issues as (i) the role of the state courts with regard to arbitral proceedings and (ii) set aside proceedings (for details see below paras 6.156 *et seq.*). Also, the city designated as the place of arbitration regularly determines **which state court has jurisdiction** pursuant to s 1062 ZPO.

2.175 Parties may find that certain places of arbitration have arbitration laws with features that they would not necessarily like. For instance, there may be mandatory provisions on the nationality of arbitrators, far-reaching possibilities for state courts to interfere with arbitral proceedings, too broad or too narrow grounds for set aside etc.[291] Further, the choice may determine a specific time zone which will affect deadlines for acts of procedure.[292] Another—and potentially even more important—consequence is that the arbitral award will be deemed to have been rendered in the chosen country, which may raise questions of **recognition and enforceability.**[293] Even if the national law does not provide any mandatory rules, the parties should consider whether by selecting a particular country as the seat,

289 Similarly Münch, in: MünchKommZPO, s 1029 para 99.
290 Münch, in: MünchKommZPO, s 1029 para 100.
291 Lachmann, para 395; Kreindler/Schäfer/Wolff, para 233.
292 Wegen/Wilske, SchiedsVZ 2003, 124, 125.
293 BT-Drucks 13/5274, p 47.

and thereby increasing the likelihood that one or more arbitrators to be selected in the future may be from that same country, they are thereby making it more or less likely that certain **approaches to procedure** including the taking of witness and documentary evidence (eg document discovery) may be applied. In practice, in international commercial transactions, the perceived **neutrality** of a place of arbitration is also often considered crucial,[294] even though this aspect is frequently overestimated. From the above, it should be clear that selecting the place of arbitration based primarily on the basis of convenience or even touristic aspects is not advisable.

In general, and without prejudice to the necessary case-by-case analysis, **selecting a German place of arbitration should not have any major drawbacks** for the parties, including non-German parties. Germany follows the Model Law, the Tenth Book of the ZPO contains only a few mandatory provisions and gives a high degree of deference to party autonomy. German state courts have limited power to interfere with arbitral proceedings; at the same time, German courts provide necessary and valuable assistance to arbitral tribunals, for instance with respect to taking of evidence (for details see below paras 4.200 *et seq.*). German law provides for limited grounds for set aside in line with international practice (for details see below paras 6.156 *et seq.*). Practical considerations, such as travel logistics, the availability of proper venues, translators, and court reporters certainly do not weigh against a German place for arbitration. **2.176**

Where the **parties fail to agree** on a place of arbitration, under the Tenth Book of the ZPO, it is upon the **arbitral tribunal** to determine the issue (s 1043 para 1 cl 2 ZPO).[295] The arbitral tribunal has **broad discretion** but shall consider the suitability under the specific circumstances (s 1043 para 1 cl 3 ZPO). An even broader rule applies in DIS proceedings (s 21.1 DIS Rules) which leaves the decision to the discretion of the arbitral tribunal without any restriction. By contrast, under the ICC, the LCIA, and the Swiss Rules, the arbitral institution decides (art 18.1 ICC Rules, 16.1 LCIA Rules, 16.1 Swiss Rules). For instance, considerations taken into account by the ICC include the arbitration law and its quality at that place, neutrality (ie different from nationalities of the parties), geography (ease of access and convenience to the arbitrators, the parties, and their counsel), and the availability of suitable facilities to conduct hearings.[296] Under art 16.2 LCIA Rules, the default seat is London, unless the LCIA Court decides otherwise. Under the Swiss Rules, the decision may also be conferred upon the arbitral tribunal. **2.177**

II. Language of the Proceedings

In a purely national context, there may be little to no need to agree on the language of the proceedings. In an international context, ie where the parties come from **2.178**

[294] Lachmann, para 397; Lionnet/Lionnet, p 209.
[295] OLG München, SchiedsVZ 2008, 307; Geimer, in: Zöller (ed), s 1043 para 3.
[296] Fry/Greenberg/Mazza, para 3-686.

different countries and/or speak different languages, the situation is different. In such a scenario, it is highly advisable to include in the arbitration clause a sentence that expressly stipulates the language of the proceedings, eg:

> The arbitral proceedings shall be conducted in the English language.

2.179 When agreeing on the language—or languages (s 1045 para 1 ZPO)—of the proceedings, various considerations can be relevant. A major aspect may be the **language of the documents** that will likely serve as evidence in future arbitral proceedings. Where the language of documents is different from the language(s) of the proceedings, the arbitral tribunal may order the submission of translations into the language(s) of the proceedings (s 1045 para 2 ZPO), which may involve a significant amount of time and cost. In addition, parties may consider the native languages of possibly important witnesses. Furthermore, language is an important consideration for the **selection of counsel and arbitrators**. Also, a party may accede to a certain language in order to obtain some other advantage in the course of the negotiations of an arbitration clause or the overall agreement at issue.

2.180 Where the parties correspond in a certain language, it may often be sensible to conduct arbitral proceedings in the same language. In transnational commercial transactions, in many instances this may mean English. The parties may also consider to allow the introduction of documents in languages other than the language of the proceedings, in particular where the core documents, such as the major agreement, use a different language. The parties thereby avoid the risk of inaccuracies where the exact wording is crucial for the interpretation and witness statements regarding the drafting history may be easier to pin down. On the other hand, this option might do more harm than good where the arbitrators do not speak this language and the interpretation of documents thus becomes significantly harder.

2.181 Where the **parties do not agree** on a language for the proceedings, but speak different languages, it is upon the **arbitral tribunal** to determine the language of the proceedings in its discretion. In doing so, the arbitral tribunal may have due regard to the **relevant circumstances**, such as the language of the **underlying contract** and of the **arbitration agreement**.[297] Additional considerations may be the language of the **pre- and post-contractual communication of the parties** as well as the **convenience** to those involved in the arbitration, including the arbitrators and parties' counsels.[298]

2.182 A decision by the arbitral tribunal is of course quite impractical from a party perspective, in particular for the claimant who may be left guessing in which language

---

[297] Article 20 ICC Rules; art 17 LCIA Rules; art 22.1 DIS Rules.

[298] Fry/Greenberg/Mazza, paras 3-734 *et seq.*; Kreindler/Schäfer/Wolff, paras 629 *et seq.;* Lionnet/Lionnet, p 334.

it should draft its request for arbitration and may find itself in the situation of having to do substantial translation work at a later stage should the tribunal order the proceedings to be conducted in a different language.[299]

III. Selection of Applicable Substantive Law

1. Party Agreement and its Limitations

In an international context, reasonably sophisticated parties nowadays will almost always include a choice of law clause into their agreements. Frequently, this is even done in agreements with a purely national nexus. It is an internationally recognized principle that contracting parties enjoy broad autonomy in their choice of law and that this choice is superior to any legal provision. For instance, this principle can be seen in Art 3 Rome I Regulation[300] and in s 1051 para 1 cl 1 ZPO. As the choice of law is not an essential element of the arbitration agreement, the form requirement of s 1031 ZPO need not be observed and even an implied agreement is sufficient. For example, this can be the case were both parties solely refer to the same substantive law in their pleadings.[301] **2.183**

It is notable that in s 1051 para 1 cl 1 ZPO the term "**rules of law**" is used whereas cl 2 contains the terms "law" and "legal system." The different terminology is meant to provide the parties with greater **flexibility** in determining the most suitable set of rules.[302] Instead of one overall legal system they can pick and choose specific regulations from one legal system and others from another. Further, they are not limited to written rules but free to agree on general principles, conventions of an international forum, or even their own regulations.[303] However, for practical reasons we would recommend not to make excessive use of this possibility. A potentially useful exercise of party choice may be to **exclude the application of ss 305 *et seq.* BGB** on general terms and conditions (AGB), at least in the context of transactions between **commercial parties**, such as M&A agreements (see above para 2.104). **2.184**

Apart from that, it is highly controversial whether this freedom of choice is limited by law and where these **limitations** should be drawn. Based on the provisions of the Rome I Regulation, there are various views advocating restrictions on the freedom of choice, such as limiting freedom of choice to cross-border cases,[304] to **2.185**

---

299 Lachmann, para 394; Lionnet/Lionnet, p 335; Kreindler/Schäfer/Wolff, para 630.

300 Martiny, in: MünchKommBGB, VO (EG) 593/2008 Art 3 Rome I Regulation para 8; Spickhoff, in: BeckOK BGB, VO (EG) 593/2008 Art 3 Rome I Regulation paras 17 *et seq.*

301 OLG Hamm, SchiedsVZ 2014, 38, 42.

302 BT-Drucks 13/5274, p 52; Münch, in: MünchKommZPO, s 1051 para 14.

303 Schmaltz, in: *Arbitration in Germany*, s 1051 para 19; Voit, in: Musielak/Voit (eds), s 1051 para 2.

304 Münch, in: MünchKommZPO, s 1051 para 22; opposing view: Voit, in: Musielak/Voit (eds), s 1051 para 3; Geimer, in: Zöller (ed), s 1051 para 2.

contractual obligations,[305] or to non-mandatory law.[306] In our view, this question should be answered on a fairly generous basis. Given that s 1051 ZPO itself provides for an unlimited choice, the only legislative restriction can be found in s 1059 para 2 ZPO, namely in the ***ordre public*** (see below paras 2.196 *et seq*.). The Rome I Regulation should not be regarded as controlling on this issue, as Art 1 para 2 lit e Rome I Regulation expressly excludes arbitration from its scope. At the very most, its rules can serve as a "persuasive authority."[307]

2.186 In particular, the choice of law and its permissibility—pursuant to the clear wording of s 1051 para 1 ZPO—are **not limited to cross-border situations** like under Art 3 para 3 Rome I Regulation. It was the clear legislative decision of the drafters of the German arbitration law to strengthen the attractiveness of Germany as a locale for arbitration, and no distinction was made between domestic and international cases. In addition, it would seem inconsistent to allow the parties to opt out of the otherwise applicable law in favor of the principles of equity and fairness (s 1051 para 3 ZPO), but to bar them from choosing other rules of law. Eventually, not even fundamental considerations like consumer protection require such an additional restriction beyond *ordre public* limitations. German arbitration is characterized by an essential role of party autonomy; should there be unacceptable results in the individual case, courts and arbitral tribunals can still refer to means like the *ordre public* or fundamental and universally accepted principles of good faith and fair dealing.[308] Thus, as an example (with significant practical importance), in our view, outside the consumer context, the parties should be allowed to exclude the **German regulations of AGB** (ss 305 *et seq.* BGB) even where a case is purely domestic.

2 Determination in the Absence of Party Agreement

2.187 Where the parties have not agreed on an applicable substantive law, it is upon the Arbitral Tribunal to make the determination. While a German state court would look to the Rome I Regulation in order to determine the applicable substantive law, pursuant to s 1051 para 2 ZPO, the arbitral tribunal shall apply the law of the state to which the subject matter of the proceedings has the **closest connection.**[309] Nevertheless, the provisions of the Rome I Regulation can be used as guidelines

305 Münch, in: MünchKommZPO, s 1051 para 21; Saenger, in: Saenger (ed), s 1051 para 1; opposing view: Voit, in: Musielak/Voit (eds), s 1051 para 3.

306 BT-Drucks 13/5274, p 52; Münch, in: MünchKommZPO, s 1051 para 20; Schmitz, in: *Arbitration in Germany*, s 1051 para 27.

307 Pfeiffer, NJW 2012, 1169, 1170; Saenger, in: Saenger (ed), s 1051 para 2.

308 Pfeiffer, NJW 2012, 1169, 1173; opposing view: Münch, in: MünchKommZPO, s 1051 para 20.

309 Section 1051 para 2 ZPO thereby uses the direct method (as opposed to referring to a set of conflict of law rules) and thus deviates from art 28 para 2 Model Law which provides that failing any designation by the parties, the arbitral tribunal shall apply the law determined by the conflict of laws rules which it considers applicable.

for the determination of the closest connection.[310] Accordingly, considerable indicators may be the **residence or central administration of the party** which is to effect the **characteristic performance** of the contract, the country where the performance has to be effected, or the place where **immovable property** related to the performance is situated. Similar provisions are contained in many institutional arbitration rules, eg s 23.2 DIS Rules, art 33.1 Swiss Rules. Article 21.1 cl 2 ICC Rules is even less specific, providing that "the arbitral tribunal shall apply the rules of law which it determines to be appropriate."

When applying the law of the state to which the subject matter of the proceedings is most closely connected, in general, the arbitral tribunal can make its determination only by applying **state law**.[311] This raises the question whether the so-called ***"lex mercatoria"***[312] (law merchant) or "general principles of international commercial law," or "transnational rules of law"[313] can be applied. There is a controversial discussion on these types of rules. The classification of the *lex mercatoria* as a transnational legal system is quite doubtful, as in the view of many authors, it is not recognized as a legal system, but seen as a collection of general, poorly defined, and elusive rules.[314] Thus, where the parties wish to authorize an arbitral tribunal to apply the *lex mercatoria*, they should expressly say so in their arbitration agreement.[315] From a practical perspective, the actual application of the *lex mercatoria* remains uncommon, as the parties to an arbitration agreement generally refer to a single national law.[316] **2.188**

In certain cases, the rules of the European Convention on International Commercial Arbitration may be relevant for the determination of the applicable law.[317] It is applicable (Art I para 1 lit a) to a dispute between natural or legal persons having their habitual place of residence or their seat in different Contracting States, provided that the arbitration agreement has been concluded for the purpose of settling disputes arising from international trade, such as cases where goods or services are delivered across borders.[318] It is not required that the party be a merchant in the sense of the HGB.[319] Unlike s 1051 ZPO, Art VII para 1 cl 2 of the Convention **2.189**

---

310 BT-Drucks 13/5274, p 53; Münch, in: MünchKommZPO, s 1051 paras 7 *et seq.*; Voit, in: Musielak/Voit (eds), s 1051 para 7.

311 Nagel/Gottwald, § 18 para 128.

312 See Berger, *The Creeping Codification of the Lex Mercatoria*, http://www.trans-lex.org/100610/ (last visited December 1, 2015).

313 Derains/Schwartz, ch 5 p 219.

314 Derains/Schwartz, ch 5 p 219, Lionnet/Lionnet, pp 379 *et seq.*; Schwab/Walter, ch 41 para 21.

315 Nagel/Gottwald, § 18 paras 129, 210.

316 Derains/Schwartz, ch 5 p 219.

317 The Convention entered into force on January 7, 1964 and was ratified by Germany on January 25, 1965; Lionnet/Lionnet, p 93.

318 Adolphsen, in: MünchKommZPO, EuÜ, Art I para 5.

319 Adolphsen, in: MünchKommZPO, EuÜ, Art I para 7; Nagel/Gottwald, § 18 para 239.

stipulates that the arbitrators shall apply the proper law under the conflict of law rules that the arbitrators deem applicable.[320]

3. *Decision Based on Equity and Fairness* (ex aequo et bono; amiable compositeur)

2.190 German law allows the parties to empower an arbitral tribunal to decide the dispute not on the basis of the applicable law, but pursuant to the principles of equity and fairness (*Billigkeit, ex aequo et bono, amiable compositeur*). Pursuant to s 1051 para 3 cl 1 ZPO, the parties need to make an **express stipulation** to this effect in order to grant such power to the arbitral tribunal.

2.191 In agreements with a purely national nexus, this is very rare; it tends to occur more often in an international context. In any event, the parties should be very cautious before submitting themselves to a decision based on *Billigkeit*. It may be an incentive for the arbitrators to take their task more lightly and to work on a more superficial basis. The result may be much less predictable for the parties. To the extent one party has insurance coverage, it should check carefully with the insurance carrier whether it endorses the concept of an arbitral decision *ex aequo et bono*. Similarly, where a party may want to seek recourse against a third party (eg a supplier), such recourse may be made more difficult.[321]

4. Ordre public *Limitations, Especially Punitive Damages*

2.192 As in state-court litigation (Arts 9, 21 Rome I Regulation), an arbitral tribunal needs to respect mandatory law, especially overriding mandatory rules.[322] Otherwise, a decision by the arbitral tribunal may be set aside and declared unenforceable for *ordre public* reasons pursuant to s 1059 para 2 no 2 and s 1060 para 2 ZPO.[323]

2.193 A prominent example in German practice are **punitive damages**. The BGH has held that an award of punitive damages would violate the German *ordre public*, because in the court's view, this type of damages is at odds with the principle of proportionality and reflects a power that is reserved for the criminal courts. In addition, the BGH is of the view that punitive damages would go beyond the field of national standards and there is no clear reason why parties of foreign nationality should be placed in a better position than parties without the instrument of punitive damages in their national legal system.[324] It is unclear whether the German Federal Constitutional Court (BVerfG) fully shares this restrictive view, and it has

---

[320] There is some criticism regarding Art VII of the Convention, as it arguably enables arbitral tribunals to manipulate the choice of applicable law; Schlosser, in: Stein/Jonas (eds), annex to s 1061 para 434.

[321] Lachmann, para 405; Kreindler/Schäfer/Wolff, paras 684 *et seq.*; Lionnet/Lionnet, pp 372 *et seq.*

[322] Horn, SchiedsVZ 2008, 209, 211, 215.

[323] Schmidt-Ahrendts/Höttler, SchiedsVZ 2011, 267.

[324] BGHZ 118, 312 = NJW 1992, 3096.

yet to fully address the issue. However, it is safe to say that the view of the BGH is still decisive for practical purposes.[325] Thus, for the parties' choice of the substantive law it is vital to consider that certain regulations might be found to be inapplicable by an arbitral tribunal seated in Germany.

IV. Institutional and ad hoc Arbitration

An important choice to make when drafting an arbitration agreement is the choice between ad hoc and institutional arbitration. When seated in Germany, ad hoc arbitration follows the Tenth Book of the ZPO, which in turn largely follows the Model Law, as explained in more detail in para 1.6. In addition, the parties can choose from various available arbitral institutions, such as the DIS, the ICC, and many others. **2.194**

1. General Considerations

Ad hoc arbitration has the advantage that it is "**easiest**" to agree on, in the sense that the parties only need to be in agreement that they want arbitration, without the need to agree on a certain institution and its rules. In addition, the parties can have a flexible agreement for their specific situation and are not tied to a strict set of rules. On the other hand, this individual drafting of a contract requires a certain experience. Where the parties lack this sophistication, they will be well advised to consult experienced counsel. Whilst it is possible to agree on ad hoc arbitration on the basis of the arbitration rules of a certain arbitral institution, we would tend to discourage such a choice. Most of the time, institutional arbitration rules are closely intertwined with the set-up and actions of the institution (eg regarding arbitrator selection, filings, further assistance in the proceedings), and the parties may find that the rules do not really "work" outside the institution.[326] **2.195**

In many instances, **institutional arbitration** may appear preferable over ad hoc arbitration.[327] Institutional arbitration rules generally cover the most relevant procedural issues without need for detailed party agreement. Arbitral institutions provide swift and efficient support in getting the proceedings going, selecting or replacing arbitrators and, in many instances, assuring the quality of the proceedings and sometimes even of an award (see ICC scrutiny of awards pursuant to art 33 ICC Rules, paras 6.104 *et seq.*). **2.196**

Where the parties choose institutional arbitration, generally the rules **in force at the time of the commencement of the proceedings** will govern, unless the parties **2.197**

---

[325] BVerfG NJW 1995, 649.

[326] Similar Lachmann, para 416; Lionnet/Lionnet, pp 200 *et seq.*; Kreindler/Schäfer/Wolff, paras 391 *et seq.*

[327] Similar probably Lachmann, paras 3042 *et seq.*; Lionnet/Lionnet, pp 200 *et seq.*; Roquette, in: Roquette/Otto (eds), para 9.

agree otherwise.[328] In most cases, it is probably not advisable to deviate from this principle, because the parties may find that the arbitral institution and the arbitrators they choose are no longer familiar with prior versions of the rules.

2.198 When selecting an arbitral institution, parties may want to consider whether it is more advisable to choose an **established institution** rather than experimenting with a **newly created institution.** At the same time, there may be situations where such new institution provides genuine benefits for the dispute at hand that outweigh the uncertainties naturally connected with a new, perhaps inexperienced arbitral institution. Notably, there is a continuing trend towards the creation of new institutions.[329] Where the parties designate an arbitral institution, they should **make sure that the designation is correct** (despite the fact that German courts have been fairly generous in helping parties who have made imprecise or unclear designations; see para 2.119). In the following, we give a brief overview of the most established institutions with a notable significance for arbitration seated in Germany.[330]

2. DIS

2.199 The German Institution of Arbitration (*Deutsche Institution für Schiedsgerichtsbarkeit*—DIS) is the most well-established arbitral institution in Germany. Founded in its present form in 1992, it currently receives well in excess of 150 new cases per year,[331] primarily in a national, but also increasingly in an international context. The service offering of the DIS includes a database of decisions on arbitration law.

2.200 Noteworthy features of the DIS Rules in the **initiation phase** of an arbitration include the following:

- Under s 3 DIS Rules, a **three-arbitrator panel is the default rule.** The chairman of the tribunal and the sole arbitrator need to be lawyers (s 2.2 DIS Rules), but not necessarily with a German law degree or bar admission.
- Only after the tribunal is constituted will it set a deadline for respondent to file its statement of defense. This **sequence differs** from many other arbitral institutions (request for arbitration, response, constitution of the tribunal, statement of claim, statement of defense).

---

[328] See, eg, s 1.2 DIS Rules; art 6. 1 ICC Rules; generally BGH WM 1986, 688, 689; Lachmann, paras 417, 3064.

[329] Lachmann, para 3068; skeptical regarding the stream of new institutions also Wilske/Markert, SchiedsVZ 2011, 57, 64.

[330] In addition, specialized arbitration in the area of international maritime law is provided by the German Maritime Arbitration Association (GMAA). For China related arbitration see the CIETAC and the CEAC. In addition, there are of course numerous very reputable arbitral institutions outside Germany, including in Austria (Vienna), Switzerland, UK (London), Sweden (Stockholm), the US, and elsewhere.

[331] See statistics available at www.disarb.org (last visited December 1, 2015).

- Under s 18.2 DIS Rules, the arbitral tribunal—and not the DIS—decides on **arbitrator challenges**. Against the decision of the arbitral tribunal, for arbitrations seated in Germany, recourse to the German state courts is available under s 1037 paras 2, 3 ZPO.
- Under s 6 DIS Rules, arbitral proceedings are commenced by filing a **statement of claim** with the DIS. Notice pleading is acceptable, but more detailed fact pleading is encouraged.[332] A separate request for arbitration is not provided for in the DIS Rules.
- Regarding fees, the DIS has a clear **fee scale driven by the amount in dispute** under which an exact amount (rather than a range) is determined both of the DIS fees and the arbitrator fees.[333] Upon filing of the complaint, the claimant has to pay the DIS fee and a provisional advance on the arbitrator fees (s 7.1 DIS Rules).

As far as the **conduct** of arbitral proceedings under the DIS Rules is concerned, noteworthy features include the following: **2.201**

- Depending on the arbitrators and counsel, the arbitral proceedings can to some extent be similar to what German practitioners are used to in German state courts (see paras 1.27 *et seq.*). For instance, the arbitral tribunal is supposed to assist the parties in formulating appropriate requests for relief and to attend to a comprehensive declaration on the facts by the parties (s 24.2 DIS Rules). The arbitral tribunal shall **investigate the facts** on its own motion (s 27.1 DIS Rule). Also, somewhat unusual for arbitration rules, the DIS Rules provide that the arbitral tribunal ought to consider **options for settlement** at all stages of the proceedings (s 32.1 DIS Rules, similar to s 278 para 1 ZPO, see para 1.28).
- Pursuant to s 43.1 DIS Rules, the parties, the arbitrators, and the persons at the DIS Secretariat involved in the administration of the arbitral proceedings shall maintain **confidentiality** towards all persons regarding the conduct of arbitral proceedings, and in particular regarding the parties involved, the witnesses, the experts, and other evidentiary materials.

3. ICC

The International Court of Arbitration of the ICC (the ICC Court) was established in 1923 and is one of the—if not the—most well-established arbitral institutions worldwide. As the ICC proudly states on its homepage, since its inception, the ICC Court has administered more than 20,000 cases involving parties and arbitrators **2.202**

---

[332] See Schilling, in: Nedden/Herzberg (eds), s 6 paras 18 *et seq.* (suggesting that the claimant should make detailed factual allegations, similar to state court proceedings).

[333] On its webpage http://www.disarb.org, the DIS provides an online calculator for determining fees (last visited December 1, 2015).

from some 180 countries. On average, it currently receives approximately 800 new cases per year.[334] Proceedings are governed by the ICC Rules of Arbitration, in its current version in force as of January 1, 2012.[335] The ICC administers a significant number of arbitrations involving German parties, 103 in 2014.[336] Thus, for arbitration practitioners in Germany, it is indispensable to be familiar with ICC proceedings.

2.203 The **ICC Court** is supported by a secretariat (the **ICC Secretariat**) that assists the parties in administering the case, especially in the initiation phase until the arbitral tribunal is constituted. It should be noted that copies of all correspondence and submissions need to be provided to the ICC Secretariat; in other words the ICC Secretariat maintains a complete file of the case throughout the conduct of the proceedings, which is different from other arbitral institutions (eg the DIS).[337]

2.204 Set forth below are noteworthy features of ICC arbitration, in particular to the extent they may be different from what German disputes practitioners may be used to. Regarding **initiation of the proceedings** the following applies:

- A claimant may start arbitral proceedings by filing a **request for arbitration** with the ICC Secretariat (art 4.1 ICC Rules). A bare bones, notice-pleading type of submission is sufficient, as long as it contains "a description of the nature and circumstances of the dispute giving rise to the claims and of the basis upon which the claims are made" (art 4.3 lit c ICC Rules). Thus, detailed, German-style fact pleading following the substantiation requirements for German state court proceedings (s 253 ZPO) is not required.
- Similarly, the **respondent's answer** may be short, as long as it fulfils the requirements of art 5.2 ICC Rules, and in particular contains respondent's "comments as to the nature and circumstances of the dispute giving rise to the claims and the basis upon which the claims are made" (art 5.1 lit c ICC Rules). It is primarily a tactical question as to how much of its case a respondent wants to disclose at this stage.
- Generally, disputes regarding the **existence, validity, or scope of the arbitration agreement** or concerning whether all of the claims made in the arbitration may be determined together in a single arbitration, are to be decided directly by the arbitral tribunal, unless the ICC Secretariat refers such issue to the ICC Court for its decision pursuant to art 6.4 ICC Rules. In such cases, the ICC Court makes a "*prima facie*" determination whether an arbitration agreement under the ICC Rules may exist with a tendency to permit arbitration.

334 http://www.iccwbo.org (last visited December 1, 2015).
335 Available at http://www.iccwbo.org (last visited December 1, 2015).
336 2014 Statistical Report, ICC Dispute Resolution Bulletin, Issue 1 2015.
337 Lachmann, para 3135; Pörnbacher/Baur, BB 2011, 2627, 2629; Reiner/Jahnel, in: Schütze (ed), II. ch 2: ICC, Art 1 para 14; ICC Art 3 paras 1 *et seq.*

Regarding the **constitution of the arbitral tribunal**, important features of the ICC Rules include the following: **2.205**

- Arbitrators nominated by a party need to be **confirmed by the ICC Court** (art 13.2 ICC Rules). The **sole arbitrator is the default** unless the parties agree otherwise or the ICC Court determines "that the dispute is such as to warrant the appointment of three arbitrators" (art 12.2 ICC Rules). Where the parties agree or the ICC Court determines a three-person arbitral panel, the default rule is that the **ICC Court appoints the chairman** of the tribunal; however, the parties can deviate from this rule (art 12.5 ICC Rules).
- The sole arbitrator or the chairman of the tribunal shall be of a **nationality** other than those of the parties; however, in suitable circumstances and provided that none of the parties objects, the sole arbitrator or the chairman of the tribunal may be chosen from a country of which any of the parties is a national (art 13.5 ICC Rules).
- The ICC Court scrutinizes the **availability of arbitrators**, who need to indicate the number of pending cases they handle and to affirm that they have sufficient time to commit to a new case (art 11.2 ICC Rules). Arbitrators thus need to provide a statement of availability, impartiality, and independence (art 11.2 ICC Rules). Qualified statements often lead the ICC Court not to confirm an arbitrator. The ICC Court does not provide reasoning where it refuses to confirm an arbitrator (art 11.4 ICC Rules).
- The **ICC Court decides on arbitrator challenges** during the proceedings. Challenges must be made by written and substantiated submission to the ICC Secretariat within 30 days from the date when the party making the challenge was informed of the facts and circumstances on which the challenge is based (art 14.2 ICC Rules). To the extent the ICC Court rejects a challenge, the defeated party may bring the challenge before the German state courts (s 1037 para 3 ZPO) if the seat of arbitration is in Germany.[338]

The ICC Rules regulate the **conduct of the proceedings** as follows: **2.206**

- One of the most noteworthy features of ICC proceedings are the so-called "**Terms of Reference.**" Article 23.1 ICC Rules provides that the arbitral tribunal shall draw up those terms immediately after receiving the file, including contact details, a summary of the parties' claims, the place of arbitration, and the applicable procedural rules. Arbitration practitioners in Germany, in particular those with a strong state-court litigation background, are often skeptical about the usefulness of the Terms of Reference process. However, the Terms of Reference can serve an important function by focusing on both the arbitral tribunal and the parties at an early stage on the core issues of the case.[339] In

[338] Lachmann, para 3118.
[339] Similarly Gaillard/Savage, paras 1229 *et seq.*

addition, the arbitral tribunal has to produce a **provisional timetable** at the outset of the proceedings (art 24.2 ICC Rules).

- Article 24.1 ICC Rules in combination with **Appendix IV** thereof provides that the arbitral tribunal shall convene a **case management conference** in connection with the Terms of Reference and the proposed provisional timetable. **Case management techniques** specifically suggested by Appendix IV include bifurcation of the proceedings or rendering partial awards on key issues, production of documentary evidence, limiting the length and scope of submissions, telephone or video conferences for procedural hearings, pre-hearing conferences, and settlement.

2.207 Importantly, the **ICC Court scrutinizes arbitral awards** before they are issued:

> Before signing any award, the arbitral tribunal shall submit it in draft form to the Court. The Court may lay down modifications as to the form of the award and, without affecting the arbitral tribunal's liberty of decision, may also draw its attention to points of substance. No award shall be rendered by the arbitral tribunal until it has been approved by the Court as to its form (art 33 ICC Rules).

This type of quality control is unique to the ICC. The scrutiny is focused on the formal aspects of the award; regarding issues on the merits, the ICC Court may only point out issues for the consideration of the arbitral tribunal.

2.208 On **costs,** the ICC Rules provide for a **framework** for arbitrator fees with minimum and maximum amounts; the ICC Court fixes the arbitrator fees based on this framework. Thus, the costs of an ICC proceeding cannot be predicted with certainty. Often, it is realistic to assume the medium amount of a given range.[340]

4. Construction Disputes

2.209 In Germany, there are three principal ways to conduct construction arbitration: (i) ad hoc arbitration; (ii) arbitration rules of an institution for general commercial arbitration (such as DIS and ICC); and (iii) construction-specific arbitration rules. The two most important construction-specific arbitration rules in Germany are the Conciliation and Arbitration Rules for Construction Disputes (SOBau) and the Regulation of Dispute Resolution for Construction (SL Bau).

2.210 Both the **SOBau and the SL Bau lean heavily on principles of German state-court litigation** and ascribe an active role to the arbitrator(s), including with respect to settlement. Further, both regulations require that the sole arbitrator and the chairman of a multi-person tribunal must be German-qualified lawyers (*Befähigung zum Richteramt*). Overall, the SOBau and the SL Bau are probably used less than originally expected. Many construction disputes are still administered either in ad hoc proceedings or through an institution such as the ICC.[341]

---

[340] Lachmann, para 3221; Derains/Schwartz, ch 7 p 304.
[341] Lachmann, paras 3517 *et seq.*

The **SOBau** provides for three types of proceedings: (i) conciliation; (ii) stand-alone evidence proceedings; and (iii) arbitration. Conciliation proceedings can be initiated during the construction phase already. Stand-alone evidence proceedings are meant to determine, by way of an expert opinion, the status of the construction, construction defects or damages, and amounts necessary to remedy a defect or damage. The institution's only task is to select an arbitrator where the parties cannot agree. The arbitrator fees are determined on the basis of the statutory fee scales for German attorneys-at-law (RVG). **2.211**

The **SL Bau** provides for a very detailed set of rules. Nevertheless, the proceedings largely follow the provisions of the Tenth Book of the ZPO, with the exception that the institution, and not the state court, appoints arbitrators where the parties cannot agree.[342] Contrary to the SOBau, the arbitrator fees shall be agreed on an hourly or daily basis. Section 2 para 3 SL Bau contains an express confidentiality provision for arbitrators and experts, but not witnesses, the parties, and their representatives. **2.212**

342 For a commentary on the SL Bau see Franke/Englert/Kuffer/Meyer-Postelt/Miernik/Halstenberg, *Kommentar zur Streitlösungsordnung für das Bauwesen, SL-Bau.*

3

THE ARBITRAL TRIBUNAL

Markus S. Rieder/Richard Kreindler

A. Overview

3.1 The constitution of the arbitral tribunal is arguably one of the most important strategic steps in any arbitration. In most cases, the parties and their counsel will tend to believe that picking the right panel is a pre-eminent precondition for achieving the desired outcome of the case. Whether there is an empirical basis for this commonly held belief is open to debate. Arbitrators often act in a way that can be vastly different from what a party may have expected when choosing the person to serve as arbitrator. Notwithstanding these limitations, energy and care should be put into the composition of the tribunal. In the present chapter, we discuss the number of arbitrators (below paras 3.2 *et seq.*), the procedure for appointing arbitrators (below 3.12 *et seq.*), the selection of arbitrators (below 3.56 *et seq.*), the challenge, termination of the office, and replacement of arbitrators (below 3.98 *et seq.*), as well as the arbitrator agreement, a topic that has more prominence in Germany than in many other jurisdictions (below 3.159 *et seq.*).

B. Number of Arbitrators

I. Legal Framework

3.2 We first address the legal framework for determining the number of arbitrators before we set forth what we think are the most relevant practical considerations in this context. In ad hoc arbitration pursuant to the Tenth Book of the ZPO, a **three-arbitrator panel** is the **statutory default** (s 1034 para 1 ZPO). The German arbitration law thereby follows art 10 Model Law. The ZPO also allows for any other number of arbitrators to be agreed on by the parties, including, of course, a sole arbitrator. The same applies for arbitral proceedings under the DIS Rules (s 3 DIS Rules). By contrast, art 12.2 ICC Rules provides for the sole arbitrator as the default in the absence of a party agreement stipulating another number of arbitrators or a finding by the ICC Court "that the dispute is such as to warrant the appointment of three arbitrators."[1] Thus, for practical purposes, most often the parties will face the choice between a panel of three arbitrators (below paras 3.3 *et seq.*) and a sole arbitrator (below paras 3.9 *et seq.*). While other options exist, they are rare in practice (below para 3.11).

II. Panel of Three Arbitrators

1. General Considerations

3.3 In practice, in arbitral proceedings seated in Germany or having otherwise a significant German nexus, the parties frequently choose a panel of three arbitrators, except for situations that, from an *ex ante* perspective, do not appear to justify the expense associated with the remuneration of three arbitrators.[2] In the view of many parties, this has a number of advantages.

3.4 First, it allows for a **balanced panel**. Each side usually gets to appoint an arbitrator, and the two party-appointed arbitrators, in coordination with the parties, usually determine the chairman of the tribunal. Even though party-appointed arbitrators must be just as neutral as the chairman, from a psychological point of view, many parties still tend to gain comfort from the fact that a person that they have chosen sits on the tribunal and has an opportunity to make heard the arguments and positions put forward by the appointing party.

3.5 Second, the **quality** of the tribunal's decisions tends to be increased by a three-person panel, as opposed to a situation with a sole arbitrator. This is particularly true where a dispute raises issues touching upon diverse factual and legal areas. For instance, a post-M&A dispute may require knowledge of M&A processes and market standards regarding specific types of contractual provisions on purchase price, closing mechanisms, representations and warranties, covenants etc. At the same time, it may raise complex issues of statutory remedies, fraud, and computation of damages. A construction case may require a specific understanding of certain types of construction defects. In such scenarios, the parties may find that a

[1] We discuss this issue in more detail below in paras 3.48 *et seq.*

[2] Lachmann, para 778; Münch, in: MünchKommZPO, s 1034 para 3 with further references; similarly in international cases, see Born, pp 1675 *et seq.*

tribunal composed of arbitrators with a combination of skills is best positioned to solve their dispute.

Third, a three-person panel obviously **avoids tied votes**, as opposed to the (rare) instances where there are panels with an even number of arbitrators. **3.6**

2. *The Role of the Chairman*

It goes without saying that the chairman of a three-person tribunal has to be **impartial and independent**. Under the German arbitration law, when it comes to decisions of the tribunal, his vote carries the **same weight** as the vote of the party-appointed arbitrators (s 1052 para 1 ZPO); unlike under some institutional rules, the Tenth Book of the ZPO does not give the chairman a casting vote, unless the parties agree otherwise. In terms of substance, the chairman can thus be described as *primus inter pares*.[3] **3.7**

From a **procedural** point of view, however, his role has more weight than that of the party-appointed arbitrators. In practice, the chairman usually conducts the correspondence with the parties, administers advances, organizes meetings, leads hearings, and drafts the award.[4] This also means that he or she usually has more **administrative tasks** than the party-appointed arbitrators and consequently a higher need for administrative support, eg from a secretary or an assistant. For the foregoing reasons, the chairman usually receives a **higher remuneration** than the party-appointed arbitrators. The fee scales of arbitral institutions take account of that.[5] The parties or the other members of the tribunal can authorize the chairman to **decide individual procedural issues alone** (s 1052 para 3 ZPO), which is generally a good idea in practice in order to accelerate the proceedings. **3.8**

III. Sole Arbitrator

A sole arbitrator may be the more appropriate option where the **amount in dispute** is limited and/or the issues to be addressed are **less complex and diverse.** In such situations, it may even be a close call whether to opt for arbitration at all or to go for state court proceedings where the other advantages of arbitration—such as enforcement abroad and confidentiality—are less important to the parties. A reported downside of sole arbitrator awards is the fact that some insurance companies do not always seem to accept them.[6] **3.9**

---

3 Lörcher/Lörcher, SchiedsVZ 2005, 179, 189; Münch, in: MünchKommZPO, Vorbem s 1034 para 61.

4 Schlosser, SchiedsVZ 2003, 1, 6 *et seq.*; Münch, in: MünchKommZPO, Vorbem s 1034 paras 63 *et seq.*; Schwab/Walter, ch 15 para 6.

5 For instance, under the DIS Rules, the chairman's remuneration is 30 percent higher than the remuneration of a party-appointed arbitrator (no 15 of Annex to s 40.5 DIS Rules). In ad hoc arbitration, the parties need to find an agreement on arbitrator compensation, or else the arbitral tribunal may fix the remuneration (ss 315, 316 BGB, see para 3.177).

6 Lionnet/Lionnet, p 237; Lachmann, para 783.

3.10 Some institutions and commentators have sought to provide **rules of thumb** as to when arbitration with a three-person panel (as opposed to a sole arbitrator) may be the preferred option, in particular with a view to amounts in dispute. For instance, the ICC tends to appoint a sole arbitrator in cases where the amount in dispute is lower than US$5 million.[7] The Swiss Rules apply a roughly comparable threshold.[8] While these may be useful rules of thumb for arbitral institutions who decide on the number of arbitrators after a specific dispute has arisen, **caution** should be applied with regard to such **numeric thresholds** where parties seek to agree on an arbitration agreement. Again, where a specific dispute has already arisen, this may be a useful approach. In situations, however, where parties negotiate a main agreement and seek to agree on an arbitration clause, these types of numbers may not be helpful guidance due to the simple fact that the parties at that point will most likely not know what will be the amount in dispute once a controversy arises. There may certainly be cases where it is highly unlikely that there will ever be a dispute under a given arbitration clause that exceeds the thresholds mentioned above. In such a case, a sole arbitrator may well be considered. Where the future amount in dispute is less clear, or there is a clear potential for counterclaims or set-off, more weight should be given to the **complexity of the issues** that are likely to arise. If in doubt, we would tend to favor a three-person panel, which seems to be in line with the thinking of the German legislator and the DIS, as both provide for the three-person panel as the default rule. Alternatively, it has been suggested that the parties can defer the decision by using a clause similar to the one recommended by the ICC which provides that all disputes should be decided "by one or more arbitrators."[9] In an ad hoc scenario, there needs to be a default rule in case the parties cannot agree once the arbitral tribunal needs to be constituted (such as the three-person panel default rule under s 1034 para 1 cl 2 ZPO).

IV. Other Options

3.11 Other options include any other conceivable number of arbitrators, eg two, four, five, and so on. Absent specific circumstances, we would recommend to be reluctant with these types of options.[10] Any even number of arbitrators has the inherent risk of a tied vote. In order to come to a decision at all, there would need to be a chairman who has a casting vote. Panels of five arbitrators (or even more) seem quite unwieldy and expensive, and there should rarely be a compelling need for them.

[7] Fry/Greenberg/Mazza, para 3-440.
[8] Bühler, in: Zuberbühler/Müller/Habegger (eds), art 6 para 10.
[9] Hantke, SchiedsVZ 2003, 269.
[10] Same view Born, pp 1674 *et seq.*

C. Procedure for the Constitution of the Arbitral Tribunal

We first address the legal framework for the appointment of arbitrators and the constitution of the arbitral tribunal under the Tenth Book of the ZPO (below paras 3.13 *et seq.*). Thereafter, we discuss the constitution process under both the DIS and the ICC Rules (below paras 3.37 *et seq.* and 3.48 *et seq.*). **3.12**

I. Legal Framework under the German Arbitration Law

1. *Introduction and Overview of the Legal Framework*

In most cases, the arbitration agreement does not yet specify who the arbitrators should be. The law would allow naming the arbitrators already in the arbitration agreement.[11] Nevertheless, it is often not recommendable to do so.[12] This is particularly true with respect to arbitration clauses which are contained in a main contract and which are usually concluded a long time before a dispute arises. Thus, it is generally hard to anticipate what the precise characteristics of a dispute will be and consequently what the qualifications of an arbitrator should be. In addition, a person chosen in an arbitration clause may no longer be available once a dispute arises or may be barred from acting due to an intervening lack of neutrality. In such situations, difficult questions may arise as to how such a gap on the tribunal should be dealt with. Does it mean that the arbitration agreement is incapable of being performed and thus state court litigation is proper?[13] Or can the arbitrator in question be replaced pursuant to the rules governing replacement in general (s 1039 ZPO; see below paras 3.155 *et seq.*)?[14] The answer may turn on issues of interpretation and the specifics of the case, and the parties may have different views thereon. Thus, they may find themselves in costly and time-consuming litigation before the arbitral proceedings can even start. At a minimum, where the parties name arbitrators in an arbitration agreement, they should also agree on clear rules as to what happens if one of these persons is not available to serve as arbitrator when the dispute arises. **3.13**

In the absence of a predetermined arbitral tribunal, the arbitrators need to be appointed in connection with the commencement of arbitral proceedings. Below, we describe the statutory mechanism of the Tenth Book of the ZPO and later compare it to the mechanisms provided for by the DIS and the ICC. **3.14**

---

11 Except unilateral nominations in general terms and conditions (AGB, see para 2.103).

12 An exception may be fast-track proceedings, eg in a post M&A context (MAC disputes), see, eg, Borris, BB 2008, 294, 296.

13 KG SchiedsVZ 2003, 185, 186.

14 Nacimiento/Abt/Stein, in: *Arbitration in Germany*, s 1035 para 6, s 1039 para 17; Schwab/Walter, ch 8 para 12; Münch, in: MünchKommZPO, s 1039 para 14.

3.15 For German ad hoc proceedings, s 1035 ZPO provides the statutory framework governing the appointment of arbitrators, which largely corresponds to art 11 Model Law. The starting point is **party autonomy**: the parties are free to agree on a procedure for the appointment of arbitrators (s 1035 para 1 ZPO). In the absence of an agreement of the parties, the provisions contained in s 1035 paras 2–5 ZPO apply. These provisions distinguish between a sole arbitrator scenario on the one hand and a panel of three arbitrators on the other.[15] Regarding a sole arbitrator situation, it is first upon the parties to agree on the person of the sole arbitrator. If they fail to reach an agreement, each party can ask the competent higher regional court (s 1062 ZPO) to make the appointment (s 1035 para 3 cl 1 ZPO).

3.16 Where a three-person panel needs to be appointed, each party has the **right to appoint one arbitrator** (s 1035 para 3 cl 2 ZPO). A party is bound by its appointment as soon as the other party has received notice thereon (s 1035 para 2 ZPO). An appointee, and in fact a person that is approached in connection with his or her possible appointment, shall **disclose** any circumstances likely to give rise to justifiable doubts as to his or her impartiality or independence (s 1036 para 1 cl 1 ZPO; for details see below paras 3.128 *et seq.*). Where a party fails to appoint an arbitrator within one month after being requested to do so, the other party can ask the competent higher regional court to make the appointment (s 1035 para 3 cl 3, s 1062 ZPO). The two party-appointed arbitrators have to **appoint the chairman** of the tribunal (s 1035 para 3 cl 2 ZPO). In case they cannot agree on a chairman within one month after their appointment, each party may again ask the competent higher regional court to make the appointment (s 1035 para 3 cl 3 ZPO).

3.17 Where the parties have agreed on certain procedures regarding the appointment of arbitrators and one party does not comply therewith, or the parties cannot find an agreement on the basis of the agreed procedure, each party may ask the competent **higher regional court to order the necessary measures** in order to achieve a constitution of the arbitral tribunal (s 1035 para 4 ZPO). The same applies where the parties have agreed that a third person shall have a role in the appointment of arbitrators, and such third person does not properly perform his or her task.

3.18 Finally, s 1035 para 5 ZPO contains **guidelines** for all of the above scenarios in which the competent higher regional court is called to make an arbitrator appointment. First, the court needs to take into account all **prerequisites** for the person of an arbitrator agreed by the parties (s 1035 para 5 cl 1 ZPO). Second, the court needs to make sure it appoints a person that is **independent and impartial** (s 1035

[15] German law does not contain any express provisions on a two-person panel. In such a case, the provisions contained in s 1035 para 3 ZPO are considered to apply by analogy, ie the competent higher regional court is to make both appointments if the parties cannot agree and one party seeks the assistance of the court. See Münch, in: MünchKommZPO, s 1035 para 41; Voit, in: Musielak/Voit (eds), s 1035 para 8. Opposing view—each party appoints one arbitrator—Saenger, in: Saenger (ed), s 1035 para 13.

para 5 cl 1 ZPO). Third, as far as the appointment of a sole arbitrator or the chairman of a three-person tribunal is concerned, the court needs to consider whether it is appropriate to appoint a person that has a **nationality** different from the parties (s 1035 para 5 cl 2 ZPO). Where the court disregards agreed prerequisites or the need for independence and impartiality, a court-appointed arbitrator is subject to challenge and replacement; by contrast, considerations of nationality are within the discretion of the court and cannot be the basis for challenging a court-appointed arbitrator.[16]

2. *Party Autonomy and Statutory Default*

Pursuant to s 1035 para 1 ZPO, the parties are free to regulate the appointment process via party agreement. Appointment generally means the determination of the person of the arbitrator and the notification of either the appointee or the other party thereof (s 1035 para 2 ZPO).[17] As long as the other party has not been notified, and in the absence of a party agreement to the contrary, the appointing party is not yet bound to its appointment (s 1035 para 2 ZPO). Pursuant to a view expressed in German legal literature, technically the consent of the appointee would not be necessary to effect the appointment as such.[18] This may sound surprising as a legal theory; anyway, in practice, it is of course highly advisable to ask a potential appointee in advance.[19] If he or she declines to accept the appointment, there will be no arbitrator agreement and another person needs to be appointed. Caution is necessary where the candidate accepts under certain conditions like government approval pursuant to s 40 para 1 German Judiciary Act (DRiG, see paras 3.83 *et seq.*). Given that the appointment is a procedural act, only legal conditions are permitted.[20] **3.19**

An agreement of the parties on the process for appointing arbitrators does not need to follow the **form requirements** of s 1031 ZPO, unless the agreed appointment process is part and parcel of the arbitration agreement (see paras 2.70 *et seq.*).[21] There are some limits as to what the parties can agree on, and such limits follow from concepts inherent to arbitration. For instance, the parties cannot waive the requirement that an arbitrator needs to be a **natural person with full legal capacity** (*volle Geschäftsfähigkeit*).[22] In addition, under German law, and in fact as a matter **3.20**

[16] Voit, in: Musielak/Voit (eds), s 1035 para 19; Münch, in: MünchKommZPO, s 1035 paras 53 *et seq.*

[17] Münch, in: MünchKommZPO, s 1035 para 11.

[18] Münch, in: MünchKommZPO, s 1035 para 13; Saenger, in: Saenger (ed), s 1035 para 8; cf Hartmann, in: Baumbach/Lauterbach/Albers/Hartmann (eds), s 1035 para 5: the appointment can be cancelled before notification to the other party, even if the appointee has already accepted.

[19] Münch, in: MünchKommZPO, s 1035 paras 16, 20.

[20] Lachmann, para 794; Nacimiento/Abt/Stein, in: *Arbitration in Germany*, s 1035 para 17.

[21] Münch, in: MünchKommZPO, s 1035 para 7; Geimer, in: Zöller (ed), s 1035 para 1; Voit, in: Musielak/Voit (eds), s 1035 para 2. Opposing view: Hartmann, in: Baumbach/Lauterbach/Albers/Hartmann (eds), s 1035 para 4.

[22] Henn, BB 1993, Beil. 27, pp 13, 14; Münch, in: MünchKommZPO, s 1035 para 8; Geimer, in: Zöller (ed), s 1035 para 6; Prütting, in: Prütting/Gehrlein (eds), s 1035 para 2; Voit, in: Musielak/Voit (eds), s 1035 para 17.

of German constitutional law and the German *ordre public*, an arbitrator must be **impartial and independent.**[23] The concept of a partial arbitrator is thus not capable of being agreed by the parties *in advance* for arbitrations seated in Germany.[24] Likewise, the parties cannot agree that a party may appoint him- or herself as an arbitrator.[25]

3.21 Examples of possible party-agreed procedures include **lists of candidates** where each party has a number of strikes or where a decision is taken by lot, or a combination thereof.[26] For instance, the AAA usually uses a list procedure that the parties can adopt or modify. Also, the parties can agree that a **third person or institution** shall make the appointment. If they do so, they need to make sure that they unequivocally designate the "appointing authority," such as the president of a certain court, the president of a certain chamber of commerce or an arbitral institution (without choosing institutional arbitration).[27] Absent a specific agreement with the parties, such institution is of course not legally bound to effect appointments (*kein Vertrag zulasten Dritter*). Thus, the parties are well advised to **check in advance** whether the institution they wish to designate, eg in the arbitration agreement, is actually prepared to make appointments.

3.22 As mentioned above, where a party-agreed mechanism for some reason does not work, s 1035 para 4 ZPO allows each party to ask the competent higher regional court to "order the necessary measures," in particular to make the appointment.[28] This may happen, for instance, where a third party tasked with making an arbitrator appointment for some reason **fails to act** (as opposed to instances of improper performance).[29] The same applies where a party fails to act or otherwise violates an agreed procedure.[30] Thus, the other party need not—and in fact cannot—sue the non-complying party (or third person) for performance of the party agreement. Instead, s 1035 para 4 ZPO provides for an easier solution, such that a court action asking for performance of the party agreement would be impermissible (*unzulässig*) for lack of a genuine need to involve the court (*fehlendes Rechtsschutzbedürfnis*).[31]

---

[23] S 1036 ZPO; Münch, in: MünchKommZPO, s 1035 para 8; Prütting, in: Prütting/Gehrlein (eds), s 1035 para 2; Blackaby/Partasides/Redfern/Hunter, para 4.39.

[24] Of course, once an arbitrator has been appointed who lacks impartiality or independence, the parties may refrain from bringing a challenge within the statutory two-week period.

[25] BGH NJW 1985, 1903, 1904; Münch, in: MünchKommZPO, s 1035 para 8; Geimer, in: Zöller (ed), s 1035 para 3.

[26] Eg BGH NJW 1992, 575, 576 = XIX Y.B. Com. Arb. 201 (1994); OLG Frankfurt, IPRspr. 2009, no 276, 709, 712; Münch, in: MünchKommZPO, s 1035 para 25.

[27] Münch, in: MünchKommZPO, s 1035 para 26; Geimer, in: Zöller (ed), s 1035 para 8; Hartmann, in: Baumbach/Lauterbach/Albers/Hartmann (eds), s 1035 para 6; Schwab/Walter, ch 10 para 3.

[28] Münch, in: MünchKommZPO, s 1035 para 29; Schwab/Walter, ch 10 para 7.

[29] OLG München, SchiedsVZ 2010, 168, 169; Münch, in: MünchKommZPO, s 1035 para 32; Geimer, in: Zöller (ed), s 1035 para 19; Voit, in: Musielak/Voit (eds), s 1035 paras 6, 14.

[30] Geimer, in: Zöller (ed), s 1035 para 19; Voit, in: Musielak/Voit (eds), s 1035 para 14.

[31] Münch, in: MünchKommZPO, s 1035 paras 27, 30; cf Geimer, in: Zöller (ed), s 1035 para 19; BayObLGZ 2000, 187, 189 ("*Reservefunktion*").

3. Panel of Three Arbitrators

Under German law, the three-person panel is the **statutory default** (s 1034 para 1 cl 2 ZPO). Thus, the appointment process for a three-person panel contained in s 1035 para 3 cl 2-3 ZPO is of particular practical importance.[32] As mentioned above, German law provides for a **two-step approach**. In the first step, each party needs to appoint one arbitrator within one month after being requested to do so by the other party.[33] German law contains no further details on such request. It may be made in any way, shape, or form. For **evidence purposes**, it is of course prudent to make the request **in writing** and to generate proof that the other side has received the request (eg by way of a letter with return receipt requested).[34] The period cannot be extended except by party agreement. In the **second step**, the two party-appointed arbitrators need to agree on the chairman. Again, a one-month period applies, and it is to be calculated in the same way as in step one. **3.23**

In order for the court to be able to appoint an arbitrator, a **party request to the court** is necessary. Pursuant to the clear wording of s 1035 para 3 cl 3 ZPO, only a party has the right to make such request. The party-appointed arbitrators may not do so, nor are they allowed to transfer the appointing authority to a third party.[35] **3.24**

The court is entitled to do a **prima facie** analysis on the **validity of the arbitration agreement**. It may reject the appointment of an arbitrator where the arbitration agreement is evidently invalid.[36] In such a scenario, when viewed properly, the requesting party already lacks the need to bring court action (*fehlendes Rechtsschutzbedürfnis*).[37] By contrast, the court is obviously not entitled to reject an application for the appointment of an arbitrator because it considers the claim to be without merits.[38] **3.25**

Under German law, it is unclear what happens if a party misses the one-month deadline, the other party files an application with the competent higher regional **3.26**

---

32 With respect to the special situation of an arbitration agreement that gives one party an unfair advantage regarding the composition of the arbitral tribunal and the corresponding right of the other party to seek appointment of the arbitrator(s) by the competent higher regional court, see s 1034 para 2 ZPO and the explanations thereon below at paras 3.35 *et seq.*

33 German law contains detailed provisions for the calculation of statutory periods that also apply to the one-month period at issue here; these provisions are to be found in s 222 ZPO, ss 186 *et seq.* BGB. They address the beginning and the end of the calculation period, the relevance of weekend days, public holidays, and the like.

34 Instructive OLG Naumburg, SchiedsVZ 2003, 235, 236 (no proof for receipt of telefax); Geimer, in: Zöller (ed), s 1035 para 14; Hartmann, in: Baumbach/Lauterbach/Albers/Hartmann (eds), s 1035 para 5.

35 OLG München, NJOZ 2009, 4781; Geimer, in: Zöller (ed), s 1035 para 16; Reichold, in: Thomas/Putzo (eds), s 1035 para 8.

36 BGH NJW-RR 2010, 425; OLG Dresden, SchiedsVZ 2009, 69; Lachmann, para 897; Kröll, NJW 2007, 743, 746; Lörcher/Lörcher, SchiedsVZ 2005, 179, 182.

37 Münch, in: MünchKommZPO, s 1035 para 49; Geimer, in: Zöller (ed), s 1035 para 17; Voit, in: Musielak/Voit (eds), s 1035 para 11.

38 Schwab/Walter, ch 10 para 25; Münch, in: MünchKommZPO, s 1035 para 49; Geimer, in: Zöller (ed), s 1035 para 17.

court to make the appointment, and **prior to the decision** of the higher regional court, the defaulting party finally **makes an appointment.** The same question arises where the party-appointed arbitrators fail to reach an agreement within the one-month period, a party files for court appointment and prior to the court's decision, the party-appointed arbitrators reach an agreement on the chairman. There are **three main views** on this topic. The first and strictest view is that the parties and the party-appointed arbitrators **lose the appointment right** once the one-month period has expired. In particular, this view has been expressed by a number of German higher regional courts.[39] A second view is that the appointment right terminates as soon as one party has **filed an application** with the court or such application has been served on the other side. This view is supported by the legislative materials to the Tenth Book, a number of German higher regional courts, and several commentators.[40] Finally, pursuant to the third view, the **appointment right continues to exist.** If an appointment is made while court proceedings are already pending, the court proceedings need to be terminated, and the appointment made by the respective party (or the appointment agreed by the party-appointed arbitrators) prevails. This view, too, is held by several higher regional courts and a number of commentators.[41]

3.27 In our opinion, the **third view is the most persuasive**. Arbitration is a creature of party autonomy. Party choice prevails. Assistance by the courts at the appointment stage should be limited to situations where without such assistance, the arbitral process would be stalled. Where court action ultimately is not necessary, the court should refrain from acting. The party who made a court request that later becomes unnecessary is sufficiently protected by the fact that it should be awarded its costs associated with instituting the court proceedings.[42] In any event, the practical differences between the three opinions outlined above should be limited. Where an appointment occurs while court proceedings are already pending, the higher regional court may simply affirm such appointment (provided it meets the required criteria under s 1035 para 5 ZPO, ie in terms of party-agreed prerequisites, independence, impartiality, and discretionary considerations of nationality).

[39] BayObLGZ 2002, 17; OLG München, MDR 2006, 1308; Münch, in: MünchKommZPO, s 1035 para 46 with further references.

[40] BT-Drucks 13/5274, p 40; RGZ 45, 382; OLG Bremen, NJW 1972, 454; OLG München, NJOZ 2011, 413; BayObLG NJW-RR 2002, 933, 934; Kröll, NJW 2007, 743, 746; Hantke, SchiedsVZ 2003, 269, 271.

[41] OLG Koblenz, BeckRS 2001, 30213028; in this direction OLG Naumburg, SchiedsVZ 2003, 235; Schwab/Walter, ch 10 para 21; Voit, in: Musielak/Voit (eds), s 1035 para 10; Münch, in: MünchKommZPO, s 1035 para 46; Geimer, in: Zöller (ed), s 1035 para 16; Reichold, in: Thomas/Putzo (eds), s 1035 para 8; Hartmann, in: Baumbach/Lauterbach/Albers/Hartmann (eds), s 1035 para 10; Lachmann, para 905; Nacimiento/Abt/Stein, in: *Arbitration in Germany*, s 1035 para 27.

[42] Münch, in: MünchKommZPO, s 1035 para 46; cf OLG Koblenz, BeckRS 2001, 30213028 (*Erledigungserklärung*).

4. Sole Arbitrator

In the absence of a party agreement on appointment procedures, in case of a sole arbitrator, the parties first need to **try and reach an agreement** on the person to be appointed. If they fail to do so, each party can ask the competent higher regional court to make the appointment (s 1035 para 3 cl 1 ZPO). The law does not contain details as to **what efforts** the parties need to make to reach an agreement and **what, if any, deadlines** need to expire before an application to the court can be made. At a minimum, the party making an application to the court needs to be able to demonstrate that there has been some effort to agree on a candidate, and that such effort was without success. For instance, the requesting party can point to the fact that it has proposed a person to the other party, and the other party has either rejected the candidate or failed to react. There are different views as to whether the requesting party has to comply with a certain **waiting period** before it can resort to the state court; some commentators propose a one month-period in analogy to s 1035 para 3 cl 3 ZPO,[43] others are more generous and allow a more or less immediate application to the state court, provided that the applicant in such application proposes a candidate which the other side can still accept.[44] We find the first view more persuasive, as it is more in line with the fundamental statutory concept that **support by state courts is a means of last resort**. Also, for practical purposes, it would seem prudent to first allow some time for finding party consensus. 3.28

Again, the court can reject the application where it finds that the arbitration agreement is evidently invalid, but not for lack of merits of the case (see para 3.25). 3.29

5. Multi-party Arbitration

German law does not expressly address the constitution of the arbitral tribunal in case of multi-party arbitration (for further issues raised by multi-party arbitration cases see paras 4.207 *et seq.*). Obviously, no issues arise in the sole arbitrator scenario, because in this case, all parties need to agree on the sole arbitrator, or, failing that, the sole arbitrator is appointed by the competent higher regional court upon request by a party.[45] By contrast, for the statutory default of a **three-person panel**, German law is silent as to how such a tribunal ought to be constituted where there are more than two parties. Possibly, and depending on the nature of the dispute at hand, the various parties can be and in fact are divided into two "camps." Where each "camp" is able to agree on a party-appointed arbitrator, the further statutory appointment mechanism (appointment of the chairman by the party-appointed arbitrators) works. 3.30

---

43 For instance Voit, in: Musielak/Voit (eds), s 1035 para 9; Kreindler/Schäfer/Wolff, para 430.

44 For instance Münch, in: MünchKommZPO, s 1035 para 38; Schlosser, in: Stein/Jonas (eds), s 1035 para 8.

45 See s 1035 para 3 cl 1 ZPO; Münch, in: MünchKommZPO, s 1035 para 67.

3.31 It is less clear what happens where one "camp" cannot agree on a party-appointed arbitrator. The Tenth Book of the ZPO does not specifically address this issue. Based on the ***Dutco* decision** of the French *Cour de Cassation*,[46] there is a strong view in arbitration practice—both domestically and internationally—that in such a case, the court (or an arbitral institution, where applicable) should appoint both arbitrators originally to be appointed by the parties, in order not to give one side an unfair advantage or disadvantage in the composition of the arbitral tribunal. The two arbitrators appointed by the court would then appoint the chairman. If they fail to do so, again the court can be asked to step in. Institutional rules usually contain specific provisions addressing multi-party situations which often reflect this or a similar approach (s 13.2 DIS Rules, art 12.8 ICC Rules; see below paras 3.45 and 3.53). In our view, for reasons of **fairness and equality** and in analogous application of s 1034 para 2 ZPO, this should also be the approach to be taken by the competent higher regional court in German ad hoc arbitration under the Tenth Book of the ZPO.[47] The alternative would be to declare the arbitration agreement incapable of being performed where the parties in multi-party situations cannot agree on the appointment of the arbitral tribunal,[48] which, however, strikes us to be much less in line with the parties' fundamental will to submit to arbitration than the majority view expressed above that grants the state court the power to make the necessary appointments.

6. *Procedure for Appointment by Court*

3.32 As already indicated above (para 3.22), where the parties or the party-appointed arbitrators cannot agree on an appointment, or where a party-agreed appointment procedure fails, s 1035 ZPO allows for an application to be made to the competent higher regional court to make the appointment or to otherwise take the necessary measures to effect a party-agreed mechanism. The proper **venue** lies with the higher regional court **agreed by the parties**, or, in the absence of party agreement, the higher regional court located in the **district in which the arbitration is seated** (s 1062 para 1 ZPO).

3.33 The higher regional court has **significant discretion** as to the conduct of the proceedings. It is **not required to hold an oral hearing.**[49] Also, it does not need to hear the person it considers to appoint. Sometimes, eg in arbitrations of very significant importance, courts do conduct oral hearings. It is even possible and occasionally happens in practice that the court invites several candidates to the hearing,

[46] Cour de Cassation, Rev arb 1992, 470.

[47] Similarly, Hantke, SchiedsVZ 2003, 269, 272; Münch, in: MünchKommZPO, s 1035 para 70; Hartmann, in: Baumbach/Lauterbach/Albers/Hartmann (eds), s 1035 para 8.

[48] Voit, in: Musielak/Voit (eds), s 1034 para 3.

[49] *Argumentum a* ***contrario*** s 1063 para 2 ZPO; Münch, in: MünchKommZPO, s 1063 paras 3 *et seq.*

questions them—possibly in the presence of the parties—and then makes its appointment decision. In making its decision, the court has wide discretion, too. It is merely bound by the parameters set forth in s 1035 para 5 ZPO, ie compliance with agreed prerequisites and appointment of a neutral person. Other than that, it is up to the court to determine who is a suitable person. German law does not impose strict nationality rules in international cases. Section 1035 para 5 ZPO merely suggests that the court takes nationality into account, without prescribing any particular outcome.

The court's decision is made by way of an **order** (*Beschluss*). Once the competent higher regional court has made an appointment, its decision is **final and binding**, and not subject to any further appeal to the BGH (s 1065 para 1 cl 2, s 1062 para 1 no 1 ZPO).[50] This is in line with art 11 para 5 cl 1 Model Law and helps accelerate the appointment process.[51] 3.34

7. Appointment by Court due to Unfair Prejudice

Where an arbitration agreement gives an unfair advantage to one party in connection with the composition of the arbitral tribunal, s 1034 para 2 cl 1 ZPO allows the prejudiced party to apply to the competent court to make a different and **balanced appointment** of arbitrator(s). This provision is without example in the Model Law and thus a true specialty of the German arbitration law. The **higher regional court** agreed by the parties or, in the absence of party agreement, of the district in which the seat of arbitration is located has jurisdiction (s 1062 para 1 no 1 ZPO). The petition must be made within **two weeks** after the requesting party has learned of the composition of the arbitral tribunal (s 1034 para 2 cl 2 ZPO). The arbitral proceedings may be continued (and concluded) pending the decision by the state court (s 1034 para 2 cl 3 ZPO). 3.35

An unfair advantage within the meaning of s 1034 para 2 ZPO means that one party has **more influence on the constitution of the arbitral tribunal** than the other. This is the case, for instance, where one party gets to appoint the entire tribunal or two out of three arbitrators, or where only one party is a member of a trade association which appoints the tribunal.[52] German courts have held that s 1034 para 2 ZPO also applies where the parties have agreed that the **right to appoint an arbitrator switches** to the other party where one party fails to appoint an arbitrator on time.[53] Section 1034 para 2 ZPO does not require proof that the party to whose 3.36

[50] BGH SchiedsVZ 2012, 281; Geimer, in: Zöller (ed), s 1065 para 1; Voit, in: Musielak/Voit (eds), s 1035 para 11.

[51] Münch, in: MünchKommZPO, s 1035 para 63; Hartmann, in: Baumbach/Lauterbach/Albers/Hartmann (eds), s 1065 para 1.

[52] Münch, in: MünchKommZPO, s 1034 para 10; Voit, in: Musielak/Voit (eds), s 1034 para 3; Saenger, in: Saenger (ed), s 1034 para 7; Reichold, in: Thomas/Putzo (eds), s 1034 para 3.

[53] OLG Neustadt, NJW 1955, 635, 636; Münch, in: MünchKommZPO, s 1034 para 10; Saenger, in: Saenger (ed), s 1034 para 10; Reichold, in: Thomas/Putzo (eds), s 1034 para 3.

advantage the agreed mechanism works actually tried to use it in a way that would increase its chances of winning the case. Instead, the objective fact that an unfair imbalance exists is sufficient to trigger the right of the prejudiced party to request a balanced appointment by the competent state court.[54] As long as only the composition of the arbitral tribunal is concerned, s 1034 para 2 ZPO is ***lex specialis*** and ss 138, 307 *et seq.* BGB do not apply.[55] Thus, an arbitration agreement that prejudices one party as defined in s 1034 para 2 ZPO is not invalid. Instead, the state court has authority, upon request of the prejudiced party, to take corrective action and to let the arbitration proceed. Thereby, the arbitration agreement is corrected such that equal treatment of the parties is assured.[56] This legislative concept should be in line with the intentions of the parties, at least as far as most cases are concerned. The parties do want arbitration; thus, invalidity of the arbitration agreement would be an inappropriate remedy.

II. DIS Rules

1. *General Principles*

3.37 The appointment process under the DIS Rules is in some respects comparable, in other respects however somewhat different and more elaborate compared to the rules laid down in the Tenth Book of the ZPO. Whilst the Tenth Book of the ZPO uses a two-step process for determining an arbitrator, consisting of the appointment by a party (or the court) and the acceptance by the appointee, the DIS Rules follow a **three-step approach:** step one is the **"nomination"** of an arbitrator by the parties or the DIS Appointing Committee (ss 6.2 para 5, 6.3 para 3, 12–14 DIS Rules), step two is the **acceptance** by the nominee (s 16 DIS Rules) which is contingent on the third step and step three is the **confirmation** of the arbitrator by the DIS Secretary General or the DIS Appointing Committee (s 17 DIS Rules).

3.38 The default rule, unless otherwise agreed by the parties, is the **three-person panel** (s 3 DIS Rules; for details see below paras 3.41 *et seq.*). Pursuant to s 2.1 DIS Rules, "the parties are free in their selection and nomination of arbitrators." A party is bound by its selection of an arbitrator once the nomination has been received by the DIS Secretariat (s 12.1 cl 5 DIS Rules), which is similar to s 1035 para 2 ZPO (binding effect once the other party has received the nomination), but takes into account that an arbitral institution exists.

3.39 The **chairman or the sole arbitrator** needs to be a **lawyer**, unless otherwise agreed by the parties (s 2.2 DIS Rules). "Lawyer" does **not necessarily** mean a

[54] Münch, in: MünchKommZPO, s 1034 para 11; Voit, in: Musielak/Voit (eds), s 1034 para 4.

[55] OLG Frankfurt SchiedsVZ 2013, 294, 296; Hanefeld/Wittinghofer, SchiedsVZ 2005, 217, 224 *et seq.*; Voit, in: Musielak/Voit (eds), s 1034 para 5; Münch, in: MünchKommZPO, s 1034 para 12. Opposing view regarding ss 307 *et seq.* BGB: Lachmann/Lachmann, BB 2000, 1633, 1638 *et seq.*; Lachmann, para 561.

[56] Münch, in: MünchKommZPO, s 1034 para 2; Reichold, in: Thomas/Putzo (eds), s 1034 para 4; Voit, in: Musielak/Voit (eds), s 1034 para 1.

German-qualified lawyer; thus, the qualification to take office as a judge (so-called *Befähigung zum Richteramt*) is not required. A foreign law degree is sufficient. It is not necessary that the person is admitted to practice as an attorney-at-law in a foreign jurisdiction.[57] "Lawyer" includes persons who have passed only the first state examination in Germany or who have obtained the degree of a **diploma in law** in Germany (*Diplomjurist*).[58] Whether it is practicable and wise to nominate someone as a chairman or sole arbitrator who does not have full qualification to practice law in at least one jurisdiction, is of course another question that is primarily left to the decision of the parties.

2. *Default Rule: Panel of Three Arbitrators*

For a three-person panel, the appointment process is as follows. The claimant needs to nominate an arbitrator in its **statement of claim** (s 6.2 para 5 DIS Rules). Where the claimant fails to do so, its statement of claim is deemed incomplete, and the DIS Secretariat will request the claimant to **supplement** the statement of claim accordingly; the DIS Secretariat will also set a **time limit** for compliance (s 6.4 DIS Rules). Where the claimant fails to comply, the proceedings are terminated without prejudice, ie the claimant may reintroduce the same claim later on in new arbitral proceedings (s 6.4 DIS Rules). Apart from that, there is an ongoing discussion regarding the further consequences of this "termination." While some commentators argue that only a proceeding which has commenced can be terminated,[59] others suggest that the expression is misleading and the claim is to be treated as never filed.[60] This difference is important for example in light of the statute of limitations and its suspension pursuant to s 204 para 1 no 11 BGB. In our view the second approach is more persuasive. Whilst it is true that under German law even an inadmissible claim is sufficient to suspend the statute of limitations,[61] it is strictly required that the claim is at least served upon the defendant. The DIS Secretariat may make delivery of the statement of claim to the respondent contingent on having received the required documents and payment (s 8 DIS Rules). In addition, s 6.4 para 2 DIS Rules clearly provides that commencement of the arbitral proceedings is not affected as long as supplementation is made within the set time limit. **3.40**

Upon delivery of the statement of claim to the respondent, the DIS Secretariat asks the respondent to nominate an arbitrator **within 30 days after receipt of** **3.41**

[57] Theune, in: Schütze (ed), DIS Rules para 20; Wagner/Klich, in: Nedden/Herzberg (eds), s 2 DIS-SchO para 21.

[58] Wagner/Klich, in: Nedden/Herzberg (eds), s 2 DIS-SchO para 21. Opposing view: Aden, p 427.

[59] Elsing, in: *Arbitration in Germany*, s 6 DIS Rules para 10; Theune, in: Schütze (ed), DIS Rules para 57; Lachmann, para 3374.

[60] Schilling, in: Nedden/Herzberg (eds), s 6 DIS-SchO para 33.

[61] Grothe, in: MünchKommBGB, s 204 para 25; Peters/Jacoby, in: Staudinger (ed), s 204 para 24; Althammer, NJW 2011, 2172, 2174.

the statement of claim by the respondent (s 12.1 cl 1 and 2 DIS Rules). If the respondent fails to comply therewith, the claimant may ask the DIS Appointing Committee to make the nomination (s 12.1 cl 2 DIS Rules). This is similar to the process under s 1035 para 3 cl 3 ZPO, where the claimant can request appointment by the state court if the respondent fails to appoint "its" arbitrator. Upon request of the respondent and after hearing the claimant, the DIS Secretariat may moderately **extend the 30-day time limit** in its discretion (s 12.1 cl 3 DIS Rules). If the claimant agrees—which is typically the case during settlement negotiations—the extension will be granted.[62] Otherwise, a party will have to put forward plausible reasons, such as the need to align with a foreign client, travel commitments or delay of the nomination itself due to an objection of the claimant pursuant to s 17 para 1 DIS Rules.[63] After the expiry of the 30-day period (or an extended period), the respondent can still make the nomination, as long as the claimant has not yet filed a request for nomination with the DIS Appointing Committee (s 12.1 cl 4 DIS Rules). Thus, the DIS Rules follow the second approach explained above (para 3.26).

3.42 Once the respondent has nominated its arbitrator, or the nomination has been effected by the DIS Appointing Committee pursuant to s 12.1 cl 2—4 DIS Rules, the **DIS Secretariat calls upon the two arbitrators to nominate the chairman** and to notify the DIS Secretariat thereof without undue delay (s 12.2 cl 1 DIS Rules). The DIS Rules expressly address and **allow for communication** between the arbitrators and the parties on the selection of the chairman; pursuant to s 12.2 cl 2 DIS Rules, the arbitrators "should take into account concurring proposals by the parties." This means that on the one hand, each arbitrator may communicate on the person of the chairman with the party by which he or she has been appointed. In fact it is not uncommon for parties to address possible chairman candidates already in the selection process for the party-appointed arbitrator. On the other hand, the above provision of the DIS Rules makes clear that the party-appointed arbitrators are not bound by proposals from the parties even where the parties are in complete agreement on the person of the chairman. In practice, in such a situation, it would however be quite unusual for party-appointed arbitrators to select a different chairman. In any event, in such a situation the parties could agree—and could indeed be deemed to have agreed—to derogate the power of the party-appointed arbitrators to appoint the chairman and to substitute such power with a party-agreed appointment of the chairman.

3.43 The two arbitrators generally have **30 days to agree on a chairman** and to inform the DIS Secretariat accordingly (s 12.2 cl 2 DIS Rules). Where the DIS Secretariat does not receive a nomination of the chairman in time, each party may request that

62 Bredow/Mulder, in: *Arbitration in Germany*, s 12 DIS Rules para 4.

63 Wagner/Klich, in: Nedden/Herzberg (eds), s 12 DIS-SchO para 9; Bredow/Mulder, in: *Arbitration in Germany*, s 12 DIS Rules para 4.

the DIS Appointing Committee nominates the chairman (s 12.2 cl 2 DIS Rules). Contrary to s 12.1 cl 3 DIS Rules the provision does not foresee an extension of the period. To avoid any delay, the DIS informs the party-appointed arbitrators shortly after their nomination about the time limit and that afterwards a party will be able to request nomination by the DIS Appointing Committee. Where the two co-arbitrators are still not able to agree on a chairman within the 30 days, it is up to them to prevent the parties from submitting such a request.[64] Again, a belated nomination is still considered timely if it is received by the DIS Secretariat before one of the parties has filed a request to the DIS Appointing Committee (s 12.2 cl 4 DIS Rules). In order for the constitution of the arbitral tribunal to be completed, the acceptance and confirmation phase of the process need to be completed (ss 16, 17 DIS Rules, see paras 3.46 *et seq.*).

3. *Sole Arbitrator*

In case of a sole arbitrator, the claimant's **statement of claim should contain proposals** for the nomination of the sole arbitrator (s 6.3 para 3 DIS Rules). If the claimant fails to do so, the DIS Secretariat may again request supplementation (s 6.4 DIS Rules). The DIS Secretariat delivers the statement of claim to the respondent (s 8 cl 1 DIS Rules), usually after payment of the DIS administration fee and a provisional advance on the arbitrator's costs (ss 8 cl 2, 7 DIS Rules). Once the respondent has received the statement of claim, the parties have **30 days to agree** on a sole arbitrator; if they fail to agree on time, each party may request nomination of the sole arbitrator by the **DIS Appointing Committee** (s 14 DIS Rules). Acceptance and confirmation again follow the provisions laid down in ss 16, 17 DIS Rules (see below paras 3.46 *et seq.*). 3.44

4. *Multi-party Arbitration*

For multi-party situations, s 13.1 DIS Rules provides that multiple claimants need to **jointly nominate one arbitrator** in the statement of claim, unless the parties agree otherwise. Where there are multiple respondents named in the statement of claim, they, too, need to jointly nominate one arbitrator for their side within 30 days after receipt of the statement of claim (s 13.2 cl 1 DIS Rules). The 30-day period is calculated by reference to the time of receipt by the respondent who last received the statement of claim (s 13.2 cl 2 DIS Rules). The 30-day period can be extended by the DIS Secretariat (s 13.2 cl 3 DIS Rules), and this frequently happens due to the complexity involved with several parties on one side. If the respondents cannot agree on an arbitrator, the **DIS Appointing Committee** consults with the parties and then nominates both arbitrators originally appointed by the parties, thereby setting aside the nomination already made by the claimant(s) (s 13.2 para 2 cl 4 and 5 DIS Rules). The **DIS appointees then need to agree** on the chairman 3.45

---

64 Bredow/Mulder, in: *Arbitration in Germany*, s 12 DIS Rules para 10; Wagner/Klich, in: Nedden/Herzberg (eds), s 12 DIS-SchO para 24.

pursuant to the general rules (ss 13.2 cls 5 and 6, 12.2 DIS Rules). Acceptance and confirmation again follow the provisions of ss 16, 17 DIS Rules (see below paras 3.46 *et seq.*).

5. Acceptance and Confirmation

3.46 Once an arbitrator is nominated, the proceedings enter the acceptance stage (s 16 DIS Rules). Section 16 DIS Rules applies to three-person tribunals, sole arbitrator situations, and multi-party arbitration. Without undue delay after his or her nomination, an arbitrator needs to **notify the DIS Secretariat** whether he or she accepts the nomination, and if yes, whether he or she fulfills the necessary **qualifications** agreed upon by the parties (s 16.1 cl 2 DIS Rules). The nominee must "**disclose** all circumstances which are likely to give rise to doubts as to his impartiality or independence" (s 16.1 cl 2 DIS Rules; for details see paras 3.128 *et seq.*). The DIS Secretariat informs the parties of the declarations received from a nominee (s 16.1 cl 3 DIS Rules). Where a nominee's declaration contains circumstances that "are likely to give rise to doubts" regarding impartiality, independence, or agreed qualifications, the DIS Secretariat gives the parties an opportunity to comment within a certain deadline (s 16.2 DIS Rules).

3.47 The final step in the appointment process and thus the constitution of the arbitral tribunal is the **confirmation of the nominees by the DIS Secretary General** (s 17 DIS Rules). The DIS Secretary General "may confirm" a nominee once the DIS Secretariat has received the nominee's declaration of acceptance pursuant to s 16 DIS Rules, and there are no circumstances likely to raise doubts regarding impartiality, independence, or agreed qualifications (s 17.1 DIS Rules). "May" in a German legal context usually means **discretion.** Neither the parties nor a nominee thus have an explicit right to request or enforce his or her confirmation. On the other hand, s 17.2 DIS Rules provides for a special procedure where not all requirements of s 17.1 DIS Rules are fulfilled. Thus, it is the prevailing view and general practice, that there is **no room for a refusal** if all the prerequisites are met.[65] Once all arbitrators are confirmed, the arbitral tribunal is constituted (s 17.3 cl 1 DIS Rules), and the DIS Secretariat informs the parties accordingly (s 17.3 cl 2 DIS Rules).

III. ICC Rules

1. General Principles

3.48 Like the DIS Rules, the ICC Rules follow a **three-step approach** consisting of **nomination, acceptance, and confirmation** (arts 11–13 ICC Rules). As will be seen from the explanations provided below, generally speaking, the **ICC Court** has a stronger role in the constitution of the arbitral tribunal than the DIS. The ICC

[65] Theune, in: Schütze (ed), DIS Rules paras 135 *et seq.*; Bredow/Mulder, in: *Arbitration in Germany*, s 17 DIS Rules para 5; Wagner/Klich, in: Nedden/Herzberg (eds), s 17 DIS-SchO para 5.

Rules, like the Tenth Book of the ZPO and the DIS Rules, only allow for **impartial and independent** arbitrators (art 11.1 ICC Rules).

2. Default Rule: Sole Arbitrator

The default provision under the ICC Rules is the sole arbitrator, unless the parties have agreed otherwise or it appears to the ICC Court that the dispute "is such as to warrant the appointment of three arbitrators" (art 12.2 cl 1 ICC Rules). This may be the case due to the factual and legal complexity and the economic value of the case, or its political sensitivity.[66] As mentioned above (para 3.10), the US$ 5 million threshold is a rule of thumb applied by the ICC. **3.49**

In the case of a sole arbitrator, the parties have the opportunity to agree on the nomination **within 30 days after receipt of claimant's request for arbitration** by the other party. The ICC Secretariat **may extend** the time limit. If the parties fail to agree, the sole arbitrator will be appointed by the ICC Court (art 12.3 ICC Rules). **3.50**

3. Panel of Three Arbitrators

Where the parties have agreed on a three-person panel, the claimant shall nominate an arbitrator **in the request for arbitration,** and the respondent shall nominate one **in its answer** (art 12.4 cl 1 ICC Rules). Where a party fails to make a nomination, the **ICC Court** will make the appointment instead (art 12.4 cl 2 ICC Rules). As a default rule, the ICC Court also appoints the chairman (which the ICC Rules call the "**president**" of the arbitral tribunal), art 12.5 cl 1 ICC Rules. The parties may, however, agree to a different procedure, such as a joint nomination by the two party-appointed arbitrators. In such case, the chairman will need to be confirmed by the ICC Court pursuant to art 13 ICC Rules. The chairman needs to be appointed within **30 days** from the confirmation or appointment of the party-appointed arbitrators (art 12.5 cl 2 ICC Rules). The time limit may be modified by party agreement and extended by the ICC Court. If there is no appointment after the time limit expires, the ICC Court will appoint the chairman (art 12.5 cl 2 ICC Rules). **3.51**

Where there is **no party agreement on the number of arbitrators** and the ICC Court decides that there shall be **three arbitrators** pursuant to art 12.2 cl 1 ICC Rules, an **accelerated timeline** applies. In this situation, the claimant will be notified of the ICC Court's decision and then has 15 days to nominate an arbitrator. The respondent, too, has 15 days to make its nomination after receipt of the notification of the nomination made by the claimant (art 12.2 cl 2 ICC Rules). If a party fails to make a nomination, the ICC Court makes the appointment (art 12.2 cl 3 ICC Rules). Regarding the chairman, the regular provisions contained in art 12.5 ICC Rules apply. **3.52**

[66] Fry/Greenberg/Mazza, para 3-439; Wagner/Herzberg, in: Nedden/Herzberg (eds), art 12 ICC-SchO para 6.

4. *Multi-party Arbitration*

3.53 In multi-party situations and a three-person tribunal, the claimants need to jointly nominate one arbitrator, and the respondents need to jointly nominate one arbitrator, too, both for confirmation (art 12.6 ICC Rules). Where one or both sides cannot agree on a nomination, the ICC Court appoints the **entire tribunal** and designates one arbitrator as the chairman (art 12.8 ICC Rules). That means that any prior nomination by one or more parties will be obsolete.[67]

5. *Acceptance and Confirmation*

3.54 Under art 11.1 cl 1 ICC Rules, a prospective arbitrator nominated by a party for confirmation by the ICC Court or otherwise to be appointed by the ICC Court must sign a "**statement of acceptance, availability, impartiality and independence.**" He or she must disclose to the ICC Secretariat in writing "any facts or circumstances which might be of such a nature as to call into question the arbitrator's independence in the eyes of the parties, as well as any circumstances that could give rise to reasonable doubts as to the arbitrator's impartiality" (art 11.2 cl 2 ICC Rules).

3.55 The final step for the constitution of the arbitral tribunal is the confirmation of an arbitrator nominated by a party (or his or her appointment in the absence of a party nomination). Appointment and confirmation decisions are within the **discretion of the ICC Court**, or, as the case may be, the ICC Secretary General, taking into account such factors as nationality, residence, other relationships with the countries of origin of the parties and other arbitrators, as well as the arbitrator's availability and ability to conduct the proceedings in accordance with the ICC Rules (arts 13.1 and 13.2 ICC Rules). In principle, the sole arbitrator or the chairman of a three-person arbitral tribunal shall be of a **nationality that is different** from the nationality of the parties (art 13.5 cl 1 ICC Rules). The ICC decides on the confirmation or appointment without communicating any reasons; the decision is final, as far as the ICC Rules are concerned (art 11.4 ICC Rules). Nevertheless, mandatory provisions of the Tenth Book of the ZPO still apply, such as, eg, the provisions on the correction of unfairly prejudicial appointments (s 1034 para 2 ZPO).

D. Selection of Arbitrators in German Practice

3.56 When it comes to selecting a specific arbitrator, the parties and their counsel will look at a series of typical selection criteria which we explore one by one (below paras 3.57 *et seq.*). In this section, we also address considerations regarding certain groups of legal professionals in Germany (below paras 3.79 *et seq.*). Finally, we turn to the selection process in practice (below paras 3.90 *et seq.*).

[67] Wagner/Herzberg, in: Nedden/Herzberg (eds), art 12 ICC-SchO para 22.

I. Typical Selection Criteria

Below we set forth a series of selection criteria that usually play a significant role in German practice, starting with a prospective arbitrator's professional background and qualifications (below paras 3.58 *et seq.*) and then turning to such factors as his or her experience in arbitration (below paras 3.67 *et seq.*), language skills (below paras 3.70 *et seq.*), soft skills and soft factors (below paras 3.72 *et seq.*), and last but not least availability (below paras 3.77 *et seq.*). **3.57**

1. Professional Background and Qualifications

The professional background, and more broadly the professional and practical qualifications of a prospective arbitrator certainly play a key role in the selection process. After all, one of the main advantages of arbitration—as opposed to state court litigation—is the fact that the parties can compose a decision-making body with qualifications that are **tailor-made** for their dispute, including complicated and complex issues requiring specialized factual and legal knowledge and skills. Two important threshold issues are whether to choose a lawyer or a non-lawyer (below paras 3.59 *et seq.*), and, if a lawyer is to be chosen, whether to go for a lawyer admitted to practice in Germany or not (below paras 3.63 *et seq.*). **3.58**

a) Lawyer v. Non-lawyer The natural choice for an arbitrator seems to be a lawyer. At the same time, it is a distinctive feature of arbitration that non-lawyers, too, can act as decision-makers. Under the Tenth Book of the ZPO, there are **no restrictions** whatsoever regarding the professional qualification of an arbitrator. The DIS Rules merely provide that a sole arbitrator and a chairman of a three-person tribunal need to be lawyers (s 2.2 DIS Rules). **3.59**

A party may conclude that its interests are served best by appointing a person who has **expertise with the factual and business background** of the dispute, and may thus appoint a construction expert in a construction case, an accounting expert in a post-M&A dispute involving accounting issues regarding purchase prices adjustments or guarantees, or a patent attorney in an IP-related dispute. For the tribunal, it can be very helpful to have that type of expertise within the panel. This increases the understanding for the factual submissions of the parties, including possible expert-witness reports. Also, it reduces the dependency on tribunal-appointed experts. **3.60**

At the same time, a party who appoints a non-lawyer needs to be aware of the fact that "its" arbitrator may have little to no understanding regarding **procedural and substantive legal issues** relevant for the decision of the case. Such expertise may then lie exclusively with the chairman (if the other side also appoints a non-lawyer) or with the chairman and the opponent's party-appointed arbitrator. The non-lawyer may not be able to contribute much to debates within the tribunal on issues of procedural or substantive law, and may have to more or less accept at face **3.61** value what the chairman and the other arbitrator tell him or her in this respect.[68] German substantive law, to the extent it applies, may certainly be just as much a "mystery" to a legal layman as any other legal system. Also, German legal thinking, eg when it comes to interpreting contracts and statutes, follows its own methodologies and standards with which non-lawyers are generally not familiar.

3.62 In addition, it is **not always easy to predict** what substantive questions will be decisive for the case. This may cause a time-consuming selection process with the result that in the end the parties still have to pay for an expert opinion.[69] Another risk arises where the losing party later may seek compensation from liability insurance. In particular, the German Insurance Association (GDV) provides a model clause whereupon arbitral awards are recognized only if at least one lawyer acted as arbitrator.[70] Thus, as a rule of thumb, we would advise to be cautious, or even reluctant, to appoint non-lawyers in arbitral proceedings seated in Germany.

3.63 **b) German-qualified Lawyer?** When it comes to choosing among lawyers, persons from different nationalities and jurisdictions can be considered. It goes almost without saying that a lawyer to be appointed as arbitrator does not necessarily need to be admitted to practice in Germany, unless the parties have agreed otherwise. Even the chairman of a three-person panel or the sole arbitrator under the DIS Rules "merely" need to be lawyers, but not necessarily German-qualified or admitted in Germany.

3.64 For a German party to an arbitration seated in Germany and governed by German substantive law, it will often seem natural to appoint a German-qualified lawyer. Nevertheless, parties should not necessarily limit their choices in that way. There are many outstanding arbitrators active in the German arbitration market who may not be German citizens or German-trained. This applies, for instance, to a number of practitioners from **Switzerland and Austria.**[71] Some are even dual-qualified and should be seriously considered, in particular where the other side may be a non-German party.

3.65 Where a non-German party finds itself in arbitration seated in Germany and subject to German substantive law, different considerations may apply. On the one hand, such a party may wish to have an arbitrator with a particularly strong German law background in order to properly counter-balance an appointment that the other side has made or will likely make. On the other hand, a foreign party may wish to purposefully give the case a more **international "touch"** by appointing a non-German lawyer, which in turn may increase the chances that the chairman, too, will not be from Germany.

68 Similar Hantke, SchiedsVZ 2003, 269, 270; Lachmann, para 815; without reservations Volze, DS 2012, 379; Blackaby/Partasides/Redfern/Hunter, para 4.57.

69 Kreindler/Schäfer/Wolff, para 489.

70 Koch, SchiedsVZ 2007, 281, 283.

71 Wilske, in: *Arbitration in Germany*, p 733 para 12.

Against the background of these considerations, and in keeping with the "**less is more**" approach, in the case of three-person panels we would generally not see a compelling reason to include in the arbitration agreement or any other party agreement a provision absolutely requiring that an arbitrator be German-qualified, even where it is clear that the case will be seated in Germany and be governed by German substantive law. It would seem that such a restriction unnecessarily limits the parties' strategic choices when they later need to constitute the arbitral tribunal.[72] **3.66**

2. Experience in Arbitration

For many parties, experience in arbitration is another key consideration when selecting an arbitrator. The advantages are obvious. Someone who has already acted as an arbitrator several, perhaps even many times, will be familiar with the procedural framework, the cross-cultural issues, and more broadly the dynamics of arbitration. Chances are also that he or she may know the chairman, the co-arbitrator, or the party representatives involved, which all in all may provide for a smoother and more efficient process. When it comes to appointing a **chairman**, parties may be especially reluctant to choose a person who has never even served as a party-appointed arbitrator.[73] Another important factor is that the parties naturally prefer to base this decision on a broad range of information, in particular regarding the organization and effectiveness of the respective candidate. This information is not available for inexperienced arbitrators and their nomination is much more risky. **3.67**

At the same time, there may be cases where it is not that important that a person has already served repeatedly as arbitrator. This may apply specifically to party-appointed arbitrators. A case may raise specific issues of substantive law that requires special expertise. Also, some parties may have a reluctance towards the arbitrator "establishment" and prefer to have someone from outside of whatever may be perceived to be the "inner circle." **3.68**

It should be noted that **experience in state court litigation**, eg on the part of an active or retired judge or an attorney specializing in state court litigation, may be considered helpful by the parties, in particular where they wish the arbitral proceedings to be conducted in a way that is by and large similar to German state court litigation. The situation may look different when it comes to international arbitration. **International cases** seated in Germany are often approached and handled by both arbitrators and parties' counsel in a way that significantly differs from state court litigation, eg regarding reduced substantiation requirements for written submissions, somewhat more generosity on document production, less inclination towards settlement, more party dominance in conducting the proceedings, **3.69**

[72] Hantke, SchiedsVZ 2003, 269, 270; Lörcher/Lörcher, SchiedsVZ 2005, 179, 181.

[73] Risse/Spehl, ZVertriebsR 2012, 151, 154; Lachmann, para 821; Blackaby/Partasides/Redfern/Hunter, para 4.59.

including the taking of evidence and the like. An arbitrator with a strong background in German state court litigation may be more irritated than anything else by these types of international approaches, and his or her state court procedural experience may be of more limited assistance in the conduct of an international case.

3. Language

3.70 Obviously, in a purely domestic context, language considerations are fairly simple. Where German parties conduct an arbitration seated in Germany with German substantive law applying, the language of the proceedings will in all likelihood be German, and it would be highly unusual to pick an arbitrator who does not speak German.

3.71 In an **international context**, more complex considerations apply. In most cases, the parties will want an arbitrator appointed by them to speak the language of the proceedings, at least as a second language.[74] This applies in particular to the **chairman**, who is responsible for much of the correspondence during the proceedings and for much of the "talking" during hearings. It is of course also helpful where an arbitrator has a sufficient command of the language in which most of the underlying documents are written and the language that the key witnesses speak. That need not necessarily be the language of the proceedings. On the other hand, it may not be possible to find otherwise sufficiently qualified and competent candidates who speak all the relevant languages. If need be, the parties and the tribunal may have to resort to **translators and interpreters**, which is not uncommon in international arbitration. Given the potential risk of losing a case due to the arbitrator's lack of language skills, these costs generally prove to be a wise investment.[75]

4. Soft Skills and Soft Factors

3.72 Besides the legal and non-legal qualifications of a candidate, the experience as an arbitrator, and sufficient language capabilities, there are a number of further, softer factors that may play an important role in selecting the "right" arbitrator, both when it comes to party-appointed arbitrators and chairmen.

3.73 In international cases, **intercultural competence** may be a key element for the smooth and efficient conduct of arbitral proceedings, both in terms of legal cultures and culture in general.[76] Where the parties come from different legal cultures, in particular where one comes from a **continental European (civil law)** and the other from an **Anglo-Saxon or Anglo-American background (common law)**, it can help tremendously when the arbitrators understand both legal cultures. They can then do a much better job in managing each party's expectations and tailor the proceedings in such a way that—hopefully—helps to bridge the gulfs

[74] Similarly Blackaby/Partasides/Redfern/Hunter, para 4.58.
[75] Karrer, SchiedsVZ 2006, 113, 114; Blackaby/Partasides/Redfern/Hunter, para 4.58.
[76] Kreindler/Schäfer/Wolff, para 504.

between legal cultures, eg when it comes to issues such as document disclosure, cross-examination, party versus court-appointed experts, tribunal-assisted settlement, and the like.

Another important characteristic of arbitrators, especially party-appointed arbitrators is the ability to effectively function as a **member of a team**. Each arbitral tribunal develops its own inner dynamics. There is a need to cooperate, to come to consensus, and to efficiently further the proceedings. Generally, a party's interests will be served better by appointing a team player to the tribunal as opposed to a loner who may be isolated quickly in cases where the chairman and the other party-appointed arbitrator get along very well. Where only a small circle of potential chairmen exists, a party should of course consider the existence and nature of any relationship to its candidate.[77] **3.74**

Finally, in the eyes of many parties, the perceived "**practical neutrality**" or "practical partiality" of an arbitrator candidate is of critical importance. As has been mentioned several times, it is a fundamental, constitutional requirement both under the Tenth Book of the ZPO and under most institutional rules (including the DIS and the ICC Rules) that party-appointed arbitrators are just as neutral as the chairman. Nevertheless, in practice, neutrality is not a concept that could be applied with mathematical precision. In particular, it is accepted that a party-appointed arbitrator may make sure that the **arguments** brought forward by the party that has appointed him or her are **properly considered** by the tribunal (see para 3.124). It is easy to imagine that different arbitrators may have different approaches to this type of task or option, and the specific approach taken by a certain person may well be known to the relevant arbitration community. Thus, it may be possible for parties to choose an arbitrator who has a reputation for being particularly "neutral" or one who takes a very active role in making the arguments of "his or her" party heard within the tribunal. **3.75**

Parties often tend to think that the latter must be the better choice.[78] In many cases, this may be true, but it need not be. A party-appointed arbitrator who always emphasizes the arguments of the party appointing him, and who almost never does the same with the arguments brought by the other party may start to look suspect to the other arbitrators. In particular, the chairman may develop the impression that said arbitrator may in fact not be as neutral as he or she could be, and the chairman may thus be inclined to actually listen more to the other party-appointed arbitrator. Thus, one arbitrator may easily be isolated by the type of conduct described above, which is the exact opposite of what the party appointing him or her would have hoped for. **3.76**

---

77 Risse/Spehl, ZVertriebsR 2012, 151, 154; Lachmann, para 830.

78 Franzen, NJW 1986, 299, 300 *et seq.*; Risse/Spehl, ZVertriebsR 2012, 151, 154; Lörcher/Lörcher, SchiedsVZ 2005, 179, 185.

5. *Availability*

3.77 Availability of arbitrators has become an issue of increasing importance in international arbitration in general; Germany is no exception. A party (or in the case of the chairman: the parties) may have selected the most qualified arbitrator—if the person does not have the necessary time to work personally and diligently on the case, the parties will likely not be satisfied with the conduct of the arbitration. Thus, arbitrators should only accept appointments that they are sure they can properly **handle in person.**[79] This applies across professions. A professional arbitrator may be overburdened with the other cases he or she already has. A practicing lawyer may find that the demands of the "daytime job" representing clients leaves not enough time to study voluminous submissions and files in person. An active judge or law professor may face similar issues.

3.78 It is obviously difficult for parties to gain control over this issue. Parties need to rely on what a candidate for arbitrator tells them about his or her availability. The ICC meanwhile requires candidates to sign a statement of availability and to fill in a form disclosing the number of other cases they currently handle.[80]

II. Considerations on Certain Groups of Legal Professionals

3.79 In the following section, we address considerations that apply more or less generally to certain groups of legal professionals in Germany, ie practicing lawyers (below paras 3.80 *et seq.*), German judges (below paras 3.83 *et seq.*), and law professors as well as other public officials (below paras 3.87 *et seq.*). These considerations are meant to provide a general overview and a starting point for a party's thinking process on specific candidates. They cannot replace a diligent analysis of every single case.

1. *Practicing Lawyers*

3.80 Attorneys-at-law admitted to practice in Germany frequently act as arbitrators. The German rules governing their profession generally only apply to their role as party representatives, but not as arbitrators.[81] Thus, they are generally free to accept arbitrator appointments. Practical restrictions may apply, however. In particular where attorneys are members of larger law firms, **conflicts of interest** play an increasingly important role, which may require a careful case-by-case analysis (see paras 3.119 and 3.121).

3.81 In addition to the ways in which the neutrality of an attorney sitting as an arbitrator can be impacted, so-called **"business conflicts"** often play an important role, too. A law firm may not be willing to accept that one of its members acts as

---

[79] Lachmann, para 822; Lörcher/Lörcher, SchiedsVZ 2005, 179, 186.

[80] Wagner, in: Nedden/Herzberg (eds), art 11 ICC-SchO para 26.

[81] Prütting, SchiedsVZ 2011, 233, 237 *et seq.*; Münch, in: MünchKommZPO, Vorbem s 1034 para 59; Lachmann, paras 4268 *et seq.*

arbitrator in a dispute for a comparatively moderate remuneration thereby "blocking" the law firm from accepting other, more lucrative matters from parties to the dispute as long as the dispute is ongoing.

To the extent an attorney-at-law is able and willing to act as an arbitrator, the parties may wish to make the following additional considerations. Practicing lawyers may have a particularly strong understanding of certain practical aspects underlying a case. For instance, an M&A lawyer will usually have a particularly quick grasp of an M&A agreement and the types of clauses typically associated with it. Also, practicing lawyers can easily access or organize support services for large and complex cases which is an advantage that should not be underestimated, especially for the chairman of an arbitral tribunal. At the same time, as is true with arbitrator candidates from any other professions, parties should carefully consider the workload of an attorney and enquire as to whether he or she has enough time to devote to the case. **3.82**

2. German Judges

Retired German judges frequently serve as arbitrators. **Active judges need government approval**, which may only be granted if the judge is appointed by both parties or by a neutral third party, s 40 para 1 cl 1 German Judiciary Act (DRiG). This is not merely a formal procedural provision but also a measure to ensure the confidence in the independence of a judge and his or her rulings. Accordingly, it is not sufficient that the parties make the common nomination just *pro forma*, but rather they have to reach an agreement with equal influence.[82] In addition, a judge must not act as an arbitrator in a case in which he or she has already been involved as a judge (s 40 para 1 cl 2 DRiG). Against this background, in practical terms, active judges most often act as sole arbitrators or as chairmen of arbitral tribunals. **3.83**

Where the necessary government approval is lacking or unlawful, the **appointment is still valid**, and a later arbitral award is not subject to set aside (s 1059 para 2 no 1 lit a ZPO);[83] however, the arbitrator agreement is considered invalid (s 134 BGB) by the majority of German scholars.[84] There is no precedent yet from the BGH[85] and German higher regional courts are split on this issue.[86] On closer inspection, however, the different approaches do not result in significant practical **3.84**

[82] KG SchiedsVZ 2003, 185, 186; Kröll, SchiedsVZ 2004, 113, 115; Nacimiento/Abt/Stein, in: *Arbitration in Germany*, s 1035 para 13; Kröll, NJW 2005, 194, 195.

[83] Kröll, SchiedsVZ 2004, 113, 116; Lachmann, para 860; Voit, in: Musielak/Voit (eds), s 1035 para 17; Geimer, in: Zöller (ed), s 1035 para 33; Münch, in: MünchKommZPO, Vorbem s 1034 para 58. Opposing view: Schwab/Walter, ch 9 para 3.

[84] See, eg, Münch, in: MünchKommZPO, Vorbem s 1034 para 58 with further references. Opposing view: Geimer, in: Zöller (ed), s 1035 para 33.

[85] Undecided in BGH NJW 1964, 593, 594.

[86] In favor of invalidity, eg OLG Hamburg, VersR 1983, 787; KG SchiedsVZ 2003, 185, 186; against invalidity eg OLG Stuttgart, SchiedsVZ 2003, 84 with concurring note from Nacimiento/Geimer.

differences. The proponents of validity argue that the approval is part of the arbitrator's sphere and it would be unfair to encumber the parties with the consequence of its absence.[87] Based on the same reasoning, the opposing view largely agrees that it would be unfair if an invalidity had any effect on the arbitral proceedings.[88]

3.85 While this result is entirely convincing, it should be founded on a more profound legal reasoning than just the principle of fairness. In our view, the better arguments support the **invalidity of the arbitrator agreement**. The approval requirement for state court judges is not a mere formality but is geared towards preserving the public interest in an independent and effective judiciary. Given this significance for the legal system, it should be considered as a legal prohibition under s 134 BGB. However, this affects only the arbitrator agreement as substantive-law agreement, but **not the appointment** of the arbitrator as a procedural act.[89] Likewise there is no room for a set aside based on the invalidity of the arbitrator agreement, because s 1059 para 2 no 1 lit d ZPO encompasses only violations of provisions under the ZPO and therefore not the lack of approval pursuant to s 40 para 1 DRiG.

3.86 From a practical point of view, there are a number of considerations that parties may want to take into account when they contemplate the appointment of an active or retired judge as an arbitrator. Obviously, one strong advantage of judges is that they are familiar with conducting judicial proceedings and **rendering decisions**. Also, they may be perceived as particularly **neutral**. Where the **language** of the proceedings is a language other than German, parties should carefully consider whether a judge has sufficient command of that language. Similar considerations may apply where the dispute has an **international or cross-cultural context**. As far as the conduct of proceedings is concerned, parties should be aware that German judges often have a tendency to conduct arbitral proceedings similar to state court proceedings, not least because this is the way they exercise their profession every day. They may lean heavily on **concepts of the ZPO** which do not apply directly in arbitration, but which the tribunal can certainly draw on within the parameters of its discretion.[90] This may apply, for instance, regarding substantiation requirements, a strong focus on the written pleadings, a reluctance to allow document disclosure requests, and an active style of questioning witnesses. Also, state courts judges may be skeptical of party expert witnesses and put more trust in court-/tribunal-appointed experts. Finally, state court judges very often have a **proactive attitude towards settlement** which is in line with their mandate in state court litigation (s 278 ZPO), but may be surprising or even alienating to parties with a common law background.

---

[87] Eg OLG Stuttgart, SchiedsVZ 2003, 84.

[88] Eg Lachmann, para 860, who argues for a unilateral application of the consequences of s 134 BGB against the arbitrator.

[89] Geimer, in: Zöller (ed), s 1035 para 2; Münch, in: MünchKommZPO, s 1035 para 11; Vorbem ss 1034 *et seq.* para 58.

[90] Lachmann, para 818.

3. *Law Professors; Public Officials*

German public officials need **government approval** in order to be able to act as arbitrator. This is provided for in ss 97 *et seq.* of the Federal Public Officials Act (BBG) for federal officials and in corresponding provisions of state legislation applying to state officials. Note that in Germany, law professors are usually state public officials (unless they work for one of the few private law schools in Germany), and thus need state government approval. Approval is to be denied where there are grounds to suspect that the activity as arbitrator will have a negative impact on the position as a government official, s 99 para 2 cl 1 BBG.[91] This can be the case where the public official uses more than 20 per cent of his or her time for arbitration (s 99 para 3 BBG).[92] **3.87**

A **German notary public** is also a kind of public official; however, s 8 para 4 of the Federal Notary Code (BNotO) expressly allows notaries to act as arbitrators without imposing any express limitations. In practice they are often appointed in legal disputes on construction, corporate, family, and inheritance law.[93] **3.88**

In German practice, **law professors** frequently act as arbitrators, less so probably notaries and to an even lesser extent public officials from other areas of government. As far as law professors are concerned, the parties may wish to bear in mind a number of considerations. First and foremost, law professors are often superb experts in specific areas of the law. Thus, where a party believes that the dispute will likely turn on difficult or complex legal issues, it may well conclude that its interests are best served by appointing a law professor as sole arbitrator or as its party-appointed arbitrator. Naturally, law professors may be less familiar with trade practices and trade usages. Also, they may have less specialized knowledge regarding technical or factual details, eg in the technology or construction area. Whether or not language and cross-cultural capabilities are important and present is a matter for case-by-case analysis. **3.89**

III. The Selection Process in German Practice

On the basis of the typical selection criteria set forth above, in this coming section we explore a number of practical considerations when it comes to nominating a specific person as arbitrator, be it a party-appointed arbitrator, a chairman or a sole arbitrator. We set forth some activities that have become common in German practice. We also try to give some useful guidance as to what parties and their counsel should not do. **3.90**

---

91 *"Die Genehmigung ist zu versagen, wenn zu besorgen ist, dass durch die Nebentätigkeit dienstliche Interessen beeinträchtigt werden."*

92 Nacimiento/Abt/Stein, in: *Arbitration in Germany*, s 1035 para 15; Lachmann, para 835.

93 Wagner, DNotZ 2000, 421 *et seq.*

1. Where to Find Arbitrator Candidates

3.91 As is probably self-evident, for commercial arbitration in Germany, there is not a single, ready-made, and comprehensive list of arbitrator candidates to choose from. Instead, the parties may rely on a number of other means and channels to find suitable candidates. One method—and probably still the most widely used one—is to ask someone who knows. Most often, this will be the counsel representing the party in the prospective arbitration. And for counsel, too, asking someone else who knows a good candidate is often the way to go. Also, the **DIS is prepared to make suggestions** for the selection of arbitrators, if a party so requests (s 2.3 DIS Rules). Furthermore, a number or arbitral institutions, such as the DIS or the German Maritime Arbitration Association (GMAA), publish **lists of members** who are prepared to act as arbitrators[94] or offer assistance in their selection like the Chambers of Industry and Commerce (IHK).

2. Research on Candidates

3.92 Once a specific person or a small group of candidates for the office of an arbitrator has been identified based on the general selection criteria outlined above, it is common practice to try and learn as much as reasonably possible about the person. Besides word of mouth, recommendations from colleagues and general knowledge about the person, it is worth checking **online resources**, such as the person's website and CV, as well as a person's publications and public speaking, in order to identify the candidate's areas of expertise and to determine whether he or she has already taken certain positions on issues that are likely to be relevant in the arbitration. Of course, a certain rule of reason needs to govern these efforts. The more important the case, the deeper the research could run. Large or specialized law firms may have their own databases or other readily available sources on experience with specific arbitrators.

3. Initial Contact

3.93 Making the initial contact with a candidate usually occurs via telephone, occasionally also by email, or a brief encounter in person. In most cases, the lawyer representing a party will make the call, possibly with the client present. In order to be able to make the required disclosure as to neutrality (s 1036 para 1 ZPO, see paras 3.128 *et seq.*), the candidate will **need to know the parties involved in the dispute**. Also, the candidate should be told in broad terms about the **nature and potential complexity of the dispute** as well as the **applicable law**. The contents of the **arbitration agreement** may be summarized, too. All this is useful for the candidate to make an honest self-assessment regarding his or her qualification, expertise, necessary time commitment, and availability. A more detailed discussion

94 http://www.disarb.org/en/15/members/overview-id0 (last visited December 1, 2015); http://gmaa.de/de/mitglieder-der-gmaa?format=html&reset=false&ordering=&orderby=&task=&search=schiedsrichter&searchfield=schiedsrichter&limit=500 (last visited December 1, 2015).

on the facts of the case and contested legal issues should be avoided as this might lead to doubts regarding the impartiality of the later arbitrator.[95] During such a call, the candidate should not take substantive positions on certain legal issues, and the persons calling should not attempt to press the candidate to do so, as this may jeopardize the candidate's neutrality.[96]

After the initial contact, the candidate will need to carefully determine whether he or she is indeed neutral, based on prior engagements, current cases, relationships with the parties and their counsel, and other relevant circumstances (for details see paras 3.113 *et seq.*). Once this check has been properly performed, the candidate will usually get back to the party or counsel interested in making the appointment and confirm his or her availability. Most often, this occurs either via phone or email. **3.94**

4. *In-person Meeting*

Once an arbitrator has confirmed that he or she would be interested and able to act in a dispute, it is possible to have a **short in-person meeting**, where the circumstances, in particular the importance of the case, warrant such effort. It is good practice for the meeting to occur at the offices of the candidate. The number of participants should be kept small, eg a counsel, the arbitrator, and potentially a party representative. The purpose of the meeting is to get to know each other on a personal level and to become comfortable with each other as persons. The purpose is **not to discuss the substance of the case**. Again, the candidate should not express any specific views on the facts or legal issues raised by the case, nor should the other participants press the candidate to do so. Also, except for a copy of the arbitration agreement, there should not be any exchange of written materials on the case. The party interested in appointing a candidate should not submit a draft statement of claim, correspondence, or legal memoranda to the candidate for review. Overall, the meeting should be short; as a rule of thumb, it should not take longer than approximately half an hour to one hour, unless particular circumstances require otherwise.[97] **3.95**

5. *Selection Decision*

Once a party has narrowed down the list of candidates to a small number, has conducted the appropriate research and in-person meetings, it comes down to selecting one specific person. As far as the party-appointed arbitrator is concerned, the party is of course under no restraints to agree with the opposing party and the **3.96**

---

[95] OLG München, BB 1971, 886; Lörcher/Lörcher, SchiedsVZ 2005, 179, 186; Lachmann, para 825; Mankowski, SchiedsVZ 2004, 304, 311.

[96] This appears to be an internationally recognized standard of behaviour, see most recently Guideline 8 of the IBA Guidelines on Party Representation in International Arbitration of May 2013.

[97] Blackaby/Partasides/Redfern/Hunter, para 4.73; Lachmann, para 827; Mankowski, SchiedsVZ 2004, 304, 311.

corresponding need for compromise. It may need to align with co-parties, however. It may make sense for a party to map the general qualification requirements it has identified with the candidates it has spoken to and done research on. Thus, a party can come to a rational decision as to whom it considers the strongest and most qualified person. Once that person is identified, the party should notify him or her as to its decision and let him or her know that the party intends to make the nomination. With respect to potential other candidates that had been contacted, a courtesy call informing them that they will not be nominated is in order.

3.97 The selection decision may be more difficult when it comes to aligning on the chairman of a three-person panel or a sole arbitrator. Each side will of course have done its own diligence based on the criteria and processes outlined above. It is common for the party-appointed arbitrators to exchange views first with the respective party that has appointed them and then among each other. It is often useful to align on a list of candidates between the party and "its" appointee, for the appointees then to confer with each other and see whether there are common candidates on both sides' lists, and then for each appointee to go back to the party that has appointed him or her.[98] It may be necessary for each side to amend and extend its list of candidates and to conduct several rounds of this exercise until a person is found that suits both sides. Often, there is a natural hesitation to accept a candidate for chairman or sole arbitrator that was originally suggested only by the other side. Parties should attempt to be rational about this and run such a proposal through their catalogue of selection criteria. Sometimes, a candidate proposed by the other side may be just as good or even better than the ideas that a party and their counsel had come up with themselves.

E. Challenge, Termination, and Replacement

3.98 We first give an overview of applicable rules for challenging arbitrators (below paras 3.99 *et seq.*). As a next step, we lay out the requirements for arbitrator impartiality in more detail (below paras 3.112 *et seq.*). A further ground for challenge is the lack of agreed prerequisites (below para 3.133). We follow this section with a detailed analysis of the challenge procedure (below paras 3.134 *et seq.*). Separately, the office of an arbitrator may be terminated as a result of inability to perform or undue delay (below paras 3.144 *et seq.*). As a result of a successful challenge or termination of office, an arbitrator may need to be replaced by a substitute arbitrator (below paras 3.155 *et seq.*).

[98] Hantke, SchiedsVZ 2003, 269, 271; Blackaby/Partasides/Redfern/Hunter, para 4.40; Mankowski, SchiedsVZ 2004, 304, 309; Lachmann, para 804.

I. Overview of Applicable Rules

As regards the rules governing the challenge, termination, and replacement of arbitrators, we first take a look at the Tenth Book of the ZPO (below paras 3.100 *et seq.*), and then turn to the DIS and the ICC Rules as two prominent examples of institutional arbitration (below paras 3.104 *et seq.*). In a third step, we address some "soft law" relevant for these issues, namely the IBA Guidelines on Conflicts of Interest in International Arbitration (below paras 3.107 *et seq.*). Finally, we outline how impartiality and independence of arbitrators, as well as the fulfilment of party-agreed requirements for arbitrators play out at the enforcement and set aside stages of the arbitral process (below paras 3.109 *et seq.*). **3.99**

1. Ad hoc Proceedings

In ss 1036–1039 ZPO, the German arbitration law addresses the challenge, the termination of office, and the replacement of arbitrators. Section 1036 para 2 cl 1 ZPO provides that an arbitrator may be challenged based on **lack of impartiality, independence, or party-agreed prerequisites.**[99] The German arbitration law thereby secures a fair trial, which is a prerequisite for arbitration to be equivalent to state court litigation. Accordingly, neutrality of arbitrators cannot be derogated or waived by party agreement in advance.[100] The German arbitration law does not contain any specific catalogues of examples to specify in more detail what impartiality and independence mean. Regarding the concept of independence, the set of examples applying to judges set forth in s 41 ZPO can serve as useful guidance.[101] Nevertheless, in the light of the peculiarities of arbitral proceedings it would be inappropriate simply to apply these criteria without further reflection. For example, the nomination of an arbitrator by a party inevitably creates an association between them and the absence of the opportunity for appeal means that decisions suffering from bias can no longer be challenged.[102] **3.100**

Section 1036 para 1 ZPO contains a corresponding **disclosure obligation** of arbitrators and arbitrator candidates to ensure that the parties can make an informed decision when accepting or rejecting a candidate as arbitrator (for details see paras 3.128 *et seq.*). Section 1037 ZPO provides for a **two-step procedure** for challenging an arbitrator based on lack of neutrality or agreed prerequisites. The first step is a **written challenge** within a two-week deadline after a party becomes aware of the underlying facts and a **decision by the arbitral tribunal** (including **3.101**

[99] For ease of reference, and in line with international practice, we speak of impartiality and independence as neutrality, and lack of impartiality or independence as lack of neutrality.

[100] Schwab/Walter, ch 14 para 2; Nacimiento/Abt/Stein, in: *Arbitration in Germany*, s 1036 para 4; Saenger, in: Saenger (ed), s 1036 para 11.

[101] BT-Drucks 13/5274, p 40.

[102] Nacimiento/Abt/Stein, in: *Arbitration in Germany*, s 1036 para 33; Henn, BB 1993, Beil. 17, pp 13, 15; Lachmann, para 970; Voit, in: Musielak/Voit (eds), s 1036 para 7; OLG Frankfurt, SchiedsVZ 2006, 329.

the challenged arbitrator) thereon (s 1037 para 2 ZPO). The parties can agree on amendments to this procedure, eg by extending the deadline or by excluding the challenged arbitrator from the tribunal's decision (s 1037 para 1 ZPO). In a second step, where the challenge in front of the arbitral tribunal is unsuccessful, the party bringing the challenge may submit the challenge to the competent higher regional court within one month (s 1037 para 3 cl 1 ZPO). The parties can amend the deadline, but they **may not exclude access to the higher regional court.**[103] Thus, the court procedure is also available in institutional cases seated in Germany. The arbitral tribunal has discretion to continue the arbitral proceedings while a challenge is pending before the higher regional court (s 1037 para 3 ZPO).

3.102 Section 1038 ZPO addresses the cases of **inability (legal or factual) to act and inactivity** of an arbitrator. In such cases, there are three options to terminate the office of an arbitrator: (i) he or she may **withdraw**; (ii) the parties may—as always and even without cause—**agree** on his or her termination; and (iii) in the absence of a withdrawal and a party agreement on termination, a party may apply to the competent higher regional **court to order the termination** of the office of an arbitrator (s 1038 para 1 cl 2 ZPO).

3.103 Where the office of an arbitrator ends, a **substitute arbitrator** needs to be appointed (s 1039 para 1 cl 2 ZPO). As a consequence, termination of the office of an arbitrator does not mean termination of the arbitral proceedings. Pursuant to s 1039 para 1 cl 2 ZPO, the rules governing the appointment of the arbitrator, whose office has been terminated, shall apply *mutatis mutandis*. Thus, in a case where the office of a party-appointed arbitrator is terminated, the party having made the original appointment gets to appoint the substitute arbitrator. Regarding the chairman of a three-person tribunal, the party-appointed arbitrators, in consultation with the parties, need to agree on a substitute. For a sole arbitrator, whose office has been terminated, the parties need to agree on his or her replacement. The parties are free to agree a different procedure (s 1039 para 2 ZPO). In each case, termination of the office of an arbitrator needs to be distinguished from the termination of the arbitrator agreement (see para 3.191).

2. Institutional Arbitration

3.104 The **DIS Rules** address the challenge, termination, and replacement of arbitrators in ss 18 and 19 which **largely follow** ss 1036–1039 ZPO. In addition, s 18.2 cl 2 DIS Rules provides that "the DIS Secretariat informs the arbitrators and the other party of the challenge and sets a reasonable time limit for comments from the challenged arbitrator and the other party." Thereafter, the arbitral tribunal shall decide (s 18.2 cl 3 DIS Rules), including the challenged arbitrator. The DIS Rules do not address the recourse to the state courts, which exists as a matter of

[103] Voit, in: Musielak/Voit (eds), s 1037 para 5; Lachmann, paras 1049, 1095; Geimer, in: Zöller (ed), s 1037 para 1; Hartmann, in: Baumbach/Lauterbach/Albers/Hartmann (eds), s 1037 para 1.

mandatory German law for arbitrations seated in Germany (s 1037 paras 1 and 3 ZPO). Section 19 DIS Rules mirrors s 1038 ZPO regarding inability to perform and failure to act. Interestingly, s 19.1 cl 2 DIS Rules also provides for an application to the competent higher regional court for termination; such termination may not be effected by the DIS. Where the office of an arbitrator is terminated, the DIS Rules, too, provide for the nomination and appointment of a substitute arbitrator (ss 18.3 and 19.2 DIS Rules), much like s 1039 ZPO does.

Articles 14 and 15 of the **ICC Rules** address the challenge, termination of office, and replacement of arbitrators. Under art 14.1 ICC Rules, a challenge for lack of impartiality or independence, or for other reasons, must be made in writing to the **ICC Secretariat**, specifying the underlying facts and circumstances. The submission must be made within **30 days** (art 14.2 ICC Rules), as opposed to the two weeks provided for by the Tenth Book of the ZPO and the DIS Rules. Article 14.3 ICC Rules provides for an opportunity to comment by the arbitrator concerned and the other party or parties. Thereafter, the **ICC Court shall decide** (as opposed to the arbitral tribunal under the Tenth Book of the ZPO and the DIS Rules) (art 14.3 ICC Rules). For arbitrations seated in Germany, subsequent **access to the competent higher regional court** pursuant to s 1037 para 3 ZPO is always open and may not be derogated by the parties (s 1037 para 1 ZPO). **3.105**

Grounds for replacement under arts 15.1 and 15.2 ICC Rules are not only death, resignation, or party agreement, but also a decision by the **ICC Court on its own initiative** finding inability or inactivity of an arbitrator. Before making such a decision, the arbitrator concerned and the parties shall be given an opportunity to comment (art 15.3 ICC Rules). Regarding replacement, the ICC Court has discretion as to whether or not to follow the original nomination process (art 15.4 cl 1 ICC Rules). Where the proceedings are already closed, the ICC Court may decide, instead of replacing an arbitrator, that the **remaining arbitrators shall continue** the arbitration and render the award (art 15.5 cl 1 ICC Rules). This is a useful means to counter obstruction tactics by arbitrators and parties who use termination of an arbitrator as a means to prevent or delay a decision which they consider unfavorable. **3.106**

3. IBA Guidelines on Conflicts of Interest in International Arbitration

In October 2014, the International Bar Association (IBA) adopted revised "Guidelines on Conflicts of Interest in International Arbitration," which replace a previous version of 2004.[104] These guidelines are the result of the efforts of a working group of numerous experts in international arbitration from more than a dozen countries, appointed by the Committee on Arbitration and ADR of the **3.107**

---

[104] In addition, in 1987, the IBA published Rules of Ethics for International Arbitrators, which also cover topics other than impartiality and independence of arbitrators. The guidelines described above supersede the IBA Rules of Ethics as to the matters treated therein (IBA Guidelines, Introduction at 8). We thus do not address the IBA Rules of Ethics in this section.

IBA. Thus, the guidelines are not the reflection of one specific set of applicable laws, much less German law alone, but "reflect the understanding of the IBA Arbitration committee as to the **best current international practice**."[105] They "are not legal provisions and do not override applicable national law or arbitral rules chosen by the parties."[106]

3.108 The guidelines follow a **two-tier approach**: on the one hand, there are **general standards** contained in part I of the guidelines. On the other hand, part II of the guidelines contain provisions on the practical application of the general standards. In this respect, the guidelines are subdivided into a total of four lists: (i) the **non-waivable red list**, containing scenarios where a person must not act as an arbitrator, irrespective of whether the parties, after full disclosure, would agree or not; (ii) the **waivable red list** with circumstances that give rise to justifiable doubts as to a person's neutrality and would thus generally exclude a person from being an arbitrator, unless the parties, after full disclosure, agree; (iii) the **orange list**, enumerating situations that in the eyes of the parties may give rise to justifiable doubts as to the arbitrator's impartiality or independence and which an arbitrator therefore ought to disclose; and (iv) the **green list**, containing situations that frequently occur in practice but do not give rise to doubts as to a person's impartiality or independence and thus do not even have to be disclosed by an arbitrator. The guidelines apply to both commercial and investment arbitration.[107] Even though the guidelines were published by a professional organization of practicing lawyers, their application is not limited to practicing lawyers acting as arbitrators. They may be applied just as well to arbitrators from other legal professions, such as active and retired judges or law professors, as well as arbitrators who are not lawyers at all.[108] We will include the guidelines in our analysis of grounds for challenge under German law as discussed below (see paras 3.118 *et seq.*).

4. *Significance at the Set Aside and Enforcement Stages*

3.109 An important issue associated with arbitrator neutrality and arbitrator challenges is the question what significance the lack of neutrality of an arbitrator (or the lack of agreed prerequisites) may have once the proceedings have reached the set aside or the enforcement stages. To the extent the competent higher regional court has rejected a challenge, its decision is final and binding (s 1065 para 1 cl 2 ZPO), and the neutrality of the challenged arbitrator is ***res judicata*** (*Rechtskraft*) as far as the underlying facts originally giving rise to the challenge are concerned.[109] Where the

---

105 IBA Guidelines, Introduction at 4.

106 IBA Guidelines, Introduction at 6.

107 IBA Guidelines, Introduction at 5.

108 IBA Guidelines, Introduction at 5; this has always been implicit in the guidelines, see, eg, the reference to former judges in Part II no 3.4.5 (formerly no 3.4.4).

109 Nacimiento/Abt/Stein, in: *Arbitration in Germany*, s 1037 para 24; Münch, in: MünchKommZPO, s 1037 para 32; Geimer, in: Zöller (ed), s 1037 para 6; Saenger, in: Saenger (ed), s 1037 para 6.

arbitral tribunal has rejected the challenge and the defeated party refrains from requesting the decision of the higher regional court, the party is **precluded** from raising the issue at the enforcement and set aside stages.[110]

Where a party refrained from bringing a challenge but could have done so because it was aware of the underlying facts, such challenge is generally again **precluded** at the enforcement and set aside stages. This is the result of the application of s 1037 para 2 cl 1 ZPO and the two-week deadline contained therein. In principle, a party who misses that deadline may no longer rely on the underlying facts, no matter whether during or after the arbitral proceedings.[111] An exception may exist based on public policy considerations: *ordre public* violations can never be precluded by missed deadlines, and they can always be brought forward in set aside and enforcement proceedings (ss 1059 para 2 no 2 lit b, 1060 para 2, 1061 para 2 ZPO). Thus, where the lack of neutrality amounts to an *ordre public* violation, it may still be relied on during enforcement or set aside proceedings, even though it may not have been raised at all or in time during the arbitral proceedings. This has been held to apply in particular with respect to grave and evident cases of partiality and lack of independence.[112] **3.110**

Finally, challenges that were still pending and that the arbitral tribunal simply overlooked or failed to decide are not precluded. At least where the time limit of s 1037 para 3 ZPO has not expired, the underlying facts can still be raised in set aside and enforcement proceedings (ss 1059 para 2 no 1 lit d, 1060 para 2 cl 1, 1061 para 2 ZPO).[113] **3.111**

II. Lack of Independence or Impartiality

Under German law, the principles of independence and impartiality are non-derogable cornerstones of any arbitral proceedings. At their core, they form part of the German procedural *ordre public* (s 1059 para 2 no 2 lit b ZPO) and are considered indispensable constitutional requirements in order for arbitral proceedings to be equivalent to state court litigation.[114] **3.112**

[110] BT-Drucks 13/5274, p 42; Mankowski, SchiedsVZ 2004, 304, 312; Voit, in: Musielak/Voit (eds), s 1037 para 6; Geimer, in: Zöller (ed), s 1037 para 6; Hartmann, in: Baumbach/Lauterbach/Albers/Hartmann (eds), s 1037 para 7.

[111] Reichold, in: Thomas/Putzo (eds), s 1037 para 9; Voit, in: Musielak/Voit (eds), s 1037 para 5; Saenger, in: Saenger (ed), s 1037 para 7.

[112] BGH NJW 1999, 2370; OLG München, BeckRS 2007, 00913; Schwab/Walter, ch 14 para 19; Münch, in: MünchKommZPO, s 1037 paras 35 *et seq.*, 39 *et seq.*; Geimer, in: Zöller (ed), s 1037 para 7; Voit, in: Musielak/Voit (eds), s 1037 para 6.

[113] OLG Stuttgart, SchiedsVZ 2003, 84, 87 with concurring note by Nacimiento/Geimer, SchiedsVZ 2003, 88, 90; Voit, in: Musielak/Voit (eds), s 1037 para 5.

[114] Münch, in: MünchKommZPO, s 1036 para 1; Schwab/Walter, ch 9 para 4; Geimer, in: Zöller (ed), s 1036 para 1; Saenger, in: Saenger (ed), s 1036 para 1. Internationally see Gaillard/Savage, paras 1022 *et seq.*

1. General Principles

3.113 Under German law, apart from the lack of agreed prerequisites (see para 3.133), an arbitrator can be challenged based on circumstances that give rise to justifiable doubts as to his or her impartiality or independence, s 1036 para 2 cl 1 ZPO. The German arbitration law does not further specify what is meant by "impartiality" and "independence." The two requirements are sometimes difficult to distinguish and are often viewed as two sides of the same coin—arbitrator neutrality. Broadly speaking, impartiality is more a subjective characteristic regarding the mental attitude of the arbitrator to the parties and the dispute, whereas independence is more an objective criterion for this connection.[115] German law requires "justifiable doubts" (s 1036 para 2 cl 1 ZPO). This means facts that are capable of triggering **suspicions in the eyes of a reasonable person**, not just in the subjective view of a party.[116] The provisions on impartiality and independence are mandatory law; there is party autonomy only with respect to prerequisites that the party may agree regarding the qualifications of an arbitrator.[117]

3.114 A party may challenge an arbitrator that it has appointed itself only on the basis of facts that the party learns after the appointment (s 1036 para 2 cl 2 ZPO). This provision can be seen as an expression of the general good faith principle that a party should not be allowed to act contrary to its own prior behaviour (*venire contra factum proprium*, s 242 BGB).[118]

3.115 The principles governing the challenge of arbitrators take precedence over the provisions of German substantive law allowing to void a contract based on errors regarding a person's qualifications (s 119 para 2 BGB). Thus, in case of a successful challenge, the arbitrator agreement is not considered void *ab initio* (s 142 para 1 BGB), but may be terminated with prospective effect (*ex nunc*) as the arbitrator is no longer able to perform his or her obligations (see para 3.203).[119]

3.116 In order to secure the parties' right to a neutral arbitrator, s 1036 para 1 cl 1 ZPO requires a prospective arbitrator to **disclose** all circumstances that may trigger doubts as to his or her impartiality or independence. Thus, the duty to disclose goes further than the grounds for challenge: in order for the disclosure duty to be triggered, "doubts"

---

[115] Lionnet/Lionnet, p 246; Born, pp 1775 *et seq.*; Blackaby/Partasides/Redfern/Hunter, paras 4.76 *et seq.*; Nacimiento/Abt/Stein, in: *Arbitration in Germany*, s 1036 para 29; similar Henn, BB 1993, Beil. 17, pp 13, 14; Rojahn/Jerger, NJW 2014, 1147.

[116] OLG Dresden, SchiedsVZ 2005, 159, 161; Münch, in: MünchKommZPO, s 1036 para 31; Hartmann, in: Baumbach/Lauterbach/Albers/Hartmann (eds), s 1036 para 3; Schwab/Walter, ch 16 para 49.

[117] Münch, in: MünchKommZPO, s 1036 para 29.

[118] BT-Drucks 13/5274, p 41; Lachmann, para 1029; Münch, in: MünchKommZPO, s 1036 para 46.

[119] BGHZ 17, 7, 8; Geimer, in: Zöller (ed), s 1037 para 2; Münch, in: MünchKommZPO, s 1036 para 27; Saenger, in: Saenger (ed), s 1037 para 4; Schwab/Walter, ch 14 para 3; Hartmann, in: Baumbach/Lauterbach/Albers/Hartmann (eds), s 1037 para 4.

suffice (see para 3.129), whereas for a successful challenge, "justifiable doubts" are necessary. The German arbitration law thereby largely follows art 12 Model Law.[120]

2. Typical Situations

The situations typically giving rise to arbitrator challenges can be grouped broadly into three categories: (a) personal relations between an arbitrator and a party or their counsel; (b) prior involvement of an arbitrator or persons close to the arbitrator in the subject matter of the dispute; and (c) an arbitrator's behaviour during the arbitral proceedings. **3.117**

a) **Personal Relations** Self-evidently, a person cannot act as an arbitrator with respect to a dispute in which the person him- or herself is involved. The same applies where the person is the **legal representative** of a party to the dispute. For instance, an active director (*Geschäftsführer*), management board member (*Vorstandsmitglied*), or supervisory board member (*Aufsichtsratsmitglied*) of a corporation is disqualified from acting as an arbitrator in a dispute in which the corporation is involved.[121] With regard to **former directors, management, and supervisory board members**, the circumstances of the individual case need to be taken into account. After a certain **"cooling off"** period, there may no longer be justifiable doubts as to a person's neutrality. What the appropriate period should be is again a question of the individual situation. The IBA Guidelines on Conflicts of Interest in International Arbitration generally take three years as a distinguishing factor. While this may be a proper rule of thumb, still each case needs to be analyzed based on its particular circumstances. For instance, where a person has served only very briefly on a corporation's supervisory board, the situation may be different from the case of a person who has been the corporation's CEO for many years. **3.118**

Likewise, **contractual and business relationships** between the arbitrator and one of the parties or its counsel can be grounds for challenge. An arbitrator should not hold shares in a party (except perhaps for very insignificant amounts), nor should an arbitrator be a tenant of a party.[122] Of high practical relevance are situations of prior or parallel **legal advice in unrelated matters**. A lawyer who regularly represents a party to the dispute in unrelated matters will likely not be considered sufficiently neutral to be able to act as an arbitrator.[123] By contrast, where an arbitrator **3.119**

---

[120] BT-Drucks 13/5274, p 40; Nacimiento/Abt/Stein, in: *Arbitration in Germany*, s 1036 para 3; Lachmann, para 967.

[121] IBA Guidelines, Part II, Non-Waivable Red List at 1.2; Münch, in: MünchKommZPO, s 1036 para 10; Schwab/Walter, ch 9 para 6; Nacimiento/Abt/Stein, in: *Arbitration in Germany*, s 1036 paras 28, 39; Voit, in: Musielak/Voit (eds), s 1036 para 5.

[122] OLG Naumburg, SchiedsVZ 2003, 134, 136; OLG Stuttgart, JW 1928, 1322; IBA Guidelines, Part II, Waivable Red List at 2.2; Münch, in: MünchKommZPO, s 1036 para 34; Mankowski, SchiedsVZ 2004, 304, 308.

[123] OLG Dresden, SchiedsVZ 2005, 159, 161; IBA Guidelines, Part II, Non-Waivable Red List at 1.4; Lachmann, para 983; Voit, in: Musielak/Voit (eds), s 1036 para 8.

or his or her law firm have advised a party on unrelated matters in the past, but have no ongoing relationship, an arbitrator may still be neutral, depending on the circumstances of the case, including, for instance, the financial volume of the prior engagement and the time that has passed since it has terminated.[124] An arbitrator may start to lack neutrality where he or she is **appointed frequently by one party**. Again, the circumstances of the individual case need to be considered. In highly specialized areas, there may only be a few very qualified arbitrators, such that repeated appointments are a practical necessity and thus may seem less suspicious than in other cases.[125] On the other hand, the fact that an arbitrator has acted together as an arbitrator with one of the co-arbitrators on several prior occasions should not impact neutrality.[126]

3.120 Finally, **close personal relationships** can raise "justifiable doubts" as to an arbitrator's neutrality. Besides the obvious cases of marriage, common-law spouses, engagement, and the like, in practice, social contacts and personal friendships are a frequently discussed topic. As a general matter, ordinary social contact, occasional invitations, occasional common leisure activities, or being on a first-name basis with someone does not suffice to challenge an arbitrator.[127] "Close" personal friendship—as well as grave hostility—is considered different. In the abstract, it is of course difficult to give a precise definition of who is a "close" friend and who is a "not so close" friend. From the perspective of the (prospective) arbitrator, the answer in a specific case may still be fairly straightforward: Can I imagine ruling against that person (or the party represented by that person) without being influenced by the fact that we know each other so well? The same applies the other way round in case of hostilities between an arbitrator and a party or its counsel. For the parties and their counsel, it is much more difficult to make these types of distinctions. They will need to rely on anecdotal evidence as to who is a "close" friend or a "special enemy" of an arbitrator and then make an informed judgment as to whether from the perspective of a reasonable party these circumstances give rise to justifiable doubts as to the neutrality of an arbitrator.

---

124 The IBA Guidelines on Conflicts of Interest in International Arbitration take the approach that services during the last three years should be disclosed (Part II, Orange List at 3.1). Further OLG Hamburg, SchiedsVZ 2006, 55, 56; Häberlein, BB 2003, Beil. 8, pp 7, 8; Nacimiento/Abt/Stein, in: *Arbitration in Germany*, s 1036 para 49; more generous Mankowski, SchiedsVZ 2004, 304, 310; Lachmann, para 986 who do not see an issue in case the representation is finally and definitely terminated, irrespective of the amount of time that has elapsed.

125 The IBA Guidelines on Conflicts of Interest in International Arbitration suggest that an arbitrator discloses that he "has within the past three years been appointed as arbitrator on two or more occasions by one of the parties or an affiliate of one of the parties" (Part II, Orange List at 3.1.3).

126 OLG Naumburg, SchiedsVZ 2003, 134, 137; Lachmann, para 1010; Münch, in: MünchKommZPO, s 1036 para 35.

127 OLG Frankfurt, NJW 2008, 1325, 1326; KG SchiedsVZ 2010, 225, 226; Münch, in: MünchKommZPO, s 1036 para 34; Voit, in: Musielak/Voit (eds), s 1036 para 8; Hartmann, in: Baumbach/Lauterbach/Albers/Hartmann (eds), s 1036 para 4; Saenger, in: Saenger (ed), s 1036 para 4. Opposing view: Lachmann, para 1003.

b) **Prior Involvement in the Subject Matter of the Dispute** It goes without saying that neither the arbitrator nor any lawyer associated with him or her in the same law firm can advise on the matter in dispute. Prior legal advice of the **arbitrator or his or her law firm on the dispute** will also disqualify in most cases.[128] Exceptions may be considered where the advice was limited to a defined and limited set of issues that are clearly not or no longer relevant to the dispute. Similarly, a person who has publicly taken a view on the merits of the case is subject to justifiable doubts as to his or her neutrality.[129] **Prior discussions of the merits of the case** as part of the communications with a party during the appointment process are likely to disqualify a candidate, whereas listening to a general description of the nature of the case and what a party views as important issues should not present a problem.[130] Similarly, prior **publications** on abstract questions of law that may be relevant to the outcome of the case generally do not impact neutrality.[131] **3.121**

Where a person has been involved in prior attempts to resolve the dispute by means of ADR, such as **mediation or conciliation**, caution is necessary. A former mediator or conciliator will generally lack neutrality.[132] Thus, where such person is asked nevertheless to act as an arbitrator on the same dispute (med/arb), it is prudent to ask for both sides' express consent to do so. The same applies where the parties agree to attempt to mediate a dispute that is already in arbitration (arb/med), and want one of the arbitrators, eg the chairman, to act as mediator. **3.122**

c) **Behavior During the Proceedings** It is in an arbitrator's best interest to make sure that his or her behavior during arbitral proceedings does not give rise to doubts as to neutrality. The parties are likely to "watch" the arbitrators closely in this respect, and in some cases, they may be particularly "nervous" about the neutrality of the arbitrator appointed by the other side. Arbitrators should not accept **gifts or invitations** from the parties.[133] It is good practice not to engage in **3.123**

128 OLG Hamburg, OLGRspr. 5 (1902), 205; DIS arbitral tribunal, SchiedsVZ 2003, 94, 96; IBA Guidelines, Part II, Waivable Red List at 2.1; Münch, in: MünchKommZPO, s 1036 para 36.

129 OLG Frankfurt, NJW-RR 2008, 801, 802; Münch, in: MünchKommZPO, s 1036 para 36; Schwab/Walter, ch 14 para 8; Voit, in: Musielak/Voit (eds), s 1036 para 8. Opposing view: Geimer, in: Zöller (ed), s 1036 para 11.

130 OLG Hamburg, OLGRspr. 5 (1902), 205; OLG Dresden, JW 1938, 2154, 2155; Lörcher/Lörcher, SchiedsVZ 2005, 179, 186; Münch, in: MünchKommZPO, s 1036 para 37.

131 OLG Naumburg, SchiedsVZ 2003, 134, 137; OLG Hamburg, JW 1918, 572; *Saenger*, in Saenger (ed), s 1036 para 8; Lachmann, para 1001; Geimer, in: Zöller (ed), s 1036 para 11; Schwab/Walter, ch 9 para 8; Mankowski, SchiedsVZ 2004, 304, 308.

132 Münch, in: MünchKommZPO, s 1036 para 36; Voit, in: Musielak/Voit (eds), s 1035 para 17. Opposing view for conciliation: OLG Frankfurt, SchiedsVZ 2006, 329, 331; Trappe, SchiedsVZ 2012, 79, 83. Section 3 para 2 German Mediation Act (MediationsG) now prohibits mediators from acting *for a party* in matters they have worked on as mediators; this should not be understood to preclude a mediator per se from acting as arbitrator, Ulrici, in: MünchKommFamFG, s 3 MediationsG para 12. Opposing view: Trappe, SchiedsVZ 2012, 79, 83, 84.

133 Henn, BB 1993, Beil. 17, pp 13, 16; Schwab/Walter, ch 14 para 8; Voit, in: Musielak/Voit (eds), s 1036 para 8; Münch, in: MünchKommZPO, s 1036 para 39; Hartmann, in: Baumbach/Lauterbach/Albers/Hartmann (eds), s 1036 para 4.

ex parte **communications** with only one party.[134] Where it occurs, the arbitrator should inform the co-arbitrators, and the tribunal should decide as to whether the other party needs to be informed. If necessary, each party ought to be admonished to communicate to the entire tribunal with notice to the other party or parties. Whether an arbitrator is indeed subject to challenge when one of the above occurs, is a different question which depends very much on the facts of the case. For instance, where an arbitrator merely listens, politely ends the communication at an early stage, reports to the other arbitrators, and the arbitral tribunal discloses to the other party, there should not be any ground for challenge. By contrast, where an arbitrator not only listens but also gives answers on topics regarding the substance of the case and does not disclose the incident to the remainder of the arbitral tribunal and the other party, a different analysis may be in place.

3.124 The conduct of the proceedings as such may also give rise to justifiable doubts as to neutrality, albeit only in particularly grave situations. It does not come as a surprise that this situation is the subject of ongoing debate, especially regarding the conduct of party-appointed arbitrators.[135] Despite the peculiarities of arbitration as a creation of party autonomy and the necessity for a case-by-case analysis, it is widely agreed that justifiable doubts arise where an arbitrator acts like a party representative for one side. However, this threshold is not exceeded where a party-appointed arbitrator merely makes sure that the tribunal duly takes into account the **arguments brought forward by "his" or "her" party**.[136] Likewise, the fact that an arbitrator asks **tough questions** only in the direction of one party, but not the other, may not be particularly good practice and will certainly be seen by the parties as an example of lacking diplomacy; nevertheless, often it will not rise to the level of justifiable doubts required for a successful challenge. The same applies where the chairman is **particularly strict** in conducting the proceedings, or where an arbitrator appears to be sloppy and unprepared.[137] Likewise, in German practice, it is not a ground for challenge where the arbitral tribunal offers **preliminary views** on the case, even if unsolicited by the parties. On the contrary, German parties and German practitioners often are very desirous of such views in order to be able to better focus their case, submissions, and arguments, as well as to explore possible ranges for a settlement.[138]

---

[134] Saenger, in: Saenger (ed), s 1036 para 10; Münch, in: MünchKommZPO, s 1036 para 39; Lachmann, para 1019; Voit, in: Musielak/Voit (eds), s 1036 para 8.

[135] Schwab/Walter, ch 14 paras 7 *et seq.*; Franzen, NJW 1986, 299 *et seq.*; Mankowski, SchiedsVZ 2004, 304, 311; Lachmann, paras 970 *et seq.*; Nacimiento/Abt/Stein, in: *Arbitration in Germany*, s 1036 paras 30 *et seq.*

[136] Lachmann, para 974.

[137] OLG Frankfurt, SchiedsVZ 2010, 52, 54; KG BeckRS 2011, 07078; Münch, in: MünchKommZPO, s 1036 para 40; Hartmann, in: Baumbach/Lauterbach/Albers/Hartmann (eds), s 1036 para 4; Geimer, in: Zöller (ed), s 1036 para 14.

[138] Mankowski, SchiedsVZ 2004, 304, 311; Schwab/Walter, ch 14 para 8; Münch, in: MünchKommZPO, s 1036 para 41; Lachmann, paras 1020 *et seq.*

A gray area exists with respect to **settlement proposals**. German state courts are at liberty to make unsolicited settlement proposals; in recent years, state court proceedings have become even more "pro-settlement" (s 278 ZPO as amended). Arbitral tribunals should be more reluctant. There is no provision equivalent to s 278 ZPO in the German arbitration law. Thus, even though an unsolicited settlement proposal as such may not necessarily be a ground for challenge per se,[139] it is still good practice in Germany that the tribunal asks for all parties' consent before doing so.[140] **3.125**

Individual **mistakes** in the conduct of the proceedings as such are generally not sufficient to justify the challenge of an arbitrator, neither with respect to procedural issues nor regarding the application of substantive law.[141] The situation may be different where there are additional circumstances clearly pointing towards bias, such as a series of "mistakes" that actually all or almost all favor one party over the other. At the other end of the spectrum, there are of course also clear grounds for challenge as a result of behavior during the proceedings, such as insults of a party or its counsel. **3.126**

Finally, it should be noted that an analysis of whether there are grounds for challenge always requires a look at the **totality of the circumstances**. Thus, where there are several individual circumstances questioning the neutrality of an arbitrator, it may well be the case that none of them, when viewed in pure isolation, would be sufficient to carry a challenge, but when viewed in combination, the totality of the circumstances may well alter the analysis.[142] **3.127**

3. *Disclosure Obligation*

The obligation to disclose circumstances that may give rise to doubts as to a prospective arbitrator's neutrality (s 1036 para 1 cl 1 ZPO) safeguards the parties' right to **impartial and independent decision-makers**. The obligation is a continuing duty **throughout the arbitral proceedings** (s 1036 para 1 cl 2 ZPO). As is common in other arbitration laws and the rules of arbitral institutions, German law expresses the disclosure obligation as a procedural duty. At the same time, under German law, the disclosure obligation could also be derived from substantive law. Despite the fact that in general parties are responsible for gathering themselves **3.128**

---

139 OLG München, SchiedsVZ 2008, 102, 104; Lachmann, paras 1021 *et seq.*; Hartmann, in: Baumbach/Lauterbach/Albers/Hartmann (eds), s 1036 para 4; Münch, in: MünchKommZPO, s 1036 para 41; Kröll, NJW 2009, 1183, 1186.

140 See, eg, IBA Rules of Ethics for International Arbitration, at 8: "*Where the parties have so requested, or consented to a suggestion to this effect by the arbitral tribunal,* the tribunal as a whole (or the presiding arbitrator where appropriate), may make proposals for settlement to both parties simultaneously, and preferably in the presence of each other" (emphasis added).

141 OLG München, BeckRS 2008, 10261; Münch, in: MünchKommZPO, s 1036 para 40; Hartmann, in: Baumbach/Lauterbach/Albers/Hartmann (eds), s 1036 para 4; Lachmann, para 1018; Kröll, NJW 2009, 1183, 1186.

142 Münch, in: MünchKommZPO, s 1036 para 40; Kröll, NJW 2009, 1183, 1186.

whatever information they deem relevant for a contract, the obligation of good faith and fair dealing (**s 242 BGB**) can trigger an unwritten obligation to disclose facts and circumstances that are of outstanding importance to the other parties as they may have the potential to frustrate the very purpose of the agreement.[143] As far as the appointment of an arbitrator is concerned, it is indeed the very purpose of an arbitrator agreement that would be frustrated if the appointee were lacking impartiality or independence.

3.129 The disclosure obligation differs from the ground for challenge in two respects. First, the disclosure obligation does not cover agreed prerequisites; in this respect, as a matter of German arbitration law, the parties need to do their own diligence.[144] Second, the disclosure obligation is already triggered by "**doubts," not only "justifiable doubts"** as to an arbitrator's neutrality. Thus, pursuant to the pure wording of s 1036 para 1 cl 1 ZPO, "any" doubts would suffice. Still, doubts must be plausible from an objective point of view; otherwise, the disclosure obligation would be without limits.[145]

3.130 In this context, it is important to **strike the right balance**. On the one hand, it is of course prudent to disclose more rather than less. On the other hand, disclosure should not be excessive. In recent years, there has been a trend to ever increasing disclosure "as a matter of precaution." At the same time, arbitral institutions sometimes refuse to appoint candidates that have made statements of impartiality and independence that contain these types of qualifications. It is difficult to give abstract guidance on this issue, as each case is likely to be different. As a very general rule of thumb, however, it would strike us as being useful to somewhat curtail disclosure back to its roots. The orange list contained in the IBA Guidelines on Conflicts of Interest in International Arbitration can serve as a good point of departure for an analysis of a specific situation. Note that these guidelines generally include not only relations and prior activities with one of the parties, but also with affiliates of a party, ie entities belonging to one group of companies (including the parent company).[146]

3.131 The disclosure obligation needs to be fulfilled **without undue delay**.[147] At a minimum, it needs to be addressed to the party suggesting the appointment of a person as arbitrator. Where the appointment is made notwithstanding a prior disclosure,

[143] Lachmann, para 1032; Emmerich, in: MünchKommBGB, s 311 para 72 with further references.

[144] Münch, in: MünchKommZPO, s 1036 para 19; Saenger, in: Saenger (ed), s 1036 para 3. Opposing view: Lachmann, paras 1046 *et seq.*

[145] Geimer, in: Zöller (ed), s 1036 para 9; Hartmann, in: Baumbach/Lauterbach/Albers/Hartmann (eds), s 1036 para 2; Lachmann, para 1036; Saenger, in: Saenger (ed), s 1036 para 4; KG SchiedsVZ 2010, 225, 227.

[146] IBA Guidelines, fn 4.

[147] Nacimiento/Abt/Stein, in: *Arbitration in Germany*, s 1036 para 10; Münch, in: MünchKommZPO, s 1036 para 17; Hartmann, in: Baumbach/Lauterbach/Albers/Hartmann (eds), s 1036 para 2.

the other party also needs to be informed.[148] Even though the law is silent as to the form of a disclosure, it is of course **prudent to do it in writing.**[149] The obligation is not limited to circumstances that form the present knowledge of a (prospective) arbitrator. Instead, the statutory wording is objective; the existence of circumstances giving rise to doubts is sufficient to trigger the disclosure obligation. Thus, a (prospective) arbitrator is well advised to do **proper research,**[150] eg by way of a conflict check that is customary in larger law firms. A (prospective) arbitrator who overlooks circumstances acts at his or her own peril.[151]

The **sanctions** for violations of the disclosure obligation can be twofold. First, it constitutes a **breach of contract** with respect to the arbitrator agreement (or a corresponding pre-contractual duty) and may thus trigger a **claim for damages** (unless the arbitrator can demonstrate that he or she acted without fault, s 280 para 1 cl 2 BGB), even though the amount of damages may be limited (eg useless expenses, and—to the extent it has already been paid—arbitrator compensation).[152] Second, a breach of the disclosure obligation may, in exceptional circumstances, be **indicative** of a lack of neutrality and thus support the challenge of an arbitrator. However, this is certainly **not an automatic consequence**. In general, the mere breach of the disclosure obligation does not equal a lack of neutrality; only clear and severe violations of the disclosure obligation may potentially trigger a right to challenge an arbitrator.[153] **3.132**

III. Lack of Agreed Prerequisites

An arbitrator may be challenged for lack of agreed prerequisites (s 1036 para 2 cl 1 ZPO). Examples for agreed prerequisites include a certain **formal legal qualification**, eg a lawyer admitted to practice in Germany. The parties may also agree on certain nationality requirements. Likewise, the parties may agree on a certain **age, number of years of practice, religion, or sex**. In the arbitration context, these criteria are not considered to constitute impermissible discrimination.[154] Whilst challenges based on lack of neutrality can be brought on the basis of "justifiable doubts," a successful challenge for lack of agreed prerequisites requires a showing that an agreed prerequisite is missing, and not merely justifiable doubts as to such **3.133**

[148] Häberlein, BB 2003, Beil. 8, pp 7, 9; Münch, in: MünchKommZPO, s 1036 para 21; Lachmann, para 1040.

[149] Lachmann, para 1042; Münch, in: MünchKommZPO, s 1036 para 22.

[150] Häberlein, BB 2003, Beil. 8, pp 7, 9; Lachmann, in: *Festschrift Geimer*, pp 513, 518.

[151] Similarly Schwab/Walter, ch 12 para 9, ch 14 para 1; Gal, pp 265 *et seq.*

[152] Schlosser, in: Stein/Jonas (eds), s 1036 para 69; Nacimiento/Abt/Stein, in: *Arbitration in Germany*, s 1036 para 22; Voit, in: Musielak/Voit (eds), s 1036 para 3; Saenger ZPO, s 1036 para 6.

[153] OLG Frankfurt, NJW 2008, 1325, 1326; KG SchiedsVZ 2010, 225, 227; OLG Karlsruhe, BeckRS 2006, 19851; OLG Naumburg, SchiedsVZ 2003, 134, 137; Lachmann, para 1043; Voit, in: Musielak/Voit (eds), s 1036 para 3; stricter Saenger, in: Saenger (ed), s 1036 para 11.

[154] Koepp, SchiedsVZ 2011, 306, 313; Münch, in: MünchKommZPO, s 1035 paras 52 *et seq.*; Voit, in: Musielak/Voit (eds), s 1035 para 18.

prerequisite.[155] Self-evidently, there can be grey areas, in particular where the parties have agreed on somewhat unspecific requirements, such as "knowledge of tax law" or "familiarity with M&A practice" and the like (which is one of the reasons why parties should be discouraged from agreeing on such unclear requirements in the first place).

IV. Challenge Procedure

3.134 Where a party declares he or she is going to challenge an arbitrator, the challenge procedure set forth in s 1037 ZPO is triggered. In other words, the declaration of a challenge as such does not terminate the office of an arbitrator.[156] The statutory challenge procedure is geared towards achieving a compromise between **safeguarding the fundamental, constitutional requirement** that the members of the arbitral tribunal are neutral, and **limiting the parties' ability to abuse** arbitrator challenges as a means to unduly delay or obstruct the arbitral proceedings.[157]

3.135 The provisions in s 1037 ZPO closely follow art 13 Model Law. As set out above (para 3.101), the parties are free to agree on the details of the challenge procedure, except for the fact that there must always be an opportunity for the party launching the challenge to bring the challenge in front of the competent higher regional court (s 1037 paras 1 and 3 ZPO).

1. Challenge Declaration and the Two-week Deadline

3.136 A party bringing a challenge must declare which arbitrator(s) it rejects for which reasons, and that **declaration, addressed to the arbitral tribunal,** must be made **in writing within the statutory two-week deadline.**[158] A challenge declared during a hearing, even if recorded verbatim, does not suffice, but must be repeated in writing in order to be effective.[159] Only parties can challenge arbitrators; arbitrators cannot challenge each other.[160] Where one arbitrator feels that another gives ground for a challenge, the only option would be to inform the parties accordingly to enable them to decide on a challenge. From a practical perspective, arbitrators doing that obviously walk a fine line between safeguarding the tribunal's neutrality, their

---

[155] Münch, in: MünchKommZPO, s 1036 para 7.

[156] Geimer, in: Zöller (ed), s 1037 para 3; Lachmann, paras 1080 *et seq.*; Reichold, in: Thomas/Putzo (eds), s 1037 para 2; Schwab/Walter, ch 14 para 3; Schlosser, in: Stein/Jonas (eds), s 1037 para 19.

[157] Nacimiento/Abt/Stein, in: *Arbitration in Germany*, s 1037 para 1; Hartmann, in: Baumbach/Lauterbach/Albers/Hartmann (eds), s 1037 para 1; Münch, in: MünchKommZPO, s 1037 para 1; Voit, in: Musielak/Voit (eds), s 1037 para 1.

[158] Hartmann, in: Baumbach/Lauterbach/Albers/Hartmann (eds), s 1037 para 4; Lachmann, para 1055; Saenger, in: Saenger (ed), s 1037 para 3; Schlosser, in: Stein/Jonas (eds), s 1037 para 3; Schwab/Walter, ch 14 para 12; Voit, in: Musielak/Voit (eds), s 1037 para 3; Zimmermann, s 1037 para 2.

[159] Cf s 1037 para 2 cl 1 ZPO; Münch, in: MünchKommZPO, s 1037 para 9; Schwab/Walter, ch 14 para 16.

[160] Münch, in: MünchKommZPO, s 1037 para 8; Lachmann, para 1054; LAG Köln, NZA-RR 2002, 270, 271.

confidentiality obligations, and exposing themselves to a challenge for lack of neutrality.[161] Thus, in most cases, such action by an arbitrator geared against another arbitrator will only be a means of last resort.

The calculation of the two-week period follows general principles of German law (s 222 ZPO, ss 187 *et seq.* BGB). The two-week period starts to run once the party has **knowledge of the underlying facts**, at the earliest, however, once the party has become aware that the arbitral tribunal has been constituted (s 1037 para 2 cl 1 ZPO).[162] The party bringing the challenge bears the burden of proof that the challenge has been brought on time. Thus, in practice, there is a tension between complying with the deadline on the one hand and not launching premature or ill-founded challenges on the other. Knowledge of the facts means knowledge of such facts that give rise to justifiable doubts as to an arbitrator's neutrality (s 1036 para 2 ZPO). Thus, in our view it should be considered—similar to the accepted principles governing the termination of service or other long-term agreements for cause[163]—to **allow a party to investigate the facts thoroughly** before it is compelled to bring a challenge. We think this should include asking an arbitrator to comment on certain circumstances that have raised a party's suspicions. The advantage of this approach would be not to force parties to **"shoot before they ask"** with the obvious collateral detrimental effects on the arbitral proceedings. Parties should be aware, however, that such an approach is not yet accepted by German courts.[164] For the time being, it is prudent to declare a challenge sooner rather than later.[165] **3.137**

2 *Withdrawal or Consent by the Other Party*

In reaction to a challenge by a party, an arbitrator may decide to withdraw voluntarily in order not to be forced to go through the challenge procedure with the arbitral tribunal, a third party called to decide upon the challenge, or even the—public—state court proceedings mandatorily provided for in s 1037 para 3 ZPO. An arbitrator may prefer the discreet withdrawal over the potentially negative publicity associated with a time-consuming and nerve-racking fight over his or her neutrality. Likewise, the other party may concur that the challenge is well-founded and thus agree with the challenge, such that the office of the arbitrator (as well as the arbitrator agreement) are terminated consensually. More often than not, however, there will be no such consensual solution, in which case the **arbitral** **3.138**

---

161 Münch, in: MünchKommZPO, s 1037 para 8.

162 Where a challenge is based on a totality of circumstances (see above para 3.127), the trigger date is the date of the individual event that tips the balance in favor of bias; similarly Schlosser, in: Stein/Jonas (eds), s 1037 para 3.

163 Henssler, in: MünchKommBGB, s 626 para 298 with further references.

164 Instructive, eg, VG Berlin, SchiedsVZ 2010, 107.

165 Münch, in: MünchKommZPO, s 1037 para 12; Hartmann, in: Baumbach/Lauterbach/Albers/Hartmann (eds), s 1036 para 6; Lachmann, para 1060; Voit, in: Musielak/Voit (eds), s 1036 para 10; OLG Dresden, SchiedsVZ 2005, 159, 162.

tribunal is called to decide, as described below (para 3.139). In case of withdrawal or party agreement, the former arbitrator will not be deemed to have acknowledged that there were proper grounds for the challenge (s 1038 para 2 ZPO). This may be important for the former arbitrator's compensation claims under the—then also terminated—arbitrator agreement (see para 3.197); the former arbitrator continues to be free to argue that he or she was actually neutral.

3. Decision by the Arbitral Tribunal

3.139 Where the arbitral tribunal is called to decide upon the challenge of an arbitrator pursuant to s 1037 para 2 cl 2 ZPO, it does so **including the person subject to the challenge.** Whilst this may be counter-intuitive to persons less familiar with the arbitral process, it is fully in line with art 13 Model Law and **international practice**, which the German legislature—after some discussion—adopted.[166] Given that there is always the option to bring the challenge in front of the competent **higher regional court** if the arbitral tribunal does not agree with the challenge, the parties' right to a neutral decision is guaranteed (s 1037 paras 1 and 3 ZPO). Thus, a sole arbitrator decides him- or herself upon the challenge, a three-person panel decides with all three arbitrators.

3.140 The parties are free to agree that instead of the arbitral tribunal, a third party or institution ought to decide on an arbitrator challenge (s 1037 para 1 ZPO), such as the ICC Court in ICC proceedings (art 14.3 ICC Rules).[167] By contrast, it is unclear whether the parties could agree to **completely dispense** with the decision of the arbitral tribunal provided for in s 1037 para 2 ZPO and thus immediately go to the higher regional court pursuant to s 1037 para 3 ZPO. The German higher regional courts that have addressed this issue appear to be split by and large equally on this issue, and so is German legal doctrine.[168] In our view, **party autonomy should prevail** on this issue. The wording of s 1037 para 1 ZPO is not entirely clear. It could be understood such that only s 1037 para 3 ZPO is absolutely mandatory, which would support our position that s 1037 para 2 ZPO can be completely dispensed with. Admittedly, the wording states that the parties may agree "on a procedure for the challenge of an arbitrator." This could be read to mean that there must at least be some "procedure" before the case goes to the higher regional court.

166 During the legislative process, the intention originally was to exclude the person subject to the challenge from the decision; later on, this concept was given up in favor of the Model Law solution; see, eg, BT-Drucks 13/5274, pp 6 *et seq.*, 41; Münch, in: MünchKommZPO, s 1037 paras 4, 16.

167 Münch, in: MünchKommZPO, s 1037 para 6; Voit, in: Musielak/Voit (eds), s 1037 para 2; Hartmann, in: Baumbach/Lauterbach/Albers/Hartmann (eds), s 1037 para 3; Zimmermann, s 1037 para 1.

168 In favor of the parties' right to completely derogate s 1037 para 2 ZPO: Schlosser, in: Stein/Jonas (eds), s 1037 para 2; Hartmann, in: Baumbach/Lauterbach/Albers/Hartmann (eds), s 1037 para 5; Voit, in: Musielak/Voit (eds), s 1037 para 2; OLG Hamburg, SchiedsVZ 2006, 55, 56; against such complete derogation: Münch, in: MünchKommZPO, s 1037 para 5; Saenger, in: Saenger (ed), s 1037 para 1; OLG München, SchiedsVZ 2006, 286, 288; BeckRS 2007, 00709.

The legislative materials can be read to support this latter position,[169] but when read properly, they do not really address the issue at hand here. Thus, the correct interpretation of the limits of party autonomy in the present context really turns on the purpose of the provisions at issue. The main purpose of s 1037 ZPO is to strike a balance between ensuring neutrality and safeguarding speed and efficiency. We are not convinced that s 1037 para 2 cl 2 ZPO has as a main purpose to keep the caseload of the higher regional court low. Thus, a party agreement that dispenses with a decision of the arbitral tribunal is fully in line with the purposes of the statute.

4 Court Review

Where the arbitral tribunal (or a third party called upon to decide) rejects the challenge, a party may request the decision of the competent higher regional court (s 1037 para 3 ZPO). The request must be made within **one month** after the petitioner becomes aware that the challenge was unsuccessful. In order for the request to be on time, filing with the higher regional court is sufficient, provided it is served upon the other party in due course (s 167 ZPO). This applies even where a higher regional court at the wrong venue received the request.[170] **3.141**

In general, the higher regional court will make a **full review of the challenge on the merits.**[171] The party requesting the decision of the court may submit new facts, provided that they fall within the **same ground for challenge**; otherwise, new facts are precluded as a result of the two-week deadline for bringing the challenge (s 1037 para 2 cl 1 ZPO).[172] The court will give the other party and possibly the challenged arbitrator an opportunity to comment (s 1063 para 1 cl 2 ZPO). Usually, it will not schedule an oral hearing. The higher regional court may reject the request where it finds that the arbitral tribunal *evidently* does not have jurisdiction for the entire case.[173] The decision of the higher regional court, whether on the merits or on procedural grounds, is **final and binding** and not subject to any further appeal or review (s 1065 para 1 cl 2 ZPO). **3.142**

5. Continued Arbitral Proceedings

Section 1037 para 3 cl 2 ZPO allows the arbitral tribunal, in its discretion, to continue the arbitral proceedings (including the challenged arbitrator) while the challenge procedure is ongoing. This provision allows the preservation of **efficiency and speed** in the arbitral process. Nevertheless, it is commonly understood that it **3.143**

169 BT-Drucks 13/5274, p 41.

170 Hartmann, in: Baumbach/Lauterbach/Albers/Hartmann (eds), s 1037 para 5; Lachmann, para 1098; Reichold, in: Thomas/Putzo (eds), s 1037 para 5; OLG Naumburg, SchiedsVZ 2003, 134, 135; OLG München, SchiedsVZ 2008, 102, 103.

171 OLG München, NJOZ 2006, 1194, 1195 *et seq.*; Mankowski, SchiedsVZ 2004, 304, 306; Münch, in: MünchKommZPO, s 1037 para 28; Geimer, in: Zöller (ed), s 1037 para 2; Lachmann, para 1102.

172 Münch, in: MünchKommZPO, s 1037 para 28.

173 Münch, in: MünchKommZPO, s 1037 para 22; OLG München, SchiedsVZ 2008, 102, 104.

should be **used with caution**. When exercising its discretion, the arbitral tribunal also needs to bear in mind the inefficiency and cost involved in case the challenge is ultimately successful. In such a case, the tribunal will have forced the parties to incur potentially useless expenses for the continuation of the proceedings with a biased arbitrator, eg an extensive evidentiary hearing, and that portion of the proceedings may need to be repeated with a substitute arbitrator. Thus, it is good practice to suspend the arbitral proceedings while a challenge is pending. A tribunal should make use of the continuation option only where it concludes that the challenge is clearly unfounded and merely brought as a means of delay tactics or for other improper reasons.[174]

V. Inability to Perform and Undue Delay

3.144 Where an arbitrator is—for legal or factual reasons—unable to perform his or her obligations, or where an arbitrator does not perform such obligations within a reasonable time, the office may end in one of three ways: (i) voluntary withdrawal by the arbitrator; (ii) party agreement; or (iii) decision by the competent higher regional court upon motion by either party (s 1038 para 1 ZPO). In scenarios (i) and (ii), an arbitrator is not deemed to have acknowledged that there were actually legally valid grounds for terminating the office (s 1038 para 2 ZPO). In all scenarios, the arbitral proceedings may be continued with a substitute arbitrator (s 1039 ZPO). Section 1038 ZPO closely mirrors art 14 Model Law.

3.145 The termination of the office of an arbitrator needs to be clearly distinguished from the **termination of the arbitrator agreement** (see para 3.191). In addition, termination pursuant to s 1038 ZPO needs to be distinguished from the **challenge procedure** contained in s 1037 ZPO. An arbitrator can be challenged pursuant to ss 1036, 1037 ZPO for lack of neutrality or agreed prerequisites; the law provides for strict deadlines and allows for the arbitral proceedings to continue while the challenge is pending. By contrast, termination of the office of an arbitrator based on inability to perform or undue delay is **not bound to statutory deadlines** (see para 3.152). Finally, there may be instances of arbitrator **misconduct that are neither sanctionable by challenge nor under s 1038 ZPO**, such as mere violations of an arbitrator's disclosure obligations (s 1036 para 1 ZPO), breaches of confidentiality, or the involvement of assistants beyond what is allowed under the law or an agreement with the parties. Unless these violations rise to a level that give grounds for termination of the arbitrator agreement for cause (see para 3.196) or grounds for set aside of an award under s 1059 ZPO, the only sanctions are a potential claim for damages under s 280 para 1 BGB, plus the potential reputational damage to the arbitrator that may reduce his or her prospects of being appointed again in the future.

[174] OLG Frankfurt, SchiedsVZ 2010, 52, 55; Schwab/Walter, ch 14 para 26; Schlosser, in: Stein/Jonas (eds), s 1037 para 17; Zimmermann, s 1037 para 3; Hartmann, Baumbach/Lauterbach/Albers/Hartmann (eds), s 1037 para 6.

1. Inability to Perform

Inability to perform may be based on **legal or factual grounds** that usually arise after the appointment of an arbitrator. Legal grounds leading to inability may be the **loss of legal capacity** or the **lack of a necessary governmental approval**, such as in the case of active judges and public officials (including law professors at state-owned universities, see paras 3.83 *et seq.*).[175] Where an arbitrator **later becomes a party or a legal representative thereof**, some courts and scholars have concluded inability,[176] even though technically, this is also a ground for challenge. Nevertheless, it is probably correct that in such a scenario an arbitrator cannot continue to serve even though the parties may have missed the two-week deadline for challenge provided for in s 1037 para 2 cl 1 ZPO. Termination of the arbitrator agreement is also sometimes seen as a scenario triggering inability to perform for legal grounds,[177] even though this appears as a construct that is not very persuasive. Instead, it should be possible to come to appropriate practical solutions by other means: where the arbitrator terminates the arbitrator agreement, his or her withdrawal (in the sense of s 1038 para 1 cl 2 alt. 1 ZPO) is implied. Where the parties jointly terminate the arbitrator agreement, they impliedly agree on the termination of the arbitrator's office (s 1038 para 1 cl 2 alt 2 ZPO). Unilateral termination of the arbitrator agreement by one of the parties is generally not possible (see para 3.198). Where an **arbitrator dies**, his office terminates *ex lege* without the need for any further action by the parties or the court. The reason is that the office of an arbitrator is a personal office that cannot be transferred to the heirs or successors.[178] As can be seen, in all of these scenarios, there is no need to resort to the provisions on inability to perform. 3.146

Factual reasons triggering inability to perform may be serious permanent illness with **no reasonable prospect of recovery** or **imprisonment** of an arbitrator for a substantial period of time.[179] Traditionally, examples such as a long trip abroad or moving to a far-away country have been considered in this context, too.[180] It should 3.147

175 Hartmann, in: Baumbach/Lauterbach/Albers/Hartmann (eds), s 1038 para 4; Lachmann, paras 1122, 1124; OLG München, BeckRS 2006, 27806; Nacimiento/Abt/Stein, in: *Arbitration in Germany*, s 1038 para 10. As stated above, in such a scenario the appointment as such is valid; thus, the office needs to be formally terminated pursuant to the provisions of s 1038 ZPO; it does not terminate automatically as a matter of law.

176 Schwab/Walter, ch 10 para 31; Münch, in: MünchKommZPO, s 1038 para 15; Saenger, in: Saenger (ed), s 1038 para 3.

177 Münch, in: MünchKommZPO, s 1038 para 15; Schwab/Walter, ch 10 para 33.

178 Similarly Münch, in: MünchKommZPO, s 1038 para 14.

179 Geimer, in: Zöller (ed), s 1038 para 2; Hartmann, in: Baumbach/Lauterbach/Albers/Hartmann (eds), s 1038 para 4; Saenger, in: Saenger (ed), s 1038 para 3; Reichold, in: Thomas/Putzo (eds), s 1038 para 3; Voit, in: Musielak/Voit (eds), s 1038 para 5; OLG Köln, April 11, 2003, 9 SchH 27/02 (unreported).

180 Nacimiento/Abt/Stein, in: *Arbitration in Germany*, s 1038 para 11; Geimer, in: Zöller (ed), s 1038 para 2; Saenger, in: Saenger (ed), s 1038 para 3; Schwab/Walter, ch 10 para 31.

be noted, however, that given modern means of transportation and communication, these examples should be much less relevant today.

3.148 Legal and factual inability must relate to circumstances that are, viewed from the present point in time, **more or less permanent**. Where it is foreseeable that the circumstances presently inhibiting an arbitrator will go away in the future, the case is probably not one of inability, but potentially one of undue delay.[181] Importantly, in all of the above scenarios (except death of an arbitrator), inability to perform does not automatically excuse the arbitrator or terminate his or her office. For reasons of legal certainty, the potentially applicable general civil law provisions (s 275 BGB) are superseded by s 1038 para 1 cl 2 ZPO, requiring a clearly communicated decision by the arbitrator, the parties, or the court.[182]

2. *Undue Delay*

3.149 Undue delay covers scenarios where the arbitrator is, in principle, able to act (as opposed to the cases of inability, see paras 3.146 *et seq.*), but does not act or acts only at a "speed" that is unacceptably slow. Whether and when delay is unacceptable is a **matter of the individual case and all its circumstances**. What is acceptable under the circumstances not only depends on the factual and legal complexities of the case, but also the behavior of the other constituents, namely the parties, and the overall duration of the proceedings thus far.[183] Termination of the office of an arbitrator for undue delay is clearly intended to be an exceptional remedy of last resort. It must not be (ab)used by a party to try and micro-manage how an arbitrator, or for that matter the entire arbitral tribunal, handles the case.[184] Against this background, in a complex and long-running case, a delay of a further few months may be entirely acceptable, whereas in a small-scale, simple matter it may not.[185]

3. *Voluntary Withdrawal*

3.150 Where a ground for termination within the meaning of s 1038 para 1 cl 1 ZPO exists—and in fact irrespective of the existence of such a ground[186]—the arbitrator concerned may voluntarily and unilaterally withdraw from office by declaration towards all parties; none of the parties can veto such withdrawal.[187] Generally,

---

[181] Münch, in: MünchKommZPO, s 1038 paras 16 *et seq.*; Schwab/Walter, ch 10 para 31.
[182] Münch, in: MünchKommZPO, s 1038 paras 20 *et seq.*; Voit, in: Musielak/Voit (eds), s 1038 paras 2 *et seq.*
[183] OLG München, SchiedsVZ 2011, 107; Hartmann, in: Baumbach/Lauterbach/Albers/Hartmann (eds), s 1038 para 4; Geimer, in: Zöller (ed), s 1038 para 3; Münch, in: MünchKommZPO, s 1038 paras 17 *et seq.*; Saenger, in: Saenger (ed), s 1038 para 4; Voit, in: Musielak/Voit (eds), s 1038 para 6.
[184] Münch, in: MünchKommZPO, s 1038 para 19.
[185] OLG München, SchiedsVZ 2011, 107; OLG Düsseldorf, BeckRS 2008, 20508.
[186] BT-Drucks 13/5274, p 42.
[187] Nacimiento/Abt/Stein, in: *Arbitration in Germany*, s 1038 para 16; Schwab/Walter, ch 13 para 17; Altenkirch, SchiedsVZ 2014, 113, 116.

withdrawal from office will also need to be viewed to be an **implied termination of the arbitrator agreement** (see paras 3.199 *et seq.*).[188] Pursuant to s 1038 para 2 ZPO, the withdrawing arbitrator will not be deemed to have formally acknowledged that there was in fact inability to perform or undue delay. To the extent there arises a dispute over this issue, eg in connection with the termination of the arbitrator agreement and the question what remuneration the withdrawing arbitrator receives, the issue can therefore be litigated *de novo.*

4. *Termination by Party Agreement*

The parties can jointly terminate the office of an arbitrator **at any time**; this is an expression of their fundamental right to party autonomy. Thus, the right to jointly terminate exists irrespective of whether an arbitrator is actually unable to perform or has been unduly late in performing his or her obligations.[189] At the same time, inability or undue delay are certainly scenarios where termination by party agreement is particularly appropriate in case the arbitrator concerned does not withdraw voluntarily. The parties may do so informally by declaring termination towards the arbitrator concerned.[190] For reasons of legal certainty and proof, it is of course advisable to act in writing. Termination of office by joint party action will in all likelihood also imply a termination of the arbitrator agreement (see para 3.198).[191] In this scenario, again s 1038 para 2 ZPO applies. **3.151**

5. *Termination by Court Decision*

As a means of last resort (*ultima ratio*), a party may request the competent higher regional court to terminate the office of an arbitrator where he or she is unable to perform or acts with undue delay. Such party must first try and ask the arbitrator to **withdraw voluntarily** or the other party to **agree to terminate**; where a party fails to try that, the request to court is not (yet) permissible.[192] Only parties may ask the court for termination, not co-arbitrators.[193] There is **no statutory deadline** for the request (unlike for challenges, where a strict two-week period applies, s 1037 para 2 cl 1 ZPO). However, in exceptional cases, where a party waits for an extended **3.152**

---

[188] Geimer, in: Zöller (ed), s 1038 para 4; Münch, in: MünchKommZPO, s 1038 para 22; Voit, in: Musielak/Voit (eds), s 1038 para 3; Schwab/Walter, ch 13 para 17.

[189] BT-Drucks 13/5274, p 42; Geimer, in: Zöller (ed), s 1038 para 4; Lachmann, para 1130; Münch, in: MünchKommZPO, s 1038 para 12; Saenger, in: Saenger (ed), s 1038 para 1; Voit, in: Musielak/Voit (eds), s 1038 para 4.

[190] Münch, in: MünchKommZPO, s 1038 para 23; Schwab/Walter, ch 13 para 8.

[191] Geimer, in: Zöller (ed), s 1038 para 4; Nacimiento/Abt/Stein, in: *Arbitration in Germany*, s 1038 para 17; Münch, in: MünchKommZPO, s 1038 para 23; Schwab/Walter, ch 13 para 8; Voit, in: Musielak/Voit (eds), s 1038 para 4.

[192] BT-Drucks 13/5274, p 42; Münch, in: MünchKommZPO, s 1038 para 25 (lack of need for court action—*fehlendes Rechtsschutzbedürfnis*), concurring Voit, in: Musielak/Voit (eds), s 1038 para 7. Opposing view: Lachmann, para 1136; KG BeckRS 2013, 03449.

[193] Saenger, in: Saenger (ed), s 1038 para 5; Prütting/Schneider, in: Prütting/Gehrlein (eds), s 1038 para 4; Münch, in: MünchKommZPO, s 1038 para 25.

period of time and has actually given the other party reason to believe that it would not seek termination, the request may be time-barred based on general principles of **good faith** (estoppel-*Verwirkung*).[194]

3.153 The court's decision is **final and binding without further remedy** to the BGH (s 1065 para 1 cl 2 ZPO). By its plain wording, s 1038 para 2 ZPO does not apply. Thus, in a subsequent litigation on his or her remuneration, an arbitrator would be free to argue that there was actually no ground for termination; he or she would, however, face a high factual burden of persuasion given the previous decision of the higher regional court.

3.154 It is unclear whether the parties may agree to **exclude the resort to the court** to terminate the office of an arbitrator.[195] The wording of s 1038 ZPO is neutral. Compared to s 1037 para 1 ZPO, there is no express provision prohibiting such a party agreement. The legislative materials appear to allow party autonomy.[196] In our view, in principle this is in line with the purpose of s 1038 ZPO, at least as long as the parties agree on a **substitute neutral mechanism** to terminate an arbitrator, such as by way of decision by the arbitral institution (see, eg, art 15.2 ICC Rules).[197] Whereas s 1037 ZPO is concerned primarily with the fundamental, constitutional requirement of arbitrator neutrality and therefore provides for court control as a must (s 1037 paras 1 and 3 ZPO), s 1038 ZPO deals with mostly external reasons that prevent an arbitrator from performing in the way he or she should. There is thus less need for mandatory court control. Nevertheless, the law clearly shows that there must be some mechanism to terminate an arbitrator where an arbitrator does not withdraw and the parties cannot agree. In the latter case, termination of the arbitrator agreement for cause is not an option, because the parties can only terminate the arbitrator agreement jointly (see para 3.198). However, we do not see a compelling need for state court action; thus, where the parties provided for termination by an arbitral institution, this fulfills the statutory purpose just as well.

VI. Replacement

3.155 Where the office of an arbitrator ends pursuant to a successful challenge for lack of neutrality or agreed prerequisites (ss 1036, 1037 ZPO), or where the office ends as a result of inability or undue delay (s 1038 ZPO), the arbitral proceedings may continue nevertheless, and a substitute arbitrator may be appointed (s 1039 para 1 cl 1 ZPO). Such appointment **follows the same rules** that applied to the appointment

[194] Lachmann, para 1135; Münch, in: MünchKommZPO, s 1038 para 26; Voit, in: Musielak/Voit (eds), s 1038 para 7.

[195] In favor of party autonomy BT-Drucks 13/5274, p 42; Schlosser, in: Stein/Jonas (eds), s 1038 para 5; Geimer, in: Zöller (ed), s 1039 para 1; Nacimiento/Abt/Stein, in: *Arbitration in Germany*, s 1038 para 7; against party autonomy: Münch, in: MünchKommZPO, Vorbem s 1038 para 11; Hartmann, in: Baumbach/Lauterbach/Albers/Hartmann (eds), s 1039 para 4.

[196] BT-Drucks 13/5274, p 42.

[197] Münch, in: MünchKommZPO, s 1038 para 12.

of the arbitrator whose office has been terminated (s 1039 para 1 cl 2 ZPO). The German arbitration law thereby follows art 15 Model Law.

Once the substitute arbitrator is validly appointed and has acquired the relevant information, the arbitral proceedings may continue. Given that the purpose of s 1039 ZPO is to avoid unnecessary delay and costly repetitions, the new tribunal is **generally not required to repeat the proceedings or parts of it *de novo*.**[198] In particular, the right to be heard does not mandate a repetition as long as it is ensured that the substitute arbitrator receives all relevant information and the legal arguments of the parties. A **different** situation may arise where **witnesses have already been heard**. Still, it may not be mandatory for the substitute arbitrator to get a personal impression of a witness where there are other means to assess his or her credibility, eg by a verbatim transcript of the witness examination or by a consistent assessment of a witness by the other arbitrators. Where the new arbitrator nevertheless prefers to obtain a personal impression of the credibility of witnesses, the evidence taking will need to be repeated.[199] **3.156**

Special situations may arise where the rules applying to the appointment of the arbitrator being replaced are no longer operable. This may be the case where the original arbitrator was appointed by a third party or institution that no longer exists. Similarly, the arbitrator being replaced may have already been named in the arbitration agreement.[200] In these situations, the parties ought to try and resolve the situation by interpretation of the arbitration agreement. If they cannot agree, as a last resort, appointment by the competent higher regional court should be the solution (s 1035 paras 4 and 5 ZPO).[201] **3.157**

The parties are free to agree different rules in case an arbitrator needs to be replaced (s 1039 para 2 ZPO). Hence, they could agree that the arbitral proceedings shall terminate where the office of an arbitrator terminates,[202] even though this would generally appear to be an impractical solution. The parties may also agree to **continue the proceedings with the remaining arbitrators** only.[203] Alternatively, it would be possible to name a substitute from the very beginning, and to allow the **3.158**

[198] Nacimiento/Abt/Stein, in: *Arbitration in Germany*, s 1039 para 20; Lachmann, paras 1145 *et seq.*; Münch, in: MünchKommZPO, s 1039 para 15.

[199] Lachmann, para 1148; Münch, in: MünchKommZPO, s 1039 para 16.

[200] BT-Drucks 13/5274, p 43.

[201] Nacimiento/Abt/Stein, in: *Arbitration in Germany*, s 1039 para 20; Münch, in: MünchKommZPO, s 1039 paras 13 *et seq.*; Saenger, in: Saenger (ed), s 1039 para 2; Voit, in: Musielak/Voit (eds), s 1039 para 3.

[202] Hartmann, in: Baumbach/Lauterbach/Albers/Hartmann (eds), s 1039 para 3; Geimer, in: Zöller (ed), s 1039 para 1; Münch, in: MünchKommZPO, s 1039 para 18; Reichold, in: Thomas/Putzo (eds), s 1039 para 4.

[203] Lachmann, para 1143; Prütting/Schneider, in: Prütting/Gehrlein (eds), s 1039 para 2; Voit, in: Musielak/Voit (eds), s 1039 para 3. Opposing view based on the principle of equality in the tribunal: Nacimiento/Abt/Stein, in: *Arbitration in Germany*, s 1039 para 5.

substitute to participate in the proceedings from the beginning.[204] This would obviate the need to repeat parts of the proceedings once the substitution actually kicks in, but is of course a costly alternative which German practice does not make use of.

F. The Arbitrator Agreement

3.159 We start our analysis with the legal nature of the arbitrator agreement (below paras 3.160 *et seq.*). We then address applicable law (below para 3.165) and conclusion of the arbitrator agreement (below paras 3.166 *et seq.*), before we look in detail at the rights and obligations of the parties to the agreement (below paras 3.170 *et seq.*). Term and termination are a further focus of our analysis (below paras 3.191 *et seq.*).

I. Legal Nature of the Arbitrator Agreement

3.160 Under German law and practice, the arbitrator agreement is understood to be an agreement between the parties of the arbitration on the one hand and the arbitrator(s) on the other regarding the conduct of the arbitral proceedings. It is to be distinguished from (i) the arbitration agreement; (ii) the appointment of an arbitrator; and (iii) the agreement with an arbitral institution (*Schiedsorganisationsvertrag*):[205]

- The **arbitration agreement** is an agreement solely between the parties to submit certain disputes to the final and binding decision of an arbitral tribunal, without usually knowing at the time of the arbitration agreement who the arbitrators will be.
- The **appointment** of an arbitrator is an act by a party, a co-arbitrator, an arbitral institution, a state court, or another third party vesting the office of an arbitrator with the appointee (see paras 3.19 and 3.33 *et seq.*).
- The **agreement with an arbitral institution** is an agreement that the parties—in most instances impliedly—conclude with the arbitral institution administering the proceedings. Its main effect is the obligation of the parties to pay the institution's administrative fees, if any, and the institution's obligation to assist the parties in the conduct of the proceedings as per the rules of the institution.[206]

3.161 The arbitrator agreement, by contrast, is a **multi-party agreement** including the parties to the arbitral proceedings and the arbitrator or arbitrators. The Tenth Book

[204] Schwab/Walter, ch 6 para 2; Münch, in: MünchKommZPO, s 1039 para 21; Voit, in: Musielak/Voit (eds), s 1039 para 3.
[205] Böckstiegel/Kröll/Nacimiento, in: *Arbitration in Germany*, p 30 para 78; Münch, in: MünchKommZPO, Vorbem s 1034 para 3; Saenger, in: Saenger (ed), Vorbem ss 1025-1066 para 11.
[206] Geimer, in: Zöller (ed), s 1035 para 23; Münch, in: MünchKommZPO, Vorbem s 1034 para 72; Lachmann, para 3064.

of the ZPO does not contain any provisions thereon. It is thus no surprise that there are different views as to its legal nature, which range from an agreement under substantive law, to a procedural law agreement, to a hybrid agreement.[207] Similar to the arbitration agreement (see para 2.12), we think the legal nature is captured best by qualifying the arbitrator agreement as a **substantive law agreement on the conduct of arbitral proceedings.**[208] Arbitration is a creature of party autonomy and freedom of contract. In a first step, the parties, by private agreement, opt out of the state court system, and in a second step, they agree with their privately chosen decision-makers on the mutual rights and obligations in order to conduct the arbitration within the framework of the German arbitration law and any further agreements of the parties.

As a consequence, as with the arbitration agreement and assuming German law to govern, the **BGB rules** on the formation, validity, interpretation, and termination of contracts apply (ss 104 *et seq.* BGB), see below paras 3.166 *et seq.*[209] As with the ZPO, the arbitrator agreement is not addressed specifically in the BGB, either. The further qualification of the contents of an arbitrator agreement is thus subject to some uncertainty and controversy. Given that the main content of an arbitrator agreement is the conduct of arbitral proceedings by the arbitrator(s) chosen by the parties, it could be argued to qualify the arbitrator agreement as a type of service agreement (*Dienstvertrag*, ss 611 *et seq.* BGB), mandate (*Auftrag*, ss 662 *et seq.* BGB), or agency (*Geschäftsbesorgung*, s 675 BGB).[210] However, none of these **contract types** properly and fully captures the essence of an arbitrator agreement: first and foremost, the main obligation is to conduct the arbitral proceedings and to render a decision by way of an award or to otherwise terminate the proceedings.[211] However, unlike in cases of services agreement, mandates, or agency relationships, as far as the decision of the dispute is concerned, arbitrators are completely independent in performing their activities and not subject to any instructions from the 3.162

[207] BGHZ 98, 32, 34 = NJW 1986, 3077 *et seq.* (private-law agreement); BGHZ 42, 313, 315 = NJW 1965, 298 (private law agreement); Hartmann, in: Baumbach/Lauterbach/Albers/Hartmann (eds.), Anh s 1035 para 1 (private law agreement); Prütting, SchiedsVZ 2011, 233, 234 *et seq.* (private law agreement); Reichold, in: Thomas/Putzo (eds), Vorbem s 1029 para 8 (private law agreement); Schwab, in: *Festschrift Schiedermair*, pp 499, 509 *et seq.* (procedural law agreement); Altenkirch, SchiedsVZ 2014, 113, 114; Münch, in: MünchKommZPO, Vorbem s 1034 para 4; Schwab/Walter, ch 11 para 9; Voit, in: Musielak/Voit (eds), s 1035 para 20.

[208] Similar BGHZ 98, 32, 34 = NJW 1986, 3077; BGHZ 42, 313, 315 = NJW 1965, 298 (obiter dictum); Münch, in: MünchKommZPO, Vorbem s 1034 para 4; Voit, in: Musielak/Voit (eds), s 1035 para 20.

[209] Münch, in: MünchKommZPO, Vorbem s 1034 para 4; Saenger, in: Saenger (ed), Vorbem ss 1025-1066 para 11; Schwab/Walter, ch 11 para 8.

[210] Hantke, SchiedsVZ 2003, 269, 272; Böckstiegel/Kröll/Nacimiento, in: *Arbitration in Germany*, p 30 para 79.

[211] BGH NJW 1986, 3077, 3079 ("*allgemeine Verpflichtung…, an dem Schiedsverfahren nach besten Kräften mitzuwirken und den Streitfall nach Maßgabe der Schiedsvereinbarung in einem geordneten, rechtsstaatlichen Grundsätzen entsprechenden Verfahren einer alsbaldigen Erledigung zuzuführen.*"); Hartmann, in: Baumbach/Lauterbach/Albers/Hartmann (eds),Anh s 1035 para 5.

parties. They may have ancillary obligations outside the key area of conducting the proceedings and making a decision, such as properly administering and accounting for advances on costs, and it may be that these obligations can be captured appropriately with legal concepts known from agency or mandate agreements. However, it would not seem appropriate to qualify an entire agreement on the basis of such ancillary items.

3.163 Thus, we are of the view that an arbitrator agreement should be qualified as an **agreement *sui generis***, and its contents and its application are primarily a matter of interpretation of the individual agreement.[212] With regard to some additional and ancillary obligations, the BGB provisions on service, mandate, or agency agreements may be used by analogy.[213] This applies for instance to issues of compensation (ss 612 *et seq.* BGB), personal service (s 613 BGB), termination (ss 626 *et seq.* BGB), and reimbursement for costs (ss 669, 670 BGB).

3.164 In **ad hoc proceedings**, the arbitrator agreement is particularly important. It is the place to address a number of issues that would otherwise be addressed by the rules of an arbitral institution, most notably the compensation of the arbitrators, their liability, the right to request advances on arbitrator compensation, and confidentiality.

II. Applicable Law

3.165 Given that the arbitrator agreement is a substantive law agreement, the **Rome I Regulation** provides for the applicable conflict of law rules.[214] The exclusion contained in Art 1 para 2 lit e of the Rome I Regulation does not apply, because the arbitrator agreement needs to be distinguished from the arbitration agreement. Pursuant to Art 3 para 1 Rome I Regulation, the parties are free to choose the law applicable to the arbitrator agreement. The parties are well advised to do so where there is an international nexus, ie where the parties and the arbitrators do not all reside in the country of the seat of the arbitration. In case the parties fail to make an explicit choice, Art 4 Rome I Regulation applies. It is questionable whether an arbitrator agreement falls under one of the specific contract categories enumerated in Art 4 para 1 Rome I Regulation. Even if one were to qualify an arbitrator agreement as a service agreement, the designation of the law of the arbitrator's residence (Art 4 para 1 lit e Rome I Regulation) does not seem particularly appropriate, especially where there are several arbitrators from different countries or where the

[212] Similarly BGH LM s 1025 ZPO prior version no 5 (p 2) = ZZP 66 (1953), 152, 155; Prütting, SchiedsVZ 2011, 233, 235; Altenkirch, SchiedsVZ 2014, 113, 115. From an international perspective Gaillard/Savage, paras 1113 *et seq.*

[213] LG Köln, NJW-RR 2013, 1273; Münch, in: MünchKommZPO, Vorbem s 1034 para 5; Schwab/Walter, ch 11 para 8. Opposing view: Hartmann, in: Baumbach/Lauterbach/Albers/Hartmann (eds), Anh s 1035 para 1.

[214] Hartmann, in: Baumbach/Lauterbach/Albers/Hartmann (eds), Anh s 1035 para 2; Münch, in: MünchKommZPO, Vorbem s 1034 para 10; Voit, in: Musielak/Voit (eds), s 1035 para 21.

seat of the arbitration is different from the residence of the arbitrator(s). The same applies to Art 4 para 2 Rome I Regulation (place of residence of the party whose obligations are characteristic of the contract). Thus, it is most appropriate to look to Art 4 para 3 Rome I Regulation and thereby to the country which has the **closest connection** to the arbitrator agreement. In most cases, this should be the country in which the arbitration is **seated.**[215] Thus, unless the parties agree otherwise, usually **German substantive law** should govern arbitrator agreements related to **arbitrations seated in Germany.**

III. Conclusion of the Arbitrator Agreement

The conclusion of the arbitrator agreement follows the provisions of the BGB for the conclusion of contracts (ss 145 *et seq.* BGB), because the arbitrator agreement is a substantive law agreement. In practice, the arbitrator agreements for a three-person panel are **often collapsed into one document** signed by all parties to the arbitration and all arbitrators. The text of the arbitration agreement is often repeated in the arbitrator agreement. In such case, there are no issues regarding contract formation. Likewise, it would be possible to conclude three separate arbitrator agreements, with all parties to the arbitration signing each arbitrator agreement. **3.166**

The law does **not require any specific** form for an arbitrator agreement. Thus, it can be concluded orally and it can even be **implied by conduct.**[216] In this case, the construction of the arbitrator agreement is more complex. In German practice, in the absence of a written arbitrator agreement, the party appointing an arbitrator is deemed, by virtue of the arbitration agreement, to have an **implied power of attorney** from the opposing party to conclude the arbitrator agreement with the appointee. The appointee only needs to accept towards the appointing party, who is deemed to have power of attorney to receive such acceptance also for the opposing party. Regarding the chairman, the party-appointees are deemed to have implied power of attorney to conclude the arbitrator agreement and to receive the chairman's acceptance also for the other persons involved.[217] The content of the arbitration agreement is deemed to be part of the arbitrator agreement.[218] This construct may sound artificial, and to some extent it certainly is. This may be one of the reasons why other jurisdictions place much less emphasis on the arbitrator agreement. **3.167**

---

[215] Similarly Geimer, in: Zöller (ed), s 1035 para 23; Münch, in: MünchKommZPO, Vorbem s 1034 para 10; Voit, in: Musielak/Voit (eds), s 1035 para 21.

[216] Hartmann, in: Baumbach/Lauterbach/Albers/Hartmann (eds), Anh s 1035 para 3; Geimer, in: Zöller (ed), s 1035 para 1; Münch, in: MünchKommZPO, Vorbem s 1034 para 13; Saenger, in: Saenger (ed), s 1035 para 4. Opposing view: Lachmann, para 4129.

[217] Münch, in: MünchKommZPO, Vorbem s 1034 para 12; Schwab/Walter, ch 11 para 5.

[218] Similarly Münch, in MünchKommZPO, Vorbem s 1034 para 8; OLG München, NJOZ 2011, 413, 418.

3.168 In principle, an arbitrator agreement may be invalid for the same reasons that can render any agreement invalid. For instance, an agreement concluded under the influence of **fraudulent misrepresentation or duress** may be voidable under ss 123, 142 BGB. The same applies in case of certain types of errors (s 119 para 1 BGB). **Errors related to personal characteristics of an arbitrator** (s 119 para 2 BGB) can, however, not justify the voidance of an arbitrator agreement. Instead, the German arbitration law contains special provisions addressing these issues (ss 1036 *et seq.* ZPO), derogating the general provision of s 119 para 2 BGB (see also above para 3.115).[219]

3.169 When it comes to grounds for invalidity, the arbitrator agreement and the arbitration agreement need to be analyzed separately. Even where an arbitration agreement is null and void or incapable of being performed, the arbitrator agreement may still be valid.[220] For instance, the case may concern the contestation of a shareholder resolution, one party then brings arbitration, the parties conclude an arbitration agreement, and the arbitral tribunal then finds the arbitration agreement to be invalid because it does not satisfy the *Schiedsfähigkeit II* requirements of the BGH (see para 1.78). In such a scenario, despite the invalidity of the arbitration agreement, the arbitrator agreement is and remains valid and binding, at least where the parties and the arbitrator(s) concluded an express written arbitrator agreement (or arbitrator agreements).[221] Importantly, it continues to serve as the legal basis for **remuneration of the arbitrators**. There may of course be cases where both agreements are invalid for the same reason. For instance, one party may lack legal capacity when concluding both the arbitration agreement and the arbitrator agreement.

IV. Rights and Obligations of the Arbitrators and the Parties

3.170 Below we address some of the typical rights and obligations of the arbitrators and the parties arising from an arbitrator agreement.

1. Efficient Conduct of the Proceedings

3.171 The main obligation for an arbitrator resulting from the arbitrator agreement is the obligation to **conduct the arbitral proceedings** and to **render a decision by**

---

[219] Voit, in: Musielak/Voit (eds), s 1035 para 22; Münch, in: MünchKommZPO, Vorbem s 1034 para 14; see also BGH NJW 1955, 709 (concerning arbitration agreement).

[220] BGH LM s 1025 ZPO prior version no 5 (p 2) = ZZP 66 (1953), 152, 155; Breetzke, NJW 1968, 1113, 1115; Geimer, in: Zöller (ed), s 1034 para 13; Münch, in: MünchKommZPO, Vorbem s 1034 para 6 with further references.

[221] The situation may of course be different where there is no express arbitrator agreement. An implied arbitrator agreement pursuant to the principles laid out above (para 3.167) is more difficult to construct, because such construct relies on an implied power of attorney derived from the arbitration agreement. Where there is no valid arbitration agreement, it is hard to see a basis for an implied power of attorney. The result could be an incomplete arbitrator agreement between the appointing party and the respective appointee only.

way of an award or to otherwise **terminate the proceedings** (see para 3.162). This obligation is similar to the duties of a state court judge. An arbitrator is therefore obliged to read the file, to analyze the applicable law, to participate in deliberations of the tribunal and oral hearings, to participate in the drafting of an award and its reasoning, and to sign the award.[222] In addition, arbitrators are obliged to take all reasonable steps such as to ensure that an award is enforceable and not subject to set aside.[223]

These obligations are both important and—at times—cumbersome. The parties have, however, only **limited means to enforce these obligations**. They are not entitled to bring a court action or arbitral proceedings seeking to compel fulfillment of the above-mentioned duties; otherwise, such court action could be (ab)used easily to fundamentally derail the arbitral process.[224] The parties have only **indirect means** to "enforce" the above obligations. In case all parties to the arbitration are in agreement, they can terminate the office of an arbitrator and the corresponding arbitrator agreement at any time. Where only one party is dissatisfied with the way an arbitrator performs, the party is limited to the grounds for challenging or terminating an arbitrator under ss 1036 *et seq.* ZPO (in particular for a lack of neutrality, lack of required characteristics, inability to perform, persistent non-performance, see paras 3.112 *et seq.*, 3.133 and 3.144 *et seq.*). In theory, damage claims may arise, too (within the parameters of possible limitations of liability, see paras 3.189 *et seq.*). However, from a practical point of view, such claims will usually be fairly illusory.[225] This may seem unsatisfactory, for instance where a claimant is faced with an arbitrator appointed by the respondent who clearly "drags his feet." On the other hand, giving a party readily available remedies against allegedly "non-performing" arbitrators would be a dangerous tool in the hands of rogue parties to derail the arbitral process. 3.172

2. *Personal Obligation and the Use of Assistants*

Arbitrators have to perform their obligations in person. Frequently, this result is derived from ss 613 cl 1, 664 para 1 cl 1 BGB, two provisions that require "in case of doubt" that services and mandates be **performed in person.**[226] However, for arbitrators, this does not only apply "in case of doubt" but generally. This obligation already follows from the nature of their mandate as appointees of the parties 3.173

[222] Geimer, in: Zöller (ed), s 1035 paras 29 *et seq.*; Münch, in: MünchKommZPO, Vorbem s 1034 para 19; similarly Voit, in: Musielak/Voit (eds), s 1035 paras 23 *et seq.*

[223] BGH NJW 1986, 3077, 3078; Voit, in: Musielak/Voit (eds), s 1035 paras 23 *et seq.*; Münch, in: MünchKommZPO, Vorbem s 1034 para 20.

[224] Bruns, ZRP 1968, 528; Münch, in: MünchKommZPO, Vorbem s 1034 para 21.

[225] Similarly Münch, in: MünchKommZPO, Vorbem s 1034 para 22; Geimer, in: Zöller (ed), s 1035 para 30.

[226] Münch, in: MünchKommZPO, Vorbem s 1034 para 17; Hartmann, in: Baumbach/Lauterbach/Albers/Hartmann (eds),Anh s 1035 para 7; similarly Geimer, in: Zöller (ed), s 1035 para 23.

entrusted with the private adjudication of a dispute that would otherwise have to be decided by state court judges. The provisions of the Tenth Book regarding appointment and replacement of arbitrators are geared towards personal service, eg as regards neutrality, qualifications, and ability to perform.

3.174 Arbitrators may receive support from assistants, but their **activities must not be substituted by assistants**. Obviously, it is difficult to state a bright-line test as to what is support and what is substitution. Clearly, research regarding abstract questions of law raised by the case in front of an arbitrator would be a support activity. Similarly, summarizing the facts of the case in preparation of a hearing qualifies as pure support, as long as the arbitrator has also read the complete file him- or herself. By contrast, applying the facts of the case to the applicable law is clearly the core prerogative of the arbitrator. Assistants may be asked to make suggestions in this regard or to **prepare drafts**.[227] However, the arbitrator still must do the work him- or herself and therefore review any drafts from assistants very carefully.[228]

3.175 As a general matter, arbitrators should be very reluctant regarding the use of assistants beyond mere research and preparatory work. Not only may they endanger the enforceability of an award if they take too much of a "hands-off" approach. They also harm their own reputation and may do a disservice to arbitration as such. Where an arbitrator does not have the time to work on the case more or less in person, he or she should decline the appointment.

3. Instructions by the Parties

3.176 As far as the core duty of an arbitrator to further and terminate the proceedings is concerned, an arbitrator is not subject to any instructions by the parties.[229] This is one of the main reasons why an arbitrator agreement cannot be qualified as a service agreement, an agency relationship, or a civil law mandate, but needs to be regarded as an agreement *sui generis* (see paras 3.160 *et seq.*). Outside the judge-like duties to apply the law to the case, decide the case, and terminate the proceedings, to a certain limited extent, party instructions are permissible. For instance, the parties may agree on procedural issues pursuant to s 1042 para 3 ZPO, and the arbitrators will, in principle, be bound to follow such agreement.[230]

---

[227] Münch, in: MünchKommZPO, s 1054 para 21 with further references; instructive BGHZ 110, 104, 107 = NJW 1990, 2199 = XVII Y.B. Com. Arb. 504 (1992).

[228] Stürner, SchiedsVZ 2013, 322, 323; Münch, in: MünchKommZPO, s 1054 para 21.

[229] Münch, in: MünchKommZPO, Vorbem s 1034 para 16; Hartmann, in: Baumbach/Lauterbach/Albers/Hartmann (eds),Anh s 1035 paras 6, 8; Voit, in: Musielak/Voit (eds), s 1035 para 24.

[230] Münch, in: MünchKommZPO, s 1042 para 82 (pointing out the arbitrator's right to terminate the arbitrator agreement where it would be unreasonable (*unzumutbar*) for the arbitrator to be bound to such party agreement); Schlosser, in: Stein/Jonas (eds), Vor s 1025 para 23; Voit, in: Musielak/Voit (eds), s 1035 para 24.

4. Remuneration

a) **General Principles** Arbitrators have the right to be compensated for their services; their activities are not pro bono.[231] The remuneration of arbitrators is a key item for any arbitrator agreement, in particular in ad hoc arbitrations. In institutional arbitration, the rules of the institution usually regulate arbitrator compensation (see, eg, the fee scales of the DIS and the ICC, paras 2.206 and 2.214). Thus, there is little room and indeed little need for additional party agreement. Institutional fee scales may also serve as a useful guideline for parties and arbitrators negotiating on arbitrator compensation in ad hoc cases. Otherwise, under German law, there is **no directly applicable fee scale** for ad hoc cases. Similar to services agreements, in the absence of a party agreement, the arbitrator has the right to request the "usual compensation" (*übliche Vergütung*, cf s 612 para 2 BGB). Where there is no "usual compensation" or it is not possible to determine it, under general principles of German law, the person rendering the services—in our case the arbitrator—is empowered to determine the compensation in his or her discretion, subject to the limitations of equity (*Leistungsbestimmung nach billigem Ermessen*, ss 315, 316 BGB).[232] **3.177**

Traditionally, there has been a strong view in Germany looking towards the statutory fee scales for attorneys-at-law in order to determine the compensation of arbitrators.[233] Originally, these fee scales were regulated in the Federal Code on Attorneys' Fees (BRAGO) which was later replaced by the **Attorney Compensation Act (RVG).** On this basis, the German Attorneys' Association (DAV) and the German Association of Judges (DRB) have published recommendations for arbitrator compensation.[234] We are skeptical of this approach. The above-mentioned statutory fee scales are geared towards the professional services of attorneys-at-law representing clients in all sorts of situations, both in and out of state court. The scales applicable to state court litigation distinguish between the various levels of appeal. Thus, they are not readily transferrable to arbitration. Arbitration is "private justice," and the activities of an arbitrator may be comparable to those of a state court judge, but certainly not a party representative. In arbitration, there is only one instance and no appeal. Many arbitrators are not German attorneys-at-law, but active or retired judges, law professors, foreign lawyers, or not even lawyers at all. Also, it is our observation that in practice, there are many cases where the parties do not seek inspiration from the RVG. Thus, we do not think that an RVG-based **3.178**

[231] Buchwaldt, NJW 1994, 638; Münch, in: MünchKommZPO, Vorbem s 1034 para 31; Voit, in: Musielak/Voit (eds), s 1035 para 26.

[232] Müller-Glöge, in: MünchKommBGB, s 612 para 31; likewise specifically for arbitrators Münch, in: MünchKommZPO, Vorbem s 1034 para 31.

[233] See eg OLG Koblenz KTS 1957, 94; LG Mönchengladbach, SchiedsVZ 2007, 104; Schwab/Walter, ch 12 para 12.

[234] Textmuster für eine Vereinbarung über die Vergütung der Schiedsrichter, dated March 10, 2006, available at http://anwaltverein.de/downloads/praxis/mustervertrag/Schiedsrichterverguetung DAV-DRiB.pdf (last visited December 1, 2015).

arbitrator compensation can still be regarded as the "usual compensation" in the sense of s 612 para 2 BGB.[235]

3.179 Therefore, unless there is some other form of "usual compensation," where the parties and the arbitrators cannot agree on arbitrator compensation in ad hoc cases seated in Germany, arbitrators will usually be empowered to fix their compensation in their "equitable discretion" (ss 315, 316 BGB). In general, in our view arbitrators will not act against the principles of equity if they base their compensation on the **DIS fee scales**. In fact, for arbitrations seated in Germany, we would recommend that arbitrators actively look to the fee scales of the DIS (Appendix to s 40.5 DIS Rules) as far as their compensation is concerned (obviously, the DIS administrative fee does not apply in ad hoc arbitration). The parties, when considering what fees to agree with an arbitrator, may still find that the DIS fee scales do not entirely fit their purpose, eg in cases with very large amounts in dispute, because the DIS scales do not contain any cap. Nevertheless, we believe they are a better starting point generally than the RVG.

3.180 While it is true that arbitrators must not be judges in their own affairs (*nemo iudex in causa propria*), fixing their own fees is not a violation of this principle, as the BGH has recently held.[236] What would not be possible for arbitrators is to render an award against a party demanding payment of arbitrator fees; in order to obtain an enforceable title on fees, arbitrators would need to bring action against a party in state court (or—to the extent the arbitrator agreement contains an arbitration agreement—before another arbitral tribunal). Obviously, arbitrators may still fix and award costs among the parties (s 1057 ZPO).

3.181 As between the parties and the arbitrators, the parties are **jointly and severally liable** for arbitrator compensation.[237] Usually, in the arbitral award, the tribunal will make a specific determination as to who bears how much of the costs (s 1057 ZPO). The compensation claims of arbitrators exist irrespective of the validity of the arbitration agreement (as opposed to the arbitrator agreement) and, in principle, irrespective of defects of the arbitral proceedings or a later set aside or lack of enforceability; an exception may exist where the arbitrator acted with fault (usually limited to intentional misconduct, see below paras 3.189 *et seq.*).[238] Outside such exceptional cases, there is **no basis**—neither under German contract law nor under the Tenth Book of the ZPO—**to reduce arbitrator fees or to hold back** on

[235] Similarly Münch, in: MünchKommZPO, Vorbem s 1034 para 34; LG Arnsberg, August 7, 2006, 2 O 83/06 (unreported), http://www.disarb.org (last visited December 1, 2015).

[236] BGHZ 193, 38, 40 *et seq.* = SchiedsVZ 2012, 154, 155 *et seq.*; Münch, in: MünchKommZPO, Vorbem s 1034 para 31; Voit, in: Musielak/Voit (eds), s 1035 para 26.

[237] Münch, in: MünchKommZPO, Vorbem s 1034 para 32; Voit, in: Musielak/Voit (eds), s 1035 para 26; Geimer, in: Zöller (ed), s 1035 para 24.

[238] BGH ZZP 66 (1953), 152, 154; Voit, in: Musielak/Voit (eds), s 1035 para 26; Münch, in: MünchKommZPO, Vorbem s 1034 para 32. Where an arbitrator acted with fault, compensation claims may be reduced by damages claims of the parties resulting from such fault.

them on the basis of "improper performance" by the arbitrators. Any such dispute would almost certainly derail the arbitral process and would lend itself to manipulation and abuse. Instead, the remedies against arbitrators who violate their duties are governed exclusively by ss 1036 *et seq.* ZPO, the right of the parties to (jointly) terminate the arbitrator agreement (see paras 3.196 *et seq.*), and potentially damages claims (as far as those are not excluded by applicable limitations of liability, see paras 3.189 *et seq.*). In practice, to avoid any such tactics (and for other reasons), arbitrators are well advised to request a full advance on costs and expenses, as they are entitled to (see paras 3.184 *et seq.*).

b) **Reimbursement of Expenses** Arbitrators have the right to seek reimbursement for **reasonable expenses**. This is a generally recognized principle of law derived from s 670 BGB. The provision covers all expenses that the arbitrator "could consider necessary under the circumstances." Thus, arbitrators have a considerable amount of discretion.[239] For instance, this covers general office supplies, postage, telecommunications costs, costs for a secretary, costs for hearing minutes, travel and lodging expenses, rent for hearing rooms, advances on witness compensation, court fees (in the case of judicial aid pursuant to s 1050 ZPO), and the like.[240] **3.182**

Despite the fairly generous discretion bestowed upon arbitrators regarding expenses, in practice arbitrators are well advised to act in a **commercially reasonable** manner, taking into account the overall situation of the parties. Arbitrators should avoid the impression that they indulge in a luxurious lifestyle at the expense of the parties, or that they view reimbursement of expenses as a source of additional compensation. In most cases, where the parties appoint a person frequently acting as an arbitrator, they will have a natural expectation that the person has an office with professional and state-of-the-art equipment. To find items of this sort on a list of reimbursement requests may be much more irritating to the parties than anything else—irrespective of whether technically, as a matter of law, such items may be covered by s 670 BGB. **3.183**

c) **Advances on Arbitrator Compensation and Expenses** It is well established under German law that arbitrators can request advances on both their compensation and possible expenses. Regarding expenses, this can already be derived from s 669 BGB, a provision applying to civil law mandates and considered to be applicable by way of analogy to comparable situations, including arbitrator agreements.[241] **3.184**

[239] Schwab/Walter, ch 12 para 12; Münch, in: MünchKommZPO, Vorbem s 1034 para 41; similarly Hartmann, in: Baumbach/Lauterbach/Albers/Hartmann (eds), Anh s 1035 para 11; Wilske, in: *Arbitration in Germany*, p 745 para 46.

[240] Lachmann, paras 1934 *et seq.*; Schlabrendorff/Sessler, in: *Arbitration in Germany*, s 1057 paras 6 *et seq.*; Münch, in: MünchKommZPO, Vorbem s 1034 para 40.

[241] BGHZ 94, 92; Schwab/Walter, ch 12 para 16; Münch, in: MünchKommZPO, Vorbem s 1034 para 42; Geimer, in: Zöller (ed), s 1035 para 26.

3.185 As far as the arbitrator compensation is concerned, the legal reasoning is less obvious. On the contrary, those qualifying the arbitrator agreement as a services agreement would need to "explain away" s 614 BGB, which requires that the person rendering the services has to render the services in advance, and can only demand compensation once he or she is "done." However, as stated above, when viewed properly, the arbitrator agreement should not be qualified as a services agreement, but as an **agreement *sui generis*** on the conduct of arbitral proceedings. Given the nature of arbitral proceedings and the corresponding nature of an arbitrator agreement, it would be highly risky for an arbitrator to be obliged to perform in advance and to seek payment once the proceedings are completed. By its very nature, an arbitral award or other form of dispute resolution will almost inevitably be unsatisfactory to one party, maybe even both parties. Arbitrators would frequently be left with the unpleasant choice of having to sue one or both of the parties before a state court or another arbitral tribunal for their compensation. Thus, it is recognized under German law that as a matter of the specific nature of the arbitrator agreement, arbitrators have a right to request a **full advance on their expected compensation.**[242]

3.186 Both parties are obliged to pay an **equal share** of the advance on compensation and costs. As the BGH has held, this is a direct result of the arbitration agreement and the substantive-law obligation of both parties to further the proceedings.[243] As the BGH has also held, where one party fails to pay its share of the advance, the arbitral tribunal may suspend the proceedings and the other party may sue the defaulting party in state court.[244] Alternatively, the non-defaulting party may pay the entire advance and then request the arbitral tribunal to render an award ordering the defaulting party to reimburse the non-defaulting party. This is not in violation of the prohibition to adjudicate one's own affairs, because in this case, the tribunal does not rule on claims of the arbitrators, but orders payment to or on behalf of the party that had paid the full advance (similar to what it would do in an award of costs).

5. Confidentiality

3.187 The arbitrator agreement obliges **arbitrators** to keep the arbitral proceedings and their contents strictly confidential. Thus, unless the parties agree otherwise, an arbitrator may not even disclose publicly that he or she acts in a certain case.[245] This

242 Lachmann, para 1273; Voit, in: Musielak/Voit (eds), s 1035 para 27; Münch, in: MünchKommZPO, Vorbem s 1034 para 43.

243 BGHZ 193, 38, 41 = SchiedsVZ 2012, 154, 155 ("*Da die Parteien eines Schiedsvertrags die Pflicht trifft, die Durchführung des Verfahrens zu fördern und hierbei, soweit erforderlich, mit der anderen Partei zusammenzuwirken, damit es zum Abschluss des Verfahrens durch einen Schiedsspruch kommt, sind die Parteien grundsätzlich zu gleichen Anteilen zum Vorschuss verpflichtet.*"); Münch, in: MünchKommZPO, Vorbem s 1034 para 44; Lachmann, para 1276.

244 BGHZ 193, 38, 41 = SchiedsVZ 2012, 154, 155; BGHZ 94, 92, 95 = NJW 1985, 1903.

245 Münch, in: MünchKommZPO, Vorbem s 1034 para 26; similarly BGH NJW 1986, 3077, 3078; Geimer, in: Zöller (ed), s 1052 para 5.

can pose challenges for arbitrators where there are press reports on an arbitration that are clearly false or even disturbing the proceedings. It is questionable whether arbitrators, in an act of "self defense," may address the public in such a scenario, eg by way of a counter-publication in the press. One way that tribunals have dealt with this is a (written) declaration addressed to the parties clarifying what was wrong in the press, and allowing each party to publish such declaration if it wishes to do so.

6. *Accounting*

Arbitrators—in particular the chairman—need to properly account for money received from the parties, especially advances on fees and expenses. Generally, the chairman will **administer advances** on a trust account.[246] By contrast, arbitrators need not—and must not—inform the parties on the details of their deliberations, which remain secret. Where arbitrators use assistants as agreed with and compensated by the parties, arbitrators need to inform the parties as to the activities of the assistants with sufficient specificity such that the parties can verify whether the expense is justified, while at the same time observing the secrecy of the tribunal's "inner works" and deliberations. **3.188**

7. *Liability*

Given that the arbitrator agreement is a substantive-law agreement, any breach of duty would trigger damages obligations under ss 280 *et seq.* BGB even in case of slight negligence (s 276 BGB). It is commonly understood that such liability would be inappropriate for arbitrators. To the extent arbitrators perform **judge-like duties**, their liability is reduced in the same way the liability of state court judges is reduced by s 839 para 2 BGB, ie liability exists only to the extent the breach of duty is a **criminal offence** (*Spruchrichterprivileg*).[247] This privilege extends to **fact-finding, legal analysis, application of the law to the facts and the conduct of the proceedings** as such. By contrast, it does not apply, for instance, to the administration of funds received from the parties (eg advances on fees and expenses), breaches of confidentiality, and "improper refusal or delay in the conduct of the proceedings" (s 839 para 2 cl 2 BGB).[248] Where the privilege applies, liability may only be found in case of criminal misconduct, ie perversion of justice (*Rechtsbeugung*) pursuant to s 339 German Criminal Code (StGB) or corruption (ss 331 *et seq.* StGB).[249] **3.189**

Most **institutional rules** contain express provisions limiting arbitrator liability in a similar way. For instance, s 44.1 DIS Rules excludes liability with respect to the **3.190**

[246] Lachmann, para 1271; Münch, in: MünchKommZPO, Vorbem s 1034 para 25; Hartmann, in: Baumbach/Lauterbach/Albers/Hartmann (eds), Anh s 1035 para 9.

[247] BGHZ 15, 12, 15; 42, 313, 316; Prütting, SchiedsVZ 2011, 233, 237; Götz, SchiedsVZ 2012, 311 *et seq.*; Münch, in: MünchKommZPO, Vorbem s 1034 para 29; Voit, in: Musielak/Voit (eds), s 1035 para 25; *Saenger*, in: Saenger (ed), Vorbem s 1025 para 13.

[248] Altenkirch, SchiedsVZ 2014, 113, 118; Nacimiento/Abt/Stein, in: *Arbitration in Germany*, Introduction to ss 1034–1039 para 29; Lachmann, para 4324.

[249] Münch, in: MünchKommZPO, Vorbem s 1034 para 30; Schwab/Walter, ch 24 para 52.

judge-like duties referred to above unless there is an intentional breach of duty. Given the commonly accepted application of s 839 para 2 BGB, this provision does not add much in terms of protecting arbitrators. However, s 44.2 DIS Rules contains a further exclusion of liability regarding obligations outside the scope of judge-like duties. For those, there is no liability either, unless there is willful action or gross negligence. Furthermore, it is not uncommon to have a similar clause in an arbitrator agreement in ad hoc arbitration.

V Term and Termination

3.191 The term and termination of the arbitrator agreement need to be distinguished from the term and termination of the office that an arbitrator holds. The latter is regulated in ss 1036–1038, 1056 para 3 ZPO (see paras 3.100 *et seq.*). Termination of the office does not automatically terminate the agreement, and vice versa. Each **follows its own rules**, much like the situation of directors of a German corporation that hold both an office and are bound by a services agreement.[250] Below, we address the most common scenarios for termination of arbitrator agreements.

1. *Effect of the Termination of the Arbitral Proceedings*

3.192 Generally, arbitrator agreements do not have a fixed term. Once the arbitral proceedings are terminated, by award or otherwise, the office of the arbitrator ends (s 1056 para 3 ZPO). This does not necessarily mean that the arbitrator agreement ends, too. Instead, the better view is to regard the arbitrators' main obligations—efficient conduct of the proceedings—as **fulfilled** (s 362 BGB).[251] The parties are still obliged under the arbitrator agreement to pay the arbitrator compensation and to reimburse arbitrators for their reasonable expenses.[252] The arbitrators continue to be obliged to render a proper accounting as to their compensation, expenses, and possible advances.[253] Also, the arbitrators continue to be bound by the confidentiality obligations resulting from the arbitrator agreement.[254] An arbitrator agreement may contain further duties extending beyond the termination of the arbitral proceedings, such as an expressly agreed obligation of the chairman to keep the files of the case for a specified period of time. Once all these obligations have been fulfilled—whereby the confidentiality obligation may extend indefinitely unless specifically limited to a certain period of time—the arbitrator agreement may no longer be the source of rights or obligations of the parties towards each other, but it still exists as an agreement.[255]

250 Cf s 84 para 3 cl 5 German Stock Corporation Act (AktG).
251 Schwab/Walter, ch 13 para 1.
252 Münch, in MünchKommZPO, Vorbem s 1034 para 45; Henn, para 205; Gal, p 327.
253 Gal, p 340.
254 Gal, pp 328 *et seq.*
255 Similarly regarding the foregoing Münch, in: MünchKommZPO, Vorbem s 1034 para 45; Voit, in: Musielak/Voit (eds), s 1035 para 28. Opposing view: Schwab/Walter, ch 13 para 1.

2. Termination by Mutual Agreement

3.193 An arbitrator agreement may be terminated by mutual agreement. "Mutual" in this case means **all the parties on the one hand and the respective arbitrator(s) on the other.**[256] Thus, it may be possible to terminate the arbitrator agreement with only one out of several arbitrators, or to terminate the agreements with all arbitrators. The first scenario may occur where an arbitrator becomes unable to perform, eg because of serious illness (s 1038 para 1 ZPO, see para 3.147), and the parties agree with the sick arbitrator on the termination of his office and the arbitrator agreement with him.

3.194 As part of their mutual agreement, the parties and the arbitrator(s) should also address the **remuneration of the terminated arbitrator(s)**. Section 628 BGB does not apply directly to this situation, as this provision only addresses cases of unilateral termination and technically only applies to services agreements, whereas the arbitrator agreement is an agreement *sui generis*. Thus, where the parties fail to address the issue, their agreement in fact contains a gap that needs to be filled by means of **supplementary contract interpretation**. The question thus is what reasonable parties would have agreed had they contemplated the issue.[257] This obviously depends on the facts of the case, including at what stage the proceedings are, what sums the respective arbitrator has already received, to what extent the proceedings or parts thereof may need to be repeated, and to what extent the parties or the arbitrator have contributed to the cause leading to the termination.

3. Unilateral Termination

3.195 Both the parties and the arbitrator may have the right to terminate the arbitrator agreement unilaterally. However, different standards apply depending on whether termination is declared by the parties or the arbitrator.

3.196 **a) Termination by the Parties** The parties to the proceedings—**acting jointly**—can terminate the arbitrator agreement **at any time and without giving reasons**. This is a result of the fact that the parties may at any time terminate the office of an arbitrator (see para 3.151). Frequently, the termination right is based on an analogy to s 627 BGB, which allows the termination of services agreements at any time where high-quality services are rendered that require a special level of trust between the parties.[258]

3.197 Regarding compensation of the terminated arbitrator, the model contained in s 628 BGB may be looked at for guidance. This would mean that the arbitrator is

---

256 Münch, in: MünchKommZPO, Vorbem s 1034 para 46; similarly Lachmann, paras 1855 *et seq.*

257 BGH NJW 1998, 450; NJW 2004, 2449; Ellenberger, in: Palandt (ed), s 157 para 7; Busche, in: MünchKommBGB, s 157 para 47 with further references.

258 BGH DB 1980, 967, 968; Münch, in: MünchKommZPO, Vorbem s 1034 para 49; Voit, in: Musielak/Voit (eds), s 1035 para 30; Hartmann, in: Baumbach/Lauterbach/Albers/Hartmann (eds), Anh s 1035 para 15; Schwab/Walter, ch 13 para 8; Henn, para 203.

compensated for what he or she has done so far, unless the arbitrator has set the cause for termination, in which case he or she gets compensated only to the extent his or her services are **still of use** to the parties. From a practical view, this model will often run into difficulties: how to quantify what an arbitrator has done so far in relation to the entire proceedings may be quite a mystery. Likewise, quantifying which parts of prior services are still of use and which not, may be equally difficult. In many cases, the introduction of a new arbitrator or the repetition of parts of the hearing may have the effect that there may be seemingly little use to what the predecessor arbitrator had done.[259] At least for attorney fees it is recognized that they are not to be paid if the new attorney will be allowed to demand the same fees again.[260] Thus, in practice, it is generally **recommendable to seek an agreement** between the parties and the respective arbitrator on his or her remuneration and any modifications from what was originally agreed in the arbitrator agreement.

3.198 It is **not possible for one party only** to terminate the arbitrator agreement for cause. The arbitrator agreement is a multi-party agreement between the parties on the one hand and the arbitrator on the other. Thus, where a party wants to "get rid" of an arbitrator in a unilateral fashion, it is confined to the mechanisms contained in ss 1036–1038 ZPO, ie it can challenge an arbitrator for lack of neutrality or lack of agreed prerequisites, or it can request a decision by the state court to terminate the office of an arbitrator based on inability or undue delay (s 1038 para 1 cl 2 ZPO). If the party is successful, the arbitrator is no longer able to perform his or her obligations (s 275 para 1 BGB), and the further consequences, eg relating to compensation, are to be derived from ss 275 paras 4, 280 *et seq.*, 326, 628 BGB (see para 3.204).

3.199 **b) Termination by Arbitrators** Unilateral termination by arbitrators follows different rules. As far as the office of an arbitrator is concerned, an arbitrator can effectively **withdraw at any time** (see para 3.150). Termination of the arbitrator agreement, however, requires cause. While it is true that an arbitrator offers high-quality services comparable to those contemplated by s 627 BGB regarding services agreements, this provision does not—or at least not beyond the scope of s 1037 ZPO[261]—allow for a termination without cause. It is generally recognized that such an unconditioned right would be incompatible with the mandate of an arbitrator because the termination renders the whole proceeding obsolete.[262] Thus, the general rules of ss 314, 626 BGB apply, and an arbitrator may terminate the arbitrator agreement only if there is an **important reason**

[259] Altenkirch, SchiedsVZ 2014, 113, 119; LG Köln, NJW-RR 2013, 1273, 1276.

[260] BGH NJW-RR 2012, 294, 295; NJW 1982, 437, 438; OLG Karlsruhe, NJW-RR 1994, 1084, 1085.

[261] Lachmann, para 4371.

[262] LG Köln, NJW-RR 2013, 1273, 1275; Schwab/Walter, ch 13 para 10; Voit, in: Musielak/Voit (eds), s 1035 para 29; Hantke, SchiedsVZ 2003, 269, 273. Opposing view: Altenkirch, SchiedsVZ 2014, 113, 116.

(*wichtiger Grund*) that renders it **unacceptable** (***unzumutbar***) for the arbitrator to continue to be bound by the arbitrator agreement. Where no such important reason exists, the arbitrator continues to be bound by the arbitrator agreement, and the rights and remedies of the parties derive from ss 275 paras 4, 280 *et seq.*, 326 BGB (see para 3.204).

Cause for termination by an arbitrator can exist where **advances on costs are not paid**, where an arbitrator is **physically threatened** by one of the parties or third persons in connection with the arbitration, where the parties have concluded an agreement on the conduct of the proceedings that is unacceptable to the arbitrator, the arbitrator for unforeseen reasons has **no longer the time necessary** to conduct the arbitral proceedings, or where there are specific and concrete grounds to suspect that the arbitral proceedings are used as a **cover-up for illegal activity**, such as bribery or money laundering.[263] **3.200**

On the other hand, **disagreement among the arbitrators** as to the right decision(s) is not a ground for termination, because in this situation, the ZPO provides for majority vote (s 1052 para 1 ZPO), and an arbitrator is required to accept that he or she may be "defeated" in such a vote. Likewise, **breaches of duties**, even serious ones, by another arbitrator must generally be addressed via the means provided for in the ZPO, in particular the termination of the office of such arbitrator, eg based on a challenge by a party, but are not grounds for another arbitrator to terminate the arbitrator agreement.[264] **3.201**

Where an arbitrator terminates the arbitrator agreement for cause, again the question of **remuneration** arises. Section 314 BGB does not contain any specific provisions regarding this issue. Generally speaking, the consequence of s 314 BGB would be that each party is entitled to keep what it has already received, and advances would need to be returned pursuant to either the provisions of ss 346 *et seq.* BGB or ss 812 *et seq.* BGB (via s 628 para 1 cl 3 BGB).[265] This is clearly not appropriate for the provision of services such as the services of an arbitrator. Instead, the model contained in s 628 BGB appears to be more appropriate, which means that the arbitrator is entitled to a **compensation commensurate with the part of the services already rendered.**[266] Again, this may be difficult to quantify (see para 3.197). **3.202**

---

[263] Münch, in: MünchKommZPO, Vorbem s 1034 paras 52 *et seq.* with further references; Rieder/Schoenemann, NJW 2011, 1169, 1174; Hartmann, in: Baumbach/Lauterbach/Albers/Hartmann (eds), Anh s 1035 para 15.

[264] OLG Kiel, JW 1927, 1656; Münch, in: MünchKommZPO, Vorbem s 1034 para 54.

[265] Gaier, in: MünchKommBGB, s 314 para 23.

[266] Hartmann, in: Baumbach/Lauterbach/Albers/Hartmann (eds), Anh s 1035 para 16; Schwab/Walter, ch 13 para 14; Henn, para 205.

4. *Termination of the Office of an Arbitrator*

3.203 As outlined above, the termination of the arbitrator agreement needs to be distinguished from the termination of the office of arbitrator. Apart from termination of the arbitral proceedings (s 1056 para 3 ZPO, see para 3.192), the office of the arbitrator may terminate pursuant to ss 1036–1038 ZPO, ie based on a successful challenge for lack of neutrality or lack of agreed prerequisites (ss 1036, 1037 ZPO), or based on inability to perform or undue delay (s 1038 ZPO). Once the office of the arbitrator ends, he or she is no longer able to perform the main obligation of the arbitrator agreement, namely to participate in the conduct and termination of the arbitral proceedings. Some commentators qualify this as a situation where the arbitrator agreement has lost its purpose and thereby terminates.[267] However, this analysis does not seem fully in line with general principles of German contract law. Impossibility to perform the main obligation means that the arbitrator is relieved of such obligation pursuant to s 275 para 1 BGB. The parties may have damages claims pursuant to ss 275 paras 4, 280 *et seq.* BGB. They may also jointly terminate the arbitrator agreement vis-à-vis the arbitrator pursuant to s 314 BGB for cause.

3.204 Irrespective of the termination, the remuneration claims of the arbitrator may be reduced proportionately pursuant to ss 326 para 1, 441 para 3 BGB or as a result of ss 314, 628 BGB (see para 3.197). In each scenario, the circumstances of the individual case need to be taken into account and the court can estimate the amount of the remaining remuneration.

---

267 Schwab/Walter, ch 13 para 1; Lachmann, para 66; Münch, in: MünchKommZPO, Vorbem s 1034 para 47.

4

THE ARBITRAL PROCEEDINGS

Markus S. Rieder/Richard Kreindler

A. Overview

4.1 In this chapter, we first address the legal framework applicable to proceedings before arbitral tribunals seated in Germany (below paras 4.2 *et seq.*). On this basis, we address the typical structure and frequent steps of arbitral proceedings (below paras 4.37 *et seq.*). Finally, we discuss a wide range of special situations, such as multi-party arbitration, parallel litigation and arbitration, arbitrations involving sovereigns, fast-track arbitration, as well as issues of fraud, money laundering, and corruption (below paras 4.206 *et seq.*).

B. Legal Framework

4.2 We first address the hierarchy of applicable procedural rules (below paras 4.3 *et seq.*) before we turn to important general legal principles for the conduct of arbitral proceedings (below paras 4.18 *et seq.*).

I. Hierarchy of Applicable Procedural Rules

4.3 The legal framework governing arbitral proceedings before tribunals seated in Germany can be derived from s 1042 ZPO:[1]

[1] BT-Drucks 13/5274, pp 46 *et seq.*

- First, mandatory rules of German arbitration law always prevail, such as the right to be heard, the right to equal treatment, and the right to be represented by counsel (s 1042 paras 1 and 2 ZPO, below paras 4.4 *et seq.*).
- Second, apart from such mandatory rules, the parties are free to regulate the arbitral proceedings by party agreement or by joint reference to the rules of an arbitral institution (s 1042 para 3 ZPO, below para 4.6).
- Third, next in the hierarchy of applicable rules are the non-mandatory provisions of German arbitration law (s 1042 para 4 cl 1 ZPO, below para 4.7).
- Fourth and finally, the arbitral proceedings are determined by the arbitral tribunal in its "free discretion" (*freies Ermessen*), s 1042 para 4 cl 1 ZPO (below paras 4.8 *et seq.*).

1. Mandatory Law

4.4 Whether a provision of the German arbitration law is mandatory can be derived in many cases from the **wording** of the provision. German arbitration law often contains expressions such as **"unless otherwise agreed by the parties"** or the like. Where such a phrase is absent, this may be taken as an indication for a mandatory rule. Nevertheless, the wording as such is not the only criterion for the analysis, and other criteria, such as the legislative history and, most importantly, the purpose of the provision, must be analyzed.[2]

4.5 Against this background, the provisions on equal treatment, the right to be heard, and the right to be represented by counsel (s 1042 paras 1 and 2 ZPO) are certainly mandatory. The same applies to provisions governing certain procedural principles like the preliminary *Kompetenz-Kompetenz* of the arbitral tribunal (s 1040 paras 1 and 2 ZPO), the final *Kompetenz-Kompetenz* of the state courts (s 1040 para 3 cl 2 ZPO), the requirement of independent and impartial arbitrators (ss 1036 *et seq.* ZPO), the various options for terminating arbitral proceedings (s 1056 ZPO), the final and binding character of arbitral awards (s 1055 ZPO), and the provisions on set aside and enforcement of arbitral awards (ss 1059 *et seq.* ZPO).[3] In addition, there are certain mandatory unwritten rules governing the conduct of arbitrations that follow from the fact that arbitration is a substitute for state court litigation, such as the requirement for arbitrators to act and decide in person.[4]

2. Party Agreement

4.6 An agreement of the parties regarding the conduct of arbitral proceedings may be found in the arbitration agreement, in procedural agreements, including by reference to the rules of an arbitral institution or on an ad-hoc basis. Party agreement,

[2] BT-Drucks 13/5274, p 46; Münch, in: MünchKommZPO, s 1042 para 15; see also: Saenger, in: Saenger (ed), s 1042 para 14; Reichold, in: Thomas/Putzo (eds), s 1042 para 5.

[3] Cf Münch, in: MünchKommZPO, s 1042 para 16, s 1059 para 1, s 1060 paras 1 *et seq.*, s 1061 para 1; Horn, SchiedsVZ 2008, 209, 216.

[4] Münch, in: MünchKommZPO, s 1042 paras 17 *et seq.*

as long as not in violation of public policy or other mandatory norms, takes **precedence over the discretion of the tribunal**. Despite the parties' far-reaching autonomy, limited only by mandatory law, an arbitration agreement or a procedural agreement—at least in German practice—is typically not the place to rewrite or otherwise seek to improve upon the arbitration law ("less is more"). We have already addressed the typical optional components of an arbitration agreement, such as the place of arbitration, the language of the proceedings or the reference to the rules of an arbitral institution (see paras 2.177, 2.181, and 2.200 *et seq.*). Practical examples of potentially useful further items for party agreement include reference to certain provisions for state court litigation,[5] as well as provisions on document disclosure and the taking of evidence more generally (eg by reference to the **IBA Rules on the Taking of Evidence in International Arbitration**).

3. Derogable Law

In the absence of mandatory law and party agreement on an issue, the derogable rules of German arbitration law apply. Where the law uses expressions like "unless otherwise agreed by the parties" or the like, it is easy to conclude that the corresponding provision of the German arbitration law is not mandatory, but derogable by party agreement. It is important to remember that it is solely the Tenth Book of the ZPO that contains the German arbitration law. The provisions of the ZPO outside the Tenth Book, in particular those governing state court litigation, do not apply in arbitration. Where parties wish provisions of the ZPO outside the Tenth Book to apply, they should explicitly so provide. **4.7**

4. Discretion of the Tribunal

In a first step, we discuss general principles governing the discretion of the arbitral tribunal pursuant to s 1042 para 4 ZPO (below paras 4.9 *et seq.*). Thereafter, we specifically address an issue that has become a highly debated one in recent German practice: the relationship and potential tension between party agreement on the one hand and the discretion of the arbitral tribunal on the other (below paras 4.14 *et seq.*). **4.8**

a) General Principles Where there is neither law—be it mandatory or non-mandatory—nor party agreement on a certain issue, the arbitral tribunal has "**free discretion**" to determine the conduct of the proceedings (s 1042 para 4 cl 1 ZPO). "Free" obviously does not mean that a tribunal would be allowed to act in an arbitrary or impermissible manner. The discretion of the tribunal exists only within the parameters of the fundamental principles of arbitral proceedings, such as equal treatment and the right to be heard.[6] Whilst the parties can further limit **4.9**

[5] Eg agreed venue for state court action (to the extent not excluded by the arbitration agreement), application of service of process rules under the ZPO (even though potentially burdensome in a cross-border context).

[6] Hartmann, in: Baumbach/Lauterbach/Albers/Hartmann (eds), s 1042 para 8; Geimer, in: Zöller (ed), s 1042 para 28; Münch, in: MünchKommZPO, s 1042 para 102; Reichold,

the tribunal's discretion by party agreement on certain issues, the parties cannot flatly eliminate the tribunal's discretion as such.[7] The tribunal has discretion only with respect to the conduct of the proceedings; regarding the merits of the case, it is bound by the applicable substantive law (unless it is expressly authorized to decide *ex aequo et bono*, s 1051 para 3 ZPO, or to the extent the parties have otherwise granted discretion to the arbitral tribunal, eg by providing for application of the conflict of law rules deemed most appropriate by the arbitral tribunal).[8]

4.10 Thus, an arbitral tribunal acting under the German arbitration law is free to adopt a **procedural style** that is akin to or "borrows from" German state court litigation, and many German arbitrators (especially active or retired judges) do exactly that.[9] This is one of the reasons why a certain knowledge of German legal traditions and state court litigation (see paras 1.13 *et seq.*) can be highly useful to an international practitioner involved in arbitral proceedings seated in Germany. At the other end of the spectrum, an arbitral tribunal acting under the German arbitration law would be just as free to conduct the proceedings in the style of Anglo-American litigation, where the tribunal often adopts a more passive and "receiving" role, often lets the parties conduct extensive document disclosure, permits the parties to drive the taking of evidence, and may allow elaborate and even contentious cross-examination of fact and expert witnesses. This happens much less frequently in Germany. Nevertheless, a number of German arbitrators take the different nationalities and legal traditions of the parties into account in shaping the proceedings. The German law is flexible enough to accommodate such endeavors.

4.11 In our view, at least in international cases, unless there is a clear desire on the part of both sides to have the proceedings conducted in a state court litigation type manner, arbitral tribunals should generally be reluctant to do so. It is the express intent of the drafters of the German arbitration law to strengthen Germany as a seat for international arbitration (without distinction between domestic and international arbitration cases).[10] At least as far as international cases are concerned, this legislative intent is better served by choosing a procedural style that is akin to the emerging international practice, which can be described as a merger of the civil and common law traditions (best of both worlds approach).

4.12 Examples of individual measures within the discretion of the tribunal include the **bifurcation or trifurcation of the proceedings** (eg in a jurisdiction, liability, and quantum phase),[11] the setting of **deadlines** for submissions and document requests,

in Thomas/Putzo (eds), s 1042 para 7; Saenger, in: Saenger (ed), s 1042 para 15; OLG Celle, OLGR Celle 2004, 396.

[7] Münch, in: MünchKommZPO, s 1042 para 94.

[8] Münch, in: MünchKommZPO, s 1042 para 96.

[9] Berger, SchiedsVZ 2009, 289, 291; Münch, in: MünchKommZPO, s 1042 para 93.

[10] BT-Drucks 13/5274, pp 1, 23, 25.

[11] RG JW 1928, 1496; Münch, in: MünchKommZPO, s 1042 para 99; similarly: Saenger, in: Saenger (ed), s 1042 para 15.

details for drafting of **submissions** and the production of **exhibits**, the sequence and the style for **questioning witnesses**, the exclusion of a person from a hearing due to unacceptable behavior,[12] or—as far as permitted by s 1042 para 2 ZPO (see below paras 4.33 *et seq.*)—the exclusion of a party representative who is incapable of performing his or her obligations.[13]

In practice, arbitral tribunals will often lay down such decisions in one or more **procedural orders**. In particular, the first order of such kind is an important tool for the initial overall structuring of the proceedings and the framing of party and tribunal expectations of the procedure.[14] **4.13**

b) Party Agreement and Tribunal Discretion Given that party autonomy is such an important cornerstone of arbitration, arbitral tribunals will usually seek agreement of the parties on procedural issues and prior to the rendering of procedural decisions. This has considerable advantages both from a legal and a psychological point of view. From the legal standpoint, where a party has consented to an act of the arbitral tribunal, there is no room for later complaints, neither within the arbitral proceedings nor at the set aside or enforcement stages. In addition, from a psychological point of view, reaching consensus on procedural issues can considerably facilitate and pacify the overall proceedings and may even contribute to paving the way to settlement or achieving a higher degree of "buy-in" for later decisions that are seen as adverse to one of the parties. **4.14**

This raises the issue, however, whether the arbitral tribunal is still free to unilaterally change procedural decisions that it has previously reached with the consensus of the parties. In other words, does party consensus mean that the issue is now one of a binding agreement of the parties which the arbitral tribunal cannot supersede unilaterally? This is precisely the issue that the **Higher Regional Court of Frankfurt/Main** had to address recently, and it did so in a manner that stirred considerable debate in the German arbitration community. **4.15**

In this case, an arbitral tribunal had issued a procedural order regarding the form of expert reports which stated that in the order "the arbitral tribunal documents the parties' agreement" on such form issues. An expert report submitted later on in the proceedings failed to comply with these form requirements, but the arbitral tribunal accepted it nevertheless over the respondent's objection. Additionally, and independent from the procedural order, the tribunal had issued terms of reference for a tribunal-appointed expert based on a draft produced by the tribunal and written comments by the parties. Again, the tribunal stated that it thereby "documents the parties' agreement," including a requirement that the expert effectively conduct his or her own investigation of facts and documents instead of simply relying **4.16**

---

[12] Münch, in: MünchKommZPO, s 1042 para 99; RGZ 47, 424, 426.

[13] Münch, in: MünchKommZPO, s 1042 para 99.

[14] In ICC cases, the terms of reference are an important tool for structuring the proceedings, see below paras 4.90 *et seq.*

on the reports of the party-appointed experts. The subsequent expert report did not meet this requirement, but nevertheless the arbitral tribunal accepted it over the respondent's objection. The respondent, who lost the case before the arbitral tribunal, successfully applied for set aside of the award. The Higher Regional Court of Frankfurt/Main found the arbitral tribunal had violated a party agreement pursuant to s 1059 para 2 no 1 lit d ZPO both with respect to the procedural order and the terms of reference.[15] The German Federal Supreme Court (BGH) did not accept the complaint on a point of law against the decision, effectively affirming the set aside of the award.[16]

4.17 The Frankfurt court decision has been the object of considerable and even sharp criticism.[17] In any event, in future it is quite possible that other higher regional courts will take similar positions when hearing set aside petitions. Against this background, arbitral tribunals seated in Germany should be careful to retain control over their procedural decisions and should avoid slipping inadvertently into negotiations with the parties and memorializing them as such. It may be useful to use **cautionary language in procedural orders** to underline this approach. One commentator has proposed the following wording:

> The parties were accorded the chance to comment on the draft of this procedural order and to propose changes and additions. In a procedural hearing held on ___ the draft was discussed with the parties together with their proposals. The following sections of this order have been modified upon the suggestion of either or both parties: ___
>
> As discussed with the parties at the beginning of the procedural hearing, the arbitral tribunal reserves the right to modify or supplement the present procedural order in due course and after hearing the parties, if it resolves that such changes are warranted in light of the development of the proceedings. The arbitral tribunal has also made it clear that it expects any agreement which purports to restrain this right to be in writing and signed by both parties.[18]

II. General Principles for the Conduct of Arbitral Proceedings

4.18 In this section, we discuss a number of general principles for the conduct of arbitral proceedings seated in Germany. The two most fundamental principles are the parties' right to equal treatment (s 1042 para 1 cl 1 ZPO, below paras 4.19 *et seq.*) and each party's right to be heard (s 1042 para 1 cl 2 ZPO, below paras 4.22 *et seq.*). In addition, the German arbitration law contains important further guideposts that

---

[15] OLG Frankfurt, SchiedsVZ 2013, 49 *et seq.* with comments from Wagner/Bülau, SchiedsVZ 2013, 6 *et seq.* For further discussion of the decision see: Wolf/Hasenstab, RIW 2011, 612; Schmeel, IBR 2011, 1241; Kröll, NJW 2013, 3135, 3140 *et seq.;* Wilske/Markert, in: BeckOK ZPO, s 1042 para 19, s 1059 para 48; Voit, in: Musielak/Voit (eds), s 1042 para 33.

[16] BGH October 2, 2012, III ZB 8/11 (unreported).

[17] Cf Wagner/Bülau, SchiedsVZ 2013, 6, 13; in favor of the decision: Wolf/Hasenstab, RIW 2011, 612, 617.

[18] Wagner/Bülau, SchiedsVZ 2013, 6, 15. Of course, where there is truly a party agreement, such cautionary language by the arbitral tribunal would be to no avail. Nevertheless, such language may help the parties *ex ante* in determining whether to conclude a party agreement, and a court *ex post* in a set aside proceeding in interpreting the conduct of the parties and the arbitral tribunal.

merit to be discussed in advance before we go into the details of what the typical structure and frequent steps in German-seated arbitrations are. Namely, regarding fact-finding by the arbitral tribunal, German law follows the principle of limited investigation by the arbitral tribunal (*beschränkter Untersuchungsgrundsatz*, below paras 4.27 *et seq.*). Furthermore, German law recognizes the duty both on the part of the arbitrators and the parties to further the proceedings (below paras 4.30 *et seq.*), and more generally the principle of procedural good faith (below paras 4.31 *et seq.*). Finally, as s 1042 para 2 ZPO explicitly provides, the parties have a non-derogable right to be represented by counsel (below paras 4.33 *et seq.*).

1. *Equal Treatment of the Parties*

German law mentions equal treatment of the parties first, even before the parties' right to be heard (s 1042 para 1 cl 1 v. cl 2 ZPO). It thereby follows **art 18 Model Law**. Even though this is not meant to express any form of priority, equal treatment is a cardinal principle for arbitral proceedings. Unequal treatment is most likely going to trigger a massive loss of trust on the part of the disadvantaged party towards the arbitral tribunal and the arbitral proceedings. An arbitrator who does not observe equal treatment will almost inevitably be viewed as biased. Equal treatment in arbitration is thus part of the **German *ordre public***, and its violation subjects an arbitral award to possible set aside (s 1059 para 2 no 2 lit b ZPO).[19] **4.19**

Equal treatment means equality of the parties in the conduct of the proceedings (*Waffengleichheit*).[20] This requires comparable situations to be treated the same; different situations need to be treated differently pursuant to their specific circumstances.[21] Besides being inspired by the Model Law, equal treatment in arbitral proceedings is a statutory implementation of the constitutional equal treatment requirement contained in art 3 para 1 of the German Constitution (GG).[22] **4.20**

As an example, the arbitral tribunal must **not conduct hearings without all parties being present**, unless there are specific circumstances justifying unequal treatment (such as a party having deliberately left the hearing or not having appeared in the first place despite being duly notified).[23] Furthermore, the parties are entitled to have the **same level of information**; communications from a party to the arbitral tribunal must be forwarded to all other parties.[24] Equal treatment requires **4.21**

---

[19] Lachmann, paras 1290, 1294; Münch, in: MünchKommZPO, s 1042 para 19; Schwab/Walter, ch 15 para 1; Reichold, in: Thomas/Putzo (eds), s 1042 para 2; Voit, in: Musielak/Voit (eds), s 1042 para 2.

[20] Hartmann, in: Baumbach/Lauterbach/Albers/Hartmann (eds), s 1042 para 3.

[21] Münch, in: MünchKommZPO, s 1042 para 25.

[22] Hartmann, in: Baumbach/Lauterbach/Albers/Hartmann (eds), s 1042 para 3; Lachmann, para 1294; Münch, in: MünchKommZPO, s 1042 para 25.

[23] Cf s 1048 para 3 ZPO; Münch, in: MünchKommZPO, s 1042 para 22.

[24] Geimer, in: Zöller (ed), s 1042 para 2; Lachmann, para 1290; Münch, in: MünchKommZPO, s 1042 para 22; Saenger, in: Saenger (ed), s 1042 para 3. Of course, this can also be seen as a requirement resulting from the right to be heard.

comparable deadlines for both sides.[25] A special case of equal treatment is regulated in **s 1034 para 2 ZPO**: where an arbitration agreement unfairly prejudices one party regarding the constitution of the arbitral tribunal, the prejudiced party may ask the competent higher regional court to reconstitute the arbitral tribunal.

2. Right to be Heard

4.22 The right to be heard, guaranteed for arbitral proceedings in s 1042 para 1 cl 2 ZPO, is a further fundamental right of the parties. Here, too, the German arbitration law is in conformity with the Model Law (art 18) as well as foreign arbitration legislation.[26] The right to be heard is a necessary requirement in order for arbitral proceedings to be considered **principally equal to state court proceedings**, as can be seen from art 103 para 1 GG.[27] Violations of the right to be heard make an arbitral award based on such violations subject to **set aside** (s 1059 para 1 nos 1 lit b, 1 lit d and 2 lit b ZPO; for details see paras 6.207 *et seq.*).[28]

4.23 The right to be heard applies at all stages of the arbitral proceedings.[29] There are a number of provisions in the German arbitration law that are an expression of the right to be heard, such as s 1046 ZPO (statement of claim and statement of defense), s 1047 ZPO (right to oral hearing, equal information of all parties), and s 1049 ZPO (right to ask questions to a tribunal-appointed expert). At the same time, the law contains limitations that are necessary to preserve the efficiency of arbitral proceedings, for instance provisions on the waiver of rights for failure to properly object (ss 1027, 1040 para 2 ZPO) and default (s 1048 ZPO).[30] Whether or not to make use of the right to be heard is of course up to the parties.[31]

---

[25] Hartmann, in: Baumbach/Lauterbach/Albers/Hartmann (eds), s 1042 para 2; Lachmann, para 1290; Saenger, in: Saenger (ed), s 1042 para 3; Voit, in: Musielak/Voit (eds), s 1042 para 2; for a more detailed solution: Münch, in: MünchKommZPO, s 1042 para 22; a different view is held by Schlosser, in: Stein/Jonas (eds), s 1042 para 40.

[26] Sachs/Lörcher, in: *Arbitration in Germany*, s 1042 para 6; Münch, in: MünchKommZPO, s 1042 para 27; Schlosser, in: Stein/Jonas (eds), annex to s 1061 para 168.

[27] Lachmann, para 1295; Münch, in: MünchKommZPO, s 1042 para 2; Saenger, in: Saenger (ed), s 1042 para 4; Schlosser, in: Stein/Jonas (eds), s 1042 paras 37, 38; BGH NJW 1983, 867; NJW 1959, 2213, 2214.

[28] BT-Drucks 13/5274, p 46; Münch, in: MünchKommZPO, s 1042 para 58; Hartmann, in: Baumbach/Lauterbach/Albers/Hartmann (eds), s 1042 para 3; Saenger, in: Saenger (ed), s 1042 para 2; Reichold, in: Thomas/Putzo (eds), s 1042 para 2; Voit, in: Musielak/Voit (eds), s 1042 para 6; subject to certain conditions also: Lachmann, para 1358. By contrast, violations of s 1042 para 1 cl 2 ZPO cannot be brought in front of the German Federal Constitutional Court (BVerfG) by means of a constitutional challenge (*Verfassungsbeschwerde*). Constitutional challenges can be brought only against state actions, which is not the case with regard to the acts of an arbitral tribunal; see BVerfG NVwZ-RR 1995, 323; Geimer, in: Zöller (ed), s 1042 para 18; Münch, in: MünchKommZPO, s 1042 para 60; Voit, in: Musielak/Voit (eds), s 1042 para 6; Wilske/Markert, in: BeckOK ZPO, s 1042 para 2.

[29] Münch, in: MünchKommZPO, s 1042 para 29; Saenger, in: Saenger (ed), s 1042 para 5.

[30] BT-Drucks 13/5274, p 46.

[31] Sachs/Lörcher, in: *Arbitration in Germany*, s 1042 para 10; Geimer, in: Zöller (ed), s 1042 para 4; Münch, in: MünchKommZPO, s 1042 para 46; Voit, in: Musielak/Voit (eds), s 1042 para 5.

As a result of the right to be heard, each party has the **right to present the case** and to respond to the submissions of the opposing side before the arbitral tribunal ultimately decides.[32] The tribunal must not base its decision on factual submissions of a party of which the opposing party has not been made aware; the same applies mutatis mutandis to facts researched and developed by the tribunal itself. Procedural decisions must be **notified to all parties.**[33] Deadlines for submissions or comments by the parties must be commensurate to the individual circumstances; the deadlines governing state court litigation (eg ss 132, 274, 276, 277 ZPO) do not apply in arbitration.[34] Parties have a **right to request an oral hearing** (s 1047 para 1 ZPO). Where a party and its counsel are not able to attend a hearing, the tribunal is generally required to postpone it,[35] unless the tribunal has clear indications that the request to postpone is actually unfounded and a mere means to delay the proceedings.[36] All parties must be given an opportunity to participate in the **taking of evidence** and to comment on its outcome.[37] Generally, the tribunal is not required to allow post-hearing briefs, but can request that the parties immediately comment on the taking of evidence (closing statements), unless the evidentiary hearing has brought to light new facts which a party cannot be expected to comment on immediately.[38] **4.24**

The tribunal needs to **take note of the parties' submissions**, review them, and consider them in rendering its decision.[39] This does not mean that the tribunal is required to address each and every factual and legal argument of each party in the reasoning of the award.[40] Thus, in order to demonstrate a violation of the right to be heard, there must be clear evidence that the tribunal did not consider certain arguments at all that would have been capable of resulting in a different outcome.[41] **4.25**

---

[32] Hartmann, in: Baumbach/Lauterbach/Albers/Hartmann (eds), s 1042 para 4; Geimer, in: Zöller (ed), s 1042 para 6; Münch, in: MünchKommZPO, s 1042 paras 34 *et seq.*, 40 *et seq.*; Saenger, in: Saenger (ed), s 1042 para 6; Voit, in: Musielak/Voit (eds), s 1042 para 3.

[33] See, eg, for hearings and takings of evidences 1047 para 2 ZPO; Münch, in: MünchKommZPO, s 1042 para 44. Opposing view: Voit, in: Musielak/Voit (eds), s 1042 para 4.

[34] Hartmann, in: Baumbach/Lauterbach/Albers/Hartmann (eds), s 1042 para 11; Saenger, in: Saenger (ed), s 1042 para 19; Voit, in: Musielak/Voit (eds), s 1042 para 15.

[35] Münch, in: MünchKommZPO, s 1042 para 54; Voit, in: Musielak/Voit (eds), s 1042 para 15.

[36] Lachmann, paras 2590 *et seq.*

[37] See s 1047 paras 2 and 3 ZPO; Geimer, in: Zöller (ed), s 1042 para 9; Sachs/Lörcher, in: *Arbitration in Germany*, s 1042 paras 13, 18; Voit, in: Musielak/Voit (eds), s 1042 para 3.

[38] Münch, in: MünchKommZPO, s 1042 para 53. Opposing view: Schlosser, in: Stein/Jonas (eds), annex to s 1061 para 222; regarding new documents in foreign language see BGH WM 1977, 948.

[39] Münch, in MünchKommZPO, s 1042 para 49; Voit, in: Musielak/Voit (eds), s 1042 para 5; Wilske/Markert, in BeckOK ZPO, s 1042 para 8.

[40] BGH NJW 1990, 2199 = XVII Y.B. Com. Arb. 503 (1992); OLG München, SchiedsVZ 2011, 230, 232; Saenger, in: Saenger (ed), s 1042 para 7; Münch, in: MünchKommZPO, s 1042 para 49.

[41] Schlosser, in: Stein/Jonas (eds), annex to s 1061 para 201.

4.26 By contrast, the parties do not have a right to learn the arbitral tribunal's (**preliminary) views** prior to a decision.[42] Likewise, the arbitral tribunal—unlike a German state court (s 139 ZPO)—is not required to point to specific factual or **legal issues** that the tribunal finds relevant and that a party may have overlooked or on which it has a different view, as long as the party was on sufficient notice of the issue, eg as a result of the pleadings submitted by the other party.[43] Where a tribunal **disregards an offer of evidence,** this may be regarded as a mistake in the conduct of the proceedings, but this mistake as such may not necessarily rise to the level of a violation of the right to be heard (for details see paras 6.207 *et seq.*).[44]

3. Limited Investigation

4.27 Even though the mandate of arbitral tribunals to investigate the facts to some extent on its own motion applies only to the fact-finding stage of the proceedings, it is of sufficient fundamental importance to be discussed here in advance, as it can have significant impacts on the overall strategy and tactics to be considered and applied by the parties and their representatives in structuring the case and making their written and oral submissions. Section 1042 para 4 cl 2 ZPO authorizes the arbitral tribunal "to determine the admissibility of taking evidence, take evidence and assess freely such evidence." This provision follows art 19 para 2 cl 2 Model Law, and together with other provisions of the Tenth Book of the ZPO, it is understood by a majority of scholars in Germany to enshrine what is called the "principle of **limited investigation**."[45] This would mean that the arbitral tribunal is **not only authorized but also obliged** to establish the facts of the case on its own motion, similar to what German law provided for prior to the reform of the Tenth Book (s 1034 para 1 cl 1 ZPO prior version). Obviously, an arbitral tribunal does not have an inquisitorial mandate like a criminal court or even a prosecutor. Thus, it would not need to go beyond the four corners of the case as presented by the parties. However, within this framework, the tribunal would be tasked with establishing the facts to a certain extent separate and apart from the efforts of the party bearing the burden of proof.[46]

4.28 In our view, this position should be handled with some **circumspection**. In the absence of a party agreement to the contrary, the tribunal is certainly authorized

[42] BGH NJW 1959, 2213; NJW 1990, 3211; Lachmann, para 1300; Schwab/Walter, ch 15 para 3.

[43] Hartmann, in: Baumbach/Lauterbach/Albers/Hartmann (eds), s 1042 para 11; Münch, in: MünchKommZPO, s 1042 para 38; Voit, in: Musielak/Voit (eds), s 1042 para 13.

[44] See BGH NJW 1966, 549; Münch, in: MünchKommZPO, s 1042 paras 56, 109 and 117 with further references; Voit, in: Musielak/Voit (eds), s 1042 para 13. Opposing view: Schwab/Walter, ch 15 para 9.

[45] Lachmann, para 1281; Münch, in: MünchKommZPO, s 1042 paras 107 *et seq.*, 114; Saenger, in: Saenger (ed), s 1042 para 16; Voit, in: Musielak/Voit (eds), s 1042 para 13; Hamann/Lennarz, BB 2007, 1009, 1011; Quinke, SchiedsVZ 2013, 129, 132; Hilger, BB 2000, Beil. 8, pp 1 *et seq.*

[46] Schlosser, in: Stein/Jonas (eds), s 1042 para 44; Hartmann, in: Baumbach/Lauterbach/Albers/Hartmann (eds), s 1042 para 10.

to act according to the principle of limited investigation; this follows already from s 1042 para 4 cl 1 ZPO (see paras 4.9 *et seq.*). We do not think, however, that it is strictly required to do so. The wording of the Tenth Book does not mandate an inquisitorial approach. The provisions on default contained in s 1048 ZPO underline the discretion of the arbitral tribunal.[47] Section 1042 para 4 cl 2 ZPO expressly provides for an **empowerment of the tribunal and not a duty**. The legislative materials are silent on this issue.[48] The parties are free to limit the power of the tribunal or to establish it as a duty by agreement even during the proceedings; there is no need and no purpose to protect them by an implied duty contrary to the wording of the statute. The fact that inexperienced persons may appear before an arbitral tribunal[49] is not unique to arbitration; it can occur just as well in state court litigation, where there is no obligation of limited investigation.[50] Thus, in light of the principal equivalence of state court litigation and arbitration, there is no need to oblige an arbitral tribunal to conduct limited investigation.

The parties are of course free to agree to limited investigation, and certain institutional rules take a similar approach. For instance, under **s 27.1 cl 1 DIS Rules**, "the arbitral tribunal shall establish the facts underlying the dispute." Similarly, under **art 25.1 ICC Rules**, "The arbitral tribunal shall proceed within as short a time as possible to establish the facts of the case by all appropriate means." These standards are similar to the previous version of s 1034 para 1 cl 1 ZPO, which indeed contained a mandate for limited investigation. **4.29**

4. Procedural Efficiency and Duty to Further the Proceedings

The tribunal's duty to conduct the proceedings efficiently follows, among other things, from the arbitrator agreement (see para 3.172). It is also a general principle inherent in arbitration.[51] The same obligation lies with the parties as a result of the substantive law character of the arbitration agreement (see para 2.148). As stated earlier (paras 3.171 *et seq.*), the principal sanctions for violations of these duties are to be found within the procedural framework governing arbitral proceedings. Parties cannot sue arbitrators in state court to oblige them to act more efficiently or quickly. Rather, arbitrators who do not perform their obligations without undue delay are subject to termination and replacement (ss 1038, 1039 ZPO). Likewise, **4.30**

47 Contrary to Hilger, BB 2000, Beil. 8, pp 1, 4; Münch, in: MünchKommZPO, s 1042 para 114.

48 BT-Drucks 13/5274, p 46.

49 Münch, in: MünchKommZPO, s 1042 para 115.

50 Admittedly, there are heightened obligations of state courts to provide notice of certain issues to the parties (*Hinweispflicht*, s 139 ZPO). An arbitral tribunal may follow a similar approach where inexperienced parties are concerned; in fact, to some extent it may even be required to do so to ensure equal treatment and the right to be heard. Nevertheless, we do not see that from such a situation a mandate for factual investigation could be derived.

51 Münch, in: MünchKommZPO, s 1042 para 107; Lachmann, paras 214 *et seq.*; Blackaby/Partasides/Redfern/Hunter, para 6.275; regarding the responsibility of the chairman for the coordination and efficiency of the proceedings see Wilske/Markert, in: BeckOK ZPO, s 1042 para 23; Lörcher, BB 1996, Beil. 15, pp 9 *et seq.*

one party cannot sue the other for efficient and speedy conduct, nor can it enjoin a party from dilatory actions. Instead, it needs to turn to the arbitral tribunal and ask for sanctions against unduly inefficient or dilatory conduct by a party. This may include the application of provisions on preclusion (see below paras 4.64 *et seq.*) and default (see below paras 4.67 *et seq.*).

5. *Procedural Good Faith*

4.31 The duty of good faith and fair dealing (s 242 BGB) is an overarching principle of German law applying to all areas of the law. Thus, despite the lack of an express provision on procedural good faith, as a result of both the arbitration agreement and the arbitrator agreement, the principle also applies to arbitral proceedings and the way the parties have to conduct themselves in arbitration.[52] As an example, as a result of the principle of good faith, it is broadly recognized that in arbitral proceedings the parties are required to **plead truthfully**;[53] for state court litigation, this is expressly stipulated in s 138 ZPO. At the same time, it is to be recognized that arbitral proceedings are adversarial proceedings. Thus, a party is generally **not required to lend its hand** to help the other party win.[54] For instance, where one party makes a mistake in its submissions, or overlooks an issue, the other party is not required to point that out.

4.32 In addition, in Germany the traditional view is that a party is generally **not required to divulge information or documents** that are harmful to its case unless the law contained a specific provision allowing the court to order production of a document (ss 421 *et seq.* ZPO).[55] However, even in state court litigation this has changed over recent years, in particular with the amendment of s 142 ZPO (para 1.25). In arbitration, the issue does not arise in the first place, since the tribunal is entitled—pursuant to a strong view in legal literature even obligated—to conduct limited investigation of the facts anyway (see above paras 4.27 *et seq.*) and thus has broad discretion to order the production of documents.

6. *Right to be Represented by Counsel*

4.33 A party is not required to be represented by a lawyer in arbitral proceedings. At the same time, pursuant to s 1042 para 2 ZPO each party has a **non-derogable right** to be represented by counsel, a right which does not have a corresponding provision in the Model Law. This includes both German attorneys-at-law and persons admitted as attorney-at-law in a foreign jurisdiction.[56] A party is bound by the acts of its

---

[52] Münch, in: MünchKommZPO, s 1042 para 104; Siegert, KTS 1956, 33, 36.

[53] Münch, in: MünchKommZPO, s 1042 para 104; Saenger, in: Saenger (ed), s 1046 para 22; Lachmann, paras 455 *et seq.* points out that this obligation is unenforceable; leaving open BGH NJW 1957, 589.

[54] Implicitly: Kaufmann-Kohler/Bärtsch, SchiedsVZ 2004, 13, 16 *et seq.*

[55] Kaufmann-Kohler/Bärtsch, SchiedsVZ 2004, 13, 16 *et seq.*

[56] BT-Drucks 13/5274, p 46; Hartmann, in: Baumbach/Lauterbach/Albers/Hartmann (eds), s 1042 para 6; Geimer, in: Zöller (ed), s 1042 para 19; Lachmann, para 1367; Saenger, in: Saenger (ed), s 1042 para 11; Voit, in: Musielak/Voit (eds), s 1042 para 7.

counsel, including mistakes or omissions (eg missed deadline).[57] A counsel may be served with legal papers on behalf of the party that he or she represents.[58] Besides attorneys-at-law, a party can use other persons as its representatives or for assistance. Unlike the right to be represented by counsel, **other representatives or assistants** can be excluded by party agreement. The arbitral tribunal may exclude party representatives who are not legal counsel where such representative is incapable of properly representing the party, including grossly inappropriate behavior.[59] By contrast, improper exclusion of counsel may subject an award to challenge based on s 1059 para 2 nos 1 lit b, 1 lit d, and 2 lit b ZPO.[60]

As a matter of German law, there are **no specific qualification requirements** for counsel representing a party in arbitral proceedings. Nevertheless, at least as far as disputes with a certain significance are concerned, parties are of course well advised to select counsel with experience in arbitration. Clearly, arbitral proceedings differ significantly from regular state court litigation, especially by virtue of the tribunal's wide discretion regarding the conduct of the proceedings. **4.34**

The compensation of German attorneys-at-law is regulated by the Attorney Compensation Act (RVG). Unless the parties otherwise agree, the RVG provides for a **statutory fee scale** which is based on the amount in dispute and which also applies to party representation in arbitral proceedings.[61] A party and its counsel are free to agree on a different fee structure, such as hourly rates, fixed fees, or budgets for different phases of an arbitration. In practice, this occurs frequently. As far as cost awards are concerned (s 1057 ZPO), those are not limited to attorney fees based on the RVG scale; instead, tribunals frequently award costs on the basis of hourly rates (see paras 6.80 *et seq.*).[62] **4.35**

Unlike in German state court proceedings, there is **no statutory legal aid** (ss 114 *et seq.* ZPO) for arbitral proceedings. A party that cannot afford arbitral **4.36**

---

57 See s 85 ZPO together with BGH NJW 94, 2155; Schwab/Walter, ch 16 para 22; Saenger, in: Saenger (ed), s 1042 para 11.

58 Lachmann, para 1778; Münch, in: MünchKommZPO, s 1042 para 65; Reichold, in: Thomas/Putzo (eds), s 1054 para 9.

59 Münch, in: MünchKommZPO, s 1042 para 73, correctly pointing out that in such case the arbitral tribunal needs to give the affected party sufficient time to select a new representative.

60 Geimer, in: Zöller (ed), s 1042 para 19; Münch, in: MünchKommZPO, s 1042 para 69; Voit, in: Musielak/Voit (eds), s 1042 para 7. For efforts, in particular in international arbitration, to establish ethics rules for party representatives and corresponding sanctions by the arbitral tribunal, see IBA Guidelines on Party Representation in International Arbitration, 2013 (available at http://www.ibanet.org, last visited December 1, 2015) as well as recent amendments to the LCIA Rules, in particular their amended art 18 and newly added Annex (General Guidelines for the Parties' Legal Representatives); Park, (2014) 30 Arb. Int'l 409; Cummins, (2014) 30 Arb. Int'l 429; Rau, (2014) 30 Arb. Int'l 457; Waincymer, (2014) 30 Arb. Int'l 513.

61 See s 36 para 1 RVG; Bernuth, SchiedsVZ 2013, 212; Münch, in: MünchKommZPO, s 1042 para 70; Lachmann, para 1946.

62 Risse/Altenkirch, SchiedsVZ 2012, 5, 9 *et seq.*; Saenger/Uphoff, NJW 2014, 1412, 1416; OLG München, SchiedsVZ 2012, 282, 286. Opposing view: Lachmann, para 1947.

proceedings may be allowed to **terminate the arbitration agreement for cause** (see para 2.161) and bring action in state court, thereby gaining access to legal aid.[63]

C. Typical Structure and Frequent Steps of Arbitral Proceedings

4.37 In this section, we address the typical structure of arbitral proceedings conducted in Germany, as well as frequently encountered steps in such proceedings. It goes without saying that our description cannot be exhaustive but can merely address what we consider particularly relevant in German practice. We start with the initiation of the proceedings (below paras 4.38 *et seq.*), then turn to initial submissions, and possible counterclaims (below paras 4.55 *et seq.*) before we address the initial structuring of the proceedings (below paras 4.87 *et seq.*) and initial determinations by the arbitral tribunal (below paras 4.93 *et seq.*). We also address further written submissions (below paras 4.110 *et seq.*), document disclosure (below paras 4.113 *et seq.*), the oral hearing (below paras 4.126 *et seq.*), the taking of evidence (below paras 4.146 *et seq.*), and post-hearing steps (below paras 4.203 *et seq.*). In Chapter 6, we explain how arbitral proceedings may be terminated by final award or other than by final award (below paras 6.126 *et seq.*).

I. Commencement of the Proceedings

4.38 We first describe the means and methods of initiation both under the German arbitration law and in institutional arbitration (below paras 4.39 *et seq.*), before we address the legal effects thereof (below paras 4.52 *et seq.*).

1. Means and Methods of Initiation

4.39 **a) German ad hoc Proceedings** Regarding the initiation of arbitral proceedings, the German arbitration law follows a **three-step model** consisting of (i) **request** for arbitration s 1044 cl 1 ZPO), (ii) **constitution** of the arbitral tribunal (ss 1034 *et seq.* ZPO, see Chapter 3); and (ii) **initial pleadings** by claimant (statement of claim) and respondent (statement of defense), s 1046 ZPO. German law thereby closely follows arts 21, 23 Model Law. In this present section, we discuss step one, the request for arbitration in more detail. German law contains **few mandatory formalities** for the request for arbitration; pursuant to s 1044 cl 2 ZPO its **minimum contents**[64] are (i) designation of the parties; (ii) designation of the subject matter of the dispute; and (iii) reference to the applicable

[63] See Court of Arbitration of the Hamburg Chamber of Commerce, SchiedsVZ 2010, 173, 175; Münch, in: MünchKommZPO, s 1042 para 72.

[64] Geimer, in: Zöller (ed), s 1044 para 2; Saenger, in: Saenger (ed), s 1044 para 3; Wilske/Markert, in: BeckOK ZPO, s 1044 para 2.

arbitration agreement. Unless otherwise agreed by the parties, arbitral proceedings on a certain dispute commence on the day on which the respondent receives the request for arbitration (s 1044 cl 1 ZPO).

As regards the minimum content for a proper request for arbitration, the claimant first needs to **designate the parties.** The most practical way is to set forth the names and addresses of the claimant(s) and the respondent(s). In the absence thereof, a designation may still be proper where it is clear and unequivocal from the circumstances who the parties are.[65] **4.40**

Second, the claimant must **designate the subject matter** of the dispute. In German civil procedure law, as far as state court litigation is concerned, much has been written on the notion of the subject matter of the dispute, and there are a number of theories how to properly define it. The prevailing view in Germany today is that the subject matter of the dispute is defined by two elements: (i) the relief sought; and (ii) the facts supporting such claim.[66] This definition is also implied by s 1046 para 1 cl 1 ZPO. For purposes of the request for arbitration, s 1044 cl 2 ZPO merely requires a "designation" of the subject matter, whereas in the statement of claim (s 1046 para 1 cl 1 ZPO) the claimant is required to substantiate claim and underlying facts. Thus, for purposes of s 1044 ZPO, in the request for arbitration a **fairly minimal description** of the claim and the underlying facts suffices. It must be sufficient to **put the respondent on notice** as to which claim and which set of facts will now be the subject matter of arbitral proceedings with the claimant.[67] Additional requirements may follow from **other legal grounds**. For instance, in disputes regarding the validity of corporate resolutions, typically the challenge procedure needs to be commenced within a certain deadline, which is one month in case of stock corporations (s 246 para 1 AktG).[68] The deadline is a substantive-law deadline and it is complied with only where the claimant, within the deadline, specifies "the core facts" that give rise to grounds for contestation.[69] **4.41**

The third minimum requirement is a **reference to the applicable arbitration agreement**. The arbitration agreement needs to be designated with clarity. Where there **4.42**

[65] Münch, in: MünchKommZPO, s 1044 para 15; Saenger, in: Saenger (ed), s 1044 para 3.

[66] BGH NZG 2014, 110, 112; NJW-RR 2006, 1502, 1503; Saenger, in: Saenger (ed), introduction para 101; Vollkommer, in: Zöller (ed), Einleitung para 83.

[67] Geimer, in: Zöller (ed), s 1044 para 2; Sachs/Lörcher, in: *Arbitration in Germany*, s 1044 para 12; Hartmann, in: Baumbach/Lauterbach/Albers/Hartmann (eds), s 1044 para 2; Voit in: Musielak/Voit (eds), s 1044 para 2; Schwab/Walter, ch 16 para 6.

[68] For German limited liability companies (*Gesellschaften mit beschränkter Haftung—GmbH*), the law is silent on applicable contestation deadlines. Pursuant to German precedent and the prevailing view in German legal literature, the one-month periods set forth for stock corporations does not apply directly, but should be used as guidance; see eg BGH GmbHR 1999, 714; NZG 2005, 551; BGHZ 101, 113, 117; Wertenbruch, in: MünchKommGmbHG, appendix s 47 para 209; Roth, in: Roth/Altmeppen, s 47 para 144.

[69] BGHZ 137, 378, 386; see also BGH NJW 1995, 260, 261; AG 2005, 613, 614; Hüffer, in: MünchKommAktG, s 246 para 44; K Schmidt, in: Großkomm AktG, s 246 paras 22 *et seq.*; Semler, in: Münchener Handbuch des Gesellschaftsrechts, Vol 4, § 41 para 73.

is only one arbitration agreement between the claimant and the respondent, there should be no doubts. Otherwise, a more specific reference may be necessary, eg by reference to a certain date or contract.[70] It is not necessary to include a copy of the arbitration agreement in the request for arbitration, but it is good practice to do so.

4.43 A request for arbitration that does not satisfy the above-described minimum requirements is invalid.[71] It is incapable of suspending the statute of limitations.[72] An arbitral award based thereon would be subject to set aside (s 1059 para 2 no 1 lit b ZPO),[73] unless the parties have reduced the minimum requirements by valid and binding party agreement. The parties are of course free to agree on additional necessary contents for the request for arbitration (eg nomination of an arbitrator, more particularized pleadings, etc).[74]

4.44 The minimum contents of the request for arbitration are designed to put the respondent on notice as to the subject matter of the dispute.[75] This type of notice is necessary to preserve the respondent's right to fair proceedings (s 1059 para 2 no 1 lit b ZPO). The claimant must express clearly and unequivocally that it **requests** a certain dispute to be **presented to an arbitral tribunal**. The wording chosen by the claimant is relevant but not exclusively material; in practice, it is of course advisable to use the wording of s 1044 ZPO or the words "request for arbitration." Where these terms are not used, the matter becomes one of interpretation. Mere threats or non-binding announcements to take a case to arbitration will not suffice.[76] In case of doubt, an important element of interpretation may be how the recipient understood it and reacted to it. Where the recipient clearly understood it to be a request for arbitration and acted accordingly, eg by nominating its arbitrator or otherwise participating in the constitution of the arbitral tribunal, a communication that may seem unclear on its face may be interpreted nevertheless as a request for arbitration.[77]

4.45 The respondent needs to **receive the request**. Any form of receipt is sufficient; formal service of process is not necessary.[78] In case the whereabouts of a party are unknown, s 1028 para 1 ZPO permits the use of the addressee's last-known

---

[70] Similarly: Lachmann, para 760.

[71] Hartmann, in: Baumbach/Lauterbach/Albers/Hartmann (eds), s 1044 para 2; Münch, in: MünchKommZPO, s 1044 para 13; Saenger, in: Saenger (ed), s 1044 para 3.

[72] Peters/Jacoby, in: Staudinger, s 204 para 101; Grothe, in: MünchKommBGB, s 204 para 54.

[73] Saenger, in: Saenger (ed), s 1044 para 3; Münch, in: MünchKommZPO, s 1059 paras 23 *et seq.*

[74] Münch, in: MünchKommZPO, s 1044 para 28; Saenger, in: Saenger (ed), s 1044 para 3.

[75] Münch, in: MünchKommZPO, s 1044 para 5; Voit, in: Musielak/Voit (eds), s 1044 para 2; Wilske/Markert, in: BeckOK ZPO, s 1044 para 3.

[76] Sachs/Lörcher, in: *Arbitration in Germany*, s 1044 para 5; Münch, in: MünchKommZPO, s 1044 para 7.

[77] Implicitly: Schlosser, in: Stein/Jonas (eds), s 1044 para 3.

[78] Hartmann, in: Baumbach/Lauterbach/Albers/Hartmann (eds), s 1044 para 2; Geimer, in: Zöller (ed), s 1044 para 2; Münch, in: MünchKommZPO, s 1044 para 11; Voit, in: Musielak/Voit (eds), s 1044 para 2.

mailing address, place of business, or habitual residence in order to effect service by way of registered mail/return receipt requested or any other means which provides a record of the attempt to deliver it there. Apart from this special situation, since the law does not prescribe any form for the request for arbitration, even an oral communication could be sufficient; for obvious reasons of legal certainty and proof, parties should be strongly discouraged from initiating arbitral proceedings orally.[79] By contrast, in today's world, initiation by email could be proper.[80] Nevertheless, from a practical perspective, a claimant is well advised to choose a means of communication that enables clear proof of receipt. Thus, in many cases, a traditional letter with return receipt requested will still be the method of choice, unless the statute of limitations is about to expire, in which case a telefax with transmission report should be considered.[81]

The claimant can **combine** the request for arbitration and the statement of claim into one document.[82] This frequently happens in German practice, as it is in line with the approach taken in state court litigation, where the complaint needs to contain all reasonable particulars and offers of evidence (ss 253, 130 ZPO, para 1.18). A combined approach is less common for international parties coming from other legal traditions. Which approach is preferable is a matter for case-by-case analysis. Incorporating a full-blown statement of claim in the request for arbitration may demonstrate the preparedness and seriousness of a claimant in pursuing its case. It requires, on the other hand, that the claimant be reasonably certain about the full case strategy, a large part of the facts of the case and the relief to be sought. Where a claimant's analysis and strategy are less advanced, eg due to lack of access to information on the case, the two-step approach underlying the German arbitration law may be more appropriate. **4.46**

b) DIS Proceedings For the initiation of arbitral proceedings, the DIS Rules follow approaches that slightly differ from the Tenth Book of the ZPO. The DIS Rules do **not provide for a separation or distinction** between the request for arbitration and the statement of claim. Instead, under s 6.1 DIS Rules: **4.47**

> [t]he claimant shall file the statement of claim with a DIS Secretariat. Arbitral proceedings commence upon receipt of the statement of claim by a DIS Secretariat.

The mandatory **minimum requirements** for a statement of claim under s 6.2 DIS Rules are (i) identification of the parties; (ii) specification of the relief sought; **4.48**

---

79 Schwab/Walter, ch 16 para 2; Voit, in: Musielak/Voit (eds), s 1044 para 2; oral initiation even excluded (because of the wording *Empfang*) according to Hartmann, in: Baumbach/Lauterbach/Albers/Hartmann (eds), s 1044 para 2.

80 Schlosser, in: Stein/Jonas (eds), s 1044 para 3; Münch, in: MünchKommZPO, s 1044 para 11.

81 Münch, in: MünchKommZPO, s 1044 para 12.—Regarding evidentiary value of telefaxes see OLG München, NJW 1994, 527; CR 1999, 368; more restrictive: BGH NJW 1995, 665, 666 *et seq.*; BeckRS 2011, 21743; OLG Köln, NJW-RR 1995, 1463 *et seq.*; OLG Brandenburg, BB 2008, 901.

82 Lachmann, para 761; Münch, in: MünchKommZPO, s 1044 para 4.

(iii) particulars regarding the facts and circumstances which give rise to the claim(s); (iv) reproduction of the arbitration agreement; and (v) nomination of an arbitrator, unless the parties have agreed on a decision by sole arbitrator. Thus, in several respects, the DIS Rules are somewhat stricter than s 1044 ZPO. Whereas the latter requires only a "designation" of the subject matter of the dispute, under the DIS Rules particulars on the facts giving rise to the claim are necessary already at the commencement stage. Likewise, a mere reference to the arbitration agreement is not enough; it needs to be reproduced. Section 6.3 DIS Rules recommends as additional content for the statement of claim (i) particulars regarding the amount in dispute; (ii) proposals for the nomination of an arbitrator, where the parties have agreed on a decision by sole arbitrator; and (iii) particulars regarding the place of arbitration, the language of the proceedings, and the rules applicable to the substance of the dispute. Notably, under the DIS Rules, the next step is the constitution of the arbitral tribunal, and only thereafter will the respondent be required to file its statement of defense (s 9 DIS Rules). Accordingly, the claimant party will be obligated to participate in the constitution of the arbitral tribunal without the benefit of receipt of respondent's initial defense.

4.49 c) **ICC Proceedings** The ICC Rules again take a somewhat modified approach. As with s 1044 ZPO, arbitral proceedings commence with a **request for arbitration**, which shall however be sent to the ICC Secretariat, and the ICC Secretariat then notifies the claimant and the respondent of the receipt of the request and the date of such receipt (art 4.1 ICC Rules). This date is the date of commencement of arbitration (art 4.2 ICC Rules).

4.50 The **minimum content** for the request is set forth in art 4.3 ICC Rules: (a) the name in full, description, address, and other contact details of each of the parties; (b) the name in full, address, and other contact details of any person(s) representing the claimant in the arbitration; (c) a description of the nature and circumstances of the dispute giving rise to the claims and of the basis upon which the claims are made; (d) a statement of the relief sought, together with the amounts of any quantified claims and, to the extent possible, an estimate of the monetary value of any other claims; (e) any relevant agreements and, in particular, the arbitration agreement(s); (f) where claims are made under more than one arbitration agreement, an indication of the arbitration agreement under which each claim is made; (g) all relevant particulars and any observations or proposals concerning the number of arbitrators and their choice in accordance with the provisions of arts 12 and 13 ICC Rules, and any nomination of an arbitrator required thereby; and (h) all relevant particulars and any observations or proposals as to the place of the arbitration, the applicable rules of law, and the language of the arbitration. It goes without saying that this is again more detailed than the minimum requirements under s 1044 ZPO.

4.51 Once the claimant has initiated the proceedings, under art 5 ICC Rules, the next step is the **answer by the respondent**, containing similar particulars, and to be submitted to the ICC Secretariat, which then transmits it to the claimant. With its answer, the respondent is to nominate an arbitrator, and the **constitution of the tribunal** shall then be completed (art 12 ICC Rules). Once constituted, the arbitral tribunal takes over the proceedings and establishes the terms of reference (arts 16, 23 ICC Rules).

2. *Legal Effects*

In state court proceedings, commencing an action triggers the pendency of the case (*Rechtshängigkeit*). The German arbitration law does not formally mirror this concept for arbitral proceedings. Nevertheless, commencing arbitral proceedings has similar effects, and some refer to this situation as **pendency of the arbitration** (*Schiedshängigkeit*).[83] The main substantive-law effect (under German law) of commencing arbitration is the **interruption of the statute of limitations** on the claim subject to the dispute, s 204 para 1 no 11 BGB. Commencing arbitration thus has the same effect as bringing an action in state court (s 204 para 1 no 1 BGB).[84] Generally, suspension is effective even if the arbitral tribunal later finds that it does not have jurisdiction, for instance because it determines that the arbitration agreement is invalid, does not cover the subject matter of the dispute or does not bind one of the parties; only where the reference to an arbitration agreement is entirely frivolous does s 204 para 1 no 11 BGB not apply.[85] **4.52**

The suspension is effective for "**six months** after the final and binding decision or other termination of the instituted proceedings" (s 204 para 2 cl 1 BGB). Even though technically the arbitral proceedings are usually terminated by final award or order of the tribunal pursuant to s 1056 ZPO, a different reading encompassing potential set aside proceedings has been suggested for purposes of s 204 para 2 cl 1 BGB.[86] Otherwise, where the arbitral tribunal rejects a claim, a claimant may be successful in achieving the setting aside of the award; nevertheless, the claimant would be barred from continuing the proceedings or bringing a new arbitration because the statute of limitations would no longer be suspended, and would have expired in the meantime. Alternatively, and probably more persuasively, the set aside proceedings should be considered to suspend the statute of limitations.[87]—Where the proceedings come to a standstill due to lack of activity on the part of the parties, the six-month period starts with the last procedural action of the parties or the arbitral tribunal, and the suspension starts again once one of the parties resumes conducting the proceedings (s 204 para 2 cl 2 and 3 BGB). **4.53**

---

[83] Schlosser, in: Stein/Jonas (eds), s 1044 paras 4 *et seq.*; Hartmann, in: Baumbauch/Lauterbach/Albers/Hartmann (eds), s 1044 para 3; Lachmann, para 1450.

[84] Geimer, in: Zöller (ed), s 1044 para 4; Münch, in: MünchKommZPO, s 1044 para 31.

[85] Lachmann, paras 767 *et seq.*; Münch, in: MünchKommZPO, s 1044 para 35; similar: Voit, in: Musielak/Voit (eds), s 1044 para 5.

[86] Münch, in: MünchKommZPO, s 1044 para 31.

[87] Grothe, in: MünchKommBGB, s 204 para 103; similarly Ellenberger, in: Palandt (ed), s 204 para 43 (for annex procedures under s 1058 ZPO).

4.54 A further substantive-law effect (under German law) of commencing arbitration is to trigger the respondent's obligation to **pay interest** in analogous application of ss 291, 288 BGB in an amount of five (or nine) percentage points above the base interest rate per annum.[88]

II. Initial Submissions; Counterclaims

4.55 In this section, we address some ground rules for initial submissions under the Tenth Book of the ZPO. Specifically, once arbitral proceedings have been commenced and the arbitral tribunal has been constituted as described in Chapter 3, the claimant will be required, within the deadline agreed by the parties or set by the arbitral tribunal, to file its statement of claim, substantiating its claim and the underlying facts (s 1046 para 1 cl 1 ZPO, see below paras 4.57 *et seq.*). As a next step, the respondent has to file its statement of defense, again within the agreed or tribunal-ordered deadline; in its statement of defense the respondent needs to "comment" on the statement of claim, s 1046 para 1 cl 1 ZPO (see below para 4.59). Legal issues frequently playing an important role at this stage of the proceedings are burden of substantiation and proof (see below paras 4.60 *et seq.*), preclusion (see below paras 4.64 *et seq.*), as well as deadlines and default (see below paras 4.67 *et seq.*).

4.56 Also in this section, we deal with a number of procedural issues frequently relevant at this stage of the proceedings, namely amendments to the initial submissions (below paras 4.73 *et seq.*), issues raised by counterclaims, set-off, and the exercise of retention rights (below paras 4.78 *et seq.*). We conclude this section with some drafting considerations (see below paras 4.84 *et seq.*).

1. Statement of Claim

4.57 The statement of claim does **not require any specific form**; in theory, it could be rendered orally,[89] which is, however, entirely impractical. In practice, some way of written documentation is the norm, which includes such means as telefax and email. In order to substantiate its claim, the claimant needs to make plausible factual allegations which, under the applicable law, would be capable of justifying the relief sought.[90] A legal analysis is not required; the arbitral tribunal is deemed to know the law (***iura novit curia***),[91] which is an interesting concept, given that the

[88] Lachmann, para 763; Münch, in: MünchKommZPO, s 1044 para 36; Voit, in: Musielak/Voit (eds), s 1044 para 6. The base interest rate is a floating interest rate that is adjusted every six months based on the refinancing interest rates of the European Central Bank (s 247 BGB).

[89] Schwab/Walter, ch 16 para 2; Münch, in: MünchKommZPO, s 1046 para 7. Opposing view: Lachmann, para 1442 (written form required).

[90] Hartmann, in: Baumbach/Lauterbach/Albers/Hartmann (eds), s 1046 para 2; Lachmann, para 1443; Geimer, in: Zöller (ed), s 1046 para 1; Münch, in: MünchKommZPO, s 1046 para 5; Saenger, in: Saenger (ed), s 1046 para 2.

[91] Lachmann, para 1445; Münch, in: MünchKommZPO, s 1046 para 4.

arbitrators neither need to be lawyers nor do they need to have any other form of legal training (see para 3.59).

The concept of conclusiveness known from German state court litigation is usually not applied strictly in arbitration, indeed sometimes not at all.[92] As explained (para 1.19), this concept means that particularized fact-pleading and detailed offers of evidence are necessary to substantiate a claim. The court then needs to conduct a detailed legal analysis as to whether these facts, if proven, would support the claim sought. Only if the answer is yes would the court proceed to the taking of evidence with regard to those facts only that are relevant for the decision and disputed (***Relationstechnik***, see para 1.21). Whilst German practitioners often view this concept as a compelling tool to further procedural economy, it is within the arbitral tribunal's discretion whether to follow it.[93] Furthermore, it should be noted that in practice, the concept of conclusiveness is not always followed strictly in German state court litigation, either. **4.58**

2. Statement of Defense

The statement of defense contains the **respondent's "comments"** to the statement of claim, which may be denials of facts, additional factual allegations, defenses, and pieces of evidence that the respondent intends to use, as well as, of course, respondent's legal arguments.[94] German law expressly provides that with their initial submissions, the parties may—but are not required to—submit relevant documents; they may also designate further pieces of evidence that they intend to use (s 1046 para 1 cl 2 ZPO). Section 1046 ZPO is inspired by art 23 Model Law. **4.59**

3. Burden of Substantiation and Proof

From a German perspective, burden of substantiation and burden of proof need to be distinguished. **Burden of substantiation** addresses the **level of specificity** with which facts need to be pleaded.[95] It is a **procedural issue** that is left to the discretion of the arbitral tribunal, unless the parties have made specific agreements thereon (which is rare).[96] As stated in paras 1.17 *et seq.*, from state court litigation, German practitioners are accustomed to fairly stringent substantiation requirements. In German state court litigation, a party is required, in its written submissions, to make its factual allegations as precise and detailed as reasonably possible (who did **4.60**

[92] Voit, in: Musielak/Voit (eds), s 1046 para 2; Schlosser, in: Stein/Jonas (eds), s 1046 para 3.

[93] Prevailing view, see eg Geimer, in: Zöller (ed), s 1046 para 1; Voit, in: Musielak/Voit (eds), s 1046 para 2; Quinke, SchiedsVZ 2013, 129, 132. Opposing view (*"weitgehende Schlüssigkeit"* [by and large conclusiveness] required): Münch, in: MünchKommZPO, s 1046 para 5.

[94] Lachmann, paras 1463 *et seq.*; Münch, in: MünchKommZPO, s 1046 para 10; Saenger, in: Saenger (ed), s 1046 para 4.

[95] Foerste, in: Musielak/Voit (eds), s 286 paras 17 *et seq.*; Prütting, in: MünchKommZPO, s 286 paras 28 *et seq.*; Bacher, in: BeckOK ZPO, s 286 paras 2 *et seq.*

[96] Implicitly: Münch, in: MünchKommZPO, s 1049 para 6; Schlosser, in: Stein/Jonas (eds), s 1051 para 7.

what, when, and why?). In addition, for each allegation for which the party bears the burden of proof and which is likely to be denied by the other party, an offer of evidence is required. Substantiation of factual allegations may not be left to an oral hearing or the taking of evidence. Instead, where factual allegations are not pleaded with sufficient specificity and substantiation, a German state court may dismiss the claim as inconclusive and unsubstantiated (see paras 1.18 *et seq.*).

4.61 Arbitral tribunals are not bound by these standards, but they are free to use them. The stronger the nexus of arbitral proceedings to Germany and German legal traditions, the more likely it is that an arbitral tribunal may seek inspiration from this approach, and the more likely it is that a party will urge the arbitral tribunal to do so if it benefits therefrom (typically the respondent).

4.62 By contrast, **burden of proof** under German law is understood to be an issue determined by **substantive law**.[97] The basic principle is that each party bears the burden of proof for those issues from which it would benefit in the arbitration or litigation (***Günstigkeitsprinzip***).[98] In order to determine which issues are beneficial to which party, the arbitral tribunal needs to look at the cause(s) of action brought in the proceedings and the elements constituting the cause of action as well as the elements constituting the defenses raised by the respondent. German substantive law is very artful in formulating the elements of a cause of action and possible defenses. Thus, a close look at the statute book is necessary to find out who has the burden of proof for which element. For instance, regarding contractual damage claims the claimant creditor bears the burden of proof for the breach of duty, causation, and damages (s 280 para 1 cl 1 BGB), whereas the respondent debtor bears the burden of proof that it acted without fault (s 280 para 1 cl 2 BGB). This can be derived from the wording: "This does not apply where the debtor is not responsible for the breach."

4.63 Against this background, we address these issues already here, in the context of the parties' written submissions. Depending on the approach taken by an arbitral tribunal sitting in Germany, they may be relevant a long time before an oral hearing or an evidentiary hearing. In many proceedings, they are eminently important already at the stage of written submissions.

4. Preclusion

4.64 The rules governing preclusion are examples of provisions implementing the principle of **procedural efficiency** (see above para 4.30). Where a non-mandatory procedural provision of the German arbitration law or a requirement agreed upon by the parties has not been complied with, a party **must object** within the deadline

[97] Greger, in: Zöller (ed), Vor s 284 para 15; Münch, in: MünchKommZPO, s 1042 para 120.
[98] BGH NJW-RR 2010, 1378, 1379; NJW 2005, 2395, 2396; NJW 1991, 1052, 1053; Laumen, in: Prütting/Gehrlein, s 286 para 62; Reichold, in: Thomas/Putzo (eds), Vorbem s 284 para 23; Prütting, in: MünchKommZPO, s 286 para 111.

provided for by law or party agreement, or otherwise without undue delay; if it fails to do so, the right to object will be precluded, unless the party was not aware of the non-compliance (**s 1027 ZPO**). German law thereby follows art 4 Model Law, which serves the interests of procedural economy and legal certainty.[99]

Section 1027 ZPO does not apply where it is superseded by **special provisions**. For instance, regarding the **form** required for an arbitration agreement, **s 1031 para 6 ZPO** contains a special provision which takes precedence over s 1027 ZPO.[100] Pursuant to s 1031 para 6 ZPO, form defects of an arbitration agreement are cured where a party participates in the merits phase of the arbitration without objecting as to form. Similarly, objections to the **tribunal's jurisdiction** are regulated separately in **s 1040 para 2 ZPO**, requiring such objection to be made at the latest with the response to the request for arbitration. For state court proceedings, s 295 ZPO contains a similar but somewhat different provision. On the one hand, s 295 ZPO is stricter in the sense that even the party that is negligently ignorant of the non-compliance is precluded. On the other hand, s 295 ZPO does not require action without undue delay, but only an objection in the next oral hearing. **4.65**

Apart from such special provisions, s 1027 ZPO applies to all non-mandatory procedural or party-agreed requirements. For practical purposes, objection without undue delay means the next oral hearing or, where no hearing is scheduled, by way of a brief to be filed immediately.[101] The only excuse that s 1027 ZPO recognizes is lack of knowledge, for which the person making the late objection bears the burden of proof.[102] **4.66**

5. Deadlines and Default

Section 1048 ZPO addresses **four scenarios** of party default: **4.67**

- First, failure by the claimant to submit its statement of claim within the deadline ordered by the arbitral tribunal (s 1046 para 1 ZPO, see below para 4.68).
- Second, failure by the respondent to submit its statement of defense within the deadline ordered by the arbitral tribunal (s 1046 para 1 ZPO, see below para 4.68).
- Third, failure of a party to appear at an oral hearing without proper excuse (s 1048 para 3 alt 1 ZPO: arbitral tribunal may continue the proceedings and render an award based on the available evidence).
- Fourth, failure of a party to produce a document within a defined deadline without proper excuse (s 1048 para 3 alt 2 ZPO; arbitral tribunal may continue the proceedings and render an award based on the available evidence).

99 Hartmann, in: Baumbach/Lauterbach/Albers/Hartmann (eds), s 1027 para 1; Münch, in: MünchKommZPO, s 1027 para 1; Saenger, in: Saenger (ed), s 1027 para 1; Voit, in: Musielak/Voit (eds), s 1027 para 1.

100 Schlosser, in: Stein/Jonas (eds), s 1027 para 1; Voit, in Musielak/Voit (eds), s 1027 para 2; Saenger, in: Saenger (ed), s 1027 para 1.

101 BT-Drucks 13/5274, p 32; Münch, in: MünchKommZPO, s 1027 para 10.

102 Lachmann, para 1433; Wagner, in: *Arbitration in Germany*, s 1027 para 10; Voit, in: Musielak/Voit (eds), s 1027 para 4.

4.68 Deadlines ordered by the tribunal for the statement of claim and the statement of defense need to be **reasonable and appropriate**, so as to preserve the party's rights to equal treatment and to be heard. In case the claimant misses the deadline without satisfactory excuse, the tribunal orders the termination of the proceedings (ss 1048 para 1, 1056 para 2 no 1 lit a ZPO; likewise s 6.4 DIS Rules and art 4.4 ICC Rules), whereas if the respondent misses the deadline without proper excuse the tribunal continues the proceedings without considering the respondent to have admitted the claimant's factual allegations (which would be the regular consequence in German state court litigation) (s 1048 para 2 ZPO).[103] Thus, the view has been expressed that missing the deadline is largely without sanction for the respondent.[104]

4.69 Apart from these specific examples of default, a party may be in default with **other deadlines** set by the arbitral tribunal, and unless the party properly excuses its default, the arbitral tribunal has discretion to disregard submissions of a party that occur thereafter, where it has clearly communicated that such will be the consequences of default.[105] This applies both to factual allegations and offers of evidence.[106] By contrast, legal arguments are generally not precluded as a result of missing a deadline, as the applicable law is a matter to be known by the arbitral tribunal (*iura novit curia*).[107]

4.70 In all of the above scenarios, the party that has missed the deadline may attempt to **excuse its failure**, and it has the burden of proof for any excuse on which it wishes to rely.[108] A recognized example may be a sudden change of legal counsel.[109]

4.71 The arbitral tribunal may also order the **closing of the proceedings** (cut-off date), which means that there shall be no further submissions thereafter.[110] Article 27 ICC Rules is a good example (similar s 31 DIS Rules):

> As soon as possible after the last hearing concerning matters to be decided in an award or the filing of the last authorized submissions concerning such matters, whichever is later, the arbitral tribunal shall:
> a) declare the proceedings closed with respect to the matters to be decided in the award; and
> b) inform the Secretariat and the parties of the date by which it expects to submit its draft award to the Court for approval pursuant to Article 33.

---

[103] The same rule is contained in s 30.1 DIS Rules; similarly art 5.2 ICC Rules.

[104] Voit, in: Musielak/Voit (eds), s 1048 para 3.

[105] Geimer, in: Zöller (ed), s 1046 para 3; Schlosser, in: Stein/Jonas (eds), annex to s 1061 para 234; Sachs/Lörcher, in: *Arbitration in Germany*, s 1046 para 10; Lachmann, para 1254; Wilske/Markert, in: BeckOK ZPO, s 1046 para 6. Opposing view: Hartmann, in: Baumbach/Lauterbach/Albers/Hartmann (eds), s 1048 para 5.

[106] Lachmann, paras 1649, 1665; Münch, in: MünchKommZPO, s 1046 paras 5, 12, 15.

[107] Münch, in: MünchKommZPO, s 1046 para 4; Voit, in: Musielak/Voit (eds), s 1042 para 4.

[108] Münch, in: MünchKommZPO, s 1046 para 29; Hartmann, in: Baumbach/Lauterbach/Albers/Hartmann (eds), s 1046 para 6; Saenger, in: Saenger (ed), s 1046 para 8.

[109] Münch, in: MünchKommZPO, s 1046 para 29; Sachs/Lörcher, in: *Arbitration in Germany*, s 1046 para 11.

[110] Internationally see Born, p 2263.

> After the proceedings are closed, no further submission or argument may be made, or evidence produced, with respect to the matters to be decided in the award, unless requested or authorized by the arbitral tribunal.

By contrast, where no specific deadlines or closing dates have been specified, arbitral tribunals should be careful when precluding submissions on the mere basis that they are made in violation of the obligation to **conduct proceedings efficiently** and without proper excuse. While in theory arbitral tribunals have the power to do so (s 1046 para 2 ZPO),[111] in practice it is often a matter of considerable **uncertainty** whether a party has actually committed such a violation, or whether it is able to furnish a sufficient excuse for such failure. Thus, arbitral tribunals are often reluctant to preclude factual allegations or offers of evidence by applying s 1046 para 2 ZPO.[112] If the arbitral tribunal errs on the wrong side of this issue, it risks set aside of the award on the grounds of a violation of the party's right to be heard.[113] This makes it even more important to structure the proceedings efficiently, including by clearly defined deadlines, clearly communicated consequences of missing such deadlines without proper excuse, and possibly a closing date for the proceedings. **4.72**

6. *Amendments to Statement of Claim and Statement of Defense*

Unless otherwise agreed by the parties, **each party may amend or supplement** its case, except where the arbitral tribunal rejects such amendment or supplement due to unexcused delay (s 1046 para 2 ZPO). The claimant may adduce additional facts and legal arguments to support its claim; likewise, the respondent may do so to support its defense. In addition, the claimant can bring an additional claim provided that it is arbitrable and encompassed by the arbitration agreement.[114] Contrary to the prevailing view under the previous law, ss 263, 264 ZPO governing **amendments in state court litigation** do not apply;[115] instead, s 1046 para 2 ZPO provides for its own limitation in the form of unexcused delay. Thus, unless otherwise agreed by the parties, there is no need for an appropriateness test (*Sachdienlichkeit*) or consent by respondent or the arbitral tribunal.[116] On the other hand, where the opposing party agrees to the amendment, the principle of party autonomy prevails **4.73**

---

[111] Münch, in MünchKommZPO, s 1046 paras 27 *et seq.*; Schlosser, in: Stein/Jonas (eds), s 1046 para 12; Saenger, in: Saenger (ed), s 1046 para 9; Wilske/Markert, in: BeckOK ZPO, s 1046 para 6.

[112] Wilske/Markert, in: BeckOK ZPO, s 1046 para 6.

[113] Geimer, in: Zöller (ed), s 1046 para 3; Hartmann, in: Baumbach/Lauterbach/Albers/Hartmann (eds), s 1046 para 6; Lachmann, para 1452; Münch, in: MünchKommZPO, s 1046 para 27; Saenger, in: Saenger (ed), s 1046 paras 8 *et seq.*; Voit, in: Musielak/Voit (eds), s 1046 para 10.

[114] BT-Drucks 13/5274, p 49; Lachmann, para 1452; Münch, in: MünchKommZPO, s 1046 paras 21 *et seq.*; Reichold, in: Thomas/Putzo (eds), s 1046 para 8; Schwab/Walter, ch 16 para 29.

[115] Saenger, in: Saenger (ed), s 1046 para 8; Voit, in: Musielak/Voit (eds), s 1046 para 11; Münch, in: MünchKommZPO, s 1046 para 22. Opposing view: BT-Drucks 13/5274, p 49 (analogous application); Lachmann, para 1452; Schwab/Walter, ch 16 para 29.

[116] Hartmann, in: Baumbach/Lauterbach/Albers/Hartmann (eds), s 1046 para 6; Münch, in: MünchKommZPO, s 1046 para 22; Reichold, in: Thomas/Putzo (eds), s 1046 para 8; Saenger, in Saenger (ed), s 1046 para 8; Voit, in: Musielak/Voit (eds), s 1046 para 11; Wilske/Markert, in: BeckOK ZPO, s 1046 para 5.

and there is no basis for rejection by the tribunal based on delay.[117] The same applies if the amended part exceeds the arbitration agreement but the other party at least impliedly agrees to this extension of the arbitration agreement.[118]

4.74 The only way for the arbitral tribunal to limit an ever-increasing scope of the case is to exercise its discretion and impose a **time limit** beyond which, in the absence of a valid excuse, such supplements are no longer admissible, in particular new facts and offers of evidence.[119] In the absence of such a deadline, the arbitral tribunal would be entitled to reject amendments and supplements only if it finds that they are delayed without proper excuse when measured against the general obligation of the parties to promote the proceedings, which may be a high-risk option for the arbitral tribunal (see above para 4.72).

4.75 An amendment can also take the form of a partial or complete **withdrawal of a claim.**[120] Where the entire claim is (or all claims are) withdrawn, the arbitral tribunal may order the termination of the proceedings, unless the respondent objects and the arbitral tribunal finds that the respondent has a legitimate interest in a decision on the merits (s 1056 para 2 no 1 lit b ZPO). Where there is such objection and a legitimate interest, the tribunal will render an arbitral award on the merits (s 1056 para 1 ZPO).[121]

4.76 The **DIS Rules** do not contain any specific provisions on amendments by the parties; thus, in general, the above principles apply. By contrast, the guiding principle under the **ICC Rules** is that the parties are limited to what is set forth in the terms of reference:

> After the Terms of Reference have been signed or approved by the Court, no party shall make new claims which fall outside the limits of the Terms of Reference unless it has been authorized to do so by the arbitral tribunal, which shall consider the nature of such new claims, the stage of the arbitration and other relevant circumstances (art 23.4 ICC Rules).

4.77 Article 27 ICC Rules not only allows for a closing of the proceedings, but expressly instructs the arbitral tribunal ("shall") to order the closing of the proceedings (see para 4.71).

7. Counterclaims, Set-off, and Retention Rights

4.78 Section 1046 para 3 ZPO **broadly allows counterclaims.** Obviously, a counterclaim must be **arbitrable** and encompassed by the **arbitration agreement**. Where

[117] Hartmann, in: Baumbach/Lauterbach/Albers/Hartmann (eds), s 1046 para 6; Saenger, in Saenger (ed), s 1046 para 9; Voit, in: Musielak/Voit (eds), s 1046 para 13.

[118] Sachs/Lörcher, in: *Arbitration in Germany*, s 1046 para 9; Lachmann, para 1452; Voit, in: Musielak/Voit (eds), s 1046 para 11.

[119] Münch, in: MünchKommZPO, s 1046 para 28; Sachs/Lörcher, in: *Arbitration in Germany*, s 1046 para 10.

[120] Münch, in: MünchKommZPO, s 1046 para 25.

[121] Münch, in: MünchKommZPO, s 1056 para 22—for a detailed discussion see below (para 6.134).

it is not encompassed by the arbitration agreement, but the claimant does not object in its statement of defense, the claimant may be precluded from objecting later (s 1040 para 2 cl 1 ZPO).[122] The counterclaim must be substantiated in the same way as the main claim (s 1046 paras 3, 1 ZPO); the original claimant then has an opportunity to comment. The arbitrator fees may be increased, depending on any agreement in or amending the arbitrator contract, and as a consequence advances ordered by the arbitral tribunal may also increase.[123]

A special situation arises where the counterclaim is brought **against a third party**, either in addition to the claimant or independently. While some institutional rules provide for a specific regulation (eg art 7 ICC Rules), the Tenth Book of the ZPO remains silent on this issue. Given the personal scope and limitations of arbitration agreements (see paras 2.121 *et seq.*), the consent of all parties is required to include a third party into the arbitral proceedings (including such third party's consent), which can be achieved on the basis of a previously concluded arbitration agreement or after the counterclaim was filed (for details on multi-party arbitration see paras 4.207 *et seq.*).[124] **4.79**

German arbitration law does not expressly address the issue of **set-off**. Under the prevailing view, set-off is similar to a counterclaim. Thus, set-off is permissible only if the claim that is to be set off is **arbitrable and encompassed by the arbitration agreement.**[125] **4.80**

The same applies to **retention rights**; there, however, the issue should have less practical relevance because retention rights will often arise from the same main agreement and should thus often be encompassed by the same arbitration agreement.[126] **4.81**

The **DIS Rules** are somewhat more restrictive regarding counterclaims. Section 10.2 DIS Rules gives the arbitral tribunal discretion to decide on the admissibility of counterclaims. Any counterclaim must be filed with the DIS Secretariat and comply with the same minimum content requirements that apply to the statement of claim (ss 10.1, 6.1–4 DIS Rules). As the DIS Rules do not expressly address set-off and retention rights, the above principles apply. **4.82**

The **ICC Rules** may be seen as taking an even more restrictive approach. Pursuant to art 5.5 ICC Rules, any counterclaims made by the respondent shall be submitted **4.83**

122 Hartmann, in: Baumbach/Lauterbach/Albers/Hartmann (eds), s 1046 para 7; Münch, in: MünchKommZPO, s 1046 para 35; Saenger, in: Saenger (ed), s 1046 para 11; Lachmann, para 497.

123 Münch, in: MünchKommZPO, s 1046 para 34; Schwab/Walter, ch 16 para 31.

124 KG NJW 2008, 2719, 2720; Kleinschmidt, SchiedsVZ 2006, 142, 150; Hamann/Lennarz, SchiedsVZ 2006, 289, 293; Voit, in: Musielak/Voit (eds), s 1046 para 14.

125 Hartmann, in: Baumbach/Lauterbach/Albers/Hartmann (eds), s 1046 para 7; Münch, in: MünchKommZPO, s 1046 para 36; Saenger, in: Saenger (ed), s 1046 para 13; Voit, in: Musielak/Voit (eds), s 1029 para 24.

126 Lachmann, para 500; Münch, in: MünchKommZPO, s 1046 para 37; Voit, in: Musielak/Voit (eds), s 1029 para 23.

with the answer and shall provide details comparable to the minimum required contents of the request for arbitration.

8. Drafting Considerations

4.84 Not surprisingly, the German arbitration law does not contain any specific provisions on the structure, style, or contents of written submissions. The provisions governing briefs in **state court litigation** (s 130 ZPO) do not apply in arbitration. Specifically, the **designation of pieces of evidence** provided for in s 1046 para 1 cl 2 ZPO allows for more flexibility than in state court proceedings. The provision allows—but does not require—reference to pieces of evidence; and where such reference is included, it need not be related specifically to individual factual allegations. A list summarizing documents and witnesses on which a party intends to rely would suffice.

4.85 Nevertheless, parties from outside Germany should not be surprised to find that written submissions in German arbitrations often follow the style of briefs in German state court litigation. Some typical features of this German "style" are the following:

- requests for relief are placed at the beginning of the submission, not at the end (as is more typical in an Anglo-American and international context);
- facts and legal analysis are usually contained in separate sections; and
- facts are pleaded with specificity. For each factual allegation that is likely to be denied by the opponent, offers of evidence are included.

4.86 Historically, it was not the norm to include copies of **legal source materials.** This is still true in purely domestic cases. By contrast, in international cases, it is often prudent to provide such copies to the arbitrators, especially where non-lawyers or non-German lawyers are members of the tribunal.

III. Initial Structuring of the Proceedings

4.87 The German arbitration law does not provide specific guidance regarding how to structure the arbitral proceedings. Thus, in the absence of an agreement by the parties, the matter is up to the **discretion of the arbitral tribunal.**

4.88 As a first step, **organizational hearings** have proven to be a very useful tool in arbitration, irrespective of whether the case is an international or domestic one. The main reason is that the conduct of arbitral proceedings is generally much less predetermined and predictable than state court litigation. This applies both from the parties' and the tribunal's perspective. Thus, it is highly recommendable for arbitral tribunals to consider holding such a hearing at an early stage. Often, an appropriate point in time may be soon after the constitution of the arbitral tribunal. Such a hearing can be held by telephone conference or video conference, and thus does not require a physical meeting of the parties. It can be an appropriate platform to agree on deadlines for the statement of claim and the statement of defense, as well as further deadlines. Also, to the extent the arbitral tribunal wishes to establish certain procedural ground rules (**Procedural Order no 1**), the initial organizational hearing is an appropriate opportunity to do so. Often, the arbitral tribunal will circulate a draft of Procedural Order no 1 prior to the organizational hearing, consult with the parties and then issue the order after the hearing. In doing so, the arbitral tribunal should be mindful to maintain control over the order and not to slip inadvertently into negotiations with the parties, which may have the unintended consequence of resulting in what could be deemed to be a party agreement and not a disposition of the tribunal (see paras 4.16 *et seq.* on the "Frankfurt surprise").

In addition, as regards the further structuring of the proceedings an arbitral tribunal may look to the **structure of state court litigation cases**. In this context, German civil procedure offers two basic approaches: (i) the early merits hearing (*früher erster Termin*); and (ii) preliminary written proceedings (*schriftliches Vorverfahren*), ss 275, 276 ZPO. Early merits hearing typically means that a hearing on the merits occurs after the parties have exchanged the statement of claim and the statement of defense. It may or may not involve the taking of evidence. Preliminary written proceedings mean that the parties typically exchange (at least) one further round of written submissions, and then a hearing on the merits occurs, often including the taking of evidence. Overall, choosing between these two basic approaches may be useful, and is in fact often used, in domestic cases with parties accustomed to the state court litigation approach. Structuring the proceedings in this way does not involve an overall time plan, but proceeds step by step. This is appropriate in cases with limited complexity where the arbitral tribunal expects the facts to be "put on the table" in due course without much need from the arbitral tribunal to structure complex issues. The early merits hearing may be appropriate for cases in which the factual scope is limited and the legal issues are straightforward, or where the arbitral tribunal sees a concrete prospect of settlement at an early stage. By contrast, where the factual and legal issues need further development after the initial round of pleadings, it is often useful to order a further round of written submissions and then schedule an oral hearing on the merits. **4.89**

Another source of inspiration may be **institutional rules**. While the DIS Rules are intentionally largely silent on the structuring of the proceedings, the ICC Rules now contain a detailed set of tools and techniques, in particular the **terms of reference**, the **procedural timetable**, the case management conference, and case management techniques. The terms of reference are a detailed document including, among other items, a description of the issues in dispute, which must be drawn up at the beginning of the case once the arbitral tribunal has been constituted (art 23 ICC Rules). The procedural timetable, which is to be established roughly at the same time (art 24.2 ICC Rules), is intended to cover the entire arbitral proceedings. The case management conference is similar to what is traditionally called an organizational hearing (art 24.1 ICC Rules). The arbitral tribunal is encouraged **4.90** to choose from a variety of case management techniques listed in Appendix IV of the ICC Rules, such as:

a) Bifurcating the proceedings or rendering one or more partial awards on key issues...
b) Identifying issues that can be resolved by agreement between the parties or their experts.
c) Identifying issues to be decided solely on the basis of documents rather than through oral evidence or legal argument at a hearing.
d) Production of documentary evidence...
e) Limiting the length and scope of written submissions and written and oral witness evidence...
f) Using telephone or video conferencing for procedural and other hearings where attendance in person is not essential...
g) Organizing a pre-hearing conference with the arbitral tribunal at which arrangements for a hearing can be discussed and agreed and the arbitral tribunal can indicate to the parties issues on which it would like the parties to focus at the hearing.
h) Settlement of disputes...

4.91 While some practitioners (in particular in Germany) are not convinced that establishing formal terms of reference is a useful technique, establishing a procedural timetable is something that arbitral tribunals should consider seriously, irrespective of whether the ICC Rules apply, in particular in more complex cases. Otherwise, the overall duration of arbitral proceedings may slip out of the tribunal's control. Likewise, the case management techniques suggested in **Appendix IV of the ICC Rules** offer a variety of common-sense methods to effectively structure and conduct the proceedings. Specifically, bifurcating proceedings for monetary claims, in particular damage claims, into a liability and a quantum phase is an approach often taken by arbitral tribunals inside and outside the ICC framework. Likewise, it is often sensible to establish early on the ground rules for the production of documents such that there are no surprises at a later stage.

4.92 Finally, there are other non-binding sources providing guidance on the structuring and conduct of arbitral proceedings. Regarding specifically the topic of evidence taking, pursuant to **art 2 of the IBA Rules on the Taking of Evidence in International Arbitration** the arbitral tribunal "shall" consult with the parties at an early stage in order to have efficient, economical, and fair proceedings regarding the taking of evidence. Such consultation may cover witness statements, expert reports, oral testimony at a hearing, formalities regarding the production of documents, as well as privilege and confidentiality issues. In addition, in 1996, **UNCITRAL** published **"Notes on Organizing Arbitral Proceedings"** which contain a 19-item "list of matters for possible consideration in organizing arbitral proceedings."[127] The

[127] Available at http://www.uncitral.org (last visited December 1, 2015) and, covering issues such as the applicable set of arbitration rules, the language of the proceedings, the place of arbitration, administrative services for the tribunal, advances on costs, confidentiality, means of

Notes may be viewed as useful guidance on a variety of organizational and procedural matters that typically arise in arbitral proceedings, in particular where the parties come from different legal backgrounds. Nevertheless, the Notes have not experienced wide acceptance or use.

IV. Initial Determinations

1. Amount in Dispute

German law does not require the arbitral tribunal to determine the amount in dispute at the outset of the proceedings. Likewise, even at the stage of determining the costs of the arbitration and making a cost award (s 1057 ZPO) it may not be necessary to define the amount in dispute. The arbitrator fees need not necessarily depend on the amount in dispute, but may be agreed freely with the parties. Similarly, the fees of counsel may be calculated on an hourly basis, such that there is no need to know an amount in dispute as a basis for calculation. **4.93**

Nevertheless, in many cases the amount in dispute is relevant for both the **arbitrator fees** and the **fees of counsel** (or possibly the **fees of an arbitral institution**). In such a scenario, it is advisable, if not necessary, to determine the amount in dispute at an early stage of the proceedings. The arbitrators will have an interest in this determination to the extent they wish to order an advance on costs (see paras 3.185 *et seq.*). Likewise, under German law counsel have a right to request advances from their clients,[128] and to the extent they apply the statutory fee scale, they should know the amount in dispute. **4.94**

German arbitration law does not provide any guidance as to how the amount in dispute should be determined. In the absence of an agreement of the parties, the arbitral tribunal thus has **discretion** (s 1042 para 4 cl 1 ZPO, and, to the extent the arbitrator fees may be concerned, ss 317 *et seq.* BGB).[129] In many instances, arbitral tribunals may look to the provisions governing the determination of the amount in dispute in **state court litigation** (ss 2 *et seq.* ZPO), including the wealth of precedent in this area. These provisions again allow for broad discretion; the most important guiding principle is to look to the interest in the matter from the perspective of the person bringing the claim (*Angreiferinteresse*).[130] **4.95**

---

communication, scheduling and details of written submissions, defining points at issue, settlement discussions, documentary, witness and expert evidence, the conduct of oral hearings, multi-party arbitration, and the delivery of the final award.

[128] See s 9 German Law on the Remuneration of Attorneys (RVG).

[129] Schlosser, in: Stein/Jonas (eds), s 1057 para 17; specifically regarding arbitrator fees depending on the amount in dispute see Wolff, SchiedsVZ 2006, 131 *et seq.*

[130] BGH NJW 1994, 735; Hartmann, in: Baumbach/Lauterbach/Albers/Hartmann (eds), s 3 para 4; Heinrich, in: Musielak/Voit (eds), s 3 para 6; Ralf/Bendtsen, in: Saenger (ed), s 3 para 2; Wöstmann, in: MünchKommZPO, s 3 paras 4 *et seq.*

4.96 This means for the most common case of a claim for payment (*Zahlungsklage*) that the interest corresponds to the amount the claimant seeks. Such a rule of thumb is missing for other cases, where the claim is directed to specific performance by the respondent. In particular, there is a dispute as to whether the amount shall reflect only the claimant's interest in this performance or also consider the potential costs for the respondent.[131] Where the claim is brought for a declaratory award (*Feststellungsklage*), the interest is usually somewhat less than a correlating claim for payment would be.[132] In the case of a counterclaim by the respondent (*Widerklage*), the interests of both claims are added together, unless they concern—from an economic point of view—an identical subject matter.[133] The same rule applies where the respondent alternatively declares set-off (*Aufrechnung*) if and to the extent that a later award contains a binding decision on the contested set-off claim.[134] Thus, the addition is limited to the amount of the principal claim.

4.97 The determination of the amount in dispute is **not set in stone** for the entire duration of the arbitral proceedings. Where new claims are brought that increase the amount in dispute, or where new facts arise shedding a better light on the interest in the dispute, the arbitral tribunal may at any time adjust the amount in dispute and correct requested advances on costs accordingly.[135]

2. Advance on Costs

4.98 As mentioned above (paras 3.185 *et seq.*), arbitrators have the right to request the parties to pay advances on the likely fees of the arbitrators and expenses for the conduct of the arbitral proceedings (including costs for witnesses, experts, hearings, court-reporters, interpreters etc). Arbitrators are well advised to make use of this right. Thus, typically, the arbitral tribunal will request the parties to pay advances to a **trust account** held by the chairman. Unless otherwise agreed by the parties, and unless otherwise ordered by the arbitral tribunal, each side is generally required **to pay half** of the advance. This contrasts with state court litigation, where the plaintiff must pay the entire advance of the court fees.[136]

4.99 In case one party—often the respondent—fails to pay its share of the advance, the claimant may step in, fund the respondent's share and wait for the cost award to

[131] For limitation to the claimant's interest: Ralf/Bendtsen, in: Saenger (ed), s 3 para 15; Hüßtege, in: Thomas/Putzo (eds), s 3 para 82; for both criteria: Herget, in: Zöller (ed), s 3 para 16; Wöstmann, in: MünchKommZPO, s 3 para 133.

[132] BGH NJW 1997, 1241; NZM 2009, 51; NJW-RR 2012, 1107; Hüßtege, in: Thomas/Putzo (eds), s 3 para 65; Wöstmann, in: MünchKommZPO, s 3 para 72 (20 percent discount).

[133] BGH NJW-RR 2005, 506; Lappe, NJW 2006, 270, 272; Herget, in: Zöller (ed), s 3 para 16; Wöstmann, in: MünchKommZPO, s 5 para 35; Heinrich, in: Musielak/Voit (eds), s 5 para 15.

[134] BGH NJW-RR 1997, 1157; Schneider, NJW-Spezial 2010, 475 *et seq.*; Herget, in: Zöller (ed), s 3 para 16; Ralf/Bendtsen, in: Saenger (ed), s 3 para 15; Heinrich, in: Musielak/Voit (eds), s 3 para 23.

[135] Implicitly: Henn, para 327.

[136] Section 12 German Court Costs Act (GKG).

be rendered by the arbitral tribunal or bring action against the respondent for repayment, either before the state courts or the arbitral tribunal seized with the main matter (for details see para 3.187).

3. *Jurisdiction*

The jurisdiction of the arbitral tribunal is an important initial determination in arbitral proceedings, whether it is confirmed in an award confined to that issue or whether the arbitral tribunal decides for itself that it has jurisdiction and thus carries on with the proceedings. After summarizing the legal framework governing the jurisdiction of the arbitral tribunal under German law (below paras 4.101 *et seq.*), we turn to the issue of *Kompetenz-Kompetenz* (below para 4.104). In a next step, we distinguish lack of jurisdiction and lack of arbitrability (below paras 4.105 *et seq.*), before we address the procedural practicalities of challenging the tribunal's jurisdiction (below para 4.107), interim awards on jurisdiction, and the state court review of such interim awards (below paras 4.108 *et seq.*). **4.100**

a) Summary of Legal Framework Pursuant to s 1040 para 1 cl 1 ZPO, the arbitral tribunal is empowered to decide on its jurisdiction, it has **(preliminary) *Kompetenz-Kompetenz***; in doing so, it may also decide on the existence and the validity of the arbitration agreement. For purposes of such analysis, an arbitration clause is to be regarded as separate from the remainder of an agreement (s 1040 para 1 cl 2 ZPO—principle of separability). A party must object to jurisdiction no later than with the statement of defense (s 1040 para 2 cl 1 ZPO), except where the arbitral tribunal finds that there is a proper excuse for a later objection (s 1040 para 2 cl 4 ZPO). The fact that a party participates in the constitution of the arbitral tribunal is not considered a waiver of the jurisdictional objection (s 1040 para 2 cl 2 ZPO). Where the arbitral tribunal exceeds its jurisdiction with respect to a specific issue during the arbitral proceedings, a party who wishes to object must do so as soon as there are deliberations on the said issue (s 1040 para 2 cl 3 ZPO). Again, a later objection requires a proper excuse, or otherwise it will be barred (s 1040 para 2 cl 4 ZPO). **4.101**

Where the arbitral tribunal finds that it has jurisdiction, it generally ought to hold so by means of a **preliminary ruling** (s 1040 para 3 cl 1 ZPO), which is subject to challenge in front of the competent higher regional court within one month after written service of the preliminary ruling (s 1040 para 3 cl 2 ZPO). While such a challenge is pending, the arbitral tribunal may continue the arbitral proceedings and render a (final) award on the merits (s 1040 para 3 cl 3 ZPO). **4.102**

In addition, German law provides for **two further mechanisms** in order to determine the jurisdiction of an arbitral tribunal. First, where an action is filed with the state court and a party objects on the basis that there is an arbitration agreement, the **state court** needs to determine the existence, validity, and enforceability of the arbitration agreement and on that basis determine its jurisdiction (s 1032 para 1 ZPO, see para 2.142). Second, prior to the constitution of the arbitral tribunal, a **4.103** party can request the competent state court to rule on whether arbitral proceedings are permissible as between the plaintiff and the defendant (s 1032 para 2 ZPO, see paras 2.144 *et seq.*). As mentioned above (para 3.25), the existence and validity of an arbitration agreement may also be examined by the state court as a threshold issue in connection with certain proceedings, such as the challenge and replacement of arbitrators; the same applies where the state court is called upon to assist an arbitral tribunal in the taking of evidence (s 1050 ZPO, see below para 4.200).

4.104 **b) Preliminary Kompetenz-Kompetenz** German law follows a concept of preliminary *Kompetenz-Kompetenz* of the arbitral tribunal.[137] The arbitral tribunal has the power to determine its own jurisdiction as a matter of the German arbitration law; there is no need for further party agreement in order to confer that power upon an arbitral tribunal. At the same time, German law provides for a **review by the state courts**; thus, it is the state courts that have the final say over whether the parties have validly waived the jurisdiction of the state courts in favor of arbitration. Pursuant to the case law of the BGH, this allocation of powers is mandatory; the **parties may not derogate** the review by the state courts; they may thus not confer full *Kompetenz-Kompetenz* on an arbitral tribunal.[138]

4.105 **c) Lack of Jurisdiction and Limits of Party Autonomy** Section 1040 para 1 ZPO is concerned with the jurisdiction of the arbitral tribunal in general, including the question whether there is a valid and binding arbitration agreement. Issues such as lack of arbitrability lead to the invalidity of the arbitration agreement and thus lack of jurisdiction of the arbitral tribunal. Section 1040 para 2 ZPO requires that the other party object based on lack of jurisdiction. The need to object relates only to those issues that are subject to party autonomy; where a dispute lacks arbitrability, the lack of a timely objection cannot confer jurisdiction upon an arbitral tribunal.[139] In such a case, the tribunal needs to dismiss the case *ex officio*, irrespective of whether one of the parties has brought a timely challenge to the jurisdiction of the tribunal.[140]

4.106 This may apply, for instance, with respect to arbitral proceedings related to the validity of corporate resolutions. Pursuant to the precedent of the BGH, arbitration agreements that do not follow four requirements pronounced by the BGH in its decision ***Schiedsfähigkeit II*** are to be considered unconscionable pursuant to

---

[137] Hartmann, in: Baumbach/Lauterbach/Albers/Hartmann (eds), s 1040 para 1; Geimer, in: Zöller (ed), s 1040 para 1; Lachmann, paras 688 *et seq.*; Münch, in: MünchKommZPO, s 1040 para 2; Voit, in: Musielak/Voit (eds), s 1040 para 2.

[138] BGH NZG 2014, 1155, 1156; BGHZ 162, 9, 14; Geimer, in: Zöller (ed), s 1040 para 1; Lachmann, paras 692 *et seq.*; Münch, in: MünchKommZPO, s 1040 paras 51 *et seq.*; Voit, in: Musielak/Voit (eds), s 1040 para 2; Schwab/Walter, ch 6 para 9; Lachmann, paras 692 *et seq.*

[139] Münch, in: MünchKommZPO, s 1040 para 16; Voit, in: Musielak/Voit (eds), s 1040 para 5.

[140] Münch, in: MünchKommZPO, s 1040 para 16; Huber/Bach, in: *Arbitration in Germany*, s 1040 para 23.

s 138 BGB because they do not satisfy the fundamental constitutional due process requirements with respect to the rights and interests of other shareholders (see para 1.78). Since (and to the extent) the lack of jurisdiction is based on the rights of other shareholders—who are generally not party to the proceedings—there is no room for a waiver by the parties (no waiver to the detriment of third parties).[141] By contrast, where all shareholders and parties concerned actually participate in the arbitral proceedings, a valid waiver pursuant to s 1040 para 2 ZPO can be considered.[142]

d) **Objection in Statement of Defense** German arbitration law allows the respondent to defer its jurisdiction objection until filing its statement of defense (ss 1040 para 2 cl 1, 1046 para 1 ZPO). This **may be significantly after the constitution** of the arbitral tribunal (s 1040 para 2 cl 2 ZPO). An objection at this stage may be highly inopportune to the claimant, who by then may have invested a significant amount of time, effort, and money into the arbitration (including, in most cases, its share of advances on cost). Nevertheless, the respondent is allowed to wait until that point of time. Indeed, the respondent may want to observe what the specific issues of the case are, how the tribunal is composed and whether the respondent concludes that the case should go forward in arbitration despite lack of the tribunal's jurisdiction.[143] **4.107**

e) **Interim Award and State Court Review** Where a party has challenged the tribunal's jurisdiction, and the tribunal finds that the challenge is timely and has merit, it must dismiss the case by final award including a decision on costs. To the extent the tribunal does find jurisdiction despite a party's objection, the tribunal is generally meant to render a preliminary ruling (s 1040 para 3 cl 1 ZPO) in order to allow the parties to have the competent higher regional court review the finding of jurisdiction (s 1040 para 3 cl 2 ZPO). A tribunal that does not render a preliminary ruling but proceeds on the merits may violate the "spirit" of s 1040 para 3 cl 1 ZPO, albeit without much sanction. The parties have no means to compel compliance with the preliminary ruling requirement.[144] The party objecting to the jurisdiction can only await the final award and then seek set aside for lack of jurisdiction (s 1059 para 2 no 1 lit a or c ZPO). **4.108**

The competent higher regional court, when petitioned by a party to annul a preliminary ruling by the arbitral tribunal respecting jurisdiction, has the power to **4.109**

[141] Implicitly: Lachmann, para 2844.

[142] Implicitly: Lachmann, paras 2843 *et seq.*

[143] Hartmann, in: Baumbach/Lauterbach/Albers/Hartmann (eds), s 1040 para 3; Geimer, in: Zöller (ed), s 1040 para 5; Münch, in: MünchKommZPO, s 1040 para 21; Saenger, in: Saenger (ed), s 1040 para 4.

[144] Geimer, in: Zöller (ed), s 1040 para 16; Lachmann, para 725; Münch, in: MünchKommZPO, s 1040 paras 26 *et seq.*; Saenger, in: Saenger (ed), s 1040 para 11; a different view is held by Voit, in: Musielak/Voit (eds), s 1040 para 10 for a few exceptional cases.

finally and bindingly determine the tribunal's jurisdiction. The higher regional court may schedule an oral hearing, but need not necessarily do so (s 1063 para 1 ZPO). The opposing party must be given an opportunity to comment (s 1063 para 1 cl 2 ZPO). The court's decision is subject to a complaint on a point of law to the BGH (s 1065 para 1 cl 1, 1062 para 1 no 2 ZPO). The court decision is binding upon the parties and the arbitral tribunal.[145]

V. Further Written Submissions

1. General Principles

4.110 Whether or not there are further written submissions after the initial round of pleadings (ie request for arbitration, statement of claim, and statement of defense) is a matter for party agreement or, in the absence thereof, **tribunal discretion**. Often, the arbitral tribunal's initial procedural order will contain provisions on the number of further written submissions and their content, including the necessity for witness statements, expert reports, the submission of documentary evidence, and the like. Where the initial procedural order does not contain such provisions, the arbitral tribunal will need to decide as part of its general discretion whether it wants to request or allow further rounds of briefs before moving to the next stage of the proceedings. In case of default, the arbitral tribunal may preclude further factual submissions. As explained above (see paras 4.69 *et seq.*), apart from the rare cases where a party has violated its general obligation to further the proceedings (s 1046 para 2 ZPO), this requires that the tribunal have first set a deadline for the submission and specified that the deadline has preclusive effect.

2. Submission of Written Witness Statements

4.111 We will address witness statements in more detail below, when we discuss the taking of witness evidence (below paras 4.164 *et seq.*). However, it is worth noting already at this stage that in German practice, in line with international standards,[146] arbitral tribunals increasingly request that the parties submit written witness statements together with their written submissions, or at least invite and encourage the parties to do so. For the parties and their counsel, this has important implications in terms of **timing and organization**. Witnesses need to be contacted, and the facts need to be established in interviews with witnesses. In order for witness statements not to contradict documentary evidence, the relevant documents need to be available and analyzed before a witness statement is submitted. Thus, the submission of witness statements at an early stage of the proceedings requires a considerable amount of upfront work. Parties and their counsel should bear this in mind when they consider and negotiate timelines for submissions.

[145] Huber/Bach, in: *Arbitration in Germany*, s 1040 para 37; Münch, in: MünchKommZPO, s 1040 para 49; Voit, in: Musielak/Voit (eds), s 1040 para 12.
[146] Born, pp 2257 *et seq.*

3. Submission of Reports of Party-appointed Experts

Likewise, we will address evidence from party-appointed experts in detail below (see paras 4.180 *et seq.*)). The important issue in the present context is once more timing and organization. Depending on when reports from party-appointed experts need to be submitted at the very latest, a **significant amount of work** may need to be done upfront, including the selection of experts, their instruction, the review of relevant documents, interviews with witnesses, reviews of draft reports, and the like. **4.112**

VI. Document Disclosure

Regarding document disclosure, a number of general principles need to be considered (below paras 4.114 *et seq.*). The IBA Rules on the Taking of Evidence in International Arbitration may provide particularly useful guidance (below paras 4.115 *et seq.*). Confidentiality and privilege play an important role in limiting document disclosure (below paras 4.122 *et seq.*). **4.113**

1. General Principles

Document disclosure is a **stage of the proceedings** that has become increasingly common in international arbitration,[147] including in cases seated in Germany. Often, it occurs **after** one or two rounds of **written submissions** and before the (main) oral hearing. Document disclosure has also found its way into proceedings with a more domestic character. Views on the usefulness and efficiency of document disclosure vary widely in the German arbitration community. Against this background, it is worth remembering that the issue of document disclosure, under German arbitration law, is not regulated specifically, but rather is left to the discretion of the arbitral tribunal unless the parties have agreed otherwise (s 1042 para 4 ZPO). Section 1048 ZPO even addresses certain aspects of document disclosure: where a party, without proper excuse, fails to produce a document by a deadline ordered by the arbitral tribunal, the tribunal may continue the proceedings and decide the case based on the information available to it (s 1048 para 3 ZPO, similarly s 30.2 DIS Rules). Thus, German arbitration law clearly presupposes that an arbitral tribunal may, in principle, order the production of documents.[148] Where the party bearing the burden of proof fails to produce a document—irrespective of an order from the arbitral tribunal—it risks losing the case (*non liquet*). Where the opposing party fails to produce a document even though production has been ordered by the arbitral tribunal, such party risks negative inferences; as in state court litigation, the arbitral tribunal may, in its discretion, assume the opponent's factual allegations with regard to such document to be true (cf s 427 ZPO) and in any event as confirmed.[149] **4.114**

[147] Born, pp 2249 *et seq.*

[148] Münch, in: MünchKommZPO, s 1048 para 35; Quinke, SchiedsVZ 2013, 129, 134 *et seq.*

[149] Geimer, in: Zöller (ed), s 1048 para 3; Lachmann, para 1665; Münch, in: MünchKommZPO, s 1048 para 37.

2. IBA Rules on the Taking of Evidence in International Arbitration

4.115 The IBA Rules on the Taking of Evidence in International Arbitration ("IBA Rules"), adopted by the International Bar Association on May 29, 2010,[150] address document disclosure in some detail in their art 3 as the first means of evidence, before addressing witnesses, experts, and the like. They thus clearly recognize the potential importance of document disclosure and the timing thereof in international arbitration. They seek to provide a **compromise** between the far-reaching discovery traditions of the Anglo-American legal systems and the reluctance and skepticism towards document disclosure in many continental European jurisdictions as well as jurisdictions inspired by the civil law system.[151]

4.116 As a basic principle, under art 4.2 IBA Rules each party may request the other party to produce documents. Pursuant to art 4.3, such a request needs to contain:

> (a) *(i)* a description of each requested Document sufficient to identify it, or *(ii)* a description in sufficient detail (including subject matter) of a narrow and specific requested category of Documents that are reasonably believed to exist; in the case of Documents maintained in electronic form, the requesting Party may, or the Arbitral Tribunal may order that it shall be required to, identify specific files, search terms, individuals or other means of searching for such Documents in an efficient and economical manner;
> (b) a statement as to how the Documents requested are relevant to the case and material to its outcome; and
> (c) *(i)* a statement that the Documents requested are not in the possession, custody or control of the requesting Party or a statement of the reasons why it would be unreasonably burdensome for the requesting Party to produce such Documents, and *(ii)* a statement of the reasons why the requesting Party assumes the Documents requested are in the possession, custody or control of another Party.

4.117 Importantly, as this text shows, the IBA Rules do allow references to categories of documents, but only if they are "narrow and specific." Likewise, they allow for the disclosure of electronic documents, such as emails. At the same time, they provide means to the parties and the arbitral tribunal to limit the burden associated with e-discovery, such as the identification of specific electronic files, the use of search terms, and the identification of document custodians. With respect to data hosted within the EU, special care may be necessary to observe data protection provisions.[152] Regarding Germany, additional limitations may follow from German telecommunications law, in particular where emails of employees are concerned and the company has allowed the private use of company email.[153]

---

[150] Available at http://www.ibanet.org (last visited December 1, 2015). The author Kreindler chaired the IBA subcommittee drafting the revised rules.

[151] Böckstiegel, SchiedsVZ 2009, 3, 7. On the different traditions in general: Kaufmann-Kohler/Bärtsch, SchiedsVZ 2004, 13, 14 *et seq.*; Weigand, RIW 1992, 361, 362 *et seq.*; Born, pp 2319 *et seq.*

[152] Burianski/Reindl, SchiedsVZ 2010, 187, 191 *et seq.*

[153] LAG Berlin-Brandenburg, BB 2011, 2298 *et seq.* with comments from Fülbier/Splittgerber, NJW 2012, 1995 *et seq.*; Geis, ZD 2013, 591, 593; Walther/Zimmer, BB 2013, 2933, 2934.

The opposing party may object to a request to produce if the request fails to satisfy the requirements of art 3.3 IBA Rules. Furthermore art 9.2 IBA Rules contains grounds for objection to production and/or refusal by the tribunal to order production for such reasons as lack of sufficient relevance to the case or materiality to its outcome, legal privilege, unreasonable burden, loss or destruction of the document, compelling grounds of confidentiality, compelling grounds of political or institutional sensitivity (including evidence that has been classified as secret by a government or a public international institution), as well as considerations of procedural economy, proportionality, fairness, or equality. **4.118**

In practice, including in Germany, often certain types of tables and schedules are used to list document requests and pertaining objections, such as the so-called ***Redfern* Schedule.**[154] Where the parties cannot agree on the production of a document, the arbitral tribunal can make a corresponding ruling. In doing so, the arbitral tribunal shall not only consider whether the requirements of art 3.3 IBA Rules are met and whether there are any valid objections pursuant to art 9.2 IBA Rules, but most fundamentally the arbitral tribunal shall decide whether "the issues that the requesting Party wishes to prove are relevant to the case and material to its outcome" (art 3.7 cl 3 IBA Rules). **4.119**

In other words, the IBA Rules do not in principle permit document requests where the requesting party merely shows that the request is reasonably believed to lead to relevant evidence. Instead, more stringently, relevance and materiality need to be established to the satisfaction of the arbitral tribunal before it will order production of a document. **4.120**

The IBA Rules contain further provisions on the disclosure of documents in the possession, custody, or control of third parties, as well as provisions on the form of document production (arts 3.9, 3.12 IBA Rules). **4.121**

3. Confidentiality and Privilege

The arbitral tribunal has **discretion to limit** document disclosure and production with a view to confidentiality and privilege issues.[155] Again, the German arbitration law does not contain any specific provisions on this issue. The IBA Rules, which the parties may have agreed on, or which may in any event serve as a source of guidance to arbitral tribunals, contain two mechanisms to protect confidentiality and privilege. **4.122**

First, art 3 para 8 IBA Rules allows for assessment of issues of commercial confidentiality (trade secrets and the like) by submitting a document to an independent expert who reviews whether a document should be protected from disclosure by looking at the document and reporting back to the arbitral tribunal without the arbitral tribunal itself having to look at the document. This mechanism is meant to be limited to "exceptional circumstances." **4.123**

---

154 Ashford, p 208; Gusy/Illmer, SchiedsVZ 2008, 284, 288.
155 Similarly: Kaufmann-Kohler/Bärtsch, SchiedsVZ 2004, 13, 17 *et seq.*

4.124 Second, and in addition, art 9 para 2 lit b IBA Rules allows the arbitral tribunal to exclude from evidence or from document production any document for reasons of "legal impediment or privilege under the legal or ethical rules determined by the Arbitral Tribunal to be applicable." Article 9 para 3 IBA Rules expressly addresses legal privilege, settlement negotiations, waiver of privilege, as well as the need to maintain fairness and equality as between the Parties, particularly if they are subject to different legal or ethical rules.

4.125 In addition, or in the alternative, arbitral tribunals may also **seek guidance from other sets of rules**, including those governing state court litigation, which are, however, by far not as elaborate. For instance, the basic provision on document disclosure in state court litigation, s 142 ZPO, does not contain any specifics regarding confidentiality or privilege as far as disclosure by a party is concerned. Instead, the prevailing view is that this is entirely a matter for the court's discretion.[156] Only regarding disclosure by third parties, s 142 para 2 ZPO regulates that the provisions on the refusal of testimony shall apply *mutatis mutandis*. Thus, we submit that arbitral tribunals and parties are generally well advised to seek guidance from the more elaborate provisions contained in the IBA Rules.

VII. Oral Hearing

4.126 We first address some general principles with respect to the necessity, usefulness, and timing of oral hearings (paras 4.127 *et seq.*) before we turn specifically to a number of organizational issues frequently relevant in German arbitration practice (paras 4.132 *et seq.*), such as venue, participants, privacy, minutes, the use of court reporters, interpreters, and time management.

1. General Principles: Necessity, Usefulness, Timing

4.127 For arbitral proceedings seated in Germany, oral hearings are **not mandatory** pursuant to the German arbitration law itself. Instead, unless otherwise agreed by the parties the arbitral tribunal has discretion as to whether it wishes to conduct an oral hearing or to decide on the basis of documents and information submitted to the arbitral tribunal (s 1047 para 1 cl 1 ZPO). The parties are free both to mandate an oral hearing and to agree to exclude an oral hearing. This decision is generally binding for the tribunal but in rare cases a party's right to be heard can exceptionally require an oral hearing.[157] Where there is no such exclusion, each party has the right to demand an oral hearing. In case of such demand, the arbitral tribunal must

[156] Hartmann, in: Baumbach/Lauterbach/Albers/Hartmann (eds), s 142 para 5; Greger, in: Zöller (ed), s 142 para 8; Stadler, in: Musielak/Voit (eds), s 142 para 7; Reichold, in: Thomas/Putzo (eds), s 142 para 3.

[157] BT-Drucks 13/5274, p 49; Sachs/Lörcher, in: *Arbitration in Germany*, s 1047 para 4. This may be the case for reasons of the right to be heard where a party would otherwise be precluded from reasonably presenting its case, eg where a party relies exclusively on witness evidence. Opposing view: Lachmann, para 1589.

conduct an oral hearing, but it has discretion at which stage of the proceedings it does so (s 1047 para 1 cl 2 ZPO; likewise s 28 DIS Rules). The arbitral tribunal must give the parties **sufficient advance notice** prior to any oral or evidentiary hearing (s 1047 para 2 ZPO), which is an expression of the party's right to be heard and its right to equal treatment.[158]

In German practice, oral hearings are the norm.[159] If nothing else, it is an important psychological aspect for the parties to "have their day in court." A decision based only on written materials is likely to be much less persuasive to the unsuccessful party. Also, from the arbitral tribunal's perspective, oral hearings are often useful. Many times, factual or even legal issues become clearer when discussed orally with the parties and their counsel. Thus, even where none of the parties requests an oral hearing, arbitrators should often consider scheduling one. **4.128**

In terms of the appropriate **timing** for an oral hearing, the specific circumstances of the case need to be considered. Generally, it would not seem advisable to have an oral hearing before both the statement of claim and the statement of defense have been filed. Beforehand, it is usually not yet clear what the main issues of the case are, and an oral hearing could be of only limited use.[160] It may be advisable to have an oral hearing after the statement of defense has been filed, similar to an "early merits hearing" in state court litigation. Circumstances where an early hearing may be appropriate are cases with limited complexity and/or cases where there may be a realistic chance for an early settlement (para 4.89). By contrast, where the issues are more complex and an early settlement seems unlikely, it may be more useful to conduct a second round of written submissions and then have an oral hearing. In case the procedural timetable provides for document disclosure, a full merits hearing should generally be conducted only thereafter. This does not exclude, however, that an early merits hearing can be useful. In particular, it may be in the tribunal's own interest to focus the parties on certain key issues before they embark on the exchange of far-flung document requests. **4.129**

Where a party **fails to appear** at an oral hearing without sufficient excuse even though it has had sufficient advance notice of the hearing, the arbitral tribunal may **continue the proceedings** and render a final award based on the facts before it (s 1048 para 3 ZPO, likewise s 30.2 DIS Rules, art 26.2 ICC Rules). The tribunal may establish further facts based on its own motion (limited investigation, paras 4.27 *et seq.*) to the extent it considers this necessary in order to make a decision on the merits.[161] Scheduling conflicts or merely "being busy" may not be **4.130**

[158] Hartmann, in: Baumbach/Lauterbach/Albers/Hartmann (eds), s 1047 para 1; Münch, in: MünchKommZPO, s 1047 para 2; Saenger, in: Saenger (ed), s 1047 para 1; Voit, in: Musielak/Voit (eds), s 1047 para 1.

[159] Lachmann, para 1586; Münch, in: MünchKommZPO, s 1047 para 3; Saenger, in: Saenger (ed), s 1047 para 1.

[160] Münch, in: MünchKommZPO, s 1047 para 6.

[161] Quinke, SchiedsVZ 2013, 129, 134; Sachs/Lörcher, in: *Arbitration in Germany*, s 1048 para 12; Voit, in: Musielak/Voit (eds), s 1048 para 5; Saenger, in: Saenger (ed), s 1042 para 16.

a sufficient excuse, to the extent it would be possible for a party to send another representative.[162] Where both parties fail to appear, the tribunal should ask the parties to progress the proceedings; if they fail to do so, it may order the termination of the proceedings based on s 1056 para 2 no 3 ZPO.[163]

4.131 As can be seen from the previous paragraph, the consequences of not appearing to an oral hearing differ vastly between German state court litigation and German-seated arbitration. In **state court litigation**, failure to appear usually results in a **default decision on the merits** (*Säumnisurteil*), in particular where the defendant fails to appear. In this case, the plaintiff's factual allegations will be deemed true (s 331 ZPO). The parties are at liberty to agree on similar consequences in arbitral proceedings,[164] which, however, only rarely happens.

2. Venue

4.132 Oral hearings need not be held at the seat of the arbitration; instead, unless otherwise agreed by the parties, the arbitral tribunal can determine an appropriate venue in its discretion (s 1043 para 2 ZPO). Usually, the arbitral tribunal should be guided by various aspects of convenience, eg the necessity for travel by the arbitrators, the parties, their counsel, witnesses, and experts, the availability of suitable locations, eg at the offices of the chairman, at an arbitral institution, or in hotels or conference centers, considerations of neutrality of the venue, and even the inhospitability of the agreed seat due to political, military, or other factors.[165]

4.133 In most cases, oral hearings are an event where the participants **meet physically** in one location. Nevertheless, German law does not limit oral hearings to such a set-up. **Telephone or video conferences** can qualify just as well as oral hearings, but not mere virtual "meetings" (eg internet chats).[166] The arbitral tribunal should carefully consider which set-up is suitable for which type of hearing. Discussions of organizational or procedural issues may well be done via telephone. By contrast, the taking of evidence (especially the examination of witnesses and experts) ought to be done at an in-person meeting, unless there are compelling circumstances that require otherwise.

3. Participants and Privacy

4.134 The arbitral tribunal must give sufficient advance notice to the parties (s 1047 para 2 ZPO). It may do so by any means it deems appropriate; there is no need for formal summons as in state court proceedings. Thus, the arbitral tribunal can

162 OLG Karlsruhe, SchiedsVZ 2006, 335, 336 = XXXII Y.B. Com. Arb. 342 (2007); Münch, in: MünchKommZPO, s 1048 para 15.

163 Münch, in: MünchKommZPO, s 1048 para 16; different view: Lachmann, para 1664.

164 Hartmann, in: Baumbach/Lauterbach/Albers/Hartmann (eds), s 1048 para 4; Geimer, in: Zöller (ed), s 1048 para 5; Lachmann, para 1670; Münch, in: MünchKommZPO, s 1048 para 28; Voit, in: Musielak/Voit (eds), s 1048 para 9; Saenger, in: Saenger (ed), s 1048 para 6.

165 Saenger, in: Saenger (ed), s 1043 para 5; Schwab/Walter, ch 15 para 43.

166 Münch, in: MünchKommZPO, s 1047 paras 8 *et seq.*; Voit, in: Musielak/Voit (eds), s 1047 para 2. Opposing view: Lachmann, para 1588.

communicate the hearing date via simple letter, telephone, or email.[167] It is good practice for arbitral tribunals to request the parties to communicate to the arbitral tribunal in advance who from each side will participate (by name and function).

German law does not contain any provisions on the publicity or privacy of oral hearings in arbitral proceedings. However, it is generally understood—both internationally and as a matter of German arbitration practice—that unlike state court proceedings, oral hearings in arbitral proceedings are **not open to the public** but rather are private.[168] Thus, ordinarily only the parties and their counsel will be admitted to oral hearings. Witnesses and experts are admitted for their appearance. It is within the discretion of the arbitral tribunal whether to admit them to the hearing before and/or after they testify. The German tradition, inspired by the rules governing state court proceedings, would be not to have them present before their testimony, and to allow them to remain in the hearing room once they have testified. **4.135**

In addition, there may be a (limited) number of **further participants** in the hearing who have the status of observers or spectators. Whether this is allowed is a matter for the agreement of the parties, or, in the absence of such agreement, the discretion of the arbitral tribunal. There may be persons who have a legitimate interest in sitting in on a hearing and observing what happens, for instance representatives from the main shareholder of a party, from a regulatory authority, or a consortium partner. **4.136**

The principle of **privacy** needs to be clearly distinguished from the principle of **confidentiality**, which is not a generally recognized characteristic of arbitration (see paras 1.51 *et seq.*). Thus, if a party expects the other participants and especially witnesses not to disclose any information about the case, it needs to conclude a specific agreement.[169] But even where such an agreement exists, a party is well advised to check whether it provides for confidentiality under the specific circumstances. For example, there may be exceptions for the opposing party due to prevailing public interests or adverse contractual obligations.[170] **4.137**

4 Minutes; Court Reporter

Different from state court proceedings (s 160 ZPO), the German arbitration law does **not contain express provisions** on hearing minutes or transcripts.[171] **4.138**

[167] Münch, in: MünchKommZPO, s 1047 para 12; Lachmann, para 1595; Voit, in: Musielak/Voit (eds), s 1042 para 15; Schwab/Walter, ch 16 paras 34 *et seq.*; Hartmann, in: Baumbach/Lauterbach/Albers/Hartmann (eds), s 1042 para 12.

[168] Blackaby/Partasides/Redfern/Hunter, para 2.148; Lachmann, para 1602; Oldenstam/v Pachelbel, SchiedsVZ 2006, 31, 21.

[169] Kreindler/Rust, in: Beck'sches Rechtsanwaltshandbuch, § 7 para 28.

[170] For a profound discussion see Leisinger, pp 192 *et seq.*

[171] In German state court proceedings, there is either a court reporter provided by the court who produces a summary record, as instructed or dictated by the chairman, or the chairman uses a dictaphone to create a summary record of the hearing. Importantly, there is generally no verbatim transcript of oral hearings in German state court proceedings.

Nevertheless, for practical purposes it is highly advisable for an arbitral tribunal to ensure establishment of a record of an oral hearing.[172] In that vein, s 29 DIS Rules specifies that "[a] record shall be made of all oral hearings. The record shall be signed by the chairman. The parties shall each receive a copy of the record."

4.139 In practice, in larger cases or cases of significant importance it is not uncommon to use the services of a court reporter to create a **verbatim transcript**. A major advantage of this approach is that it relieves all participants of the need to engage in constant note-taking themselves and thus has a considerable convenience aspect. In addition, it is certainly much more reliable than other forms of creating minutes and provides an unambiguous record of due process and equal treatment of the parties. On this basis, both counsel and the tribunal have a common source for future reference, be it for closing argument, post-hearing submissions or the drafting of the award.

4.140 It is a matter for agreement between the parties and the tribunal who organizes the court reporter and who pays the person. Arbitral tribunals often expect that the parties will assume that task. Otherwise, the tribunal may do so; if it does so, it may want to obtain sufficient advances on costs to be able to pay the court reporter.

5. Interpreter

4.141 Oral hearings are to be conducted in the language of the proceedings (s 1045 para 1 cl 3 ZPO). An interpreter may be needed where not everyone in a hearing speaks that same language. This may be the case for witnesses of fact and expert witnesses who do not have sufficient command of the language of the proceedings. Since the arbitral tribunal cannot force witnesses to appear and testify (see para 4.161), it has even less power to compel testimony in a language that the witness is not willing to testify in. To the extent the parties have access to or influence over witnesses, they should carefully consider the **pros and cons** of using an interpreter where the witness has at least some familiarity with the language of the proceedings. For instance, the fact that an interpreter steps in to translate may be a significant advantage where parties and their counsel expect forceful, or even aggressive and intense cross-examination. On the other hand, witnesses who have conducted the relevant contract negotiations in, say, English, but refuse to testify in English may appear uncooperative, which, together with other circumstances, might possibly have an impact on their credibility in the eyes of the arbitral tribunal.

4.142 Again, arbitral tribunals often appreciate where parties take care of organizing an interpreter and paying the interpreter directly. Otherwise, again, the arbitral tribunal may want to make sure it obtains sufficient advances on costs from the parties.

[172] Hartmann, in: Baumbach/Lauterbach/Albers/Hartmann (eds), s 1042 para 13; Münch, in: MünchKommZPO, s 1047 para 10; Voit, in: Musielak/Voit (eds), s 1042 para 14; Schwab/Walter, ch 15 para 17; Lachmann, paras 1598 *et seq.*

6. Time Management

German law does not contain any provisions regarding time management in hearings before an arbitral tribunal. Arbitral tribunals frequently **encourage the parties to seek and reach agreement** on time allocations for a hearing, eg specified and usually equal times for opening statements, certain time allotments for individual witnesses and experts, as well as time slots for closing arguments where appropriate. In the absence of party agreement, it is up to the discretion of the arbitral tribunal to manage timing during hearings, both in terms of an advance time schedule and during the hearing on an ad hoc basis. Where hearings are more complex and involve a number of issues and/or witnesses, advance planning may be strongly advisable. By contrast, in simpler and more straightforward matters, it may suffice for the arbitral tribunal to set a time frame for the overall duration of the hearing and nothing more. **4.143**

Where the arbitral tribunal makes time allocations to the parties, witnesses, experts, and the like, it must **treat the parties equally** (s 1042 para 1 cl 1 ZPO). This does not mean that each party needs to be allocated the same amount of time by hour and minute as the other. Instead, the arbitral tribunal may differentiate if there are valid reasons to do so (see para 4.20). For instance, where one party brings only one witness and the other ten, it would be unfair that the one party receives ten times as much time for questioning a witness. **4.144**

Equally important is the **right to be heard** (s 1042 para 1 cl 2 ZPO). The time management of the arbitral tribunal must be such that each party has a reasonable opportunity to present its case. It should be noted, however, that an oral hearing is generally not the right venue for making new factual allegations or to make first-time legal arguments; instead, the parties are generally supposed to do that in their prior written submissions. Thus, the most relevant issues are again witnesses and experts. Where the arbitral tribunal has adopted an "international style" for the overall proceedings, it will likely have required written witness statements. As a consequence, there should be no need for extensive direct examination of a witness. In this case, the right to be heard relates particularly to sufficient time for cross-examination and redirect examination of a witness.[173] **4.145**

VIII. Taking of Evidence

The taking of evidence in a hearing of the tribunal is at the heart of many arbitral proceedings. Oftentimes, the arbitral tribunal will not be able or willing to decide a case solely on the basis of the law and the documents in front of it without testing them in a hearing with the parties, witnesses, and experts. Thus, the hearing where the taking of evidence takes place can be crucial for the outcome of the case. We **4.146**

[173] Implicitly: Lachmann, para 1508.

first address the framework of applicable rules (below paras 4.147 *et seq.*) and then turn to the various means of evidence, ie witness evidence and party examination (below paras 4.159 *et seq.*), expert evidence (below paras 4.177 *et seq.*), documentary evidence (below paras 4.193 *et seq.*), and inspection of objects (below para 4.197). We also address the securing of evidence (below paras 4.198 *et seq.*), and the assistance by German state courts in the taking of evidence, including located abroad (below paras 4.200 *et seq.*). There may be additional means of taking evidence, such as seeking information from a government agency, which, however, rarely occurs in practice and is not further addressed herein.[174]

1. Framework of Applicable Rules

4.147 We start with some general principles under German law (below paras 4.148 *et seq.*) and then turn to institutional arbitration (below paras 4.154 *et seq.*) as well as the IBA Rules on the Taking of Evidence in International Arbitration (below paras 4.156 *et seq.*).

4.148 a) **General Principles** The basic provision for the taking of evidence in German arbitration law is s 1042 para 4 cl 2 ZPO, which follows art 19 para 2 cl 2 Model Law and authorizes the arbitral tribunal to **determine the admissibility** of taking of evidence, **take evidence**, and **assess freely** such evidence (see para 4.27). Apart from that, there are two further provisions in the German arbitration law that deal with selected issues of evidence taking: s 1049 ZPO addresses **expert evidence** and s 1050 ZPO concerns **assistance by state courts** in the taking of evidence. In principle, all other issues are left to **party agreement** and, in its absence, the **discretion** of the arbitral tribunal. This applies, eg to the hearing of witnesses and party representatives, the production of documents, the inspection of objects, and the gathering of information from other sources.

4.149 The procedure for the taking of evidence in arbitral proceedings is **less formalized** than in German state court proceedings. The arbitral tribunal is not required to issue an evidence order setting forth the allegations to be proven and the means of evidence to be used to prove them.[175] At the same time, the arbitral tribunal certainly has discretion to use the technique of an evidence order and often this will further the efficiency of the proceedings. Likewise, the arbitral tribunal is not required to make formal rulings on offers of evidence that it does not wish to pursue.[176] The tribunal may decide based on its analysis of the case which allegations it thinks need to be proven and by what means, or it may even let the party representatives decide which issues they wish to prove, and then decide in the

[174] See Münch, in: MünchKommZPO, s 1049 para 78.
[175] Münch, in: MünchKommZPO, s 1042 para 116; Schwab/Walter, ch 15 para 8; Voit, in: Musielak/Voit (eds), s 1042 para 22. Opposing view: Lachmann, para 1483.
[176] OLG Köln, RIW 1993, 499, 501 = XXI Y.B. Com. Arb. 535, 540 (1996); Geimer, in: Zöller (ed), s 1042 para 11; Voit, in: Musielak/Voit (eds), s 1042 para 21.

course of making the award what it considers relevant for the case and material for its outcome.

Regarding the conduct of evidence taking, again the arbitral tribunal has **wide discretion**. It is not bound to apply the traditional means of proof generally employed in state court litigation.[177] In particular, it is not bound to follow the distinction in German state court litigation between examination of witnesses and party representatives.[178] Instead, arbitral tribunals frequently treat **witnesses and party representatives alike** and consider the closeness of a person to a party when assessing the credibility of that person's testimony.[179] Given the ZPO's authorization of limited investigation (see paras 4.27 *et seq.*) the arbitral tribunal is at liberty to consider items of evidence that none of the parties has offered.[180] **4.150**

In **assessing the evidence**, the arbitral tribunal has discretion much like a state court judge (s 286 ZPO). The issue that arises here is the applicable **standard of proof**. Neither German nor international arbitration law provides a definition of this standard. As far as state court litigation is concerned, the Anglo-American tradition applies a lower standard of "preponderance of the evidence," while the civil law systems—including Germany—typically require a conviction "beyond a reasonable doubt." There is an ongoing discussion whether the arbitral tribunal has discretion as to which standard it applies or whether has to use the same "beyond a reasonable doubt" standard that German state courts are required to follow.[181] **4.151**

In international cases the trend clearly goes towards allowing a **wider discretion** for the tribunal.[182] This view allows arbitral tribunals to take a **flexible approach** and link the standard of proof to the gravity of the issue to be proven.[183] For instance, where issues of willful or criminal misconduct are concerned, arbitral tribunals will often be reluctant to draw conclusions based on a standard of mere preponderance of the evidence, but instead would seek to be satisfied beyond a reasonable doubt.[184] By contrast, regarding the amount of damages, arbitral tribunals may take a more generous approach and resort to estimates based on **4.152**

[177] Münch, in: MünchKommZPO, s 1042 para 118; Reichold, in: Thomas/Putzo (eds), s 1042 para 7; Saenger, in: Saenger (ed), s 1042 para 17; Schwab/Walter, ch 15 paras 8 *et seq.*; Voit, in: Musielak/Voit (eds), s 1042 para 22.

[178] Schlosser, in: Stein/Jonas (eds), s 1042 para 58; Wilske/Markert, in: BeckOK ZPO, s 1042 para 25; Lachmann, para 1490.

[179] Implicitly: Lachmann, para 1504.

[180] BGH NJW 1964, 593, 595; Lachmann, para 1282; Saenger, in: Saenger (ed), s 1042 para 16; Schwab/Walter, ch 15 paras 8 *et seq.*

[181] For discretion, eg Elsing, SchiedsVZ 2011, 114, 121; Born, p 2314; for state court standard, eg Münch, in: MünchKommZPO, s 1042 para 119; Saenger, in: Saenger (ed), s 1042 para 18; Schlosser, in: Stein/Jonas (eds), s 1042 para 67; Rieder/Schoenemann, NJW 2011, 1169, 1174.

[182] Blackaby/Partasides/Redfern/Hunter, para 6.94; Born, p 2314; Elsing, SchiedsVZ 2011, 114, 121.

[183] Elsing, SchiedsVZ 2011, 114, 121; Blackaby/Partasides/Redfern/Hunter, paras 6.94 *et seq.*; Schlosser, in: Stein/Jonas (eds), s 1042 para 43.

[184] Elsing, SchiedsVZ 2011, 114, 121; Blackaby/Partasides/Redfern/Hunter, para 6.95.

reasonable probabilities (which is incidentally in conformity with German state court litigation, see eg s 287 ZPO and s 252 BGB).[185] However, at the time of writing there is no certainty on this issue. Conversely, the stronger the nexus of the case, the parties or the arbitrators to the civil law tradition, the more likely the tribunal will be expected—at least in this respect—to act **"equivalent"** to state court litigation and hence to apply the same standard of proof customary in state court litigation.

4.153 Under German law, the **burden of proof** is considered an issue of substantive law (see para 4.62).[186] Whether the arbitral tribunal considers and applies **alleviations** with respect to the burden of proof is again a procedural issue within the discretion of the tribunal. Thus, an arbitral tribunal may resort to the principles known from German state court litigation, such as *res ipsa loquitur* (*Anscheinsbeweis*), frustration of proof (*Beweisvereitelung*), and reversed burden of proof (*Umkehr der Beweislast*).[187] Also, a tribunal may seek inspiration from the principles of **secondary burden** of substantiation and proof (*sekundäre Darlegungs- und Beweislast*), which is a technique developed by German state courts to allow for the fact that there is in principle no discovery in German state court litigation and thus a party bearing the burden of proof may not have access to information necessary to make its case. This technique, when applied by a court or arbitral tribunal, may require a party that does not bear the burden of proof to make substantiated counter-allegations and disclose relevant facts where (i) the party bearing the burden of proof has no means of knowing such facts; and (ii) making such disclosures is not an undue burden to the obligated party.[188] An arbitral tribunal should bear in mind, however, that there may be less justification for this technique where the tribunal allows substantial **document disclosure**,[189] a context that is sometimes overlooked by German practitioners.

4.154 **b) Institutional Arbitration** For the taking of evidence, the DIS Rules closely follow ss 1042 para 3, 1049 ZPO. **Section 27.1 DIS Rules** tasks the arbitral tribunal with establishing the facts underlying the dispute, without being bound by the parties' applications for the admission of evidence. Section 27 DIS Rules further addresses witness and expert evidence, in the latter case very similar to s 1049 ZPO.

4.155 The ICC Rules take a comparable approach, also mandating the arbitral tribunal with establishing the facts "within as short a time as possible" (**art 25.1 ICC Rules**).

---

185 OLG Frankfurt, IPRspr. 2008, no 203, 646 = XXXIV Y.B. Com. Arb. 527 (2009).

186 Greger, in: Zöller (ed), Vor s 284 para 15; Münch, in: MünchKommZPO, s 1042 para 120.

187 Hartmann, in: Baumbach/Lauterbach/Albers/Hartmann (eds), s 1042 para 10; Geimer, in: Zöller (ed), s 1042 para 29; Münch, in: MünchKommZPO, s 1042 para 120.

188 BGH NJW 2009, 2199; NJW 1999, 2887, 2888; BGHZ 145, 170, 183 *et seq*.

189 On this context see Rieder/Schoenemann, TDM 3 2013, p 8.

Article 25 ICC Rules further addresses witnesses, experts, and documentary evidence.

c) IBA Rules on the Taking of Evidence in International Arbitration The IBA Rules are meant to be: 4.156

> a resource to parties and to arbitrators to provide an efficient, economical and fair process for the taking of evidence in international arbitration... [They] reflect procedures in use in many different legal systems, and they may be particularly useful when the parties come from different legal cultures.[190]

The parties can adopt the IBA Rules as part of their arbitration agreement or at a later stage. In the absence of an agreement of the parties to use these "rules," an arbitral tribunal, in exercising its discretion, may still **seek inspiration** from the IBA Rules. Three important general principles of the IBA Rules are (i) conducting the taking of evidence in good faith (Preamble at 3); (ii) avoiding surprises to the other party (Preamble at 3); and (iii) early consultations among the parties and between the parties and the arbitral tribunal on issues related to the taking of evidence (art 2). The IBA Rules contain detailed provisions on the disclosure of documents (art 3), witnesses of fact (art 4), party-appointed experts (art 5), tribunal-appointed experts (art 6), inspections of property, goods, processes, or documents (art 7), the conduct of evidentiary hearings (art 8), as well as the admissibility and assessment of evidence (art 9). 4.157

In **German arbitration practice**, it is our experience that the IBA Rules are more used as a source of inspiration rather than as agreed-upon and binding "rules." In line with their purpose, they are used most often in arbitral proceedings with an **international nexus**. In seeking inspiration from the IBA Rules, different tribunals take different approaches; some apply them more strictly than others. For practitioners, especially counsel representing a party in arbitral proceedings, the IBA Rules are a useful source of possible approaches and arguments, especially as they are considerably more detailed than the provisions of the German arbitration law or rules of an arbitral institution. For arbitral tribunals, the solutions offered by the IBA Rules may serve as a good compromise between views originating from different legal systems and cultures. We will address the provisions of the IBA Rules in more detail below when we discuss the various means of evidence. 4.158

2. *Witness Evidence and Party Examination*

We first turn to some general principles in connection with the examination of witnesses and party representatives (below paras 4.160 *et seq.*). We then address issues of witness statements (below paras 4.164 *et seq.*) and witness preparation (below paras 4.167 *et seq.*), and the examination in front of the arbitral tribunal (below 4.159

[190] IBA Rules, Foreword, p 2.

paras 4.169 *et seq.*). Finally, we address the assistance that state courts may provide in the taking of witness evidence (below 4.175 *et seq.*).

4.160 a) **Legal Framework and General Principles** Witnesses are **natural persons** who can speak to **facts** that they have experienced, without drawing any conclusions or providing any (expert) analysis thereon. Any person that can somehow express him- or herself can be a witness.[191] The German arbitration law does not contain specific provisions on witness evidence. The parties are free to agree on the details for the examination of witnesses. In the absence of such agreement, the matter is left to the discretion of the arbitral tribunal (s 1042 para 4 ZPO).

4.161 An arbitral tribunal does **not have any power of coercion** over witnesses. Thus, anyone who testifies as a witness does so voluntarily. As a consequence, an arbitral tribunal cannot summon a witness, but merely make an invitation to appear.[192] As a further consequence, since any testimony is voluntary, technically there is no need to consider rights to refuse testimony. Nevertheless, in order to be able to properly assess the credibility of a witness' testimony or refusal to testify, it may be recommendable that the arbitral tribunal explore whether there are grounds for a refusal or not.[193] With regard to witnesses who do not appear or testify voluntarily, an arbitral tribunal may seek the **assistance of the competent state court** (s 1050 ZPO), which may compel the appearance and testimony of a witness before the state court (but not in front of the arbitral tribunal; see para 4.175).

4.162 In German state court litigation, there is a strict distinction between witness examination (ss 373 *et seq.* ZPO) and **party examination** (ss 445 *et seq.* ZPO). By law, party examination is a minor form of evidence that is available only in certain circumstances and generally carries less weight than witness testimony.[194] Whether these distinctions still make sense in state court litigation, or whether they should be abolished, is a question that is open to debate. As far as arbitral proceedings are concerned, the law does not contain any such distinction. An arbitral tribunal has discretion how to address the issue. In today's **arbitration practice**, there is **less and less distinction** made between witnesses and parties or their representatives. Thus, art 4.2 IBA Rules provides that "[a]ny person may present evidence as a witness, including a Party or a Party's officer, employee or other representative."

4.163 How close a person is to the claimant or the respondent, and how strong his or her personal interest is in the outcome of the proceedings, is a matter to be considered

[191] Münch, in: MünchKommZPO, s 1049 para 49.

[192] Lachmann, para 1493; Geimer, in: Zöller (ed), s 1042 para 32; Schwab/Walter, ch 15 para 13; Münch, in: MünchKommZPO, s 1049 para 54.

[193] Voit, in: Musielak/Voit (eds), s 1042 para 27; Lachmann, paras 1493 *et seq.*; Münch, in: MünchKommZPO, s 1049 paras 50 *et seq.*

[194] Similarly: Hartmann, in: Baumbach/Lauterbach/Albers/Hartmann (eds), Übers s 445 para 7; Schreiber, in: MünchKommZPO, s 445 para 6.

when assessing the evidence.[195] A person who is technically a witness (eg a newly hired employee with substantial personal debt) may be much less "independent" than a person who is technically considered a party representative (eg a long-time managing director with independent wealth shortly before retirement).

b) Written Witness Statements German law does not specifically address written witness statements, whether in arbitration or even in state court litigation.[196] Nevertheless, written witness statements have also become **common** in arbitral proceedings in Germany. Many arbitrators view them as a means to efficiently structure and streamline the proceedings. Article 4.5 IBA Rules is a useful point of reference for the **suggested content** of written witness statements, addressing as essential elements (i) the identification of the witness by name and address, relationships with the parties, background, qualifications, training, and experience; (ii) the necessity for a full and detailed description of the facts, and the source of the witness's information as to those facts; and (iii) an affirmation of the truth of the witness statement. **4.164**

Providing a written witness statement is, however, generally **not a substitute for appearing** at an evidentiary hearing. Where a witness whose appearance has been requested fails without a valid reason to appear for testimony, art 4.7 IBA Rules provides that the arbitral tribunal generally shall disregard a witness statement by that witness. **4.165**

From a practical point of view, many arbitrators will usually not consider it particularly useful where witness statements merely repeat the written submissions of a party. Instead, they will expect the witness to provide more factual detail as to what the author personally experienced when and where and how. In international arbitration, it is generally not considered improper for counsel to assist in the **drafting of a witness statement.**[197] The important point is that the witness carefully reviews any such suggestions from counsel to verify whether those are a true and complete rendition of the relevant facts and a faithful expression of its own recollection, thoughts, or opinion as the case may be.[198] **4.166**

c) Witness Preparation Traditionally, German practice in state court litigation has been characterized by considerable reluctance regarding contacts between a **4.167**

195 Lachmann, para 1504; Münch, in: MünchKommZPO, s 1049 para 60.

196 In injunction proceedings, it is common to use affidavits which are written witness statements whose correctness is averred "in lieu of oath." Since arbitral tribunals are not proper addressees of such assurances "in lieu of oath" (Münch, in: MünchKommZPO, s 1049 para 79; Schwab/Walter, ch 15 paras 24 *et seq.*; Voit, in: Musielak/Voit (eds), s 1042 para 23), they are generally not relevant in arbitration; where they occur, they should not be treated differently from regular witness statements.

197 See eg IBA Guidelines on Party Representation in International Arbitration (2013), para 20: "A Party Representative may assist Witnesses in the preparation of Witness Statements...."

198 IBA Guidelines on Party Representation in International Arbitration (2013), p 15.

party or its counsel and witnesses to be examined, in particular in the case of witnesses outside a party's immediate control. The **traditional view** was that such contacts may significantly impact the credibility of a witness.[199] Whether that is still true in state court litigation is an evolving issue.[200] As far as arbitral proceedings are concerned, it seems that many practitioners do not per se object to such contacts. We believe that in arbitral proceedings it should **not be considered improper** to meet a witness in advance of an evidentiary hearing, to explain to the witness how the hearing will likely be conducted and what the witness' duties and obligations are.[201] In our view, it is also appropriate to discuss the **substance of a witness' testimony** as long as there are no improper attempts to influence such substance.[202] In that vein, a witness may be asked **test questions** and provide corresponding answers (**mock examination**).[203] This is particularly true—and necessary—where a party and its counsel expect that there will be some type of US-style or otherwise intense **cross-examination**, which is a situation with which most people are not familiar and can pose significant traps for the unwary.

4.168 The above is encapsulated in **art 4.3 IBA Rules**, which provides that it is not considered improper for a party or its representatives to interview its witnesses or potential witnesses and to discuss their prospective testimony with them.

4.169 **d) Witness Examination** It is within the arbitral tribunal's **discretion** how witnesses are to be examined. The tribunal may be inspired by the rules governing witness examinations in German state court litigation (ss 394 *et seq.* ZPO), which frequently happens in a domestic German arbitration setting. In such a case, usually the arbitral tribunal will **take the lead** in questioning the witness. Based on the model contained in s 396 ZPO, it will ask the witness to "tell the story" comprehensively and then ask additional questions. Only then will the parties and their representatives be allowed to ask supplemental questions (see s 397 ZPO). Generally, the party that has named a witness goes first (direct examination), and afterwards, the opposing party has the opportunity for cross-examination. It should be noted, however, that arbitrators with a significant background in the German legal system and German legal traditions often disapprove the type of vigorous, perhaps even aggressive cross-examination that is an important cornerstone in US and UK litigation.

4.170 Apart from the approach described above, an arbitral tribunal may decide to take a **different approach** and to let the parties and their counsel take the lead in

---

199 See Lachmann, para 1513.

200 Bertke/Schroeder, SchiedsVZ 2014, 80; Schlosser, SchiedsVZ 2004, 225, 228 *et seq.*; Ullrich, NJW 2014, 1341 *et seq.*; Voser, SchiedsVZ 2005, 113, 117; Wirth, SchiedsVZ 2003, 9, 13.

201 Bertke/Schroeder, SchiedsVZ 2014, 80, 82 *et seq.*; Schlosser, SchiedsVZ 2004, 225, 229; Ullrich, NJW 2014, 1341, 1345.

202 Bertke/Schroeder, SchiedsVZ 2014, 80, 83 *et seq.*; Schlosser, SchiedsVZ 2004, 225, 229.

203 For recent comprehensive discussions of witness preparation in German state court litigation and arbitration, see Bertke/Schroeder, SchiedsVZ 2014, 80 *et seq.;* Ullrich, NJW 2014, 1341 *et seq.*

examining witnesses. This is often done in an international context, in particular where (at least) one party has a common law background. Where written witness statements have been submitted, arbitral tribunals often limit the direct examination of a witness to a minimum, such as a confirmation of the witness' personal background and the correctness of his or her witness statement. In such a case, a more active type of cross-examination may occur, too. Nevertheless, again, most arbitral tribunals sitting in Germany do not appreciate overtly aggressive cross-examination questions and tactics.

There are various methods of **time management** during witness hearings. It is advisable for an arbitral tribunal to consult with the parties on how much time is considered to be necessary for each witness, and to allot the time fairly between the parties in order to ensure equal treatment (s 1042 para 1 cl 1 ZPO). Various techniques have been developed in practice, including such rigid methods as the "**chess clock.**"[204] **4.171**

In German practice, witnesses are usually examined **one by one**. Generally, the other witnesses are not present while a witness is examined, unless the parties agree otherwise and the arbitral tribunal does not insist on the absence of the other witnesses. In certain cases, it may be useful for an arbitral tribunal to confront witnesses with someone else's testimony or to confront two witnesses with each other. In addition, there may be cases where it is useful for witnesses to be heard together in the first place (**witness conferencing**). **4.172**

Under German law, an arbitral tribunal does **not** have the power to **administer oaths.**[205] Nevertheless, a witness who willingly provides false testimony can be criminally liable for (attempted) procedural fraud. As a matter of German law, an arbitral tribunal could request the **assistance of the competent state court** to put a witness under oath (s 1050 ZPO), see para 4.176. **4.173**

Witnesses have a right to be compensated for their out-of-pocket **expenses.**[206] Under German doctrine, it is the parties (not the arbitral tribunal) who owe remuneration of expenses to the witnesses.[207] Nevertheless, an arbitral tribunal may consider requesting that the parties make appropriate advance payments to the arbitral tribunal covering the likely expenses of witnesses in order to increase the likelihood that witnesses actually appear. In the alternative, the arbitral tribunal may leave it to the initiative of the parties which witnesses they wish to call. Thus, as a practical matter, it will be up to the party to ensure that a witness offered by it **4.174**

---

[204] Cf Elsing, SchiedsVZ 2011, 114, 119.

[205] Münch, in: MünchKommZPO, s 1049 para 52; Schwab/Walter, ch 17 para 1; Wilske/Markert, in: BeckOK ZPO, s 1042 para 27.

[206] Münch, in: MünchKommZPO, s 1049 para 56; Lachmann, para 1939; Voit, in: Musielak/Voit (eds), s 1042 para 23, s 1049 para 8.

[207] Geimer, in: Zöller (ed), s 1042 para 36; Lachmann, para 1939; Münch, in: MünchKommZPO, s 1049 para 56; Voit, in: Musielak/Voit (eds), s 1042 para 23.

appears, and the willingness of the witness to appear may be linked with the preparedness of the party calling him or her to compensate for expenses.

4.175 e) **State Court Assistance** If a witness fails to appear, the arbitral tribunal may ask the competent state court—generally the local court (AG) of the district **where the witness resides**[208]—for assistance; likewise, a party—with the approval of the arbitral tribunal—may make such request (ss 1050 cl 1, 1062 para 4 ZPO). The state court may then question the witness. If the witness also fails to appear before the state court, it can **compel appearance** by means of monetary penalties or incarceration (s 390 ZPO). The **arbitrators may be present** when the state court questions a witness (s 1050 cl 3 ZPO). Likewise, as a result of their right to be heard, the **parties may be present** and be asking questions, too, pursuant to s 1042 para 1 cl 2 and s 357 para 1 ZPO.[209]

4.176 The state court may also assist an arbitral tribunal in **administering oaths.**[210] As mentioned (para 4.173), under German law arbitral tribunals are not empowered to put witnesses under oath. Thus, where an arbitral tribunal decides that a witness should be put under oath, it may ask the competent state court to do so (s 1050 ZPO). In our experience, however, this is rarely done in German practice.

3. Expert Evidence

4.177 We first address certain general principles and legal traditions in connection with expert evidence (below paras 4.178 *et seq.*). We then turn to party-appointed and tribunal-appointed experts (below paras 4.180 *et seq.* and paras 4.182 *et seq.*). In a next step, we deal with the written expert report (below para 4.189) and the oral examination of experts, including expert conferencing (below paras 4.190 *et seq.*). Finally, we address the challenge of experts (below para 4.192).

4.178 a) **General Principles and Legal Traditions** Expert evidence is the only means of evidence that the German arbitration law addresses with some specificity in **s 1049 ZPO**, which closely follows art 26 Model Law. Section 1049 para 1 cl 1 ZPO provides that unless otherwise agreed by the parties, the arbitral tribunal may appoint one or more experts to render an expert opinion on certain issues defined by the arbitral tribunal. The arbitral tribunal may request a party to provide the court-appointed expert with all relevant information, documents, or objects (s 1049 para 1 cl 2 ZPO). The tribunal-appointed expert is to render

[208] RG JW 1912, 305; Münch, in: MünchKommZPO, s 1050 para 13. Exceptions may exist where it is more efficient to resort to a different local court, eg where several witnesses residing in different places need to be examined by the state court. In such a case, it may be more efficient for one local court to examine all witnesses instead of having each witness examined by another court.

[209] Geimer, in: Zöller (ed), s 1050 para 7; Voit, in: Musielak/Voit (eds), s 1050 para 7; Münch, in: MünchKommZPO, s 1050 para 31; Hartmann, in: Baumbach/Lauterbach/Albers/Hartmann (eds), s 1050 para 4.

[210] Saenger, in: Saenger (ed), s 1050 para 3; Schwab/Walter, ch 17 para 1; Voit, in: Musielak/Voit (eds), s 1050 para 2; Wilske/Markert, in: BeckOK ZPO, s 1050 para 4.

a written or oral report (s 1049 para 2 cl 1 ZPO). If a party so requests or if the tribunal considers it necessary, the tribunal-appointed expert shall participate in an oral hearing in order to be questioned by the arbitral tribunal and the parties (s 1049 para 2 cl 1 and 2 ZPO). For such hearing, the parties may also rely on party-appointed experts and have them speak to the questions at issue (s 1049 para 2 cl 2 ZPO). Regarding neutrality of tribunal-appointed experts, the same principles apply as with respect to arbitrators (ss 1049 para 3, 1036, 1037 ZPO).

Thus, German law, at least on the face of it, expresses a certain **preference for tribunal-appointed** versus party-appointed **experts**, which is in conformity with the approach taken in German **state court litigation**. Party-appointed experts are mentioned only in passing. The IBA Rules take a more balanced approach; art 5 contains detailed provisions for party-appointed experts; art 6 addresses tribunal-appointed experts. We will address these provisions in more detail next. **4.179**

b) Party-appointed Experts While the German arbitration law mentions party-appointed experts only in passing, they play a **significant role** in arbitration practice both internationally and in Germany. Parties may instruct experts on issues of law and fact, and it is not uncommon to do so in arbitral proceedings in Germany. Parties will furnish their experts with the necessary facts and documents. Parties conclude the required engagement agreements with their party-appointed experts, and they need to remunerate them. Costs for a party-appointed expert may be included in costs of the arbitral proceedings, and the arbitral tribunal may decide who should bear such costs (s 1057 para 1 ZPO).[211] **4.180**

German practitioners, in particular those with a strong state court litigation background (eg active or retired judges sitting as arbitrators) can have a certain skepticism toward party-appointed experts and may tend, as a matter of principle, to consider tribunal-appointed experts to be more credible and persuasive.[212] We do not think that such skepticism is in principle warranted. There are highly credible and qualified party-appointed experts; at the same time, there are tribunal-appointed experts who do not line up to their appointed task. The issue is thus one for careful case-by-case analysis, looking at the credentials and the persuasiveness of the opinions of both party-appointed and tribunal-appointed experts. **4.181**

c) Tribunal-appointed Experts Tribunal-appointed experts are typically tasked with issues of fact or specific (non-legal) expertise, whereas the application of the law to the facts is and remains the core task of the arbitral tribunal **4.182**

[211] Lachmann, paras 1979 *et seq.*; Münch, in: MünchKommZPO, s 1049 para 37; Schwab/Walter, ch 15 para 12; Voit, in: Musielak/Voit (eds), s 1049 para 9; Blackaby/Partasides/Redfern/Hunter, para 9.90.

[212] For this view, see eg Münch, in: MünchKommZPO, s 1049 para 37; Voit, in: Musielak/Voit (eds), s 1049 para 11.

(*iura novit curia*).[213] Arbitrators may have specialized knowledge such that there is no need for a tribunal-appointed expert, eg with respect to certain business, industry, or technical issues (see also para 1.49).[214]

4.183 The arbitral tribunal is **free to choose an expert** or experts it deems sufficiently qualified unless the parties have limited its discretion by specific requirements or certain names.[215] It may consider available lists of publicly appointed and sworn experts,[216] but need not limit itself to these lists. As a result of the tribunal's appointment and the expert's corresponding acceptance emerges a **contract for works** (*Werkvertrag*) under substantive law on rendering the expert opinion.[217] There is no consensus in German legal doctrine on the mechanics for concluding this contract. In particular, it is disputed whether the tribunal is **authorized by the arbitrator agreement** on behalf of the parties,[218] or instead acts on behalf of the party bearing the burden of proof,[219] or rather acts in its own name with the parties benefitting therefrom only as third-party beneficiaries.[220] The differences of opinion are of practical relevance in particular for the question of liability for remuneration of the expert.

4.184 In the first place, the issue is of course determined by what has been agreed expressly between the parties, the tribunal, and the expert. In the absence of an agreement on the issue, in our opinion, the first view—which is also followed by German courts—best reflects the interests of all involved parties and provides for an efficient practical solution. Distinguishing along the lines of burden of proof fails where the expert opinion concerns numerous questions on both parties' sides. As between the first and the last view, we consider the first more persuasive because, eventually, arbitration is a dispute resolution mechanism based on private party agreement, which is in line with required experts being mandated by the parties as well. The arbitral tribunal itself—be it a one-person or a three-person panel—has no legal personality, such that the individual arbitrators or the chairman would need to be considered parties to the engagement agreement with an

[213] Lachmann, paras 1981 *et seq.*; Geimer, in: Zöller (ed), s 1049 para 3; Münch, in: MünchKommZPO, s 1049 para 11.

[214] Münch, in: MünchKommZPO, s 1049 para 13; Blackaby/Partasides/Redfern/Hunter, para 4.55; Voit, in: Musielak/Voit (eds), s 1042 para 18.

[215] Lotz, SchiedsVZ 2011, 203, 206; Geimer, in: Zöller (ed), s 1049 para 1; Voit, in: Musielak/Voit (eds), s 1049 para 2; Hartmann, in: Baumbach/Lauterbach/Albers/Hartmann (eds), s 1049 para 2.

[216] Hartmann, in: Baumbach/Lauterbach/Albers/Hartmann (eds), s 1049 para 2; Münch, in: MünchKommZPO, s 1049 para 21; Lotz, SchiedsVZ 2011, 203, 206.

[217] Müller-Glöge, in: MünchKommBGB, s 611 para 141; Sachs/Lörcher, in: *Arbitration in Germany*, s 1049 para 18; Hartmann, in: Baumbach/Lauterbach/Albers/Hartmann (eds), s 1049 para 1; Saenger, in: Saenger (ed), s 1049 para 2; Schwab/Walter, ch 15 para 18.

[218] BGH NJW 1965, 298, 299; Lotz, SchiedsVZ 2011, 203, 207; Lachmann, paras 1162 *et seq.*; Schwab/Walter, ch 15 para 13; Sachs/Lörcher, in: *Arbitration in Germany*, s 1049 para 19; Voit, in: Musielak/Voit (eds), s 1049 para 8; Saenger, in: Saenger (ed), s 1049 para 2.

[219] Hartmann, in: Baumbach/Lauterbach/Albers/Hartmann (eds), s 1049 para 1.

[220] Münch, in: MünchKommZPO, s 1049 paras 22, 31.

expert. Given the potentially substantial costs for expert reports, this would seem inappropriate to us.

4.185 The expert's main obligation is to **answer the question**(s) asked by the arbitral tribunal, which should be asked with precision and specificity. Possibly, it makes sense for the arbitral tribunal to confer with the expert on the proper wording of his or her instructions. In addition, conferring with the parties about this issue may be a good idea (see art 6.1 IBA Rules). In rendering the expert opinion, the expert is bound by the arbitral tribunal's instructions. Further obligations of the expert are to appear at an oral hearing and to answer questions from the arbitral tribunal and the parties (s 1049 para 2 ZPO). Also, the expert must be and remain neutral; he or she must disclose facts that could give rise to doubts as to neutrality (ss 1049 para 3, 1036 ZPO). The expert is not required to take an oath, since an arbitral tribunal under German law is not empowered to administer oaths.[221] In theory, the arbitral tribunal could request the assistance of the competent state court to put an expert under oath (s 1050 ZPO). However, this should be very rare in practice.

4.186 Although the arbitral tribunal is usually not party to the contract and therefore not obliged to **remunerate the expert**, in practice it regularly requests an **advance on the expert's costs** from the parties to ensure a smooth process and to relieve the expert of the risk and burden of having to look after his or her money.[222] The arbitral tribunal and the expert should agree expressly on the remuneration of the expert. The arbitral tribunal should consult with the parties on this issue. Where there is no agreement, existing fee scales may be applied; if none exist, the "usual" remuneration is deemed to be agreed (s 632 para 2 BGB). Where there is no "usual" remuneration, the expert would have the power to determine the remuneration (s 316 BGB).[223]

4.187 Tribunal-appointed experts need to render their expert work in person; they may **involve assistants** without the need for specific approval to a limited extent, such as for clerical or preparatory work. Still, they remain solely responsible for the opinion rendered.[224] The parties are required to assist tribunal-appointed experts to the extent ordered by the arbitral tribunal to do so, eg by **providing relevant information, documents, or access to objects** (s 1049 para 1 cl 2 ZPO, similar art 6.3 cl 1 IBA Rules). Where a party fails to provide the required assistance and cooperation, the arbitral tribunal may draw negative inferences from such behavior (s 1042

221 Sachs/Lörcher, in: *Arbitration in Germany*, s 1046 para 8; Lotz, SchiedsVZ 2011, 203, 208; Schwab/Walter, ch 15 para 15; Voit, in: Musielak/Voit (eds), s 1042 para 23.

222 Lachmann, para 1167; Sachs/Lörcher, in: *Arbitration in Germany*, s 1049 para 19; Lotz, SchiedsVZ 2011, 203, 207. However, there is no obligation to do so, RGZ 74, 321, 324 *et seq.*

223 BGH NJW 2006, 2472; Münch, in: MünchKommZPO, s 1049 para 29; Müller-Glöge, in: MünchKommBGB, s 612 para 31.

224 Münch, in: MünchKommZPO, s 1049 para 16; Stürner, SchiedsVZ 2013, 322, 322 *et seq.*

para 4 cl 2 ZPO).[225] By contrast, the arbitral tribunal has **no power to order third parties** to assist and cooperate with tribunal-appointed experts.[226]

4.188 Under the prevailing view in Germany, tribunal-appointed experts benefit from an **implied limitation of liability**; their liability towards the arbitral tribunal and the parties is limited to willful misconduct and gross negligence, equivalent to the principles applicable to experts appointed by a court in state court litigation (s 839a BGB).[227]

4.189 d) **Written Expert Report** Notwithstanding the fact that s 1049 ZPO allows for an oral expert report, in practice experts—whether party- or tribunal-appointed—almost always render a written report on the questions raised in their instructions. German law does not contain any further specifics on written expert reports. Arts 5.3 and 6.4 IBA Rules may be looked at for useful practical guidance.

4.190 e) **Oral Examination of Experts and Expert Conferencing** As set out above, German law provides for each party's right to request a tribunal-appointed expert to appear at an oral hearing and to answer questions from the parties (s 1049 para 2 ZPO, see also art 6.6 IBA Rules). Regarding party-appointed experts, in order to assess their credibility and the persuasiveness of the views expressed by them, it is at least as important to confront them in an oral hearing and to ask them questions. Article 5.5 IBA Rules even suggests to disregard the written reports of a party-appointed expert who does not appear at an oral hearing.

4.191 A tool that has become more and more popular in arbitration, including in Germany, is **expert conferencing**. It can be applied to both party-appointed and tribunal-appointed experts. With regard to party-appointed experts, art 5.4 IBA Rules provides as follows:

> The Arbitral Tribunal in its discretion may order that any Party-Appointed Experts who will submit or who have submitted Expert Reports on the same or related issues meet and confer on such issues. At such meeting, the Party-Appointed Experts shall attempt to reach agreement on the issues within the scope of their Expert Reports, and they shall record in writing any such issues on which they reach agreement, any remaining areas of disagreement and the reasons therefore.

4.192 f) **Challenge of Experts** Pursuant to ss 1049 para 3, 1037 ZPO, tribunal-appointed experts can be challenged for lack of neutrality. The **same principles apply as to arbitrators**. In particular, the two-week deadline provided for in

[225] Saenger, in: Saenger (ed), s 1049 para 2; Schlosser, in: Stein/Jonas (eds), s 1049 para 8; Schwab/Walter, ch 15 paras 24 *et seq*.; Voit, in: Musielak/Voit (eds), s 1049 para 4.

[226] Sachs/Lörcher, in: *Arbitration in Germany*, s 1042 para 44; Münch, in: MünchKommZPO, s 1049 para 17.

[227] BGHZ 42, 313, 316 *et seq*.; Münch, in: MünchKommZPO, s 1049 para 31; Schwab/Walter, ch 15 para 18; Voit, in: Musielak/Voit (eds), s 1049 para 10; Sachs/Lörcher, in: *Arbitration in Germany*, s 1049 para 20; different view: Lachmann, para 1544.

s 1037 para 2 cl 1 ZPO needs to be observed. The arbitral tribunal decides on the challenge. Unlike with arbitrator challenges, for expert challenges there is no resort to the state court once the arbitral tribunal has decided.[228] Article 6.2 IBA Rules contains similar provisions on the challenge of tribunal-appointed experts. By contrast, there is no possibility to challenge a party-appointed expert for lack of neutrality.[229] Instead, where a party-appointed expert is particularly close to the party instructing him or her, or expresses views and behaves in a way such as to suggest lack of neutrality, the arbitral tribunal will need to consider this aspect in assessing the credibility of such expert's views.[230]

4. *Documentary Evidence*

Documents are important pieces of evidence in most arbitral proceedings. Increasingly, parties wish to rely on documents that they intend to obtain from the other side or third parties (document disclosure, see paras 4.113 *et seq.*). The German arbitration law does not contain any specific provisions on documentary evidence. Thus, in the absence of an agreement by the parties, documentary evidence is a matter for the discretion of the arbitral tribunal (s 1042 para 4 ZPO). Documentary evidence is taken by providing the document to the arbitral tribunal and by the arbitral tribunal taking note of its contents. As a result of the right to be heard (ss 1042 para 1 cl 2, 1047 para 3 ZPO), documents must also be **made available to the other party or parties.**[231] Documents may be traditional hard-copy documents or electronic documents, including emails.[232] Whether the original of the document needs to be produced is again a matter for the discretion of the arbitral tribunal. Where the other party does not deny that a copy submitted as evidence conforms to the original, arbitral tribunals will often be satisfied with copies. Of course, the arbitral tribunal has discretion to request an original.[233] As far as electronic documents are concerned, the distinction between original and copy does not make sense. **4.193**

The arbitral tribunal has **discretion on how to assess documentary evidence** in relation to the allegations to be proven. The strict evidence rules governing **4.194**

[228] Geimer, in: Zöller (ed), s 1049 para 4; Lachmann, para 1534; Münch, in: MünchKommZPO, s 1049 para 34; Hartmann, in: Baumbach/Lauterbach/Albers/Hartmann (eds), s 1049 para 4; Schwab/Walter, ch 15 para 21; Voit, in: Musielak/Voit (eds), s 1049 para 7; Sachs/Lörcher, in: *Arbitration in Germany*, s 1049 para 16.

[229] Hartmann, in: Baumbach/Lauterbach/Albers/Hartmann (eds), s 1049 para 4; Lachmann, para 1534; Münch, in: MünchKommZPO, s 1049 para 37; Saenger, in: Saenger (ed), s 1049 para 6; Schwab/Walter, ch 15 para 21; Reichold, in: Thomas/Putzo (eds), s 1049 para 8; Sachs/Lörcher, in: *Arbitration in Germany*, s 1049 para 21.

[230] Schlosser, in: Stein/Jonas (eds), s 1049 paras 1, 3; Münch, in: MünchKommZPO, s 1049 para 37; Voit, in: Musielak/Voit (eds), s 1049 para 11.

[231] Article 3 para 1 IBA Rules; Münch, in: MünchKommZPO, s 1049 para 68; Hartmann, in: Baumbach/Lauterbach/Albers/Hartmann (eds), s 1047 para 4; Saenger, in: Saenger (ed), s 1047 para 4.

[232] Münch, in: MünchKommZPO, s 1049 para 65.

[233] Article 3 para 12 lit a IBA Rules.

documentary evidence in German state court litigation (ss 415 *et seq.*, 437 *et seq.* ZPO) do not apply in arbitration.[234] Arbitral tribunals may, however, seek inspiration from these rules, and some arbitrators, in particular those with a strong state court litigation background, may be strongly inclined to do so. Other than that, tribunals should be guided by common sense when exercising their discretion. For instance, the fact and content of an email or a presentation does not necessarily constitute full proof that the writing is actually true and correct, in particular when it comes to complex issues, views, and opinions. In such situations, arbitral tribunals are well advised to hear the persons involved in the genesis of such documents as witnesses to the extent they are available. Arbitral tribunals may do so even where none of the parties has offered a relevant person as a witness (principle of limited investigation, see paras 4.27 *et seq.*).

4.195 Where a party **fails to produce a document** that the arbitral tribunal has ordered to be produced, the arbitral tribunal has discretion to draw negative inferences from such behavior. This principle is broadly accepted, both in German state court litigation (s 427 ZPO) and in art 9 para 5 IBA Rules. Importantly, negative inferences are within the discretion of the arbitral tribunal; they are not a must.

4.196 Where a **third party** ordered to produce a document does not comply, the arbitral tribunal can seek the **assistance from the competent state court** pursuant to s 1050 ZPO, which may order a third party to produce and may impose sanctions where the third party fails to comply with a court order, including monetary penalties and incarceration (ss 142 para 2, 390 ZPO), which is, of course, a rare and extreme remedy.

5. *Inspection*

4.197 The German arbitration law does not contain any specific provisions on the inspection of property, goods, processes, or other objects. There will rarely be an advance party agreement on this issue. Thus, in most cases, inspection as a means of taking evidence will be within the discretion of the arbitral tribunal. The arbitral tribunal will require the parties' cooperation to conduct an inspection; it cannot force it. Failure to cooperate may trigger negative inferences by the arbitral tribunal in assessing the evidence.[235] In addition, the arbitral tribunal could seek the assistance of the competent state court to force an inspection (s 1050 ZPO).[236] Article 7 IBA Rules also addresses inspection. In cl 3, it provides that the parties and their representatives shall have the right to attend any such inspection.

[234] Münch, in: MünchKommZPO, s 1049 paras 66 *et seq.*; Geimer, in: Zöller (ed), s 1042 para 30; Schwab/Walter, ch 15 para 22; Voit, in: Musielak/Voit (eds), s 1042 para 22.

[235] Münch, in: MünchKommZPO, s 1049 para 47; Saenger, in: Saenger (ed), s 1042 para 18; Voit, in: Musielak/Voit (eds), s 1042 para 27.

[236] Münch, in: MünchKommZPO, s 1049 para 48.

6. *Securing of Evidence*

A party may be concerned that certain pieces of evidence which it does not have in its immediate possession, custody, or control may disappear or be destroyed and thus no longer be available in the arbitral proceedings when needed. Thus, a party may feel the need to preserve evidence. For instance, documents may need to be preserved from routine destruction (or intentional destruction by the other party who possesses them). The appropriate remedy here is to ask either the state courts or the arbitral tribunal for interim measures to protect evidence. We discuss this issue in more detail below in Chapter 5. **4.198**

Importantly, the German arbitration law does **not mandate document hold procedures** that are common in litigation in common law legal systems. Likewise, in German state court litigation, there are no such document hold requirements. Thus, to make sure the other party is prevented from destroying documents, it is not sufficient to rely on the expectation that the other party will issue document holds, but such party needs to take affirmative steps to secure evidence, such as by injunction and other forms of interim relief discussed in Chapter 5 below. **4.199**

7. *Procedure for Assistance by State Courts and Taking of Evidence Abroad*

As mentioned several times, the German arbitration law provides for assistance by state courts to arbitral tribunals and the parties in the taking of evidence pursuant to s 1050 ZPO. The competent court is the **local court (AG) in the district in which the taking of evidence is meant to occur** (s 1062 para 4 ZPO). The state court needs to verify the **admissibility** of such a request and, provided the request is admissible, to comply with the request by applying the procedural rules for the taking of evidence applicable in state court litigation (s 1050 cl 2 ZPO).[237] Section 1050 ZPO is inspired by **art 27 Model Law**. Beyond the examples already discussed above (compelling witnesses to testify, putting witnesses under oath, ordering third parties to produce documents),[238] further measures may be to seek information from public authorities or permission to testify by public officials.[239] **4.200**

---

[237] It is disputed to what extent the state court has to verify whether there is a valid arbitration agreement. While some argue that the arbitral tribunal has (preliminary) *Kompetenz-Kompetenz*, thereby excluding a further analysis by the state court (eg Geimer, in: Zöller (ed), s 1050 para 6; Münch, in: MünchKommZPO, s 1050 para 21), the prevailing—and more persuasive—view is still that the state court needs to analyze the validity of the arbitration agreement, at a minimum for obvious grounds for invalidity (see, eg, Lachmann, para 1634; Schlosser, in: Stein/Jonas (eds), s 1050 para 13; Voit, in: Musielak/Voit (eds), s 1050 para 5; in favor of full review Wolff, 19 Am. Rev. Int'l Arb. 145, 165 *et seq.* (2008).

[238] Hartmann, in: Baumbach/Lauterbach/Albers/Hartmann (eds), s 1050 para 1; Geimer, in: Zöller (ed), s 1050 para 8; Lachmann, para 1621; Münch, in: MünchKommZPO, s 1050 para 6; Reichold, in: Thomas/Putzo (eds), s 1050 para 1; Saenger, in: Saenger (ed), s 1050 para 3; Voit, in: Musielak/Voit (eds), s 1050 para 2.

[239] Geimer, in: Zöller (ed), s 1050 para 8; Münch, in: MünchKommZPO, s 1050 para 9; Reichold, in: Thomas/Putzo (eds), s 1050 para 1; Saenger, in: Saenger (ed), s 1050 para 3; Voit, in: Musielak/

4.201 In addition, the competent state court can be asked to assist with the taking of evidence abroad by using the rules and mechanisms of applicable instruments and treaties between Germany and the relevant foreign state on judicial assistance in the taking of evidence, such as the Council Regulation (EC) No 1206/2001 on Cooperation between the Courts of the Member States in the Taking of Evidence in Civil or Commercial Matters ("EU Evidence Regulation") and the Hague Convention on the Taking of Evidence Abroad in Civil and Commercial Matters ("Hague Evidence Convention").[240] Even though an arbitral tribunal, unlike a state court, is not per se prevented from taking evidence abroad, there may still be a need for court assistance. This applies, in particular, to measures that the tribunal has not the power to conduct, such as forcing witnesses to appear or documents to be produced.

4.202 Finally, it should be noted that s 1050 ZPO is **not limited to arbitral proceedings seated in Germany**. German state courts may provide assistance also where the seat of the arbitral tribunal is abroad or not yet determined (s 1025 para 2 ZPO). Thus, s 1050 ZPO may be an attractive tool for practitioners in international arbitration who seek to access evidence located in Germany, eg the examination of witnesses who do not appear voluntarily before the arbitral tribunal or to compel the production of documents (within the fairly strict limitations for document production in German state court litigation, see paras 1.24 *et seq.*).[241]

IX. Post-hearing Steps

1. Post-hearing Briefs

4.203 As mentioned above (para 4.24), unless specifically agreed by the parties it is within the arbitral tribunal's **discretion** to have oral closing arguments immediately after the taking of evidence or post-hearing briefs. German law does not contain any specific provisions thereon. Different practitioners have different approaches, and there is no uniform practice. In some cases, there is both. From the point of view of counsel and the parties, it is a matter for **case-by-case assessment** whether one's interests are served better by one or the other approach, depending on such circumstances as the complexity of the testimony, whether new issues have arisen

Voit (eds), s 1050 para 2; Hartmann, in: Baumbach/Lauterbach/Albers/Hartmann (eds), s 1050 para 1. Judicial measures outside the taking of evidence may be assistance with service of process, in particular abroad. However, since the German arbitration law does not contain any specific service provisions, judicial assistance is usually not required. Instead, a transmission by letter with return receipt or courier will often be the means of choice; see Münch, in: MünchKommZPO, s 1050 para 10; Schwab/Walter, ch 16 para 34.

[240] Geimer, in: Zöller (ed), s 1050 para 5; Münch, in: MünchKommZPO, s 1050 para 7; Voit, in: Musielak/Voit (eds), s 1050 para 2.

[241] For a comprehensive discussion see Wolff, 19 Am. Rev. Int'l Arb. 145–171 (2008) with further references.

that require some consideration before a firm position can be taken and the level of preparedness compared to the other side.[242]

2. *Cost Submissions*

In order for the arbitral tribunal to make an award on costs (s 1057 ZPO), the parties need to submit their respective costs to the arbitral tribunal. The German arbitration law does **not contain provisions on the form or content** of cost submissions. Thus, again, the matter is one for party agreement (which is rare) or tribunal discretion (which is the rule). Often, arbitral tribunals will not set any specific rules for cost submissions. Thus, it is **left to the parties and their counsel to consider** what is necessary to properly substantiate a claim for costs. At a minimum, a cost submission will need to specify the amount sought, and break it down into the relevant different categories, such as advances to the arbitral tribunal, payments to the arbitral institution, fees for counsel, expenses in connection with a hearing, expenses for witnesses and experts, and the like. Whether or not the submission of invoices is necessary is a matter for the discretion of the arbitral tribunal. **4.204**

Parties are well advised to provide a **reasoning** in their cost submissions for the entitlement to an award of costs, both as a matter of principle and with respect to the reasonableness and connectedness of individual items, cf s 1057 para 1 cl 2 ZPO. We will discuss the award on costs in detail in paras 6.48 *et seq.* **4.205**

D. Special Situations

At the conclusion of this chapter, we address a number of specific situations that arise time and again in arbitration, and sometimes during several stages of the proceedings, such as multi-party issues (below paras 4.207 *et seq.*), consolidation of cases (below paras 4.219 *et seq.*), parallel litigation and arbitration (below paras 4.221 *et seq.*), arbitral proceedings involving sovereigns (below paras 4.223 *et seq.*), fast-track arbitration (below paras 4.227 *et seq.*) as well as issues of illegality, such as fraud, money laundering, and corruption (below paras 4.229 *et seq.*). Given the size limitations of this work, our analysis is necessarily confined to some major topics and issues; for more detailed discussions, specialized literature may need to be consulted. **4.206**

I. Multi-party Arbitrations

1. *General Principles*

In practice, the need to involve multiple parties often arises out of **contracts with multiple parties** or out of a **chain of different contracts** which is often found **4.207**

[242] Kreindler/Schäfer/Wolff, para 875.

in trading or construction disputes. Furthermore, disputes regarding the validity of **corporate resolutions** (*gesellschaftsrechtliche Beschlussmängelstreitigkeiten*, see paras 1.78 *et seq.*) are almost by definition multi-party cases. German arbitration law does not contain any express provisions for multi-party arbitration.[243] Thus, issues such as multiple claimants, multiple respondents, intervention by third parties, counterclaims against third parties or by third parties, as well as recourse claims against third parties are not explicitly addressed in the Tenth Book of the ZPO. The **rules governing state court litigation** (ss 59 *et seq.* ZPO) **do not apply**, at least not directly.[244] However, significant guidance can be derived from the BGH decision *Schiedsfähigkeit II* on the arbitrability of challenges to corporate resolutions (see paras 1.78 *et seq.*). The principles underlying *Schiedsfähigkeit II* are widely shared in German literature.

4.208 First, the most fundamental principle governing multi-party cases is that arbitration is a matter of **party autonomy**.[245] Participation in an arbitration requires a valid agreement to do so by way of an arbitration agreement. Likewise, the parties to an arbitration agreement are not required to accept the participation of a person in an arbitration with whom they have not concluded an arbitration agreement.[246] This becomes particularly evident where arbitration is chosen for reasons of confidentiality because the third party would get access to all related information. On the other hand, as long as there is no arbitration agreement, the third party has not waived its constitutional right to conduct state court litigation over disputes arising out of or in connection with a legal relationship to one of the parties.

4.209 Thus, in principle, multiple persons can be co-claimants only to the extent they and the respondent(s) are parties to the same arbitration agreement.[247] The same applies *mutatis mutandis* to co-respondents.[248] As a matter of course this agreement can be concluded impliedly and even on an ad hoc basis after a dispute has arisen. A counterclaim against a third party or by a third party follows the same rule.

---

[243] For a comprehensive discussion see Böckstiegel/Berger/Bredow (eds).

[244] For inapplicability: Elsing, SchiedsVZ 2004, 88, 91; Lachmann, paras 2826 *et seq.*; for an application *mutatis mutandis*: Schwab/Walter, ch 16 paras 18 *et seq.*; Hartmann, in: Baumbach/Lauterbach/Albers/Hartmann (eds), s 1042 para 14; Münch, in: MünchKommZPO, s 1029 para 56; Voit, in: Musielak/Voit (eds), s 1042 para 11.

[245] Thus, not surprisingly, the first requirement under *Schiedsfähigkeit II* is that all shareholders have consented to the arbitration agreement, see para 1.78.

[246] Lachmann, para 2806; Münch, in: MünchKommZPO, s 1029 paras 56 *et seq.*; Voit, in Musielak/Voit (eds), s 1029 para 9. From an international perspective Blackaby/Partasides/Redfern/Hunter, paras 2.52 *et seq.*

[247] Implicitly: Schlosser, in: Stein/Jonas (eds), s 1034 para 39; Schwab/Walter, ch 16 paras 16 *et seq.*; Münch, in: MünchKommZPO, s 1029 paras 59 *et seq.*; Lachmann, paras 2806, 2808 *et seq.* Regarding arts 6.4, 9 ICC Rules pursuant to which mutually compatible arbitration agreements are sufficient, see below para 4.217. In the absence of such a rule, which may be agreed by all parties concerned, it is necessary that there be the same underlying arbitration agreement.

[248] Implicitly: Schlosser, in: Stein/Jonas (eds), s 1034 para 39; Schwab/Walter, ch 16 paras 16 *et seq.*; Münch, in: MünchKommZPO, s 1029 paras 59 *et seq.*; Lachmann, paras 2806, 2808 *et seq.*

Second, **equality of the parties** regarding the composition of the arbitral tribunal is key.[249] As explored in detail above (paras 3.30 *et seq.*), in today's practice, multiple parties are usually grouped into "camps," and each camp has an opportunity to agree on one arbitrator; failing that, usually a third party (eg an arbitral institution or a court) appoints the entire tribunal. **4.210**

Third, there is a strong view that the **consent of the arbitrators** is necessary, too.[250] This is of course no issue where the arbitration is commenced with multiple parties and each arbitrator is aware of this situation when accepting the appointment. Where further parties are added at a later stage, the difference of opinion should not make much of a difference, either, because in any event the arbitrator agreement contains an implied duty to consent unless there are good reasons for a rejection, eg where the additional party would impact the independence and impartiality of the arbitrator.[251] **4.211**

2. *Intervention* (Nebenintervention) *and Third-party Notice* (Streitverkündung)

An intervention by a third party in support of the claimant(s) or the respondent(s) requires an arbitration agreement between and among all of them, because in the absence of such an agreement, no party to the arbitration is required to **tolerate the participation of a third person**, including the likely consequences of such participation in terms of learning confidential information and potential for obstructive behavior.[252] **4.212**

Where a notice of dispute to a third party (*Streitverkündung*) is supposed to trigger the same **binding effects** as in state court litigation (*Interventionswirkung*, ss 74, 68 ZPO),[253] again an **agreement of all parties concerned** to such effect is required.[254] **4.213**

---

[249] Lachmann, para 2806; Schlosser, in: Stein/Jonas (eds), s 1034 paras 27 *et seq.*; Hartmann, in: Baumbach/Lauterbach/Albers/Hartmann (eds), s 1034 para 6. As discussed in para 1.78, the BGH requires in *Schiedsfähigkeit II* that all shareholders are put on notice regarding the dispute and have an opportunity to participate in the constitution of the arbitral tribunal.

[250] In favor of this requirement: Hartmann, in: Baumbach/Lauterbach/Albers/Hartmann (eds), s 1042 para 14; Lachmann, paras 2811 *et seq.*, 2826; Elsing, SchiedsVZ 2004, 88, 92. Opposing view: Münch, in: MünchKommZPO, s 1029 para 59; Hamann/Lennarz, SchiedsVZ 2006, 289, 291. The issue of arbitrator consent is not addressed in *Schiedsfähigkeit II* because the underlying case did not give rise to a discussion of this issue.

[251] Geimer, in: Böckstiegel/Berger/Bredow, pp 81 *et seq.*; Lachmann, paras 2806, 2811 *et seq.*

[252] Hamann/Lennarz, SchiedsVZ 2006, 289, 291; Schwab/Walter, ch 16 para 20; Münch, in: MünchKommZPO, s 1029 paras 60 *et seq.*; Hartmann, in: Baumbach/Lauterbach/Albers/Hartmann (eds), s 1042 para 14; Voit, in: Musielak/Voit (eds), s 1042 para 11. For an instructive case where there was an agreement on the intervention of a third party see OLG Stuttgart, SchiedsVZ 2003, 84 *et seq.*

[253] Ie the third party, in a follow-on dispute, may not question the correctness of the decision in the first case, and has only limited opportunity to allege that the first case was litigated improperly; see generally Schultes, in: MünchKommZPO, s 68 para 6.

[254] Müller/Keilmann, SchiedsVZ 2007, 113, 119; Elsing, SchiedsVZ 2004, 88, 92; Voit, in: Musielak/Voit (eds), s 1042 para 11; Lachmann, para 2832.

For instance, the claimant customer may have prevailed in an arbitration against the respondent seller on the theory that the product sold by the respondent was defective and caused the claimant to suffer a certain amount of damages. During the arbitral proceedings, the respondent seller may have provided a dispute notice to its supplier on the theory that it would seek recourse against the supplier in case it turned out the product was defective. In the second case on such recourse claims, the supplier may be tempted to re-argue issues of defect, causation, and damages. The seller will have an interest in asserting that these issues have been determined during the first proceeding with binding effect also towards the supplier. In the absence of party agreement, such binding effect may not be achieved.

3. Effect of Awards

4.214 Regarding the effects of multiple parties participating in an arbitration, an arbitral award has *res judicata* effect with regard to all of them, as far as such effects exist (s 1055 ZPO, see para 6.111). Thus, where for example a third party in consequence of a counterclaim became a party to the arbitration, it is bound by the award in the same way as by a judgment. Whether there are additional effects comparable to interventions and dispute notices in German state court litigation (ie binding with regard to factual and legal determinations[255]) is, as set out above (paras 4.212 *et seq.*), a matter of **party agreement.**[256] Where the parties expressly agree on such effects, factual and legal determinations contained in an arbitral award will be binding in follow-on proceedings either before an arbitral tribunal or before a state court.[257] In practice, parties should make sure such an agreement exists as an integral part of the inclusion of the third party.[258]

4.215 In the absence of a specific party agreement on such effects, the only source to be considered for binding effects with respect to factual or legal determinations could, in theory, be the discretion of the arbitral tribunal presiding over the *first* or *second* case. This would raise the question whether an arbitral tribunal has the power to order such effect, in particular whether s 1042 para 4 cl 1 ZPO confers such power by authorizing the arbitral tribunal "to determine the rules of the proceedings." In our view, however, this can no longer be considered a rule of the proceedings, but is instead a rule on the effects of an award, which is not something that the arbitral tribunal can determine in its discretion. Where the second case is in front of a state court, it is even more evident that such state court, in the absence of a legal provision or a party agreement to such effect, cannot simply order that the results of the first proceedings shall have binding effect on the parties to the second proceedings.

---

[255] For state court scenarios see Schultes, in: MünchKommZPO, s 68 para 6.

[256] Voit, in: Musielak/Voit (eds), s 1042 para 11; Hartmann, in: Baumbach/Lauterbach/Albers/Hartmann (eds), s 1042 para 14; Müller/Keilmann, SchiedsVZ 2007, 113, 119; Elsing, SchiedsVZ 2004, 88, 92.

[257] Kreindler/Schäfer/Wolff, paras 1035 *et seq.*

[258] Lachmann, para 2833.

Thus, again, for practical purposes, parties need to make sure they have an express agreement on this core issue.

4. *Multi-party Situations in Institutional Arbitration*

The DIS Rules address multi-party disputes only very briefly in their s 13.3 which provides that the "arbitral tribunal decides on the admissibility of the multi-party proceedings." **4.216**

By contrast, the ICC Rules now contain elaborate provisions on multi-party cases (arts 7–10 ICC Rules). Article 7 ICC Rules allows for the joinder of additional parties before the confirmation of the arbitrators; thereafter, joinder is possible only with the consent of all parties, including the additional one. In an arbitration with multiple parties, pursuant to art 8 ICC Rules, in principle claims may be made by any party against any other party, provided however that no new claims may be made after the terms of reference have been established unless the arbitral tribunal authorizes otherwise. Article 9 ICC Rules allows claims arising out of or in connection with more than one contract to be made in a single arbitration, irrespective of whether such claims are made under one or more than one arbitration agreement under the ICC Rules, as long as the different arbitration agreements are "**compatible**" (art 6.4(ii)(a) ICC Rules). Compatibility requires, at a minimum, the same place of arbitration and the same number of arbitrators.[259] **4.217**

5. *Class Arbitrations*

Class arbitrations, a phenomenon thus far mainly encountered in the US,[260] are largely unknown in Germany. In German state court litigation, there are no US-style class actions. Certain forms of collective redress exist in specialized areas, such as with respect to stock market disclosures and corresponding securities litigation (KapMuG). German arbitration law does not contain any specific provisions on class arbitrations. Thus, the ordinary rules apply, requiring that every party to be brought into an arbitration must have entered into the same arbitration agreement and must have an opportunity to participate both in the constitution of the arbitral tribunal and the conduct of the proceedings, much like the BGH has held in *Schiedsfähigkeit II* with respect to the inclusion of other shareholders in disputes between a shareholder and the corporation regarding the validity of corporate resolutions (see paras 1.78 *et seq.*). **4.218**

II. Consolidation of Cases

As is the case with issues of intervention and dispute notices, there are **no specific rules** regarding consolidation of cases. The provisions governing consolidation in state court litigation (eg s 147 ZPO) do not apply directly in arbitration.[261] **4.219**

---

[259] Fry/Greenberg/Mazza, para 3-243.

[260] Born, pp 1506 *et seq.*

[261] Section 147 ZPO allows consolidation where several cases are pending with the same court, irrespective of whether they are between the same or different parties, as long as the claims

Especially where two (or more) arbitrations are pending between the same parties, the arbitral tribunals are composed of the same persons and the proceedings are governed by the same arbitration agreement, consolidation of the cases may seem sensible. However, under the prevailing principle of party autonomy, this requires an **agreement of all parties**, either as a provision in the initial arbitration agreement or ad hoc after the dispute has arisen.[262] With the consent of all participants even a consolidation of proceedings with different parties is possible.[263] By contrast, the tribunal's discretion to "determine the rules of the proceedings" does not generally include the power to consolidate separate arbitral proceedings.[264]

4.220 Article 10 ICC Rules contains an elaborate provision on consolidation of cases:

> The Court may, at the request of a party, consolidate two or more arbitrations pending under the Rules into a single arbitration, where:
> a) the parties have agreed to consolidation; or
> b) all of the claims in the arbitrations are made under the same arbitration agreement; or
> c) where the claims in the arbitrations are made under more than one arbitration agreement, the arbitrations are between the same parties, the disputes in the arbitrations arise in connection with the same legal relationship, and the Court finds the arbitration agreements to be compatible.
>
> In deciding whether to consolidate, the Court may take into account any circumstances it considers to be relevant, including whether one or more arbitrators have been confirmed or appointed in more than one of the arbitrations and, if so, whether the same or different persons have been confirmed or appointed.
>
> When arbitrations are consolidated, they shall be consolidated into the arbitration that commenced first, unless otherwise agreed by all parties.

III. Parallel Litigation and Arbitration

4.221 A party may seek to bring several disputes in front of different fora, such as an arbitration as well as parallel state court litigation. Also, there may be cases where separate arbitrations are conducted with similar underlying issues. German arbitration law does not expressly regulate such scenarios, nor does the German civil procedure law on state court litigation. Instead, from a legal point of view, the issue is primarily governed by the principles of *lis pendens*, the primacy of arbitration

brought are legally interrelated or could have been brought in one action in the first place; Voit, in: Musielak/Voit (eds), s 1042 para 13; Schwab/Walter, ch 16 para 20; for exceptions: Münch, in: MünchKommZPO, s 1029 para 62.

[262] Lachmann, para 2835; Schlosser, in: Stein/Jonas (eds), s 1034 para 41; Raeschke-Kessler/Berger, para 779.

[263] Voit, in: Musielak/Voit (eds), s 1042 para 13; Hamann/Lennarz, SchiedsVZ 2006, 289, 294; Lachmann, para 2835; Hartmann, in: Baumbach/Lauterbach/Albers/Hartmann (eds), s 1042 para 15; Geimer, in: Zöller (ed), s 1042 para 44.

[264] Implicitly: Voit, in: Musielak/Voit (eds), s 1042 para 13; Hartmann, in: Baumbach/Lauterbach/Albers/Hartmann (eds), s 1042 para 15.

over litigation where a valid and binding arbitration agreement exists (s 1032 para 1 ZPO) and the (preliminary) *Kompetenz-Kompetenz* of arbitral tribunals seated in Germany (see para 4.104). Thus, where the subject matters or the parties of the disputes are technically different, parallel proceedings are admissible.[265]

In addition, it is a **tactical consideration** whether and how to initiate and conduct parallel proceedings. Of course, there may be many options in a given case, such as resorting to the state courts in parallel to arbitral proceedings, starting two parallel arbitral proceedings or seeking to compel compliance with an arbitration agreement where one party has disregarded it by starting state court litigation.[266] Also, parallel litigation and arbitration may be a valid strategy for a claimant/plaintiff in order to create additional pressure or nuisance value. Parallel proceedings may also serve to obtain information needed in another proceeding, eg by enforcing information and disclosure rights based on contract or otherwise applicable law. At the same time, on a very general note, there is always a risk of backlash. The parallel proceedings may fail, and they may fail in a way such as to impact the main proceedings, eg because of the reasoning, including *obiter dicta*, of the tribunal or court in the parallel proceedings. For the respondent/defendant, tactical considerations may involve issues such as whether the proceedings may be combined, whether the same arbitrator(s) should be appointed in parallel proceedings (or not), starting additional parallel proceedings on its own and the like. **4.222**

IV. Arbitrations Involving Sovereigns

Arbitration in Germany may at times involve sovereigns. This is obvious in **investment arbitration**, even though thus far investment cases in front of arbitral tribunals seated in Germany have been rare in practice. In addition, there may be arbitration cases resulting from **public–private partnerships** with a governmental entity in dispute with a private entity.[267] Likewise, **M&A transactions** may involve sovereigns, eg where the purchaser or the seller is a sovereign wealth fund.[268] **4.223**

German arbitration law does not contain any specifics regarding sovereigns; the fact that **arbitral proceedings against sovereigns** are as such admissible is implied, as far as German law is concerned, in ss 168 para 1 no 5, 173 German Code of Administrative Court Procedure (VwGO), which allow arbitral proceedings in administrative matters, and by their very nature, these matters typically involve government entities, including the Federal Republic of Germany, as parties. **4.224**

265 Implicitly: Kersting, SchiedsVZ 2013, 297, 300.

266 For instructive analyses, see, eg, Gaillard/Pinsolle, in: Bishop/Kehoe (eds), pp 173 *et seq.*; Kreindler, in: Cremades/Lew (eds.), pp 153 *et seq.*

267 A prominent German example are the widely publicized arbitration cases triggered by the *Toll Collect* project, a German infrastructure project on the implementation of an innovative and complex system for truck tolls on German highways.

268 This was the case, for instance, in the prominent *Ferrostaal* DIS case where the seller was a German company and the purchaser a sovereign wealth fund from the Middle East.

Whether a sovereign is capable of entering into a valid and binding arbitration agreement is a matter of **subjective arbitrability** and needs to be determined based on the law governing such sovereign entity (see para 2.65).

4.225 In addition to the legal limitations, arbitral proceedings with or among sovereign entities often also raise a number of **practical and tactical issues**. As in many other instances, service of documents may be a concern with respect to sovereigns, just as with other foreign entities. Since the German arbitration law does not contain formal service of process requirements, all means of service can be applied, including by letter with return receipt requested. Where a party contracting with a foreign sovereign entity is concerned that even such type of service may not succeed, it can consider requesting the appointment of a domestic process agent, eg by putting a provision to this effect into the agreement with the sovereign entity. Issues of sovereign immunity may arise when it comes to the enforcement of an award.

4.226 Further, there may be certain peculiarities regarding the proceeding with sovereigns as such. For instance, governmental entities may need more time to react and respond than corporations or private persons because they often have a **complex system of decision-making**. Also, it may be **more difficult to settle** a dispute involving a sovereign, in particular where the sovereign entity is on the respondent side. An incisive issue is the question of confidentiality. In many cases there is a strong public interest on both the non-sovereign and the sovereign side regarding the proceedings as well as the outcome because such transparency is deemed to be the cornerstone of any democratic control.[269] Accordingly, there is always a need to balance these interests with the conflicting interest for confidentiality of the opposing party.

V. Fast-track Arbitration

4.227 German law does not contain any specific provisions on fast-track arbitration, ie arbitral proceedings that occur on an accelerated time schedule. Nor do the ICC Rules contain such mechanisms. By contrast, the DIS has set up, as an Annex to the DIS Rules, **DIS Supplementary Rules for Expedited Proceedings**[270] which aim at concluding arbitral proceedings within six months (in the case of a sole arbitrator) or nine months (in the case of a three-person tribunal), *inter alia* by (i) adhering to a regime of four-week deadlines for submissions, scheduling an oral hearing, and rendering an award; (ii) providing for only two rounds of written submissions, one oral hearing and no post-hearing submissions; and (iii) allowing for awards that do not contain a statement of the facts. Furthermore, the revised **Swiss Rules** in their art 42 now provide for an expedited procedure with only one

269 Leisinger, pp 209 *et seq.*; Schorkopf, NVwZ 2003, 1471 *et seq.*
270 Available at http://www.disarb.org (last visited December 1, 2015).

round of full written submissions, a single oral hearing, an award with a summary reasoning only, and the rendering of the award within six months after the arbitral tribunal has received the file from the secretariat.

Whether or not to agree to fast-track arbitration is for the parties to consider. There may be types of scenarios which require a swift resolution. For instance, some commentators have proposed that a dispute over whether a **material adverse change (MAC)** has occurred and whether consequently the sale and purchase agreement over a company or its shares need or need not be closed may be a proper one for fast-track arbitration, while others are skeptical about this approach.[271] It should be noted that fast-track entails considerable risk for the party bearing the burden of proof. It may not be able to assemble and present all the available and required evidence within the short time available and thus effectively have its right to be heard correspondingly circumscribed. The consequence may be a challenge to the award based on an alleged violation of the right to be heard (s 1059 para 2 no 1 lit d ZPO). **4.228**

VI. Fraud, Money Laundering, and Corruption

Issues of illegality, such as fraud, money laundering, and corruption may arise in arbitral proceedings. In fact, the parties may have chosen arbitration over state court litigation precisely because they did not want such issues to arise in a public court proceeding. The German arbitration law does not contain specific provisions dealing with such instances of illegality. Thus, a number of more general principles and provisions need to be applied, which are summarized briefly below. For more detailed discussions, we refer our readers to specialized literature.[272] **4.229**

As a general matter, under the German arbitration law the **validity of an arbitration agreement** is not impacted by the fact that the parties to the arbitration may have otherwise engaged in illegal activity in connection with the subject matter of the dispute. This follows from the separability doctrine enshrined in s 1040 para 1 cl 2 ZPO. As discussed above (para 2.47), by way of exception, the illegality may also impact the arbitration agreement itself, for instance where the arbitral proceedings are meant to be used as a disguise for actually performing illegal acts, such as the payment of a bribe or the laundering of money. Also, in investment arbitration, there is established case law that bribery by the investor undermines already the jurisdiction of the arbitral tribunal, not only the merits of the case.[273] **4.230**

[271] For a brief discussion, see Rieder, in: Schütze/Weipert/Rieder (eds), p 365; Borris, BB 2008, 294; Blackaby/Partasides/Redfern/Hunter, paras 2.133 *et seq.*

[272] For a more detailed discussion and further references, see eg Kreindler, *Competence-Competence in the Face of Illegality in Contracts and Arbitration Agreements*; Rieder/Schoenemann, NJW 2011, 1169 *et seq.*

[273] Kreindler, SchiedsVZ 2010, 2, 5 with further references; Rieder/Schoenemann, NJW 2011, 1169, 1173 *et seq.* with further references.

4.231 Under German law, arbitrators are generally **not required to report illegal activity** of the parties (or suspicions of such activity) to German law enforcement authorities. It is unclear and controversial under German law whether arbitrators are allowed to make such reporting.[274] Thus, the safest course of action is for arbitrators to **withdraw** from their office and to terminate the arbitrator agreement (s 627 BGB, see paras 3.151 and 3.201) if they consider it inappropriate for themselves to continue to serve the parties despite the evidence of illegality (or suspicion thereof) in relation to the subject matter of the dispute.[275]

4.232 As far as the **merits of the case**, in particular the **validity and enforceability** of agreements under substantive German law are concerned, it is by now well established that agreements on the conduct of illegal activity, such as the payment of bribes, are null and void.[276] Likewise, agreements induced by illegal activities, such as a delivery contract or a construction project awarded as a result of bribery, will often be null and void.[277] Long-term agreements may be terminated where one party engages in illegal conduct; termination may even be possible in case of a **suspicion grounded on specific facts** that there was or is illegal conduct (*Verdachtskündigung*).[278] Suspicion of illegal activity may also be considered a defect of a company subject to an M&A transaction, thereby potentially triggering claims for unwinding of the transaction and/or damages.[279]

4.233 All the issues addressed above raise **difficult questions of proof**, including the availability of evidence, burden of proof, and standard of proof. Especially where the arbitral tribunal is concerned with issues of jurisdiction and the termination of the arbitration agreement, it may find that neither of the parties has an interest in supporting the tribunal's efforts to get to the bottom of potentially illegal acts. Thus, the arbitral tribunal may need to inquire itself, which it is allowed to do under the German approach of limited investigation.[280]

---

[274] Rieder/Schoenemann, NJW 2011, 1169, 1173 *et seq.* with further references.

[275] Rieder/Schoenemann, NJW 2011, 1169, 1174 with further references.

[276] BGH NJW 1999, 2266; OLG Karlsruhe, BB 2000, 635 *et seq.*; Harbst, SchiedsVZ 2007, 22, 24; Armbrüster, in: MünchKommBGB, s 134 para 59; Sack/Fischinger, in: Staudinger (ed), s 138 para 635; Looschelders, in: Heidel/Hüßtege/Mansel/Noack (eds), s 134 para 254.

[277] Rieder/Schoenemann, NJW 2011, 1169, 1169 *et seq.* with further references.

[278] Rieder/Schoenemann, NJW 2011, 1169, 1170 *et seq.* with further references.

[279] Rieder/Schoenemann, NJW 2011, 1169, 1170 *et seq.* with further references.

[280] For a further detailed discussion of these issues, see Kreindler, pp 252 *et seq.*

5

INTERIM RELIEF

Reinmar Wolff

A. Overview

Time and again whether a party finally achieves its requested legal protection will depend on interim measures of protection: the disclosure of a trade secret, for example, cannot be undone even if an award or judgment later finds that the trade secret was disclosed illegally. Interim measures at the same time represent one of the most difficult areas in arbitration: such measures can be issued both by the state court and by the arbitral tribunal. While state court interim measures per se follow the general rules of civil procedural law at the place of their issuance, they pose a number of challenges at the interface between these general local civil procedure rules and the particularities of arbitration, particularly in cross-border disputes (paras 5.3 *et seq.*). Arbitral interim measures are characterized by the tribunal's broad discretion and the need for a grant of enforcement by the state court (paras 5.64 *et seq.*). Finally, the parallel competence of the state court and the arbitral tribunal for issuance of interim measures raises the question of how these approaches interrelate and how the parties can make best use of the freedom granted to them (paras 5.115 *et seq.*). **5.1**

B. Interim Relief Before the State Courts

Section 1033 ZPO stipulates that **interim measures of state courts are not incompatible with an arbitration agreement** (paras 5.3 *et seq.*). This allows for application **5.2** to the German state courts for all interim measures that would be available under the civil procedure law, including seizure (paras 5.16 *et seq.*), injunctions (paras 5.41 *et seq.*) and independent evidence proceedings (paras 5.51 *et seq.*).

I. Access to State Courts Despite an Arbitration Agreement (s 1033 ZPO)

1. Rationale

5.3 Section 1033 ZPO allows for interim measures rendered by state courts despite an arbitration agreement. The provision deviates from the directly preceding s 1032 ZPO, pursuant to which a claim brought before the state courts notwithstanding the existence and application of an arbitration agreement is to be dismissed (cf paras 2.136 *et seq.*). Section 1033 ZPO adopts almost word for word art 9 Model Law.

5.4 By foreseeing the possibility of interim measures rendered by state courts notwithstanding an arbitration agreement, s 1033 ZPO aims to **ensure effective legal protection**[1] which the German constitution guarantees equivalent to a fundamental right.[2] The need for such protection is obvious in the case of interim measures prior to the full constitution of the arbitral tribunal:[3] in view of the deadlines for the appointment of arbitrators as stipulated by s 1035 para 3 ZPO, the constitution of a three-member tribunal may well take several months even where all respective deadlines are met. Leaving the parties without any forum for petitioning for interim measures during that time would result in the denial of effective legal protection in that time window. Section 1033 ZPO also aims to establish an equilibrium respecting the restrictions on the ability of the arbitral tribunal itself to grant interim relief under s 1041 ZPO, ie on the one hand its discretion (s 1041 para 1 ZPO, below para 5.76) and on the other hand the linking of enforcement of the measure to a granting of leave by a state court (s 1041 para 2 ZPO, below paras 5.94 *et seq.*).[4]

2. Scope of Application

5.5 **a) Temporal Scope of s 1033 ZPO** Pursuant to the wording of s 1033 ZPO, interim measures may be granted "**before or during** arbitral proceedings" (cf para 5.4; for independent evidence proceedings see paras 5.9 *et seq.*). While this wording covers the typical fact situations for interim measures, it is not exhaustive. Interim measures can also be granted **after** the arbitral proceedings have been concluded, but only to the extent that they do not interfere with the *res judicata*

[1] Government bill, BT-Drucks 13/5274, p 38.
[2] Jarass, in: Jarass/Pieroth (eds), art 20 paras 91 *et seq.*
[3] Government bill, BT-Drucks 13/5274, p 38.
[4] Government bill, BT-Drucks 13/5274, pp 38 *et seq.*

effect of the arbitral award.[5] Interim enforcement of the award may be granted under s 1063 para 3 ZPO, but only limited to measures of protection (para 6.283).

5.6 **b) Irrelevance of the Seat of Arbitration** Access is granted to state courts for interim measures notwithstanding an existing arbitration agreement regardless of the place of arbitration and even if the place of arbitration is not yet determined (s 1025 para 2 ZPO). However, s 1025 para 2 ZPO does not substitute the international jurisdiction of the German courts, which has to be established in any case with an international nexus (para 5.21).

3. Applicability of General Rules on Interim Measures and Their Modification

5.7 Section 1033 ZPO is silent on which interim measures can be obtained from the state courts and which procedural rules govern applications for such measures. Hence, the rules of civil procedure governing such applications generally apply as if no arbitration agreement had been concluded between the parties. However, the fact that the main action is to be brought before an arbitral tribunal rather than before a state court results in a **number of modifications**. A short overview of state court proceedings for interim measures which reflects these modifications follows.

5.8 The German Code of Civil Procedure provides for two remedies for interim relief, namely seizure and injunction. **Seizure** (ss 916–934 ZPO, paras 5.17 *et seq.*) is basically a remedy serving to secure compulsory enforcement against property for a monetary claim (s 916 para 1 ZPO) while **injunctions** (ss 935–942 ZPO, paras 5.41 *et seq.*) are designed to secure other claims. Although injunctions have gained greater practical relevance, the ZPO has chosen seizure as the standard model. The provisions on seizure also apply to injunctions to the extent that the law does not provide otherwise (s 936 ZPO).

5.9 Section 1033 ZPO also covers **independent evidence proceedings** (*selbständige Beweisverfahren*, ss 485 *et seq.* ZPO),[6] which aim to preserve evidence for later use in court proceedings (paras 5.51 *et seq.*). However, the extent to which such proceedings are admissible is a matter of dispute. While the prevailing view allows for independent evidence proceedings before the state courts at any stage,[7] a minority view contends that such state court proceedings are inadmissible once the arbitral tribunal has been established[8] or indeed if it can easily be established.[9] For the

[5] OLG Frankfurt, SpuRt 2013, 206 *et seq.*; Kreindler/Schäfer/Wolff, para 1117; Voit, in: Musielak/Voit (eds), s 1033 para 3; see also Münch, in: MünchKommZPO, s 1033 para 14; dissenting LG Braunschweig, SchiedsVZ 2015, 292, 294.

[6] OLG Brandenburg, BauR 2011, 1533, 1534; OLG Koblenz, MDR 1999, 502 *et seq.*; LG Berlin, BeckRS 2012, 09512; Government bill, BT-Drucks 13/5274, pp 38 *et seq.*; Münch, in: MünchKommZPO, s 1033 para 7; dissenting Lachmann, para 2892.

[7] OLG Koblenz, MDR 1999, 502, 503; Knoblach, p 129; Rojahn, in: *Festschrift Meibom*, pp 395, 401; Steinbrück, pp 407 *et seq.*

[8] Münch, in: MünchKommZPO, s 1033 paras 8 *et seq.*

[9] Schlosser, para 646; Schwab/Walter, ch 7 para 14.

latter position, the reasoning is that no state court jurisdiction is needed to preserve evidence if the arbitral tribunal can be approached for the same purpose without much ado.[10] However, the general availability of arbitral interim measures under s 1041 ZPO is never decisive for s 1033 ZPO, which explicitly permits state court interim measures during arbitral proceedings.

5.10 Contrary to the prevailing view, it makes more sense to hold that independent evidence proceedings are excluded from s 1033 ZPO once the tribunal is constituted. Section 1042 para 4 cl 2 ZPO explicitly empowers the arbitral tribunal to decide on the admissibility of taking evidence and on the taking of evidence itself. Furthermore, s 1050 ZPO makes "court assistance in taking evidence" contingent upon the tribunal's consent and imposes other restrictions such as the lack of the tribunal's empowerment or the arbitrators' right to participate in any judicial taking of evidence and to ask questions. These restrictions are irreconcilable with allowing independent evidence proceedings to be available to each party without the tribunal's consent and participation.[11] Independent evidence proceedings that have been commenced prior to constitution of the arbitral tribunal remain admissible even after its constitution; the evidence taken in such proceedings is of the same (limited) effect as evidence secured before constitution of the arbitral tribunal (para 5.63).

4. Mandatory Nature of s 1033 ZPO?

5.11 It is disputed whether the parties can waive state court jurisdiction under s 1033 ZPO. No recent case law exists on this point.[12] Article 9 Model Law, which is the basis for s 1033 ZPO, is intentionally silent on its (non-) mandatory character.[13] The German legislative documents on s 1033 ZPO do not address this question at all.[14] The prevailing scholarly view relies on the gap in efficient legal protection that would result from a waiver (para 5.4) and concludes that s 1033 ZPO has a mandatory character.[15] The minority view reasons that no party is in need of protection against consequences resulting from its own voluntary waiver.[16]

---

[10] Schlosser, para 646; Schwab/Walter, ch 7 para 14.

[11] Münch, in: MünchKommZPO, s 1033 paras 8 *et seq.*

[12] Tending to waivabilty ("substantial arguments") OLG München, NJW-RR 2001, 711, 712 = SpuRt 2001, 64, 65; for mandatory nature OLG Köln, IPRspr. 2002, no 209, 540, 541; tending to non-mandatory nature OLG Frankfurt, NJW-RR 2000, 1117, 1119 (without raising the issue).

[13] Cf Holtzmann/Neuhaus, p 346 (with p 333); UNCITRAL Commission Report, A/40/17, p 346 para 97.

[14] See Government bill, BT-Drucks 13/5274, pp 38 *et seq.*

[15] LG Berlin, CaS 2006, 73; LG München I, IPRspr. 2000, no 182a, 396, 398 = SpuRt 2000, 155, 156 (obiter); Cherkeh/Schroeder, SpuRt 2007, 101, 103; Lachmann, para 2853; Münch, in: MünchKommZPO, s 1033 para 18; Reichold, in: Thomas/Putzo (eds), s 1033 para 2; Scheef, p 151; Schlosser, in: Stein/Jonas (eds), s 1033 para 1 (if no specific arbitral interim measures are available); Thümmel, DZWIR 1997, 133, 134 *et seq.*; Voit, in: Musielak/Voit (eds), s 1033 para 3; Wolf, DB 1999, 1101, 1103.

[16] Adolphsen, SpuRt 2000, 159; Berninger/Theißen, SpuRt 2008, 185, 186 *et seq.*; Rojahn, in: *Festschrift Meibom*, pp 395, 404; Schütze, BB 1998, 1650 and IPRax 2006, 442, 443; Schwab/Walter, ch 17a para 24; Steinbrück, IPRax 2010, 424, 427.

The better grounds speak in favor of s 1033 ZPO's non-mandatory character since no public interest is concerned. It is indeed true that only the judicial enforcement of rights as guaranteed by the right to effective legal protection allows for the ban on self-redress, which in turn is of public interest.[17] However, the unavailability of judicial enforcement (due to a party's waiver or for other reasons) does not result in a revival of a right to self-redress.[18] The right to effective legal protection primarily serves the individual's interests rather than general public interests.[19] **5.12**

Certain authors restrict the waivability of s 1033 ZPO to the same degree to which German law restricts choice of forum clauses.[20] The rationale behind this analogy is that the limits to modification of the place of jurisdiction (which does not restrict effective legal protection) should apply all the more to the waiver of any effective (interim) legal protection.[21] This argument has only surface appeal. It relies on idiosyncrasies of German domestic law (see also para 2.68) while the 1998 reform of the German arbitration law precisely aimed at making German arbitration law more accessible particularly to international parties.[22] **5.13**

The extrapolation *a fortiori* from choice of forum clauses to interim measures under s 1033 ZPO is also inapposite for other reasons: German law generally recognizes *pacta de non petendo* by which the parties exclude the actionability of claims.[23] If such far-reaching waivers of legal protection are permitted, the exclusion of interim protection must be all the more permissible. If a party needs to be protected against its own waiver, such protection is sufficiently effectuated by the general limits of party autonomy,[24] eg invalidity of contracts that violate the law or good morals (ss 134, 138 BGB). The rules on general terms and conditions (ss 305 *et seq.* BGB, paras 2.95 *et seq.*) will often provide for further protection. Finally, reliance on the choice of forum provisions does not and cannot take into account that a waiver of s 1033 ZPO does not necessarily deprive parties of any legal protection, in particular if they have agreed on (institutional) rules that provide for an emergency arbitrator or equivalent instruments.[25] **5.14**

Given the serious risks accompanying a contractual waiver of court-ordered interim measures, such waiver **cannot be assumed lightly**. The mere stipulation **5.15**

---

17 Dütz, p 158.
18 Bandel, p 324.
19 Bandel, p 324; Wagner, p 91.
20 Bandel, pp 325 *et seq.*
21 Bandel, pp 329 *et seq.*
22 Government bill, BT-Drucks 13/5274, p 23.
23 BGH NJW-RR 1989, 1048, 1049.
24 Similarly from a Swiss perspective Haas, ZZPInt 17 (2012), 347, 358 *et seq.*
25 Cf Kreindler/J Schmidt, in: *Arbitration in Germany*, s 1033 para 9; Kreindler/Schäfer/Wolff, para 899.

that the arbitral tribunal may grant measures of interim protection simply repeats s 1041 ZPO, but does not exclude state court competence.[26]

II. Seizure

5.16 By way of seizure, compulsory enforcement against property for a monetary claim can be secured, be it by way of an attachment (seizure against the debtor's assets, *dinglicher Arrest*) or by way of an arrest (seizure against the debtor personally, *persönlicher Arrest*). The requirements for such an application (paras 5.17 *et seq.*), the court proceedings (paras 5.30 *et seq.*), and the enforcement of court decisions ordering seizure (paras 5.38 *et seq.*) are governed by ss 916–934 ZPO. The following overview of these general issues will highlight the issues which arise in the context of the particularities of arbitration.

1. Request for Writ of Seizure

a) Admissibility

5.17 *aa) General Prerequisites* As in the case of any other court action, the request for a writ of seizure must comply with the general prerequisites for admissibility of an action.[27] These general prerequisites can be separated into those relating to the court, the parties, and the matter in dispute respectively.[28] Court-related requirements include German jurisdiction (*deutsche Gerichtsbarkeit*, ie excluding exterritorial persons and bodies), jurisdiction of the ordinary courts (*Rechtswegzuständigkeit*), and international, local, subject matter and functional jurisdiction (*internationale, örtliche, sachliche und funktionale Zuständigkeit*). Among the party-related requirements are the admissibility of a party to an action (*Parteifähigkeit*), the capacity to be a party to a legal action (*Prozessfähigkeit*), and the right to appear in court (*Prozessführungsbefugnis*). Requirements relating to the matter in dispute include the correct commencement of the action (*ordnungsgemäße Klageerhebung*), absence of *res judicata* (*keine entgegenstehende Rechtskraft*), absence of alternative pendency (*keine anderweitige Rechtshängigkeit*), and the presence of a legitimate reason to take legal action (*Rechtsschutzbedürfnis*, para 5.23). The latter requires the plaintiff to have a legitimate interest in availing itself of court proceedings. It is to be denied only in exceptional cases, including if either the plaintiff can achieve legal protection more easily or more effectively by other means or if the claim is brought abusively.[29] For a detailed explanation of these general criteria, reference is made to legal literature on civil procedure law.[30]

---

[26] OLG Frankfurt, SpuRt 2013, 206; Kreindler/J Schmidt, in: *Arbitration in Germany*, s 1033 para 10; Voit, in: Musielak/Voit (eds), s 1033 para 3.

[27] Foerste, in: Musielak/Voit (eds), Vorbem s 253 para 3.

[28] Foerste, in: Musielak/Voit (eds), Vorbem s 253 paras 4 *et seq.*

[29] Greger, in: Zöller (ed), Vor s 253 paras 18 *et seq.*

[30] For further references see Greger, in: Zöller (ed), Vor s 253 paras 9 *et seq.*

bb) Request The request for a writ of seizure must include the parties, the court, precise information on the subject matter and grounds for filing the request, and a precisely specified request for relief (s 253 para 2 ZPO), ie the request to protect a precisely identified claim including its amount or value (s 920 para 1 ZPO) by way of seizure against the property of the debtor (cf s 916 para 1 ZPO). The request must also include the ground for a writ of seizure (paras 5.26 *et seq.*), s 920 para 1 ZPO. **5.18**

cc) Competent Court Under general rules of civil procedure, two **courts are competent** for issuing a writ of seizure: the court before which the main action is to be pursued and the local court (*Amtsgericht*) where the object to be seized or the person to be incarcerated is located (s 919 ZPO). If the main action is subject to an arbitration agreement, the "court before which the main action is to be pursued" cannot refer to the arbitral tribunal—arbitral interim measures are exhaustively governed by s 1041 ZPO (paras 5.64 *et seq.*).[31] The prevailing view suggests that the court of the main action is the state court which would have jurisdiction if no arbitration agreement had been concluded[32] or the competent state court at the place of arbitration if such place is within Germany.[33] At first glance, it seems logical not to assume any state court jurisdiction where no state court will hear the main claim and thus to restrict state court competence to the second case mentioned in s 919 ZPO, ie where the object to be seized is situated.[34] Such solution, however, would restrict jurisdiction to the location of previously identified property and thus would significantly impair effective legal protection in a significant number of cases. **5.19**

The place of arbitration, on the other hand, cannot be decisive for territorial jurisdiction: the seat neither indicates the place where the decision is actually made (s 1043 para 2 ZPO) nor does it play any role for state court jurisdiction as long as the seat is within the district of a higher regional court (s 1062 para 1 ZPO).[35] Finally, for international proceedings, s 1025 para 2 ZPO explicitly decouples the place of arbitration and state court competence for interim measures. The better argument is therefore that of the enduring competence of the state court competent in the absence of an arbitration agreement. These fora are **exclusive** (s 802 ZPO), ie exclude otherwise applicable general fora (s 12 ZPO) and are not open to a deviating party agreement (s 40 para 2 cl 1 no 2 ZPO). The parties can, however, **5.20**

[31] Münch, in: MünchKommZPO, s 1033 para 19.

[32] OLG Köln, IPRspr. 2002, no 209, 540, 541; Bandel, p 286; LG Berlin, BeckRS 2012, 09512 (on independent evidence proceedings); Lachmann, para 2876.

[33] OLG Hamburg, NJW 1997, 749 = RIW 1996, 857 with concurring case note Trappe; Münch, in: MünchKommZPO, s 1033 para 20; Reichold, in: Thomas/Putzo (eds), s 1033 para 2; Voit, in: Musielak/Voit (eds), s 1033 para 3; see also OLG Köln, IPRspr. 2002, no 209, 540, 541 (assuming jurisdiction of the state courts at the place of arbitration alongside the jurisdiction under general rules); now dissenting Schlosser, in: Stein/Jonas (eds), s 1033 para 5.

[34] Cf ECJ ECR 1998, I-7091, para 24 – *Van Uden Maritime* = EuZW 1999, 413, 415.

[35] Concurring Lachmann, para 2875; Landbrecht, SchiedsVZ 2013, 241, 244.

indirectly determine the fora for interim measures by choosing the forum for the main action.[36] This includes a state court forum agreed upon subsidiary to arbitral proceedings.[37]

5.21 Court competence finally requires **international jurisdiction**, ie jurisdiction of the German courts as opposed to foreign courts. International jurisdiction is primarily governed by EU regulations (including the Brussels I Regulation[38]) and international conventions. In the remaining cases, local jurisdiction of a German court indicates its international jurisdiction.[39] As with other aspects of jurisdiction, international jurisdiction is subject to deviating party agreements. The mere agreement on a foreign place of arbitration does, however, not include a choice of forum clause for interim measures.[40] Such interpretation would considerably restrict effective legal protection and thus would not comply with the parties' will (cf para 5.15). Moreover, it would be inconsistent with s 1033 ZPO's applicability regardless of the place of jurisdiction (s 1025 para 2 ZPO) and with the understanding that s 1033 ZPO allows for state court interim measures as if no arbitration agreement had been concluded (para 5.7).[41]

5.22 *dd) Representation Before Court* Even if the request for a writ of seizure is filed with a district court (*Landgericht*), there is **no requirement** that the parties be represented by a lawyer admitted to the German bar (s 78 para 3, s 920 para 3 ZPO).

5.23 *ee) Legitimate Reason to Take Legal Action* No request for a writ of seizure can be filed if the plaintiff is otherwise protected, eg by a reservation of title.[42] In such cases, the plaintiff lacks legitimate reason to take legal action (*Rechtsschutzbedürfnis*, para 5.17).

5.24 **b) Merits** In order to succeed on the merits, a request for a writ of seizure needs to conclusively substantiate and furnish *prima facie* evidence (para 5.29) both for the claim to seizure (para 5.25) and the grounds for a writ of seizure (paras 5.26 *et seq.*).

5.25 *aa) Claim to Seizure* (Arrestanspruch) Only monetary claims and claims that may evolve to become monetary claims qualify as claims to seizure (s 916 para 1 ZPO). There is no necessity for a claim to seizure to have matured and such claims can also be conditional (s 916 para 2 ZPO). Accordingly, seizure may also secure a

36 Kreindler/Schäfer/Wolff, para 964.
37 Landbrecht, SchiedsVZ 2013, 241, 247.
38 Magnus, in: Magnus/Mankowski, Introduction paras 12 *et seq.*
39 BGHZ 188, 373, 383 para 26 = NJW 2011, 2515, 2518 with further references; Landbrecht, SchiedsVZ 2013, 241, 242.
40 Geimer, SchiedsVZ 2005, 52; Kröll, IHR 2005, 142, 144 *et seq.*; Reichold, in: Thomas/Putzo (eds), s 1033 para 2; Schlosser, SchiedsVZ 2008, 261; Schütze, IPRax 2006, 442, 443 *et seq.*; Steinbrück, IPRax 2010, 424, 427; Voit, in: Musielak/Voit (eds), s 1033 para 3; dissenting OLG Düsseldorf, SchiedsVZ 2008, 258, 260; OLG Nürnberg, SchiedsVZ 2005, 50, 51 *et seq.*
41 Kröll, IHR 2005, 142, 144 *et seq.*
42 See generally Greger, in: Zöller (ed), Vor s 253 paras 18 *et seq.*

future claim to reimbursement of costs of an arbitration.[43] Most claims can evolve into monetary claims, be it if the performance is defective (ss 280 *et seq.* BGB) or by way of enforcement (ss 887, 893 ZPO).[44] If a need for security exists for both the claim that can evolve to become a monetary claim and the future monetary claim (in particular a claim for damages), the current claim can be protected by way of an injunction and the future claim by way of seizure.[45]

bb) Grounds for a Writ of Seizure (Arrestgrund) Only endangered claims to seizure justify a seizure. The degree of endangerment depends on the kind of seizure, ie attachment or arrest. 5.26

***(1) Attachment* (dinglicher Arrest)** An attachment is available in those cases where there exists a concern that without such attachment the enforcement of a later judgment would be frustrated or considerably aggravated (s 917 para 1 ZPO). The attachment is not designed to improve the financial situation of the creditor, rather to protect against its deterioration.[46] Situations that threaten a deterioration typically include wastefulness, dissipation, or frequent change of normal residence.[47] It is deemed to be sufficient grounds for attachment if the judgment would need to be enforced in a foreign country with which reciprocity is not guaranteed (s 917 para 2 ZPO). 5.27

***(2) Arrest* (persönlicher Arrest)** The grounds for arrest are even more restricted: the debtor can be arrested only if enforcement against the debtor's property cannot be ensured otherwise (s 918 ZPO). Arrest can only be the last resort; typical examples are cases in which the debtor refuses to disclose the whereabouts of its property[48] or threatens to misappropriate it. Arrest is rare in practice. 5.28

cc) Prima facie *Evidence for Claim to Seizure and Grounds for Writ of Seizure* Whereas under general civil procedural rules any disputed fact needs to be proven by evidence to a degree that fully convinces the judge (cf s 286 ZPO), the threshold is lower for interim measures. For both the claim and the grounds for a writ of seizure, *prima facie* evidence is sufficient (s 920 para 2 ZPO). This standard requires the judge to be convinced of the predominant probability of the underlying facts in dispute,[49] ie that the existence of the fact is of higher probability than its non-existence. *Prima facie* evidence can be furnished by the regularly admissible means of evidence and additionally by an affidavit (*Versicherung an Eides statt*); all means of evidence, however, need to be readily available (s 294 ZPO). As an 5.29

[43] Pörnbacher/Thiel, SchiedsVZ 2010, 14, 16.
[44] Seiler, in: Thomas/Putzo (eds), s 916 para 4.
[45] Seiler, in: Thomas/Putzo (eds), Vorbem s 916 para 8.
[46] Seiler, in: Thomas/Putzo (eds), s 917 para 1.
[47] Seiler, in: Thomas/Putzo (eds), s 917 para 1.
[48] OLG Karlsruhe, NJW-RR 1997, 450, 451; Seiler, in: Thomas/Putzo (eds), s 917 para 1.
[49] Huber, in: Musielak/Voit (eds), s 920 para 10; Hartmann, in: Baumbach/Lauterbach/Albers/Hartmann (eds), s 920 para 11.

exception, the court can order seizure even if no *prima facie* evidence has been furnished for the underlying facts in dispute. However, this applies only if security is provided for the prejudice that the opponent is at risk of incurring (s 921 cl 1 ZPO).

2. Procedure, Decisions, and Remedies

5.30 Once the request for a writ of seizure has been filed, the procedure is dependent upon the initial assessment of the court: it can order an oral hearing or directly grant the seizure or dismiss the request without a hearing, ie *ex parte* (cf s 922 para 1 ZPO). When making this assessment, the court will in particular weigh the urgency of legal protection and the opposing party's right to be heard.[50]

5.31 a) **Dismissal Without Oral Hearing** If the court dismisses the request without an oral hearing, its order (*Beschluss*) will not be communicated to the opposing party (s 922 para 3 ZPO). The expectation of an unsuccessful request remaining secret will often incentivize the filing of a request, in particular if the element of surprise is at stake. The requesting party may file an immediate appeal (*sofortige Beschwerde*, s 567 para 1 no 2 ZPO) as a remedy against this decision.

5.32 b) **Order of Seizure Without Oral Hearing** If the court grants the seizure without an oral hearing, the order (*Beschluss*) will not be served to the opposing party on the court's own motion (s 922 para 2 ZPO; for the necessity of service by a party see para 5.39). The winning requesting party can take advantage of these *ex parte* proceedings and surprise the opposing party with simultaneous service (s 922 para 2 ZPO) and enforcement (ss 928 *et seq.* ZPO). As a remedy against this order, the opposing party may file a reasoned protest (*Widerspruch*, s 924 para 1 ZPO) at any time.[51] Upon such protest, the court will schedule an oral hearing (s 924 para 2 ZPO) in which the opposing party will be heard. The further proceedings follow the same rules as if the court had initially scheduled an oral hearing (paras 5.34 *et seq.*).

5.33 In any order of seizure, the court will on its own motion include an **amount of money** which, if deposited, will suspend the enforcement of the seizure or, if it has already been enforced, will entitle the debtor to file a petition for the enforced seizure to be set aside (s 923 ZPO).

5.34 c) **Dismissal Following an Oral Hearing** If the court schedules an oral hearing—be it on its own motion (para 5.30), be it upon protest (para 5.32)—the **proceedings** follow the general rules for court proceedings which are modified only to the extent required by the proceedings' summary nature: the parties are to be summoned at least three days before the hearing (s 217 ZPO); the period for filing a defense (generally two weeks, s 274 para 3 cl 1 ZPO) does not apply.[52]

---

50 Cf Huber, in: Musielak/Voit (eds), s 921 para 3.
51 Thümmel, in: Wieczorek/Schütze (ed), s 924 para 5.
52 Seiler, in: Thomas/Putzo (eds), s 922 para 2.

Taking of evidence is limited to present means of evidence (s 294 para 2 ZPO, para 5.29). Counterclaims cannot be filed in seizure proceedings.[53]

Following the oral hearing, the court decides by way of a **judgment** (as opposed to a court order if no oral hearing was held, paras 5.31 *et seq.*). This judgment can be appealed against subject to s 511 ZPO. No further remedy is available against the appellate decision (s 542 para 2 ZPO). **5.35**

d) Judgment Ordering Seizure Following an Oral Hearing The court ordering seizure following an oral hearing will do so by way of a judgment which is subject to **appeal** (para 5.35). Similar to an order of seizure (para 5.33), such judgment provides for an **amount of money** which, if deposited, will suspend the enforcement of the seizure (s 923 ZPO). If the court has granted seizure at least partially, the law provides the seizure debtor with **two additional remedies**: first, the debtor can apply for an order—which the court must grant—that the seizure creditor is to file the main action by a deadline to be specified by the court if the main action is not yet pending (s 926 para 1 ZPO). In case of non-compliance with this order and upon further application, the court will set aside the seizure (s 926 para 2 ZPO). Second, the debtor can apply to set aside the seizure due to a change in circumstances (s 927 ZPO), eg if the debtor has obtained a favorable judgment in the main action or the grounds for a writ for seizure have otherwise ceased to exist.[54] **5.36**

Since the parties have agreed on arbitration, the **order to file the main action under s 926 para 1 ZPO** (para 5.36) can be complied with by commencing arbitral proceedings as required under s 1044 ZPO.[55] However, the main action can also be filed with the state court, even if the validity of the arbitration agreement is not in question.[56] If the opposing party does not raise the objection under s 1032 para 1 ZPO timely, such claim will be fully admissible, so that its filing is to be considered sufficient under s 926 para 1 ZPO.[57] In that case, however, the creditor runs the risk that the award debtor may successfully apply to set aside the seizure under s 926 para 2 ZPO once the main action is dismissed due to the arbitration objection.[58] Even if the parties have concluded an arbitration agreement, only the state court can set aside the seizure due to a change in circumstances (s 927 ZPO).[59] **5.37**

---

53 Seiler, in: Thomas/Putzo (eds), s 922 para 2.

54 Thümmel, in: Wieczorek/Schütze (ed), s 927 para 1.

55 Münch, in: MünchKommZPO, s 1033 para 25; Schlosser, in: Stein/Jonas (eds), s 1033 para 6; Schwab/Walter, ch 7 para 13; Voit, in: Musielak/Voit (eds), s 1033 para 4.

56 Cf Schlosser, in: Stein/Jonas (eds), s 1033 para 6.

57 Voit, in: Musielak/Voit (eds), s 1033 para 4.

58 Cf Seiler, in: Thomas/Putzo (eds), s 926 para 13.

59 Schlosser, in: Stein/Jonas (eds), s 1033 para 8; Schwab/Walter, ch 7 para 13.

3. *Enforcement of a Writ of Seizure*

5.38 a) **Prerequisites** Attachments are enforced like any other executory title subject to only a few modifications (ss 928 *et seq.* ZPO). As a general rule, any enforcement requires an executory title (*Titel*), an enforcement clause (*Klausel*), and service (*Zustellung*) of both. For the enforcement of attachments, however, generally no enforcement clause is needed (s 929 para 1 ZPO). Similarly, prior service is not required to enforce an attachment (s 929 para 3 cl 1 ZPO); service, however, needs to be conducted within one week following the attachment's enforcement (s 929 para 3 cl 2 ZPO).

5.39 One specific requirement for the enforcement of attachments regularly causes difficulties for unwary parties: the writ of seizure needs to be enforced **within one month** after it has been declared or served on the requesting party (s 929 para 2 ZPO). This deadline aims to avoid ambush enforcement under changed circumstances.[60]

5.40 b) **Means of Enforcement and Claim for Damages** The attachment can be enforced in movable property and claims (s 930 ZPO), registered ships (s 931 ZPO) and real estate (s 932 ZPO). It can be enforced abroad under the Brussels I Regulation.[61] However, if upon remedy the seizure proves to have been unfounded from the start, the creditor of the seizure will be liable for all damages to the debtor of the seizure that it has suffered from enforcement (s 945 ZPO). This claim for damages, which does not require fault on the part of the creditor, is the price that the creditor pays for enforcement of a summary executory title.[62] If the arbitration agreement encompasses the claim under s 945 ZPO, be it explicitly or by way of interpretation, it can be brought in arbitral proceedings.[63]

III. Injunctions

1. *Procedure*

5.41 Whenever **seizure is not available**, an injunction is the proper means of interim protection.[64] Since only monetary claims and claims that may evolve to become monetary claims can be secured by way of seizure (s 916 para 1 ZPO, para 5.25), injunctions are the proper remedy for any other interim request. Injunctions are governed by the **provisions on seizure** to the extent that ss 937 *et seq.* ZPO do not expressly deviate (s 936 ZPO).

---

60 Seiler, in: Thomas/Putzo (eds), s 929 para 2.

61 BGH SchiedsVZ 2009, 174, 175 *et seq.* paras 6 *et seq.*; Schlosser, IPRax 2009, 416 *et seq.*; Voit, in: Musielak/Voit (eds), s 1033 para 3.

62 Fischer, in: Prütting/Gehrlein (eds), s 945 para 1.

63 Bandel, p 269; Schlosser, in: Stein/Jonas (eds), s 1033 para 8; dissenting Kreindler/J Schmidt, in: *Arbitration in Germany*, s 1033 para 39 (claim under s 945 ZPO can be brought in arbitration proceedings).

64 Hartmann, in: Baumbach/Lauterbach/Albers/Hartmann (eds), Vorbem s 916 para 3.

The main deviation from seizure proceedings is divergent **court jurisdiction.** Whereas both the court before which the main action is to be pursued and the local court (*Amtsgericht*) where the object to be seized is located have jurisdiction in matters of seizure (paras 5.19 *et seq.*), the court before which the main action is to be pursued has primary jurisdiction for injunctions (s 937 para 1 ZPO). This court is determined under general rules of civil procedure, as if no arbitration agreement had been concluded between the parties (paras 5.19 *et seq.*). The local court where the object in dispute is located has jurisdiction only in cases of urgency (s 942 para 1 ZPO) or if the injunction's content relates to entries in the land register or ship's register (s 942 para 2 ZPO). Urgency requires that requesting the injunction from the court of the main action would delay the proceedings and endanger legal protection, which nowadays in times of electronic communication is seldom the case.[65] **5.42**

The court before which the main action is to be pursued will **regularly hold an oral hearing** except in case of (specific) urgency, or if the injunction is dismissed (s 937 para 2 ZPO). In urgent cases even the presiding judge can alone decide on the injunction application (s 944 ZPO). The local court where the object in dispute is located will on its own motion set a deadline within which the applicant must file the main action with the competent court (s 942 para 1 ZPO). Since it is not the aim of an injunction to secure the enforcement of a monetary claim, it can, unlike a writ of seizure (s 923 ZPO, para 5.33), usually not be set aside against provision of **security** (s 939 ZPO). **5.43**

2. *Types of Injunctions*

The law distinguishes between security orders (s 935 ZPO, paras 5.45 *et seq.*) and regulatory orders (s 940 ZPO, paras 5.47 *et seq.*). In practice, however, this distinction is difficult to draw and the courts regularly base injunctions on "ss 935, 940 ZPO."[66] Performance of the claim can generally not be granted as an interim measure since it is contrary to the principle that the main action may not be pre-judged (*keine Vorwegnahme der Hauptsache*). Case law, however, has identified a number of factual situations in which ordering performance of the claim is permissible (paras 5.49 *et seq.*). **5.44**

a) Security Order (*Sicherungsverfügung*), s 935 ZPO Security orders are **available** for creditors of a claim whose realization might be frustrated or considerably endangered by a change of the status quo (s 935 ZPO). The claim may be any non-monetary claim; monetary claims can be secured by way of seizure (paras 5.25 *et seq.*). *Prima facie* evidence must be provided both for the claim and its endangerment (para 5.29). **5.45**

The court determines in its sole discretion the **content** of the order as it deems necessary to achieve the intended purpose (s 938 para 1 ZPO). Any measure can **5.46**

65 Huber, in: Musielak/Voit (eds), s 942 para 2.
66 Fischer, in: Prütting/Gehrlein (eds), s 938 para 2.

be ordered that facilitates the security of the applicant's claim. Section 938 para 2 ZPO names two examples of such orders: sequestration, ie custody and maintenance by a neutral person, and an order to take an action or to be prohibited from taking it, in particular by prohibiting sale, encumbrance, or pledge of real estate, of a registered ship, or of a ship under construction. Other typical examples include injunctions that prevent the beneficiary of a bank guarantee from illegally drawing on that guarantee,[67] that grant the building contractor a mortgage for securing its contractual claims under s 648 BGB[68] or that prevent a limited liability company from executing invalid shareholder resolutions.[69] The court cannot compel non-parties by way of injunction; for example, the land registry can be requested but can never be ordered to make an entry. Since injunctions are granted in summary proceedings in which it suffices to provide *prima facie* evidence rather than to prove the relevant facts, such injunctions cannot grant performance of the claim which would pre-judge the main action (*keine Vorwegnahme der Hauptsache*; for exceptions see paras 5.49 *et seq.*). The claim for damages under s 945 ZPO (para 5.40) cannot be seen as full compensation, because at minimum the debtor bears the applicant's solvency risk.

5.47 **b) Regulatory Order (*Regelungsverfügung*), s 940 ZPO** By way of a regulatory order, a temporary status regarding a **legal relationship** in dispute can be regulated, in particular in case of long-term legal relationships, to avert significant disadvantages, or to prevent impending force or for other reasons (s 940 ZPO). As compared to the security order, the applicant's claim is replaced by the legal relationship and its endangerment by the necessity to prevent detrimental changes. The legal relationship needs to exist between the parties;[70] examples include corporate authorities to act, rights to use, infringement of patent and similar rights, and employment.[71] The necessity to prevent detrimental changes is determined from the creditor's perspective. It is, however, limited by the debtor's interests: the debtor's disadvantage must not be disproportionate to the creditor's advantage.[72] The application lacks urgency (ie will fail) if the applicant is aware of all relevant factors but does not file its application in good time.[73] Examples of regulatory orders include the preliminary withdrawal of a general partner's management authority for a commercial partnership[74] or ordering to hand over construction material at the construction site to the customer.[75]

67 Cf Kreindler/J Schmidt, in: *Arbitration in Germany*, s 1033 para 18.

68 See OLG Hamm, BauR 1982, 285 (injunction denied in the specific case); OLG Saarbrücken, BauR 1993, 348.

69 Wolff, in: Münchener Handbuch des Gesellschaftsrechts, Vol 3, § 40 para 109 with further references.

70 OLG Düsseldorf, WM 1978, 359, 360.

71 Seiler, in: Thomas/Putzo (eds), s 940 para 4.

72 Seiler, in: Thomas/Putzo (eds), s 940 para 5.

73 Seiler, in: Thomas/Putzo (eds), s 940 para 5.

74 BGHZ 33, 105, 107 = NJW 1960, 1997, 1998.

75 OLG Stuttgart, MDR 2012, 212.

Just as with a security order, the content of a regulatory order is within the court's full discretion (s 938 ZPO). Since performance of the claim can generally not be granted as an interim measure (para 5.46), regulatory orders are to be made subject to a specific period in a way that the previous legal situation automatically revives once the regulatory order expires.[76] **5.48**

c) **Order for Performance of a Claim (*Leistungsverfügung*)** Neither a security order (para 5.46) nor a regulatory order (para 5.48) may grant performance of the claim. While granting performance of a claim as such is not alien to the German legal system, it can be requested only in regular court proceedings which allow for full due process rights. Interim proceedings shall not create accomplished facts. **5.49**

This rule, however, is not without exception. The courts may issue orders for performance of the claim under **strict conditions**: the applicant must be in urgent need of immediate performance, the requested performance must be provided in such time that awaiting the outcome of regular court proceedings would frustrate the enforcement of the duty, and the disadvantages threatening the applicant must be severe and disproportionate when compared to the damage that the opposing party may suffer.[77] In some situations, orders for performance of the claim are allowed for by law, eg s 247 FamFG for the maintenance of a newborn child or s 12 para 2 UWG for unfair competition claims. Other examples include an employee's claim for a reference from an employer[78] or the temporary prohibition from publishing a libellous text.[79] **5.50**

IV. Independent Evidence Proceedings (*selbständiges Beweisverfahren*)

Independent evidence proceedings as governed by ss 485 *et seq.* ZPO provide for means of anticipating the taking of evidence outside or within pending court proceedings. While German courts will normally take evidence only if and to the extent that the facts to be proven are relevant for the court's decision, independent evidence proceedings allow for securing evidence regardless of its (future) relevance.[80] Independent evidence proceedings before state courts are available as long as the arbitral tribunal has not yet been constituted (paras 5.9 *et seq.*). A typical scenario for independent evidence proceedings is when defects arise in the course of an ongoing construction project. In order to mitigate damages, construction projects cannot wait for a final decision of the dispute. It would, however, put evidence at risk of destruction to continue with the construction project. In this case, independent evidence proceedings allow for the preservation of evidence and for the postponement of the main dispute to a later stage. **5.51**

[76] Drescher, in: MünchKommZPO, s 938 para 8.
[77] Huber, in: Musielak/Voit (eds), s 940 para 14.
[78] Huber, in: Musielak/Voit (eds), s 940 para 17.
[79] OLG München, NJW-RR 1996, 926.
[80] BGH NJW 2000, 960, 961.

1. Admissibility

5.52 The admissibility of independent evidence proceedings is contingent on the underlying facts: s 485 para 1 ZPO sets out the general rules for consensual or preservative independent evidence proceedings regardless of whether court proceedings are pending (paras 5.53 *et seq.*). Section 485 para 2 ZPO additionally allows for independent evidence proceedings if legal proceedings are not yet pending (paras 5.56 *et seq.*). Under these circumstances, independent evidence proceedings may also aim at preventing legal proceedings.

5.53 a) **Consensual or Preservative Independent Evidence Proceedings** Section 485 para 1 ZPO sets out the procedure for independently taking evidence in its "traditional" shape. Such proceedings can be initiated both within and outside of pending legal proceedings. Filing an application within pending court proceedings is a sensible approach if the proceedings are stayed or not yet at an advanced enough stage for the taking of evidence[81]—the usual relevance requirement for the decision of the court is superfluous in independent evidence proceedings (para 5.51). If the main dispute is subject to an arbitration agreement, independent evidence proceedings can be initiated in parallel to a pending main claim only if the main claim (despite the arbitration agreement) is pending before a state court (cf paras 5.9 *et seq.*).

5.54 *aa) Requirements* Section 485 para 1 ZPO requires either **the other party's consent** (which in practice may be difficult to obtain) or alternatively a **concern that evidence might be lost** or that it will become difficult to use. Examples for such a concern include the infirmity of a witness, old age or serious illness, a threatened extinction or spoilage of an item, as well as forthcoming changes to an item including repairs and construction progress.[82]

5.55 *bb) Means of Evidence* Under s 485 para 1 ZPO, the court can order the judicial examination of the scene, the examination of witnesses or expert opinions. Other means of evidence, including interviewing a party, cannot be pursued within independent evidence proceedings.[83] The party can, however, record its statement in writing and submit it in later arbitral proceedings in which it is subject to the arbitral tribunal's free assessment (para 4.148). Affidavits (*Versicherungen an Eides statt*) including those of a party do not bear specific legal relevance in arbitration (para 5.78).

5.56 b) **Independent Evidence Proceedings for the Avoidance of Legal Proceedings or Other Legitimate Interests** Section 485 para 2 ZPO provides for an alternative route for independent evidence proceedings which may be entered into independent of s 485 para 1 ZPO. It allows for independent evidence proceedings

81 Huber, in: Musielak/Voit (eds), s 485 para 2.
82 Huber, in: Musielak/Voit (eds), s 485 para 10.
83 OLG Hamm, MDR 1994, 307.

prior to a pending dispute particularly in order to avoid future litigation or arbitration (cf s 485 para 2 cl 2 ZPO). This remedy aims to facilitate settlement in cases in which the parties' dispute is primarily fact-related[84] as is often the case in construction disputes.

aa) Requirements Section 485 para 2 ZPO requires the applicant's legitimate interest in establishing the state of a person or the state or value of an object, in the reason of personal injury, property damage or a material defect, or in the effort required to remedy a personal injury, property damage, or material defect. Such legitimate interest is to be assumed if the establishment of these facts may avoid litigation (s 485 para 2 cl 2 ZPO). The required legal interest can be established relatively easily; it is not present, for example, if it is clear that the expert report has no bearing on the settling or deciding of the dispute.[85] **5.57**

bb) Means of Evidence Only a written expert report on the factual questions listed in s 485 para 2 ZPO can be requested under this provision. Further forms of evidence may be secured only under the provisions of s 485 para 1 ZPO (paras 5.53 *et seq.*). **5.58**

2. *Competent Court*

Under **general rules**, the court competent to conduct independent evidence proceedings is either the court before which the matter is pending (s 486 para 1 ZPO) or the court that is to be competent for the applicant's claim based on the applicant's submission (s 486 para 2 ZPO). The local court in the district of which the evidence is located has jurisdiction only in cases of imminent danger (s 486 para 3 ZPO). As for seizure (paras 5.19 *et seq.*), the determination of the state court competent for independent evidence proceedings remains unaffected by the parties' **arbitration agreement.**[86] The competent state court is therefore to be determined as if no arbitration agreement had been concluded. However, this holds true only to the extent that the state courts' jurisdiction is not excluded from the start (paras 5.9 *et seq.*). **5.59**

3. *Representation Before Court*

In independent evidence proceedings, there is **no requirement** that the parties be represented by a lawyer admitted to the German bar (s 78 para 3, s 486 para 4 ZPO). Although not required, such representation is, however, advisable. **5.60**

4. *Application*

Independent evidence proceedings are never initiated on the court's own motion. The application must include the opposing party, the facts about which evidence is **5.61**

84 Government bill, BT-Drucks 11/3621, p 23.
85 Cf Reichold, in: Thomas/Putzo (eds), s 485 para 7a.
86 OLG Köln, IPRspr. 2002, no 209, 540, 541.

to be taken, the designation of the evidence to be taken and *prima facie* evidence for the facts on which the admissibility of the proceedings and the court's jurisdiction is based (s 487 ZPO). The applicant does not need to name the opposing party if it cannot do so without fault (s 494 para 1 ZPO).

5. Procedure

5.62 The court rules on the application by way of an order (*Beschluss*, s 490 para 1 ZPO). If the application is granted, the order is comparable to a regular order to take evidence (cf s 490 para 2 ZPO). The court will usually summon the opposing party so that it can present its case (s 491 ZPO). The taking of evidence in independent evidence proceedings is governed by the general provisions that apply in any court proceedings (s 492 para 1 ZPO). The independent evidence proceedings end once the evidence has been taken; the proceedings are not concluded by court decision.[87] The costs incurred are to be allocated within the subsequent main action;[88] they form part of the arbitral tribunal's award on costs (para 6.75). Upon the opposing party's application, the court can set a deadline to file the main action (s 494a ZPO) including by commencement of arbitral proceedings (cf para 5.37).

6. Effects

5.63 If a party in subsequent litigation relies on facts as to which evidence was taken in independent evidence proceedings, this evidence has the **same effect as evidence taken in the subsequent litigation** (s 493 para 1 ZPO). In the event of subsequent arbitral proceedings, the arbitral tribunal is in any event free in its consideration of evidence taken (s 1042 para 4 cl 2 ZPO). It is therefore a solely academic question as to whether s 493 para 1 ZPO has a similar binding effect for a subsequent arbitral tribunal. Under German substantive law, the **limitation period** is suspended by the service of an application for independent evidence proceedings (s 204 para 1 no 7 BGB).

C. Interim Relief Before the Arbitral Tribunal (s 1041 ZPO)

5.64 The parties to an arbitration can request interim relief not only from the state court (paras 5.3 *et seq.*) but also from the arbitral tribunal (s 1041 ZPO). Such interim measures are governed by a set of rules different from those applicable to interim measures ordered by the state courts. However, arbitral tribunals seated in Germany will often consider applications for interim measures in light of the considerably more detailed provisions on interim proceedings applicable before the state courts.

[87] BGH NJW 2011, 594, 595 para 11.
[88] BGH NJW-RR 2011, 931 paras 7 *et seq.*

I. Preliminary Remarks

1. *Legislative History*

With the adoption of **art 17 Model Law 1985** almost word for word in the form of s 1041 para 1 ZPO in 1998, competence of an arbitral tribunal in respect of interim relief was established for the first time[89] under German law. This competence was complemented by an enforcement mechanism which at that time had no counterpart in the Model Law.[90] The **2006 Model Law** revision that replaced the former art 17 with arts 17–17J has not yet been adopted in Germany and the government has no current plans to implement these provisions. Nevertheless, the 2006 Model Law provisions on interim measures may serve as guidance for the understanding of s 1041 ZPO.[91] Such guidance is all the more welcome as both tribunals and state courts enjoy considerable discretion under s 1041 ZPO. **5.65**

2. *Non-mandatory Nature*

As expressly provided by s 1041 para 1 ZPO, the parties can jointly deprive the arbitral tribunal of its power to grant interim measures of protection. The competence of state courts to enforce such measures (s 1041 para 2 ZPO) cannot be waived separately[92] but becomes moot if the parties have excluded the tribunal's competence under s 1041 para 1 ZPO.[93] **5.66**

3. *Applicability to Foreign Proceedings*

Section 1041 ZPO applies to arbitral proceedings seated in Germany (s 1025 para 1 ZPO). It is a matter of dispute, however, whether German courts can also enforce interim measures rendered by arbitral tribunals with a foreign seat. Section 1062 para 2 ZPO speaks in favor of such an extension: the provision expressly determines a court of local jurisdiction also for cases of s 1041 ZPO in which no German place of arbitration has been established and thus implies that German courts will decide on the enforcement of interim measures ordered by foreign tribunals.[94] However, the determination of a competent court under s 1062 ZPO is technically irrelevant since s 1025 ZPO excludes both s 1041 ZPO and s 1062 ZPO (insofar as the recognition and enforcement of foreign arbitral awards is not concerned) for foreign places of arbitration. Section 1062 ZPO does therefore not establish a basis for the enforcement of foreign interim measures. **5.67**

However, the provisions on state court enforcement of domestic arbitral interim measures in **s 1041 para 2 ZPO can be applied by way of analogy to foreign** **5.68**

---

[89] Government bill, BT-Drucks 13/5274, pp 44 *et seq.*
[90] Cf Government bill, BT-Drucks 13/5274, p 45.
[91] Kreindler/Schäfer/Wolff, para 925.
[92] Münch, in: MünchKommZPO, s 1041 para 10; dissenting Schlosser, in: Stein/Jonas (eds), s 1041 para 17.
[93] Münch, in: MünchKommZPO, s 1041 para 8.
[94] Cf Schäfer, in: *Arbitration in Germany*, s 1041 para 34.

arbitral measures.[95] The place of arbitration does not make a difference for the enforcement of arbitral interim measures: since s 1041 para 1 ZPO does not restrict the types of interim measures that a tribunal seated in Germany may order (paras 5.79 *et seq.*), it is not apparent how interim measures of foreign tribunals could cause additional issues.[96]

5.69 Whether the German legislature has deliberately restricted s 1041 ZPO to domestic interim measures is more difficult to determine. The legislative documents are silent. While the German legislature's arbitration-friendliness (para 1.6) may be invoked in favor of an unintentional omission, the express extension of other provisions to foreign arbitrations (eg s 1050 ZPO, see s 1025 para 2 ZPO)[97] counters this argument. In this situation, the 2006 amendments to the Model Law tip the scales in favor of an analogy: its art 17H para 1 now expressly allows for the recognition and enforcement of an interim measure issued by an arbitral tribunal irrespective of the country in which it was issued. It is in line with the German legislature's aim of a modern, harmonized, and arbitration-friendly arbitration regime[98] to adhere to such an emerging standard to the extent that it is consistent with the existing German arbitration law.[99] Such consistency can be achieved by applying s 1041 ZPO to foreign interim measures by way of analogy.

4. Emergency Arbitrators

5.70 Interim measures granted by arbitral tribunals are to be distinguished carefully from so-called emergency arbitrators. Emergency arbitrators have been introduced in particular by institutional rules (eg art 29 ICC Rules) to bridge the time gap until the constitution of the arbitral tribunal. Emergency arbitrators are not arbitral tribunals and their orders cannot be enforced under s 1041 ZPO. The emergency arbitrator's order is binding on the parties only because they have contractually agreed so, in particular by agreeing on institutional arbitration rules which include emergency arbitrator provisions. Under the ICC Rules, the emergency arbitrator is appointed by the president of the ICC Court within two days and shall make its order within 15 days.

II. The Arbitral Tribunal's Order of Interim Relief (s 1041 para 1 ZPO)

5.71 The arbitral tribunal has broad discretion whether to grant interim measures of protection and which ones (paras 5.76 *et seq.*) upon request by a party (para 5.72). The procedure leading to this decision is likewise within the arbitral tribunal's

[95] Schlosser, in: Stein/Jonas (eds), s 1041 para 41; dissenting Voit, in: Musielak/Voit (eds), s 1041 para 6.
[96] Bandel, p 364.
[97] Government bill, BT-Drucks 13/5274, p 31.
[98] See Government bill, BT-Drucks 13/5274, p 1.
[99] Kreindler/Schäfer/Wolff, para 938.

discretion (paras 5.73 *et seq.*). Form (paras 5.87 *et seq.*) and effects (paras 5.90 *et seq.*) of tribunal-ordered interim measures, however, are pre-defined by law.

1. *Request by a Party*

The arbitral tribunal may never issue an interim measure on its own initiative. It instead requires a party's request for which, however, the mere indication that interim protection is needed suffices.[100] The request does not need to indicate the measure by which the sought-after legal protection is to be pursued[101] because s 1041 para 1 ZPO entrusts the determination of the measure to the arbitral tribunal's discretion. **5.72**

2. *Procedure*

Since the law does not set out specific procedural requirements, the arbitral tribunal is free to determine its procedure (cf s 1042 para 4 ZPO) to the extent that the parties did not agree on stipulations including by reference to institutional rules. The tribunal is, however, limited by the mandatory provisions, in particular the parties' right to be heard (s 1042 para 1 cl 2 ZPO). In recent decades, it has been a hotly debated issue (both internationally and in Germany) to what extent arbitral tribunals may issue interim measures ***ex parte***, ie without previously notifying the other party of the pending request and without giving it the chance to present its case. The prevailing view in Germany acknowledges *ex-parte* arbitral interim measures:[102] state courts are permitted to issue *ex-parte* measures (para 5.32) and the due process standard for arbitral tribunals is not deemed to be higher than for state courts.[103] As must state courts (para 5.32), arbitral tribunals must inform the opposing party, provide it with the opportunity to comment and take into consideration these comments after the measure has been issued.[104] This is possible since the arbitral tribunal is free to set aside or to amend its measures (para 5.93). The admissibility of *ex-parte* arbitral interim measures under German law is confirmed by s 1063 para 3 cl 1 ZPO according to which leave of enforcement of an interim measure may be granted *ex parte* by the state court.[105] This interpretation of s 1041 **5.73**

---

[100] Münch, in: MünchKommZPO, s 1041 para 7.

[101] Münch, in: MünchKommZPO, s 1041 para 7; Voit, in: Musielak/Voit (eds), s 1041 para 2.

[102] Bandel, p 99; Lachmann, para 2907; Laukemann, ZZP 126 (2013), 175, 184; Leitzen, pp 115 *et seq.*; Reichold, in: Thomas/Putzo (eds), s 1041 para 2; Schäfer, in: *Arbitration in Germany*, s 1041 para 2; Schlosser, in: Stein/Jonas (eds), s 1041 para 21; Schwab/Walter, ch 17a para 20; Voit, in: Musielak/Voit (eds), s 1041 para 3; see also Hobeck/Weyhreter, SchiedsVZ 2005, 238 (emphasizing the need for *ex-parte* measures); dissenting Gottwald/Adolphsen, DStR 1998, 1017, 1020; Münch, in: MünchKommZPO, s 1041 para 25; Schütze, BB 1998, 1650, 1651; Thümmel, DZWIR 1997, 133, 135; Wolf, DB 1999, 1101, 1102 (if not allowed for by the parties).

[103] Voit, in: Musielak/Voit (eds), s 1041 para 3.

[104] Bandel, p 99; Kreindler/Schäfer/Wolff, para 920; Schlosser, in: Stein/Jonas (eds), s 1041 para 21; Schwab/Walter, ch 17a para 20; Voit, in: Musielak/Voit (eds), s 1041 para 3.

[105] Voit, in: Musielak/Voit (eds), s 1041 para 3.

para 1 ZPO is also in conformity with the 2006 amendments to the Model Law (art 17B).[106]

5.74 Including in cases of great urgency, the **chairman** of a three-member tribunal cannot grant or deny interim measures alone even if he or she has been authorized by the co-arbitrators.[107] Section 1052 para 3 ZPO does not cover such authorization:[108] interim measures are more than a mere question of procedure and the parties have for valid reasons established a three-member tribunal rather than a sole arbitrator. The parties, however, can authorize the chairman to decide requests to grant an interim measure without the co-arbitrators. Such authorization is nothing but the establishment of a separate tribunal consisting of the chairman only.[109]

3. Interim Measures of Protection

5.75 The types of interim measures (paras 5.76 *et seq.*) and the prerequisites under which they are issued (paras 5.79 *et seq.*) are largely in the discretion of the arbitral tribunal. Security, conversely, has found express mention in s 1041 ZPO (para 5.86).

a) Prerequisites for Issuing Interim Measures

5.76 *aa) The Arbitral Tribunal's Discretion* Section 1041 para 1 ZPO is remarkably taciturn as regards the requirements for interim measures of protection: the arbitral tribunal may order such measures "as the arbitral tribunal may consider necessary in respect of the subject matter of the dispute." The law neither contains a definition of interim measures nor remarks on the prerequisites for its issuance. The tribunal enjoys **broad procedural discretion**[110] which corresponds to its general procedural discretion under s 1042 para 4 ZPO.

5.77 A tribunal should, however, generally require **three elements** which are reflected both in the German law of civil procedure and in the Model Law: first, a threat of harm of some intensity without which no urgency is justified (cf ss 917 *et seq.*, 935, 940 ZPO [paras 5.26 *et seq.*, 5.45, 5.47] and art 17A para 1 lit a Model Law), second, a prospect of success of the applicant's claim (including the tribunal's **jurisdiction**[111]) to some degree as a necessary object to be secured (cf ss 916, 935, 940 ZPO [paras 5.25, 5.45, 5.47] and art 17A para 1 lit b Model Law), and third, demonstration of the underlying facts to a certain degree (cf s 920 para 2 ZPO

---

[106] See Zekoll/Giessen, SchiedsVZ 2010, 137; Barona Vilar, in: *Festschrift Leipold*, pp 853, 861 *et seq.*; Matsuura, in: *Festschrift Leipold*, pp 933, 939 *et seq.*

[107] Lachmann, para 2899; Leitzen, pp 125 *et seq.*; Voit, in: Musielak/Voit (eds), s 1041 para 3; dissenting Schlosser, in: Stein/Jonas (eds), s 1041 para 22; Schwab/Walter, ch 17a para 17.

[108] Lachmann, para 2899; Leitzen, pp 125 *et seq.*; Voit, in: Musielak/Voit (eds), s 1041 para 3; dissenting Schlosser, in: Stein/Jonas (eds), s 1041 para 22; Schwab/Walter, ch 17a para 17.

[109] Bandel, pp 80 *et seq.*; Lachmann, para 2899; Leitzen, p 126; Voit, in: Musielak/Voit (eds), s 1041 para 3.

[110] Münch, in: MünchKommZPO, s 1041 para 22; Schäfer, in: *Arbitration in Germany*, s 1041 para 10; Schlosser, in: Stein/Jonas (eds), s 1041 para 21.

[111] Kreindler/Schäfer/Wolff, para 917; Schäfer, in: *Arbitration in Germany*, s 1041 para 8; dissenting Schwab/Walter, ch 17a para 19.

[para 5.29] and art 17A para 1 Model Law). The tribunal may want to accept the requirements either under the German law of civil procedure or under the Model Law as **guidance** when exercising its discretion; the former is typical in domestic arbitrations in Germany.[112] However, the tribunal remains free to deviate from each of the three elements set out above.[113]

bb) In Particular: Standard of Proof Although German law does not describe a **standard of proof** applicable in interim arbitral proceedings, it is sensible for arbitral tribunals to lower the standard of proof (cf para 5.29) since time is of the essence for interim measures. **Affidavits** (*Versicherungen an Eides statt*), which play a major role in interim proceedings before state courts (para 5.29), can sometimes also be seen in arbitral proceedings. Legally, however, they have no effect in arbitral proceedings beyond that of any written statement:[114] their probative value is substantially determined by the fact that issuing an incorrect affidavit vis-à-vis a state court constitutes a criminal offence (s 156 StGB) while issuance in arbitral proceedings does not give rise to criminal liability under German law beyond that for any incorrect fact allegation. **5.78**

b) Types of Interim Measures

aa) Interim Measures as the Arbitral Tribunal May Consider Necessary The types of interim measures that the tribunal can issue are predefined by law just as sparsely as is the procedure to issue such measures (paras 5.76 *et seq.*). The tribunal enjoys a **broad procedural discretion** as to the type of measure which it issues. This discretion, however, is subject to deviating **party agreement**: since the parties can fully exclude the tribunal's competence to issue interim measures (para 5.66), they can all the more restrict this power.[115] Although such agreements are rare in practice, the parties could, for example, narrow the types of interim measures to allow only those permitted before the state courts. **5.79**

The types of interim measures that a tribunal may issue under s 1041 para 1 ZPO include the measures **available before German state courts**, ie seizure (paras 5.17 *et seq.*; see also art 17 para 2 lit c Model Law), injunctions (paras 5.41 *et seq.*; see also art 17 para 2 lit a Model Law), and preservation of evidence (paras 5.51 *et seq.*; see also art 17 para 2 lit d Model Law). The tribunal may also order an arrest (*persönlicher Arrest*) as stipulated in s 918 ZPO.[116] The constitutional requirement that only **5.80**

112 Schäfer, in: *Arbitration in Germany*, s 1041 para 20.

113 Cf Schlosser, in: Stein/Jonas (eds), s 1041 para 22; apparently dissenting Schütze, para 482; Schwab/Walter, ch 17a paras 18 *et seq.*

114 OLG Saarbrücken, SchiedsVZ 2007, 323, 326; Lachmann, para 2902; Münch, in: MünchKommZPO, s 1041 para 24; Schäfer, in: *Arbitration in Germany*, s 1041 para 17; Schlosser, in: Stein/Jonas (eds), s 1041 para 21; Voit, in: Musielak/Voit (eds), s 1041 para 3; in favor of an increased evidentiary value Leitzen, pp 148 *et seq.*

115 Cf Schlosser, in: Stein/Jonas (eds), s 1041 para 17; Schroth, SchiedsVZ 2003, 102, 103; dissenting Münch, in: MünchKommZPO, s 1041 para 9.

116 Bandel, p 168; Geimer, in: Zöller (ed), s 1041 para 2; Lachmann, para 2890; Voit, in: Musielak/Voit (eds), s 1041 para 4; dissenting Kreindler/Schäfer/Wolff, para 927; Münch,

a judge shall decide on the admissibility of a detention and its continuation (art 104 para 2 cl 1 GG) is complied with by the leave of enforcement decision under s 1041 para 2 ZPO.

5.81 The arbitral tribunal, however, is not restricted to the types of measures that a German state court could issue.[117] This is particularly relevant for the protection of monetary claims otherwise than through seizure.[118] Measures **not available before the German state courts** include those common in foreign jurisdictions and those which the tribunal considers necessary although they are not admissible before any state court. The tribunal may also issue interim measures which have no prospect of being granted leave of enforcement under s 1041 para 2 ZPO[119] and which do not even comply with German public policy:[120] leave of enforcement of these measures may well be granted in another jurisdiction[121] and even without any enforcement the measures remain binding between the parties (para 5.90).

5.82 **Examples** of interim measures that the arbitral tribunal can order under s 1041 para 1 ZPO are maintenance of the property in dispute, prohibitions of disposal, deposition of the property in dispute, the order to furnish a bank guarantee, the preliminary withdrawal of a shareholder's power of attorney, the preliminary prohibition to make use of a bank guarantee or of specific actions, freezing orders, use and maintenance of machines, and completion of a construction phase.[122]

5.83 Similar to a state court (para 5.46), an arbitral tribunal can never bind a **third party** that is not a party to the arbitration.[123] While a lack of a valid arbitration agreement covering the dispute may be overcome if such agreement exists *prima facie* (para 5.77), it would be contrary to basic notions of due process if a tribunal (or court) could encumber a non-party. Thus a tribunal cannot order a land register to make entries or a bank to withhold payments under a guarantee as long as these entities are not parties to the arbitration.

---

in: MünchKommZPO, s 1041 para 14; Scheef, p 42; Schlosser, in: Stein/Jonas (eds), s 1041 para 11 (contrary to the 22nd edn, para 5); Schwab/Walter, ch 17a para 4.

117 Bandel, pp 133 *et seq.*; Schäfer, in: *Arbitration in Germany*, s 1041 para 21; Scheef, p 50; Schlosser, in: Stein/Jonas (eds), s 1041 para 7; Schwab/Walter, ch 17a para 5; dissenting Reichold, in: Thomas/Putzo (eds), s 1041 para 2 (orientation towards ss 916 *et seq.* ZPO); Schütze, para 482 (ss 915 *et seq.* ZPO apply by way of analogy).

118 Leitzen, pp 77 *et seq.*; Schlosser, in: Stein/Jonas (eds), s 1041 para 7.

119 Schwab/Walter, ch 17a para 5; Voit, in: Musielak/Voit (eds), s 1041 para 4.

120 Schwab/Walter, ch 17a para 5; Voit, in: Musielak/Voit (eds), s 1041 para 4.

121 Schwab/Walter, ch 17a para 5.

122 Münch, in: MünchKommZPO, s 1041 paras 13 *et seq.*; Schlosser, in: Stein/Jonas (eds), s 1041 paras 9 *et seq.*; Schwab/Walter, ch 17a paras 4 *et seq.*; more detail on freezing orders: Schroeder, SchiedsVZ 2004, 26.

123 Government bill, BT-Drucks 13/5274, p 45; Lachmann, para 1426; similar (no party to the arbitration agreement): Kronke, RIW 1998, 257, 264; Schäfer, in: *Arbitration in Germany*, s 1041 para 9.

bb) In Respect of the Subject Matter of the Dispute The tribunal may order interim measures only in respect of the subject matter of the dispute. This wording, which is in line with art 17 Model Law 1985, does not cover interim measures that aim to secure the arbitral proceedings as such (as opposed to the claim brought in these proceedings). Therefore, s 1041 para 1 ZPO does not entitle the arbitral tribunal to issue interim measures to prevent a party from initiating state court proceedings in the matter covered by the arbitration agreement (**anti-suit injunctions**).[124] Although a party's future claim for reimbursement of costs also does not pertain to the subject matter of the dispute, the prevailing view acknowledges that the arbitral tribunal may order **security for costs** as an interim measure to secure that claim.[125] Security for costs, however, is granted reluctantly and only if new facts occurred after the conclusion of the arbitration agreement that have increased the risk of a loss of the claim.[126] Article 17 para 1 Model Law 2006, which has not been transformed into German law, has broadened the definition of interim measures by deleting the reference to the subject matter of the dispute and explicitly listing measures protecting the arbitral process itself (art 17 para 2 lit b Model Law 2006). **5.84**

cc) Pre-judgment of the Main Action It is said that an arbitral tribunal, just like a German state court (para 5.44), may generally not order performance of the claim if that pre-judges the main action (*keine Vorwegnahme der Hauptsache*).[127] However, s 1041 para 1 ZPO does not transfer the limitations of state court interim proceedings to arbitral interim proceedings (paras 5.79 *et seq.*). The fact that measures ordered under s 1041 para 1 ZPO may also serve as a basis for enforcement abroad and that pre-judging of the main action in interim proceedings is allowed in jurisdictions outside Germany[128] also speaks against such a strict limitation. However, the arbitral tribunal will be well advised to use interim measures only as temporary measures; this restriction is also contained in art 17 para 2 Model Law 2006's definition. **5.85**

c) **Security (s 1041 para 1 cl 2 ZPO)** The arbitral tribunal may require any party to provide appropriate security in connection with an interim measure (s 1041 para 1 cl 2 ZPO). This can apply to either party, ie the applicant and its counterparty. The applicant can in particular be ordered to provide security **5.86**

---

124 Bandel, p 187; Kreindler/Schäfer/Wolff, para 893; Münch, in: MünchKommZPO, s 1041 para 21; Schäfer, in: *Arbitration in Germany*, s 1041 para 13; dissenting Schlosser, in: Stein/Jonas (eds), s 1041 para 13.

125 Geimer, in: Zöller (ed), s 1042 para 40; Pörnbacher/Thiel, SchiedsVZ 2010, 14, 17; Voit, in: Musielak/Voit (eds), s 1042 para 12.

126 Pörnbacher/Thiel, SchiedsVZ 2010, 14, 18 *et seq.* with further references.

127 Kreindler/Schäfer/Wolff, paras 929 *et seq.*; Lachmann, para 2895; Schäfer, in: *Arbitration in Germany*, s 1041 para 14; Schroth, SchiedsVZ 2003, 102, 103; see also OLG Frankfurt, NJW-RR 2001, 1078; Leitzen, pp 58 *et seq.*; Voit, in: Musielak/Voit (eds), s 1041 para 2; dissenting Bandel, pp 189 *et seq.*; Schlosser, in: Stein/Jonas (eds), s 1041 para 11.

128 Kreindler/Schäfer/Wolff, para 931.

which compensates for the measure and/or subsequent damages that the counterparty incurs although the order later turns out to have been unjustified.[129] The counterparty, on the other hand, can be ordered to provide security in particular to avert the interim measure (cf s 1041 para 4 cl 1 ZPO).[130] The arbitral tribunal's competence to order security does not require a specific request (see also para 5.72).[131]

4. Form of Interim Measures

5.87 a) **Form of Decision** The arbitral tribunal issues interim measures in the form of an **order** rather than of an arbitral award.[132] This is obvious from the existence of a specific procedure to grant leave of enforcement (s 1041 para 2 ZPO) which would be futile if interim measures could be enforced as arbitral awards under ss 1060, 1061 ZPO. The broader definition in art 17 para 2 Model Law according to which an interim measure is any temporary measure, "whether in the form of an award or in another form," refers to jurisdictions in which interim measures are classified as arbitral awards.[133] Germany is not such a jurisdiction.

5.88 Arbitral tribunals can, however, render so-called **interim awards** which contain a final decision for a fixed term.[134] Such interim awards are not interim measures as regulated in s 1041 ZPO[135] but regular arbitral awards. Unlike interim measures, interim awards gain a *res judicata* effect (s 1055 ZPO) and cannot be repealed by the arbitral tribunal. Due to this binding nature, interim awards cannot be rendered in summary proceedings but require full proceedings complying with all due process rights of the parties.[136] German arbitration practice is well acquainted with interim awards since under the former arbitration law in force until 1998, these were the only interim decisions an arbitral tribunal could issue (cf para 5.65).[137]

5.89 b) **Formal Requirements for Orders of Interim Measures** Since interim measures are not arbitral awards, s 1054 ZPO (paras 6.87 *et seq.*) does not govern the formal requirements. This provision can also not be applied by way of analogy.[138] While the arbitral tribunal may find guidance in this provision, an analogous application would unnecessarily burden the issuance of interim measures and

---

[129] Münch, in: MünchKommZPO, s 1041 para 28; Schütze, BB 1998, 1650, 1652.

[130] Bandel, p 112; Leitzen, p 102 (security for the claim for damages under s 1041 para 4 ZPO); Voit, in: Musielak/Voit (eds), s 1041 para 4.

[131] Münch, in: MünchKommZPO, s 1041 para 27; Voit, in: Musielak/Voit (eds), s 1041 para 4.

[132] Schütze, SchiedsVZ 2009, 241, 244.

[133] Report of the Working Group on Arbitration on the work of its thirty-sixth session, A/CN.9/508, para 68 (p 18).

[134] Geimer, in: Zöller (ed), s 1041 para 6; Voit, in: Musielak/Voit (eds), s 1041 para 5.

[135] Münch, in: MünchKommZPO, s 1041 para 4; Voit, in: Musielak/Voit (eds), s 1041 para 5.

[136] Voit, in: Musielak/Voit (eds), s 1041 para 5; dissenting Geimer, in: Zöller (ed), s 1041 para 7.

[137] Münch, in: MünchKommZPO, s 1041 para 4 with further references.

[138] Münch, in: MünchKommZPO, s 1041 para 26; Schlosser, in: Stein/Jonas (eds), s 1041 para 22; Voit, in: Musielak/Voit (eds), s 1041 para 4; dissenting Bandel, pp 68 *et seq.*; Geimer, in: Zöller (ed), s 1041 para 2; Leitzen, pp 167 *et seq.*

cause the risk of formal invalidity. The interim measure may be issued orally.[139] However, if leave of enforcement of the interim measure is to be granted under s 1041 para 2 ZPO, the measure at least needs to be in writing.[140]

5. *Effects*

a) Binding but not Compelling Effect for the Parties The law is silent on the effects of an interim measure issued by an arbitral tribunal. It is clear from s 1041 para 2 ZPO that any enforcement of such an interim measure requires the state court's leave of enforcement. Even if the arbitral tribunal has included a disciplinary fine for violation of its order, such violation cannot be sanctioned as long as leave of enforcement has not been granted previously.[141] Although the interim measure cannot be enforced against the parties prior to the state court's leave of enforcement (s 1041 para 2 ZPO), it has a binding effect on the parties comparable to that of a procedural order. Since the interim measure has no compelling effect before leave of enforcement has been granted, the request for repeal (paras 5.110 *et seq.*) is a sufficient remedy. **5.90**

Although interim measures are non-compelling, the arbitral tribunal may design certain **self-enforceable measures.**[142] Violation of these measures has an immediate (inner-procedural) effect on the parties even if they have not been declared enforceable under s 1041 para 2 ZPO. Examples of such effects include taking the violation into consideration within the allocation of the burden of proof, within the consideration of evidence, within a decision *ex aequo et bono* (if the parties allowed for such a decision)[143] or within the award's cost decision. **5.91**

Violation of a tribunal-ordered interim measure for which leave of enforcement has not yet been granted under s 1041 para 2 ZPO can furthermore be sanctioned by a **contractual penalty**. Such a penalty, however, needs to be agreed upon between the parties and cannot be ordered unilaterally by the arbitral tribunal.[144] **5.92**

b) No Binding Effect for the Tribunal Unlike an arbitral award, the *res judicata* effect of which immunizes it against repeal and amendment by the arbitral tribunal (para 6.122), the interim measure is always exposed to such changes by the tribunal.[145] While issuance of an interim measure always requires a party's application, the arbitral tribunal can repeal and amend an interim measure on **5.93**

---

[139] Schlosser, in: Stein/Jonas (eds), s 1041 para 22; Voit, in: Musielak/Voit (eds), s 1041 para 4; dissenting Bandel, pp 69 *et seq.*

[140] Schlosser, in: Stein/Jonas (eds), s 1041 para 22; Voit, in: Musielak/Voit (eds), s 1041 para 4.

[141] Voit, in: Musielak/Voit (eds), s 1041 para 4.

[142] Dissenting Lachmann, para 2893.

[143] Münch, in: MünchKommZPO, s 1041 para 19; Schwab/Walter, ch 17a para 2.

[144] Voit, in: Musielak/Voit (eds), s 1041 para 4; unclear Münch, in: MünchKommZPO, s 1041 para 18.

[145] OLG Jena, BB 2000, Beil. 12, p 22; Bandel, pp 224 *et seq.*; Schlosser, in: Stein/Jonas (eds), s 1041 para 25; see also Schwab/Walter, ch 17a para 38.

its own motion, in particular in light of a change of circumstances.[146] This gains particular importance if the tribunal had issued an *ex-parte* measure.

III. The Enforcement by the State Courts

5.94 Similar to arbitral awards (ss 1055, 1060 ZPO), interim measures issued by an arbitral tribunal are binding but as such not enforceable (paras 5.90 *et seq.*): the arbitral tribunal lacks the power to enforce its own decisions.[147] Since the German legislature has recognized enforcement as being often essential for the effectiveness of interim measures, it completed its framework of tribunal competence based on the Model Law to issue interim measures with an enforcement mechanism (para 5.65). The state court may grant (s 1041 para 2 ZPO, paras 5.95 *et seq.*), repeal and amend leave of enforcement (s 1041 para 3 ZPO, paras 5.110 *et seq.*). If the interim measure turns out to have been unjustified from the outset, the affected party has a claim for damages (s 1041 para 4 ZPO, paras 5.112 *et seq.*).

1. Leave of Enforcement (s 1041 para 2 ZPO)

5.95 a) **Admissibility** In order to be admissible, a request under s 1041 para 2 ZPO requires an interim measure issued by an arbitral **tribunal seated in Germany** (s 1025 para 1 ZPO, para 5.67). However, the provision applies by way of analogy to interim measures issued by **foreign arbitral tribunals** (paras 5.68 *et seq.*).

5.96 Any leave of enforcement requires a **party request**; the state court will never enforce an arbitral interim measure on its own motion. The request can be filed by either party[148] although the party burdened by the interim measure will in practice have no incentive to request enforcement.[149] The request does not need to specify how leave of enforcement shall be granted;[150] the state court will recast the measure on its own motion if necessary (para 5.105).

5.97 The **competent court** where the request is to be filed is the *Oberlandesgericht* (higher regional court) which the parties have stipulated in the arbitration agreement or, in the absence of such stipulation, in the district of which the seat of arbitration is located (s 1062 para 1 no 3 ZPO). The *Oberlandesgericht* competent for the enforcement of interim measures issued by foreign arbitral tribunals (paras 5.68 *et seq.*) is determined under s 1062 para 2 ZPO.

---

[146] Schlosser, in: Stein/Jonas (eds), s 1041 para 25; dissenting Bandel, p 224.
[147] Schwab/Walter, ch 17a para 2.
[148] Münch, in: MünchKommZPO, s 1041 para 31; dissenting Lachmann, para 2913.
[149] Concurring Lachmann, para 2913. It is doubtful to see the enforcement request as a compensation for the lack of a remedy for setting aside the interim measure (Münch, in: MünchKommZPO, s 1041 para 31): The burdened party would need to request enforcement although it aims at the contrary. And even a declined request would not affect the existence and bindingness of the interim measure (different for arbitral awards, s 1060 para 2 cl 1 ZPO). See Schwab/Walter, ch 17a para 39.
[150] Cf Münch, in: MünchKommZPO, s 1041 para 31.

No **application for a corresponding interim measure** must have been made to a court (s 1041 para 2 cl 1 ZPO).[151] This requirement shall prevent parallel court proceedings which ultimately pursue the same aim of legal protection and entail the risk of contradictory decisions.[152] Since the application to the state court does not need to specify the demanded measure precisely, but may be limited to the mere aim of legal protection, it already "corresponds" to the arbitral interim measure if both share the same aim of legal protection.[153] The request for leave of enforcement is precluded once the application for a corresponding interim measure has been filed regardless of whether that court has decided on the application[154] and whether that filing took place before or after leave of enforcement was requested.[155] **5.98**

The request under s 1041 para 2 ZPO does not require the opposing party's refusal to **voluntarily comply** with the interim measure.[156] Similar to the enforcement of an arbitral award (paras 6.246 *et seq.*), each party is entitled to extend the effects of an arbitral interim measure by requesting its enforcement.[157] The deviating view can not be reconciled with the fact that also the party burdened by an interim measure may request its enforcement (para 5.96) and the beneficiary's "voluntary compliance" would be difficult to determine. **5.99**

b) Merits While the admissibility of an enforcement request follows clear rules (paras 5.95 *et seq.*), the law furnishes little guidance on the decision on the merits. Section 1041 para 2 cl 1 ZPO, according to which the court "may... grant leave of enforcement," provides the court with discretion but with no criteria for how to exercise it. **5.100**

aa) Standard of Review The arbitral tribunal is not bound to apply specific criteria when issuing an interim measure, in particular not the criteria that a state court would apply when approached for such a measure (paras 5.76 *et seq.*). It would be irreconcilable with the tribunal's broad discretion (para 5.76) if the state court applied a strict standard of review, in particular the standard that it would apply if it were approached with the initial request to issue the interim measure. The state court therefore generally needs to respect the tribunal's decision that an interim measure was issued and the kind of measure issued.[158] **5.101**

151 But see also Schäfer, in: *Arbitration in Germany*, s 1041 para 29 (discretion).
152 Government bill, BT-Drucks 13/5274, p 45; Münch, in: MünchKommZPO, s 1041 para 41.
153 Münch, in: MünchKommZPO, s 1041 para 41; Voit, in: Musielak/Voit (eds), s 1041 para 6; narrower OLG Saarbrücken, SchiedsVZ 2007, 323, 325 (identical measures).
154 Voit, in: Musielak/Voit (eds), s 1041 para 6.
155 Voit, in: Musielak/Voit (eds), s 1041 para 6.
156 Schäfer, in: *Arbitration in Germany*, s 1041 para 28; Voit, in: Musielak/Voit (eds), s 1041 para 6; dissenting Schwab/Walter, ch 17a para 28.
157 Voit, in: Musielak/Voit (eds), s 1041 para 6.
158 OLG Frankfurt, NJW-RR 2001, 1078; OLG Saarbrücken, SchiedsVZ 2007, 323, 325; Schäfer, in: *Arbitration in Germany*, s 1041 para 33; Voit, in: Musielak/Voit (eds), s 1041 para 8; dissenting Schütze, SchiedsVZ 2009, 241, 244.

5.102 The state court's review standard therefore needs to be more generous. It will not grant enforcement if the arbitral tribunal's interim procedure or the interim measure itself violates **public policy**.[159] The application is also to be denied if the interim measure is **incompatible with the German law of enforcement** and such incompatibility cannot be cured by recasting the measure (para 5.105). The arbitral interim measure is not subject to review respecting urgency, appropriateness, pre-judging of the main action, etc.[160]

5.103 If the arbitral tribunal is not **competent** to decide the main dispute—whether on grounds of lack of an arbitration agreement, invalidity, lack of scope of an arbitration agreement vis-à-vis the dispute or lack of arbitrability—it also lacks competence to issue interim measures of protection (para 5.77). This is to be taken into account by the state court if enforcement is requested under s 1041 para 2 ZPO.[161] The tribunal's competence is subject to full review, ie the state court is not bound by the tribunal's assessment (similar to s 1059 para 2 no 1 lit a ZPO). For the underlying facts, however, only *prima facie* evidence needs to be furnished (cf s 920 para 2, s 294 ZPO) since the leave of enforcement functionally forms part of the interlocutory procedure.[162] If it becomes obvious in the course of this review that the opposing party is precluded from raising an objection of lack of competence under s 1040 para 2 cl 1 ZPO or for other reasons, the state court cannot deny the leave of enforcement because of a lack of jurisdiction.[163] If the arbitral interim measure later turns out to suffer from the tribunal's lack of jurisdiction, the burdened party may file a repeal request (paras 5.110 *et seq.*) and have a claim for damages (paras 5.112 *et seq.*).

5.104 Although the state court has discretion to grant or deny enforcement (para 5.100), a decision that does not follow these guidelines will amount to an incorrect exercise of its discretionary power.[164]

5.105 *bb) Recast* The state court may recast (ie reformulate) the arbitral order of interim measures if necessary for the purpose of enforcing the measure (s 1041 para 2

[159] Lachmann, para 2917; Schäfer, in: *Arbitration in Germany*, s 1041 para 33; Schwab/Walter, ch 17a para 30; Voit, in: Musielak/Voit (eds), s 1041 para 8; broader (anticipation of enforceability of a future award) OLG Saarbrücken, SchiedsVZ 2007, 323, 325; Münch, in: MünchKommZPO, s 1041 para 39.

[160] Dissenting OLG Saarbrücken, SchiedsVZ 2007, 323, 326; Government bill, BT-Drucks 13/5274, p 45; Münch, in: MünchKommZPO, s 1041 para 40; Lachmann, para 2919.

[161] OLG Saarbrücken, SchiedsVZ 2007, 323, 325; Government bill, BT-Drucks 13/5274, p 45; Reichold, in: Thomas/Putzo (eds), s 1041 para 3; Schäfer, in: *Arbitration in Germany*, s 1041 para 32; Schütze, para 486; Thümmel, DZWIR 1997, 133, 136; Voit, in: Musielak/Voit (eds), s 1041 para 7; dissenting (no court review for validity of the arbitration agreement) Hartmann, in: Baumbach/Lauterbach/Albers/Hartmann (eds), s 1041 para 4.

[162] Bandel, pp 89, 218; Voit, in: Musielak/Voit (eds), s 1041 para 7.

[163] Geimer, in: Zöller (ed), s 1041 para 3; Schäfer, in: *Arbitration in Germany*, s 1041 para 32; dissenting Voit, in: Musielak/Voit (eds), s 1041 para 7.

[164] Voit, in: Musielak/Voit (eds), s 1041 para 8; see also Government bill, BT-Drucks 13/5274, p 45.

cl 2 ZPO). This competence to recast allows in particular for ensuring that the order conforms with the principle of certainty (*Bestimmtheitsgrundsatz*) governing German enforcement law, which requires any executory title to exhibit a high degree of specificity.[165] Recasting does not include a "translation" of the arbitral tribunal's interim measure into another measure that the state court would have granted.[166]

c) **Procedure** The *Oberlandesgericht* will usually **hear** the opposing party before it decides on the enforcement request (s 1063 para 1 cl 2 ZPO). Section 1063 para 2 ZPO, according to which an **oral hearing** is to be scheduled if grounds for setting aside an arbitral award are to be considered in setting aside or enforcement proceedings, does not apply to the enforcement of interim measures.[167] However, grounds for refusal of leave of enforcement are to be taken into account by the state court when deciding whether to hold an oral hearing. The presiding judge may preliminarily allow enforcement of the interim measure pending a court senate decision on the request **without prior hearing** of the party opposing the application (s 1063 para 3 ZPO). The opposing party is sufficiently protected by being heard subsequently and by its right to bring a claim for damages pursuant to s 1041 para 4 ZPO (paras 5.112 *et seq.*). **5.106**

d) **Effect** The enforcement request is decided by way of a court order (*Beschluss*, s 1063 para 1 cl 1 ZPO) against which no remedy is available (s 1065 para 1 ZPO). Once leave of enforcement of the interim measure has been granted, the regular provisions on the enforcement of titles apply. The executory title as a general prerequisite for enforcement (para 5.38) lies within the leave of enforcement although it is not enumerated in ss 794 *et seq.* ZPO, which contain a list of executory titles. These provisions, however, are not exhaustive.[168] **5.107**

The regular provisions on enforcement assign a number of tasks to the **court of first instance hearing the case** (*Prozessgericht des ersten Rechtszugs*), eg authorizing substitute performance (s 887 ZPO) or imposing a coercive penalty payment if the action may not be taken by others (s 888 ZPO). In the case of arbitral interim measures, these tasks are not carried out by the arbitral tribunal—which lacks coercive powers (para 5.94)—but by the *Oberlandesgericht* that had granted leave of enforcement.[169] **5.108**

---

165 Government bill, BT-Drucks 13/5274, p 45; Schäfer, in: *Arbitration in Germany*, s 1041 para 36.

166 OLG Saarbrücken, SchiedsVZ 2007, 323, 327; Voit, in: Musielak/Voit (eds), s 1041 para 9; broader Scheef, p 53 (state court's comprehensive "right to transformation"); unclear Münch, in: MünchKommZPO, s 1041 para 48.

167 Dissenting Münch, in: MünchKommZPO, s 1041 para 34.

168 Münch, in: MünchKommZPO, s 1041 para 30; Voit, in: Musielak/Voit (eds), s 1041 para 8.

169 Lachmann, paras 2929 *et seq.*; Schlosser, in: Stein/Jonas (eds), s 1041 para 33; dissenting Münch, in: MünchKommZPO, s 1041 para 36 (fictitious court of first instance).

5.109 While state court interim measures need to be enforced **within one month** after they have been pronounced or served to the requesting party (s 929 para 2 ZPO, para 5.39), no such provision exists for arbitral interim measures. This one-month deadline cannot be applied by way of analogy:[170] arbitral interim measures operate in a different legal setting than interim measures issued by state courts including *ex-officio* service of the state court's leave of enforcement.

2. Repeal and Amendment (s 1041 para 3 ZPO)

5.110 The state court may repeal or amend its leave of enforcement (s 1041 para 3 ZPO). This **procedure** is generally governed by the same rules that also apply to the leave of enforcement under s 1041 para 2 ZPO (paras 5.95 *et seq.*). As expressly stated in s 1041 para 3 ZPO, the state court will neither repeal nor amend its leave of enforcement on its own motion but rather only upon **request** of one of the parties.

5.111 The law is silent on the **substantive prerequisites** under which the arbitral interim measure may be repealed or amended. The challenge in determining these rules is that the state court must respect the arbitral tribunal's decision on interim measures when granting leave of enforcement under s 1041 para 2 ZPO and is not permitted to replace the tribunal's decision with its own (para 5.101). It would be inconsistent with these principles if the state court were allowed to substitute the tribunal's decision when repealing or amending the leave of enforcement.[171] The state court must therefore apply the same limited review standard under s 1041 para 3 ZPO as it must under s 1041 para 2 ZPO (paras 5.102 *et seq.*). The court may therefore repeal or amend its leave of enforcement if the arbitral tribunal has repealed or amended its interim measure (para 5.93)[172] or if, due to another change in circumstances, the state court could now deny leave of enforcement.

3. Claim for Damages (s 1041 para 4 ZPO)

5.112 **a) Claim** The enforcement of an interim measure is an undertaking **at the applicant's own risk**. If a measure issued by a state court turns out to have been unjustified from the outset, the opposing party has a claim for damages regardless of whether the applicant is at fault (s 945 ZPO). This claim for damages has been transformed into s 1041 para 4 cl 1 ZPO for arbitral interim measures.

5.113 The claim for damages requires that the interim measure issued by the arbitral tribunal "proves to have been **unjustified from the outset**." This requires that either the factual or the legal prerequisites for issuing the measure have not been met at the

[170] Dissenting Münch, in: MünchKommZPO, s 1041 paras 42 *et seq.*; Thümmel, DZWIR 1997, 133, 136.

[171] Cf OLG Jena, BB 2000, Beil. 12, pp 22, 23; Voit, in: Musielak/Voit (eds), s 1041 para 12; critically Thümmel, DZWIR 1997, 133, 137.

[172] OLG Jena, BB 2000, Beil. 12, pp 22, 23; Lachmann, paras 2924 *et seq.*; Thümmel, DZWIR 1997, 133, 137.

time it was issued[173]—a finding that will often be difficult to make in view of the arbitral tribunal's broad discretion under s 1041 para 1 ZPO (para 5.76).[174] The claim for damages moreover requires that the party against whom the claim is asserted has obtained the measure's **enforcement**. Enforcement is more than leave of enforcement under s 1041 para 2 ZPO, it is the actual commencement of this decision's enforcement.[175] Finally, the party seeking damages must have suffered **damages** from the enforcement of such measure or from providing security. It does not suffice for the arbitral tribunal's interim measure to have been complied with voluntarily even if leave of enforcement was given under s 1041 para 2 ZPO. Voluntary compliance suffices only if it was done under pressure of enforcement.[176] It is disputed whether the parties can **waive** the claim for damages in the arbitration agreement.[177]

b) **Enforcement** The claim for damages may be asserted in the pending arbitral proceedings (s 1041 para 4 cl 2 ZPO). The debtor cannot raise the objection under s 1040 para 2 ZPO even if the claim is not encompassed by the arbitration clause.[178] The creditor, on the other hand, can also bring the claim before the state court ("may").[179] While some recommend the latter course of action,[180] no general guidance is available for this tactic. As is often the case in arbitration and particularly in the context of interim proceedings, the choice can be made only under consideration of the details of an individual case. **5.114**

D. Relation Between Interim Relief Before the State Court and the Arbitral Tribunal

The availability of interim measures of protection issued by the state court (s 1033 ZPO, paras 5.3 *et seq.*) and by the arbitral tribunal (s 1041 ZPO, paras 5.64 *et seq.*) raises two questions in particular: pursuant to which guidelines shall the choice of proper forum be made (paras 5.116 *et seq.*)? And how do arbitral tribunals and state courts interact where both are simultaneously approached for interim measures (paras 5.121 *et seq.*)? **5.115**

[173] Cf BGH NJW 1988, 3268, 3269 (on s 945 ZPO).
[174] Münch, in: MünchKommZPO, s 1041 para 52.
[175] Münch, in: MünchKommZPO, s 1041 para 51; Voit, in: Musielak/Voit (eds), s 1041 para 14.
[176] BGHZ 120, 261, 270 = NJW 1993, 593, 595 (on s 945 ZPO); Münch, in: MünchKommZPO, s 1041 paras 50 *et seq.*
[177] Pro: Risse/Frohloff, SchiedsVZ 2011, 239, 241; con: Münch, in: MünchKommZPO, s 1041 para 49 (differently para 10); Voit, in: Musielak/Voit (eds), s 1041 para 14.
[178] Leitzen, p 219; Münch, in: MünchKommZPO, s 1041 para 58; Voit, in: Musielak/Voit (eds), s 1041 para 13.
[179] Dissenting Schütze, BB 1998, 1650, 1653 (exclusive jurisdiction of the arbitral tribunal).
[180] Risse/Frohloff, SchiedsVZ 2011, 239, 247; Voit, in: Musielak/Voit (eds), s 1041 para 13.

I. Freedom of Choice for Interim Relief

1. Forum Selection by Party Agreement

5.116 The applicant's freedom of choice exists only to the extent that the parties have not restricted this choice. The tribunal's jurisdiction to issue interim measures is explicitly non-mandatory (para 5.66) and the state court's competence can be excluded at least to the extent that effective legal protection is otherwise guaranteed (paras 5.11 *et seq.*). If at all, a forum selection for interim measures is agreed in the arbitration agreement—later agreements are unlikely, especially in case of urgency.[181]

5.117 Agreements restricting the choice of forum for interim measures typically aim at strengthening the arbitral tribunal's competence. Valid motivations for such agreements can be an extended confidentiality of the proceedings or a greater independence from the imponderables of national civil procedural law, especially for international parties. Article 28 para 2 cl 1 ICC Rules restricts access to the state courts after transmission of the file to the tribunal to "appropriate circumstances" for these reasons. If the parties wish to increase the effectiveness of any arbitral interim measures of protection, they can provide for a sanction of any violation of such measures by way of a contractual penalty (para 5.92). In view of the unpredictability of potential future developments that may call for interim measures of protection for either party, the parties will often be well advised not to narrow the freedom of forum selection already in the arbitration agreement.

2. Forum Selection by the Applicant

5.118 To the extent that the applicant can choose whether to approach the arbitral tribunal or the state court for interim measures, the more frequent recommendation is to apply to the state court.[182] The effectiveness of legal protection favors this approach: the arbitral tribunal's availability and thus power commences only with its constitution and even already constituted tribunals will often not act with the speed of some German state courts, which may decide urgent applications within hours. Above all, arbitral interim measures depend on a leave of enforcement from the state court, so that directly approaching the state court for an interim measure will often be the faster route.

5.119 There are, however, also good grounds for requesting interim measures from the arbitral tribunal on a case-by-case basis. Not every interim measure needs to be enforced and not every party will frivolously violate an interim order of a tribunal that will later decide the main claim. For an arbitral interim measure the same grounds may argue as for the overall arbitration (paras 1.48 *et seq.*): the arbitrator's substantive

---

[181] Kreindler/Schäfer/Wolff, para 911.

[182] Lachmann, para 2933; Schlosser, in: Stein/Jonas (eds), s 1041 paras 3 *et seq.*; Schroth, SchiedsVZ 2003, 102, 104; Voit, in: Musielak/Voit (eds), s 1041 para 3.

or technical appreciation of the complexities of the dispute, the parties' trust in the tribunal, the potential confidentiality of the proceedings, and the procedural flexibility.[183] The decision finally depends on the particularities of the individual case.

From a strategic perspective, filing requests for interim relief with the state court and with the arbitral tribunal simultaneously (paras 5.121 *et seq.*) or consecutively should also be taken into consideration. Since any application under s 1033 ZPO blocks the remit of a court to enforce an arbitral interim measure (s 1041 para 2 cl 1 ZPO), a party making the most of its options may consider filing the application with the arbitral tribunal before, in case of failure, the application is filed with the state court. This avenue, however, is more time-consuming than directly approaching the state court (para 5.118). **5.120**

II. Parallel Requests for Interim Relief

A party may file parallel requests for interim relief with both the arbitral tribunal and the state court. It is understood that contradictory decisions on such parallel requests should be avoided.[184] Some propose that the state court, when approached with a request under s 1033 ZPO, should carefully examine whether to assume that a legitimate ground for taking legal action exists even in the event that a parallel request has been filed with the arbitral tribunal.[185] Others assume that once a state court has been approached, the application to the arbitral tribunal is to be dismissed due to a lack of legitimate grounds for taking legal action (*Rechtsschutzbedürfnis*).[186] **5.121**

The solution, however, is to be found in the sole provision that governs the interaction between s 1033 ZPO and s 1041 ZPO: s 1041 para 2 cl 1 ZPO gives preference to an application under s 1033 ZPO over an enforcement application under s 1041 para 2 ZPO (para 5.98). In light of this legislative decision, the state court when approached under s 1033 ZPO can give no preference to arbitral interim measures.[187] Section 1041 para 2 cl 1 ZPO efficiently avoids contradictory enforceable interim measures. The parallel existence of a non-enforceable tribunal-issued interim measure (s 1041 para 1 ZPO) and a court-ordered interim measure (s 1033 ZPO) is not prejudicial. **5.122**

---

[183] Kreindler/Schäfer/Wolff, para 910; Schlosser, in: Stein/Jonas (eds), s 1041 para 3 (flexibility).

[184] Cf Government bill, BT-Drucks 13/5274, p 45.

[185] Steinbrück, p 442.

[186] Lachmann, para 2865; Reichold, in: Thomas/Putzo (eds), s 1041 paras 2, 3.

[187] Münch, in: MünchKommZPO, s 1041 para 41; Schroth, SchiedsVZ 2003, 102, 105; Voit, in: Musielak/Voit (eds), s 1033 para 5; Rojahn, in: *Festschrift Meibom*, pp 395, 401.

6

THE ARBITRAL AWARD

Reinmar Wolff

A. Overview

Arbitration is characterized by, on the one hand, largely flexible arbitral proceedings (Chapter 4) and, on the other hand, an outcome, the award, that not only is tantamount to a state court judgment (paras 6.108 *et seq.*), but also is equipped with restricted remedies (paras 6.145 *et seq.* and 6.156 *et seq.*) and facilitated means of enforcement both domestically (paras 6.246 *et seq.*) and internationally (paras 6.287 *et seq.*). Before the making of an award is discussed (paras 6.86 *et seq.*), the different ways to resolve the dispute—by decision of the arbitral tribunal and by settlement of the parties (paras 6.2 *et seq.*)—and the rules which the arbitral tribunal applies when deciding on the merits and on costs (paras 6.46 *et seq.*) are described. In some cases, the arbitral proceedings end with a termination order instead of an award (paras 6.128 *et seq.*). **6.1**

B. Procedures of Dispute Resolution

The standard procedure for the resolution of the dispute that the parties have brought before the arbitral tribunal is the tribunal's decision on that dispute **6.2** (paras 6.3 *et seq.*) by way of an arbitral award. Alternatively, the parties may amicably settle the case (paras 6.19 *et seq.*) and relieve the tribunal of the duty to render a decision on the dispute. In conformity with German court tradition, arbitral tribunals in Germany often encourage the parties to consider making a settlement. To facilitate enforcement of the terms of any such settlement, it may be recorded by the arbitral tribunal in the form of an award on agreed terms.

I. Resolution by Decision of the Arbitral Tribunal

6.3 If the arbitral tribunal is to decide the dispute, it will typically follow a two-step procedure, consisting of deliberations (paras 6.4 *et seq.*) followed by voting (paras 6.16 *et seq.*).

1. Deliberation

6.4 The tribunal's deliberation is at the heart of the decision-making process. While the structure and conduct of any deliberation are not legally prescribed (paras 6.5 *et seq.*), the process is protected by the secrecy of deliberations (paras 6.8 *et seq.*) and restrictions on the participants (paras 6.13 *et seq.*).

6.5 **a) Form and Style** The **style of deliberations** may vary considerably without being limited to specific forms. The arbitrators may deliberate in a physical meeting, by telephone conference, by correspondence, by exchange of emails, etc.[1] The exchange of views and arguments is as little standardized as the design and effectiveness of the deliberations. If the arbitrators disagree on these questions of style, it will be for the chairman to decide.[2] In practice, however, the style of deliberations often depends more on the personalities of the arbitrators (including the chairman) than on the formal right to determine the style of deliberations. This is one of the core reasons why a careful selection of arbitrators can hardly be emphasized sufficiently (cf paras 3.56 *et seq.*). As a matter of law, the parties may agree on stipulations regarding the tribunal's deliberations.[3] Again, owing to the dominant influence of the arbitrators' respective personalities, such party agreements would be of limited effect and are rare in practice.

6.6 It is **best practice** to conduct the deliberations promptly after the oral hearing of witnesses has concluded and the arbitrators' recollection is still fresh.[4] Often the chairman will lead and structure the deliberations but ask the co-arbitrators for their views before voicing his or her own opinion. Occasionally, arbitrators adopt the court practice of circulating a full assessment of the case (*Votum*), sometimes

---

[1] Münch, in: MünchKommZPO, s 1052 para 2; Nedden/Büstgens, SchiedsVZ 2015, 169, 173 *et seq.*; Voit, in: Musielak/Voit (eds), s 1052 para 1.

[2] Dissenting (entire tribunal) Geimer, in: Zöller (ed), s 1052 para 2; Lachmann, para 1680; Münch, in: MünchKommZPO, s 1052 para 2; Voit, in: Musielak/Voit (eds), s 1052 para 1.

[3] Voit, in: Musielak/Voit (eds), s 1052 para 1.

[4] Concurring Nedden/Büstgens, SchiedsVZ 2015, 169, 174.

even in the form of a draft award.[5] While the arbitrators may base their deliberations on such full-fledged draft, its unannounced circulation may also be perceived as inappropriate, in particular if it is issued by a co-arbitrator.

The prevailing view restricts the scope of deliberations to the **outcome of the case** and assumes that the legal reasoning need not be deliberated.[6] Since, however, at least the majority of the arbitrators must sign the award and will likely refuse to do so if not comfortable with its reasoning, the deliberations will invariably extend to the reasoning leading to the agreed outcome of the case. In addition, differences of opinion that may exist between and among the arbitrators will often relate not to the outcome of the case only but rather also to the underlying reasoning. **6.7**

b) Secrecy of Deliberations

aa) Relevance and Protective Function The arbitrators are under an **obligation of secrecy** regarding the content and course of the deliberations.[7] This duty is usually rooted in the arbitrator contract even if not expressly stipulated there.[8] Similar to the conflict disclosure obligation (paras 3.128 *et seq.*), it should also be understood as a duty that is directly attached to the arbitrator's office and that exists regardless of the validity of the arbitrator contract.[9] **6.8**

The secrecy of deliberations does not only protect the arbitrators (whose conduct and position during the deliberations shall not be disclosed), but also the **integrity of the arbitral process** as such.[10] Since arbitration is deemed to be a dispute resolution mechanism equivalent to state court proceedings, it must be ensured that the arbitrators decide according to their best knowledge. This again requires an open discussion of the case, including an equally open exchange of pros and cons and frank addressing of the respective strengths and weaknesses. Such an open atmosphere could be seriously endangered if the arbitrators had to take into consideration that the parties or other third persons would become privy to the content of the deliberations. **6.9**

bb) Waivability and Constraints Since the secrecy of the deliberations also aims to protect the integrity of the proceedings, it is not within the parties' or the arbitrators' power to **abandon** such secrecy.[11] It is therefore somewhat incongruous that the prevailing view allows for the parties to agree that the deliberations be held in their presence (para 6.15). **6.10**

---

5 See Nedden/Büstgens, SchiedsVZ 2015, 169, 174.

6 KG OLGRspr. 27 (1913), 196, 198; Münch, in: MünchKommZPO, s 1052 para 2.

7 BGHZ 23, 138, 140 = NJW 1957, 592; Bartels, SchiedsVZ 2014, 133, 134; Münch, in MünchKommZPO, s 1052 para 3; Schwab/Walter, ch 19 para 5.

8 BGHZ 98, 32, 35 = NJW 1986, 3077, 3078.

9 Prütting, in: *Festschrift Schwab*, pp 409, 413 *et seq.*; Voit, in: Musielak/Voit (eds), s 1035 para 24.

10 BGHZ 23, 138, 141 = NJW 1957, 592; Prütting, in: *Festschrift Böckstiegel*, pp 629, 632 *et seq.*

11 Prütting, in: *Festschrift Schwab*, pp 409, 419; dissenting Lachmann, para 1695; Münch, in: MünchKommZPO, s 1052 para 5; Nedden/Büstgens, SchiedsVZ 2015, 169, 173; Schwab/Walter, ch 19 para 5.

6.11 The secrecy of deliberations is **constrained** by law, in particular by s 1052 para 2 ZPO (para 6.18). It is further acknowledged that the secrecy of deliberations does not bar an arbitrator from informing the parties of evident bias on the part of another arbitrator.[12] Although such bias will often become apparent only in the deliberations, the secrecy of the deliberations cannot yield to any ground for challenge (s 1036 para 2 ZPO, paras 3.112 *et seq.*) or even any ground that is to be disclosed under s 1036 para 1 ZPO (paras 3.116 *et seq.*) even if the respective party is thereby deprived of its right to challenge. In light of its significance for the arbitral procedure as such (para 6.9), the secrecy of deliberations may allow at best for the disclosure of such grounds for challenge that would also qualify as grounds for setting aside the award (cf para 6.215). Any further allowance would serve to demote the arbitrators to agents of a party's procedural remedies.

6.12 *cc) Consequences* An obvious consequence of the arbitrator's duty to keep deliberations confidential is his or her **right to refuse to give evidence** in court proceedings.[13] At the same time, a breach of the confidentiality obligation is not a criminal offence under s 203 StGB inasmuch as this provision does not address arbitrators. It is a matter of dispute whether it is impermissible in light of the arbitrator's secrecy obligation to issue a **dissenting opinion** (paras 6.102 *et seq.*).[14] The more elegant solution may in any event be to make clear within the award that certain issues are the result of a majority decision.[15]

6.13 c) **Presence of Third Persons** Third persons may attend the deliberations if all arbitrators agree and the third persons do not influence the outcome of the case.[16] Uncontroversial examples of such attendance include secretaries (performing administrative tasks like taking notes)[17] and trainees.[18] Tribunal-appointed experts or **advisers** must not attend deliberations since such attendance would run the risk of influencing the outcome of the case.[19] Nevertheless, the prevailing view is more generous and allows for the attendance of advisers if the tribunal leaves neither the factual nor the legal assessment of the case to the adviser[20] or at least

---

[12] Münch, in: MünchKommZPO, s 1052 para 7; Voit, in: Musielak/Voit (eds), s 1052 para 3.

[13] BGHZ 23, 138, 141 = NJW 1957, 592 *et seq.*; Geimer, in: Zöller (ed), s 1052 para 5; Hartmann, in: Baumbach/Lauterbach/Albers/Hartmann (eds), s 1052 para 5; Münch, in: MünchKommZPO, s 1052 para 4; Schwab/Walter, ch 19 para 5; Voit, in: Musielak/Voit (eds), s 1052 para 3.

[14] Pro: Münch, in: MünchKommZPO, s 1052 para 3; con: Bartels, SchiedsVZ 2014, 133; Lionnet/Lionnet, pp 395 *et seq.*; Wagner, in: Weigand (ed), 1st edn, Part 4: Germany, para 331.

[15] Dissenting Bartels, SchiedsVZ 2014, 133, 135 *et seq.* (emphasizing the advantages of dissenting opinions).

[16] BGH ZZP 71 (1958), 427, 435; Schwab/Walter, ch 19 para 3; Voit, in: Musielak/Voit (eds), s 1052 para 2.

[17] KG JW 1928, 735, 736; OLG Düsseldorf, BB 1976, 251; Münch, in: MünchKommZPO, s 1052 para 5.

[18] Münch, in: MünchKommZPO, s 1052 para 5.

[19] Nedden/Büstgens, SchiedsVZ 2015, 169, 177; Voit, in: Musielak/Voit (eds), s 1052 para 2; see also Münch, in: MünchKommZPO, s 1052 para 5.

[20] BGH ZZP 71 (1958), 427, 435; Geimer, in: Zöller (ed), s 1049 para 3; Münch, in: MünchKommZPO, s 1052 para 6; Schwab/Walter, ch 19 para 3.

if the tribunal maintains a critical stance and does not merely adopt the adviser's decision.[21] This view, however, deprives the parties of their right to be heard.[22] If the tribunal seeks to include third-party advice, it may appoint its own expert and question the expert in the oral hearing. The parties' right to comment on the expert's views cannot be circumvented by making the expert the tribunal's private adviser.

To what extent **(administrative) secretaries** may be involved in the decision-making process has been subject to a lively discussion during the last few years. Internationally, a number of institutional[23] and best practice guidelines[24] have been released on this topic. German law will take no offence as long as the secretary's duties are limited to purely administrative tasks like organizing the files, arranging hearing logistics, typing the award etc.[25] Conversely, it is clear that a secretary must not act as a fourth arbitrator:[26] the parties have mandated the arbitrators in person to decide the dispute and the arbitrators cannot delegate this task to a secretary.[27] The exact borderline, however, is difficult to determine. The prevailing view allows for the secretary to draft the award based on the tribunal's decision of the dispute.[28] In international arbitrations, the secretary is even deemed to be permitted to submit a draft award which only in a second step is subject to the tribunal's deliberation.[29] Such procedure, however, entails the risk that the tribunal abdicates its duties by merely rubber-stamping the secretary's draft without forming an own opinion. It is in any event not best practice for a responsible tribunal to transfer its core duties to a secretary in such way. **6.14**

The prevailing view allows for the attendance of the **parties** during the deliberations if all arbitrators and parties agree.[30] However, since the secrecy of deliberations also protects the integrity of the arbitral process (para 6.9), the better arguments suggest that the parties' attendance constitutes a ground for setting aside the award under s 1059 para 2 no 1 lit d ZPO, and in actual best practice attendance of the parties in the deliberations is essentially unheard of, and rightly so. **6.15**

---

[21] Schlosser, in: Stein/Jonas (eds), s 1042 para 2.

[22] Voit, in: Musielak/Voit (eds), s 1052 para 2.

[23] Eg the ICC Note on the Appointment, Duties and Remuneration of Administrative Secretaries of August 1, 2012.

[24] Eg the Young ICCA Guide on Arbitral Secretaries of 2014.

[25] Cf Münch, in: MünchKommZPO, s 1052 para 5; Stürner, SchiedsVZ 2013, 322, 327.

[26] Term tracing back to Partasides, "The Fourth Arbitrator? The Role of Secretaries to Tribunals in International Arbitration," (2002) 18(2) Arb. Int'l 147.

[27] Münch, in: MünchKommZPO, s 1052 para 6.

[28] OLG Düsseldorf, BB 1976, 251; Kreindler/Schäfer/Wolff, para 1092; Voit, in: Musielak/Voit (eds), s 1054 para 5; more generous Stürner, SchiedsVZ 2013, 322, 327.

[29] Münch, in: MünchKommZPO, s 1052 para 5; Raeschke-Kessler/Berger, para 955; see generally Menz, SchiedsVZ 2015, 210 *et seq.*

[30] Nedden/Büstgens, SchiedsVZ 2015, 169, 176; Schlosser, in: Stein/Jonas (eds), s 1042 para 37; Schwab/Walter, ch 19 para 2; dissenting Voit, in: Musielak/Voit (eds), s 1052 para 1.

2. Voting (s 1052 ZPO)

6.16 If the arbitral tribunal consists of a sole arbitrator, the arbitrator simply applies the law to the facts (para 6.47). With more than one arbitrator, the **specific procedure** needed for making the decision is enshrined in s 1052 ZPO. This provision adopts art 29 Model Law and adds rules on the refusal of an arbitrator to participate in the voting (para 6.18).

6.17 If the parties have not agreed on a **voting procedure**, the content and order of voting proposals is to be determined by the chairman.[31] In practice, the voting is often not a formalized act, but rather an iterative process in the course of the deliberations. Each arbitrator has one vote and the decision is taken by the **absolute majority** of votes.[32] In case of a tie, ie if the arbitrators cannot reach a decision, the arbitration agreement becomes incapable of being performed (s 1032 para 1 ZPO)[33] and the arbitral tribunal issues a termination order under s 1056 para 2 no 3 ZPO.[34] The parties can agree that in case of a tie the chairman's vote shall be decisive[35] or that another procedure shall apply.

6.18 As the arbitrators are appointed to decide the dispute, each arbitrator is under a **duty to vote**; to abstain from voting violates this duty.[36] If an arbitrator abstains from voting, the other arbitrators can take the **decision without the abstaining arbitrator** (s 1052 para 2 cl 1 ZPO). Even in that case, any decision is to be taken with the absolute majority of all members of the arbitral tribunal (para 6.17).[37] The remaining arbitrators must give the parties **advance notice** of their intention to make the award without the abstaining arbitrator (s 1052 para 2 cl 2 ZPO). Therewith, the parties shall be given an opportunity to exert influence on the refusing arbitrator,[38] eg by reminding him or her to adhere to his or her duties and threatening to jointly remove him or her from office as arbitrator (cf para 3.172). If no such notice is given or if it is given at too short notice as to allow for influencing the arbitrator, the award is subject to setting aside under s 1059 para 2 no 1 lit d ZPO.[39]

II. Resolution by Settlement (s 1053 ZPO)

6.19 Since the parties are the masters of the arbitral proceedings, they can at any time end their dispute including by agreeing on a settlement (paras 6.20 *et seq.*). While

[31] Voit, in: Musielak/Voit (eds), s 1052 para 5.
[32] Government bill, BT-Drucks 13/5274, p 53.
[33] Münch, in: MünchKommZPO, s 1052 para 9; Voit, in: Musielak/Voit (eds), s 1052 para 9.
[34] Government bill, BT-Drucks 13/5274, p 53; Schwab/Walter, ch 8 para 14; dissenting Prütting, in: Prütting/Gehrlein (eds), s 1052 para 3 (dismissal of claim).
[35] Government bill, BT-Drucks 13/5274, p 54.
[36] Münch, in: MünchKommZPO, s 1052 para 8; Voit, in: Musielak/Voit (eds), s 1052 para 6.
[37] Government bill, BT-Drucks 13/5274, p 54; Geimer, in: Zöller (ed), s 1052 para 6.
[38] Government bill, BT-Drucks 13/5274, p 54.
[39] OLG Saarbrücken, SchiedsVZ 2003, 92, 93.

a settlement puts an end to the dispute, it is not an executory title. The parties can, however, request the arbitral tribunal to transform the settlement into an award on agreed terms, which allows for enforcement of the terms of the settlement in the same way as any contested arbitral award (paras 6.34 *et seq.*). With these stipulations, s 1053 ZPO implements art 30 Model Law, the sole modification being that the tribunal is in principle not at liberty to decline to issue an award on agreed terms (para 6.37). German law also attributes advanced effects to an award on agreed terms (s 1053 paras 3 and 4 ZPO, paras 6.43 *et seq.*).

1. Settlement (s 1053 para 1 cl 1 ZPO)

a) Conclusion of a Settlement Section 1053 para 1 cl 1 ZPO merely requires that the parties (para 6.22) settle (para 6.21) the dispute (paras 6.23 *et seq.*) during the arbitral proceedings (para 6.25). **6.20**

aa) Settlement A settlement in any event requires a contractual agreement under the law chosen by the parties or otherwise applicable under conflict of law rules.[40] Beyond this basic prerequisite, it is disputed whether a settlement always requires mutual concessions as demanded under German substantive law (s 779 para 1 cl 1 BGB)[41] or whether one party's concession suffices.[42] The prevailing view apparently is in favor of such requirement. The better view, however, speaks for making a distinction between the procedural requirements for a settlement (as defined in s 1053 ZPO) and the substantive requirements under the law governing the settlement (eg s 779 BGB).[43] While s 779 BGB may indeed invalidate settlements to the extent that it applies (para 6.28), there is little reason why the "settlement" under s 1053 para 1 cl 1 ZPO (and, subsequently, the award on agreed terms) should be available only if the parties compromise.[44] The wording of s 1053 ZPO is flexible enough to accommodate the practical need to extend the provision to acknowledging claims, and the drafting history of art 30 Model Law, the provision's blueprint, provides no support for such restriction either.[45] **6.21**

bb) Settlement Between the Parties The settlement must be concluded between the parties, ie the parties to the arbitral proceedings, not necessarily the parties to the arbitration agreement.[46] As long as at least two parties to the arbitral **6.22**

40 Cf Voit, in: Musielak/Voit (eds), s 1053 para 4.
41 OLG München, GmbHR 2005, 1568, 1570; Münch, in: MünchKommZPO, s 1053 para 9; Schwab/Walter, ch 23 para 7; Spohnheimer, in: *Festschrift Kaissis*, pp 933, 935 *et seq.*
42 Bredow, SchiedsVZ 2010, 295, 297; v Schlabrendorff/Sessler, in: *Arbitration in Germany*, s 1053 para 9; Schlosser, in: Stein/Jonas (eds), s 1053 para 8; Schroeter, SchiedsVZ 2006, 298, 302 *et seq.*
43 See Voit, in: Musielak/Voit (eds), s 1053 para 4.
44 v Schlabrendorff/Sessler, in: *Arbitration in Germany*, s 1053 para 9.
45 Bredow, SchiedsVZ 2010, 295, 297; Holtzmann/Neuhaus, pp 822 *et seq.*; v Schlabrendorff/Sessler, in: *Arbitration in Germany*, s 1053 para 9.
46 Münch, in: MünchKommZPO, s 1053 para 11.

proceedings are parties to the settlement, additional third parties can also join the settlement.[47] Not all parties to the arbitral proceedings need to be involved in the settlement;[48] the arbitral proceedings can, however, be terminated only with regard to the parties to the settlement.

6.23 *cc) Settlement of the Dispute* The parties need to settle **the dispute**. Similar to the involvement of the parties (para 6.22), the settlement needs to encompass at least partially the matter in dispute[49] but may also go beyond it.[50] The arbitral tribunal can terminate the proceedings only to the extent that the matter in dispute is settled.[51] A full settlement of "the dispute" which allows for a termination of the proceedings consists of a substantive law solution plus the procedural law agreement that the arbitral proceedings shall be terminated.[52] Without the latter, the tribunal cannot terminate the proceedings as stipulated by s 1053 para 1 cl 1 ZPO (cf s 1056 para 2 no 2 ZPO).[53]

6.24 The "dispute" to be settled also comprises the allocation of **costs**. If the parties fail to agree on an allocation of costs, the tribunal must render an (adversarial) arbitral award on costs under the standard of s 1057 ZPO (paras 6.48 *et seq*.). Section 98 ZPO, according to which in case of a settlement before the state courts the costs shall be deemed to have been cancelled against each other absent any agreement of the parties to the contrary, applies neither directly nor by way of analogy.[54] However, this cost allocation may be reached by way of interpretation of the settlement or as a standard for inspiration of the arbitral tribunal when allocating the costs under s 1057 ZPO.

6.25 *dd) Settlement During the Arbitral Proceedings* Section 1053 ZPO furthermore requires the settlement to be reached during arbitral proceedings, ie after the commencement of the proceedings (s 1044 ZPO).[55] Some authors extend the scope of the provision to pre-arbitral settlements, arguing with the practical need for transforming a settlement reached within a mediation or elsewhere into an arbitral award.[56] However, the constitution of an arbitral tribunal (and the remuneration

---

[47] v Schlabrendorff/Sessler, in: *Arbitration in Germany*, s 1053 para 11; Voit, in: Musielak/Voit (eds), s 1053 para 5.

[48] v Schlabrendorff/Sessler, in: *Arbitration in Germany*, s 1053 para 11.

[49] Mankowski, ZZP 114 (2001), 37, 62 *et seq*.; Münch, in: MünchKommZPO, s 1053 para 16; v Schlabrendorff/Sessler, in: *Arbitration in Germany*, s 1053 para 14.

[50] Münch, in: MünchKommZPO, s 1053 para 17; Voit, in: Musielak/Voit (eds), s 1053 para 4.

[51] Münch, in: MünchKommZPO, s 1053 paras 16, 37; v Schlabrendorff/Sessler, in: *Arbitration in Germany*, s 1053 para 14.

[52] Cf v Schlabrendorff/Sessler, in: *Arbitration in Germany*, s 1053 para 16.

[53] Cf v Schlabrendorff/Sessler, in: *Arbitration in Germany*, s 1053 para 7.

[54] Dissenting Münch, in: MünchKommZPO, s 1053 para 43; v Schlabrendorff/Sessler, in: *Arbitration in Germany*, s 1053 para 18.

[55] Münch, in: MünchKommZPO, s 1053 para 13; v Schlabrendorff/Sessler, in: *Arbitration in Germany*, s 1053 paras 13, 25 *et seq*.; F Schmidt, SchiedsVZ 2013, 32, 34.

[56] Voit, in: Musielak/Voit (eds), s 1053 para 3; dissenting F Schmidt, SchiedsVZ 2013, 32, 34.

of its members) will usually not be a viable option for the parties, whether in terms of time or cost, in particular since s 796a ZPO allows for the enforcement of settlements reached between attorneys. Absent a relevant practical need, the scope of s 1053 para 1 cl 1 ZPO should not be extended to pre-arbitral agreements. Section 1053 ZPO applies to settlements reached outside and within the arbitral proceedings, be it with or without the assistance of the arbitral tribunal.[57] Such assistance can often be observed in domestic arbitrations seated in Germany since it is a distinct feature of German civil procedural law to actively encourage the parties to settle the case (para 1.28). In particular in international proceedings, however, the arbitral tribunal must carefully avoid giving rise to grounds for a later challenge (para 3.125).

b) **Validity of the Settlement** Only a valid settlement has legal effects. The **6.26**
validity of the settlement is to be assessed under the **law** chosen by the parties or otherwise applicable to it under choice of law rules[58] with the exception of form requirements if the settlement is transformed into an award on agreed terms (paras 6.43 *et seq.*).[59] Some authors contend that the parties' freedom to choose the law applicable to the settlement is even extended as under s 1051 ZPO (cf paras 2.183 *et seq.*).[60] At first sight, it is indeed plausible that s 1051 ZPO could be extended by way of analogy from the substantive law governing the merits of the case to the substantive law governing the settlement of the case. While, however, the arbitral tribunal's decision on the merits is not subject to further review in setting aside proceedings (para 6.187), the validity of the settlement can be reviewed under s 1059 para 2 no 1 lit d ZPO (para 6.32). Extending the scope of s 1051 ZPO would therefore make sense only if the state court were bound by s 1051 ZPO (which is not the case). Section 1051 ZPO applies directly to the parties' choice of law if any dispute about the validity of the settlement is submitted to an arbitral tribunal.

No valid settlement can be concluded if the law thus determined does not **6.27**
entitle the parties to conclude such a settlement even if the matter in dispute is nonetheless arbitrable (cf s 1030 para 1 cl 1 ZPO, paras 2.49 *et seq.*).[61] Neither can the requirements under the applicable contract law be ignored nor can the mere fact that arbitral proceedings are pending between the parties extend the parties' ability to settle a dispute.[62]

[57] Münch, in: MünchKommZPO, s 1053 para 4.
[58] Voit, in: Musielak/Voit (eds), s 1053 para 4.
[59] Münch, in: MünchKommZPO, s 1053 para 9.
[60] Voit, in: Musielak/Voit (eds), s 1053 para 4.
[61] Bilda, DB 2004, 171, 175; Mankowski, ZZP 114 (2001), 37, 61 *et seq.*; v Schlabrendorff/Sessler, in: *Arbitration in Germany*, s 1053 para 28; see also Voit, in: Musielak/Voit (eds), s 1053 para 1.
[62] Cf Voit, in: Musielak/Voit (eds), s 1053 para 1.

6.28 If German substantive law governs the settlement, **s 779 BGB** contains **specific grounds for invalidity**. The provision requires that the dispute be resolved by way of mutual concession; minor concession is considered sufficient, including on the allocation of costs.[63] If the fact situation (or the realization of a claim) that the parties had considered as definite turns out not to comport with reality and if the dispute would not have arisen had the facts been known, then the settlement is invalid under s 779 BGB.

6.29 Settlements before German courts are often concluded with the reservation of a **right to revoke** within a defined time frame. Such reservation is usually to be interpreted as a condition precedent to the validity of the settlement.[64] Only once the time frame has lapsed without revocation does the settlement become valid and can it serve as the basis for an award on agreed terms.[65]

6.30 **c) Legal Effects** While the settlement reshapes the substantive legal situation, it does not directly terminate the arbitral proceedings. Rather, the arbitral tribunal will terminate the proceedings (s 1053 para 1 cl 1 ZPO) in a separate procedural step, be it by making an award on agreed terms under ss 1053, 1054 ZPO (paras 6.34 *et seq.*) or, if the procedural prerequisites for an award on agreed terms are not met, by issuing a termination order under s 1056 para 2 no 2 ZPO (para 6.135). Such termination order requires that the parties have agreed on the termination of the proceedings, which will usually be part of the settlement. Even if the settlement is silent on the termination of the proceedings, such agreement can usually be derived by way of (supplementary) interpretation. If exceptionally the parties have made clear that they did not agree on the termination of the proceedings and no other termination ground under s 1056 para 2 ZPO exists, the arbitral tribunal must decide the dispute by way of an (adversarial) award based on the substantive legal situation as it has been reshaped by the settlement.[66]

6.31 **d) Effects of Invalid Settlements** The arbitral tribunal must examine the validity of the settlement **before taking further procedural steps.**[67] If it turns out to be invalid, the arbitral tribunal cannot terminate the arbitral proceedings. Until the arbitral tribunal has terminated the arbitral proceedings, the parties can urge the invalidity of the settlement before the arbitral tribunal.

---

63 BGHZ 39, 60, 63 = NJW 1963, 637; Münch, in: MünchKommZPO, s 1053 para 9.

64 BGHZ 88, 364, 366 *et seq.* = NJW 1984, 312; R Fischer, in: BeckOK BGB, s 779 para 89.

65 Bredow, SchiedsVZ 2010, 295, 297; Geimer, in: Zöller (ed), s 1053 para 3; Münch, in: MünchKommZPO, s 1053 para 23; v Schlabrendorff/Sessler, in: *Arbitration in Germany*, s 1053 para 35; Schwab/Walter, ch 23 para 13; Voit, in: Musielak/Voit (eds), s 1053 para 10; dissenting Mankowski, ZZP 114 (2001), 37, 70.

66 Cf Busse, SchiedsVZ 2010, 57, 59 *et seq.*; Gerstenmaier, SchiedsVZ 2010, 281, 284; v Schlabrendorff/Sessler, in: *Arbitration in Germany*, s 1053 para 16.

67 Münch, in: MünchKommZPO, s 1053 para 24; Voit, in: Musielak/Voit (eds), s 1053 para 10; Waßmuth, pp 53 *et seq.*

6.32 If the arbitral tribunal has issued an **award on agreed terms** (paras 6.34 *et seq.*), the invalidity of the settlement can be asserted only as a ground for setting aside the award. Beyond this (time-limited) remedy, the award is protected by its *res judicata* effect.[68] The setting aside application can be based on the irregularity of the procedure (s 1059 para 2 no 1 lit d ZPO).[69] A lack of jurisdiction (s 1059 para 2 no 1 lit c ZPO) can be invoked if the tribunal has ruled on the validity of the settlement principally and the arbitration agreement does not encompass this subject matter. Jurisdiction is not at issue, however, if the validity of the settlement has been tested only as a preliminary question.[70] If in their arbitration agreement the parties have empowered the arbitral tribunal to decide on the validity of the settlement, then an award principally doing so has binding effect in setting aside proceedings (s 1055 ZPO).[71]

6.33 If the arbitral tribunal has issued a **termination order** under s 1056 para 2 no 2 ZPO (para 6.135), this order serves to terminate the arbitral proceedings (s 1056 para 1 ZPO), including the office of the arbitrators (s 1056 para 3 ZPO), regardless of the validity of the settlement.[72] If an incorrect termination does not render the arbitration agreement incapable of being performed under s 1032 para 1 ZPO (para 2.158), the arbitration agreement remains in force in its original scope.[73] The legal situation is similar to the arbitration agreement surviving the setting aside of an arbitral award rendered on this basis (s 1059 para 5 ZPO).[74] Whether the invalidity of the settlement must be claimed before an arbitral tribunal or a state court depends on whether the arbitration agreement also encompasses the validity of the settlement.[75] The original dispute can in any event be brought before a (newly constituted) arbitral tribunal, which will examine the validity of the settlement as a preliminary question.

2. *Award on Agreed Terms*

6.34 Elevating the party settlement to an award on agreed terms pursues mainly one aim, namely facilitating enforcement. If a party does not comply with a settlement voluntarily, it must be enforced before the competent state court or arbitral tribunal before it can actually be executed against the debtor. An award on agreed terms has the same effect as any other award (s 1053 para 2 cl 2 ZPO) and can be enforced similarly, including abroad under the New York Convention (para 6.302). International enforcement was decisive for the legislature's decision to replace the former "arbitral settlement," a discrete executory title that was not

[68] Münch, in: MünchKommZPO, s 1053 para 40.
[69] Voit, in: Musielak/Voit (eds), s 1053 para 15.
[70] Cf Voit, in: Musielak/Voit (eds), s 1053 para 17.
[71] Voit, in: Musielak/Voit (eds), s 1053 para 17.
[72] Cf Voit, in: Musielak/Voit (eds), s 1056 para 1.
[73] Voit, in: Musielak/Voit (eds), s 1053 para 16.
[74] Cf Voit, in: Musielak/Voit (eds), s 1053 para 16 (analogous application of s 1059 para 5 ZPO).
[75] Voit, in: Musielak/Voit (eds), s 1053 para 16.

recognized internationally, by the award on agreed terms.[76] It is generally advisable for the parties to request an award on agreed terms and appropriate for the arbitral tribunal to suggest such requests.

6.35 **a) Procedure for Issuing an Award on Agreed Terms (s 1053 para 1 cl 2 ZPO)** The award on agreed terms is issued by the arbitral tribunal upon a request by the parties (paras 6.36 *et seq.*). If the tribunal considers that the settlement is valid (paras 6.31 *et seq.*)[77] and complies with German public policy (para 6.38), the arbitral tribunal issues the award on agreed terms without further scrutiny.

6.36 *aa) Request by the Parties* An award on agreed terms can be issued only if both **parties** so request, although not necessarily jointly.[78] The request will often already be included in the settlement.[79] All parties to the settlement need to request that the (full) settlement be recorded as an award on agreed terms.[80] If only some of these parties file the request, then the award on agreed terms must be limited to the requesting parties. Once filed, the request cannot be withdrawn unilaterally.[81]

6.37 An award on agreed terms can be issued only between at least two parties to the arbitration. While **third parties** can readily become party to the settlement agreement (para 6.22), they cannot be included in an award unless they have previously acceded to the arbitration agreement and become party to the arbitration.[82] The third party's joinder and its accession to the arbitration agreement is impliedly contained in the request to render an award on agreed terms.[83] Each request to issue an award on agreed terms similarly includes the submission to the jurisdiction of the arbitral tribunal of any additional **matter** not encompassed by the arbitration agreement.[84]

---

[76] Government bill, BT-Drucks 13/5274, p 54.

[77] v Schlabrendorff/Sessler, in: *Arbitration in Germany*, s 1053 para 30.

[78] Mankowski, ZZP 114 (2001), 37, 70 *et seq.*; Münch, in: MünchKommZPO, s 1053 para 20; v Schlabrendorff/Sessler, in: *Arbitration in Germany*, s 1053 para 32; Voit, in: Musielak/Voit (eds), s 1053 para 8.

[79] Cf Bredow, SchiedsVZ 2010, 295, 296.

[80] Geimer, in: Zöller (ed), s 1053 para 2; v Schlabrendorff/Sessler, in: *Arbitration in Germany*, s 1053 para 34; Voit, in: Musielak/Voit (eds), s 1053 para 8.

[81] Mankowski, ZZP 114 (2001), 37, 73 *et seq.*; Schütze, in: *Festschrift Lorenz*, pp 275, 277; Voit, in: Musielak/Voit (eds), s 1053 para 8; dissenting Münch, in: MünchKommZPO, s 1053 para 20 with further references.

[82] Bilda, DB 2004, 171, 172; Lachmann, para 1809; Münch, in: MünchKommZPO, s 1053 para 12; v Schlabrendorff/Sessler, in: *Arbitration in Germany*, s 1053 para 24; requiring only submission to the arbitration agreement: Voit, in: Musielak/Voit (eds), s 1053 para 5.

[83] Cf Bredow, SchiedsVZ 2010, 295, 296; Schwab/Walter, ch 23 para 8; see also Schlosser, in: Stein/Jonas (eds), s 1053 para 17.

[84] Mankowski, ZZP 114 (2001), 37, 62 *et seq.*; Münch, in: MünchKommZPO, s 1053 para 17; v Schlabrendorff/Sessler, in: *Arbitration in Germany*, s 1053 para 27; Schlosser, in: Stein/Jonas (eds), s 1053 para 4; Voit, in: Musielak/Voit (eds), s 1053 para 4.

bb) No Public Policy Violation Under art 30 para 1 Model Law, the settlement is recorded as an arbitral award if not objected to by the arbitral tribunal. The German legislature found this requirement too broad and too unspecific.[85] It was thus replaced by the requirement that the contents are not in violation of public policy (s 1053 para 1 cl 2 ZPO). The standard for (domestic) public policy is the same as under s 1059 para 2 no 2 lit b ZPO (paras 6.225 *et seq.*).[86] **6.38**

b) Form and Content of an Award on Agreed Terms (s 1053 para 2 cl 1 ZPO) Form and content of the award on agreed terms follow the **same general rules** that govern form and content of any other award (s 1053 para 2 cl 1 ZPO). It is in particular to be signed by the arbitrators (s 1054 para 1 ZPO). Additional signatures by the parties do not invalidate the award on agreed terms but may question the arbitral tribunal's intention to issue an award.[87] **6.39**

Two exceptions to the rule exist: first, the award on agreed terms must **state that it is an award** (s 1053 para 2 cl 1 ZPO). This serves to avoid confusion with a protocol taken by the arbitral tribunal.[88] Second, the award on agreed terms does not need to give **reasons** upon which it is based (s 1054 para 2 ZPO) and in fact cannot, since the tribunal did not make the decision but merely transformed the parties' decision. For this reason, it is advisable to state in the award that it is an award on agreed terms although such declaration is not legally required.[89] **6.40**

c) Effects of an Award on Agreed Terms

aa) Same Effect as any Other Award (s 1053 para 2 cl 2 ZPO) The award on agreed terms has the same effect as any other award on the merits of the case (s 1053 para 2 cl 2 ZPO), ie the same effect as a **final and binding court judgment** (s 1055 ZPO, paras 6.108 *et seq.*). Like any other award, the award on agreed terms can be **enforced** in Germany after it has been declared enforceable (s 1060 ZPO).[90] For recognition and enforceability abroad, the award on agreed terms constitutes an award under the New York Convention as under most other enforcement regimes.[91] **6.41**

Like any other award, the award on agreed terms is subject to **setting aside proceedings** under s 1059 ZPO.[92] The content of the award, however, is not the result **6.42**

---

[85] Government bill, BT-Drucks 13/5274, p 55; critical Münch, in: MünchKommZPO, s 1053 para 25.

[86] v Schlabrendorff/Sessler, in: *Arbitration in Germany*, s 1053 para 36; Voit, in: Musielak/Voit (eds), s 1053 para 10; Waßmuth, p 38; see also Government bill, BT-Drucks 13/5274, p 55; dissenting Bilda, DB 2004, 171, 174 *et seq.*; Mankowski, ZZP 114 (2001), 37, 44 *et seq.*

[87] v Schlabrendorff/Sessler, in: *Arbitration in Germany*, s 1053 para 22; stricter Münch, in: MünchKommZPO, s 1053 para 31 (parties must not sign).

[88] See OLG München, NZBau 2007, 311; Voit, in: Musielak/Voit (eds), s 1053 para 9: no enforcement of a simple protocol.

[89] Geimer, in: Zöller (ed), s 1053 para 6; v Schlabrendorff/Sessler, in: *Arbitration in Germany*, s 1053 para 21; Voit, in: Musielak/Voit (eds), s 1053 para 9.

[90] Münch, in: MünchKommZPO, s 1053 para 38.

[91] Government bill, BT-Drucks 13/5274, p 54.

[92] Münch, in: MünchKommZPO, s 1053 para 38; Spohnheimer, in: *Festschrift Kaissis*, pp 933, 940.

of legal proceedings before the arbitral tribunal, but rather traces back directly to the parties. Procedural deficiencies during the arbitral proceedings before the settlement, including the constitution of the arbitral tribunal, will therefore usually not affect the award.[93] The arbitral tribunal likewise cannot interpret the award on agreed terms (s 1058 para 1 no 2 ZPO), since it did not make (but rather only issue) the decision.[94]

6.43 *bb) Substitution of Form Requirements (s 1053 para 3 ZPO)* If a settlement in state court proceedings is recorded in the court record, this recording **substitutes for notarial certification** (s 127a BGB) which German substantive law requires for a number of contracts, including on the transfer of real estate (s 311b para 1 BGB) and of shares in a limited liability company (s 15 para 4 GmbHG). Section 1053 para 3 ZPO extends this effect to awards on agreed terms.[95] However, the prevailing view—in light of s 1055 ZPO: unconvincingly—requires the award on agreed terms to be declared enforceable (s 1060 ZPO) before the land registry (*Grundbuchamt*) registers a transfer of title (para 6.256).

6.44 Section 1053 para 3 ZPO does not apply to **sham awards on agreed terms.** Such "awards" stem from arbitral proceedings which were initiated for the sole purpose of saving notarization costs.[96] While case law has thus far been called upon to address only clear-cut cases, the borderline between "real" and "sham" arbitrations will often be somewhat blurred.

6.45 **d) Declaration of Enforceability (s 1053 para 4 ZPO)** Since an award on agreed terms is tantamount to an adversarial award (s 1053 para 2 cl 2 ZPO, paras 6.41 *et seq.*), it can be declared enforceable by the higher regional court like any other award (s 1060 ZPO). Moreover, in light of the consensual content of the award on agreed terms,[97] the parties can agree to have the award on agreed terms declared enforceable by a public notary. The notary's declaration as enforceable serves as an executory title[98] for which lower fees are due than for proceedings for a declaration of enforceability before the higher regional courts.[99] As opposed to the state court which performs a full review of the award on agreed terms pursuant to all six grounds under s 1060 para 2 cl 1, s 1059 para 2 ZPO, the notary's review is restricted to violations of public policy (s 1053 para 4 cl 2, para 1 cl 2 ZPO). The notary's declaration of enforceability in turn does

---

[93] Münch, in: MünchKommZPO, s 1053 para 40.
[94] Lachmann, para 1829; Münch, in: MünchKommZPO, s 1053 para 47.
[95] Government bill, BT-Drucks 13/5274, p 55.
[96] OLG München, GmbHR 2005, 1568, 1570; Voit, in: Musielak/Voit (eds), s 1053 para 13.
[97] Government bill, BT-Drucks 13/5274, p 55.
[98] Voit, in: Musielak/Voit (eds), s 1053 para 14; dissenting Münch, in: MünchKommZPO, s 1053 paras 53 *et seq.*
[99] Münch, in: MünchKommZPO, s 1053 para 52; v Schlabrendorff/Sessler, in: *Arbitration in Germany*, s 1053 para 41; Voit, in: Musielak/Voit (eds), s 1053 para 14.

not preclude grounds for setting aside the award; s 1059 para 3 cl 4 ZPO does not apply.[100]

C. Rules Applicable to the Arbitral Tribunal's Decision on the Merits and on Costs

If the arbitral tribunal is to decide the dispute, it will first determine its jurisdiction over the dispute. To the extent that the arbitral tribunal lacks jurisdiction (paras 2.3 *et seq.*), it cannot decide on the merits and will dismiss the claim. Only if the arbitral tribunal finds that it has jurisdiction will it decide the dispute under the applicable rules (para 6.47) and render an award on the merits, either granting or dismissing the claim. If the parties settle the case, the arbitral tribunal's decisions are replaced by the parties' agreement; the arbitral tribunal's tasks are then significantly reduced (paras 6.19 *et seq.*). **6.46**

I. Decision on Substance (s 1051 ZPO)

The arbitral tribunal will decide the dispute on the merits by applying the rules of law that the parties have chosen (s 1051 para 1 cl 1 ZPO). By submitting to arbitration, the parties broaden their freedom to choose the applicable law as compared to dispute resolution before German state courts. This includes the right to agree on rules of law other than national laws (s 1051 para 1 cl 1 ZPO), the right to agree on an *ex aequo et bono* decision under s 1051 para 3 ZPO, and the extended freedom from substantive law limits. If the parties have not elected a substantive law, the arbitral tribunal applies the law of the state with which the subject matter of the proceedings is most closely connected (s 1051 para 2 ZPO). For details on the legal rules which the arbitral tribunal shall apply to the merits of the dispute, see paras 2.183 *et seq.* **6.47**

II. Decision on Costs (s 1057 ZPO)

1. *General Overview*

While it may at first sight seem uneventful, the decision on costs often belongs to the more challenging tasks of an arbitral tribunal. Remarkably, a provision addressing the decision on costs is one of the few additions that the German legislature made to the Model Law, inasmuch as costs are of importance at the termination of **6.48**

[100] Münch, in: MünchKommZPO, s 1053 para 52; Schlosser, in: Stein/Jonas (eds), s 1053 para 32; v Schlabrendorff/Sessler, in: *Arbitration in Germany*, s 1053 para 42; Voit, in: Musielak/Voit (eds), s 1053 para 14; dissenting Hartmann, in: Baumbach/Lauterbach/Albers/Hartmann (eds), s 1053 para 10.

any arbitral proceedings and the parties frequently do not enter into cost-related stipulations.[101]

6.49 a) **Procedure on Costs in State Court Proceedings** Since the particularities of cost procedures in German arbitration are easier to understand when contrasted with the cost procedures in German state court arbitration, a **short overview** over the former will be given as background information.

6.50 In German state court proceedings, two cost decisions are to be taken: the first one **allocates the costs** between the parties and is taken by the court as part of the judgment. Although the court allocates the costs *sua sponte* (s 308 para 2 ZPO), parties usually request a cost decision in their favor. Pursuant to the general rule of s 91 para 1 cl 1 ZPO, the party that has not prevailed in the dispute is to bear the costs of the legal dispute. This general rule is supplemented by rules for specific procedural settings including costs for unsuccessful appellate remedies (s 97 ZPO), costs for withdrawn claims (s 269 para 3 cl 2 and 3 ZPO), and costs incurred as a result of default by a party (s 344 ZPO). The decision on cost allocation rendered by the court does not determine any amounts, but rather indicates which party has to bear the costs fully or in which portion.

6.51 The **amounts** to be borne by a party are determined in a second step. The party that is entitled under the court's cost allocation decision must apply to the court registrar (*Rechtspfleger*) and request fixing of the amounts due based on the court's cost allocation (ss 103 *et seq.* ZPO). The registrar will fix only such costs as the party is entitled to receive under s 91 ZPO, in particular costs that were necessitated to appropriately bring or defend against the court action. Lawyer's fees are to be refunded only up to the amounts of the statutory lawyer's fees (s 91 para 2 cl 1 ZPO, see also para 3.178). Lawyer's fees as well as court fees depend on the amount in dispute, which is to be determined by court order.

6.52 b) **Procedure on Costs in Arbitral Proceedings** The provision on costs in arbitral proceedings, s 1057 ZPO, takes up on the distinction between allocation of costs and fixing the amount of costs. For both steps, however, the **arbitral tribunal is in charge** since arbitral tribunals do not have registrars for fixing the costs and the state court registrars are not competent to determine costs based on arbitral awards.[102]

6.53 In the first step, the arbitral tribunal will **allocate** the costs between the parties to the arbitration. Unlike a German state court, the arbitral tribunal enjoys broad discretion as to the criteria for cost allocation (paras 6.60 *et seq.*).

[101] Government bill, BT-Drucks 13/5274, p 57.

[102] BGHZ 193, 38, 42 para 9 = SchiedsVZ 2012, 154, 155; 2014, 31, 33 para 10; Government bill, BT-Drucks 13/5274, p 57; Münch, in: MünchKommZPO, s 1057 para 4.

The second step again consists of **fixing the amount of costs** to be awarded. The arbitral tribunal can indeed issue a separate cost award for this purpose. If it does so, it can restrict the main award to the allocation of costs and then collect the relevant figures only after the main award has been issued. The procedurally more efficient and more often chosen route, however, is to request the parties' cost submissions towards the end of the proceedings.[103] This route, which is mandatory in ICC proceedings (art 37 para 4 ICC Rules), allows the arbitral tribunal to render one final award which already includes the complete cost decision. Regardless of which route the arbitral tribunal chooses, it has equally broad discretion to determine the amount of costs to be borne by each party (para 6.68). **6.54**

c) **Jurisdiction of the Arbitral Tribunal** The arbitral tribunal has jurisdiction to decide on costs **unless the parties have excluded** this jurisdiction fully or in part. This follows from the explicit wording of s 1057 para 1 cl 1 ZPO, which is referenced by the provision's second paragraph ("also"). While it is rare in practice for parties to exclude the tribunal's jurisdiction to allocate costs, certain institutional rules such as the ICC Rules entrust the institution with fixing at least some kinds of costs, in particular the arbitrator's fees and expenses. To the extent that the arbitral tribunal has jurisdiction to rule on costs, it will decide ***sua sponte***, ie even if the parties have not requested a cost decision.[104] **6.55**

A specific issue arises in the event the **arbitral tribunal declines its jurisdiction** due to the lack of a valid arbitration agreement encompassing the dispute. In that case, the parties have not validly empowered the arbitral tribunal to issue binding decisions on them. This would generally also include decisions on costs;[105] under that approach, the parties would need to bring claims for cost recovery under substantive law before the state courts.[106] The prevailing view under German law, however, assumes a residual jurisdiction stemming from the (invalid or otherwise insufficient) arbitration agreement.[107] **6.56**

d) **Relevant Relationship for Cost Decisions** It is important to identify which exact relationship is encompassed by the arbitral tribunal's cost decision.[108] The arbitration agreement as the source of the arbitral tribunal's jurisdiction empowers it to make rulings only with effect **between the parties** to the arbitration (s 1055 ZPO). Therefore, the sole contents of the cost decision are how the costs **6.57**

[103] v Schlabrendorff/Sessler, in: *Arbitration in Germany*, s 1057 para 39.

[104] Münch, in: MünchKommZPO, s 1057 para 3; Schlosser, in: Stein/Jonas (eds), s 1057 para 1.

[105] Reichold, in: Thomas/Putzo (eds), s 1057 para 9; Voit, in: Musielak/Voit (eds), s 1057 para 2.

[106] Voit, in: Musielak/Voit (eds), s 1057 para 2.

[107] BGHZ 151, 79, 84 = SchiedsVZ 2003, 39, 40; Lachmann, para 1879; Münch, in: MünchKommZPO, s 1057 para 24; Reichold, in: Thomas/Putzo (eds), s 1057 para 9; v Schlabrendorff/Sessler, in: *Arbitration in Germany*, s 1057 para 36; Schlosser, in: Stein/Jonas (eds), s 1057 para 4; Schwab/Walter, ch 33 para 4.

[108] Explicitly KG SchiedsVZ 2011, 110, 111.

are allocated between the parties and which amount shall be borne by each party, again only with regard to the other party.

6.58 It follows from the cost decision's confinement to the relationship between the parties that the cost decision cannot and does not govern the relationship between the parties and **third persons** including the arbitrators, the arbitral institution, the parties' lawyers, experts, witnesses, translators, court reporters, and others.[109]

6.59 If the cost decision, for example, fixes a certain amount as an **arbitrator's fees**, it only obliges one party vis-à-vis the other either to pay its share of the arbitrator's fees to the arbitrator or to refund such payments as were already made by the other party.[110] Such cost decision does not have any legal effect on the relationship between the parties and the arbitrator.[111] Neither does it entitle the arbitrator vis-à-vis the parties nor provide for an executory title for the arbitrator's fee claim.[112] It does not even fix the amount due to the arbitrator with binding effect for the arbitrator (para 6.72). Any dispute arising between the parties and the arbitrator regarding his or her fees must be settled before the competent state court (unless the arbitrator agreement exceptionally provides for an arbitration agreement itself).[113] In these proceedings, the state court is not bound by the cost decision contained in the arbitral award.

2. Allocation of Costs

6.60 a) **Standard for Allocation** The arbitral tribunal allocates the costs of the arbitration as between the parties (s 1057 para 1 cl 1 ZPO). It enjoys **broad discretion** as to the standard under which the allocation shall be made (s 1057 para 1 cl 2 ZPO). The law does not provide for a specific standard under which the allocation is to be made, but instead merely stipulates that the circumstances of the case, in particular the outcome of the proceedings, shall be taken into consideration. This solution provides for the necessary flexibility.[114] At the same time, it expresses the expectation that the principle of **"cost follows the event,"** with its statutory modifications as defined in ss 91 *et seq.* ZPO, will in most cases be followed.[115] German arbitration practice indeed puts specific weight on this

---

109 Kreindler/Schäfer/Wolff, para 1207; Münch, in: MünchKommZPO, s 1057 para 12; v Schlabrendorff/Sessler, in: *Arbitration in Germany*, s 1057 para 41; Schlosser, in: Stein/Jonas (eds), s 1057 para 1; Schwab/Walter, ch 33 para 2; Voit, in: Musielak/Voit (eds), s 1057 para 5; Wolff, SchiedsVZ 2006, 131, 133 *et seq.*

110 Münch, in: MünchKommZPO, s 1057 para 8.

111 KG SchiedsVZ 2011, 110, 111.

112 Münch, in: MünchKommZPO, s 1057 para 8.

113 BGHZ 193, 38, 41 para 7 = SchiedsVZ 2012, 154, 155; KG SchiedsVZ 2011, 110, 111; Voit, in: Musielak/Voit (eds), s 1057 para 5.

114 Government bill, BT-Drucks 13/5274, p 57.

115 Government bill, BT-Drucks 13/5274, p 57.

principle, in particular in domestic cases.[116] Arbitral tribunals seated in Germany likewise often apply the cost rules for specific procedural settings in state court proceedings (para 6.50) by way of analogy.[117]

6.61 It is less common but still within the arbitral tribunal's discretion to apply a **totally different standard** for the allocation of costs,[118] including the so-called American Rule whereby each party bears its own costs regardless of the outcome of the case.[119]

6.62 More often, arbitral tribunals seated in Germany will modify the "cost follows the event" rule rather than fully replace it.[120] **Criteria for such modifications** include the legal and factual decisiveness of the decision[121] and in particular the conduct of the parties during the arbitral proceedings (cf art 37 para 5 ICC Rules).[122] Although some tribunals are still reluctant to impose cost sanctions for dilatory or even so-called guerrilla tactics, it is recommended[123] and has proven effective to use the allocation of costs to encourage efficient conduct of the proceedings. In doing so, the arbitral tribunal can take into account failure or delay to pay advances on costs, abusive requests for or responses to requests for evidence, excessive submissions or exhibits, excessive document requests, or failure to comply with procedural orders.[124]

6.63 The arbitral tribunal's discretion is limited by **party agreements** on a cost allocation standard.[125] The parties can in particular bind the arbitral tribunal to apply the cost allocation rules for state court proceedings (ss 91 *et seq.* ZPO).[126] Such party agreements are not rare in domestic proceedings. They have the advantage that from the outset the parties can better assess the cost risks associated with an arbitration.[127] However, the price paid for such foreseeability is the lack of flexibility when it comes to finding a suitable cost allocation for a specific case.

6.64 **b) Form of Decision and Remedies** The arbitral tribunal decides on the cost allocation by means of an arbitral award (s 1057 para 1 cl 1 ZPO), be it a final

116 Kreindler/Schäfer/Wolff, para 1193; Kühn/Gantenberg, in: DIS-Mat. X, pp 83, 89; Münch, in: MünchKommZPO, s 1057 para 14; v Schlabrendorff/Sessler, in: *Arbitration in Germany*, s 1057 para 33; see also BGHZ 193, 38, 42 para 9 = SchiedsVZ 2012, 154, 155.

117 Cf KG SchiedsVZ 2011, 110, 111 (s 269 ZPO).

118 OLG Karlsruhe, SchiedsVZ 2012, 101, 106 = XXXVIII Y.B. Com. Arb. 379, 383 (2013); Kühn/Gantenberg, in: DIS-Mat. X, pp 83, 88; Münch, in: MünchKommZPO, s 1057 para 12; Schlosser, in: Stein/Jonas (eds), s 1057 para 6; Schwab/Walter, ch 33 para 1.

119 See Born, p 3090.

120 See Kreindler/Schäfer/Wolff, para 1195.

121 Kreindler/Schäfer/Wolff, para 1195; Schlosser, in: Stein/Jonas (eds), s 1057 para 8.

122 v Schlabrendorff/Sessler, in: *Arbitration in Germany*, s 1057 para 34.

123 See eg the ICC Commission Report Techniques for Controlling Time and Costs in Arbitration, 2nd edn, 2012, para 82.

124 ICC Commission Report Techniques for Controlling Time and Costs in Arbitration, 2nd edn, 2012, para 82; Kreindler/Schäfer/Wolff, para 1195.

125 Voit, in: Musielak/Voit (eds), s 1057 para 3.

126 Government bill, BT-Drucks 13/5274, p 57.

127 Kreindler/Schäfer/Wolff, paras 1203 *et seq.*

award or a separate cost award (cf s 1057 para 2 cl 2 ZPO). A cost award must fully comply with the formal requirements of s 1054 ZPO (paras 6.91 *et seq.*) and is subject to setting aside and declarations of enforceability.[128]

6.65 The main award and the cost decision are closely connected. If the **cost decision is set aside** (with or without the main arbitral award) and the case is not remitted to the arbitral tribunal under s 1059 para 4 ZPO (para 6.244), the parties can rely only on a substantive law cost recovery claim which they must bring either before the arbitral tribunal or the state court (s 1059 para 5 ZPO, para 6.243).[129]

6.66 If **only the main award is set aside**, the prevailing view assumes that the cost decision shares this fate, regardless of whether the main award is set aside fully or in part and of whether the cost decision was rendered as a separate cost award.[130] In fact, main award and cost decision are interrelated. An award can therefore be set aside in part only if the defective part is separable from the remaining award. The main decision and cost decision are also not separable irrespective of whether the cost decision is part of the main award or has been issued as a separate cost award. An application for setting aside must therefore refer to both the main award and the cost decision (in the same award or in a separate cost award). By way of interpretation, an application to set aside a main award is to be extended to encompass its cost decision including in a separate cost award. If, however, only the main award has been set aside, the prevailing view may be supported by the parallel legal situation before German state courts, in which the order fixing the costs becomes baseless once the cost allocation decision is quashed or amended.[131]

3. Amount of Costs

6.67 **a) Fixed Costs** The decision on which amounts are to be borne by each party can be made only for such amounts as are "fixed." Costs are fixed if the arbitral tribunal knows the amount in which they were incurred.[132] The arbitral tribunal cannot itself fix the amount in which costs were incurred since this would be beyond its jurisdiction (paras 6.57 *et seq.*). It needs to await cost submissions from the parties (para 6.54) if the costs are not its own or otherwise already known.

6.68 **b) Standard for Decision on the Amount to be Borne** The arbitral tribunal has **broad discretion** to determine in which amount costs are to be borne by a

[128] Voit, in: Musielak/Voit (eds), s 1057 para 4.

[129] BGH NJW-RR 1998, 234, 235; Münch, in: MünchKommZPO, s 1057 para 28; Schlosser, in: Stein/Jonas (eds), s 1057 para 24; Schwab/Walter, ch 33 para 12; Voit, in: Musielak/Voit (eds), s 1057 para 4.

[130] BGHZ 179, 304, 314 para 37 = SchiedsVZ 2009, 176, 179; OLG München, SchiedsVZ 2012, 156, 158 (even a declaration of enforceability would lose its effect [p 159]) = XXXIX Y.B. Com. Arb. 389, 391 (2014); OLG Stuttgart, NJW-RR 2003, 1438, 1439; Münch, in: MünchKommZPO, s 1057 para 28; Reichold, in: Thomas/Putzo (eds), s 1057 para 8; v Schlabrendorff/Sessler, in: *Arbitration in Germany*, s 1057 para 42; Schlosser, in: Stein/Jonas (eds), s 1057 para 24.

[131] BGH NJW-RR 2007, 784 para 3; Lackmann, in: Musielak/Voit (eds), s 104 para 40.

[132] Wolff, SchiedsVZ 2006, 131, 138 *et seq.*

party. The law does not restrict this discretion—with one exception: the costs incurred by the parties are compensable only to the extent that they were necessary for the proper pursuit of their claim or defense (s 1057 para 1 cl 1 ZPO). Costs incurred by the parties include costs for legal representation and expenses of the parties (paras 6.79 *et seq.*). As the case may be, costs for taking evidence (paras 6.77 *et seq.*) may also be incurred by the parties. The determination of which party costs are necessary in a given case is again in the hands of the arbitral tribunal. As a general rule, costs which are refundable under the (rather strict) rules for state court proceedings will not be unnecessary in arbitral proceedings.[133] The arbitral tribunal is at liberty to acknowledge higher costs, in particular for legal representation (para 6.80). Costs which are not incurred by a party and the reimbursement of which is not limited by necessity include arbitrators' fees and expenses (paras 6.71 *et seq.*), fees of the arbitral institution (para 6.74), and court fees (paras 6.75 *et seq.*).

The arbitral tribunal's discretion also allows it to take into account the broader **6.69** picture, in particular to **compare the amounts** spent by the parties overall and for specific cost items such as lawyer's fees or experts. If both parties have spent high amounts, the arbitral tribunal may more easily regard these costs as compensable than in the case that one party has limited its expenses to a more reasonable amount.[134] Conversely, there may be valid reasons why one side has spent significantly more money on the pursuit of its case than the other, eg where there are multiple parties on one side, necessary translations, or one side had significantly more work in making its case for reasons of sustaining its burden of proof.

The rules on compensable costs are subject to **deviating party agreements**. The **6.70** parties can tie the arbitral tribunal's decision to the statutory rules for state court proceedings (even though this will often not be advisable), can—either directly or, more commonly, by reference to institutional rules (eg the ICC Note on Personal and Arbitral Tribunal Expenses or the DIS Guidelines for the Reimbursement of Arbitrators Expenses)—define a standard at least for some types of costs like travel and accommodation costs, or can include or exclude specific cost items from refund.[135] The parties can even agree to exclude refunding of costs entirely.[136] Finally, in particular institutional rules commonly bind the arbitral tribunal to an amount determined as refundable at least for some cost items, for example the fees and expenses of the arbitrators and the ICC administrative expenses under art 37 para 1 ICC Rules.

---

133 For potential exceptions, see Münch, in: MünchKommZPO, s 1057 para 21; v Schlabrendorff/Sessler, in: *Arbitration in Germany*, s 1057 para 19.

134 Kreindler/Schäfer/Wolff, para 1244.

135 Kühn/Gantenberg, in: DIS-Mat. X, pp 83, 88; Münch, in: MünchKommZPO, s 1057 para 1.

136 Münch, in: MünchKommZPO, s 1057 para 13; Voit, in: Musielak/Voit (eds), s 1057 para 6.

c) Individual Types of Costs

6.71 *aa) Arbitrators' Fees and Expenses* The amount of the arbitrators' fees results from the **fee arrangement** in the arbitrator contract (para 3.177). Besides some other fee schemes, the most common calculation methods for arbitrators' fees depend on the amount in dispute which, in turn, is to be determined by the arbitral tribunal. Institutional rules like the ICC Rules or the DIS Rules also follow this approach.

6.72 Since the cost decision does not go beyond the relationship between the parties (paras 6.57 *et seq.*), the **amount of the arbitrators' fee claim** remains unaffected by their cost decision.[137] The arbitral tribunal's determination of the amount in dispute serves as a specification of the performance under the arbitrator contract by one of the parties to that contract.[138] Such specification is to be made at the reasonably exercised discretion of the arbitral tribunal (s 315 para 1 BGB).[139] If the determination is not equitable, the parties to the arbitration can apply to the state courts to revise the specification (s 315 para 3 BGB).[140] The cost decision in the award is binding (only) between the parties to the arbitration (s 1055 ZPO). Each party can, however, have a cost decision in an award set aside under s 1059 para 2 no 1 lit d ZPO if it is based on a non-equitable amount in dispute.[141] Such non-equitable determination is not binding on the parties to the arbitration (s 315 para 3 cl 1 BGB) so that the amount of the arbitrators' fees is not yet fixed as required by s 1057 para 2 cl 1 ZPO.

6.73 The Federal Supreme Court's earlier case law had mistakenly invoked the notion that **nobody shall judge on one's own behalf** and that an arbitral tribunal that determines the amount in dispute and includes its fees calculated on that basis in the cost decision in its award violates public policy.[142] According to the court, the only exception was if the arbitrators' fees thus established were fully covered by advances on costs already.[143] While it is true that the arbitral tribunal would indeed violate public policy if it ruled on its own fee claim in its arbitral award,[144] it in fact does not do so (para 6.72). In a landmark decision of 2012, the Federal Supreme Court has rightfully given up this restriction.[145]

137 Cf BGHZ 193, 38, 43 para 10 = SchiedsVZ 2012, 154, 155 *et seq.*; Government bill, BT-Drucks 13/5274, p 58 ("decision has not the quality of an award"); Wolff, SchiedsVZ 2006, 131, 134.

138 Wolff, SchiedsVZ 2006, 131, 136.

139 Voit, in: Musielak/Voit (eds), s 1057 para 5; Wolff, SchiedsVZ 2006, 131, 136.

140 BGHZ 193, 38, 43 para 10 = SchiedsVZ 2012, 154, 156; Wolff, SchiedsVZ 2006, 131, 137.

141 Voit, in: Musielak/Voit (eds), s 1057 para 5; Wolff, SchiedsVZ 2006, 131, 140; dissenting Münch, in: MünchKommZPO, s 1057 para 9 fn 18.

142 BGH WM 1977, 319, 320; similar OLG Hamburg, MDR 1965, 54, 55.

143 BGH WM 1977, 319, 320 *et seq.*; similar OLG Dresden, SchiedsVZ 2004, 44; OLG Hamburg, MDR 1965, 54, 55; Government bill, BT-Drucks 13/5274, p 58.

144 See BGHZ 193, 38, 40 *et seq.* para 6 = SchiedsVZ 2012, 154, 155; Wolff, SchiedsVZ 2006, 131, 133.

145 BGHZ 193, 38 = SchiedsVZ 2012, 154; for foreign arbitral awards OLG München, SchiedsVZ 2012, 287, 288.

bb) Fees of the Arbitral Institution Arbitral institutions charge fees for their services, in particular for administering the case under the institution's rules. The fee schedules of the institutions usually determine the fees as a certain fraction of the amount in dispute. These fees form part of the reimbursable costs.[146] **6.74**

cc) Court Fees Court fees form part of the costs of the arbitration if the court's cost decision did not result from contentious proceedings that on the merits resolved a dispute.[147] This is in particular the case if the court proceedings merely supported the arbitral proceedings, as it is particularly evident for judicial assistance proceedings under s 1050 ZPO (paras 4.200 *et seq.*): it cannot make a difference whether for example the taking of evidence was accomplished in arbitral proceedings or instead outsourced to a state court.[148] Fees for a court decision under s 1032 para 2 ZPO, on the other hand, result from a self-contained dispute in which both parties take opposing positions.[149] No need exists to correct the cost allocation of these contentious proceedings by adding their costs to the costs of the arbitration. The fees for a court appointment of an arbitrator under s 1035 paras 3 or 4 ZPO will be costs of the arbitration at least if the appointment was not due to a party's failure: if the party-appointed arbitrators cannot agree on a chairman, his or her appointment by the court does not resolve a dispute between the parties. Moreover, it is random which party files the court application and thus "wins" the court appointment procedure. **6.75**

Costs stemming from **court proceedings in a matter that is encompassed by the arbitration agreement** are not costs of the arbitration and can therefore not be included in the cost decision under s 1057 ZPO even if the court, like US courts under the American Rule, does not order reimbursement of costs.[150] Bringing such claim may, however, be a violation of the arbitration agreement and give rise to a substantive law claim for damages. Such a claim for damages needs to be brought in the arbitration as a main claim, not only in the cost submission. **6.76**

dd) Costs for Taking Evidence The costs for taking evidence belong to the costs of the arbitration, which may be incurred by the parties or may pertain to the general costs of the arbitration. If they belong to the **general costs of the arbitration**, the costs for taking of evidence are fully recoverable subject to the arbitral tribunal's cost decision (para 6.68). These costs include any costs that were triggered by the **6.77**

[146] Elsing, in: DIS-Mat. X, pp 3, 5; Münch, in: MünchKommZPO, s 1057 para 9; v Schlabrendorff/Sessler, in: *Arbitration in Germany*, s 1057 para 15.

[147] Cf Schwab/Walter, ch 33 para 18.

[148] Kreindler/Schäfer/Wolff, para 1217; see also Münch, in: MünchKommZPO, s 1057 para 19; v Schlabrendorff/Sessler, in: *Arbitration in Germany*, s 1057 paras 29 *et seq.*

[149] Cf Münch, in: MünchKommZPO, s 1057 para 19; v Schlabrendorff/Sessler, in: *Arbitration in Germany*, s 1057 para 30.

[150] Münch, in: MünchKommZPO, s 1057 para 19; dissenting Geimer, in: Zöller (ed), s 1057 para 8; Sandrock, IDR 2004, 106, 109; v Schlabrendorff/Sessler, in: *Arbitration in Germany*, s 1057 para 31.

arbitral tribunal, eg costs for hearing venues, court reporters, tribunal-appointed experts, reimbursement of witness expenses promised by the arbitral tribunal or the arbitral tribunal's travel expenses for taking evidence.[151] The costs for tribunal-appointed experts form part of the general costs of the arbitration irrespective of whether the expert contract was concluded with members of the arbitral tribunal or with the parties to the arbitration.

6.78 Costs for taking evidence that were **incurred by the parties** are recoverable only to the extent that they were necessary (para 6.68). These costs include the fees and expenses for party-appointed experts (cf s 1049 para 2 cl 2 ZPO) as well as fees and expenses for witnesses. The latter may be promised and paid by a party if their amount stays within reasonable limits and the witness is not contractually committed to a specific testimony.[152]

6.79 *ee) Costs for Legal Representation* As party-incurred expenses, the costs for legal representation can be recovered by the parties only to the extent that they were "necessary for the proper pursuit of their claim or defense" (para 6.68). This phrase is inspired by s 91 para 1 cl 1 ZPO, which applies to state court proceedings and restricts the reimbursable lawyer's fees and expenses to the **statutory fees and expenses** as set out in the German Law on the Remuneration of Attorneys (s 91 para 2 cl 1 ZPO). It is therefore not unusual for arbitral tribunals to adopt this standard for their cost decision and it is indeed common that an arbitral tribunal will align its cost decision with ss 91 *et seq.* ZPO, in particular in domestic or smaller proceedings.[153]

6.80 However, for larger disputes commonly lawyers are engaged on the basis of hourly rates or other **fee arrangements**. Moreover, the German Law on the Remuneration of Attorneys does from the outset not apply to lawyers from foreign jurisdictions who frequently act in international arbitrations. In recognizing these facts, it is accepted that arbitral tribunals do not exceed their discretion when they include lawyer's fees beyond the statutory standard in their cost decision.[154]

6.81 Costs for **inhouse counsel** replacing or complementing external counsel are not refundable in German state court proceedings.[155] Again, the arbitral tribunal's discretion covers both consideration and non-consideration of such costs.[156] An

[151] Kreindler/Schäfer/Wolff, para 1220; Münch, in: MünchKommZPO, s 1057 para 6; v Schlabrendorff/Sessler, in: *Arbitration in Germany*, s 1057 para 6.

[152] Schlosser, RIW 2005, 81, 83.

[153] Lörcher/Lörcher, para 314; even stricter Lachmann, paras 1947 *et seq.* (refundability limited by ss 91 *et seq.* ZPO).

[154] OLG München, SchiedsVZ 2012, 282, 286; Kühn/Gantenberg, in: DIS-Mat. X, pp 83, 90; Risse/Altenkirch, SchiedsVZ 2012, 5, 10; v Schlabrendorff/Sessler, in: *Arbitration in Germany*, s 1057 para 28; Schroth, in: DIS-Mat. X, pp 41, 44.

[155] BGH NJW-RR 2004, 856, 857; Bork, in: Stein/Jonas (eds), s 91 paras 35 *et seq.*

[156] Risse/Altenkirch, SchiedsVZ 2012, 5, 12; dissenting Voit, in: Musielak/Voit (eds), s 1057 para 5.

argument in favor of a deviation from the rules in state court proceedings is that inhouse counsel may well assume parts of the work that otherwise would have to be done by outside counsel. In particular if one party has significantly involved inhouse counsel while the other party has not, the cost decision may otherwise become imbalanced.[157] It may, however, be difficult or undesirable to calculate and disclose the inhouse counsel's salary that is to be allotted to the arbitral proceedings.[158]

The arbitral tribunal may also include the costs for a **party's employees** who are not lawyers, again deviating from the practice of German state courts. Again, well-prepared documents and other facts can significantly reduce the workload (and fees) of outside counsel and thus contribute to cost-efficient proceedings.[159] **6.82**

ff) Other Expenses of the Parties The arbitral tribunal can include other necessary (para 6.68) expenses of the parties in its cost decision, *inter alia* travel and accommodation costs, postal and courier fees, costs for copies and telecommunication.[160] In order not to jeopardize an otherwise good impression that a party may have made on the tribunal, parties and their counsel are well advised to refrain from including excessive costs in their cost submission. **6.83**

gg) Interest on Costs German state courts may award interest on costs based either on a substantive or procedural basis. Substantive law claims may be based on s 291 BGB, which grants interest on payment claims as of their pendency in the amount of five percentage points above base rate. Procedurally, s 104 para 1 cl 2 ZPO allows for interest in the same amount from the filing of a request to that effect or the pronouncement of the judgment, whichever is later. A claim based on s 291 BGB can be awarded by the arbitral tribunal if German substantive law applies (s 1051 ZPO) and the prevailing party has so requested.[161] Whether s 104 para 1 cl 2 ZPO applies by way of analogy under German arbitration law is a matter of dispute.[162] **6.84**

d) Form of Decision and Remedies The arbitral tribunal determines the amount of costs that are to be reimbursed by one party to the other by means of an award, be it in the main award or a subsequent cost award. Procedural efficiency calls for only one award, but if costs can be fixed only later, then a separate cost award is necessary (s 1057 para 2 cl 2 ZPO). The cost award must meet the **6.85**

157 v Schlabrendorff/Sessler, in: *Arbitration in Germany*, s 1057 para 20.

158 Bühler/Jarvin, in: Weigand (ed), 2nd edn, para 15.1142; Kreindler/Schäfer/Wolff, para 1224.

159 Kreindler/Schäfer/Wolff, para 1225; v Schlabrendorff/Sessler, in: *Arbitration in Germany*, s 1057 para 20 fn 40.

160 Kreindler/Schäfer/Wolff, para 1226; Lachmann, paras 1962 *et seq.*; Münch, in: MünchKommZPO, s 1057 para 7.

161 Gerstenmaier, SchiedsVZ 2012, 1, 2 *et seq.*; Voit, in: Musielak/Voit (eds), s 1057 para 5.

162 Pro: Gerstenmaier, SchiedsVZ 2012, 1, 3; con: Lachmann, paras 1907 *et seq.*; Risse/Altenkirch, SchiedsVZ 2012, 5, 14; Voit, in: Musielak/Voit (eds), s 1057 para 5; undecided Saenger/Uphoff, MDR 2014, 192, 196.

formal requirements of s 1054 ZPO and is subject to the same remedies as any other award (para 6.64). For specific issues resulting from the close connection between the main award and the cost decision, see paras 6.65 *et seq.*

D. Making of the Arbitral Award

6.86 The formal requirements for making an award under s 1054 ZPO are manageable, in particular if compared to the strict rules that govern the making of a judgment under German civil procedural rules. With the lowering of the formal requirements, the German legislature intended to meet the practical needs of international arbitration.[163] Not even all of the few formal requirements affect the arbitral award if violated: while some requirements are essential for the notion of an award with its *res judicata* and other effects (para 6.92), the violation of others results in a ground for setting aside only (para 6.99) or does not have any effect on the award (para 6.101).

I. Scope of Applicability: Notion of an Arbitral Award

6.87 The formal rules of s 1054 ZPO apply only to awards, not to other decisions of the arbitral tribunal like procedural orders. While no abstract definition exists for what an arbitral award is, it is understood from its legal effect (s 1055 ZPO, paras 6.112 *et seq.*) that arbitral awards are characterized by an **element of finality.**[164] Arbitral awards therefore include awards on agreed terms (s 1053 para 2 cl 1 ZPO; paras 6.34 *et seq.*), separate cost awards (s 1057 para 2 cl 2 ZPO),[165] partial awards deciding a part of the dispute in a final manner, for instance one of several requests,[166] partial awards ordering reimbursement of the other party's cost advances that have been voluntarily paid,[167] and interim awards containing a final decision for a fixed term (para 5.88). Section 1054 ZPO does not apply to preliminary rulings under s 1040 para 3 ZPO (para 4.102)[168] or to interim measures under s 1041 ZPO (para 5.89). If the arbitral tribunal finds that it does not have jurisdiction, the prevailing view allows the tribunal to decide by means of an arbitral award although the parties did not empower the tribunal (para 6.56).[169]

---

[163] Government bill, BT-Drucks 13/5274, p 55.

[164] Cf BGH NJW-RR 2007, 1008 para 6 = XXXIII Y.B. Com. Arb. 506, 507 (2008).

[165] OLG Köln, SchiedsVZ 2004, 269.

[166] BGH NJW-RR 2007, 1008 para 6 = XXXIII Y.B. Com. Arb. 506, 507 (2008); Geimer, in: Zöller (ed), s 1054 para 3; Schlosser, in: Stein/Jonas (eds), s 1054 para 3; Voit, in: Musielak/Voit (eds), s 1054 para 2.

[167] Buchwitz/Schütt, SchiedsVZ 2015, 1, 6 *et seq.*

[168] Münch, in: MünchKommZPO, s 1054 para 4; Voit, in: Musielak/Voit (eds), s 1054 para 2.

[169] BGHZ 151, 79, 80 = SchiedsVZ 2003, 39 *et seq.*; v Schlabrendorff/Sessler, in: *Arbitration in Germany*, s 1054 para 4; dissenting OLG Hamburg, NJW-RR 2000, 806; Voit, in: Musielak/Voit (eds), s 1054 para 2.

The most difficult area is that of **interlocutory decisions** including interlocutory awards (*Zwischenschiedssprüche*), ie decisions on individual issues in dispute that are preliminary to the parties' requests like jurisdiction and liability.[170] Such interlocutory decisions may have *res judicata* effect under s 1055 ZPO (paras 6.112 *et seq.*) and may be set aside and enforced, they may bind only the arbitral tribunal for the subsequent proceedings or they may not even have such a binding effect. Compliance with s 1054 ZPO is required only in the first case, ie if the award has the effects under s 1055 ZPO.[171] While some authors also apply s 1054 ZPO to interlocutory decisions binding the arbitral tribunal,[172] this view unnecessarily needs to postulate different notions of an award for its form (s 1054 ZPO) and effects (s 1055 ZPO). Interlocutory decisions which do not qualify as awards therefore do not need to comply with s 1054 ZPO (or with other form requirements) regardless of whether they bind the arbitral tribunal.[173] **6.88**

Interlocutory decisions are awards if the parties have empowered the arbitral tribunal to decide the interlocutory question only while the remaining dispute is to be decided by the state courts.[174] This is because in such cases the arbitral tribunal's decision must also be final and binding for the state court. Since the parties can choose another forum for the remaining part of the dispute, they can also agree that the arbitral tribunal may issue an interlocutory award if the arbitral tribunal has jurisdiction to decide the entire dispute.[175] In other cases, the arbitral tribunal cannot issue an interlocutory award.[176] Whether such decision of an interlocutory question is binding for the arbitral tribunal depends on the arbitral tribunal's will as it becomes evident from its decision.[177] If the arbitral tribunal (incorrectly) labels its decision as an (interlocutory) award, this indicates its will to be bound by it.[178] **6.89**

Awards under the **reservation** that the arbitral tribunal is still to decide on a set-off defense (paras 2.134 *et seq.*) are not deemed to be awards under s 1054 ZPO[179] while they are classified as awards if a state court is to decide on such defense.[180] If **6.90**

170 For the notion, see v Schlabrendorff/Sessler, in: *Arbitration in Germany*, s 1055 para 12; for an apparently simple solution (interlocutory decisions are always awards) F Schmidt, SchiedsVZ 2013, 32, 35, 40.

171 Voit, in: Musielak/Voit (eds), s 1054 para 2.

172 Münch, in: MünchKommZPO, s 1056 para 8.

173 Voit, in: Musielak/Voit (eds), s 1054 para 2.

174 Münch, in: MünchKommZPO, s 1055 para 6; Voit, in: Musielak/Voit (eds), s 1055 para 4.

175 Kremer/Weimann, SchiedsVZ 2007, 238, 242 *et seq.*; Voit, in: Musielak/Voit (eds), s 1055 para 4; dissenting OLG Frankfurt, SchiedsVZ 2007, 278, 279 (interlocutory decision on liability not capable of becoming *res judicata*); Münch, in: MünchKommZPO, s 1055 para 6 (interlocutory award not capable of becoming *res judicata*).

176 Schwab/Walter, ch 18 paras 9 *et seq.*; Voit, in: Musielak/Voit (eds), s 1054 para 2.

177 Voit, in: Musielak/Voit (eds), s 1054 para 2.

178 Voit, in: Musielak/Voit (eds), s 1054 para 2.

179 OLG Frankfurt, SchiedsVZ 2007, 278, 279; Schwab/Walter, ch 18 para 7; Voit, in: Musielak/Voit (eds), s 1054 para 2.

180 Schlosser, in: Stein/Jonas (eds), s 1054 para 9; Schwab/Walter, ch 18 para 8; Voit, in: Musielak/Voit (eds), s 1054 para 2.

the arbitration agreement stipulates that the parties can appeal against the award to a **supreme arbitral tribunal**, the first arbitral tribunal's decision is an arbitral award only if the appeal was not filed or if it was dismissed by the supreme arbitral tribunal.[181]

II. Form and Content of the Arbitral Award (s 1054 paras 1 to 3 ZPO)

1. *Typical Elements of an Arbitral Award*

6.91 An arbitral award will typically consist of a cover page also identifying the parties to the arbitration and the arbitral tribunal, a table of contents, a table of abbreviations, the procedural history, the facts of the case and the parties' requests, the arbitral tribunal's legal reasoning, the dispositive part, and the signatures of the arbitrators. The exact composition of the arbitral award and its elements is subject to the arbitrators' background; in particular in domestic proceedings it is not rare that an arbitral award's structure closely mirrors that of a German state court judgment. This diversity, however, does no harm, as only few elements are legally required under s 1054 ZPO.[182] For successful enforcement, however, the court will need to identify two elements that are not mandatory under this provision, namely the parties to the arbitration[183] and the dispositive part.[184] For DIS arbitrations, s 34.2 DIS Rules is more demanding as it requires full identification of the parties to the arbitral proceedings and their legal representatives and the names of the arbitrators who have rendered the award. The award is to be made in the language determined under s 1045 ZPO.[185]

2. *Form (s 1054 para 1 ZPO)*

6.92 The arbitral award needs to be made in writing and to contain the arbitrators' signatures (s 1054 para 1 ZPO). As long as these form requirements are not complied with, the award is **legally not in existence**, does not have *res judicata* effect (s 1055 ZPO), does not terminate the arbitral proceedings (s 1056 para 1 ZPO), and cannot be set aside (s 1059 ZPO) or declared enforceable (s 1060 ZPO).[186] As can be concluded from s 1054 para 2 ZPO, all of the requirements under s 1054 para 1 ZPO are not susceptible to a party agreement to the contrary.[187]

6.93 a) **Written Form** Written form in practice means physical production of a paper document although legally written form can be substituted by electronic

[181] Kreindler/Schäfer/Wolff, para 1013.

[182] Cf KG SchiedsVZ 2011, 110, 111 (facts dispensable).

[183] Lachmann, para 1755; Münch, in: MünchKommZPO, s 1054 paras 6, 25; v Schlabrendorff/Sessler, in: *Arbitration in Germany*, s 1054 para 6.

[184] OLG München, SchiedsVZ 2012, 217, 218 (although not legally necessary); Münch, in: MünchKommZPO, s 1054 para 6; Voit, in: Musielak/Voit (eds), s 1054 para 3.

[185] Münch, in: MünchKommZPO, s 1054 para 18; v Schlabrendorff/Sessler, in: *Arbitration in Germany*, s 1054 para 5.

[186] Kreindler/Schäfer/Wolff, para 1014.

[187] Government bill, BT-Drucks 13/5274, p 56 (for the requirement of the majority of signatures).

form for which a qualified electronic signature under the German Signature Act is needed (s 126 para 3, s 126a BGB).[188] Pronouncing the award orally is in any event insufficient.[189]

b) Signatures The arbitrators must **sign the arbitral award** (s 1054 para 1 cl 1 ZPO). Any signature needs to be made by the arbitrator in person and can, like most duties of an arbitrator (para 3.173), not be delegated to a proxy.[190] All arbitrators need to sign one and the same document, and be it on different pages.[191] The arbitrators can provide a blank signature[192] and agreed amendments can be made to the award after signature.[193] Often, after the arbitrators have agreed on the award, only the signature pages will be circulated and signed while the chairman finally assembles the full copies of the award. **6.94**

However, the **majority of signatures** suffices if an award states the reason for the omitted signature (s 1054 para 1 cl 2 ZPO). Different from the parallel provision for deliberations (s 1052 para 2 ZPO), s 1054 ZPO does not require refusal (or even obstruction) on the side of the arbitrator[194] even though this was the primary motive for the provision.[195] In fact, indicating the reason why signatures have been omitted merely allows for distinguishing between drafts which are not yet fully signed and final awards.[196] Even an incorrect reason stated in the award does not affect its validity.[197] It is, however, good practice to have the award signed by all arbitrators whenever possible.[198] The majority of signatures is sufficient regardless of the number of missing signatures[199] and regardless of whether the chairman has signed the award.[200] **6.95**

The prevailing view allows the arbitrators to **re-enter into the deliberations** until the award is signed by all arbitrators if a majority of them decides to do so.[201] Once **6.96**

188 Dissenting Münch, in: MünchKommZPO, s 1054 para 5.

189 Münch, in: MünchKommZPO, s 1054 para 5.

190 OLG München, SchiedsVZ 2013, 230, 233 *et seq.*; Münch, in: MünchKommZPO, s 1054 para 8; v Schlabrendorff/Sessler, in: *Arbitration in Germany*, s 1054 para 17; Schwab/Walter, ch 12 para 6.

191 OLG München, SchiedsVZ 2013, 230, 233 *et seq.*; Münch, SchiedsVZ 2013, 235, 236 *et seq.*; Voit, in: Musielak/Voit (eds), s 1054 para 6; dissenting v Schlabrendorff/Sessler, in: *Arbitration in Germany*, s 1054 para 17.

192 OLG München, SchiedsVZ 2013, 230, 234 (*obiter dictum*); Münch, in: MünchKommZPO, s 1054 para 12; Schlosser, in: Stein/Jonas (eds), s 1054 para 12; for general rules on blank signatures see RGZ 78, 28, 29; BGHZ 40, 65, 68 = NJW 1963, 1971; BGHZ 53, 11, 15 = NJW 1970, 324, 326.

193 Münch, in: MünchKommZPO, s 1054 para 13; Voit, in: Musielak/Voit (eds), s 1054 para 6.

194 Cf Kreindler/Schäfer/Wolff, para 1015; Voit, in: Musielak/Voit (eds), s 1054 para 6.

195 Government bill, BT-Drucks 13/5274, p 56.

196 Münch, in: MünchKommZPO, s 1054 para 15; v Schlabrendorff/Sessler, in: *Arbitration in Germany*, s 1054 para 18.

197 Münch, in: MünchKommZPO, s 1054 para 15; Schlosser, in: Stein/Jonas (eds), s 1054 para 17.

198 Cf Münch, in: MünchKommZPO, s 1054 para 15.

199 Government bill, BT-Drucks 13/5274, p 55.

200 Government bill, BT-Drucks 13/5274, p 56.

201 v Schlabrendorff/Sessler, in: *Arbitration in Germany*, s 1054 para 22; Voit, in: Musielak/Voit (eds), s 1054 para 10.

the award has been signed by all arbitrators, amendments to the award can be made only by unanimous decision.[202] If the award has been delivered to at least one party (paras 6.105 *et seq.*), the arbitrators can no longer amend their decision.[203]

3. Reasons (s 1054 para 2 ZPO)

6.97 The award **must state the reasons** upon which it is based (s 1054 para 2 ZPO). These reasons do not need to meet a high standard;[204] in particular they do not need to be correct in a way that they legally justify the arbitral tribunal's decision.[205] Such high standard would not take into account the fact that the parties have entrusted solely the arbitral tribunal with the decision of the dispute. The reasons must, however, not be contradictory and need to comment at least along general lines on the principal points of the parties' arguments.[206] Although they should sensibly do so, the reasons do not need to demonstrate that the arbitral tribunal has fully granted both parties the right to present their case.[207]

6.98 The **reasons are dispensable** if either the award is an award on agreed terms (s 1053 ZPO, paras 6.34 *et seq.*) or if the parties have waived this requirement (s 1054 para 2 ZPO). Given the weight of the award's reasons for its acceptance, such waiver should not be assumed lightly. An agreed waiver of remedies against the award does not suffice for that purpose.[208]

6.99 If under these rules reasons are necessary but **fail to meet the required standard**, this does not deprive the decision of its qualification as an arbitral award. The prevailing view acknowledges a ground for setting aside under s 1059 para 2 no 1 lit d ZPO[209] although this ground requires a causal link between the procedural deficiency and the outcome of the proceedings, and such link will hardly ever exist in case of insufficient reasons. Classification as a ground for setting aside and an

---

[202] v Schlabrendorff/Sessler, in: *Arbitration in Germany*, s 1054 para 22; Schlosser, in: Stein/Jonas (eds), s 1054 para 20; dissenting (majority decision) Geimer, in: Zöller (ed), s 1054 para 7.

[203] Lachmann, paras 1780 *et seq.*; Schlosser, in: Stein/Jonas (eds), s 1054 para 32; Voit, in: Musielak/Voit (eds), s 1054 para 10.

[204] In particular lower than that for state court judgments, see BGHZ 30, 89, 92 = NJW 1959, 1438, 1439; BGHZ 96, 40, 47 = NJW 1986, 1436, 1437; OLG München, December 20, 2006, 34 Sch 16/06 (unreported), http://www.disarb.org (last visited December 1, 2015); SchiedsVZ 2011, 159, 167; Münch, in: MünchKommZPO, s 1054 paras 28 *et seq.*; Schwab/Walter, ch 19 para 11; Schlosser, in: Stein/Jonas (eds), s 1054 para 17.

[205] RGZ 23, 432, 436; RG JW 1896, 434 (no 14); LZ 17 (1923), 649, 650; BGHZ 96, 40, 47 = NJW 1986, 1436, 1437; v Schlabrendorff/Sessler, in: *Arbitration in Germany*, s 1054 para 10; Schwab/Walter, ch 19 paras 11 *et seq.*

[206] BGHZ 96, 40, 47 = NJW 1986, 1436, 1437 *et seq.*; Schwab/Walter, ch 19 para 12; Voit, in: Musielak/Voit (eds), s 1054 para 4.

[207] Schlosser, in: Stein/Jonas (eds), s 1054 para 17.

[208] Schwab/Walter, ch 19 para 13; dissenting Hartmann, in: Baumbach/Lauterbach/Albers/Hartmann (eds), s 1054 para 4.

[209] Lachmann, para 2281; Münch, in: MünchKommZPO, s 1054 para 18; v Schlabrendorff/Sessler, in: *Arbitration in Germany*, s 1054 para 9; Schlosser, in: Stein/Jonas (eds), s 1054 para 17; Schwab/Walter, ch 19 para 12.

extension of s 1059 para 2 no 1 lit d ZPO are, however, the lesser evil compared to no sanction at all.[210]

4. Date and Place of Arbitration (s 1054 para 3 ZPO)

6.100 The date of the award and the place of arbitration (s 1043 para 1 ZPO, paras 2.174 *et seq.*) must be stated in the arbitral award (s 1054 para 3 cl 1 ZPO). Section 1054 para 3 cl 2 ZPO stipulates a **fiction** against which no counter-evidence can be brought:[211] the award is deemed to have been made at that date and at that place. The place of arbitration is decisive for the arbitral award's nationality and the jurisdiction of the higher regional court under s 1062 para 1 ZPO (paras 6.174 *et seq.*). By contrast, the date of the award—to which the fiction was extended without a template in the Model Law[212]—has no legal relevance since the deadline for the setting aside application under s 1059 para 3 ZPO starts with receipt of the arbitral award and not with its making.[213]

6.101 At first sight, s 1054 para 3 ZPO reads as if the indication of date and place of arbitration, which are both mandatory requirements, were an integral part of the arbitral award. However, the failure to indicate the place of arbitration was not understood to be sanctioned under the German arbitration law in force before 1998 and the reform explicitly aimed at alleviating (rather than tightening) the form requirements for arbitral awards.[214] **Omission** of date or place of arbitration therefore results neither in a non-award nor in a ground for setting aside the award.[215]

III. Dissenting Opinions

6.102 It is a matter of dispute under German law whether issuance of dissenting opinions is **reconcilable with the secrecy of deliberations** (para 6.12). The German legislature refrained from implementing a provision on dissenting opinions and indicated that the prevailing view under former German law allowed dissenting opinions.[216]

---

[210] Voit, in: Musielak/Voit (eds), s 1054 para 5.

[211] Government bill, BT-Drucks 13/5274, p 56; Münch, in: MünchKommZPO, s 1054 para 34; Voit, in: Musielak/Voit (eds), s 1054 para 8; dissenting Schütze, para 431.

[212] Government bill, BT-Drucks 13/5274, p 56.

[213] OLG Karlsruhe, SchiedsVZ 2012, 101, 106 = XXXVIII Y.B. Com. Arb. 379, 383 (2013); Voit, in: Musielak/Voit (eds), s 1054 para 8; dissenting (relevance for binding effect on the arbitral tribunal) v Schlabrendorff/Sessler, in: *Arbitration in Germany*, s 1054 para 16.

[214] Government bill, BT-Drucks 13/5274, p 55.

[215] OLG München, SchiedsVZ 2011, 167, 168 (at least if the place of arbitration can be identified by way of interpretation); 2013, 230, 233; OLG Stuttgart, NJW-RR 2003, 1438, 1439; Hartmann, in: Baumbach/Lauterbach/Albers/Hartmann (eds), s 1054 para 5; v Schlabrendorff/Sessler, in: *Arbitration in Germany*, s 1054 para 13; Schwab/Walter, ch 20 para 13; Voit, in: Musielak/Voit (eds), s 1054 para 7; dissenting Münch, in: MünchKommZPO, s 1054 para 35; Münch, SchiedsVZ 2013, 235, 236.

[216] Government bill, BT-Drucks 13/5274, p 56.

Regardless of their general admissibility, it is recognized that dissenting opinions should be avoided whenever possible and that implementation of dissenting views in the reasons of the award is preferable, not least for the sake of an increased acceptance of the award by the parties.[217]

6.103 If dissenting opinions are considered admissible at all, they must not disclose the course and content of the **deliberations**.[218] It will be subject to a **majority decision** of the arbitral tribunal whether the (admissible) dissenting opinion is delivered alongside the award to the parties.[219] Issuance of an inadmissible dissenting opinion does not constitute a **ground for setting aside** the award, but may give rise for a claim for damages against the defaulting arbitrator.[220] Some of these issues may be avoided if the arbitral tribunal seeks the parties' consent on the delivery of dissenting opinions.

IV. Scrutiny of an ICC Award by the ICC Court of Arbitration (art 33 ICC Rules)

6.104 Before an ICC arbitral award is signed and delivered to the parties, it must undergo the scrutiny process by the ICC Court of Arbitration (art 33 ICC Rules). This scrutiny aims to ensure a high quality (and an increased likeliness of enforceability) of the award and it is a distinctive feature under the ICC Rules.[221] Article 33 cl 2 ICC Rules distinguishes between questions of form and of substance: questions of form include typographical, clerical, and computational issues[222] as well as missing information under the ICC Award Checklist and others.[223] The Court can instruct the arbitral tribunal to adjust the arbitral award according to its comments on form. Questions of substance are treated differently, as the Court will solely draw the arbitral tribunal's attention to such issues. Whether or not the arbitral tribunal makes amendments to its draft accordingly is left to its own decision; art 33 cl 2 ICC Rules explicitly confirms that the arbitral tribunal's liberty of decision shall not be affected. Questions of substance may include whether the tribunal has neglected any issues or has decided issues not raised by the parties, has given reasons for all decisions, whether the dispositive section of the award is clearly formulated, and whether costs and interests are properly addressed.[224]

---

[217] v Schlabrendorff/Sessler, in: *Arbitration in Germany*, s 1054 para 20.
[218] v Schlabrendorff/Sessler, in: *Arbitration in Germany*, s 1054 para 20.
[219] v Schlabrendorff/Sessler, in: *Arbitration in Germany*, s 1054 para 20.
[220] RG JW 1932, 2877 (no 25); Münch, in: MünchKommZPO, s 1054 para 22; Schlosser, in: Stein/Jonas (eds), s 1054 para 20; dissenting Schütze, para 437; Schütze, in: *Festschrift Nakamura*, pp 525, 535 *et seq.*; SchiedsVZ 2008, 10, 13 *et seq.*
[221] Fry/Greenberg/Mazza, para 3-1181.
[222] Fry/Greenberg/Mazza, para 3-1182.
[223] Fry/Greenberg/Mazza, para 3-1209.
[224] Fry/Greenberg/Mazza, para 3-1210.

V. Delivery of the Arbitral Award (s 1054 para 4 ZPO)

A copy of the award signed by the arbitrators is to be delivered to each party (s 1054 para 4 ZPO). **Delivery** has replaced deposit under the former German law;[225] such deposit with a German state court nowadays is not even any longer possible.[226] Delivery must be made to the party, its counsel, or any other authorized receiving agent.[227] While the law does not prescribe a specific form of delivery, a registered letter with return receipt or a courier are advisable as they provide for evidence of the date of delivery, which in turn is dispositive under s 1059 para 3 ZPO.[228] Section 1054 para 4 ZPO also allows electronic transmission,[229] though this practice has not been made broad use of. Often arbitral tribunals distribute the award via complementary email in addition to its hard-copy delivery. The parties can agree on a specific form of delivery including by registered letter with return receipt to the parties' counsel.[230] **6.105**

It is important to note that each party is to receive an award with the **original signatures** of (the majority of) the arbitrators.[231] A simple copy of an originally signed award does not suffice even if it was certified by the chairman, the arbitral institution, or any other body.[232] The parties cannot **waive** the requirements under s 1054 para 4 ZPO.[233] As long as no award with original signatures has been delivered to a party, the deadline for setting aside applications under s 1059 para 3 ZPO does not commence. **6.106**

Under institutional rules, usually the **arbitral institution** rather than the arbitral tribunal will deliver the award to the parties (art 34 para 1 ICC Rules, s 36.2 DIS Rules). The award will not be delivered until the costs of the arbitral proceedings have been fully addressed (art 34 para 1 ICC Rules, s 36.3 DIS Rules). Arbitral tribunals in ad hoc proceedings will usually also withhold the arbitral award until the costs have been fully paid.[234] **6.107**

---

225 Government bill, BT-Drucks 13/5274, p 56.

226 Münch, in: MünchKommZPO, s 1054 para 45.

227 Münch, in: MünchKommZPO, s 1054 para 40; Schwab/Walter, ch 20 para 11; Voit, in: Musielak/Voit (eds), s 1054 para 9.

228 Hartmann, in: Baumbach/Lauterbach/Albers/Hartmann (eds), s 1054 para 6; v Schlabrendorff/Sessler, in: *Arbitration in Germany*, s 1054 para 21.

229 Government bill, BT-Drucks 15/4067, p 36; Münch, in: MünchKommZPO, s 1054 para 38.

230 BGH NJW 2015, 3234, 3238 *et seq.* para 37.

231 OLG München, SchiedsVZ 2012, 217, 218; Hartmann, in: Baumbach/Lauterbach/Albers/Hartmann (eds), s 1054 para 6; v Schlabrendorff/Sessler, in: *Arbitration in Germany*, s 1054 para 21; Schwab/Walter, ch 20 para 9; dissenting OLG Düsseldorf, SchiedsVZ 2008, 156, 159.

232 Voit, in: Musielak/Voit (eds), s 1054 para 9.

233 Münch, in: MünchKommZPO, s 1054 paras 42 *et seq.*

234 Critical Münch, in: MünchKommZPO, s 1054 para 40.

E. Effects of the Arbitral Award

6.108 The main effect of an arbitral award is addressed by s 1055 ZPO, pursuant to which the arbitral award has the same effects between the parties as a final and binding court judgment (paras 6.109 *et seq.*). As a separate effect, the arbitral award terminates the arbitral proceedings (paras 6.126 *et seq.*).

I. Effects of a Final and Binding Court Judgment (s 1055 ZPO)

6.109 The arbitral award has the same effects between the parties as a final and binding court judgment (s 1055 ZPO). This provision, which has no equivalent in the Model Law but rather was perpetuated from the former German arbitration law,[235] references a bundle of effects that German civil procedure law attaches to a state court judgment (paras 6.112 *et seq.*). These effects are transferred to any arbitral award (paras 6.110 *et seq.*).

1. Requirement of an Arbitral Award

6.110 German law distinguishes between procedural and substantive *res judicata*. Substantive *res judicata* is one of the main effects of procedural *res judicata*. A matter gains **procedural *res judicata*** effect once no remedy is available which suspends the *res judicata* effect and brings the matter before a court of higher instance (s 705 ZPO). If applied to arbitral awards, any award would instantly gain procedural *res judicata* effect, since awards are never open to a full review.[236] However, since s 1055 ZPO ties the effects of a judgment with (procedural) *res judicata* effect up to any arbitral award, it is futile to discuss the award's procedural *res judicata*.

6.111 Section 1055 ZPO rather requires an **award** (paras 6.87 *et seq.*), ie a final and binding decision which was made in writing and bears the signatures of the (majority of the) arbitrators (s 1054 para 1 ZPO, paras 6.92 *et seq.*). The effects under s 1055 ZPO moreover require the award to be delivered to each party under s 1054 para 4 ZPO (paras 6.105 *et seq.*). The effects under s 1055 ZPO occur only with the delivery to the last party[237] since a party cannot be bound by a decision of which it has not and cannot have knowledge.

2. Substantive

6.112 **a) Effects of Substantive *res judicata*** While procedural *res judicata* means formal non-appealability (para 6.110), substantive *res judicata*—as one of the

[235] Government bill, BT-Drucks 13/5274, p 56.

[236] Kreindler/Schäfer/Wolff, para 1029; Münch, in: MünchKommZPO, s 1055 para 3; v Schlabrendorff/Sessler, in: *Arbitration in Germany*, s 1055 para 5.

[237] Voit, in: Musielak/Voit (eds), s 1055 para 3; dissenting (first party) Münch, in: MünchKommZPO, s 1055 para 4; v Schlabrendorff/Sessler, in: *Arbitration in Germany*, s 1055 para 3.

main effects of procedural *res judicata*—implies that the content of the decision is **definite** between the parties.[238] This definiteness becomes obvious in subsequent proceedings: it does, on the one hand, hinder subsequent proceedings on the same matter (*res judicata* in a narrower sense) while, on the other hand, it facilitates subsequent proceedings in which the earlier decision must not be reviewed again if it becomes relevant as a preliminary issue (prejudicial effect).[239]

If, for **example**, a plaintiff has obtained a first judgment that a rent contract between the parties is valid and has not been terminated and this decision has become *res judicata*, a second claim filed by the defendant based on the same facts and requesting a declaration that the contract has been validly terminated would be inadmissible. If, however, the plaintiff initiates follow-up proceedings and requests payment under this contract, the court must not take into account the defense that the contract has been validly terminated based on the same facts. Section 1055 ZPO extends these effects to arbitral awards. **6.113**

According to the prevailing view, substantive *res judicata* of an arbitral award **differs in two respects** from that of a court judgment. Both of these differences are rooted in the understanding that access to state court justice is a scarce resource while arbitration is available against payment. First, while a state court will take into account the *res judicata* effect of an earlier judgment on its own motion, it will consider the *res judicata* effect of an arbitral award only upon a party's objection.[240] Second, while the parties to a judgment cannot jointly waive its *res judicata* effect, the parties to an arbitral award are legally allowed to waive the award's *res judicata* effect.[241] **6.114**

b) Objective Scope of *res judicata* German law is restrictive when it comes to the scope of which elements of a decision are covered by the *res judicata* effect. This effect is limited to the matter in dispute (*Streitgegenstand*) as it has been decided in the decision's **dispositive part** (s 322 para 1 ZPO)[242] and its opposite, eg the non-existence of the claim that has been awarded (*kontradiktorisches Gegenteil*).[243] It neither covers the reasoning (which may be relevant only for **6.115**

238 BGH NJW 2004, 1805, 1806; Vollkommer, in: Zöller (ed), Vor s 322 paras 14 *et seq.*

239 BGH NJW 1989, 2133, 2134; 1995, 2993; 2003, 3058, 3059; Musielak, in: Musielak/Voit (eds), s 322 paras 9 *et seq.*; Vollkommer, in Zöller (ed), Vor s 322 para 35.

240 BGH NJW 1958, 950; Government bill, BT-Drucks 13/5274, pp 56 *et seq.*; Münch, in: MünchKommZPO, s 1055 para 12; Schlosser, in: Stein/Jonas (eds), s 1055 para 8; dissenting Schwab/Walter, ch 21 para 6; Voit, in: Musielak/Voit (eds), s 1055 para 5.

241 BayObLG BB 1984, 746; OLG Bremen, NJW 1957, 1035, 1036; Reichold, in: Thomas/Putzo (eds), s 1055 para 2; v Schlabrendorff/Sessler, in: *Arbitration in Germany*, s 1055 para 24; Schlosser, in: Stein/Jonas (eds), s 1055 para 5; dissenting Schwab/Walter, ch 21 para 7; Voit, in: Musielak/Voit (eds), s 1055 para 6.

242 OLG Naumburg, SchiedsVZ 2011, 228, 230; Kreindler/Schäfer/Wolff, para 1037; Münch, in: MünchKommZPO, s 1055 para 15; v Schlabrendorff/Sessler, in: *Arbitration in Germany*, s 1055 para 17; Voit, in: Musielak/Voit (eds), s 1055 para 9.

243 BGHZ 123, 137, 139 = NJW 1993, 2684, 2685; NJW 2003, 3058, 3059; Kreindler/Schäfer/Wolff, para 1040.

interpretation of what is covered by the dispositive part[244]) nor—contrary to common law concepts—facts or legal consequences of facts which are essential for the cause of action or defense.[245] By way of example, a decision awarding a seller's payment claim gains *res judicata* effect only to the extent that the buyer is obligated to pay. Although such decision legally requires a sales contract to have been validly concluded, the existence and validity of such contract does not become *res judicata*. If the seller wishes to extend the *res judicata* effect to preliminary questions like the existence of a valid contract, he or she needs to request a separate decision (cf s 256 para 2 ZPO).[246]

6.116 The **matter in dispute** (***Streitgegenstand***) is defined by the request plus the underlying set of facts.[247] As an example, if payment of a specific sum of money has been requested based on a sales contract and awarded (or such claim has been dismissed) in the decision's dispositive part, only the (non-) existence of a payment claim based on these facts becomes *res judicata*. If the buyer has negotiated a bill of exchange in the same amount, a payment claim based on such bill of exchange is considered to be another matter in dispute than the contractual payment claim.[248] A seller whose request for payment based upon the contractual payment was dismissed in a final and binding decision can therefore bring another claim for the same amount based on the bill of exchange without being restricted by the first decision's *res judicata* effect.

6.117 An exception to the rule that *res judicata* does not extend to preliminary issues (para 6.115) exists for the **set-off defense**. According to s 322 para 2 ZPO, a decision that the counterclaim does not exist becomes *res judicata* up to the amount for which the set-off has been asserted. If the court or arbitral tribunal has denied the set-off defense because it found the counterclaim to be non-existent, subsequent proceedings in which payment of the counterclaim is requested would be inadmissible for reasons of *res judicata*. If, however, the set-off defense was dismissed for other reasons than the non-existence of the counterclaim, eg for grounds of a prohibition of set-off, the existence of the counterclaim does not become *res judicata*.[249]

6.118 **c) Subjective Scope of *res judicata*** The *res judicata* effect is limited to the **parties to the dispute**[250] as explicitly confirmed by s 1055 ZPO. Third parties are included only exceptionally as in the *res judicata* effect of a judgment, in

---

[244] Voit, in: Musielak/Voit (eds), s 1055 para 10.

[245] BGH NJW 1995, 967, 968; 1986, 2508, 2509; NJW-RR 2008, 1397, 1398; Musielak, in: Musielak/Voit (eds), s 322 para 17.

[246] Kreindler/Schäfer/Wolff, para 1038.

[247] BGHZ 117, 1, 5 = NJW 1992, 1172, 1173; 1993, 333, 334; 1996, 3151, 3152; 1999, 3126, 3127; 2000, 1958; 2001, 157, 158.

[248] BGHZ 157, 224, 229 = NJW 2004, 1456, 1458; OLG Saarbrücken, WM 1998, 833, 835; Schaaff, NJW 1986, 1029, 1030.

[249] BGHZ 125, 351, 354 = NJW 1994, 2769, 2770; 1984, 128, 129; 1997, 743; 2001, 3616.

[250] Münch, in: MünchKommZPO, s 1055 para 21.

particular singular and universal successors to a party and executors, insolvency administrators, or administrators of estates to a party.[251] Common law concepts like the extension to privies or the application of issue preclusion in subsequent litigation with third parties are unknown under German law.

The strict limitation of *res judicata* to the parties to the dispute time and again creates the risk to be caught between two stools. A typical situation would be where a seller is successfully sued by his or her buyer for damages due to defective goods while he or she cannot gain refund from his or her seller since he or she cannot establish the defectiveness of the goods. Similar situations often occur in chains of contractors where the *res judicata* effect of a judgment or arbitral award that the customer has obtained against the general contractor does not extend to the subcontractor. Before state courts, the third party can be included in the litigation and bound to the judgment by way of a **third-party notice** (ss 72 *et seq.* ZPO). While third-party notices generally also work in arbitration, the underlying arbitration clauses need careful drafting and need to include also the third party notice addressee (para 2.137). **6.119**

d) Temporal Scope of *res judicata* *Res judicata* cannot change the legal situation to stone. German civil procedural law allows for **remedies** terminating the binding effect (or enforceability) where new facts occur. Under s 767 ZPO, the debtor can assert objections against the claim itself as established by the judgment by filing a corresponding court action (paras 6.276 *et seq.*). Such objections, however, can be brought only if they occurred after the close of the hearing in which they could have been brought last. In case of a judgment ordering recurrent performance becoming due in the future, s 323 ZPO provides each part with a remedy for the modification of the judgment if the new facts result in a material change to the factual or legal circumstances on which the decision is based. Section 323 ZPO is also limited to grounds that have arisen after the hearing on the facts in the preceding proceedings was closed. **6.120**

These remedies are to be brought before the arbitral tribunal if they are covered by the arbitration agreement.[252] The arbitral tribunal has jurisdiction for the s 767 ZPO action if the arbitration agreement covers the new objection.[253] If under these rules the arbitral tribunal has jurisdiction, a new arbitral tribunal needs to be constituted since the office of the arbitrators had ended with their award (para 6.127).[254] **6.121**

---

[251] Schlosser, in: Stein/Jonas (eds), s 1055 paras 30 *et seq.*, 24; Schwab/Walter, ch 21 para 3; Voit, in: Musielak/Voit (eds), s 1055 para 7.

[252] Voit, in: Musielak/Voit (eds), s 1055 para 12.

[253] BGHZ 99, 143, 145 *et seq.* = NJW 1987, 651, 652 *et seq.*; NJW-RR 1996, 508; Geimer, in: Zöller (ed), s 1030 para 17; Schwab/Walter, ch 7 para 15; Voit, in: Musielak/Voit (eds), s 1030 para 7.

[254] Münch, in: MünchKommZPO, s 1055 para 27; v Schlabrendorff/Sessler, in: *Arbitration in Germany*, s 1055 para 28; Schlosser, in: Stein/Jonas (eds), s 1055 para 18; Schwab/Walter, ch 21 para 10.

3. *Other Effects*

6.122 Apart from substantive *res judicata*, procedural *res judicata* has some other effects which s 1055 ZPO also extends to arbitral awards. These effects include the **binding effect** under which the court (or arbitral tribunal) is bound to its judgment (or arbitral award) for subsequent decisions.[255] By way of exception, the arbitral tribunal can correct and interpret its arbitral award subject to s 1058 ZPO (paras 6.145 *et seq.*). The procedural *res judicata* also gives rise to the effect that **substantive law provisions tie in** with a final and binding judgment.[256] For example, under s 864 para 2 BGB certain claims of a possessor lapse if a final and binding judgment declares that the debtor has a (specific) right to the property.

6.123 For judgments, the procedural *res judicata* also triggers **enforceability** as final and binding judgments serve as executory titles (s 704 ZPO). Contrary to the wording of s 1055 ZPO, arbitral awards are not executory titles which allow for enforcement. According to s 1060 para 1 ZPO, enforcement of the award only takes place if the award has been declared enforceable. Only the higher regional court's order declaring the arbitral award enforceable serves as an executory title (s 794 para 1 no 4a ZPO). Such declaration of enforceability is also required for arbitral awards that order the respondent to make a declaration of intent. According to s 894 ZPO, such declaration shall be deemed to have been made as soon as the judgment has become final and binding. As part of the enforcement law, this fiction, however, applies only once the award has been declared enforceable (s 1060 para 1 ZPO).[257]

6.124 German law foresees a limited number of judgments changing a legal right or status; this effect occurs with procedural *res judicata*. For example, a general partnership can be dissolved by way of a judgment (s 133 HGB). While it is acknowledged that decisions changing a legal right or status can be requested from an arbitral tribunal, it is a matter of dispute whether an **award changing a legal right or status** (*Gestaltungsschiedsspruch*) must be declared enforceable under s 1060 ZPO to effectuate that change. The prevailing view postulates the need for a declaration of enforceability (para 6.255)[258] although the better grounds advocate the opposite: s 1060 para 1 ZPO pierces the full equalization of an arbitral award with a final and binding judgment (s 1055 ZPO) only as to enforcement. The effect of changing a legal right or status, however, under German law does not belong to enforcement but is a separate and independent effect.[259]

---

[255] Münch, in: MünchKommZPO, s 1055 para 36.

[256] Cf Münch, in: MünchKommZPO, s 1055 para 34.

[257] Geimer, in: Zöller (ed), s 1055 para 2; Lachmann, para 1788; Münch, in: MünchKommZPO, s 1060 para 3; Schwab/Walter, ch 28 para 18; Voit, in: Musielak/Voit (eds), s 1060 para 2; dissenting OLG Dresden, BB 2001, Beil. 7, pp 22 *et seq.*; Schlosser, in: Stein/Jonas (eds), s 1060 para 6.

[258] BayObLGZ 1984, 45, 48 = BB 1984, 746; K Schmidt, ZGR 1988, 523, 535 *et seq.*; AG 1995, 551, 554; dissenting Geimer, in: Zöller (ed), s 1055 para 2; Lachmann, para 1787; v Schlabrendorff/ Sessler, in: *Arbitration in Germany*, s 1055 para 25; Schwab/Walter, ch 21 para 12; Voit, in: Musielak/ Voit (eds), s 1055 para 11.

[259] Kreindler/Schäfer/Wolff, para 1032.

4. *Foreign Awards*

Section 1055 ZPO applies only to awards with a place of arbitration in Germany (s 1025 para 1 ZPO). For the *res judicata* effect of foreign awards, German law of civil procedure refers to the *lex arbitri*, ie to the arbitration law at the place of arbitration (para 6.290). **6.125**

II. Termination of the Proceedings (s 1056 para 1 ZPO)

Besides having the effects of a final and binding judgment (paras 6.109 *et seq.*), the arbitral award also **terminates the arbitral proceedings** (s 1056 para 1 ZPO). Just like for the effects under s 1055 ZPO (cf para 6.111), the award needs to meet the formal requirements of s 1054 para 1 ZPO and must have been delivered to all parties in order to terminate the proceedings.[260] Moreover, only the final award, ie the award deciding the last part of the matter in dispute, has terminating effect; partial awards may become *res judicata* but never terminate arbitral proceedings.[261] **6.126**

Simultaneously with the termination of the arbitral proceedings, the **arbitrators' office terminates** (s 1056 para 3 ZPO); they become *functus officio.* The law sets out only three tasks for which the arbitrators are deemed to be still in office: for a separate cost award under s 1057 para 2 ZPO (para 6.85), for correction, interpretation, and an additional award under s 1058 ZPO (paras 6.145 *et seq.*), and for remission of the case after the award has been set aside under s 1059 para 4 ZPO (para 6.244). For other newly arising arbitral tasks, a new arbitral tribunal needs to be constituted.[262] **6.127**

F. Termination Order

While the arbitral proceedings are designed to end with a final award, they can under specific circumstances also end without an award. As a second termination instrument, the law provides for a termination order (s 1056 para 1 ZPO). **6.128**

It is a matter of dispute whether arbitral proceedings can terminate only with a final award or with a termination order, in other words whether s 1056 para 1 ZPO is exhaustive. The prevailing view assumes that all arbitral proceedings need an award or a termination order to terminate.[263] While legal certainty indeed speaks in favor of this position, at least some cases exist in which arbitral proceedings must **6.129**

---

[260] v Schlabrendorff/Sessler, in: *Arbitration in Germany*, s 1055 para 5; Voit, in: Musielak/Voit (eds), s 1056 para 2.

[261] Münch, in: MünchKommZPO, s 1056 para 5; v Schlabrendorff/Sessler, in: *Arbitration in Germany*, s 1056 para 4.

[262] OLG Frankfurt, NJW-RR 2008, 590, 591; Münch, in: MünchKommZPO, s 1056 para 34.

[263] Government bill, BT-Drucks 13/5274, p 57; Busse, SchiedsVZ 2010, 57, 58; dissenting Voit, in: Musielak/Voit (eds), s 1056 para 1.

end without an award or termination order. One example would be the death of a sole arbitrator who was agreed upon in the arbitration agreement and who was decisive for the choice to arbitrate (cf para 2.165). The better reasons therefore speak in favor of s 1056 para 1 ZPO's **non-exhaustive nature.**

I. Prerequisites

6.130 Section 1056 para 2 ZPO sets out a number of grounds for termination orders, most of which have been adopted from **art 32 Model Law**. The German legislature has added the failure of the claimant to state its claim (s 1056 para 2 no 1 lit a ZPO).[264] It has furthermore transformed art 32 para 2 lit c Model Law, according to which a termination order is to be issued if the arbitral tribunal finds that the continuation of the proceedings has for any other reason become unnecessary or impossible, into the more specific provision of s 1056 para 2 no 3 ZPO.[265]

6.131 The termination order under s 1056 para 2 ZPO is mostly understood to be **constitutive** for the termination of the arbitral proceedings.[266] A termination order also ends the arbitral proceedings if none of the grounds enlisted in the law is met (para 6.143). According to the prevailing view, s 1056 para 2 ZPO is of **mandatory** nature,[267] which view is supported by the need for legal certainty.

1. Failure of Claimant to State its Claim (s 1056 para 2 no 1 lit a ZPO)

6.132 The arbitral tribunal issues a termination order if the claimant fails to submit its statement of claim within the time limit set under s 1046 para 1 ZPO and if such default has not been justified to the tribunal's satisfaction under s 1048 para 4 ZPO (s 1056 para 2 no 1 lit a ZPO). Unlike a dismissal of the claim in an award, such termination order leaves the parties with nothing but costs (paras 6.140 *et seq.*) and an unresolved dispute.[268] Whether in light of this result the arbitral tribunal needs to inform the parties before it issues a termination order[269] appears to be a more theoretical question since without such information the arbitral tribunal will not be able to determine that the default has not been justified.

2. Withdrawal of Claim (s 1056 para 2 no 1 lit b ZPO)

6.133 A termination order is also to be issued if the claimant withdraws its claim, unless the respondent objects and the arbitral tribunal recognizes a legitimate interest on

---

[264] Government bill, BT-Drucks 13/5274, p 57.

[265] Government bill, BT-Drucks 13/5274, p 57.

[266] Gerstenmaier, SchiedsVZ 2010, 281, 282; Münch, in: MünchKommZPO, s 1056 paras 3, 14, 23; Schlosser, in: Stein/Jonas (eds), s 1056 para 2; dissenting Voit, in: Musielak/Voit (eds), s 1056 para 4.

[267] v Schlabrendorff/Sessler, in: *Arbitration in Germany*, s 1056 para 3; dissenting Schlosser, in: Stein/Jonas (eds), s 1056 para 12; Voit, in: Musielak/Voit (eds), s 1056 para 1.

[268] Voit, in: Musielak/Voit (eds), s 1056 para 3; see also Münch, in: MünchKommZPO, s 1056 para 24.

[269] Pro: Voit, in: Musielak/Voit (eds), s 1056 para 3; con: Münch, in: MünchKommZPO, s 1056 para 24; v Schlabrendorff/Sessler, in: *Arbitration in Germany*, s 1056 para 7.

the part of the respondent in obtaining a final settlement of the dispute (s 1056 para 2 no 1 lit b ZPO). It is obvious that the arbitral proceedings must end if both parties are in **agreement** on the withdrawal. The arbitral tribunal will usually set a deadline for obtaining such consent.

If the **respondent objects**, the tribunal needs to decide whether the respondent has a **legitimate interest** in obtaining an award that settles the dispute in a final and binding manner. Such legitimate interest is to be assumed if the claimant could otherwise initiate proceedings anew: it is unacceptable to lose a favorable procedural situation just in order to be exposed to the same claim later again. The respondent lacks a legitimate interest in obtaining an award only if the claimant waives its claim,[270] if a new claim would be inadmissible due to a preclusive time limit, or if the claimant cannot initiate new arbitral proceedings for other reasons. Obtaining a cost award will usually not constitute a legitimate interest in continuation of the proceedings since in the event of a termination the arbitral tribunal still needs to decide on costs (para 6.141).[271] **6.134**

3. *Party Agreement on the Termination of the Proceedings (s 1056 para 2 no 2 ZPO)*

As long as they are in agreement, the parties can terminate the arbitral proceedings for any reason including settlement or performance by the respondent.[272] Upon such agreement, the arbitral tribunal will issue a termination order (s 1056 para 2 no 2 ZPO). The party agreement on the termination of the proceedings may simultaneously include a waiver of the arbitration agreement so that the state courts have jurisdiction over future disputes.[273] Whether the parties also intended to waive the arbitration agreement is subject to interpretation of their termination agreement. **6.135**

4. *Parties' Failure to Pursue the Proceedings (s 1056 para 2 no 3 option 1 ZPO)*

Another ground for a termination order is that the parties fail to pursue the arbitral proceedings (s 1056 para 2 no 3 option 1 ZPO), eg by non-payment of the advances on costs,[274] by non-appearance in a hearing,[275] or by other means.[276] The arbitral tribunal needs to request the parties to continue to pursue the proceedings before **6.136**

[270] Lachmann, paras 1460, 1841; v Schlabrendorff/Sessler, in: *Arbitration in Germany*, s 1056 para 8; Voit, in: Musielak/Voit (eds), s 1056 para 4; dissenting Münch, in: MünchKommZPO, s 1056 para 21.

[271] Lachmann, para 1849; Reichold, in: Thomas/Putzo (eds), s 1056 para 4; v Schlabrendorff/Sessler, in: *Arbitration in Germany*, s 1056 para 8.

[272] Government bill, BT-Drucks 13/5274, p 57; Münch, in: MünchKommZPO, s 1056 paras 27 *et seq.*; v Schlabrendorff/Sessler, in: *Arbitration in Germany*, s 1056 para 9.

[273] Voit, in: Musielak/Voit (eds), s 1056 para 5.

[274] Lachmann, para 1861; Schütze, para 420.

[275] v Schlabrendorff/Sessler, in: *Arbitration in Germany*, s 1056 para 11; Schlosser, in: Stein/Jonas (eds), s 1056 para 9.

[276] Münch, in: MünchKommZPO, s 1056 para 29.

it issues a termination order. For that purpose, it will make sense to set a deadline and point the parties to the legal consequences of their inactivity.[277] If the parties jointly stay the proceedings, the arbitral tribunal cannot issue a termination order under s 1056 para 2 no 3 option 1 ZPO.[278] The arbitrators may, however, terminate their arbitrator contracts for cause under appropriate circumstances (para 3.199).[279]

5. Impossibility of Continuation of the Proceedings (s 1056 para 2 no 3 option 2 ZPO)

6.137 Finally, a termination order can be issued when the continuation of the proceedings has become impossible (s 1056 para 2 no 3 option 2 ZPO). Impossibility may have legal or factual grounds;[280] oftentimes it results in the arbitration agreement becoming incapable of being performed (s 1032 para 1 ZPO).[281] Examples for impossible continuation are a tie decision in the arbitral tribunal[282] or extraordinary conditions such as war or hostilities that prevent a party from participating in the arbitral proceedings.[283] If the ground for the impossible continuation simultaneously deprives the arbitral tribunal of its jurisdiction, a termination order cannot be issued based on the prevailing view that a decision denying jurisdiction is made by means of an arbitral award (para 6.56).[284] Such grounds include the termination of the arbitration agreement, its challenge or a judgment under s 1032 para 2 ZPO. If the dispute before the arbitral tribunal is *res judicata* of a state court judgment or inadmissible on other grounds than jurisdiction, the claim in any event needs to be dismissed by means of an award.[285]

6. Other Reasons

6.138 The **parties may agree** on further reasons for issuing a termination order although s 1056 ZPO does not explicitly open that avenue (see also para 6.131 on mandatory nature).[286] However, legal certainty is not affected if the parties extend the grounds

---

[277] v Schlabrendorff/Sessler, in: *Arbitration in Germany*, s 1056 para 11; Voit, in: Musielak/Voit (eds), s 1056 para 6.

[278] Voit, in: Musielak/Voit (eds), s 1056 para 6.

[279] Münch, in: MünchKommZPO, s 1056 para 31; Voit, in: Musielak/Voit (eds), s 1056 para 6.

[280] v Schlabrendorff/Sessler, in: *Arbitration in Germany*, s 1056 para 12; Voit, in: Musielak/Voit (eds), s 1056 para 7.

[281] Voit, in: Musielak/Voit (eds), s 1056 para 7.

[282] Government bill, BT-Drucks 13/5274, p 57; Lachmann, para 1863; Münch, in: MünchKommZPO, s 1056 para 33; Voit, in: Musielak/Voit (eds), s 1056 para 7.

[283] v Schlabrendorff/Sessler, in: *Arbitration in Germany*, s 1056 para 12; Schlosser, in: Stein/Jonas (eds), s 1056 para 9.

[284] Haas, SchiedsVZ 2010, 286, 293 *et seq.*; v Schlabrendorff/Sessler, in: *Arbitration in Germany*, s 1056 para 12; consistent (termination order, but no award in cases of lack of jurisdiction) Voit, in: Musielak/Voit (eds), s 1056 para 7; inconsistent Government bill, BT-Drucks 13/5274, p 57; Münch, in: MünchKommZPO, s 1056 para 33.

[285] Haas, SchiedsVZ 2010, 286, 293 *et seq.*; v Schlabrendorff/Sessler, in: *Arbitration in Germany*, s 1056 para 12; Schlosser, in: Stein/Jonas (eds), s 1056 para 9; dissenting Münch, in: MünchKommZPO, s 1056 para 33.

[286] Gerstenmaier, SchiedsVZ 2010, 281, 285.

for terminating the proceedings. Those who posit that an arbitral tribunal **declining its jurisdiction** has no power to render its decision as an award (para 6.56) need to allow for the issuance of a termination order in these cases.[287]

II. Form and Content

There are no legal requirements as to form and content of a termination order under s 1056 ZPO. Since the termination order is not an award irrespective of its denomination,[288] s 1054 ZPO does not apply. Thus, a termination order could also be issued orally. In practice, arbitral tribunals will issue the termination order in writing and signed by at least the chairman, will specify the arbitration including parties and arbitral tribunal, will issue the termination, and will indicate the grounds on which it is based.[289] **6.139**

III. Effects

1. Termination of the Proceedings (s 1056 para 1 ZPO)

The termination order has the same **terminating effect** as an arbitral award on the arbitral proceedings (s 1056 para 1 ZPO, para 6.126) and on the office of the arbitrators (s 1056 para 3 ZPO, para 6.127). **6.140**

Similar to an award (para 6.126), the termination order terminates the proceedings only if the entire dispute including the **costs** has been resolved (cf para 6.24). This will often be the case if the parties amicably settle the dispute (para 6.24). If the parties do not resolve the allocation of costs, the arbitral tribunal needs to issue a separate cost award (paras 6.48 *et seq.*).[290] **6.141**

2. Other Effects

The termination order is furthermore relevant for the **suspension of limitation** that began to run with the commencement of the arbitral proceedings (s 204 para 1 no 11 BGB); it ends six months after the termination order has been issued (s 204 para 2 BGB).[291] Since it puts an end to the arbitration, the termination order indirectly also renders the **arbitrators' fee claims due** (s 614 cl 1 BGB).[292] **6.142**

---

287 Voit, in: Musielak/Voit (eds), s 1056 para 1.

288 v Schlabrendorff/Sessler, in: *Arbitration in Germany*, s 1056 para 5; Voit, in: Musielak/Voit (eds), s 1056 para 3.

289 Cf Lachmann, para 1865.

290 Cf v Schlabrendorff/Sessler, in: *Arbitration in Germany*, s 1056 para 8.

291 Münch, in: MünchKommZPO, s 1056 para 14; v Schlabrendorff/Sessler, in: *Arbitration in Germany*, s 1056 para 5; Schütze, para 422.

292 Münch, in: MünchKommZPO, s 1056 para 14; v Schlabrendorff/Sessler, in: *Arbitration in Germany*, s 1056 para 5.

IV. Remedies

6.143 Since the termination order is not an award (para 6.139), the remedies against an arbitral award (s 1059 ZPO) are unavailable for a termination order.[293] In fact, procedural orders are **not subject to review** at all. An arbitral award terminates the arbitral proceedings under s 1056 para 1 ZPO regardless of whether it later is successfully set aside; s 1059 para 4 ZPO only exceptionally allows for continuation of the already terminated arbitral proceedings. The terminating effect of arbitral awards irrespective of their validity and indeed future existence is justified by the need for legal certainty regarding the pendency of arbitral proceedings. As demonstrated by s 1056 para 1 ZPO, this need is the same for termination orders as for arbitral awards. At the same time, the law does not set out an option to remit the case to the arbitral tribunal as under s 1059 para 4 ZPO if the termination order was invalid. Even if a termination order was not based on a ground for termination, it therefore maintains its terminating effect.[294]

6.144 However, the parties are free to agree on a **reopening of the proceedings**.[295] Since the office of the arbitrators has ended (para 6.127), the arbitrators also need to approve the reopening.[296] Whether the arbitration agreement is affected by the termination of the proceedings is to be assessed under general rules (waiver or s 1032 para 1 ZPO).

G. Correction, Interpretation, and Supplementation of the Arbitral Award (s 1058 ZPO)

6.145 The arbitral award is binding on the tribunal (para 6.122). Once it has been delivered to the parties, the arbitral tribunal can therefore not amend its findings even if it finds that it incorrectly decided the case. Section 1058 ZPO is no exception to this rule, as the arbitral tribunal is allowed to change its word but not its will. However, s 1058 ZPO takes account of deficiencies that the award may suffer from beyond the correct application of the law to the facts. The need for such clarification is significant in light of the low requirements for an award (paras 6.91 *et seq.*). Section 1058 ZPO applies to any award that meets the requirements of s 1054 paras 1, 4 ZPO (paras 6.92 *et seq.*).[297]

---

[293] Lachmann, para 1867; Münch, in: MünchKommZPO, s 1056 para 9; v Schlabrendorff/Sessler, in: *Arbitration in Germany*, s 1056 para 5; dissenting Haas, SchiedsVZ 2010, 286, 289 *et seq.*; Schütze, SchiedsVZ 2009, 241, 247.

[294] Cf Voit, in: Musielak/Voit (eds), s 1056 para 1.

[295] Voit, in: Musielak/Voit (eds), s 1056 para 8.

[296] v Schlabrendorff/Sessler, in: *Arbitration in Germany*, s 1056 para 6; Voit, in: Musielak/Voit (eds), s 1056 para 8.

[297] Münch, in: MünchKommZPO, s 1058 para 5.

I. Correction (s 1058 para 1 no 1 ZPO)

The arbitral tribunal can correct any errors in computation, any clerical or typographical errors or any errors of similar nature in the award (s 1058 para 1 no 1 ZPO). Errors of similar nature need to be as **obvious** as computational, clerical, or typographical errors are.[298] Once there can be any doubt whether the award is incorrect, such ambiguity may be cured by way of interpretation (para 6.147) but cannot be corrected.[299] Correction is an instrument to obtain what the arbitral tribunal has decided but accidentally did not express; it is a means to correct the expression of the tribunal's decision, not the underlying decision.[300] Correction does not allow for adding legal reasoning.[301] As long as these guidelines are adhered to, the correction may significantly amend or even reverse the decision in its dispositive part (eg if the arbitral tribunal confused the party roles or omitted a "not").[302] Violation of these rules constitutes a ground for setting aside the correction award under s 1059 para 2 no 1 lit d ZPO.[303] Since correction aims at obvious errors, the arbitral tribunal can also correct errors in awards on agreed terms even though it did not make the underlying decision.[304] Otherwise, the parties would have no remedy at all to correct errors in such awards. **6.146**

II. Interpretation (s 1058 para 1 no 2 ZPO)

Similar to its correction, the (authentic) interpretation of the award under s 1058 para 1 no 2 ZPO must not amend the decision that the arbitral tribunal has reached.[305] Interpretation rather serves only to clarify ambiguous parts of the award (not the entire award[306]). Interpretation may in particular be an instrument to rephrase the dispositive part of the award in a way that it becomes enforceable.[307] If the interpretation award exceeds these limits, it is subject to setting aside under s 1059 para 2 no 1 lit d ZPO.[308] **6.147**

298 Münch, in: MünchKommZPO, s 1058 para 6; Schwab/Walter, ch 21 para 14; Voit, in: Musielak/Voit (eds), s 1058 para 2.

299 Voit, in: Musielak/Voit (eds), s 1058 para 2.

300 RG JW 1935, 2050; OLG Stuttgart, December 20, 2001, 1 Sch 13/01 (unreported), http://www.disarb.org (last visited December 1, 2015); Münch, in: MünchKommZPO, s 1058 para 6; v Schlabrendorff/Sessler, in: *Arbitration in Germany*, s 1058 para 3; Voit, in: Musielak/Voit (eds), s 1058 para 2.

301 Münch, in: MünchKommZPO, s 1058 para 6; Schwab/Walter, ch 21 para 14; dissenting Schlosser, in: Stein/Jonas (eds), s 1058 para 3.

302 Reichold, in: Thomas/Putzo (eds), s 1058 para 3; Voit, in: Musielak/Voit (eds), s 1058 para 2.

303 OLG Stuttgart, BeckRS 2001, 30229524; Schlosser, in: Stein/Jonas (eds), s 1058 para 9; Schwab/Walter, ch 21 para 14; Voit, in: Musielak/Voit (eds), s 1058 para 2.

304 Münch, in: MünchKommZPO, s 1053 para 47; Reichold, in: Thomas/Putzo (eds), s 1058 para 3; Voit, in: Musielak/Voit (eds), s 1058 para 2.

305 Voit, in: Musielak/Voit (eds), s 1058 para 3.

306 Lachmann, para 2021; Münch, in: MünchKommZPO, s 1058 para 8; v Schlabrendorff/Sessler, in: *Arbitration in Germany*, s 1058 para 6; Schlosser, in: Stein/Jonas (eds), s 1058 para 18.

307 Voit, in: Musielak/Voit (eds), s 1058 para 3.

308 OLG Stuttgart, December 20, 2001, 1 Sch 13/01 (unreported), http://www.disarb.org (last visited December 1, 2015); Kreindler/Schäfer/Wolff, para 1052.

III. Additional Award (s 1058 para 1 no 3 ZPO)

6.148 An additional award under s 1058 para 1 no 3 ZPO can be made if the arbitral tribunal has made a final award which, however, does not cover the entire matter in dispute as defined by the parties' requests. Whether these requests have been referenced in the award is irrelevant.[309] An additional award can also be made on costs if the cost decision was not included in the final award.[310] The putatively final award triggering an additional award under s 1058 para 1 no 3 ZPO is to be distinguished from a partial award in which the arbitral tribunal deliberately does not adjudicate the entire matter in dispute. The award following a partial award requires neither a party request nor observance of the deadline under s 1058 para 3 ZPO.[311]

IV. Request

1. Request by a Party (s 1058 paras 1, 4 ZPO)

6.149 The interpretation of an award and an additional award can be made by the arbitral tribunal only if requested by at least one party (s 1058 para 1 ZPO). Only the correction can likewise be made on the tribunal's own initiative (s 1058 para 4 ZPO).

2. Deadline (s 1058 para 2 ZPO)

6.150 Any **party request** under s 1058 ZPO needs to be filed within the deadline of one month after the award has been received by that party (s 1058 para 2 ZPO). This deadline runs for each party individually.[312] The parties may agree on another deadline, even after the original deadline has lapsed.[313] The arbitral tribunal, however, cannot extend the deadline; each party can legitimately rely on the fact that the award is subject to interpretation only within the set time frame and that an additional award can be rendered only within that time frame as well.[314] If the arbitral tribunal interprets the award or renders an additional award although the request did not meet the relevant deadline, its decision is subject to being set aside under s 1059 para 2 no 1 lit c and d ZPO.[315] A belated request for correction can be understood as a suggestion for a correction on the tribunal's own initiative;[316]

---

[309] Schwab/Walter, ch 21 para 16; Voit, in: Musielak/Voit (eds), s 1058 para 4.

[310] OLG Stuttgart, NJW-RR 2003, 1438, 1439; Münch, in: MünchKommZPO, s 1058 para 14.

[311] v Schlabrendorff/Sessler, in: *Arbitration in Germany*, s 1058 para 7; Voit, in: Musielak/Voit (eds), s 1058 para 4.

[312] Voit, in: Musielak/Voit (eds), s 1058 para 5.

[313] Christ, pp 220 *et seq.*; Münch, in: MünchKommZPO, s 1058 para 18; v Schlabrendorff/Sessler, in: *Arbitration in Germany*, s 1058 para 8; Voit, in: Musielak/Voit (eds), s 1058 para 5.

[314] Voit, in: Musielak/Voit (eds), s 1058 para 5.

[315] For lit c only: Voit, in: Musielak/Voit (eds), s 1058 para 5; for lit d only: Münch, in: MünchKommZPO, s 1058 para 21; Osterthun, pp 260 *et seq.*; Schlosser, in: Stein/Jonas (eds), s 1058 para 9.

[316] Kröll, SchiedsVZ 2006, 203, 208; v Schlabrendorff/Sessler, in: *Arbitration in Germany*, s 1058 para 8; Schlosser, in: Stein/Jonas (eds), s 1058 para 16; Voit, in: Musielak/Voit (eds), s 1058 para 5; dissenting Münch, in: MünchKommZPO, s 1058 para 7.

a correction issued upon a belated request is therefore not subject to setting aside for that reason.

Only the party request is subject to the deadline set out by s 1058 para 2 ZPO. If the **arbitral tribunal** corrects its award on its own motion, it is not bound by a deadline.[317] This is in compliance with the wording of the provision and meets a practical need for correction that becomes obvious only later. **6.151**

V. Procedure

1. *Right to be Heard*

The procedure follows the general rules of ss 1042 *et seq.* ZPO.[318] Before the arbitral tribunal renders a decision on the interpretation or on an additional award, it needs to give all parties the opportunity to present their case (s 1042 para 1 cl 2 BGB). While it is best practice to grant the parties the right to be heard also for the correction of obvious mistakes, this is not legally necessary[319] since a state court would not need to hear the parties before such decision[320] and the due process standard in arbitral proceedings is not higher than in German state court proceedings. **6.152**

2. *Deadline (s 1058 para 3 ZPO)*

The arbitral tribunal should make the correction or give the interpretation within one month and make an additional award within two months (s 1058 para 3 ZPO). This deadline serves only as a guideline for the arbitral tribunal; if it exceeds the deadline, the tribunal's decision is not subject to setting aside or other sanctions.[321] **6.153**

3 *Form of Decision (s 1058 para 5 ZPO)*

Section 1054 ZPO applies to the correction or interpretation of the award and to an additional award (s 1058 para 5 ZPO). Any decision under s 1058 ZPO that does not dismiss the request therefore has to meet the **form requirements of an award** (paras 6.92 *et seq.*). **6.154**

As it contains a separate decision, an **additional award** (s 1058 para 1 no 3 ZPO) is indeed an award and subject to the same remedies including setting aside.[322] **6.155**

---

[317] v Schlabrendorff/Sessler, in: *Arbitration in Germany*, s 1058 para 9; dissenting Münch, in: MünchKommZPO, s 1058 para 7.

[318] Government bill, BT-Drucks 13/5274, p 58.

[319] Voit, in: Musielak/Voit (eds), s 1058 para 6; see also (with incorrect reference to s 1058 para 4 ZPO) OLG Frankfurt, SchiedsVZ 2005, 311, 312; dissenting Government bill, BT-Drucks 13/5274, p 58; Lachmann, para 2011; Reichold, in: Thomas/Putzo (eds), s 1058 para 4; v Schlabrendorff/Sessler, in: *Arbitration in Germany*, s 1058 para 4.

[320] BVerfGE 34, 1, 7 *et seq.*

[321] Hartmann, in: Baumbach/Lauterbach/Albers/Hartmann (eds), s 1058 para 3; Münch, in: MünchKommZPO, s 1058 para 19; v Schlabrendorff/Sessler, in: *Arbitration in Germany*, s 1058 para 8; see also Government bill, BT-Drucks 13/5274, p 58; dissenting Kreindler/Schäfer/Wolff, para 1060; Schwab/Walter, ch 21 para 17 (s 1059 para 2 no 1 lit d ZPO).

[322] Government bill, BT-Drucks 13/5274, p 58; Voit, in: Musielak/Voit (eds), s 1058 para 7.

Interpretation and correction, conversely, become part of the original award so that both decisions can be set aside and enforced only together.[323] Only if interpretation or correction exceed their borders, eg amend the underlying award, can they be set aside separately.[324] The deadline for a request to set aside the award is extended by s 1059 para 3 cl 3 ZPO (para 6.179).

H. Setting Aside of Arbitral Awards (s 1059 ZPO)

I. Spirit and Purpose

6.156 The setting aside application as set out in s 1059 ZPO is one of the most important elements in German arbitration for a number of reasons. First, it provides for a state court review of the arbitral award without (the possibility of) which the effects of a state court judgment could not be attached to an arbitral award. Section 1059 ZPO therefore serves as a—constitutionally required[325]—**counterpart to s 1055 ZPO.**[326] Notably, the effects of an award under s 1055 ZPO are not contingent on an actual court review. Although the review under s 1059 ZPO at least in part serves public interests, it cannot be initiated by the court on its own motion. The application is rather solely in the hands of the parties. The law could establish such mechanism since at least one party will usually be interested in filing the setting aside application ("private enforcement").

6.157 Second, s 1059 ZPO sets out an exhaustive list of criteria for state court review which **balance the powers** between the arbitral tribunal and the state court. As s 1059 ZPO does not go beyond an internationally recognized set of grounds for setting aside an arbitral award which the courts do not apply in an unduly extensive interpretation, it is also the essential provision for establishing the arbitration-friendliness of German law.

6.158 Third, although the number of setting aside applications in Germany is small as compared to the number of arbitral proceedings, the grounds for setting aside legally limit the broad discretion that the arbitral tribunal enjoys in procedural matters. Moreover, having one's own award set aside for the violation of procedural standards does not contribute to an arbitrator's good reputation. The sanction that the setting aside proceedings provide will, even if the parties do actually not make use of this remedy, often **admonish the arbitrators** to comply with their duties.

---

[323] KG SchiedsVZ 2011, 110, 111; Government bill, BT-Drucks 13/5274, p 58; v Schlabrendorff/Sessler, in: *Arbitration in Germany*, s 1058 para 10; Voit, in: Musielak/Voit (eds), s 1058 para 7.

[324] Voit, in: Musielak/Voit (eds), s 1058 para 7.

[325] Kröll/Kraft, in: *Arbitration in Germany*, s 1059 para 1; Sonnauer, pp 32 *et seq.*; Schütze, SchiedsVZ 2009, 241 *et seq.*

[326] Kröll/Kraft, in: *Arbitration in Germany*, s 1059 para 1; Voit, in: Musielak/Voit (eds), s 1059 para 1.

II. Application for Setting Aside as the Only Recourse (s 1059 para 1 ZPO)

1. *Binding Effect of an Arbitral Award not yet Set Aside*

An arbitral award (preliminarily) has the same effect as a final and binding state court judgment (s 1055 ZPO) regardless of how defective the arbitral proceedings have been. Only if successfully set aside does the arbitral award cease to be binding with retrospective effect (para 6.242). **6.159**

2. *No Incidental Review of an Arbitral Award*

In order to protect its legal effects under s 1055 ZPO, the arbitral award can be reviewed by a state court for grounds for setting aside (and can consequently be treated as non-binding) only within setting aside proceedings under s 1059 ZPO. Outside setting aside proceedings, no court may review the arbitral award for grounds for setting aside. Unless the award has been set aside, no court may disregard the effects of the award. In particular the award debtor cannot raise the defense that the arbitral award suffers from grounds for setting aside in subsequent proceedings.[327] **6.160**

3. *Other Remedies Against the Arbitral Award*

German law recognizes two procedural remedies which only apparently seem to violate the rule that the setting aside application is the only remedy against an arbitral award (para 6.160). The first of these is the **application for a declaration of enforceability** under s 1060 ZPO which, if unsuccessful, results in a refusal of the declaration of enforceability and the setting aside of the award (s 1060 para 2 cl 1 ZPO). While the proceedings for a declaration of enforceability indeed mirror the setting aside proceedings, they are not a remedy against the award but rather a remedy to enhance the effects of an award (para 6.247). **6.161**

The second seeming exception is the **request to declare that an award does not meet the requirements of s 1054 ZPO** (paras 6.92 *et seq.*) and thus does not have the effects of an arbitral award. This request for declaratory relief under general rules of civil procedure (s 256 ZPO) is not barred by s 1059 para 1 ZPO[328] since s 1059 ZPO applies only to arbitral awards that meet the requirements of s 1054 ZPO. Relief against an award that fails to meet these requirements therefore is beyond the scope (and the exhaustive character) of s 1059 ZPO. **6.162**

As the only remaining exception from s 1059 para 1 ZPO, the prevailing view under German law acknowledges a substantive law **claim for damages under s 826** **6.163**

[327] Hausmann, in: *Festschrift Stoll*, pp 593, 616; Kröll/Kraft, in: *Arbitration in Germany*, s 1059 para 101; Schlosser, in: Stein/Jonas (eds), s 1059 para 62.

[328] Hausmann, in: *Festschrift Stoll*, pp 593, 616; Voit, in: Musielak/Voit (eds), s 1059 para 2; dissenting Kröll/Kraft, in: *Arbitration in Germany*, s 1059 para 101.

BGB.[329] Pursuant to this provision, a person who intentionally inflicts damage on another person against good morals is liable for damages. Case law approves liability under this provision if executory titles are misused in particularly severe cases.[330] This requires the award to be incorrect on the merits and that such incorrectness not be due to the negligence of the award debtor.[331] Furthermore, special circumstances must apply for the award creditor's conduct to violate good morals.[332] The award creditor must usually have obtained the award by fraud; in cases without such fraud, it must have been highly unfair and almost intolerable to utilize the award.[333] The award creditor is generally not liable if the award debtor can make use or could have made use of remedies without further ado or has failed to do so.[334] The award creditor must act at least with qualified intent regarding all other prerequisites including the damage occurring.[335] The claim under s 826 BGB aims at restoring the position that would exist if the circumstances giving rise to damages had not occurred (s 249 para 1 BGB), in particular omission of any enforcement actions and compensation for already completed enforcement actions.[336]

6.164 Although it is generally questionable to allow for a substantive law claim for damages to complement procedural law remedies,[337] the better grounds speak in favor of the prevailing view[338] that applies s 826 ZPO to arbitral awards, at least on the basis that this provision is applied to executory titles in any event. It is irrelevant that in all cases covered by s 826 ZPO German public policy is likewise violated.[339] A public policy violation will not affect the arbitral award once the three-month deadline under s 1059 para 3 ZPO has lapsed and a setting aside application can no longer be filed.[340] Arbitral awards violating public policy can indeed not be declared enforceable even after this deadline has lapsed. However, reliance on this option is useless in the case of arbitral awards that do not need to be declared enforceable, eg declaratory awards.[341] The claim under s 826 BGB is

[329] BGHZ 145, 376, 381 = NJW 2001, 373, 374; Government bill, BT-Drucks 13/5274, p 60; Boecker, EWiR 2001, 345, 346; Schwab/Walter, ch 24 para 2a; Voit, ZZP 114 (2001), 355, 357 *et seq.*; dissenting Eckstein-Puhl, pp 273 *et seq.*; Gaul, in: *Festschrift Leipold*, pp 881, 907 *et seq.*, 911 *et seq.*; Kröll/Kraft, in: *Arbitration in Germany*, s 1059 para 103.

[330] BGH NJW 2006, 154, 156 (not reproduced in BGHZ 164, 87); OLG Köln, SchiedsVZ 2015, 295, 297 (for an arbitral award); Sprau, in: Palandt (ed), s 826 para 52.

[331] BGH NJW-RR 1988, 957, 959.

[332] BGH NJW 1999, 1257, 1258 *et seq.*

[333] BGHZ 26, 391, 396 *et seq.* = NJW 1958, 826; BGHZ 112, 54, 57 = NJW 1991, 30, 31; 2005, 2991, 2994; OLG Köln, SchiedsVZ 2015, 295, 297 (for an arbitral award).

[334] OLG Köln, NJW-RR 2009, 1074, 1075.

[335] Sprau, in: Palandt (ed), s 826 paras 10 *et seq.*

[336] BGHZ 13, 71, 72 *et seq.* = NJW 1954, 880; BGHZ 26, 391, 394 = NJW 1958, 826; OLG Köln, SchiedsVZ 2015, 295, 299 (for an arbitral award).

[337] Walker, in: 50 Jahre Bundesgerichtshof, Festgabe aus der Wissenschaft, Vol 3, pp 367, 373 *et seq.* with further references.

[338] OLG Köln, SchiedsVZ 2015, 295, 297 *et seq.*

[339] Dissenting Kröll/Kraft, in: *Arbitration in Germany*, s 1059 para 103.

[340] See Voit, in: Musielak/Voit (eds), s 1059 para 26; Voit, ZZP 114 (2001), 355, 358.

[341] Voit, in: Musielak/Voit (eds), s 1059 para 26 fn 86; overlooked by Weigand, LM s 1053 ZPO no 1 p 4.

to be brought before an arbitral tribunal if it is covered by an arbitration agreement. If the arbitration clause refers to "all disputes arising out of or in connection with this contract," it is decisive whether the s 826 BGB claim as a dispute arising out of a party's conduct in the arbitration is still "in connection" with the underlying contract. Since the claim aims to rectify the incorrect decision on substance (which is in the hands of the arbitral tribunal), the better grounds speak in favor of a broad interpretation of the clause which constitutes the arbitral tribunal's jurisdiction.[342]

4. Waiver of Remedies

According to the prevailing view, a party **cannot wholly waive its right** to apply for setting aside of an arbitral award.[343] A party can, however, waive its right to rely on individual grounds for setting aside, but only after the award has been rendered and in awareness of the ground for setting aside[344] and, moreover, only the grounds under s 1059 para 2 no 1 ZPO. The grounds under s 1059 para 2 no 2 ZPO are said to be non-waivable since they serve public interests.[345] This, in turn, is said to be indicated by the fact that the grounds under s 1059 para 2 no 2 ZPO are to be considered on the courts' own motion, regardless of whether the party relied on them.[346] **6.165**

While s 1059 para 2 no 2 ZPO indeed serves public interests, denial of waivability is difficult to reconcile with the private enforcement approach underlying s 1059 ZPO (para 6.156): no public interest obliges a party to apply for setting aside of an award even if grounds under s 1059 para 2 no 2 ZPO exist[347] and letting the application deadline lapse has the same effect as waiving grounds for setting aside. The reason for restricting waivability therefore cannot be a public interest, but rather the **protection of the party and/or the integrity of the arbitral process**. **6.166**

[342] Feldmann, pp 108 *et seq.*; dissenting OLG Köln, SchiedsVZ 2015, 295, 297; see also Schlosser, in: Stein/Jonas (eds), annex to s 1061 para 353.

[343] BGHZ 96, 40, 42 = NJW 1986, 1436; BayObLG EWiR 2000, 199, 200; OLG Frankfurt, NJW 1984, 2768; Geimer, in: Zöller (ed), s 1059 para 79; Hausmann, in: *Festschrift Stoll*, pp 593, 595; Lachmann, para 2346; Münch, in: MünchKommZPO, s 1059 para 53; Schwab/Walter, ch 24 para 53.

[344] BayObLG BB 2000, Beil. 12, pp 16, 17; Schwab/Walter, ch 24 para 53; Voit, in: Musielak/Voit (eds), s 1059 para 39; see also (waivability also before the award has been rendered if only the ground for setting aside is known before) Kröll/Kraft, in: *Arbitration in Germany*, s 1059 para 7; Schlosser, in: Stein/Jonas (eds), s 1059 para 2.

[345] Kröll/Kraft, in: *Arbitration in Germany*, s 1059 para 7; Münch, in: MünchKommZPO, s 1059 para 53; Schlosser, in: Stein/Jonas (eds), s 1059 para 2; Schwab/Walter, ch 24 para 53; more restrictive (not waivable only if public interests are directly affected) Geimer, in: Zöller (ed), s 1059 para 82.

[346] Voit, in: Musielak/Voit (eds), s 1059 para 39.

[347] Concurring Kröll/Kraft, in: *Arbitration in Germany*, s 1059 para 9.

III. Admissibility

6.167 The requirements for filing a claim under German civil procedural law also apply to the application to set aside an arbitral award to the extent that the German arbitration law in ss 1025 *et seq.* ZPO does not contain more specific diverging provisions. While the general requirements are described in paras 5.17 *et seq.*, the following comments focus on the specific rules for the setting aside procedure.

6.168 Setting aside proceedings are to be conducted **in German** as the official language used in court (s 184 cl 1 GVG). This holds true regardless of the language in which the award has been drafted.

1. Domestic Award

6.169 The setting aside application is available only for decisions qualifying as arbitral awards (paras 6.170 *et seq.*), including void awards (para 6.172), with a place of arbitration in Germany (para 6.173).

6.170 a) **Limitation to Arbitral Awards** A setting aside application is admissible only against arbitral awards. This remedy is neither available against other decisions of arbitral tribunals like procedural orders, interim measures (s 1041 ZPO), or preliminary rulings (s 1040 para 3 ZPO) nor against any decisions of bodies that are not arbitral tribunals, including association courts (*Vereinsgerichte*, para 2.40). The notion of the arbitral award is the same as in s 1054 ZPO and s 1055 ZPO;[348] for more detail see paras 6.87 *et seq.* Like s 1055 ZPO (para 6.111), s 1059 ZPO requires the award to be made in writing and to bear the signatures of the (majority of the) arbitrators (s 1054 para 1 ZPO, paras 6.92 *et seq.*). Unlike under s 1055 ZPO, s 1059 ZPO does not require the award to be delivered to each party under s 1054 para 4 ZPO but only to the party filing the setting aside application (see s 1059 para 3 ZPO).

6.171 The prevailing view rightfully denies the opportunity to challenge decisions that only appear to be arbitral awards: a non-award (or pseudo-award) cannot be set aside[349] and the state courts will test this requirement on their own motion in every instance.[350] Doubts as to whether a decision qualifies as an arbitral award may be clarified by way of a **request under s 256 ZPO to declare that a decision is not an award** (cf para 6.162), be it that the decision was not rendered by an arbitral tribunal or that it does not meet the formal requirements under s 1054 para 1 ZPO.

---

[348] Schwab/Walter, ch 25 para 2; Voit, in: Musielak/Voit (eds), s 1059 para 3.

[349] BGHZ 159, 207, 210 = SchiedsVZ 2004, 205, 207; Geimer, in: Zöller (ed), s 1059 para 16; Voit, in: Musielak/Voit (eds), s 1059 para 3; dissenting OLG Frankfurt, September 6, 2001, 3 Sch 02/00 (unreported), http://www.disarb.org (last visited December 1, 2015); Kröll/Kraft, in: *Arbitration in Germany*, s 1059 para 20.

[350] BGHZ 85, 288, 290 = NJW 1983, 867 (on the deposit requirement under former German arbitration law); NJW 1980, 1284; BGHZ 159, 207, 210 = SchiedsVZ 2004, 205, 206 *et seq.*; Schwab/Walter, ch 25 para 3; Voit, in: Musielak/Voit (eds), s 1059 para 3.

Such declaratory request can be brought before the higher regional court; s 1062 para 1 no 4, para 5 ZPO applies by way of analogy.[351] The jurisdiction of the same court that is competent for setting aside an award allows for requesting setting aside as an alternative request to a declaratory request under s 256 ZPO and vice versa. Since alternative requests are sufficient to meet the deadline for filing the setting aside application under s 1059 para 3 ZPO, the party burdened by a decision the classification of which is unclear is well advised to file such an alternative request.

b) Void Awards As an exception to the rule that any award is binding until it is successfully set aside (para 6.159), German law recognizes the existence of void awards. Awards are considered void if they so obviously suffer from such severe defects that they cannot even have a preliminary binding effect until the award is set aside.[352] Examples of void awards are awards that assume jurisdiction contrary to a court decision under s 1032 para 2 ZPO,[353] awards that decide an obviously non-arbitrable matter,[354] or awards that have been rendered by a "man in the street" without any indication of an arbitration agreement between the parties[355]. Although void awards do not have effects that need to be terminated by setting them aside, the setting aside application is also considered admissible against void awards.[356] Contrary to its usual effect, the setting aside of a void arbitral award is only declaratory in nature.[357] **6.172**

c) Limitation to Domestic Awards In line with the Model Law, German courts do not assume jurisdiction for setting aside foreign awards. To the contrary, only domestic awards can be challenged with the setting aside application. This requirement is not contained in the wording of s 1059 ZPO, but follows from s 1025 para 1 ZPO. As set out in this provision, s 1059 ZPO applies only if the place of arbitration is located in Germany.[358] **6.173**

2. *Competent Court (s 1062 ZPO)*

The competent court for setting aside an arbitral award is the **higher regional court at the place of arbitration** (s 1062 para 1 no 4 ZPO). The place of arbitration is deemed to be the one that is indicated in the arbitral award (s 1054 para 3 ZPO, **6.174**

---

351 Voit, in: Musielak/Voit (eds), s 1059 para 3.

352 Kröll/Kraft, in: *Arbitration in Germany*, s 1059 para 18; Voit, in: Musielak/Voit (eds), s 1059 para 5.

353 Münch, in: MünchKommZPO, s 1059 para 86; Schlosser, in: Stein/Jonas (eds), s 1059 para 7; Schlosser, in: *Festschrift Nagel*, pp 352, 360.

354 Geimer, in: Zöller (ed), s 1059 para 15; Kröll/Kraft, in: *Arbitration in Germany*, s 1059 para 18; Schlosser, in: Stein/Jonas (eds), s 1059 para 7; Voit, in: Musielak/Voit (eds), s 1059 para 5; dissenting Münch, in: MünchKommZPO, s 1059 para 86.

355 Kröll/Kraft, in: *Arbitration in Germany*, s 1059 para 18; Voit, in: Musielak/Voit (eds), s 1059 para 5.

356 Geimer, in: Zöller (ed), s 1059 para 16; Kröll/Kraft, in: *Arbitration in Germany*, s 1059 para 18; Münch, in: MünchKommZPO, s 1059 para 66; Schlosser, in: Stein/Jonas (eds), s 1059 para 8.

357 Geimer, in: Zöller (ed), s 1059 para 16; Münch, in: MünchKommZPO, s 1059 para 66; Schlosser, in: Stein/Jonas (eds), s 1059 para 8; Voit, in: Musielak/Voit (eds), s 1059 para 5.

358 Münch, in: MünchKommZPO, s 1059 para 68; Voit, in: Musielak/Voit (eds), s 1059 para 3.

para 6.100).[359] While the parties can agree on the (local) jurisdiction of another higher regional court in their arbitration agreement (s 1062 para 1 ZPO) or by later amendment to the arbitration agreement[360], they cannot agree on the (subject matter) jurisdiction of the court of another level.[361] The higher regional courts usually do not serve as courts of first instance in civil matters; by s 1062 para 1 ZPO the legislature acknowledged that setting aside an arbitral award is more similar to an appeal than to proceedings of first instance.[362]

6.175 If several higher regional courts exist in the territory of a federal state, that federal state may **concentrate the competence** with one higher regional court (s 1062 para 5 ZPO). Bavaria has provided the Oberlandesgericht München (Munich Higher Regional Court) with competence for the entire federal state,[363] while Rhineland-Palatinate has concentrated setting aside competence with the Oberlandesgericht Koblenz (Koblenz Higher Regional Court).[364] The higher regional courts that have been deprived of their competence by such concentration cannot again be provided jurisdiction by agreement of the parties.[365] If the parties agree on such a court in their arbitration agreement, such agreement is regularly to be interpreted as denominating the court at which jurisdiction was concentrated.[366]

3. Proper Representation (s 1063 para 4, s 78 para 3 ZPO)

6.176 Parties generally need to be represented before higher regional courts by a lawyer admitted to the German bar (s 78 para 1 cl 1 ZPO). For arbitration-related court proceedings, however, s 1063 para 4 ZPO allows for an exception: as long as no oral hearing has been ordered by the court, applications and declarations may be put on record at the court registry and for such filings no party needs to be represented by a lawyer (s 78 para 3 ZPO). Since the court has to order an oral hearing in all setting aside proceedings (s 1063 para 2 ZPO), parties need to mandate a lawyer at a later stage of the setting aside proceedings in any event. Not least since s 1059 para 3 ZPO sets limits to later submissions (para 6.191), parties are well advised to retain a lawyer from the very beginning of such proceedings.

---

359 OLG München, SchiedsVZ 2008, 307, 308; 2010, 336; Voit, in: Musielak/Voit (eds), s 1062 para 3.

360 OLG München, SchiedsVZ 2010, 336; Münch, in: MünchKommZPO, s 1062 paras 25 *et seq.*; Voit, in: Musielak/Voit (eds), s 1062 para 3.

361 OLG München, BeckRS 2010, 08692; Voit, in: Musielak/Voit (eds), s 1062 para 2.

362 Government bill, BT-Drucks 13/5274, p 63.

363 Ordinance of June 15, 1998, GVBl 1998, 356.

364 Ordinance of April 28, 1998, GVBl 1998, 134.

365 OLG München, SchiedsVZ 2012, 96, 99.

366 OLG München, October 29, 2009, 34 Sch 15/09 (unreported), http://www.disarb.org (last visited December 1, 2015); Voit, in: Musielak/Voit (eds), s 1062 para 3.

4. Specified Request for Relief

As its specified request for relief (s 253 para 2 no 2 ZPO), the setting aside application needs to request the full or partial setting aside of an arbitral award. The award must be sufficiently specified in the request, eg by indicating parties, date, and arbitrators.[367] While only s 1059 para 2 no 1 lit c ZPO explicitly allows for setting aside only parts of an arbitral award, this option is available for all grounds for setting aside if only the part of the award which is affected by the ground for setting aside is separable.[368] The setting aside application cannot contain a request to amend the arbitral award.[369] **6.177**

5. Application Deadline (s 1059 para 3 cls 1–3 ZPO)

The setting aside application must be filed within **three months** if the parties have not agreed on another deadline (s 1059 para 3 cl 1 ZPO). The deadline **starts to run** for each party separately once it has received an arbitral award that meets the requirements of s 1054 paras 1, 4 ZPO.[370] A setting aside application that has been filed after this deadline has lapsed will not be successful, whether based on the grounds under s 1059 para 2 no 1 ZPO or under s 1059 para 2 no 2 ZPO. Only the former are, however, also precluded as objections in proceedings for a declaration of enforceability (s 1060 para 2 cl 3 ZPO). **6.178**

If a **request under s 1058 ZPO** has been made, the deadline is extended to the extent that the applicant has at least one month after receipt of the decision on that request (s 1059 para 3 cl 3 ZPO).[371] If, however, the arbitral tribunal has made a decision on an additional award (s 1058 para 1 no 3 ZPO) or has exceeded the limits of correction or interpretation (para 6.155), the applicant must be given the full application deadline under s 1059 para 3 ZPO.[372] **6.179**

A setting aside application can exceptionally be filed **after the deadline** has lapsed if the applicant would be entitled to damages under s 826 BGB since the other party has intentionally inflicted damage against good morals by obtaining the arbitral award (paras 6.163 *et seq.*).[373] **6.180**

---

[367] Cf Kreindler/Schäfer/Wolff, para 1163.

[368] BGHZ 179, 304, 313 para 30 = SchiedsVZ 2009, 176, 178; VersR 1982, 92 *et seq.*; KG NJW 1976, 1357 *et seq.*; Geimer, in: Zöller (ed), s 1059 para 6; Voit, in: Musielak/Voit (eds), s 1059 para 32.

[369] Geimer, in: Zöller (ed), s 1059 para 6; Kröll/Kraft, in: *Arbitration in Germany*, s 1059 para 27; Voit, in: Musielak/Voit (eds), s 1059 para 32.

[370] OLG Düsseldorf, SchiedsVZ 2008, 156, 158; Münch, in: MünchKommZPO, s 1059 para 60; Voit, in: Musielak/Voit (eds), s 1059 para 36.

[371] Government bill, BT-Drucks 13/5274, p 60; Lachmann, para 2375; Münch, in: MünchKommZPO, s 1059 para 56; Voit, in: Musielak/Voit (eds), s 1059 para 36.

[372] Voit, in: Musielak/Voit (eds), s 1059 para 36.

[373] BGHZ 145, 376, 380 *et seq.* = NJW 2001, 373, 374.

6. No Declaration of Enforceability (s 1059 para 3 cl 4 ZPO)

6.181 Setting aside an award cannot be requested if the award has been declared enforceable by a German court (s 1059 para 3 cl 4 ZPO). Since all grounds for setting aside could have been brought in these proceedings for a declaration of enforceability (s 1060 para 2 cl 1 ZPO), no need exists for another opportunity to make submissions on these grounds.[374]

7. Grievance

6.182 It is disputed whether only a party that is burdened by the arbitral award can file a setting aside application.[375] While a prevailing party theoretically may have an interest in setting aside an incorrect award, such parties are rare in practice.

8. Legitimate Reason to Take Legal Action

6.183 As any other court action, the setting aside application requires a legitimate reason to take legal action (*Rechtsschutzbedürfnis*). The applicant has no such reason *inter alia* if it can achieve legal protection more easily or more effectively by other means (para 5.17). Since **pending proceedings to declare the award enforceable** allow for submitting all grounds for setting aside within these pending proceedings (s 1060 para 2 cl 1 ZPO), no legitimate reason for filing a setting aside application exists.[376]

6.184 If within pending setting aside proceedings a **counter-application for declaring the award enforceable** is filed, this counter-application pursues the more extensive aim since it may lead to declaring the award enforceable or to setting it aside (s 1060 para 2 cl 1 ZPO). Once the application for declaring the arbitral award enforceable has been filed, the party that had applied for setting aside the award loses any legitimate reason to take legal action and the setting aside application will be dismissed as inadmissible for that reason.[377] To avoid this result and the cost decision associated with it, the applicant may declare the main issue settled (*Erledigung der Hauptsache*) and therewith obtain a cost decision as if the counter-application had not been filed.[378]

---

[374] Government bill, BT-Drucks 13/5274, p 60.

[375] Pro: Geimer, in: Zöller (ed), s 1059 para 3; Kröll/Kraft, in: *Arbitration in Germany*, s 1059 para 33; Münch, in: MünchKommZPO, s 1059 para 55; Schwab/Walter, ch 25 para 11; con: Hartmann, in: Baumbach/Lauterbach/Albers/Hartmann (eds), s 1059 para 4; Kreindler/Schäfer/Wolff, para 1165; Voit, in: Musielak/Voit (eds), s 1059 para 32.

[376] OLG Frankfurt, October 14, 2010, 26 Sch 6/10 and 26 Sch 22/10 (unreported), http://www.disarb.org (last visited December 1, 2015); OLG Hamburg, SchiedsVZ 2003, 284, 286; OLG Naumburg, May 21, 2004, 10 Sch 06/03 (unreported), http://www.disarb.org (last visited December 1, 2015); Geimer, in: Zöller (ed), s 1059 paras 4, 22; Kröll/Kraft, in: *Arbitration in Germany*, s 1059 para 25; Schwab/Walter, ch 25 para 4; Voit, in: Musielak/Voit (eds), s 1059 para 33.

[377] Kreindler/Schäfer/Wolff, para 1171; Voit, in: Musielak/Voit (eds), s 1059 para 33; dissenting (stay in analogous application of s 148 ZPO) Geimer, in: Zöller (ed), s 1059 para 23; Hartmann, in: Baumbach/Lauterbach/Albers/Hartmann (eds), Grundz s 1059 para 2; Schwab/Walter, ch 25 para 4.

[378] Kreindler/Schäfer/Wolff, para 1171; Voit, in: Musielak/Voit (eds), s 1059 para 33.

IV. Merits

The setting aside application will be successful on the merits if it is brought against the correct opposing party (para 6.186), if a ground for setting aside exists, and if it is not excluded (paras 6.187 *et seq.*). **6.185**

1. *Party Opposing the Application*

The application for setting aside an award is to be brought against the **other party to the arbitration or its legal successor.**[379] In case of singular succession after the award has been rendered, the setting aside application can be filed either against the opposing party in the arbitration or its successor.[380] If the arbitral award's *res judicata* effect is extended to non-parties, the setting aside application is to be filed against all parties to the arbitration.[381] **6.186**

2. *Grounds for Setting Aside (s 1059 para 2 ZPO)*

a) General

aa) Exhaustive Character The grounds for setting aside are exhaustively listed in s 1059 para 2 ZPO as the wording ("only") demonstrates.[382] The exhaustive character of s 1059 para 2 ZPO distinguishes setting aside applications from appeals as it in particular excludes the incorrect decision of the dispute as a ground for setting aside (no *révision au fond*).[383] The parties cannot add additional grounds for setting aside by agreement.[384] Individual grounds can, however, be waived by party agreement (paras 6.165 *et seq.*). **6.187**

bb) No Mutual Exclusivity The grounds for setting aside are not mutually exclusive. Rather, one and the same factual situation can constitute various grounds for setting aside, for example a violation of the right to be heard may result in grounds for setting aside under s 1059 para 2 no 1 lit b and no 2 lit b ZPO.[385] **6.188**

cc) Burden of Proof The burden of proof that a ground for setting aside exists lies with the applicant, both for grounds under s 1059 para 2 no 1 and no 2 ZPO.[386] An **6.189**

---

[379] Kröll/Kraft, in: *Arbitration in Germany*, s 1059 para 34; Voit, in: Musielak/Voit (eds), s 1059 para 34.

[380] Geimer, in: Zöller (ed), s 1059 para 5; Hartmann, in: Baumbach/Lauterbach/Albers/Hartmann (eds), s 1059 para 4; Schwab/Walter, ch 25 para 8; dissenting (only against the successor) Schlosser, in: Stein/Jonas (eds), s 1059 para 9.

[381] Geimer, in: Zöller (ed), s 1059 para 5; Voit, in: Musielak/Voit (eds), s 1059 para 34.

[382] Government bill, BT-Drucks 13/5274, p 58.

[383] BGH NJW 1999, 2974, 2975; BGHZ 151, 79, 82 = SchiedsVZ 2003, 39, 40; Government bill, BT-Drucks 13/5274, pp 58 *et seq.*; OLG Köln, SchiedsVZ 2012, 161, 166; OLG Stuttgart, SchiedsVZ 2011, 49, 52; Geimer, in: Zöller (ed), s 1059 para 74; Voit, in: Musielak/Voit (eds), s 1059 para 18.

[384] Kröll/Kraft, in: *Arbitration in Germany*, s 1059 para 41; see also Wolff, 26(3) ASA Bull. 626, 631 *et seq.* (2008).

[385] Kröll/Kraft, in: *Arbitration in Germany*, s 1059 para 46; Schwab/Walter, ch 15 para 1; Voit, in: Musielak/Voit (eds), s 1042 para 2.

[386] Kröll/Kraft, in: *Arbitration in Germany*, s 1059 para 49; Lachmann, para 2381; Voit, in: Musielak/Voit (eds), s 1059 para 10 (for grounds under s 1059 para 2 no 1 ZPO).

exception is discussed for the (non-)existence of a valid arbitration agreement.[387] While it is true that the arbitration agreement forms the basis of the entire arbitration and that claimant has the burden to prove its existence in the arbitral proceedings, no need exists to extend this burden of proof to the setting aside proceedings.[388] An exception is to be made only if the applicant was not informed of the arbitral proceedings or did not otherwise have a sufficient opportunity to raise its objection during the arbitral proceedings.[389]

6.190 *dd) No Binding Effect of the Arbitral Tribunal's Findings* In order to allow for an effective review of the arbitral award, the court is not bound by the arbitral tribunal's factual findings[390] and legal assessment.[391] While the arbitral tribunal's decision on the merits cannot be reviewed by the court (para 6.187), its decision assuming jurisdiction is subject to a full court review. Clauses that expressly waive or limit this review are considered null and void, but do not affect the validity of the arbitration agreement.[392]

6.191 *ee) Sufficient Cause for Grounds for Setting Aside Under s 1059 para 2 no 1 ZPO* The court will consider a lack of arbitrability and a public policy violation on its own motion (s 1059 para 2 no 2 ZPO) since they also involve public interests. By contrast, the applicant must show sufficient cause for the grounds under s 1059 para 2 no 1 ZPO. To show sufficient cause, the applicant must designate the specific procedural irregularities on which it bases the application.[393] The designation as one particular ground or several of the grounds under s 1059 para 2 no 1 ZPO, conversely, is not required.[394] Since these irregularities define the matter that is in dispute,[395] any later addition amounts to an amendment of the application which can be brought only within the deadline under s 1059 para 3 ZPO.[396]

---

[387] OLG München, December 16, 2011, 34 Sch 30/11 (unreported), http://www.disarb.org (last visited December 1, 2015); LG Hamburg, RIW 1991, 419, 420; Schlosser, in: Stein/Jonas (eds), s 1059 para 10.

[388] Kröll/Kraft, in: *Arbitration in Germany*, s 1059 para 50.

[389] Cf (for cases in which the respondent had not participated in the arbitral proceedings) Voit, in: Musielak/Voit (eds), s 1059 para 10.

[390] BGHZ 30, 89, 92 = NJW 1959, 1438, 1439; KTS 1964, 172, 174; BGHZ 46, 365, 370 = NJW 1967, 1178, 1179; NJW 1972, 2180, 2181; WM 1983, 1207, 1208; Schlosser, in: Stein/Jonas (eds), s 1059 para 10; Schwab/Walter, ch 24 para 46; Voit, in: Musielak/Voit (eds), s 1059 para 30.

[391] BGHZ 27, 249, 254 = NJW 1958, 1538, 1539; 1972, 2180, 2181; WM 1983, 1207, 1208; Kröll/Kraft, in: *Arbitration in Germany*, s 1059 para 52.

[392] BGHZ 162, 9, 14 = SchiedsVZ 2005, 95, 96 *et seq.*

[393] Schlosser, in: Stein/Jonas (eds), s 1059 para 4; Voit, in: Musielak/Voit (eds), s 1059 para 35.

[394] OLG München, SchiedsVZ 2005, 308, 309; Voit, in: Musielak/Voit (eds), s 1059 para 35; dissenting Kröll/Kraft, in: *Arbitration in Germany*, s 1059 para 30 (but see para 32); Schlosser, in: Stein/Jonas (eds), s 1059 para 4.

[395] Lachmann, para 2379; Voit, in: Musielak/Voit (eds), s 1059 para 35; indecisive Schwab/Walter, ch 25 para 10.

[396] RGZ 23, 432, 433; KG SchiedsVZ 2009, 179, 180; Kröll/Kraft, in: *Arbitration in Germany*, s 1059 para 32; Schlosser, in: Stein/Jonas (eds), s 1059 para 4; Voit, in: Musielak/Voit (eds), s 1059 para 35.

Subsequently, another distinction is made: while in the fact situations underlying some grounds for setting aside, the arbitral tribunal has **not been sufficiently empowered** by the parties to decide the dispute (paras 6.193 *et seq.*), the remaining grounds for setting aside describe **egregious procedural flaws** (paras 6.206 *et seq.*). **6.192**

b) Lack of Legitimation of the Arbitral Tribunal The first group of grounds for setting aside consists of grounds in which the arbitral tribunal **lacked jurisdiction** to decide the dispute, be it that the parties had not concluded an arbitration agreement at all or that it is invalid (paras 6.194 *et seq.*), including for reasons of a party's incapacity (para 6.201) or the subject matter's lack of arbitrability (para 6.202),[397] or that a valid arbitration agreement exists but does not encompass the dispute between the parties (paras 6.203 *et seq.*). By contrast, the **incorrect denial of jurisdiction** by an arbitral tribunal does not constitute a ground for setting aside under the clear wording of s 1059 para 2 ZPO[398] even if such decision is to be classified as an arbitral award (paras 6.56, 6.87). **6.193**

aa) Invalidity of the Arbitration Agreement (s 1059 para 2 no 1 lit a option 2 ZPO) **6.194**
(1) General Grounds for Invalidity The arbitral award can be set aside if the underlying arbitration agreement is invalid (s 1059 para 2 no 1 lit a ZPO); this holds true all the more if an arbitration agreement has not even been concluded.[399] Both questions are **governed by the law** that the parties have chosen for the validity of the arbitration agreement or, failing such agreement, German law (s 1059 para 2 no 1 lit a ZPO). For details on the validity of an arbitration agreement governed by German law, see paras 2.44 *et seq.*

The decisive **point in time** for determining whether the arbitral award was based on a valid arbitration agreement is when the arbitral tribunal has last granted an opportunity to comment.[400] The parties can, however, even subsequently conclude an agreement (or approve the previous conclusion of an arbitration agreement by an agent without authority), thus subsequently providing the necessary jurisdiction.[401] **6.195**

(2) Lack of Form The lack of form is not only particularly important as a ground for setting aside, but is also subject to specific rules including for the **governing law**. Section 1059 para 2 no 1 lit a option 1 ZPO references "the arbitration agreement referred to in ss 1029 and 1031" and therewith presupposes an arbitration **6.196**

[397] Cf Government bill, BT-Drucks 13/5274, p 59 (split into several grounds for setting aside is explained by differing conflict of law rules).
[398] BGHZ 151, 79, 82 = SchiedsVZ 2003, 39, 40; Government bill, BT-Drucks 13/5274, p 44; dissenting Schlosser, in: Stein/Jonas (eds), s 1059 para 32 (s 1059 para 2 no 1 lit a ZPO); Schwab/Walter, ch 24 para 15a (s 1059 para 2 no 1 lit c ZPO).
[399] Münch, in: MünchKommZPO, s 1059 paras 15 *et seq.*; Schwab/Walter, ch 24 para 7.
[400] Lachmann, para 2185; Schlosser, in: Stein/Jonas (eds), s 1059 para 17; Schwab/Walter, ch 24 para 8; Voit, in: Musielak/Voit (eds), s 1059 para 9; dissenting (rendering of the award) Münch, in: MünchKommZPO, s 1059 para 17.
[401] Schlosser, in: Stein/Jonas (eds), s 1059 para 9; Voit, in: Musielak/Voit (eds), s 1059 para 9.

agreement that meets the (German) form requirements under s 1031 ZPO (for details on these requirements, see paras 2.67 *et seq.*).[402] While the wording of option 2 ("arbitration agreement") is less clear than in art 34 para 2 lit a (i) Model Law ("said agreement"),[403] the German legislator intended to generally exclude the form requirement from the parties' choice of law and to generally submit it to German law.[404] According to an alternative view, the arbitration agreement needs to comply with the form requirements of both German law and the law applicable to the arbitration agreement.[405]

6.197 The arbitration agreement does not lack its required form if such lack is **cured** by entering into argument on the substance of the dispute in the arbitral proceedings (s 1031 para 6 ZPO). Since, as a result, the arbitration agreement is not invalid due to a lack of form, the arbitral award cannot be set aside under s 1059 para 2 no 1 lit a option 2 ZPO.

6.198 *(3) No Exclusion of the Ground for Setting Aside* The applicant can also be barred from relying on the invalidity of the arbitration agreement (caused by whatever defect) for a number of reasons. First, a party cannot rely on the invalidity of the arbitration agreement if doing so would be contrary to **good faith** (s 242 BGB), in particular if it acted contrary to prior conduct (*venire contra factum proprium*).[406] Examples include that the applicant who relies on the invalidity of the arbitration agreement had previously initiated the arbitral proceedings, had invoked the arbitration agreement in preceding state court proceedings (s 1032 para 1 ZPO),[407] or had explicitly relied on the validity of the arbitration agreement before the other party had initiated arbitral proceedings.[408]

6.199 The respondent must **object to the arbitral tribunal's jurisdiction** at the latest in its statement of defense (s 1040 para 2 cl 1 ZPO). If the objection has not been filed timely (and with reference to the specific facts that are in question in the setting aside proceedings[409]), the respondent is precluded from relying on the invalidity of the arbitration agreement in setting aside proceedings.[410] The same holds true if the arbitral tribunal has assumed its jurisdiction by means of a preliminary ruling

402 Münch, in: MünchKommZPO, s 1031 para 20.

403 Münch, in: MünchKommZPO, s 1031 para 21.

404 Government bill, BT-Drucks 13/5274, p 36.

405 Voit, in: Musielak/Voit (eds), s 1059 para 7, s 1031 para 17.

406 BGH SchiedsVZ 2008, 196, 197 para 12; 2009, 287, 288 para 9; Kröll/Kraft, in: *Arbitration in Germany*, s 1059 para 60; Voit, in: Musielak/Voit (eds), s 1059 para 7.

407 RGZ 40, 401, 403; BGH SchiedsVZ 2009, 287, 288 para 9; OLG Naumburg, JurBüro 2003, 389, 390; Geimer, in: Zöller (ed), s 1059 para 39; Schlosser, in: Stein/Jonas (eds), s 1059 para 20; Voit, in: Musielak/Voit (eds), s 1059 para 7.

408 BGH NJW-RR 1987, 1194, 1195.

409 BGH SchiedsVZ 2005, 259, 260.

410 OLG Koblenz, SchiedsVZ 2005, 260, 261; Borges, ZZP 111 (1998), 487, 490; Münch, in: MünchKommZPO, s 1040 paras 41 *et seq.*; Schwab/Walter, ch 16 para 11; dissenting Hartmann, in: Baumbach/Lauterbach/Albers/Hartmann (eds), s 1059 para 6.

(s 1040 para 3 cl 1 ZPO) and the respondent has failed to request a court ruling under s 1040 para 3 cl 2 ZPO.[411]

If a court has already decided on the jurisdiction of the arbitral tribunal and this **state court decision has become *res judicata*,** it also has binding effect for setting aside proceedings. Relevant state court decisions may have been rendered upon request prior to the constitution of the arbitral tribunal (s 1032 para 2 ZPO) or against the arbitral tribunal's preliminary ruling (s 1040 para 3 cl 2 ZPO).[412] **6.200**

bb) Incapacity of a Party (s 1059 para 2 no 1 lit a option 1 ZPO) A party that is incapable of concluding an arbitration agreement cannot validly conclude such an agreement (para 2.64). An arbitral award based on such invalid arbitration agreement is therefore subject to setting aside under s 1059 para 2 no 1 lit a option 1 ZPO. The provision goes beyond its Model Law template[413] by providing the law governing the capability, ie the law applicable to the party. The law applicable to a party is determined by the citizenship of natural persons (arts 7, 12 EGBGB), by the seat for corporations within the scope of the right of establishment under Arts 49, 54 TFEU, Art 31 EEA Agreement, and under Art XXV para 5 German-American Friendship Treaty, and by the law under which the corporation has been established for all other corporations.[414] For details on the (fairly rare) incapacity of a party under German law, see paras 2.64 *et seq.* **6.201**

cc) Lack of Arbitrability (s 1059 para 2 no 2 lit a ZPO) An arbitral award that decides a non-arbitrable matter on the merits is to be set aside under s 1059 para 2 no 2 lit a ZPO. Since it is of public interest that non-arbitrable matters are not decided in arbitration, the court will find this ground on its own motion even if the applicant has not pleaded it. For similar reasons, arbitrability is not included in the choice of law provision under s 1059 para 2 no 1 lit a option 2 ZPO (para 6.194) but regardless of the parties' choice to be determined under German law.[415] Arbitrability under German law is defined by s 1030 ZPO (for details, see paras 2.48 *et seq.*) and likewise rarely an issue. **6.202**

dd) Award Exceeding the Scope of the Arbitration Clause (s 1059 para 2 no 1 lit c ZPO) An arbitral award can be set aside if it **exceeds the scope** of the arbitration clause, as s 1059 para 2 no 1 lit c ZPO stipulates. As opposed to the aforementioned grounds for setting aside, here a (valid) arbitration clause exists which, however, does not cover the dispute. As with the determination of whether a valid arbitration agreement exists, the arbitral tribunal's determination of the scope of such agreement is subject to full review (para 6.190). **6.203**

411 BGH SchiedsVZ 2003, 133, 134; Borges, ZZP 111 (1998), 487, 490; Münch, in: MünchKommZPO, s 1059 para 11; Voit, in: Musielak/Voit (eds), s 1040 para 13.

412 Voit, in: Musielak/Voit (eds), s 1059 para 11.

413 Government bill, BT-Drucks 13/5274, p 59.

414 For details see Wolff, in: BeckOGK, s 24 BGB paras 46 *et seq.*

415 Government bill, BT-Drucks 13/5274, p 59.

6.204 Some assume that **decisions *ultra petita***, ie beyond what has been requested by the parties, can also be set aside under s 1059 para 2 no 1 lit c ZPO.[416] While it is clear that the arbitral tribunal cannot award more than has been requested, this procedural rule is detached from the arbitral tribunal's (contractual) legitimation, which is the rationale underlying awards exceeding the scope of the arbitration clause (para 6.203). This can also be derived from the fact that state courts are similarly concerned with the prohibition of decisions *ultra petita*. While decisions exceeding the request may be set aside under s 1059 para 2 no 1 lit d ZPO (para 6.220) or even under s 1059 para 2 no 2 lit b ZPO (para 6.228), they do not constitute a ground for setting aside under lit c.[417]

6.205 If the arbitral award exceeds the scope of the arbitration agreement only in **separable parts**, setting aside can be restricted to the affected part while the unaffected part remains in force. This stipulation in s 1059 para 2 no 1 lit c ZPO expresses a general rule (para 6.177).

6.206 c) **Severe Irregularities** The second group of grounds for setting aside is concerned with serious irregularities in the arbitral proceedings, including a party's inability to fully present its case (paras 6.207 *et seq.*), the incorrect composition of the arbitral tribunal (paras 6.213 *et seq.*), the violation of procedural rules (paras 6.219 *et seq.*), and, finally, the violation of public policy (paras 6.225 *et seq.*). These grounds for setting aside overlap significantly (see para 6.188).

6.207 *aa) Party's Inability to Present its Case (s 1059 para 2 no 1 lit b ZPO)* Section 1059 para 2 no 1 lit b ZPO makes the inability of a party to present its case a ground for setting aside the award. That the party was not given proper notice of the appointment of an arbitrator or of the arbitral proceedings are merely **examples** ("otherwise") that the provision names. The ability to present one's case is synonymous with the **right to be heard** as guaranteed by s 1042 para 1 cl 2 ZPO (see paras 4.22 *et seq.*). The right to be heard is at least at its core part of German public policy (para 6.229) so that often fact situations in which a ground under s 1059 para 2 no 1 lit b ZPO is given simultaneously constitute a ground under s 1059 para 2 no 2 lit b ZPO.

6.208 The right to be heard is usually understood to consist of **three parts**, namely notice to the party, opportunity to comment, and consideration of comments.[418] First, proper **notice** must be given to the party in advance of any decision. Violation of

[416] Hausmann, in: *Festschrift Stoll*, pp 593, 600; Kröll/Kraft, in: *Arbitration in Germany*, s 1059 para 67; Lachmann, para 2243; Schwab/Walter, ch 24 para 15.

[417] Kreindler/Schäfer/Wolff, para 1089; Münch, in: MünchKommZPO, s 1059 para 19; Voit, in: Musielak/Voit (eds), s 1059 para 14.

[418] BVerfGE 107, 395, 409 = NJW 2003, 1924, 1926 *et seq.*; OLG Frankfurt, SchiedsVZ 2013, 49, 60; OLG München, SchiedsVZ 2011, 159, 165; 2012, 43, 46 = XXXVII Y.B. Com. Arb. 231, 233 (2012); SchiedsVZ 2012, 156, 159 = XXXIX Y.B. Com. Arb. 389, 391 (2014); OLG Naumburg, SchiedsVZ 2011, 228, 229; Pieroth, in: Jarass/Pieroth, art 103 GG paras 9 *et seq.*

this requirement includes the two examples explicitly provided for in s 1059 para 2 no 1 lit b ZPO (para 6.207), namely that no proper notice of the appointment of an arbitrator or of the arbitral proceedings was given. No proper notice is also given to the respondent if the statement of claim is not delivered to it,[419] if a party is not invited to attend the taking of evidence,[420] or if the respondent is incapable of suing.[421] While the arbitral tribunal is not under a duty to discuss its views with the parties prior to rendering the arbitral award,[422] it must refrain from issuing "surprise decisions,"[423] ie deviate from previously voiced views or rely on views that are entirely different from those discussed during the arbitral proceedings.[424] If its requirements are met, the fiction provided for by s 1028 ZPO allows for the sufficiency of a notice which has not been received.[425]

Second, no **opportunity to comment** may be granted if insufficient time for preparation is granted in case of an exchange in legal representation,[426] if no oral hearing is held despite a party request,[427] if an interpreter is rejected,[428] or if a final decision on a plea is made without having invited comments.[429] The arbitral tribunal must take evidence that is relevant to the case, but such relevance is to be determined by the arbitral tribunal alone.[430] No opportunity to comment is given if a motion to admit evidence is dismissed arbitrarily and without substantive discussion.[431] By contrast, it does not constitute a ground for setting aside if the arbitral tribunal provides no reasons for dismissing a motion to admit evidence or if such reasons are incorrect.[432] **6.209**

419 OLG Hamburg, November 8, 2001, 6 Sch 04/01 (unreported), http://www.disarb.org (last visited December 1, 2015).

420 OLG Hamburg, MDR 1968, 1018.

421 OLG Frankfurt, FamRZ 2008, 1978, 1979.

422 OLG Karlsruhe, SchiedsVZ 2012, 101, 105 = XXXVIII Y.B. Com. Arb. 379, 383 (2013); OLG Köln, SchiedsVZ 2012, 161, 166; OLG München, SchiedsVZ 2011, 159, 165; 2011, 230, 232; 2012, 43, 46 = XXXVII Y.B. Com. Arb. 231, 233 (2012); OLG Stuttgart, SchiedsVZ 2011, 49, 54.

423 OLG Köln, SchiedsVZ 2012, 161, 166; Münch, in: MünchKommZPO, s 1059 para 27.

424 OLG München, SchiedsVZ 2011, 159, 165; 2011, 230, 232; October 29, 2009, 34 Sch 15/09 (unreported), http://www.disarb.org (last visited December 1, 2015); OLG Stuttgart, SchiedsVZ 2011, 49, 53; Kröll/Kraft, in: *Arbitration in Germany*, s 1059 para 65.

425 OLG Dresden, SchiedsVZ 2006, 166; Kröll/Kraft, in: *Arbitration in Germany*, s 1059 para 64; Münch, in: MünchKommZPO, s 1059 para 23.

426 BGHZ 27, 163, 165 *et seq.* = NJW 1958, 1186 *et seq.*

427 OLG Naumburg, NJW-RR 2003, 71, 72 (denied *in concreto*); Münch, in: MünchKommZPO, s 1047 para 2; Schwab/Walter, ch 16 para 32; Voit, in: Musielak/Voit (eds), s 1047 para 2.

428 Münch, in: MünchKommZPO, s 1059 para 27; dissenting OLG München, SchiedsVZ 2010, 169, 172 = XXXV Y.B. Com. Arb. 371, 373 (2010).

429 RGZ 119, 29, 32.

430 OLG Köln, SchiedsVZ 2012, 161, 168; OLG München, SchiedsVZ 2011, 230, 232.

431 BGH NJW 1992, 2299; OLG Saarbrücken, SchiedsVZ 2012, 47, 52; Berger, EWiR 2000, 199; Voit, in: Musielak/Voit (eds), s 1059 para 13; dissenting Schwab/Walter, ch 24 para 14.

432 BGH NJW 1992, 2299; OLG Frankfurt, SchiedsVZ 2013, 49, 60; OLG München, SchiedsVZ 2011, 230, 232; 2012, 156, 159 = XXXIX Y.B. Com. Arb. 389, 391 (2014); critical Geimer, in: Zöller (ed), s 1042 paras 11 *et seq.*; Schwab/Walter, ch 15 para 9.

6.210 Third, the arbitral tribunal must **consider the comments** provided by the parties. The right to be heard may therefore be violated if the arbitral tribunal precludes party submissions although the delay has been sufficiently justified[433] or if it classifies disputed facts as undisputed.[434] By contrast, the arbitral tribunal is not obliged to comment on any party submission in the arbitral award's reasons.[435]

6.211 Although the wording of s 1059 para 2 no 1 lit b ZPO does not require a **causal link** between the violation of the right to be heard and the content of the arbitral award, the better grounds speak in favor of such requirement. As under lit d (para 6.216), a potentially existing causal connection suffices; a ground for setting aside is to be denied only if the violation cannot have had an effect on the outcome of the proceedings.[436]

6.212 A party **cannot rely** on a violation of its right to be heard if such reliance contradicts previous conduct (*venire contra factum proprium*).[437] For that reason, a party cannot rely on s 1059 para 2 no 1 lit b ZPO if, upon inquiry by the arbitral tribunal, it confirmed that it had sufficient opportunity to present its case.[438] The parties can also stipulate in their arbitration agreement that each party may within a given deadline file an objection with the arbitral tribunal if the arbitral award violated the party's right to be heard.[439] A party that does not make use of such remedy in time cannot rely on a violation of its right to be heard in setting aside proceedings.[440]

6.213 *bb) Flawed Composition of the Arbitral Tribunal (s 1059 para 2 no 1 lit d option 1 ZPO)* The award can be set aside if the composition of the arbitral tribunal was not in accordance with a provision of ss 1025 *et seq.* ZPO or with an admissible agreement of the parties and this presumably affected the award (s 1059 para 2 no 1 lit d option 1 ZPO). As compared to art 34 para 2 lit a (iv) Model Law, the German provision not only clarifies that the violation must have affected the award, but also simplifies the determination of the relevant rules that are violated.[441] In fact, the **applicable procedural rules** must be determined according to the hierarchy of applicable procedural rules in arbitration (paras 4.3 *et seq.*),

---

433 OLG Celle, February 19, 2004, 8 Sch 09/03 (unreported), http://www.disarb.org (last visited December 1, 2015).

434 OLG Hamburg, June 8, 2001, 11 Sch 1/01 (unreported), http://www.disarb.org (last visited December 1, 2015).

435 KG SchiedsVZ 2011, 110, 111; OLG Frankfurt, SchiedsVZ 2013, 49, 60; OLG München, SchiedsVZ 2011, 159, 165; 2011, 230, 232; 2012, 43, 46 = XXXVII Y.B. Com. Arb. 231, 233 (2012).

436 BGHZ 31, 43, 48 = NJW 1959, 2213, 2214 *et seq.*; BGH SchiedsVZ 2009, 126, 127 para 7 (Art V(1)(d) NYC); OLG Celle, February 19, 2004, 8 Sch 09/03 (unreported), http://www.disarb.org (last visited December 1, 2015); Geimer, in: Zöller (ed), s 1059 para 40; Hausmann, in: *Festschrift Stoll*, pp 593, 599; Voit, in: Musielak/Voit (eds), s 1059 para 13; dissenting Münch, in: MünchKommZPO, s 1059 para 22.

437 Spohnheimer, pp 389 *et seq.*

438 Spohnheimer, pp 391 *et seq.*

439 For details, see Wolff, LMK 2015, 374507.

440 BGH NJW 2015, 3234, 3238 paras 27 *et seq.*

441 Government bill, BT-Drucks 13/5274, p 59.

ie first mandatory law, second party agreement including arbitration rules, and third non-mandatory law.[442]

6.214 *(1) Flawed Composition* The arbitral tribunal is incorrectly constituted **if the decision is made by other than those who have been appointed as arbitrators**, ie if appointed arbitrators do not decide or if arbitrators decide who have not been appointed.[443] The latter also includes secretaries to the arbitral tribunal who have assumed decision-making tasks (para 6.14).[444] The arbitral tribunal is furthermore incorrectly constituted if the applicable **rules on constitution** (paras 6.213, 3.2 *et seq.*) have not been adhered to.[445] If both parties are aware of the incorrect composition and do not object, this may constitute an implied amendment to the arbitration agreement.[446]

6.215 Another example for the arbitral tribunal's flawed composition is the participation of a **biased arbitrator**. However, with issuance of the award the other party has an increased interest in legal certainty under the law. Therefore, not any ground that would allow for challenging an arbitrator (paras 3.112 *et seq.*) suffices for setting aside the arbitral award. Rather, the impartiality and independence must be particularly severe and evident to constitute a ground for setting aside,[447] eg judging on one's own behalf (see also para 6.228).[448] Finally, since a person who is **legally incapacitated** cannot be appointed as arbitrator (para 3.20), the composition of an arbitral tribunal that includes such person is flawed.[449]

6.216 *(2) Impact on the Arbitral Award* The incorrect composition must have presumably affected the award. This requirement avoids the setting aside of the arbitral award on grounds of mere formalities and the commencement of new arbitral proceedings that lead to the very same result.[450] The **mere possibility** that the arbitral tribunal would have decided differently in correct composition is, however, sufficient[451]—which is almost always the case: in an arbitral tribunal with more than one arbitrator, it can never be excluded that deliberations would have resulted in a different decision if another person had participated or one of the present

[442] OLG Frankfurt, SchiedsVZ 2013, 49, 55.

[443] Schlosser, in: Stein/Jonas (eds), s 1059 para 21; Schwab/Walter, ch 24 para 18; Voit, in: Musielak/Voit (eds), s 1059 para 16.

[444] Kreindler/Schäfer/Wolff, para 1092.

[445] BayObLG NJW-RR 2000, 360, 361; OLG Köln, KTS 1971, 222, 225; Voit, in: Musielak/Voit (eds), s 1059 para 16.

[446] Kreindler/Schäfer/Wolff, para 1095; Voit, in: Musielak/Voit (eds), s 1059 para 16.

[447] BGHZ 141, 90, 95 = NJW 1999, 2370, 2371 *et seq.*; OLG Frankfurt, SchiedsVZ 2010, 52, 54; Schwab/Walter, ch 14 para 19.

[448] OLG München, December 20, 2006, 34 Sch 16/06 (unreported), http://www.disarb.org (last visited December 1, 2015).

[449] BGH NJW 1986, 3079, 3080; Voit, in: Musielak/Voit (eds), s 1059 para 16.

[450] Government bill, BT-Drucks 13/5274, p 59.

[451] OLG Saarbrücken, SchiedsVZ 2003, 92, 94; Münch, in: MünchKommZPO, s 1059 para 34; Schlosser, in: Stein/Jonas (eds), s 1059 para 48; Schwab/Walter, ch 24 para 30; Voit, in: Musielak/Voit (eds), s 1059 para 22.

persons had not participated.[452] The contributions of an arbitrator to the deliberations can always influence the decision-making process.[453] This holds even more true for a sole arbitrator.

6.217 *(3) Preclusion and Binding Prior Decisions* The applicant is **precluded** from raising any ground that it could have raised in the arbitral proceedings but failed to do so. This holds true in particular for grounds that could have justified a challenge under ss 1036 *et seq.* ZPO (paras 3.112 *et seq.*). If a party fails to challenge an arbitrator within the deadline under s 1037 ZPO, it is precluded from relying on such ground in setting aside proceedings,[454] since otherwise the deadline would be futile. A party is likewise precluded from raising the ground for setting aside under s 1059 para 2 no 1 lit d option 1 ZPO if it did not request a court decision on the challenge within the deadline set out by s 1037 para 3 cl 1 ZPO.[455]

6.218 The setting aside court may be bound by **prior court decisions** that are relevant for the constitution of the arbitral tribunal and that have become *res judicata*. The setting aside court is, in particular, bound by a prior court decision accepting (or dismissing) a challenge under s 1037 para 3 cl 1 ZPO.[456]

6.219 *cc) Flawed Arbitral Procedure (s 1059 para 2 no 1 lit d option 2 ZPO)* An arbitral award can be set aside under s 1059 para 2 no 1 lit d option 2 ZPO if the arbitral procedure did not comply with the applicable procedural rules (para 6.213) and this presumably affected the award. In light of its broad scope (paras 6.220 *et seq.*), this ground for setting aside is of considerable importance. It is, however, effectively restricted by the additional requirement of an impact on the arbitral award (para 6.223) and can easily be precluded (para 6.224).

6.220 *(1) Flawed Procedure* **Examples** for the violation of procedural rules set by law or party agreement include decisions *ultra petita*, ie beyond what has been requested as relief (see also para 6.204),[457] receiving the oath,[458] unjustified

[452] BGH NJW-RR 2015, 1087, 1088 para 13.
[453] BGH NJW-RR 2015, 1087, 1088 para 13; BayObLG NJW-RR 2000, 360; OLG Saarbrücken, SchiedsVZ 2003, 92, 94; dissenting Raeschke-Kessler, in: Prütting/Gehrlein (eds), s 1059 para 44.
[454] BGHZ 3, 215, 218 *et seq.* = NJW 1952, 27; Geimer, in: Zöller (ed), s 1037 para 6; Voit, in: Musielak/Voit (eds), s 1059 para 16.
[455] OLG Frankfurt, SchiedsVZ 2010, 52, 53; OLG Köln, October 6, 2000, 9 Sch 23/00 (unreported), http://www.disarb.org (last visited December 1, 2015); Kröll/Kraft, in: *Arbitration in Germany*, s 1059 para 74.
[456] RGZ 159, 92, 98; BGH NJW-RR 2015, 1087, 1088 para 13; Münch, in: MünchKommZPO, s 1059 para 36; Voit, in: Musielak/Voit (eds), s 1059 para 16.
[457] RGZ 149, 45, 49; RG JW 1920, 703, 704; Münch, in: MünchKommZPO, s 1059 para 10; Voit, in: Musielak/Voit (eds), s 1059 para 14; dissenting Hausmann, in: *Festschrift Stoll*, pp 593, 600; Schwab/Walter, ch 24 para 24.
[458] KG JW 1926, 2219, 2220; Hartmann, in: Baumbach/Lauterbach/Albers/Hartmann (eds), s 1059 para 13; Lachmann, para 2273; Schwab/Walter, ch 24 para 24.

rejection of counsel,[459] denial of an oral hearing that has been requested (see also para 6.209),[460] or use of a report rendered by an obviously unqualified expert.[461]

According to the prevailing view, **deficient reasons** may justify setting aside the award, but only if the reasons are lacking entirely,[462] are absurd, or do not comment on the main points of the party's pleading (para 6.97).[463] The impact of deficient reasons on the award, however, is difficult to assess (para 6.99).[464] **6.221**

A flawed procedure needs to be distinguished from an **incorrect decision on the dispute**. While the former leads to setting aside the arbitral award, the latter is not subject to review by the state court (no *révision au fond*, para 6.187).[465] An incorrect application of the law to the facts concerns the decision (as opposed to the proceedings) only, even if mandatory rules under the applicable law are violated.[466] By contrast, application of an incorrect standard including of a national law other than that chosen by the parties or a decision *ex aequo et bono* without express authorization is considered a violation of procedure.[467] The determination of the applicable law by applying conflict of law rules again belongs to the decision on the dispute, which is not subject to court review.[468] **6.222**

(2) Impact on the Arbitral Award Both options of s 1059 para 2 no 1 lit d ZPO share the requirement that the violation of rules must presumably have affected the award. For both options, the mere possibility of a causal link suffices (para 6.216).[469] While, however, an incorrect constitution of the arbitral tribunal will usually be relevant for the outcome of the arbitral award (para 6.216), the need for a potential impact gains more relevance in the case of flawed arbitral proceedings. The use of a language other than the language of the proceedings (s 1045 ZPO), for example, does not even potentially influence the decision on the dispute if all persons involved are fully capable of communicating in the language actually used. A record of a hearing that was required but not made cannot influence the **6.223**

[459] Münch, in: MünchKommZPO, s 1059 para 37; Schwab/Walter, ch 24 para 24; Voit, in: Musielak/Voit (eds), s 1042 para 7.

[460] BGH NJW 1994, 2155 *et seq.*; OLG Bremen, BB 2000, Beil. 12, pp 18, 19 *et seq.*; Schlosser, in: Stein/Jonas (eds), s 1042 para 3 and s 1059 para 23.

[461] OLG München, HRR 1940, no 627; Schlosser, in: Stein/Jonas (eds), s 1059 para 23.

[462] Government bill, BT-Drucks 13/5274, pp 59 *et seq.*

[463] BGHZ 96, 40, 47 = NJW 1986, 1436, 1437; OLG Frankfurt, IHR 2003, 93, 95 *et seq.*; OLG Köln, SchiedsVZ 2012, 161, 168; Sandrock, BB 2001, 2173, 2176.

[464] See Kröll/Kraft, in: *Arbitration in Germany*, s 1059 para 76.

[465] Sandrock, BB 2001, 2173, 2179 *et seq.*; Schwab/Walter, ch 24 para 22; Voit, in: Musielak/Voit (eds), s 1059 para 18.

[466] Kreindler/Schäfer/Wolff, para 1098.

[467] BGHZ 96, 40, 44 *et seq.* = NJW 1986, 1436 *et seq.*; OLG München, SchiedsVZ 2005, 308, 309 *et seq.*; 2011, 159, 166; Geimer, in: Zöller (ed), s 1059 para 43; Hausmann, in: *Festschrift Stoll*, pp 593, 601; Lachmann, para 2276; Schwab/Walter, ch 24 para 22.

[468] Voit, in: Musielak/Voit (eds), s 1059 para 18.

[469] On lit d option 2: OLG Frankfurt, SchiedsVZ 2013, 49, 57.

outcome of the dispute.[470] If witness evidence has mistakenly not been taken, the applicant needs to submit what the witness would have testified and why this could have had an impact on the arbitral award.[471] The requirement of potential impact has replaced the restriction under former German arbitration law that only the violation of "significant" provisions constitutes a ground for setting aside.[472]

6.224 *(3) Preclusion* A party is **precluded** from relying on a violation of procedural rules if it had to object under s 1027 ZPO but failed do so.[473] The violation can furthermore be **cured** for example if the party is later given the opportunity to comment.[474]

6.225 *dd) Public Policy Violation (s 1059 para 2 no 2 lit b ZPO)* As the last ground for setting aside, s 1059 para 2 no 2 lit b ZPO defines the violation of public policy. In practice, this ground belongs to the grounds that are invoked most often and at the same time are least successful.[475] Like non-arbitrability (para 6.202), the public policy violation involves the protection of public interests and is therefore to be determined on the court's own motion (s 1059 para 2 no 2 ZPO). Again like non-arbitrability (para 6.202), public policy in s 1059 para 2 no 2 lit b ZPO serves as a safety-valve protecting specifically German interests[476] and is therefore not subject to the parties' choice of law.[477]

6.226 *(1) Standard* Public policy provides for a wide net to eliminate awards that, in the words of s 1041 para 1 no 2 ZPO's pre-reform version, **"obviously violate basic principles of German law."**[478] German public policy does not include all procedural or substantive rules (no *révision au fond*) even if they happen to be mandatory.[479] According to a common definition, public policy consists of those

[470] OLG Braunschweig, SchiedsVZ 2005, 262, 264; OLG München, SchiedsVZ 2011, 167, 168.

[471] Kröll/Kraft, in: *Arbitration in Germany*, s 1059 para 77.

[472] Borges, ZZP 111 (1998), 487, 493; Münch, in: MünchKommZPO, s 1059 para 30; Voit, in: Musielak/Voit (eds), s 1059 para 17; dissenting Schwab/Walter, ch 24 para 21.

[473] OLG München, May 7, 2008, 34 Sch 26/07 (unreported), http://www.disarb.org (last visited December 1, 2015); Geimer, in: Zöller (ed), s 1059 para 42; Münch, in: MünchKommZPO, s 1059 para 30; Schlosser, in: Stein/Jonas (eds), s 1059 para 21.

[474] Voit, in: Musielak/Voit (eds), s 1059 para 19.

[475] For Switzerland, see Dasser, 25(3) ASA Bull. 444 (2007) and 28(1) ASA Bull. 82 (2010). Reliable figures for Germany are not available.

[476] Cf Wolff, in: Wolff (ed), Art V para 481.

[477] Cf Government bill, BT-Drucks 13/5274, p 59.

[478] BGH SchiedsVZ 2014, 98 *et seq.* paras 5 *et seq.*; Baumert, SchiedsVZ 2014, 139; Kröll/Kraft, in: *Arbitration in Germany*, s 1059 para 83.

[479] BGH SchiedsVZ 2009, 66, 67 para 5; OLG Dresden, SchiedsVZ 2005, 210, 211; OLG Frankfurt, September 8, 2005, 26 Sch 06/05 (unreported), http://www.disarb.org (last visited December 1, 2015); SchiedsVZ 2014, 154, 158; OLG München, SchiedsVZ 2011, 167, 168; OLG Schleswig, SchiedsVZ 2010, 276, 277; Geimer, in: Zöller (ed), s 1059 para 55; Lachmann, paras 2302 *et seq.*; Münch, in: MünchKommZPO, s 1059 para 41; Schwab/Walter, ch 24 paras 33, 38.

rules that regulate crucial issues which affect the basis of public and economic life due to specific political or economical visions or fundamental ideas of justice.[480]

The public policy standard to be applied in s 1059 ZPO is that of so-called **national public policy.**[481] National public policy is the national standard for domestic awards as opposed to international public policy as the national standard for foreign awards. International public policy is considered even more broad than national public policy (para 6.316) as the arbitral award is rooted in another legal order with different moral values and principles.[482] In Germany, international public policy is applied only to awards with a foreign place of arbitration even if the nationality of the parties and arbitrators, the applicable substantive law, and other criteria are not German.[483] Within German national public policy, the violation of basic principles of German procedural law (procedural public policy, paras 6.228 *et seq.*) and of German substantive law (substantive public policy, paras 6.231 *et seq.*) are distinguished. **6.227**

(2) Procedural Public Policy Procedural public policy is violated if recognition of the award leads to a result which obviously violates basic principles of German procedural law,[484] ie if the arbitral proceedings violated basic principles of procedural fairness.[485] **Examples** of such basic principles include the principle of neutral administration of justice[486] including the prohibition against judging on one's own behalf (para 6.73), the proper representation of a party in the arbitral proceedings,[487] and observance of the *res judicata* effect of previous decisions.[488] An award whose content remains contradictory or unintelligible even after interpretation likewise violates procedural public policy.[489] The principle of *ne ultra petita* has **6.228**

480 BGH SchiedsVZ 2009, 66, 67 para 5 with further references; OLG Frankfurt, SchiedsVZ 2013, 49, 60; 2014, 154, 158.

481 BGHZ 179, 304, 312 para 27 = SchiedsVZ 2009, 176, 178; critical Münch, in: MünchKommZPO, s 1059 para 43.

482 Cf Kröll/Kraft, in: *Arbitration in Germany*, s 1059 para 84.

483 BGHZ 27, 249, 256 = NJW 1958, 1538, 1539; BGHZ 179, 304, 312 para 27 = SchiedsVZ 2009, 176, 178; Schwab/Walter, ch 24 paras 37 *et seq.*; Voit, in: Musielak/Voit (eds), s 1059 para 25; dissenting Borges, ZZP 111 (1998), 487, 495; Kröll/Kraft, in: *Arbitration in Germany*, s 1059 para 84; critical also Baumert, SchiedsVZ 2014, 139, 141 *et seq.*

484 OLG Köln, SchiedsVZ 2005, 163, 165.

485 BayObLG BB 2000, Beil. 12, pp 16, 18; OLG Bremen, November 10, 2005, 2 Sch 02/05 (unreported), http://www.disarb.org (last visited December 1, 2015); OLG Frankfurt, SchiedsVZ 2013, 49, 60; 2014, 154, 158; OLG Hamburg, May 14, 1999, 1 Sch 02/99 (unreported), http://www.disarb.org (last visited December 1, 2015).

486 Kröll/Kraft, in: *Arbitration in Germany*, s 1059 para 90; Voit, in: Musielak/Voit (eds), s 1059 para 26.

487 BGHZ 179, 304, 308 para 14 = SchiedsVZ 2009, 176, 177; Government bill, BT-Drucks 13/5274, p 59; Schwab/Walter, ch 24 para 48.

488 Gaul, in: *Festschrift Sandrock*, pp 285, 314 *et seq.*; Münch, in: MünchKommZPO, s 1059 para 45; dissenting Geimer, in: Zöller (ed), s 1059 para 61.

489 OLG Frankfurt, IHR 2003, 93, 96; OLG Köln, December 23, 2011, 19 Sch 27/10 (unreported), http://www.disarb.org (last visited December 1, 2015); Rechberger, SchiedsVZ 2006, 169, 175; Schlosser, in: Stein/Jonas (eds), annex to s 1061 paras 329 *et seq.*; Schwab/Walter, ch 24

also been deemed to be part of procedural public policy so that in at least one case an award holding respondents liable jointly and severally even though joint and several liability had not been requested was set aside.[490]

6.229 Another important part of procedural public policy is the **right to be heard** (paras 6.207 *et seq.* and 4.22 *et seq.*),[491] at least in its core.[492] The right to be heard is violated in its core if for example a party is disparaged to a mere object of the proceedings.[493] As under s 1059 para 2 no 1 lit b ZPO (para 6.211), the violation of the right to be heard must at least potentially have affected the arbitral award.[494]

6.230 Procedural public policy finally includes cases of procedural fraud as contained in the **grounds for an action for retrial** under s 580 nos 1 to 6 ZPO which had been referenced by the former German arbitration law as grounds for setting aside.[495] The prevailing view accepts the grounds for an action for retrial under s 580 nos 1 to 5 ZPO only if the offender has been finally convicted for its criminal offence or if criminal proceedings cannot be initiated or implemented for other reasons than the lack of evidence (s 581 ZPO).[496] This view significantly reduces the scope of the underlying grounds.

6.231 *(3) Substantive Public Policy* Substantive public policy is violated if recognition of the arbitral award violates rules that regulate the basis of public and economic life or that are **intolerably inconsistent with the German legislature's fundamental ideas of justice** and therewith lead to a blatant violation of substantive justice.[497] Not every violation of mandatory rules results in a violation of substantive public

para 42; see also OLG Karlsruhe, SchiedsVZ 2006, 335, 336 = XXXII Y.B. Com. Arb. 342, 346 (2007); dissenting Münch, in: MünchKommZPO, s 1059 para 46.

[490] OLG Köln, SchiedsVZ 2012, 161, 164 *et seq.*

[491] BGH NJW 2015, 3234, 3237 *et seq.* para 30; Government bill, BT-Drucks 13/5274, p 59; OLG Frankfurt, SchiedsVZ 2013, 49, 60.

[492] BGHZ 182, 204, 210 paras 22 *et seq.* = NJW 2010, 153, 154 (on the Hague Convention of 2 October 1973 on the Recognition and Enforcement of Decisions Relating to Maintenance Obligations); Kröll/Kraft, in: *Arbitration in Germany*, s 1059 para 63.

[493] OLG Frankfurt, IPRspr. 2001, no 205, 440, 442; Münch, in: MünchKommZPO, s 1059 para 45.

[494] BGHZ 3, 215, 218 *et seq.* = NJW 1952, 27; BGHZ 31, 43, 46 *et seq.* = NJW 1959, 2213, 2214 *et seq.*; Voit, in: Musielak/Voit (eds), s 1059 para 27; dissenting Aden, DZWIR 2013, 149, 153.

[495] BGHZ 145, 376, 381 = NJW 2001, 373, 374; BayObLG SchiedsVZ 2004, 319, 320; KG SchiedsVZ 2013, 112, 117 = XXXVIII Y.B. Com. Arb. 384, 391 (2013); Government bill, BT-Drucks 13/5274, p 59.

[496] BGHZ 145, 376, 381 = NJW 2001, 373, 374; KG SchiedsVZ 2013, 112, 118 = XXXVIII Y.B. Com. Arb. 384, 391 (2013); OLG Saarbrücken, SchiedsVZ 2012, 47, 53 *et seq.*; OLG Stuttgart, SchiedsVZ 2003, 84, 88; Münch, in: MünchKommZPO, s 1059 para 45; dissenting Kröll, NJW 2005, 194, 198; Kröll/Kraft, in: *Arbitration in Germany*, s 1059 paras 92 *et seq.*

[497] BGH NJW 1990, 3210, 3211; SchiedsVZ 2009, 66, 67 para 5; OLG Braunschweig, SchiedsVZ 2005, 262, 264; OLG Dresden, SchiedsVZ 2005, 210, 211; OLG Frankfurt, SchiedsVZ 2013, 49, 60; Schlosser, in: Stein/Jonas (eds), annex to s 1061 para 316; Voit, in: Musielak/Voit (eds), s 1059 para 29.

policy.[498] Only the result (as opposed to the reasoning) of the award can violate substantive public policy.[499]

Examples of violations of substantive public policy include where compliance with the award would constitute a criminal offence,[500] violate price fixing provisions,[501] competition law,[502] foreign currency law,[503] import or export restrictions,[504] treat insolvency creditors unequally,[505] and contravene German[506] or European[507] antitrust law. Severe commercial consequences of the award culminating in the award debtor's insolvency are of no relevance for setting aside the award.[508] **6.232**

V. Procedure

While the procedural requirements for a setting aside application have been discussed in paras 6.167 *et seq.* above, the setting aside proceedings entail certain specific rules that in part deviate from general procedural rules of civil procedure. These specific rules are discussed in this section. **6.233**

1. Right to be Heard (s 1063 para 1 cl 2 ZPO)

The right to be heard is guaranteed under the German constitution (art 103 para 1 GG). Section 1063 para 1 cl 2 ZPO confirms that the party opposing the setting aside application is to be granted the opportunity to comment before the decision is made. While it would constitutionally not be required to hear the opposing party if the court will in any event dismiss the application,[509] s 1063 para 1 cl 2 ZPO requires that the opposing party be heard regardless of the court's decision on the application.[510] **6.234**

498 BGH SchiedsVZ 2009, 66, 67 para 5; 2014, 98, 99 para 8; OLG Frankfurt, SchiedsVZ 2013, 49, 60.

499 BGH NJW 1972, 2180, 2181; OLG Dresden, SchiedsVZ 2005, 210, 211; Kreindler/Schäfer/Wolff, para 1108; Kröll, NJW 2001, 1173, 1183.

500 RGZ 57, 331, 334; OLG Hamburg, NJW 1953, 1309 *et seq.*; Schwab/Walter, ch 24 para 41; Voit, in: Musielak/Voit (eds), s 1059 para 31.

501 BGH BB 1953, 811; BGHZ 27, 249, 256 = NJW 1958, 1538, 1539.

502 BGHZ 46, 365, 373 (s 20 GWB) = NJW 1967, 1178; BGHZ 88, 314, 316 *et seq.* (GWB) = NJW 1984, 1355, 1356; 1969, 978, 979 (Art 81 para 1 TFEU); 1972, 2180, 2181 *et seq.*

503 OLG Köln, NJW 1952, 1420.

504 BGH KTS 1964, 172, 173.

505 BGHZ 179, 304, 310 paras 21 *et seq.* = SchiedsVZ 2009, 176, 177 *et seq.*

506 BGHZ 30, 89, 96 *et seq.* = NJW 1959, 1438, 1440; BGHZ 46, 365, 367 *et seq.* = NJW 1967, 1178; BGH GRUR 1966, 576, 578.

507 BGH NJW 1969, 978, 980.

508 OLG München, SchiedsVZ 2012, 107, 111.

509 Cf (right to be heard not violated if comments could not have led to a more favorable decision) BVerfGE 89, 381, 392 *et seq.* = NJW 1994, 1053, 1054; Pieroth, in: Jarass/Pieroth, art 103 GG para 12.

510 Voit, in: Musielak/Voit (eds), s 1063 para 6; dissenting Münch, in: MünchKommZPO, s 1063 paras 3 *et seq.*

2. *Oral Hearing (s 1063 para 2 ZPO)*

6.235 While proceedings that result in a court order (para 6.240) usually do not require an oral hearing to be held, this rule does not apply to setting aside proceedings (s 1063 para 2 ZPO). Once the court has ordered an oral hearing, the parties must be represented by a lawyer admitted to the German bar (para 6.176).

3. *No Default Judgments*

6.236 Under the general rules of civil procedure, severe sanctions apply if a party fails to appear in an oral hearing: if the plaintiff does not appear, its claim will be dismissed (s 330 ZPO), if the defendant fails to appear, the facts alleged by the plaintiff are deemed undisputed (s 331 ZPO). Such **default judgments** are, however, not available in setting aside proceedings and other court proceedings under the German arbitration law since the remedies available against default judgments are irreconcilable with the remedies under ss 1062 *et seq.* ZPO.[511] If either party (or both) does not appear in the oral hearing, the application must be decided by the court based on the entirety of the parties' oral and written submissions.[512]

4. *Court Fees, Lawyer's Fees, and Amount in Dispute*

6.237 The costs of setting aside proceedings including court fees and lawyer's fees are **allocated** between the parties according to ss 91 *et seq.* ZPO, ie primarily under the "costs follow the event" rule. If the other party immediately acknowledges the claim and has not given cause for the application to be brought, the applicant bears the costs of the proceedings pursuant to s 93 ZPO.[513] If the application is withdrawn, the applicant bears all costs (s 269 para 3 cl 2 ZPO).[514]

6.238 For an application for setting aside, two **court fees** are due (no 1620 KV GKG). While under s 12 GKG, a claim is serviced only after the court fees have been paid in advance, this provision does not apply to setting aside applications.[515] **Lawyer's fees** incur pursuant to nos 3100, 3104 VV RVG if the party did not agree with the lawyer on another basis for remuneration.

6.239 The amount of both the court fees and the lawyer's fees depends on the **amount in dispute** fixed by the court. The amount in dispute is fixed on the basis of the applicant's commercial interest in the application, ie the value of the (part of the) arbitral award that it applies for setting aside.

---

[511] BGHZ 166, 278, 281 para 14 = SchiedsVZ 2006, 161, 162 = XXXII Y.B. Com. Arb. 328, 335 (2007); OLG Hamm, SchiedsVZ 2013, 182, 183 *et seq.*; dissenting Schwab/Walter, ch 28 para 10; distinguishing between mandatory and discretionary oral hearing Voit, in: Musielak/Voit (eds), s 1063 para 5.

[512] Cf Schroeder/Wortmann, in: *Arbitration in Germany*, s 1063 para 6.

[513] Münch, in: MünchKommZPO, s 1063 para 25; Schroeder/Wortmann, in: *Arbitration in Germany*, s 1063 para 19.

[514] Voit, in: Musielak/Voit (eds), s 1063 para 2.

[515] Münch, in: MünchKommZPO, s 1063 para 2; Voit, in: Musielak/Voit (eds), s 1063 para 2.

VI. Decision and Remedies

1. *Form of Decision (s 1063 para 1 cl 1 ZPO)*

The court decides on the setting aside application not by means of a judgment but by means of an **order** (s 1063 para 1 cl 1 ZPO). This form of decision entails some deviations from regular court proceedings. For example, orders are to be formally pronounced only if an oral hearing had taken place (s 329 para 1 cl 1 ZPO); otherwise, informal communication to the parties suffices (s 329 para 2 cl 1 ZPO).[516] The order must identify the award, eg by stating its date and the names of the arbitrators.[517] **6.240**

2. *Effects of an Order Setting Aside the Award*

A court order setting aside the arbitral award mainly renders the award null and void from the beginning (para 6.242) but does not decide the dispute in lieu of the arbitral tribunal. For resolving the underlying dispute, either the state court or the arbitral tribunal may be competent (para 6.243). If the arbitral tribunal remains the competent forum, the final question is whether the arbitral tribunal that has rendered the award remains in office or whether it must be newly constituted (para 6.244). In any event, an arbitral award will be set aside partly if only a separable part is affected (para 6.177). **6.241**

a) Effects on the Arbitral Award Any arbitral award—with the exception of void awards (para 6.172)—has binding effect between the parties even if it suffers from grounds for setting aside (para 6.159). The order setting aside the arbitral award deprives it retroactively of its binding effect.[518] Like any other decision changing a legal right or status, this effect takes place once the court order becomes procedurally *res judicata* (para 6.109).[519] **6.242**

b) Effects on the Arbitration Agreement (s 1059 para 5 ZPO) After the arbitral award has been set aside, the dispute has to be brought before an arbitral tribunal again if a valid arbitration clause exists between the parties which encompasses the dispute. Whether the original arbitration agreement between the parties also covers arbitral proceedings following the setting aside is to be answered by way of interpretation of the original arbitration agreement.[520] If this interpretation does not return clear results, s 1059 para 5 ZPO stipulates an assumption for continuation in force of the arbitration agreement. It does for good cause, since usually the reasons why the parties have chosen arbitration (paras 1.48 *et seq.*) **6.243**

[516] Münch, in: MünchKommZPO, s 1063 para 19; Schroeder/Wortmann, in: *Arbitration in Germany*, s 1063 para 8.
[517] Cf Voit, in: Musielak/Voit (eds), s 1063 para 8.
[518] Kröll/Kraft, in: *Arbitration in Germany*, s 1059 para 3; Schlosser, in: Stein/Jonas (eds), s 1059 para 3.
[519] BGH SchiedsVZ 2008, 94, 95 para 12; generally Gottwald, in: MünchKommZPO, s 322 para 19.
[520] OLG Frankfurt, NJW-RR 2008, 590, 591; Voit, in: Musielak/Voit (eds), s 1059 para 43.

will persist.[521] The arbitration agreement can obviously not continue in force if it had not been concluded validly (including for lack of arbitrability of the subject matter or incapability of a party) or does not cover the dispute.[522]

6.244 **c) Remission of the Case (s 1059 para 4 ZPO)** Where appropriate and requested by a party, the court may pronounce along with the setting aside of the award that the matter is to be remitted to the arbitral tribunal. In this case, the (former) arbitrators continue in office (s 1056 para 3 ZPO) and no new arbitral tribunal must be constituted. Remitting the case is not appropriate if the arbitral tribunal has no jurisdiction to decide the case, if remission would give rise to additional procedural efforts, or if grounds for challenging at least one arbitrator exist.[523]

3. Remedy (s 1065 ZPO)

6.245 The appeal on a point of law is available as a remedy against the higher regional court's order on the setting aside application (s 1065 para 1 cl 1 ZPO). The appeal on a point of law must be based on the fact that the order has violated federal law or a rule whose territorial scope extends beyond the district of one higher regional court (s 576 para 1 ZPO) or that the order is based on a violation of a treaty (s 1065 para 2 cl 1 ZPO). It brings the setting aside application before the Federal Supreme Court. The appeal on a point of law is admissible only if the legal matter is of fundamental significance or if the development of the law or safeguarding uniform case law requires a decision by the Federal Supreme Court (s 574 para 1 no 1, para 2 ZPO). If these prerequisites are met, the party's grievance need not have any minimum amount in dispute.

I. Enforceability of Domestic Arbitral Awards (s 1060 ZPO)

6.246 German law distinguishes between domestic and foreign arbitral awards when it comes to recognition and enforceability. Domestic and foreign arbitral awards differ in their place of arbitration: if the place of arbitration is within Germany, the award is domestic and s 1060 ZPO governs the award's declaration of enforceability. Otherwise the award is foreign and s 1061 ZPO (paras 6.287 *et seq.*) applies to its enforceability.

6.247 As the reference to the grounds for setting aside in s 1060 para 2 ZPO demonstrates, **s 1060 ZPO closely mirrors s 1059 ZPO.** While the setting aside application is the remedy against the award (usually employed by the unsuccessful party

[521] Government bill, BT-Drucks 13/5274, p 60.

[522] See Hartmann, in: Baumbach/Lauterbach/Albers/Hartmann (eds), s 1059 para 20; Voit, in: Musielak/Voit (eds), s 1059 para 43.

[523] Wolff, SchiedsVZ 2007, 254 *et seq.*; for other criteria see OLG Köln, SchiedsVZ 2012, 161, 167; Wighardt, SchiedsVZ 2010, 252, 254 *et seq.*

to the arbitration), the application for a declaration of enforceability allows for the recognition of the arbitral award in favor of the party that has been successful in the arbitration.

I. Spirit and Purpose

1. Recognition, Enforcement, and Declaration of Enforceability

Under German law, usually a right is enforced against a debtor in two steps: first, the creditor pursues **regular court proceedings** (*Erkenntnisverfahren*) which are intended to result in a judgment. The judgment establishes with binding effect that the awarded claim exists (substantive *res judicata*). It simultaneously serves as the most prominent example of an executory title (*Vollstreckungstitel*). Only based on such executory titles may coercive **enforcement proceedings** (or execution proceedings, *Vollstreckungsverfahren*) in the debtor's assets be pursued if the debtor does not comply voluntarily with the judgment. **6.248**

A domestic arbitral award readily assumes binding effect between the parties (substantive *res judicata*). This is called **recognition.** While recognition of an arbitral award under arts 35 *et seq.* Model Law requires separate court proceedings, German law is more generous[524] and provides recognition without the need for a separate court confirmation (s 1055 ZPO). On the contrary, the award debtor must apply for setting aside in order to terminate the binding effect of the arbitral award (para 6.159). **6.249**

On the other hand and contrary to the wording of s 1055 ZPO (which is too broad in this regard), the arbitral award is not an executory title which could directly serve as a basis for enforcement proceedings into the assets of the debtor. Contrary to recognition, **enforcement** of the award takes place only if it has been declared enforceable in proceedings under s 1060 ZPO. Technically, only the decision which declares an arbitral award enforceable (rather than the award itself) serves as an executory title (s 794 para 1 no 4a ZPO). **6.250**

Since they are required in order to create an executory title, the **proceedings for a declaration of enforceability** are not enforcement proceedings but rather regular proceedings of their own kind.[525] Hence, the rules—including, for example, on state immunity—for regular proceedings apply.[526] **6.251**

Terminology in the field of recognition and enforcement is inconsistent and confusing.[527] The term "enforcement" is commonly used not only for enforcement of **6.252**

[524] Government bill, BT-Drucks 13/5274, p 61 (adoption of the Model Law would be a step back from the former law).

[525] BGH SchiedsVZ 2013, 110, 111 para 10 = XXXVIII Y.B. Com. Arb. 384, 391 (2013); OLG Naumburg, SchiedsVZ 2010, 277, 278.

[526] Cf BGH SchiedsVZ 2013, 110, 111 para 10 = XXXVIII Y.B. Com. Arb. 384, 391 (2013).

[527] Kröll, in: *Arbitration in Germany*, introduction ss 1059, 1060 paras 4 *et seq.*

an executory title in the debtor's assets but also for declaring an award enforceable. An example for such inaccurate use of terminology is s 1061 ZPO, the first paragraph of which refers to "[r]ecognition and enforcement of foreign arbitral awards" while its second paragraph continues to regulate the case "[i]f the declaration of enforceability is to be refused." Both paragraphs refer to the same thing, namely the declaration of enforceability.

2. Need for a Declaration of Enforceability

6.253 a) **Basis for Enforcement** The declaration of enforceability is required for any enforcement (ss 704 *et seq.* ZPO) of a domestic award in Germany. This is the only purpose of a declaration of enforceability set out by s 1060 para 1 ZPO. As part of the German enforcement law, s 894 ZPO, pursuant to which a declaration of will shall be deemed to have been made as soon as the judgment has become final and binding, also requires a declaration of enforceability (para 6.122).

6.254 b) **Fortification Against Grounds for Setting Aside?** The prevailing view moreover allows the declaration of enforceability of **arbitral awards that lack enforceable content.**[528] Such awards include declaratory awards, awards changing a legal right or status, awards dismissing a claim (apart from a cost decision contained therein; see also paras 6.56, 6.87), or awards that do not meet the strict requirements for certainty under German enforcement law. Enforcement proceedings cannot be initiated based on such awards even if they have been declared enforceable. A declaration of enforceability does, however, *de facto* also fortify the award against grounds for setting aside (s 1059 para 3 cl 4 ZPO, para 6.181). This is deemed a sufficient ground for invoking s 1060 ZPO by the prevailing view—not convincingly, however, since it ignores the clear wording and rationale of s 1060 para 1 ZPO[529] and satisfies a need that does not exist in light of the tight deadline under s 1059 para 3 ZPO.[530]

6.255 c) **Basis for Altering a Legal Right or Status?** The declaration of enforceability is also not a prerequisite for an award changing a legal right or status (*Gestaltungsschiedsspruch*) to gain this effect of altering of rights.[531] Since this effect

[528] BGH SchiedsVZ 2006, 278, 279 paras 11 *et seq.*; OLG München, SchiedsVZ 2009, 127, 128; 2015, 205, 206; OLG Naumburg, SchiedsVZ 2010, 277, 278 *et seq.*; OLG Stuttgart, SchiedsVZ 2014, 307, 311 *et seq.*; Hartmann, in: Baumbach/Lauterbach/Albers/Hartmann (eds), s 1060 para 5; Kröll, in: *Arbitration in Germany*, s 1060 paras 11, 22; Lachmann, paras 2403 *et seq.*; Schlosser, in: Stein/Jonas (eds), s 1060 para 6; Schwab/Walter, ch 26 para 7.

[529] Geimer, in: Zöller (ed), s 1060 paras 5 *et seq.*; Münch, in: MünchKommZPO, s 1060 paras 8, 11; Voit, in: Musielak/Voit (eds), s 1060 para 2; Wolff/Falk, SchiedsVZ 2006, 280, 281.

[530] Münch, in: MünchKommZPO, s 1060 paras 8, 11; Voit, in: Musielak/Voit (eds), s 1060 para 2; Wolff/Falk, SchiedsVZ 2006, 280.

[531] OLG Dresden, BB 2001, Beil. 7, pp 22 *et seq.*; Geimer, in: Zöller (ed), s 1060 para 7; Lachmann, para 1787; Lüke/Blenske, ZGR 1998, 253, 273 *et seq.*; Münch, in: MünchKommZPO, s 1060 para 6; Schlosser, in: Stein/Jonas (eds), s 1060 para 7; Voit, in: Musielak/Voit (eds), s 1060 para 2; Walter, in: *Festschrift Schwab*, pp 539, 544, 558 *et seq.*; dissenting K Schmidt, ZGR 1988, 523, 536 and AG 1995, 551, 554.

is distinct from enforcement, requiring a declaration of enforceability would be irreconcilable with the immediate recognition of arbitral awards by s 1055 ZPO.

d) Basis for Recognition by Public Authorities? Public authorities have to recognize an arbitral award for such purposes as entry into public registers and others regardless of whether a declaration of enforceability has been issued.[532] A diverging position was taken in pre-reform case law,[533] but is irreconcilable with s 1055 ZPO. **6.256**

3. Other Means to Enforce an Arbitral Award

a) Declaration of Enforceability of an Award on Agreed Terms by a Public Notary Awards on agreed terms can also be declared enforceable by a public notary (s 1053 para 4 ZPO, para 6.45). This provides for a faster and more cost-effective means than applying to a state court for a declaration of enforceability. **6.257**

b) Actions Based on the Duty to Comply with the Award No action can be based on the award debtor's duty to comply with the award. While such duty may indeed be derived from the arbitration agreement,[534] an **action to enforce this duty** would constitute a "shortcut" that circumvents the proceedings for a declaration of enforceability under s 1060 ZPO. These proceedings are not only the easiest means to enforce the award, but also those specifically provided by the law and those properly protecting the defenses of the award debtor.[535] **6.258**

Actions for a **declaration** that the arbitral award does not suffer from grounds for setting aside are inadmissible. They lack the legitimate reason to take legal action[536] since the arbitral award already has binding effect regardless of any grounds for setting aside (para 6.159) and enforcement in any event requires s 1060 ZPO proceedings. **6.259**

c) Actions Based on the Awarded Claim Actions to enforce the substantive law claim awarded in the arbitral award are likewise generally inadmissible by reason of the arbitral award's *res judicata* effect.[537] **6.260**

II. Admissibility

Since the proceedings for a declaration of enforceability mirror the setting aside proceedings, unsurprisingly both are admissible under similar conditions. Reference **6.261**

---

[532] Schlosser, in: Stein/Jonas (eds), s 1060 para 6; Schwab/Walter, ch 28 para 19; Voit, in: Musielak/Voit (eds), s 1060 para 3; dissenting Hartmann, in: Baumbach/Lauterbach/Albers/Hartmann (eds), s 1060 para 5.

[533] BayObLGZ 1984, 45, 47 = BB 1984, 746.

[534] Kröll, in: *Arbitration in Germany*, s 1060 para 51.

[535] Kröll, in: *Arbitration in Germany*, s 1060 para 51; Münch, in: MünchKommZPO, s 1060 para 41; Voit, in: Musielak/Voit (eds), s 1060 para 4.

[536] RGZ 99, 129, 131; Münch, in: MünchKommZPO, s 1060 para 43; Schlosser, in: Stein/Jonas (eds), s 1060 para 36.

[537] Münch, in: MünchKommZPO, s 1060 paras 41 *et seq.*; Voit, in: Musielak/Voit (eds), s 1060 para 4.

can therefore be made to the requirements for admissibility of a setting aside application (paras 6.167 *et seq.*), in particular as to the competent court (s 1062 para 1 no 4, para 5 ZPO, paras 6.174 *et seq.*) and proper representation (s 1063 para 4, s 78 para 3 ZPO, para 6.176). The particularities of an application for a declaration of enforceability will be explained subsequently. Unlike for setting aside applications (paras 6.178 *et seq.*), no deadline exists for filing the application for a declaration of enforceability.[538]

1. Domestic Award

6.262 As evidenced by its official heading, s 1060 ZPO applies only to **domestic** awards, ie to awards with a place of arbitration in Germany (s 1025 para 1 ZPO). The notion of an **arbitral award** is the same as underlies s 1059 ZPO (para 6.162), ie the award must meet the prerequisites under s 1054 para 1 ZPO.[539] Defects of form may be cured in the course of the proceedings.[540] If the arbitration clause allows for an arbitral tribunal of second instance, the decision of first instance is an award and can be declared enforceable only if appeal is no longer available by reason of a deadline passed or a waiver of the right to appeal.[541] Void awards (para 6.172) are not capable of being declared enforceable.[542]

2. Specified Request for Relief

6.263 The application for a declaration of enforceability must contain a specific **request for relief** (s 253 para 2 no 2 ZPO), namely that the award is to be declared enforceable in its entirety or in part. The award is to be sufficiently specified in the request, eg by indicating parties, date, and arbitrators, and its dispositive part should be included in the request.[543] Like setting aside applications (para 6.177), the application for a declaration of enforceability may be limited to a separate claim under the award.[544] If not otherwise indicated, an unrestricted application for a declaration of enforceability is to be understood as limited to that part of the award that is favorable to the applicant.[545]

---

538 OLG Koblenz, r+s 2010, 84, 85.

539 BayObLG BB 2003, Beil. 8, pp 26 *et seq.*; Geimer, in: Zöller (ed), s 1060 para 15; Schwab/Walter, ch 26 para 5; Voit, in: Musielak/Voit (eds), s 1060 para 5.

540 BGHZ 85, 288, 290 = NJW 1983, 867; NJW 1980, 1284; Münch, in: MünchKommZPO, s 1060 para 9.

541 Münch, in: MünchKommZPO, s 1060 para 12; Voit, in: Musielak/Voit (eds), s 1060 para 5.

542 BGH ZZP 75 (1962), 119, 120; Schlosser, in: Stein/Jonas (eds), s 1060 para 17.

543 Kröll, in: *Arbitration in Germany*, s 1060 para 27.

544 OLG München, BeckRS 2015, 09565 para 16; Schwab/Walter, ch 34 para 8.

545 KG JW 1929, 143, 144; OLG Frankfurt, June 26, 2003, 1 Sch 01/02 (unreported), http://www.disarb.org (last visited December 1, 2015); OLG Hamburg, NJW 1958, 1046, 1047; OLG Köln, KTS 1970, 52 *et seq.*; March 30, 2004, 9 Sch 02/04 (unreported), http://www.disarb.org (last visited December 1, 2015); Kröll, in: *Arbitration in Germany*, s 1060 para 28; Lachmann, para 2468.

Pursuant to s 1064 para 1 ZPO, the application must be accompanied by the **award or a certified copy of the award**. While it is advisable to attach at least such a certified copy, the failure to do so does not put the admissibility of the application at risk (para 6.281). For an award drafted in a language other than German, the court may request a **certified translation** (s 142 para 3 ZPO).[546] While some courts do so as a matter of routine even for English-language awards, others, eg the Higher Regional Court in Frankfurt, request translations of such awards only in exceptional cases. **6.264**

3 Legitimate Reason to Take Legal Action

The application for a declaration of enforceability requires a legitimate reason to take legal action (*Rechtsschutzbedürfnis*). The applicant has no such reason if it can achieve legal protection more easily or more effectively by other means or if it has no interest that is deemed worthy of protection (para 5.17). Such need for protection may also be assumed if the debtor's obligations pursuant to the award are not yet owing (cf ss 257 *et seq.* ZPO).[547] To what extent the legitimate reason to take legal action is to be denied in s 1060 ZPO proceedings depends on the purpose of s 1060 ZPO. If that purpose is rightfully (and in line with s 1060 para 1 ZPO) limited to providing a **basis for enforcement** (paras 6.253 *et seq.*), the legitimate reason to take legal action is to be denied if enforcement cannot be based on the award for other reasons including its non-enforceable content (para 6.254) or if the other party has already indisputably complied with the award.[548] **6.265**

By contrast, if the purpose of a declaration of enforceability is understood to **fortify the arbitral award against grounds for setting aside** (para 6.254), any application within the deadline under s 1059 para 3 ZPO would generally be made with legitimate reason to take legal action.[549] If the purpose of s 1060 ZPO is even understood to provide "additional moral value" to the award,[550] not even the lapse of this deadline restricts the legitimate reason to take legal action. **6.266**

Regardless of the rationale behind s 1060 ZPO, no **refusal of the award debtor** is required in order to provide the award creditor with legitimate reason to take legal action.[551] However, the applicant has to bear the costs of the proceedings if the defendant immediately acknowledges and has not given cause for the application to be brought (s 93 ZPO). Some courts have granted the award debtor a fortnight **6.267**

546 OLG München, SchiedsVZ 2012, 339, 341 = XXXIX Y.B. Com. Arb. 394, 396 (2014); Kröll, NJW 2001, 1173, 1181.

547 OLG Naumburg, SchiedsVZ 2010, 277, 278.

548 OLG München, SchiedsVZ 2009, 127, 128; dissenting Voit, in: Musielak/Voit (eds), s 1060 para 6.

549 See OLG München, SchiedsVZ 2015, 205, 206.

550 Kröll, in: *Arbitration in Germany*, s 1060 para 22.

551 OLG Stuttgart, SchiedsVZ 2009, 67, 68; Kröll, in: *Arbitration in Germany*, s 1060 para 22.

to comply with the award before he or she gives cause for the application for a declaration of enforceability.[552] Other courts hold that the award debtor has given cause for the application to be brought if his or her conduct has created the award creditor's impression prior to the filing of the application that he or she will not gain redress without the enforcement court's decision.[553] This formula is difficult to reconcile with the prevailing view that s 1060 ZPO also serves to fortify the arbitral award against grounds for setting aside (para 6.254) as it is hard to imagine how the award debtor could have accorded redress before filing of the application if, for example, the award only grants declaratory relief.[554]

6.268 Since s 1060 ZPO proceedings are more far-reaching than setting aside proceedings in terms of the effect of a court order, **pending setting aside proceedings** do not contest the legitimate reason to take legal action to initiate proceedings for a declaration of enforceability.[555]

III. Merits

6.269 The application for a declaration of enforceability is successful on the merits if it is directed against the correct opposing party (para 6.270) and if no grounds for setting aside the award exist (para 6.271) on which the opposing party can rely (paras 6.272 *et seq.*). Although not stipulated in s 1060 ZPO, the declaration of enforceability may also be denied if the opposing party raises specific substantive law objections against the claim underlying the award (paras 6.276 *et seq.*).

1. Party Opposing the Application

6.270 The correct parties to proceedings for a declaration of enforceability are generally the parties that are named in the arbitral award. In case of legal succession, the application may be filed by or against the successor. This follows from s 727 ZPO, which applies by way of analogy.[556] The applicant is, however, not restricted to the means of taking evidence as listed in that provision.[557]

2. Non-existence of Grounds for Setting Aside (s 1060 para 2 cl 1 ZPO)

6.271 The application for a declaration of enforceability is to be refused if grounds for setting aside exist (s 1060 para 2 cl 1 ZPO). This provision references s 1059 para 2

[552] OLG Frankfurt, March 30, 2010, 26 SchH 15/09 (unreported), http://www.disarb.org (last visited December 1, 2015); see also OLG München, January 5, 2010, 34 Sch 7/07 (unreported), http://www.disarb.org (last visited December 1, 2015); dissenting OLG Dresden, February 24, 2009, 11 Sch 01/09 (unreported), http://www.disarb.org (last visited December 1, 2015).

[553] OLG Frankfurt, June 21, 2013, 26 SchH 3/13 (unreported), http://www.disarb.org (last visited December 1, 2015); OLG München, SchiedsVZ 2015, 205, 206.

[554] Critical also Pörnbacher/Duncker, SchiedsVZ 2015, 207, 208.

[555] OLG Stuttgart, BB 2002, Beil. 7, pp 44, 45 (not reproduced in NJW-RR 2003, 1438).

[556] BGH NJW-RR 2007, 1366 para 12; Schlosser, in: Stein/Jonas (eds), s 1060 para 31; Schwab/Walter, ch 27 para 5; Voit, in: Musielak/Voit (eds), s 1060 para 7.

[557] OLG München, November 12, 2009, 34 Sch 17/09 (unreported), http://www.disarb.org (last visited December 1, 2015); Voit, in: Musielak/Voit (eds), s 1060 para 7.

ZPO (for details, see paras 6.187 *et seq.*). Also in s 1060 ZPO proceedings, the party invoking the grounds under s 1059 para 2 no 1 ZPO must show sufficient cause for their existence while the court assesses the grounds under s 1059 para 2 no 2 ZPO on its own motion.[558]

3. *Exclusion of Grounds for Setting Aside*

a) Final Rejection of an Application for Setting Aside (s 1060 para 2 cl 2 ZPO) Under s 1060 para 2 cl 2 ZPO, grounds for setting aside are disregarded if at the time the application for a declaration of enforceability is served an application for setting aside based on such grounds has been finally rejected. Although the court will always consider the grounds under s 1059 para 2 no 2 ZPO on its own motion, these grounds are excluded only if they had actually been made the subject matter of the setting aside proceedings.[559] If the court rejects a setting aside application after the application for a declaration of enforceability is served, the grounds considered therein are likewise excluded, this time by the setting aside decision's prejudicial effect.[560] **6.272**

b) Expiry of the Time Limit for Filing a Setting Aside Application (s 1060 para 2 cl 3 ZPO) Under s 1060 para 2 cl 3 ZPO, grounds for setting aside under s 1059 para 2 no 1 ZPO are likewise excluded if the deadline set by s 1059 para 3 ZPO has expired without an application for setting aside the award having been made. This **safeguards the deadline** for filing setting aside applications which would be rendered meaningless if the burdened party could simply await s 1060 ZPO proceedings.[561] Hence, the party opposing the declaration of enforceability can rely on the non-arbitrability and public policy violation (s 1059 para 2 no 2 ZPO) grounds only if it had not timely filed an application for setting aside the award. These two grounds, however, remain available even if the underlying facts simultaneously constitute an (excluded) ground under s 1059 para 2 no 1 ZPO.[562] This is often the case with violations of the right to be heard (s 1059 para 2 no 1 lit b ZPO), which can be brought only if they amount to a public policy violation (s 1059 para 2 no 2 lit b ZPO). **6.273**

If the proceedings under s 1060 ZPO were **commenced within the deadline** under s 1059 para 3 ZPO, s 1060 para 2 cl 2 ZPO does not apply. Once proceedings for a declaration of enforceability are pending, subsequent setting aside applications are inadmissible (para 6.183) and the opposing party cannot be requested to initiate inadmissible proceedings.[563] **6.274**

---

[558] BGHZ 142, 204, 206 *et seq.* = NJW 1999, 2974, 2975; Münch, in: MünchKommZPO, s 1060 para 20; Schlosser, in: Stein/Jonas (eds), s 1060 para 22; Schwab/Walter, ch 27 para 8.

[559] Kröll, in: *Arbitration in Germany*, s 1060 para 36; Voit, in: Musielak/Voit (eds), s 1060 para 10.

[560] Reichold, in: Thomas/Putzo (eds), s 1060 para 2; Voit, in: Musielak/Voit (eds), s 1060 para 10.

[561] Government bill, BT-Drucks 13/5274, p 61.

[562] BGHZ 145, 376, 381 = NJW 2001, 373.

[563] Voit, in: Musielak/Voit (eds), s 1060 para 11.

6.275 c) **Waiver of Grounds for Setting Aside** The party opposing application for a declaration of enforceability also cannot rely on grounds for setting aside which it had validly waived; for details on waivability of such grounds, see paras 6.165 *et seq.*

4. *Substantive Law Objections Against the Awarded Claim*

6.276 Pursuant to the wording of s 1060 para 2 ZPO, the application for a declaration of enforceability is to be rejected only if grounds for setting aside exist. Even if the award debtor has in the meantime already paid, set off, or otherwise extinguished the claim underlying the award, this objection would not affect the declaration of enforceability. The debtor would need to file for a **separate court action** under s 767 ZPO in order to have enforcement declared inadmissible. Section 767 ZPO is available for any substantive law objection that arose **only after** the debtor had the last opportunity to assert objections within the regular proceedings (s 767 para 2 ZPO). Objections that arose earlier can be brought under s 767 ZPO only if the arbitral tribunal has refrained from deciding the objection since it—rightfully or wrongfully—found that it lacked jurisdiction to do so.[564] This is particularly relevant for the set-off defense (paras 2.134 *et seq.*), which generally requires that the tribunal have jurisdiction over the counterclaim. The arbitral tribunal's finding that it lacks jurisdiction to decide on such defense does not bind the state court in s 1060 ZPO proceedings.[565]

6.277 The prevailing view permits the **raising of objections that could be brought in proceedings under s 767 ZPO** already in the proceedings for a declaration of enforceability under s 1060 ZPO.[566] This is permitted for reasons of procedural efficiency even though no such objections are foreseen in s 1060 ZPO and the higher regional court having competence over the s 1060 ZPO proceedings would not have jurisdiction over s 767 ZPO proceedings.

6.278 Depending on the content of the arbitration agreement and its interpretation, the substantive law objections under s 767 ZPO may well be within

[564] BGH SchiedsVZ 2010, 330, 331 para 8 = XXXVI Y.B. Com. Arb. 279, 280 (2011); SchiedsVZ 2014, 31, 32 para 5; OLG München, BeckRS 2015, 12786 para 20.

[565] BGH SchiedsVZ 2010, 330, 332 para 12 = XXXVI Y.B. Com. Arb. 279, 280 (2011).

[566] BGH SchiedsVZ 2008, 40, 43 para 31; 2008, 148, 150 para 18; 2010, 330, 331 para 8 = XXXVI Y.B. Com. Arb. 279, 280 (2011); SchiedsVZ 2014, 31, 32 para 5; OLG Dresden, SchiedsVZ 2005, 210 *et seq.*; OLG Düsseldorf, SchiedsVZ 2005, 214 *et seq.*; OLG Frankfurt, SchiedsVZ 2014, 154, 159; OLG Hamm, NJW-RR 2001, 1362 *et seq.*; OLG Koblenz, SchiedsVZ 2005, 260, 262; OLG Köln, SchiedsVZ 2005, 163 *et seq.*; OLG München, BeckRS 2015, 12786 para 15; Geimer, in: Zöller (ed), s 1060 para 9; Köhne/Langner, RIW 2003, 361, 368 *et seq.*; Mack, IDR 2006, 36, 37 *et seq.*; Münch, in: MünchKommZPO, s 1060 paras 33 *et seq.*; Voit, in: Musielak/Voit (eds), s 1060 para 12; dissenting BayObLG NJW-RR 2001, 1363 *et seq.*; Borris/L Schmidt, SchiedsVZ 2004, 273, 276; 2005, 254 *et seq.*; Kröll, NJW 2001, 1173, 1181; SchiedsVZ 2011, 210, 214; critical Pfeiffer, LMK 2008, 250684; Spetzler, SchiedsVZ 2011, 287, 288 (potential for obstruction).

the **jurisdiction of an arbitral tribunal.**[567] If that is the case and the applicant raises the arbitration objection, the higher regional court cannot consider the substantive law objections (s 1032 para 1 ZPO).[568] An exception applies only if the objection, in case of a set-off defense in particular the counterclaim, is undisputed[569] or if the arbitral tribunal has already rendered an award on the counterclaim.[570]

IV. Procedure

The proceedings for a declaration of enforceability follow mainly the same rules as the setting aside proceedings (paras 6.234 *et seq.*), in particular regarding the form of the decision (s 1063 para 1 cl 1 ZPO, paras 6.240 *et seq.*), court fees, lawyer's fees, and the amount in dispute (paras 6.237 *et seq.*) as well as available remedies (s 1065 ZPO, para 6.245). Below, only issues that do not arise in setting aside proceedings will be discussed. **6.279**

1. *Right to be Heard (s 1063 para 1 cl 2 ZPO)*

The party opposing the application shall be given an opportunity to comment before a decision is taken (s 1063 para 1 cl 2 ZPO). This opportunity is—contrary to the prevailing view—to be given in all cases governed by this provision even if the application is to be dismissed (para 6.234). In proceedings for a declaration of enforceability, the opposing party has a specific interest in being heard even if the court intends to dismiss the application on non-curable grounds since it can have a legitimate interest in a refusal of the declaration of enforceability and the setting aside of the arbitral award (para 6.286).[571] **6.280**

2. *Documents to Supply (s 1064 ZPO)*

At the time of the application, the award or a certified copy of the award are to be supplied (s 1064 para 1 cl 1 ZPO). The certification may also be made by counsel to the applicant (s 1064 para 1 cl 1 ZPO). This document, however, is not understood to be necessary for the proceedings for a declaration of enforceability to be admissible, but rather only to be a means of evidence if the content of the award is **6.281**

567 BGH SchiedsVZ 2008, 40, 42 para 19 (*obiter dictum*); 2010, 275 para 4 = XXXVI Y.B. Com. Arb. 277, 278 (2011); SchiedsVZ 2010, 330, 331 *et seq.* para 10 = XXXVI Y.B. Com. Arb. 279, 280 (2011); SchiedsVZ 2014, 31, 33 para 10; OLG München, SchiedsVZ 2013, 179, 180; Geimer, in: Zöller (ed), s 1030 para 17; Münch, in: MünchKommZPO, s 1029 para 80; Schwab/Walter, ch 7 para 14.

568 OLG München, SchiedsVZ 2006, 165 *et seq.*; 2008, 151, 152; BeckRS 2015, 12786 para 16; Voit, in: Musielak/Voit (eds), s 1060 para 12.

569 BGH SchiedsVZ 2010, 275 para 5 = XXXVI Y.B. Com. Arb. 277, 278 (2011).

570 OLG München, BeckRS 2015, 12786 para 20.

571 Voit, in: Musielak/Voit (eds), s 1060 para 6; dissenting Hartmann, in: Baumbach/Lauterbach/Albers/Hartmann (eds), s 1060 para 9; Münch, in: MünchKommZPO, s 1060 para 16; Schwab/Walter, ch 27 para 7.

in dispute between the parties.[572] It is in any event advisable to attach a certified copy of the award to the application (see also para 6.264).

3. Oral Hearing (s 1063 para 2 ZPO)

6.282 In proceedings for a declaration of enforceability, the court orders an oral hearing to be held if grounds for setting aside are to be considered (s 1063 para 2 ZPO). While the grounds for setting aside under s 1059 para 2 no 2 ZPO are always "to be considered," the grounds under s 1059 para 2 no 1 ZPO are "to be considered" only if they are pleaded with substantiation.[573]

4. Interim Measures (s 1063 para 3 ZPO)

6.283 Under s 1063 para 3 ZPO, the presiding judge of the court senate hearing the application may order *ex parte* interim measures which must, however, not go beyond measures of protection. By requesting such interim measures, the applicant can preserve its interest in effective enforcement, eg by prohibiting the award debtor from moving domestic assets abroad.[574] The party opposing the application can prevent enforcement by providing security even if it has not been expressly ordered (s 1063 para 3 cl 3 ZPO).

V. Effects of an Order on the Declaration of Enforceability

1. Order Granting a Declaration of Enforceability

6.284 The order declaring an arbitral award enforceable constitutes an **executory title** that serves as a basis for enforcement if this decision is final and binding or has been declared provisionally enforceable (s 794 para 1 no 4a ZPO, paras 6.250 *et seq.*). An order granting the declaration of enforceability under s 1060 ZPO is to be declared provisionally enforceable (s 1064 para 2 ZPO), thus allowing for immediate enforcement.

6.285 The **operative part** of the court order will usually include the operative part of the arbitral award that it declares enforceable.[575] While the court cannot amend the arbitral tribunal's decision as to substance,[576] it can **rephrase** the operative part in a way that it meets the strict requirements of German enforcement law.[577] If,

572 Münch, in: MünchKommZPO, s 1064 para 4.

573 BGHZ 142, 204, 207 = NJW 1999, 2974, 2975; Ehricke, ZZP 113 (2000), 453, 464; Schwab/Walter, ch 27 para 18; dissenting (probability that a ground for setting aside will be pleaded with substantiation in the oral hearing) OLG München, SchiedsVZ 2011, 167, 168; 2012, 156, 158 = XXXIX Y.B. Com. Arb. 389, 391 (2014); SchiedsVZ 2012, 287, 288; Voit, in: Musielak/Voit (eds), s 1063 para 3.

574 Cf OLG Frankfurt, SchiedsVZ 2010, 227 *et seq.*; Voit, in: Musielak/Voit (eds), s 1063 para 9.

575 Kröll, in: *Arbitration in Germany*, s 1060 para 43; Voit, in: Musielak/Voit (eds), s 1060 para 14.

576 OLG Dresden, April 20, 1999, 11 Sch 02/99 (unreported), http://www.disarb.org (last visited December 1, 2015); Kröll, in: *Arbitration in Germany*, s 1060 para 44.

577 Münch, in: MünchKommZPO, s 1060 para 24; Voit, in: Musielak/Voit (eds), s 1060 para 14.

for example, the arbitral tribunal made clear in the reasoning of the award that it intended to let the claimant participate in the distribution of respondent's assets under insolvency law, an operative part ordering payment may be rephrased to a determination of the insolvency schedule.[578] The order may limit the declaration of enforceability to a **separable part** of the arbitral award.[579]

2. Order Denying a Declaration of Enforceability

The content of an order denying a declaration of enforceability depends on the reason why the declaration was denied: if the application was inadmissible (paras 6.261 *et seq.*) or the other party successfully raised substantive law objections against the awarded claim (paras 6.276 *et seq.*), only the application is dismissed.[580] The award remains in effect.[581] If, however, the application is denied because grounds for setting aside were found, the court dismisses the application and sets aside the award (s 1060 para 2 cl 1 ZPO) even if the latter has not been requested.[582] In this case, s 1059 paras 4 and 5 ZPO (paras 6.244, 6.243) apply by way of analogy.[583] **6.286**

J. Recognition and Enforceability of Foreign Arbitral Awards (s 1061 ZPO)

Historically, recognition and enforcement of foreign arbitral awards have been one of the core elements of international arbitration. The Convention on the Recognition and Enforcement of Foreign Arbitral Awards (New York Convention, NYC, Annex B) of 1958 laid the foundation for effectively harmonizing international arbitration. Later, the grounds for denial of recognition and enforcement under Art V NYC were adopted almost verbatim in the UNCITRAL Model Law of 1985. The German legislature, however, did not adopt the provisions governing recognition and enforcement of foreign arbitral awards when Germany became a Model Law country in 1998. Rather, it considered it redundant to be a member state to the New York Convention and have a nearly identical domestic enforcement regime in its arbitration law.[584] The legislature therefore opted simply to reference the New York Convention as the applicable enforcement regime in s 1061 ZPO. The results, however, are similar to those under the Model Law. **6.287**

578 BGHZ 179, 304, 306 para 7 = SchiedsVZ 2009, 176.
579 Lachmann, para 2486.
580 Münch, in: MünchKommZPO, s 1060 paras 7, 35; Schwab/Walter, ch 28 paras 1 *et seq.*
581 Voit, in: Musielak/Voit (eds), s 1060 para 15.
582 Kröll, in: *Arbitration in Germany*, s 1060 para 41.
583 OLG Köln, SchiedsVZ 2012, 161, 166 *et seq.* (s 1059 para 4 ZPO); Münch, in: MünchKommZPO, s 1060 para 27; Voit, in: Musielak/Voit (eds), s 1060 para 15; Wighardt, SchiedsVZ 2010, 252, 253 (s 1059 para 4 ZPO).
584 Government bill, BT-Drucks 13/5274, p 62.

I. Spirit and Purpose

1. Recognition, Enforcement, and Declaration of Enforceability

6.288 The **relationship** between recognition, enforcement, and the declaration of enforceability has been explained in detail in paras 6.248 *et seq.*: recognition acknowledges the binding effect of a decision while enforcement entails coercive execution proceedings in the debtor's assets to satisfy the creditor. Enforcement is based on an executory title, which the arbitral award does not qualify as. This gap is bridged by the declaration of enforceability, which constitutes the required executory title.

6.289 Section 1061 ZPO provides, as its second paragraph sets out correctly (para 6.252), for the **declaration of enforceability** for foreign arbitral awards, which generally is to be granted on the merits if none of the grounds for denial of recognition (Art V NYC) exists. This declaration of enforceability serves as the necessary executory title (s 794 para 1 no 4a ZPO) that allows for enforcement proceedings under ss 704 *et seq.* ZPO.[585]

6.290 As s 1061 para 1 ZPO and Art V NYC indicate, the **recognition** of a foreign arbitral award is to be granted under similar prerequisites as the declaration of its enforceability. It is, however, acknowledged that recognition does not require a separate recognition procedure, but rather occurs automatically if it has become binding under the law applicable to it (para 6.313) and if no grounds under Art V NYC exist.[586] Absent a provision prohibiting the incidental review of a foreign arbitral award for the substantive requirements for recognition (as s 1059 para 1 ZPO does for domestic arbitral awards, para 6.160), any court or public authority may **incidentally** recognize the foreign award.[587] However, such incidental review has no binding effect on other courts or public authorities.[588]

6.291 Alternatively, recognition can also be granted by way of a **court order** under s 1061 para 1 cl 1 ZPO, Art V NYC. Such court order recognizes the foreign arbitral award with binding effect for any subsequent decisions.[589] Unlike the recognition of foreign judgments (s 328 para 1 no 5 ZPO), recognition of a foreign arbitral award does not require reciprocity.[590]

2. Other Court Actions in the Context of Foreign Arbitral Awards

6.292 Similar to the legal situation for domestic arbitral awards, actions cannot be based on the **duty to comply** with a foreign award (paras 6.258 *et seq.*) or on the awarded claim (para 6.260).[591]

---

585 BGH SchiedsVZ 2012, 41, 42 para 6.

586 Schwab/Walter, ch 30 para 3; Voit, in: Musielak/Voit (eds), s 1061 para 1.

587 Münch, in: MünchKommZPO, s 1061 para 3; Voit, in: Musielak/Voit (eds), s 1061 para 2.

588 Kröll, in: *Arbitration in Germany*, s 1061 para 2.

589 Kröll, in: *Arbitration in Germany*, s 1061 para 3; Voit, in: Musielak/Voit (eds), s 1061 para 2.

590 BGHZ 55, 162, 171 = NJW 1971, 986, 987 *et seq.*; Münch, in: MünchKommZPO, s 1061 para 1; Voit, in: Musielak/Voit (eds), s 1061 para 1.

591 Münch, in: MünchKommZPO, s 1061 para 35; Schwab/Walter, ch 30 para 38; Voit, in: Musielak/Voit (eds), s 1061 para 9.

As a counter-action to the recognition under s 1061 ZPO (para 6.291), the award debtor may request a **declaration that the arbitral award is not to be recognized in Germany.**[592] Such request also allows the award debtor to gain a decision on the (denial of) recognition that is as binding as the decision under s 1061 ZPO (para 6.291). This request lacks legitimate reason to take legal action if the award creditor has already applied for a declaration of enforceability as the more far-reaching action.[593] Recognition is detached from a declaration of enforceability (paras 6.288 *et seq.*) so that the request does not require the award to have enforceable content.[594] **6.293**

Since—under the preferable view—the award creditor cannot request a declaration of enforceability if the award is of non-enforceable content (para 6.254), it is permissible to file a **request for a declaration that the arbitral award be recognized in Germany.**[595] For other awards, the award creditor has no legitimate reason to take such legal action since the request under s 1061 ZPO is the more far-reaching court action. **6.294**

Although foreign declarations of enforceability may be judgments, they cannot be recognized as such in Germany by way of a **"double exequatur"** since their effect is limited to the underlying decision's enforceability in the country in which the declaration of enforceability was issued.[596] Formerly, case law had made an exception to this rule for foreign decisions declaring foreign arbitral awards enforceable if they, as under the US doctrine of merger, went beyond a declaration of enforceability and fully incorporated the award.[597] This exception has, however, properly been revoked, inasmuch as it allowed for a separate, second avenue to enforce a foreign arbitral award and thereby undermined the procedural requirements that s 1061 ZPO specifically sets up for arbitral awards (such as, for example, the denial of a declaration of enforceability on the grounds of a lack of a valid arbitration agreement).[598] **6.295**

II. Admissibility

The admissibility of a request to declare a foreign arbitral award enforceable is governed by the same rules as the admissibility of a request to declare a domestic **6.296**

592 OLG Nürnberg, KTS 1966, 111, 112 (pre-reform); for a decision by means of an order: Münch, in: MünchKommZPO, s 1061 paras 9, 28; Schlosser, in: Stein/Jonas (eds), s 1061 para 11; Voit, in: Musielak/Voit (eds), s 1061 para 9; for a decision by means of a judgment: Schwab/Walter, ch 30 para 39.

593 Münch, in: MünchKommZPO, s 1061 para 28.

594 Dissenting Kröll, in: *Arbitration in Germany*, s 1061 para 176.

595 Geimer, in: Zöller (ed), s 1061 para 18; Voit, in: Musielak/Voit (eds), s 1061 para 2.

596 BGH SchiedsVZ 2009, 285, 286 para 12 = XXXV Y.B. Com. Arb. 374, 376 (2010) with further references.

597 BGH NJW 1984, 2765 *et seq.*

598 BGH SchiedsVZ 2009, 285, 287 para 23 = XXXV Y.B. Com. Arb. 374, 376 (2010); concurring Geimer, IPRax 2010, 346 *et seq.*; Plaßmeier, SchiedsVZ 2010, 82 *et seq.*; Schütze, RIW 2009, 817, 819; Voit, in: Musielak/Voit (eds), s 1061 para 6.

arbitral award enforceable (paras 6.261 *et seq.*). However, the subject matter of the proceedings is limited to foreign (rather than to domestic) awards (para 6.303) and modifications apply for the competent court (para 6.304) and the legitimate reason to take legal action (para 6.305).

1. Foreign Award

6.297 a) **Limitation to Arbitral Awards** Section 1061 para 1 cl 1 ZPO applies only to (foreign, para 6.303) arbitral awards. The provision does not allow recognizing or declaring enforceable either decisions of dispute resolution bodies other than arbitral tribunals or other decisions of an arbitral tribunal. It is **difficult to determine** what the notion of an arbitral award for purposes of s 1061 ZPO is since that provision refers to the New York Convention. The Convention also refers to the notion of an arbitral award and both notions do not necessarily match. Moreover, it is a matter of dispute whether the notion of an arbitral award underlying Art I NYC is to be determined autonomously, by reference to the national law of the state where the award was made or where enforceability is requested, or a combination of several of these criteria.[599]

6.298 In light of the German legislature's pro-enforcement approach, it cannot be assumed that decisions that would qualify as arbitral awards if they were domestic decisions, ie that meet the **German standard** for awards (para 6.262), cannot be recognized and declared enforceable under s 1061 ZPO.[600] On the other hand, Germany is a signatory state to the New York Convention and is under a duty as a matter of public international law to recognize and declare enforceable all awards within the scope of the Convention.[601] Since Germany has withdrawn its reservation of reciprocity under Art I para 3 cl 1 NYC,[602] this duty extends to awards made in any country other than Germany.[603] Even if the notion of an arbitral award in s 1061 para 1 cl 1 ZPO were restricted to the German standard, it would need to be extended by direct application of the New York Convention.[604] In light of this, it is more elegant to broaden the term "award" in s 1061 ZPO and to include any decision that meets the **standard under Art I NYC.**[605]

6.299 Only an arbitral award that is **binding** between the parties can be successfully recognized and declared enforceable under s 1061 ZPO. While the binding effect would indeed belong to the notion of an arbitral award under German law

[599] For an overview, see Ehle, in: Wolff (ed), Art I paras 14 *et seq.*

[600] BGH NJW 1982, 1224, 1226; Geimer, in: Zöller (ed), s 1061 para 4; Schlosser, in: Stein/Jonas (eds), annex to s 1061 para 16; Voit, in: Musielak/Voit (eds), s 1061 para 3.

[601] Voit, in: Musielak/Voit (eds), s 1061 para 3.

[602] BGBl 1999 II p 7.

[603] BGH SchiedsVZ 2003, 281, 282 = XXIX Y.B. Com. Arb. 767, 768 (2004); SchiedsVZ 2006, 161, 163 para 19 = XXXII Y.B. Com. Arb. 328, 335 *et seq.* (2007) (not reproduced in BGHZ 166, 278).

[604] Voit, in: Musielak/Voit (eds), s 1061 para 3.

[605] Schwab/Walter, ch 30 para 11; Voit, in: Musielak/Voit (eds), s 1061 para 3.

(paras 6.87 *et seq.*), this cannot hold true for a foreign arbitral award: Art V para 1 lit e NYC provides for the non-binding character as a ground for denying recognition and enforceability of a foreign award (paras 6.313 *et seq.*) so that the binding effect cannot yet put into question the classification as an arbitral award.[606] What sounds merely dogmatic at first sight has the practical effect that the state court takes the non-binding character into account on the merits only if proven by the party opposing the application while the state court would review it on its own motion if it was part of the application's admissibility.[607]

By contrast, **finality** is part and parcel of the notion of the arbitral award. A decision against which ordinary means of recourse to a state court or to another arbitral tribunal are available does not qualify as an arbitral award.[608] Likewise, an arbitral tribunal's decision is not (yet) an award if under the applicable arbitration law it requires a formal recognition to become final.[609] **6.300**

The **form requirements** of an award are governed by its *lex arbitri*, ie the arbitration law of the country in which it was made.[610] Therefore, an award does not need to meet the formal requirements under s 1054 para 1 ZPO in order to be recognized and declared enforceable under s 1061 ZPO.[611] **6.301**

It is acknowledged that recognition and a declaration of enforceability can be sought for **various types of awards** including partial awards,[612] awards on agreed terms,[613] and awards on costs.[614] It is controversial whether or not s 1061 ZPO applies to interlocutory awards (*Zwischenschiedssprüche*);[615] interim awards (para 5.88) are assumed to be arbitral awards.[616] Decisions like the Italian *lodo irrituale* which have contractual force only between the parties and require subsequent **6.302**

606 Münch, in: MünchKommZPO, s 1061 para 11; Voit, in: Musielak/Voit (eds), s 1061 para 5; dissenting Schwab/Walter, ch 30 para 10.

607 Münch, in: MünchKommZPO, s 1061 para 11; Voit, in: Musielak/Voit (eds), s 1061 para 5; dissenting Schwab/Walter, ch 30 para 10.

608 BayObLG SchiedsVZ 2003, 142, 144 = XXIX Y.B. Com. Arb. 754, 757 (2004); Kröll, in: *Arbitration in Germany*, s 1061 para 16.

609 BayObLG SchiedsVZ 2003, 142, 143 = XXIX Y.B. Com. Arb. 754, 757 (2004).

610 Kreindler/Schäfer/Wolff, para 1130; Schwab/Walter, ch 30 para 13; see also (*lex arbitri* governs signature requirements) BGH SchiedsVZ 2008, 195, 196 para 10 = XXXIII Y.B. Com. Arb. 510 (2008); OLG München, SchiedsVZ 2010, 169, 171 = XXXV Y.B. Com. Arb. 371, 373 (2010).

611 OLG Celle, October 6, 2005, 8 Sch 06/05 (unreported), http://www.disarb.org (last visited December 1, 2015); OLG München, SchiedsVZ 2010, 169, 171 = XXXV Y.B. Com. Arb. 371, 373 (2010); Münch, in: MünchKommZPO, s 1061 para 9.

612 BGH NJW-RR 2007, 1008 para 6 = XXXIII Y.B. Com. Arb. 506, 507 (2008); Schlosser, in: Stein/Jonas (eds), annex to s 1061 paras 21 *et seq.*

613 BGHZ 145, 376, 381 = NJW 2001, 373; Schlosser, in: Stein/Jonas (eds), annex to s 1061 paras 34 *et seq.*

614 Kröll, in: *Arbitration in Germany*, s 1061 para 11.

615 Pro: Schlosser, in: Stein/Jonas (eds), annex to s 1061 paras 21 *et seq.*; con: Schwab/Walter, ch 30 para 11; Voit, in: Musielak/Voit (eds), s 1061 para 3.

616 Schlosser, in: Stein/Jonas (eds), annex to s 1061 para 23; Schwab/Walter, ch 30 para 12.

court action to become binding are not considered to be arbitral awards.[617] Foreign interim measures usually are not classified as arbitral awards[618] if not issued in the form of an interim award (para 5.88)[619] but can, under the preferable view, be recognized and granted leave of enforcement under s 1041 ZPO (paras 5.67 *et seq.*).

6.303 **b) Limitation to Foreign Awards** Only foreign awards can be recognized and declared enforceable under s 1061 ZPO. An award is foreign if its **place of arbitration** is outside Germany (s 1025 paras 4 and 1 ZPO).[620] The approach under the German pre-reform arbitration law to determine the nationality of an arbitral award by the arbitration law chosen by the parties or otherwise applicable to the arbitral award has been abandoned. Only by selecting the place of arbitration can the parties determine the nationality of an arbitral award.[621] So-called a-national awards that are supposedly not anchored in a national arbitration law may—if this concept is to be acknowledged—be enforced under s 1060 ZPO or s 1061 ZPO depending on their place of arbitration.[622]

2. Competent Court (s 1062 ZPO)

6.304 The application for a declaration of enforceability is to be filed with a higher regional court (s 1062 para 1 no 4, paras 2, 5 ZPO; paras 6.174 *et seq.*). The court of local jurisdiction is to be determined in a two-step procedure: first, all higher regional courts are competent in the district in which the party opposing the application has its place of business or place of habitual residence, or where assets of that party or the property in dispute or affected by the measure is located. If more than one of these courts has jurisdiction, the applicant may choose at its convenience.[623] If none of these is competent, the Berlin Higher Regional Court (*Kammergericht*) shall be competent (s 1062 para 2 ZPO). Some assume that a sufficient connection to Germany is required in order to establish the *Kammergericht's* jurisdiction[624] and that this criterion is not met if the foreign award debtor neither has assets in Germany nor is expected to have such domestic assets in the future.[625] In that case, however, the applicant has no legitimate reason to take legal action so that its

[617] BGH NJW 1982, 1224 *et seq.*; BayObLG SchiedsVZ 2003, 142, 143 *et seq.* = XXIX Y.B. Com. Arb. 754, 757 (2004); Adolphsen, in: MünchKommZPO, annex I to s 1061 Art I para 4; Lachmann, para 2516; Voit, in: Musielak/Voit (eds), s 1061 para 3.
[618] Voit, in: Musielak/Voit (eds), s 1061 para 3; dissenting Schwab/Walter, ch 30 para 12.
[619] Voit, in: Musielak/Voit (eds), s 1061 para 3.
[620] Kröll, in: *Arbitration in Germany*, s 1061 para 15; Münch, in: MünchKommZPO, s 1061 para 8.
[621] Voit, in: Musielak/Voit (eds), s 1061 para 4.
[622] Haas, in: Weigand (ed), 1st edn, Part 3, Art I para 24; Kröll, in: *Arbitration in Germany*, s 1061 para 16; Voit, in: Musielak/Voit (eds), s 1061 para 4; see also Geimer, in: Zöller (ed), s 1061 para 11.
[623] Government bill, BT-Drucks 13/5274, p 64; dissenting Münch, in: MünchKommZPO, s 1062 paras 18 *et seq.*
[624] KG SchiedsVZ 2007, 108, 112; Escher/Reichert, SchiedsVZ 2007, 71, 76; Schlosser, in: Stein/Jonas (eds), s 1062 para 6; Schwab/Walter, ch 31 para 7.
[625] KG SchiedsVZ 2007, 108, 112; OLG München, IBRRS 2015, 0349.

application would be inadmissible in any event.[626] Therefore, there is little need to deny the court jurisdiction.

3. Legitimate Reason to Take Legal Action

As in the case of any other court action, the s 1061 ZPO proceedings are admissible only if the applicant has legitimate reason to take legal action (para 5.17). The application lacks such interest if for example the award does not have enforceable content (para 6.254)[627] or if the foreign award debtor does not have and will not have property located in Germany (para 6.304). The amounts owed under the award need not yet be due.[628] **6.305**

III. Merits

The application will be successful on the merits under s 1061 ZPO if it is directed against the correct opposing party (para 6.307), if no grounds for denial of recognition and enforceability exist (paras 6.308 *et seq.*) on which the opposing party can rely (paras 6.323 *et seq.*), and if the opposing party does not successfully raise specific substantive law objections against the claim underlying the award (para 6.327). **6.306**

1. Party Opposing the Application

The correct parties to an application for the recognition and a declaration of enforceability of a foreign arbitral award are the parties named in the arbitral award or their legal successors (for details, see para 6.270).[629] **6.307**

2. Non-existence of Grounds for Denial of Recognition and Enforceability (Art V NYC)

The application under s 1061 ZPO will be denied if grounds under Art V NYC exist. While the word "**may**" in Art V paras 1 and 2 NYC internationally—including in the US, France, and Switzerland—is read to provide the court with discretion to recognize the foreign award and declare it enforceable,[630] the prevailing view in German jurisprudence and commentary is notably more restrictive and has seen fit to read "may" as "must."[631] This is in line with the fact that German law never allows for court discretion in the context of recognition and enforceability.[632] **6.308**

[626] KG SchiedsVZ 2007, 108, 112; Schroeder/Wortmann, in: *Arbitration in Germany*, s 1062 para 23; Voit, in: Musielak/Voit (eds), s 1062 para 4.

[627] KG SchiedsVZ 2007, 108, 112; dissenting Kröll, in: *Arbitration in Germany*, s 1061 para 19.

[628] OLG München, SchiedsVZ 2009, 343, 344 = XXXV Y.B. Com. Arb. 367, 368 (2010); Voit, in: Musielak/Voit (eds), s 1061 para 12.

[629] OLG Karlsruhe, SchiedsVZ 2015, 145, 147.

[630] Borris/Hennecke, in: Wolff (ed), Art V paras 74 *et seq.* with further references.

[631] OLG München, SchiedsVZ 2012, 339, 341 = XXXIX Y.B. Com. Arb. 394, 396 (2014); Schlosser, in: Stein/Jonas (eds), annex to s 1061 para 147; Schwab/Walter, ch 56 para 3; Wolff, LMK 2008, 265473.

[632] Voit, in: Musielak/Voit (eds), s 1061 para 28.

6.309 The grounds listed in Art V NYC almost literally match the grounds listed in s 1059 para 2 ZPO. This does not come as a surprise since Art V NYC served as the blueprint for art 34 Model Law, which in turn was adopted into German law in 1998.[633] German courts tend to interpret and apply the **grounds under s 1059 para 2 ZPO** and Art V NYC similarly so that reference can be made to the former (paras 6.193 *et seq.*) including the general remarks in paras 6.187 *et seq.* Specific details are, however, to be discussed with regard to the grounds for denial of recognition and enforceability under Art V para 1 lit a option 2 (paras 6.310 *et seq.*), para 1 lit e (paras 6.313 *et seq.*), and para 2 lit b (paras 6.315 *et seq.*) NYC.

6.310 **a) Invalidity of the Arbitration Agreement (Art V para 1 lit a option 2 NYC)** By expressly referencing the "agreement referred to in article II," Art V para 1 lit a option 2 NYC also incorporates the **"in writing" requirement** for arbitration agreements and the lack of such form as a ground for invalidity which would allow for denial of recognition and enforceability. Under Art II para 2 NYC, the term "agreement in writing" shall include an arbitral clause in a contract or an arbitration agreement, signed by the parties or contained in an exchange of letters or telegrams.[634] In line with no 1 of the 2006 UNCITRAL Recommendation (Annex C), this provision is to be interpreted in a **non-exhaustive** manner:[635] "include" allows for an understanding according to which the subsequently listed requirements are nothing but examples for what accounts as "in writing." Article VII para 1 NYC, which—in line with no 2 of the 2006 UNCITRAL Recommendation—is to be applied by way of analogy to arbitration agreements, furthermore allows for applying **more favorable form requirements** under national law.[636]

6.311 It is a matter of dispute under German law as to the form requirements of **which national law could apply as more favorable** by operation of Art VII para 1 NYC. The Federal Supreme Court deems it sufficient if the form requirements either under German law (s 1031 ZPO, paras 2.67 *et seq.*) or under the law determined under general German conflict of law rules (art 11 EGBGB) are met.[637] This result goes beyond the rationale of Art VII para 1 NYC: the most-favorable-law provision makes clear that the New York Convention is not to be understood as an exclusive instrument for recognizing and declaring enforceable foreign arbitral awards (or

[633] Government bill, BT-Drucks 13/5274, p 58; Schwab/Walter, ch 30 para 1.

[634] For details, see Wolff, in: Wolff (ed), Art II paras 91 *et seq.* with further references.

[635] Wolff, in: Wolff (ed), Art II paras 104 *et seq.* with further references.

[636] Wolff, in: Wolff (ed), Art II paras 177 *et seq.* with further references; dissenting OLG Schleswig, RIW 2000, 706, 707.

[637] BGH SchiedsVZ 2005, 306, 307; BGHZ 187, 126, 128 paras 5 *et seq.* = SchiedsVZ 2010, 332 *et seq.* = XXXVI Y.B. Com. Arb. 282, 283 (2011); KG SchiedsVZ 2011, 285, 286; OLG München, SchiedsVZ 2009, 340, 341 *et seq.* = XXXV Y.B. Com. Arb. 383, 385 (2010); dissenting Moller, NZG 1999, 143, 145 *et seq.*; Münch, in: MünchKommZPO, s 1061 para 14; Schwab/Walter, ch 30 para 18; Voit, in: Musielak/Voit (eds), s 1061 para 14.

recognizing foreign arbitration agreements respectively), but that the otherwise applicable rules remain applicable if they are more favorable. If Art II NYC did not exist, a German court would need to determine the law governing form requirements for arbitration agreements under its conflict of law rules, ie under Art V para 1 no 1 NYC.[638]

However, Art VII para 1 NYC does not open additional avenues such as recourse to national form provisions that the legislature had not contemplated applying to foreign arbitration agreements and, in fact, expressly excluded from application (s 1025 para 1 ZPO).[639] The Federal Supreme Court's reasoning that otherwise foreign awards would be more difficult to enforce in Germany than domestic awards[640] cannot supersede this clear rationale.[641] **6.312**

b) Non-binding Award (Art V para 1 lit e NYC) Under Art V para 1 lit e NYC, a foreign award "may" (para 6.308) not be recognized and declared enforceable if it has not yet become binding on the parties, or has been set aside or suspended by a competent authority of its country of origin. Whether the award has **not yet become binding** is to be determined autonomously taking into account the law at the place of arbitration.[642] The award is binding if it cannot be challenged before an arbitral tribunal of second instance or under the laws of its country of origin.[643] It is irrelevant whether the award is already enforceable in its country of origin[644] or may already be declared enforceable there.[645] **6.313**

If the foreign arbitral award has been **set aside in its country of origin**, this constitutes a separate ground for denial of recognition and a declaration of enforceability regardless of the grounds for which the award was set aside.[646] An exception applies within the scope of Art IX para 2 European Convention (para 6.335). The setting aside decision in the award's country of origin does not need to meet the **6.314**

---

[638] Geimer, LMK 2006, 166229.

[639] Mallmann, SchiedsVZ 2004, 152, 156; Moller, NZG 1999, 143, 145 *et seq.*; Quinke, SchiedsVZ 2011, 169, 171 *et seq.* (favoring a development of the law by judicial interpretation); Voit, in: Musielak/Voit (eds), s 1031 para 18.

[640] BGHZ 187, 126, 129 para 7 = SchiedsVZ 2010, 332, 333 = XXXVI Y.B. Com. Arb. 282, 283 (2011).

[641] Dissenting Kröll, in: *Arbitration in Germany*, s 1061 para 69.

[642] Solomon, pp 98 *et seq.*, 374; Voit, in: Musielak/Voit (eds), s 1061 para 18; dissenting Schwab/Walter, ch 57 para 20 (German law).

[643] BGHZ 52, 184, 188 = NJW 1969, 2093 *et seq.*; NJW 1984, 2763, 2764; NJW-RR 1988, 572; BayObLG SchiedsVZ 2003, 142, 144 = XXIX Y.B. Com. Arb. 754, 757 (2004); Geimer, in: Zöller (ed), s 1061 para 24; F Schmidt, SchiedsVZ 2013, 32, 36; Schwab/Walter, ch 30 para 16.

[644] Sandrock, RIW 1987, issue 5, Beil. 2, pp 1, 14; Schlosser, in: Stein/Jonas (eds), annex to s 1061 para 302.

[645] Voit, in: Musielak/Voit (eds), s 1061 para 18.

[646] OLG München, SchiedsVZ 2012, 339, 341 = XXXIX Y.B. Com. Arb. 394, 396 (2014); Schwab/Walter, ch 30 para 14; dissenting Nelle, pp 572 *et seq.*

requirements for recognition and enforceability of a foreign judgment under s 328 ZPO.[647] The mere fact that the arbitral award cannot be declared enforceable in its country of origin does not constitute a ground under Art V para 1 lit e NYC.[648]

6.315 c) **Public Policy Violation (Art V para 2 lit b NYC)** German courts will not recognize and declare as enforceable a foreign award if doing so would be contrary to German public policy (Art V para 2 lit b NYC). Similar to the public policy violation in s 1059 para 2 no 2 lit b ZPO (paras 6.225 *et seq.*), Art V para 2 lit b NYC serves the purpose of providing the member states to the New York Convention with a **safety-valve** allowing them to prevent the intrusion of awards into their legal system which they consider irreconcilable with it.[649]

6.316 *aa) Standard* According to the prevailing view, the public policy standard to be applied within Art V para 2 lit b NYC ("**international public policy**") is even more lenient for reasons of comity than the public policy standard under s 1059 para 2 no 2 lit b ZPO ("national public policy").[650] Both standards, however, are—and need to be in light of public policy's safety-valve purpose (para 6.315)—standards under German law rather than internationalized standards.[651] Under German law, the differences between both standards will be only a matter of degree.[652]

6.317 *bb) Procedural International Public Policy* Procedural international public policy takes into consideration the **remedies** that are available under the arbitration law governing the arbitral proceedings: the easier it is for the affected party to remedy an issue within the arbitration effectively, the more difficult it will be for such issue to meet the threshold of a public policy violation.[653]

6.318 The Federal Supreme Court has held that the **lack of a valid arbitration agreement** may constitute a public policy violation if that objection had been timely raised in the arbitral proceedings.[654] Public policy may also be violated if the parties have **chosen a law** (applicable on the merits, on procedure, on the validity of an arbitration clause etc) that has no connection with the dispute and that has been chosen

---

647 Münch, in: MünchKommZPO, s 1061 paras 11 *et seq.*; Schwab/Walter, ch 30 para 14; Wolff, LMK 2008, 265473.

648 Schlosser, in: Stein/Jonas (eds), annex to s 1061 para 310; Voit, in: Musielak/Voit (eds), s 1061 para 19.

649 Wolff, in: Wolff (ed), Art V para 490 with further references.

650 BGHZ 138, 331, 334 = NJW 1998, 2358; BGHZ 179, 304, 312 para 27 = SchiedsVZ 2009, 176, 178; OLG Karlsruhe, SchiedsVZ 2012, 101, 104 = XXXVIII Y.B. Com. Arb. 379, 383 (2013); Baumert, SchiedsVZ 2014, 139 *et seq.*; Schlosser, in: Stein/Jonas (eds), annex to s 1061 para 316; Voit, in: Musielak/Voit (eds), s 1061 para 23; dissenting Kornblum, in: *Festschrift Nagel*, pp 140, 149 *et seq.*; Schütze, IPRax 2009, 504 *et seq.*; Schwab/Walter, ch 30 paras 20 *et seq.*

651 Wolff, in: Wolff (ed), Art V para 497.

652 BGH SchiedsVZ 2009, 66, 67 para 5; Adolphsen, in: MünchKommZPO, annex I to s 1061 Art V para 69.

653 Kreindler/Schäfer/Wolff, para 1139; Voit, in: Musielak/Voit (eds), s 1061 para 24.

654 BGHZ 55, 162, 165 = NJW 1971, 986; BGHZ 71, 131, 136 = NJW 1978, 1744, 1745.

only in order to circumvent otherwise applicable mandatory law.[655] It has been held to be a violation of public policy if the executory title is not sufficiently specific to be enforced by the German enforcement agencies[656] if the dispositive part cannot be rephrased accordingly (para 6.331).

An arbitral award issued by a biased **arbitrator** may violate international public policy if such bias had an effect on the arbitral award[657] and if the affected party could not reasonably remedy this issue before the arbitral tribunal or before the state courts at the place of arbitration.[658] It was held that a sole arbitrator appointed by one of the parties alone pursuant to English arbitration law after the other party failed to make use of its appointment rights could permissibly render an arbitral award without violating German international public policy.[659] Consultation of a legal adviser by an arbitrator is considered to comply with international public policy,[660] as is scrutiny of the award under art 33 ICC Rules.[661] **6.319**

A violation of the **right to be heard** may also constitute a public policy violation.[662] However, exclusion of a party from the proceedings due to contempt of court has not been held to violate international public policy.[663] **6.320**

International public policy is violated if a **ground for an action for retrial** under s 580 nos 1 to 6 ZPO is present (cf para 6.230).[664] If an arbitral award does not provide **reasons** for its decision and was required to do so, international public policy may be violated.[665] **6.321**

cc) Substantive International Public Policy Substantive international public policy is a standard that is similar to, but more lenient (para 6.316) than substantive national public policy (paras 6.231 *et seq.*). Examples include the violation of **6.322**

---

655 Adolphsen, in: MünchKommZPO, annex I to s 1061 Art V para 73; Gottwald, in: *Festschrift Nagel*, pp 54, 68; Kornblum, KTS 1972, 59, 63.

656 BGH SchiedsVZ 2012, 41, 42 para 6.

657 BGHZ 98, 70, 72 *et seq.* = NJW 1986, 3027, 3028; critical on the requirement of an effect Kornblum, NJW 1987, 1105, 1107.

658 BGH NJW-RR 2001, 1059, 1060 = XXIX Y.B. Com. Arb. 700, 704 *et seq.* (2001); Schlosser, in: Stein/Jonas (eds), annex to s 1061 paras 356 *et seq.*

659 BGHZ 98, 70, 72 *et seq.* = NJW 1986, 3027, 3028 *et seq.*; NJW-RR 2001, 1059, 1060 = XXIX Y.B. Com. Arb. 700, 704 *et seq.* (2001); differently for domestic arbitrations: BGHZ 54, 392, 394 *et seq.* = NJW 1971, 139 *et seq.*

660 BGHZ 110, 104, 106 *et seq.* = NJW 1990, 2199 *et seq.* = XVII Y.B. Com. Arb. 503, 504 *et seq.* (1992).

661 Böckstiegel, NJW 1977, 463, 465 *et seq.*; Habscheid, RIW 1998, 421, 424 *et seq.*

662 OLG München, SchiedsVZ 2006, 111, 112.

663 BGHZ 48, 327, 328 *et seq.* = NJW 1968, 354, 355; differently for Australian family court proceedings BGHZ 182, 204, 215 *et seq.* paras 33 *et seq.* = NJW 2010, 153, 156 *et seq.*

664 BGHZ 145, 376, 381 = NJW 2001, 373, 374; Engelhardt, JZ 1987, 227, 230 *et seq.*; Schwab/Walter, ch 24 para 51.

665 Schlosser, in: Stein/Jonas (eds), annex to s 1061 para 438; Voit, in: Musielak/Voit (eds), s 1061 para 24.

German mandatory commercial law like competition law or price fixing law,[666] the violation of mandatory rules of European Community law,[667] an award ordering payment of punitive damages,[668] an award of claims based on a contract that is clearly against good morals (cf s 138 BGB),[669] or an award that has been obtained by intentionally inflicting damage on the opposing party against good morals (s 826 BGB, para 6.163).[670] Substantive international public policy does not allow for reviewing the correctness of the arbitral tribunal's decision on substance (no *révision au fond*).[671]

3. Exclusion of Grounds for Denial of Recognition and Enforceability

6.323 a) **Preclusion due to Inactivity in the Arbitral Proceedings** As in the case of domestic arbitral proceedings (paras 6.217 *et seq.* and 6.224), a party to foreign arbitral proceedings may not be able to invoke a ground for denial of recognition and enforceability if the ground arose during the arbitral proceedings and the party did not raise it. If under the arbitration law at the place of arbitration the party is precluded from relying on such defect, if the defect as such is cured or if the party is otherwise barred from relying on the defect, then this effect will also be acknowledged in proceedings under s 1061 ZPO.[672]

6.324 b) **Preclusion due to Inactivity After the Arbitral Proceedings** The more controversial question is whether an applicant is also precluded from relying on grounds that it could have raised in setting aside or similar proceedings which were subject to a limitation period although no such proceedings were timely initiated. The New York Convention does not stipulate such preclusion, but rather leaves the decision on preclusion to the national law.[673] The Federal Supreme Court held in a case in which the opposing party relied on the absence of a valid arbitration agreement that no such preclusion took place.[674] The court reasoned that Art VII para 1 NYC references not only the national law regime for the

[666] BGHZ 27, 249, 256 = NJW 1958, 1538, 1539 (price fixing law); BGHZ 46, 365, 367 *et seq.* = NJW 1967, 1178 (competition law); OLG München, SchiedsVZ 2015, 40, 46 (competition law); Schlosser, in: Stein/Jonas (eds), annex to s 1061 paras 345 *et seq.*

[667] ECJ EuZW 1999, 565, 567 – *Eco Swiss*; BGH NJW 1969, 978, 980; 1972, 2180, 2181 *et seq.*; Geimer, in: Zöller (ed), s 1061 para 51; Michaels, ZfRV 1999, 5, 7.

[668] BGHZ 118, 312, 334 *et seq.* = NJW 1992, 3096, 3098; Schwab/Walter, ch 30 para 22.

[669] OLG Saarbrücken, SchiedsVZ 2012, 47, 50.

[670] BGH NJW 1993, 1270, 1272; 1993, 1801, 1802 (not reproduced in BGHZ 122, 16); KG SchiedsVZ 2013, 112, 118 = XXXVIII Y.B. Com. Arb. 384, 391 (2013).

[671] OLG Brandenburg, SchiedsVZ 2016, 43, 51; OLG Frankfurt, SchiedsVZ 2014, 206, 208.

[672] Kröll, in: *Arbitration in Germany*, s 1061 para 53; Schlosser, in: Stein/Jonas (eds), annex to s 1061 para 110; Voit, in: Musielak/Voit (eds), s 1061 para 20; examples: KG SchiedsVZ 2013, 112, 117 (no objection against jurisdiction) = XXXVIII Y.B. Com. Arb. 384, 391 (2013); OLG Hamm, SchiedsVZ 2013, 182, 184; OLG Köln, SchiedsVZ 2014, 203, 205 (no objection against use of incorrect language); OLG München, SchiedsVZ 2013, 62, 64 (cure of a lack of form).

[673] BGHZ 188, 1, 5 para 10 = SchiedsVZ 2011, 105, 106.

[674] BGHZ 188, 1, 5 paras 10 *et seq.* = SchiedsVZ 2011, 105, 106; concurring Kröll, in: *Arbitration in Germany*, s 1061 para 56; Kröll, SchiedsVZ 2011, 210, 214 *et seq.*; Otto, IPRax 2012, 223, 224 *et seq.*; Schütze, RIW 2011, 417 *et seq.*

recognition and enforceability of foreign awards (ie s 1061 ZPO), but also the national law regime for the enforceability of domestic awards (ie s 1060 ZPO).[675] It further held that s 1059 para 3, s 1060 para 2 cl 3 ZPO—which stipulate such preclusion for domestic awards—were not referenced since the German legislature lacks competence to regulate the setting aside of foreign awards.[676]

While it already goes beyond the concept of Art VII para 1 NYC to allow the provision to reference the national law regime for the enforceability of domestic awards (paras 6.311 *et seq.*), it is inconsistent to exclude a detail of this regime (ie s 1059 para 3, s 1060 para 2 cl 3 ZPO) without further reasoning.[677] Since s 1060 para 2 cl 3 ZPO aims to safeguard the deadline under s 1059 para 3 ZPO (para 6.273) and this rationale also applies to foreign arbitral awards, the better grounds speak for applying s 1060 para 2 cl 3 ZPO by way of analogy.[678] **6.325**

c) Waiver of Grounds for Denial of Recognition and Enforceability A party cannot rely on a ground for denial of recognition or enforceability if that ground is subject to a valid waiver. In the context of s 1061 ZPO and the New York Convention, such waivers are similarly restricted as for domestic awards (paras 6.165 *et seq.*).[679] **6.326**

4. Substantive Law Objections Against the Awarded Claim

Although not expressly permitted in s 1061 ZPO, the prevailing view allows for raising substantive law objections against the awarded claims in these proceedings.[680] The same limits and the same concerns that have been discussed for s 1060 ZPO proceedings (paras 6.276 *et seq.*) also apply here. **6.327**

IV. Procedure

1. General

The proceedings for recognition and a declaration of enforceability of a foreign award under s 1061 ZPO are governed by the **same rules** as those for a declaration of enforceability of a domestic award under s 1060 ZPO, namely ss 1062 *et seq.* ZPO (paras 6.279 *et seq.*). An **oral hearing** (para 6.282) will more likely be ordered **6.328**

---

[675] BGHZ 188, 1, 6 para 15 = SchiedsVZ 2011, 105, 107.

[676] BGHZ 188, 1, 7 para 16 = SchiedsVZ 2011, 105, 107.

[677] Wolff, LMK 2011, 318374.

[678] Wolff, LMK 2011, 318374; similar OLG Karlsruhe, SchiedsVZ 2012, 101, 103 *et seq.* = XXXVIII Y.B. Com. Arb. 379, 383 (2013); Merkt, in: *Festschrift Stürner*, Vol II, pp 1303, 1314 *et seq.*; Voit, in: Musielak/Voit (eds), s 1061 para 20.

[679] Borris/Hennecke, in: Wolff (ed), Art V paras 71 *et seq.* with further references.

[680] BGH SchiedsVZ 2010, 275 para 3 = XXXVI Y.B. Com. Arb. 277, 278 (2011); SchiedsVZ 2010, 330, 331 para 8 = XXXVI Y.B. Com. Arb. 279, 280 (2011); OLG Brandenburg, SchiedsVZ 2016, 43, 50; OLG München, SchiedsVZ 2013, 179, 180; OLG Schleswig, SchiedsVZ 2010, 276, 277; Schwab/Walter, ch 30 para 27; Voit, in: Musielak/Voit (eds), s 1061 para 12; dissenting Kröll, in: *Arbitration in Germany*, s 1061 paras 161 *et seq.*

in s 1061 ZPO proceedings than in s 1060 ZPO proceedings, since the applicability of a foreign *lex arbitri* tends to complicate the proceedings.[681]

2. Documents to Supply (s 1064 ZPO)

6.329 Under Art IV para 1 NYC, the application must be accompanied by the duly authenticated original award or a duly certified copy thereof and by the original arbitration agreement or a duly certified copy thereof. These rules are stricter than s 1064 ZPO, pursuant to which the award or a certified copy of the award suffices (para 6.281). Although s 1064 para 3 ZPO gives preference to international treaties including the New York Convention, the more-favorable-law provision in Art VII para 1 NYC allows for the application of the more recognition- and enforcement-friendly provision of s 1064 ZPO. Therefore, only the award or a certified copy thereof need be supplied with the application under s 1061 ZPO,[682] and not a copy of the arbitration agreement.[683] Like s 1064 ZPO (para 6.281), Art IV para 1 NYC is not understood as a prerequisite for the application's admissibility but rather as a provision containing evidentiary rules in the event the content of the arbitral award is disputed.[684]

6.330 Article IV para 2 NYC, according to which the arbitral award would have to be **translated** into German and according to which that translation would need to be certified by an official or sworn translator or by a diplomatic or consular agent, is likewise superseded by the general rules of German civil procedure. Under these

---

[681] Kreindler/Schäfer/Wolff, para 1145; Kröll, in: *Arbitration in Germany*, s 1061 para 36; Schwab/Walter, ch 30 para 28.

[682] BGH SchiedsVZ 2003, 281, 282 = XXIX Y.B. Com. Arb. 767, 769 (2004); BayObLG BB 2000, Beil. 12, pp 10, 11; OLG Brandenburg, SchiedsVZ 2016, 43, 49; OLG Hamm, SchiedsVZ 2006, 106, 108; OLG München, SchiedsVZ 2012, 43, 45 = XXXVII Y.B. Com. Arb. 231, 233 (2012); SchiedsVZ 2012, 156, 158 = XXXIX Y.B. Com. Arb. 389, 391 (2014); SchiedsVZ 2012, 287, 288; 2012, 339, 341 = XXXIX Y.B. Com. Arb. 394, 396 (2014); OLG Schleswig, SchiedsVZ 2003, 237 = XXX Y.B. Com. Arb. 524, 525 (2005); Krapfl, IPRax 2001, 443, 445; Lachmann, BB 2000, Beil. 12, pp 8, 9; dissenting Moller, NZG 1999, 143, 144; Münch, in: MünchKommZPO, s 1064 para 5.

[683] BGH SchiedsVZ 2003, 281, 282 = XXIX Y.B. Com. Arb. 767, 768 (2004); OLG Frankfurt, SchiedsVZ 2014, 206, 207; OLG München, SchiedsVZ 2010, 169, 171 = XXXV Y.B. Com. Arb. 371, 373 (2010); SchiedsVZ 2010, 336; 2012, 43, 45 = XXXVII Y.B. Com. Arb. 231, 233 (2012); SchiedsVZ 2012, 156, 158 = XXXIX Y.B. Com. Arb. 389, 391 (2014); SchiedsVZ 2012, 287, 288; OLG Rostock, BB 2000, Beil. 8, pp 20, 23; Government bill, BT-Drucks 13/5274, p 65; Voit, in: Musielak/Voit (eds), s 1061 para 11; dissenting Münch, in: MünchKommZPO, s 1064 para 4.

[684] BGH NJW 2000, 3650, 3651; NJW-RR 2001, 1059 = XXIX Y.B. Com. Arb. 700, 709 (2001); NJW 2001, 1730 = XXIX Y.B. Com. Arb. 724, 728 (2004); BayObLG SchiedsVZ 2003, 142, 143 = XXIX Y.B. Com. Arb. 754, 757 (2004); OLG Frankfurt, IPRspr. 2008, no 203, 646, 647 = XXXIV Y.B. Com. Arb. 527, 532 (2009); OLG Hamm, SchiedsVZ 2006, 106, 108; OLG Karlsruhe, SchiedsVZ 2015, 145, 147; OLG München, IPRspr. 2009, no 273, 703, 704 = XXXV Y.B. Com. Arb. 365, 366 (2010); SchiedsVZ 2010, 50, 51 = XXXVI Y.B. Com. Arb. 273, 276 (2011); SchiedsVZ 2011, 337, 338; 2013, 179, 180; OLG Schleswig, SchiedsVZ 2003, 237 = XXX Y.B. Com. Arb. 524, 526 (2005); SchiedsVZ 2010, 276; Haas, IPRax 2000, 432, 433 *et seq.*; Mallmann, SchiedsVZ 2004, 152, 154 *et seq.*; dissenting Borges, ZZP 111 (1998), 487, 510; Münch, in: MünchKommZPO, s 1064 para 4.

rules, it remains in the court's discretion to request a translation (para 6.264), which is the more enforceability-friendly regulation in the sense of Art VII para 1 NYC.[685]

V. Effects of an Order on the Declaration of Enforceability

1. *Order Granting a Declaration of Enforceability*

If the declaration of enforceability is granted, the court may not amend the operative part of the arbitral award on substance, but may **rephrase** it so that it meets the German standards for enforcement (para 6.285).[686] For example, reference to a foreign statutory interest rate may be replaced by that rate as a figure.[687] Interest awarded from the delivery of the cost award may be substantiated by the specific date on which the cost award was delivered.[688] If father and son share the same name and live at the same address, an ambiguous party designation in the award's dispositive part may be clarified in the declaration of enforceability if the award's reasoning is unequivocal in this regard.[689] The order granting the declaration of enforceability under s 1061 ZPO is to be declared provisionally enforceable (s 1064 para 2 ZPO), thereby allowing for immediate enforcement (para 6.284). **6.331**

2. *Order Denying a Declaration of Enforceability (s 1061 para 2 ZPO)*

If the declaration of enforceability is to be refused since the court found a ground for denial of recognition and enforcement to apply (paras 6.308 *et seq.*), the court shall rule that the arbitral award is not to be recognized in Germany (s 1061 para 2 ZPO). This declaration takes the position of setting aside a domestic arbitral award (s 1060 para 2 cl 1 ZPO, para 6.286); such setting aside is outside the jurisdiction of the German courts if foreign awards are concerned (para 6.173). If, however, the declaration of enforceability is refused since the application was inadmissible (paras 6.296 *et seq.*) or the other party successfully raised substantive law objections against the awarded claim (para 6.327), only the application is dismissed.[690] In that case, the application may be filed again once the admissibility issues have been cured.[691] **6.332**

---

685 BGH SchiedsVZ 2003, 281, 282 = XXIX Y.B. Com. Arb. 767, 769 (2004); OLG Schleswig, SchiedsVZ 2003, 237, 238 = XXX Y.B. Com. Arb. 524, 526 (2005); Kröll, IPRax 2002, 384, 388; ZZP 117 (2004), 453, 457 *et seq.*; Schwab/Walter, ch 30 para 26; dissenting OLG Rostock, IPRax 2002, 401, 403.

686 BGH SchiedsVZ 2012, 41, 42 para 6; OLG Karlsruhe, SchiedsVZ 2015, 145, 148.

687 BGH SchiedsVZ 2012, 41, 42 para 9; OLG Koblenz, SchiedsVZ 2005, 260, 261 *et seq.*; OLG München, SchiedsVZ 2010, 169, 172 *et seq.* = XXXV Y.B. Com. Arb. 371, 373 (2010); Kröll, in: *Arbitration in Germany*, s 1061 para 167.

688 OLG München, SchiedsVZ 2012, 156, 159 = XXXIX Y.B. Com. Arb. 389, 391 (2014).

689 OLG München, SchiedsVZ 2013, 62, 63.

690 OLG Hamburg, August 27, 2002, 6 Sch 04/02 (unreported), http://www.disarb.org (last visited December 1, 2015); OLG Karlsruhe, SchiedsVZ 2015, 145, 148; Kröll, in: *Arbitration in Germany*, s 1061 para 166.

691 Kröll, in: *Arbitration in Germany*, s 1061 para 166; Münch, in: MünchKommZPO, s 1061 para 27.

VI. Setting Aside the Declaration of Enforceability (s 1061 para 3 ZPO)

6.333 A foreign arbitral award that has been set aside in its country of origin will not be recognized and declared enforceable in Germany (Art V para 1 lit e NYC). If the setting aside occurs only after the recognition and declaration as enforceable in Germany, the latter remains unaffected. However, setting aside the declaration of enforceability can be requested (s 1061 para 3 ZPO). While this provision requires the arbitral award to be finally[692] set aside in its country of origin,[693] the grounds for which the award was set aside are irrelevant even if they differ from the respective grounds under German law.[694] The request under s 1061 para 3 ZPO is not time-bound.[695]

VII. Other Treaties on the Recognition and Enforceability of Foreign Arbitral Awards

6.334 The provisions of treaties on the recognition and enforceability of arbitral awards other than the New York Convention remain applicable (s 1061 para 1 cl 2 ZPO). The **relevance** of such other regimes for recognition and enforceability, however, remains limited in practice. The **Geneva Treaties** (Geneva Protocol on Arbitration Clauses of 1923 and the Geneva Convention on the Execution of Foreign Arbitral Awards of 1927) have largely been supplanted by the New York Convention (Art VII para 2 NYC).

6.335 A (slightly) more important alternative regime for the recognition and declaration of enforceability of foreign arbitral awards is the **European Convention** on International Commercial Arbitration of April 21, 1961 (Annex D). The European Convention, pursuant to its Art X para 7, does not supersede other conventions. The European Convention's most relevant provision is Art IX para 2, which, in relation between member states to the New York Convention, notably limits Art V para 1 lit e NYC to the grounds set out by Art IX para 1 European Convention. The effect of this restriction is that if the award has been set aside in its country of origin for grounds of a lack of arbitrability or a violation of public policy, such setting aside cannot be raised as a ground for denial of recognition and a declaration of enforceability under Art V para 1 lit e NYC.[696] The members to the European Convention are not limited to European states (Art X paras 1 and 2 European Convention), and also include Azerbaijan, Burkina Faso, Cuba, and Kazakhstan.

---

[692] OLG Hamburg, SchiedsVZ 2003, 284, 286; Schlosser, in: Stein/Jonas (eds), annex to s 1061 para 306; Schwab/Walter, ch 30 para 34.

[693] Borges, ZZP 111 (1998), 487, 510 *et seq.*; Münch, in: MünchKommZPO, s 1061 para 29.

[694] Schwab/Walter, ch 30 para 34; Voit, in: Musielak/Voit (eds), s 1061 para 29.

[695] Government bill, BT-Drucks 13/5274, p 62.

[696] BGH SchiedsVZ 2013, 229 para 3 = XXXIII Y.B. Com. Arb. 510, 511 *et seq.* (2008); OLG Dresden, SchiedsVZ 2007, 327, 328 = XXXIII Y.B. Com. Arb. 510, 511 (2008).

The **most favorable law provisions** in Art VII para 1 NYC, Art X para 7 European Convention and other conventions allow for applying the regime for recognition and declaration as enforceable that is most favorable to the applicant (see also paras 6.311 *et seq.*). The courts apply the most favorable law on their own motion without the need of an election by the applicant.[697] The prevailing view does, however, allow only for the choice among (entire) regimes, not among (individual) provisions (no "cherry picking").[698] **6.336**

The Convention on the Settlement of Investment Disputes between States and Nationals of Other States (**ICSID** Convention) has established a self-contained arbitration system for investment disputes. Awards rendered under this convention do not require recognition and a declaration as enforceable under s 1061 ZPO to be enforceable in Germany (Art 54 ICSID Convention). The award may be reviewed only by an annulment committee under Art 52 ICSID Convention. Germany has been a member state to the ICSID Convention since 1969.[699] **6.337**

[697] BGH SchiedsVZ 2003, 281, 282 = XXIX Y.B. Com. Arb. 767, 768 (2004); SchiedsVZ 2006, 161, 163 para 19 = XXXII Y.B. Com. Arb. 328, 335 *et seq.* (2007) (not reproduced in BGHZ 166, 278); Voit, in: Musielak/Voit (eds), s 1061 para 7.

[698] BGH SchiedsVZ 2003, 281, 282 = XXIX Y.B. Com. Arb. 767, 768 (2004) ("in toto"); OLG Frankfurt, RIW 1989, 911; OLG Köln, ZZP 91 (1978), 318, 320; Münch, in: MünchKommZPO, s 1061 para 20; Quinke, in: Wolff (ed), Art VII paras 59 *et seq.*; Schlosser, in: Stein/Jonas (eds), annex to s 1061 para 383; Schwab/Walter, ch 42 para 25.

[699] BGBl 1969 II p 369.

Annexes

ANNEX A

German Code of Civil Procedure, Book 10: Arbitration Procedure*

Chapter 1. General provisions

Section 1025 Scope of application

(1) The provisions of this Book apply if the place of arbitration as referred to in section 1043 subs. 1 is situated in Germany.
(2) The provisions of sections 1032, 1033 and 1050 also apply if the place of arbitration is situated outside Germany or has not yet been determined.
(3) If the place of arbitration has not yet been determined, the German courts are competent to perform the court functions specified in sections 1034, 1035, 1037 and 1038 if the respondent or the claimant has his place of business or habitual residence in Germany.
(4) Sections 1061 to 1065 apply to the recognition and enforcement of foreign arbitral awards.

Section 1026 Extent of court intervention

In matters governed by sections 1025 to 1061, no court shall intervene except where so provided in this Book.

Section 1027 Loss of right to object

[1]If any provision of this Book from which the parties may derogate or any agreed requirement of the arbitral procedure has not been complied with, a party not stating his objection to such non-compliance without undue delay or, if a time-limit is provided therefor, within such period of time, may not raise that objection later. [2]This does not apply if the party did not know of the defect.

Section 1028 Receipt of written communications in case of unknown whereabouts

(1) Unless otherwise agreed by the parties, if the whereabouts of a party or of a person entitled to receive communications on his behalf are not known, any written communication shall be deemed to have been received on the day on which it could have been received at the addressee's last-known mailing address, place of business or habitual residence after proper transmission by registered mail/return receipt requested or any other means which provides a record of the attempt to deliver it there.
(2) Subsection 1 does not apply to communications in court proceedings.

Chapter 2. Arbitration agreement

Section 1029 Definition

(1) "Arbitration agreement" is an agreement by the parties to submit to arbitration all or certain disputes which have arisen or which may arise between them in respect of a defined legal relationship, whether contractual or not.
(2) An arbitration agreement may be in the form of a separate agreement ("separate arbitration agreement") or in the form of a clause in a contract ("arbitration clause").

* Based on the unofficial translation by the German Institution of Arbitration. Updated in cooperation with and reprinted with kind permission of DIS. Numbering of clauses added.

Section 1030 Arbitrability

(1) [1]Any claim involving an economic interest ("vermögensrechtlicher Anspruch") can be subject to an arbitration agreement. [2]An arbitration agreement concerning claims not involving an economic interest shall have legal effect to the extent that the parties are entitled to conclude a settlement on the issue in dispute.
(2) [1]An arbitration agreement relating to disputes over the existence of a lease of residential accommodations within Germany shall be null and void. [2]This does not apply to residential accommodations as specified in section 549 subs. 2, nos. 1 to 3 of the Civil Code.
(3) Statutory provisions outside of this Book regarding which disputes may not be submitted to arbitration, or which disputes may be submitted to arbitration only under certain conditions, remain unaffected.

Section 1031 Form of arbitration agreement

(1) The arbitration agreement shall be contained either in a document signed by the parties or in an exchange of letters, telefaxes, telegrams or other means of telecommunication which provide a record of the agreement.
(2) The form requirement of subsection 1 shall be deemed to have been complied with if the arbitration agreement is contained in a document transmitted from one party to the other party or by a third party to both parties and—if no objection was timely raised—the contents of such document are considered to be part of the contract in accordance with common usage.
(3) The reference in a contract complying with the form requirements of subsection 1 or 2 to a document containing an arbitration clause constitutes an arbitration agreement provided that the reference is such as to make that clause part of the contract.
(4) *(repealed)*
(5) [1]Arbitration agreements to which a consumer is a party must be contained in a document which has been personally signed by the parties. [2]The written form pursuant to sentence 1 may be substituted by electronic form pursuant to section 126a of the Civil Code ("Bürgerliches Gesetzbuch—BGB"). [3]No agreements other than those referring to the arbitral proceedings may be contained in such a document or electronic document; this shall not apply in the case of a notary certification.
(6) Any non-compliance with the form requirements is cured by entering into argument on the substance of the dispute in the arbitral proceedings.

Section 1032 Arbitration agreement and substantive claim before court

(1) A court before which an action is brought in a matter which is the subject of an arbitration agreement shall, if the respondent raises an objection prior to the beginning of the oral hearing on the substance of the dispute, reject the action as inadmissible unless the court finds that the arbitration agreement is null and void, inoperative or incapable of being performed.
(2) Prior to the composition of the arbitral tribunal, an application may be made to the court to declare whether or not arbitration is admissible.
(3) Where an action referred to in subsection 1 or 2 is pending, arbitral proceedings may nevertheless be commenced or continued, and an award may be made, while the issue is pending before the court.

Section 1033 Arbitration agreement and interim measures by court

It is not incompatible with an arbitration agreement for a court to grant, before or during arbitral proceedings, a provisional or conservatory measure of protection relating to the subject-matter of the arbitration upon request of a party.

Chapter 3. Composition of arbitral tribunal

Section 1034 Constitution of arbitral tribunal

(1) [1]The parties are free to determine the number of arbitrators. [2]Failing such determination, the number of arbitrators shall be three.
(2) [1]If the arbitration agreement grants preponderant rights to one party with regard to the constitution of the arbitral tribunal which place the other party at a disadvantage, that other party

may request the court to appoint the arbitrator or arbitrators in deviation from the nomination made, or from the agreed nomination procedure. [2]The request must be submitted at the latest within two weeks of the party becoming aware of the constitution of the arbitral tribunal. [3]Section 1032 subs. 3 applies mutatis mutandis.

Section 1035 Appointment of arbitrators

(1) The parties are free to agree on a procedure of appointing the arbitrator or arbitrators.

(2) Unless otherwise agreed by the parties, a party shall be bound by his appointment of an arbitrator as soon as the other party has received notice of the appointment.

(3) [1]Failing an agreement between the parties on the appointment of the arbitrators, a sole arbitrator shall, if the parties are unable to agree on his appointment, be appointed, upon request of a party, by the court. [2]In an arbitration with three arbitrators, each party shall appoint one arbitrator, and the two arbitrators thus appointed shall appoint the third arbitrator who shall preside over the arbitral tribunal. [3]If a party fails to appoint the arbitrator within one month of receipt of a request to do so from the other party, or if the two arbitrators fail to agree on the third arbitrator within one month of their appointment, the arbitrator shall be appointed, upon request of a party, by the court.

(4) Where, under an appointment procedure agreed upon by the parties, a party fails to act as required under such procedure, or if the parties, or two arbitrators, are unable to reach an agreement expected of them under such procedure, or a third party fails to perform any function entrusted to it under such procedure, any party may request the court to take the necessary measure, unless the agreement on the appointment procedure provides other means for securing the appointment.

(5) [1]The court, in appointing an arbitrator, shall have due regard to any qualifications required of the arbitrator by the agreement of the parties and to such considerations as are likely to secure the appointment of an independent and impartial arbitrator. [2]In the case of appointment of a sole or third arbitrator, the court shall take into account as well the advisability of appointing an arbitrator of a nationality other than those of the parties.

Section 1036 Challenge of an arbitrator

(1) [1]When a person is approached in connection with his possible appointment as an arbitrator, he shall disclose any circumstances likely to give rise to doubts as to his impartiality or independence. [2]An arbitrator, from the time of his appointment and throughout the arbitral proceedings, shall without delay disclose any such circumstances to the parties unless they have already been informed of them by him.

(2) [1]An arbitrator may be challenged only if circumstances exist that give rise to justifiable doubts as to his impartiality or independence, or if he does not possess qualifications agreed to by the parties. [2]A party may challenge an arbitrator appointed by him, or in whose appointment he has participated, only for reasons of which he becomes aware after the appointment has been made.

Section 1037 Challenge procedure

(1) The parties are free to agree on a procedure for challenging an arbitrator, subject to the provisions of subsection 3.

(2) [1]Failing such agreement, a party who intends to challenge an arbitrator shall, within two weeks after becoming aware of the constitution of the arbitral tribunal or after becoming aware of any circumstance referred to in section 1036 subs. 2, send a written statement of the reasons for the challenge to the arbitral tribunal. [2]Unless the challenged arbitrator withdraws from his office or the other party agrees to the challenge, the arbitral tribunal shall decide on the challenge.

(3) [1]If a challenge under any procedure agreed upon by the parties or under the procedure of subsection 2 is not successful, the challenging party may request, within one month after obtaining knowledge of the decision rejecting the challenge, the court to decide on the challenge; the parties may agree on a different time-limit. [2]While such a request is pending, the arbitral tribunal, including the challenged arbitrator, may continue the arbitral proceedings and make an award.

Section 1038 Failure or impossibility to act

(1) [1]If an arbitrator becomes de jure or de facto unable to perform his functions or for other reasons fails to act without undue delay, his mandate terminates if he withdraws from his office or if the parties agree on the termination. [2]If the arbitrator does not withdraw from his office or if the parties cannot agree on its termination, any party may request the court to decide on the termination of the mandate.

(2) If, under subsection 1 or section 1037 subs. 2, an arbitrator withdraws from his office or a party agrees to the termination of the mandate of an arbitrator, this does not imply acceptance of the validity of any ground for withdrawal referred to in subsection 1 or section 1036 subs. 2.

Section 1039 Appointment of substitute arbitrator

(1) [1]Where the mandate of an arbitrator terminates under sections 1037, 1038 or because of his withdrawal from office for any other reason or because of the revocation of his mandate by agreement of the parties, a substitute arbitrator shall be appointed. [2]The appointment shall follow the rules that were applicable to the appointment of the arbitrator being replaced.

(2) The parties are free to agree on another procedure.

Chapter 4. Jurisdiction of arbitral tribunal

Section 1040 Competence of arbitral tribunal to rule on its jurisdiction

(1) [1]The arbitral tribunal may rule on its own jurisdiction and in this connection on the existence or validity of the arbitration agreement. [2]For that purpose, an arbitration clause shall be treated as an agreement independent of the other terms of the contract.

(2) [1]A plea that the arbitral tribunal does not have jurisdiction shall be raised not later than the submission of the statement of defence. [2]A party is not precluded from raising such a plea by the fact that he has appointed, or participated in the appointment of, an arbitrator. [3]A plea that the arbitral tribunal is exceeding the scope of its authority shall be raised as soon as the matter in which this is alleged is raised during the arbitral proceedings. [4]The arbitral tribunal may, in either case, admit a later plea if it considers that the party has justified the delay.

(3) [1]If the arbitral tribunal considers that it has jurisdiction, it rules on a plea referred to in subsection 2 in general by means of a preliminary ruling. [2]In this case, any party may request, within one month after having received written notice of that ruling, the court to decide the matter. [3]While such a request is pending, the arbitral tribunal may continue the arbitral proceedings and make an award.

Section 1041 Interim measures of protection

(1) [1]Unless otherwise agreed by the parties, the arbitral tribunal may, at the request of a party, order such provisional or conservatory measures of protection as the arbitral tribunal may consider necessary in respect of the subject-matter of the dispute. [2]The arbitral tribunal may require any party to provide appropriate security in connection with such measure.

(2) [1]The court may, at the request of a party, grant leave of enforcement of a measure referred to in subsection 1, unless application for a corresponding interim measure has already been made to a court. [2]It may recast such an order if necessary for the purpose of enforcing the measure.

(3) The court may, upon request, repeal or amend the decision referred to in subsection 2.

(4) [1]If a measure ordered under subsection 1 proves to have been unjustified from the outset, the party who obtained its enforcement is obliged to compensate the opposing party for damage resulting from the enforcement of such measure or from his providing security in order to avoid enforcement. [2]This claim may be put forward in the pending arbitral proceedings.

Chapter 5. Conduct of arbitral proceedings

Section 1042 General rules of procedure

(1) [1]The parties shall be treated with equality. [2]Each party shall be given a full opportunity of presenting his case.

(2) Lawyers ("Rechtsanwälte") may not be excluded from acting as authorised representatives.

(3) Otherwise, subject to the mandatory provisions of this Book, the parties are free to determine the procedure themselves or by reference to a set of arbitration rules.

(4) [1]Failing an agreement by the parties, and in the absence of provisions in this Book, the arbitral tribunal shall conduct the arbitration in such manner as it considers appropriate. [2]The arbitral tribunal is empowered to determine the admissibility of taking evidence, to take evidence and assess freely such evidence.

Section 1043 Place of arbitration

(1) [1]The parties are free to agree on the place of arbitration. [2]Failing such agreement, the place of arbitration shall be determined by the arbitral tribunal. [3]In this respect, regard is to be had to the circumstances of the case, including the suitability of the place for the parties.
(2) Notwithstanding the provisions of subsection 1, the arbitral tribunal may, unless otherwise agreed by the parties, meet at any place it considers appropriate for an oral hearing, for hearing witnesses, experts or the parties, for consultation among its members or for inspection of property or documents.

Section 1044 Commencement of arbitral proceedings

[1]Unless otherwise agreed by the parties, the arbitral proceedings in respect of a particular dispute commence on the date on which a request for that dispute to be referred to arbitration is received by the respondent. [2]The request shall state the names of the parties, the subject-matter of the dispute and contain a reference to the arbitration agreement.

Section 1045 Language of proceedings

(1) [1]The parties are free to agree on the language or languages to be used in the arbitral proceedings. [2]Failing such agreement, the arbitral tribunal shall make this determination. [3]This agreement or determination, unless otherwise specified therein, shall apply to any written statement by a party, any oral hearing and any award, other decision and other communication by the arbitral tribunal.
(2) The arbitral tribunal may order that any documentary evidence shall be accompanied by a translation into the language or languages agreed upon by the parties or determined by the arbitral tribunal.

Section 1046 Statements of claim and defence

(1) [1]Within the period of time agreed by the parties or determined by the arbitral tribunal, the claimant shall state his claim and the facts supporting the claim, and the respondent shall state his defence in respect of these particulars. [2]The parties may submit with their statements all documents they consider to be relevant or may add a reference to other evidence they will submit.
(2) Unless otherwise agreed by the parties, either party may amend or supplement his claim or his means of attack and defence during the course of the arbitral proceedings, unless the arbitral tribunal does not allow so having regard to the delay in making it without sufficient justification.
(3) Subsections 1 and 2 apply mutatis mutandis to a counter-claim.

Section 1047 Oral hearings and written proceedings

(1) [1]Subject to agreement by the parties, the arbitral tribunal shall decide whether to hold oral hearings or whether the proceedings shall be conducted on the basis of documents and other materials. [2]Unless the parties have agreed that no oral hearings shall be held, the arbitral tribunal shall hold such hearings at an appropriate stage of the proceedings, if so requested by a party.
(2) The parties shall be given sufficient advance notice of any hearing and of any meeting of the arbitral tribunal for the purpose of taking evidence.
(3) All statements, documents or other information supplied to the arbitral tribunal by one party shall be communicated to the other party; any expert report or evidentiary document on which the arbitral tribunal may rely in making its decision shall be communicated to both parties.

Section 1048 Default of a party

(1) If the claimant fails to communicate his statement of claim in accordance with section 1046 subs. 1, the arbitral tribunal shall terminate the proceedings.
(2) If the respondent fails to communicate his statement of defence in accordance with section 1046 subs. 1, the arbitral tribunal shall continue the proceedings without treating such failure in itself as an admission of the claimant's allegations.
(3) If any party fails to appear at an oral hearing or to produce documentary evidence within a set time-limit, the arbitral tribunal may continue the proceedings and make the award on the evidence before it.
(4) [1]Any default which has been sufficiently justified to the tribunal's satisfaction will be disregarded. [2]Apart from that, the parties may agree otherwise on the consequences of default.

Section 1049 Expert appointed by arbitral tribunal

(1) [1]Unless otherwise agreed by the parties, the arbitral tribunal may appoint one or more experts to report to it on specific issues to be determined by the arbitral tribunal. [2]It may also require a party to give the expert any relevant information or to produce, or to provide access to, any relevant documents or property for his inspection.
(2) [1]Unless otherwise agreed by the parties, if a party so requests or if the arbitral tribunal considers it necessary, the expert shall, after delivery of his written or oral report, participate in an oral hearing. [2]At the hearing, the parties shall have the opportunity to put questions to him and to present expert witnesses of their own in order to testify on the points at issue.
(3) Sections 1036 and 1037 subs. 1 and 2 apply mutatis mutandis to an expert appointed by the arbitral tribunal.

Section 1050 Court assistance in taking evidence and other judicial acts

[1]The arbitral tribunal or a party with the approval of the arbitral tribunal may request from a court assistance in taking evidence or performance of other judicial acts which the arbitral tribunal is not empowered to carry out. [2]Unless it regards the application as inadmissible, the court shall execute the request according to its rules on taking evidence or other judicial acts. [3]The arbitrators are entitled to participate in any judicial taking of evidence and to ask questions.

Chapter 6. Making of award and termination of proceedings

Section 1051 Rules applicable to substance of dispute

(1) [1]The arbitral tribunal shall decide the dispute in accordance with such rules of law as are chosen by the parties as applicable to the substance of the dispute. [2]Any designation of the law or legal system of a given State shall be construed, unless otherwise expressed, as directly referring to the substantive law of that State and not to its conflict of laws rules.
(2) Failing any designation of the applicable rules of law by the parties, the arbitral tribunal shall apply the law of the State with which the subject-matter of the proceedings is most closely connected.
(3) [1]The arbitral tribunal shall decide ex aequo et bono or as amiable compositeur only if the parties have expressly authorized it to do so. [2]The parties may so authorize the arbitral tribunal up to the time of its decision.
(4) In all cases, the arbitral tribunal shall decide in accordance with the terms of the contract and shall take into account the usages of the trade applicable to the transaction.

Section 1052 Decision-making by panel of arbitrators

(1) In arbitral proceedings with more than one arbitrator, any decision of the arbitral tribunal shall be made, unless otherwise agreed by the parties, by a majority of the votes of all its members.
(2) [1]If an arbitrator refuses to take part in the vote on a decision, the other arbitrators may make the decision without him, unless otherwise agreed by the parties. [2]The parties shall be given advance notice of the intention to make an award without the arbitrator refusing to participate in the vote. [3]In the case of other decisions, the parties shall be informed of the refusal to participate in the vote subsequent to the decision.

(3) Individual questions of procedure may be decided by a presiding arbitrator alone if so authorized by the parties or the other members of the arbitral tribunal.

Section 1053 Settlement

(1) [1]If, during arbitral proceedings, the parties settle the dispute, the arbitral tribunal shall terminate the proceedings. [2]If requested by the parties, it shall record the settlement in the form of an arbitral award on agreed terms, unless the contents of the settlement are in violation of public policy (ordre public).
(2) [1]An award on agreed terms shall be made in accordance with section 1054 and shall state that it is an award. [2]Such an award has the same effect as any other award on the merits of the case.
(3) If notarial certification is required for declarations to be effective, it will be substituted, in the case of an arbitral award on agreed terms, by recording the declarations of the parties in the award.
(4) [1]An award on agreed terms may, upon agreement between the parties, also be declared enforceable by a notary whose notarial office is in the district of the court competent for the declaration of enforceability according to section 1062 subs. 1, 2. [2]The notary shall refuse the declaration of enforceability, if the requirements of subsection 1, sentence 2 are not complied with.

Section 1054 Form and contents of award

(1) [1]The award shall be made in writing and shall be signed by the arbitrator or arbitrators. [2]In arbitral proceedings with more than one arbitrator, the signatures of the majority of all members of the arbitral tribunal shall suffice, provided that the reason for any omitted signature is stated.
(2) The award shall state the reasons upon which it is based, unless the parties have agreed that no reasons are to be given or the award is an award on agreed terms under section 1053.
(3) [1]The award shall state the date on which it was made and the place of arbitration as determined in accordance with section 1043 subs. 1. [2]The award shall be deemed to have been made on that date and at that place.
(4) A copy of the award signed by the arbitrators shall be delivered to each party.

Section 1055 Effects of arbitral award

The arbitral award has the same effects between the parties as a final and binding court judgment.

Section 1056 Termination of proceedings

(1) The arbitral proceedings are terminated by the final award or by an order of the arbitral tribunal in accordance with subsection 2.
(2) The arbitral tribunal shall issue an order for the termination of the arbitral proceedings when
   1. the claimant
      a) fails to state his claim according to section 1046 subs. 1 and no case referred to in section 1048 subs. 4 exists, or
      b) withdraws his claim, unless the respondent objects thereto and the arbitral tribunal recognizes a legitimate interest on the part of the respondent in obtaining a final settlement of the dispute; or
   2. the parties agree on the termination of the proceedings, or
   3. the parties fail to pursue the arbitral proceedings despite requests by the arbitral tribunal or when the continuation of the proceedings has for any other reason become impossible.
(3) The mandate of the arbitral tribunal terminates with the termination of the arbitral proceedings, subject to the provisions of section 1057 subs. 2 and sections 1058, 1059 subs. 4.

Section 1057 Decision on costs

(1) [1]Unless the parties agree otherwise, the arbitral tribunal shall allocate, by means of an arbitral award, the costs of the arbitration as between the parties, including those incurred by the parties necessary for the proper pursuit of their claim or defence. [2]It shall do so at its discretion and take into consideration the circumstances of the case, in particular the outcome of the proceedings.

(2) [1]To the extent that the costs of the arbitral proceedings have been fixed, the arbitral tribunal shall also decide the amount to be borne by each party. [2]If the costs have not been fixed or if they can only be fixed once the arbitral proceedings have been terminated, the decision shall be taken by means of a separate award.

Section 1058 Correction and interpretation of award; additional award

(1) Any party may request the arbitral tribunal
   1. to correct in the award any errors in computation, any clerical or typographical errors or any errors of similar nature;
   2. to give an interpretation of specific parts of the award;
   3. to make an additional award as to claims presented in the arbitral proceedings but omitted from the award.

(2) Unless the parties did agree on another time-limit, the request shall be made within one month of receipt of the award.

(3) The arbitral tribunal should make the correction or give the interpretation within one month and make an additional award within two months.

(4) The arbitral tribunal may make a correction of the award even without request.

(5) Section 1054 shall apply to a correction or interpretation of the award or to an additional award.

Chapter 7. Recourse against award

Section 1059 Application for setting aside

(1) Recourse to a court against an arbitral award may be made only by an application for setting aside in accordance with subsections 2 and 3.

(2) An arbitral award may be set aside only
   1. if the applicant shows sufficient cause that
      a) a party to the arbitration agreement referred to in sections 1029 and 1031 was under some incapacity pursuant to the law applicable to him; or the arbitration agreement is not valid under the law to which the parties have subjected it or, failing any indication thereon, under German law; or
      b) he was not given proper notice of the appointment of an arbitrator or of the arbitral proceedings or was otherwise unable to present his case; or
      c) the award deals with a dispute not contemplated by or not falling within the terms of the submission to arbitration, or contains decisions on matters beyond the scope of the submission to arbitration; provided that, if the part of the award relating to matters submitted to arbitration can be separated from the part relating to matters not so submitted, only the latter part of the award may be set aside; or
      d) the composition of the arbitral tribunal or the arbitral procedure was not in accordance with a provision of this Book or with an admissible agreement of the parties and this presumably affected the award; or
   2. if the court finds that
      a) the subject-matter of the dispute is not capable of settlement by arbitration under German law; or
      b) recognition or enforcement of the award leads to a result which is in conflict with public policy (ordre public).

(3) [1]Unless the parties have agreed otherwise, an application to the court for setting aside must be made within a three month time-limit. [2]The time-limit shall commence on the date on which the party making the application had received the award. [3]If a request had been made under section 1058, the time-limit shall be extended by not more than one month from receipt of the decision on the request. [4]No application for setting aside the award may be made once the award has been declared enforceable by a German court.

(4) The court, when asked to set aside an award, may, where appropriate, upon request of a party set aside the award and remit the case to the arbitral tribunal.

(5) Setting aside the arbitral award shall, in the absence of any indication to the contrary, result in the arbitration agreement becoming operative again with respect to the subject-matter of the dispute.

Chapter 8. Recognition and enforcement of awards

Section 1060 Domestic awards

(1) Enforcement of the award takes place if it has been declared enforceable.
(2) [1]An application for a declaration of enforceability shall be refused and the award set aside if one of the grounds for setting aside under section 1059 subs. 2 exists. [2]Grounds for setting aside shall not be taken into account, if at the time when the application for a declaration of enforceability is served, an application for setting aside based on such grounds has been finally rejected. [3]Grounds for setting aside under section 1059 subs. 2, no. 1 shall also not be taken into account if the time-limits set by section 1059 subs. 3 have expired without the party opposing the application having made an application for setting aside the award.

Section 1061 Foreign awards

(1) [1]Recognition and enforcement of foreign arbitral awards follows the Convention on the Recognition and Enforcement of Foreign Arbitral Awards of 10 June 1958 (Bundesgesetzblatt [BGBl.] 1961 Part II p. 121). [2]The provisions of other treaties on the recognition and enforcement of arbitral awards shall remain unaffected.
(2) If the declaration of enforceability is to be refused, the court shall rule that the arbitral award is not to be recognized in Germany.
(3) If the award is set aside abroad after having been declared enforceable, application for setting aside the declaration of enforceability may be made.

Chapter 9. Court proceedings

Section 1062 Competence

(1) The Higher Regional Court ("Oberlandesgericht") designated in the arbitration agreement or, failing such designation, the Higher Regional Court in whose district the place of arbitration is situated, is competent for decisions on applications relating to
   1. the appointment of an arbitrator (sections 1034, 1035), the challenge of an arbitrator (section 1037) or the termination of an arbitrator's mandate (section 1038);
   2. the declaration of the admissibility or inadmissibility of arbitration (section 1032) or the decision of an arbitral tribunal confirming its competence in a preliminary ruling (section 1040);
   3. the leave of enforcement, setting aside or amendment of an order for provisional or conservative measures of protection by the arbitral tribunal (section 1041);
   4. the setting aside (section 1059) or the declaration of enforceability of the award (sections 1060 et seqq.) or the setting aside of the declaration of enforceability (section 1061).
(2) If the place of arbitration in the cases referred to in subsection 1, no. 2, first alternative, nos. 3 or 4 is not in Germany, competence lies with the Higher Regional Court ("Oberlandesgericht") where the party opposing the application has his place of business or place of habitual residence, or where assets of the party opposing the application or the property in dispute or affected by the measure is located, failing which the Berlin Higher Regional Court ("Kammergericht") shall be competent.
(3) In the cases referred to in section 1025 subs. 3, the Higher Regional Court ("Oberlandesgericht") in whose district the claimant or the respondent has his place of business or place of habitual residence is competent.
(4) For assistance in the taking of evidence and other judicial acts (section 1050), the Local Court ("Amtsgericht"), in whose district the judicial act is to be carried out, is competent.
(5) [1]Where there are several Higher Regional Courts ("Oberlandesgerichte") in one state, the government of that state may transfer the competence by ordinance to one Higher Regional Court, or to the Highest Regional Court ("oberstes Landesgericht"); the state government may transfer such authority to the Department of Justice of the state concerned by ordinance. [2]Several states may agree on cross-border competence of a Higher Regional Court.

Section 1063 General provisions

(1) [1]The court shall decide by means of an order. [2]The party opposing the application shall be given an opportunity to comment before a decision is made.

(2) The court shall order an oral hearing to be held, if the setting aside of the award has been requested or if, in an application for recognition or declaration of enforceability of the award, grounds for setting aside in terms of section 1059 subs. 2 are to be considered.

(3) [1]The presiding judge of the civil court senate ("Zivilsenat") may issue, without prior hearing of the party opposing the application, an order to the effect that, until a decision on the request has been made, the applicant may pursue enforcement of the award or enforce the provisional or conservatory measure of protection of the arbitral tribunal pursuant to section 1041. [2]In the case of an award, enforcement of the award may not go beyond measures of protection. [3]The party opposing the application may prevent enforcement by providing an amount corresponding to the amount that may be enforced by the applicant as security.

(4) As long as no oral hearing is ordered, applications and declarations may be put on record at the court registry.

Section 1064 Particularities regarding the enforcement of awards

(1) [1]At the time of the application for a declaration of enforceability of an arbitral award the award or a certified copy of the award shall be supplied. [2]The certification may also be made by counsel authorised to represent the party in the judicial proceedings.

(2) The order declaring the award enforceable shall be declared provisionally enforceable.

(3) Unless otherwise provided in treaties, subsections 1 and 2 shall apply to foreign awards.

Section 1065 Legal remedies

(1) [1]An appeal on a point of law is permitted for decisions mentioned under section 1062 subs. 1, nos. 2 and 4. [2]Otherwise, decisions in the proceedings specified in section 1062 subs. 1 may not be challenged.

(2) [1]An appeal on a point of law may be based on the ground that the decision is based on a violation of a treaty. [2]Sections 707, 717 apply mutatis mutandis.

Chapter 10. Arbitral tribunals not established by agreement

Section 1066 Mutatis mutandis application of the provisions of the Book 10

For arbitral tribunals, established lawfully by dispositions on testamentary or other decrees not based on an agreement, the provisions of this Book apply mutatis mutandis.

ANNEX B

New York Convention

Convention on the Recognition and Enforcement of Foreign Arbitral Awards*

Article I

1. [1]This Convention shall apply to the recognition and enforcement of arbitral awards made in the territory of a State other than the State where the recognition and enforcement of such awards are sought, and arising out of differences between persons, whether physical or legal. [2]It shall also apply to arbitral awards not considered as domestic awards in the State where their recognition and enforcement are sought.
2. The term "arbitral awards" shall include not only awards made by arbitrators appointed for each case but also those made by permanent arbitral bodies to which the parties have submitted.
3. [1]When signing, ratifying or acceding to this Convention, or notifying extension under article X hereof, any State may on the basis of reciprocity declare that it will apply the Convention to the recognition and enforcement of awards made only in the territory of another Contracting State. [2]It may also declare that it will apply the Convention only to differences arising out of legal relationships, whether contractual or not, which are considered as commercial under the national law of the State making such declaration.

Article II

1. Each Contracting State shall recognize an agreement in writing under which the parties undertake to submit to arbitration all or any differences which have arisen or which may arise between them in respect of a defined legal relationship, whether contractual or not, concerning a subject matter capable of settlement by arbitration.
2. The term "agreement in writing" shall include an arbitral clause in a contract or an arbitration agreement, signed by the parties or contained in an exchange of letters or telegrams.
3. The court of a Contracting State, when seized of an action in a matter in respect of which the parties have made an agreement within the meaning of this article, shall, at the request of one of the parties, refer the parties to arbitration, unless it finds that the said agreement is null and void, inoperative or incapable of being performed.

Article III

[1]Each Contracting State shall recognize arbitral awards as binding and enforce them in accordance with the rules of procedure of the territory where the award is relied upon, under the conditions laid down in the following articles. [2]There shall not be imposed substantially more onerous conditions or higher fees or charges on the recognition or enforcement of arbitral awards to which this Convention applies than are imposed on the recognition or enforcement of domestic arbitral awards.

---

* Done at New York on June 10, 1958 and published in United Nations Treaty Series, Vol 330 (1959), p 38. Reprinted with kind permission of UNCITRAL. Numbering of clauses added.

Article IV

1. To obtain the recognition and enforcement mentioned in the preceding article, the party applying for recognition and enforcement shall, at the time of the application, supply:
   a) The duly authenticated original award or a duly certified copy thereof;
   b) The original agreement referred to in article II or a duly certified copy thereof.
2. [1]If the said award or agreement is not made in an official language of the country in which the award is relied upon, the party applying for recognition and enforcement of the award shall produce a translation of these documents into such language. [2]The translation shall be certified by an official or sworn translator or by a diplomatic or consular agent.

Article V

1. Recognition and enforcement of the award may be refused, at the request of the party against whom it is invoked, only if that party furnishes to the competent authority where the recognition and enforcement is sought, proof that:
   a) The parties to the agreement referred to in article II were, under the law applicable to them, under some incapacity, or the said agreement is not valid under the law to which the parties have subjected it or, failing any indication thereon, under the law of the country where the award was made; or
   b) The party against whom the award is invoked was not given proper notice of the appointment of the arbitrator or of the arbitration proceedings or was otherwise unable to present his case; or
   c) The award deals with a difference not contemplated by or not falling within the terms of the submission to arbitration, or it contains decisions on matters beyond the scope of the submission to arbitration, provided that, if the decisions on matters submitted to arbitration can be separated from those not so submitted, that part of the award which contains decisions on matters submitted to arbitration may be recognized and enforced; or
   d) The composition of the arbitral authority or the arbitral procedure was not in accordance with the agreement of the parties, or, failing such agreement, was not in accordance with the law of the country where the arbitration took place; or
   e) The award has not yet become binding on the parties, or has been set aside or suspended by a competent authority of the country in which, or under the law of which, that award was made.
2. Recognition and enforcement of an arbitral award may also be refused if the competent authority in the country where recognition and enforcement is sought finds that:
   a) The subject matter of the difference is not capable of settlement by arbitration under the law of that country; or
   b) The recognition or enforcement of the award would be contrary to the public policy of that country.

Article VI

If an application for the setting aside or suspension of the award has been made to a competent authority referred to in article V (1) (e), the authority before which the award is sought to be relied upon may, if it considers it proper, adjourn the decision on the enforcement of the award and may also, on the application of the party claiming enforcement of the award, order the other party to give suitable security.

Article VII

1. The provisions of the present Convention shall not affect the validity of multilateral or bilateral agreements concerning the recognition and enforcement of arbitral awards entered into by the Contracting States nor deprive any interested party of any right he may have to avail himself of an arbitral award in the manner and to the extent allowed by the law or the treaties of the country where such award is sought to be relied upon.
2. The Geneva Protocol on Arbitration Clauses of 1923 and the Geneva Convention on the Execution of Foreign Arbitral Awards of 1927 shall cease to have effect between Contracting States on their becoming bound and to the extent that they become bound, by this Convention.

Article VIII

1. This Convention shall be open until 31 December 1958 for signature on behalf of any Member of the United Nations and also on behalf of any other State which is or hereafter becomes a member of any specialized agency of the United Nations, or which is or hereafter becomes a party to the Statute of the International Court of Justice, or any other State to which an invitation has been addressed by the General Assembly of the United Nations.
2. This Convention shall be ratified and the instrument of ratification shall be deposited with the Secretary-General of the United Nations.

Article IX

1. This Convention shall be open for accession to all States referred to in article VIII.
2. Accession shall be effected by the deposit of an instrument of accession with the Secretary-General of the United Nations.

Article X

1. [1]Any State may, at the time of signature, ratification or accession, declare that this Convention shall extend to all or any of the territories for the international relations of which it is responsible. [2]Such a declaration shall take effect when the Convention enters into force for the State concerned.
2. At any time thereafter any such extension shall be made by notification addressed to the Secretary-General of the United Nations and shall take effect as from the ninetieth day after the day of receipt by the Secretary-General of the United Nations of this notification, or as from the date of entry into force of the Convention for the State concerned, whichever is the later.
3. With respect to those territories to which this Convention is not extended at the time of signature, ratification or accession, each State concerned shall consider the possibility of taking the necessary steps in order to extend the application of this Convention to such territories, subject, where necessary for constitutional reasons, to the consent of the Governments of such territories.

Article XI

In the case of a federal or non-unitary State, the following provisions shall apply:

a) With respect to those articles of this Convention that come within the legislative jurisdiction of the federal authority, the obligations of the federal Government shall to this extent be the same as those of Contracting States which are not federal States;
b) With respect to those articles of this Convention that come within the legislative jurisdiction of constituent states or provinces which are not, under the constitutional system of the federation, bound to take legislative action, the federal Government shall bring such articles with a favourable recommendation to the notice of the appropriate authorities of constituent states or provinces at the earliest possible moment;
c) A federal State Party to this Convention shall, at the request of any other Contracting State transmitted through the Secretary-General of the United Nations, supply a statement of the law and practice of the federation and its constituent units in regard to any particular provision of this Convention, showing the extent to which effect has been given to that provision by legislative or other action.

Article XII

1. This Convention shall come into force on the ninetieth day following the date of deposit of the third instrument of ratification or accession.
2. For each State ratifying or acceeding** to this Convention after the deposit of the third instrument of ratification or accession, this Convention shall enter into force on the ninetieth day after deposit by such State of its instrument of ratification or accession.

** Should read "acceding."

Article XIII

1. [1]Any Contracting State may denounce this Convention by a written notification to the Secretary-General of the United Nations. [2]Denunciation shall take effect one year after the date of receipt of the notification by the Secretary-General.
2. Any State which has made a declaration or notification under article X may, at any time thereafter, by notification to the Secretary-General of the United Nations, declare that this Convention shall cease to extend to the territory concerned one year after the date of the receipt of the notification by the Secretary-General.
3. This Convention shall continue to be applicable to arbitral awards in respect of which recognition or enforcement proceedings have been instituted before the denunciation takes effect.

Article XIV

A Contracting State shall not be entitled to avail itself of the present Convention against other Contracting States except to the extent that it is itself bound to apply the Convention.

Article XV

The Secretary-General of the United Nations shall notify the States contemplated in article VIII of the following:

a) Signatures and ratifications in accordance with article VIII;
b) Accessions in accordance with article IX;
c) Declarations and notifications under articles I, X and XI;
d) The date upon which this Convention enters into force in accordance with article XII;
e) Denunciations and notifications in accordance with article XIII.

Article XVI

1. This Convention, of which the Chinese, English, French, Russian and Spanish texts shall be equally authentic, shall be deposited in the archives of the United Nations.
2. The Secretary-General of the United Nations shall transmit a certified copy of this Convention to the States contemplated in article VIII.

ANNEX C

UNCITRAL Recommendation

Recommendation regarding the interpretation of article II, paragraph 2, and article VII, paragraph 1, of the Convention on the Recognition and Enforcement of Foreign Arbitral Awards, done in New York, 10 June 1958, adopted by the United Nations Commission on International Trade Law on 7 July 2006 at its thirty-ninth session*

The United Nations Commission on International Trade Law,

Recalling General Assembly resolution 2205 (XXI) of 17 December 1966, which established the United Nations Commission on International Trade Law with the object of promoting the progressive harmonization and unification of the law of international trade by, inter alia, promoting ways and means of ensuring a uniform interpretation and application of international conventions and uniform laws in the field of the law of international trade,

Conscious of the fact that the different legal, social and economic systems of the world, together with different levels of development, are represented in the Commission,

Recalling successive resolutions of the General Assembly reaffirming the mandate of the Commission as the core legal body within the United Nations system in the field of international trade law to coordinate legal activities in this field,

Convinced that the wide adoption of the Convention on the Recognition and Enforcement of Foreign Arbitral Awards, done in New York on 10 June 1958,[1] has been a significant achievement in the promotion of the rule of law, particularly in the field of international trade,

Recalling that the Conference of Plenipotentiaries which prepared and opened the Convention for signature adopted a resolution, which states, inter alia, that the Conference "considers that greater uniformity of national laws on arbitration would further the effectiveness of arbitration in the settlement of private law disputes,"

Bearing in mind differing interpretations of the form requirements under the Convention that result in part from differences of expression as between the five equally authentic texts of the Convention,

Taking into account article VII, paragraph 1, of the Convention, a purpose of which is to enable the enforcement of foreign arbitral awards to the greatest extent, in particular by recognizing the right of any interested party to avail itself of law or treaties of the country where the award is sought to be relied upon, including where such law or treaties offer a regime more favourable than the Convention,

Considering the wide use of electronic commerce,

Taking into account international legal instruments, such as the 1985 UNCITRAL Model Law on International Commercial Arbitration,[2] as subsequently revised, particularly with respect

* Issued in Official Records of the General Assembly, Sixty-first Session, Supplement No. 17 (A/61/17), annex II. Reprinted with kind permission of UNCITRAL.

1 United Nations, *Treaty Series,* vol. 330, No. 4739.

2 *Official Records of the General Assembly, Fortieth Session, Supplement No. 17* (A/40/17), annex I, and United Nations publication, Sales No. E.95.V.18.

to article 7,[3] the UNCITRAL Model Law on Electronic Commerce,[4] the UNCITRAL Model Law on Electronic Signatures[5] and the United Nations Convention on the Use of Electronic Communications in International Contracts,[6]

Taking into account also enactments of domestic legislation, as well as case law, more favourable than the Convention in respect of form requirement governing arbitration agreements, arbitration proceedings and the enforcement of arbitral awards,

Considering that, in interpreting the Convention, regard is to be had to the need to promote recognition and enforcement of arbitral awards,

1. *Recommends* that article II, paragraph 2, of the Convention on the Recognition and Enforcement of Foreign Arbitral Awards, done in New York, 10 June 1958, be applied recognizing that the circumstances described therein are not exhaustive;
2. *Recommends also* that article VII, paragraph 1, of the Convention on the Recognition and Enforcement of Foreign Arbitral Awards, done in New York, 10 June 1958, should be applied to allow any interested party to avail itself of rights it may have, under the law or treaties of the country where an arbitration agreement is sought to be relied upon, to seek recognition of the validity of such an arbitration agreement.

---

[3] Ibid., *Sixty-first Session, Supplement No. 17* (A/61/17), annex I.

[4] Ibid., *Fifty-first Session, Supplement No. 17* (A/51/17), annex I, and United Nations publication, Sales No. E.99.V.4, which contains also an additional article 5 bis, adopted in 1998, and the accompanying Guide to Enactment.

[5] Ibid., *Fifty-sixth Session, Supplement No. 17* and corrigendum (A/56/17 and Corr.3), annex II, and United Nations publication, Sales No. E.02.V.8, which contains also the accompanying Guide to Enactment.

[6] General Assembly resolution 60/21, annex.

ANNEX D

European Convention

European Convention on International Commercial Arbitration*

THE UNDERSIGNED,

DULY authorized,

CONVENED under the auspices of the Economic Commission for Europe of the United Nations,

HAVING NOTED that on 10th June 1958 at the United Nations Conference on International Commercial Arbitration has been signed in New York a Convention on the Recognition and Enforcement of Foreign Arbitral Awards,

DESIROUS of promoting the development of European trade by, as far as possible, removing certain difficulties that may impede the organization and operation of international commercial arbitration in relations between physical or legal persons of different European countries,

HAVE AGREED on the following provisions:

Article I. Scope of the Convention

1. This Convention shall apply:
   (a) to arbitration agreements concluded for the purpose of settling disputes arising from international trade between physical or legal persons having, when concluding the agreement, their habitual place of residence or their seat in different Contracting States;
   (b) to arbitral procedures and awards based on agreements referred to in paragraph 1 (a) above.
2. For the purpose of this Convention,
   (a) the term "arbitration agreement" shall mean either an arbitral clause in a contract or an arbitration agreement, the contract or arbitration agreement being signed by the parties, or contained in an exchange of letters, telegrams, or in a communication by teleprinter and, in relations between States whose laws do not require that an arbitration agreement be made in writing, any arbitration agreement concluded in the form authorized by these laws;
   (b) the term "arbitration" shall mean not only settlement by arbitrators appointed for each case (*ad hoc* arbitration) but also by permanent arbitral institutions;
   (c) the term "seat" shall mean the place of the situation of the establishment that has made the arbitration agreement.

Article II. Right of legal persons of public law to resort to arbitration

1. In the cases referred to in Article I, paragraph 1, of this Convention, legal persons considered by the law which is applicable to them as "legal persons of public law" have the right to conclude valid arbitration agreements.
2. On signing, ratifying or acceding to this Convention any State shall be entitled to declare that it limits the above faculty to such conditions as may be stated in its declaration.

---

* Done at Geneva on April 21, 1961 and published in United Nations Treaty Series, Vol 484 (1965), p 349. Reprinted with kind permission of United Nations Publications. Numbering of clauses added.

Article III. Right of foreign nationals to be designated as arbitrators

In arbitration covered by this Convention, foreign nationals may be designated as arbitrators.

Article IV. Organization of the arbitration

1. The parties to an arbitration agreement shall be free to submit their disputes:
   (a) to a permanent arbitral institution; in this case, the arbitration proceedings shall be held in conformity with the rules of the said institution;
   (b) to an *ad hoc* arbitral procedure; in this case, they shall be free *inter alia*
      (i) to appoint arbitrators or to establish means for their appointment in the event of an actual dispute;
      (ii) to determine the place of arbitration; and
      (iii) to lay down the procedure to be followed by the arbitrators.
2. [1]Where the parties have agreed to submit any disputes to an *ad hoc* arbitration, and where within thirty days of the notification of the request for arbitration to the respondent one of the parties fails to appoint his arbitrator, the latter shall, unless otherwise provided, be appointed at the request of the other party by the President of the competent Chamber of Commerce of the country of the defaulting party's habitual place of residence or seat at the time of the introduction of the request for arbitration. [2]This paragraph shall also apply to the replacement of the arbitrator(s) appointed by one of the parties or by the President of the Chamber of Commerce above referred to.
3. [1]Where the parties have agreed to submit any disputes to an *ad hoc* arbitration by one or more arbitrators and the arbitration agreement contains no indication regarding the organization of the arbitration, as mentioned in paragraph 1 of this article, the necessary steps shall be taken by the arbitrator(s) already appointed, unless the parties are able to agree thereon and without prejudice to the case referred to in paragraph 2 above. [2]Where the parties cannot agree on the appointment of the sole arbitrator or where the arbitrators appointed cannot agree on the measures to be taken, the claimant shall apply for the necessary action, where the place of arbitration has been agreed upon by the parties, at his option to the President of the Chamber of Commerce of the place of arbitration agreed upon or to the President of the competent Chamber of Commerce of the respondent's habitual place of residence or seat at the time of the introduction of the request for arbitration. [3]Where such a place has not been agreed upon, the claimant shall be entitled at his option to apply for the necessary action either to the President of the competent Chamber of Commerce of the country of the respondent's habitual place of residence or seat at the time of the introduction of the request for arbitration, or to the Special Committee whose composition and procedure are specified in the Annex to this Convention. [4]Where the claimant fails to exercise the rights given to him under this paragraph the respondent or the arbitrator(s) shall be entitled to do so.
4. When seized of a request the President or the Special Committee shall be entitled as need be:
   (a) to appoint the sole arbitrator, presiding arbitrator, umpire, or referee;
   (b) to replace the arbitrator(s) appointed under any procedure other than that referred to in paragraph 2 above;
   (c) to determine the place of arbitration, provided that the arbitrator(s) may fix another place of arbitration;
   (d) to establish directly or by reference to the rules and statutes of a permanent arbitral institution the rules of procedure to be followed by the arbitrator(s), provided that the arbitrators have not established these rules themselves in the absence of any agreement thereon between the parties.
5. Where the parties have agreed to submit their disputes to a permanent arbitral institution without determining the institution in question and cannot agree thereon, the claimant may request the determination of such institution in conformity with the procedure referred to in paragraph 3 above.
6. [1]Where the arbitration agreement does not specify the mode of arbitration (arbitration by a permanent arbitral institution or an *ad hoc* arbitration) to which the parties have agreed to submit their dispute, and where the parties cannot agree thereon, the claimant shall be entitled

to have recourse in this case to the procedure referred to in paragraph 3 above to determine the question. [2]The President of the competent Chamber of Commerce or the Special Committee, shall be entitled either to refer the parties to a permanent arbitral institution or to request the parties to appoint their arbitrators within such time-limits as the President of the competent Chamber of Commerce or the Special Committee may have fixed and to agree within such time-limits on the necessary measures for the functioning of the arbitration. [3]In the latter case, the provisions of paragraphs 2, 3 and 4 of this Article shall apply.

7. Where within a period of sixty days from the moment when he was requested to fulfil one of the functions set out in paragraphs 2, 3, 4, 5 and 6 of this Article, the President of the Chamber of Commerce designated by virtue of these paragraphs has not fulfilled one of these functions, the party requesting shall be entitled to ask the Special Committee to do so.

Article V. Plea as to arbitral jurisdiction

1. [1]The party which intends to raise a plea as to the arbitrator's jurisdiction based on the fact that the arbitration agreement was either non-existent or null and void or had lapsed shall do so during the arbitration proceedings, not later than the delivery of its statement of claim or defence relating to the substance of the dispute; those based on the fact that an arbitrator has exceeded his terms of reference shall be raised during the arbitration proceedings as soon as the question on which the arbitrator is alleged to have no jurisdiction is raised during the arbitral procedure. [2]Where the delay in raising the plea is due to a cause which the arbitrator deems justified, the arbitrator shall declare the plea admissible.
2. [1]Pleas to the jurisdiction referred to in paragraph 1 above that have not been raised during the time-limits there referred to, may not be entered either during a subsequent stage of the arbitral proceedings where they are pleas left to the sole discretion of the parties under the law applicable by the arbitrator, or during subsequent court proceedings concerning the substance or the enforcement of the award where such pleas are left to the discretion of the parties under the rule of conflict of the court seized of the substance of the dispute or the enforcement of the award. [2]The arbitrator's decision on the delay in raising the plea, will, however, be subject to judicial control.
3. Subject to any subsequent judicial control provided for under the *lex fori*, the arbitrator whose jurisdiction is called in question shall be entitled to proceed with the arbitration, to rule on his own jurisdiction and to decide upon the existence or the validity of the arbitration agreement or of the contract of which the agreement forms part.

Article VI. Jurisdiction of courts of law

1. A plea as to the jurisdiction of the court made before the court seized by either party to the arbitration agreement, on the basis of the fact that an arbitration agreement exists shall, under penalty of estoppel, be presented by the respondent before or at the same time as the presentation of his substantial defence, depending upon whether the law of the court seized regards this plea as one of procedure or of substance.
2. [1]In taking a decision concerning the existence or the validity of an arbitration agreement, courts of Contracting States shall examine the validity of such agreement with reference to the capacity of the parties, under the law applicable to them, and with reference to other questions
   (a) under the law to which the parties have subjected their arbitration agreement;
   (b) failing any indication thereon, under the law of the country in which the award is to be made;
   (c) failing any indication as to the law to which the parties have subjected the agreement, and where at the time when the question is raised in court the country in which the award is to be made cannot be determined, under the competent law by virtue of the rules of conflict of the court seized of the dispute.

   [2]The courts may also refuse recognition of the arbitration agreement if under the law of their country the dispute is not capable of settlement by arbitration.
3. Where either party to an arbitration agreement has initiated arbitration proceedings before any resort is had to a court, courts of Contracting States subsequently asked to deal with

the same subject-matter between the same parties or with the question whether the arbitration agreement was non-existent or null and void or had lapsed, shall stay their ruling on the arbitrator's jurisdiction until the arbitral award is made, unless they have good and substantial reasons to the contrary.

4. A request for interim measures or measures of conservation addressed to a judicial authority shall not be deemed incompatible with the arbitration agreement, or regarded as a submission of the substance of the case to the court.

Article VII. Applicable law

1. [1]The parties shall be free to determine, by agreement, the law to be applied by the arbitrators to the substance of the dispute. [2]Failing any indication by the parties as to the applicable law, the arbitrators shall apply the proper law under the rule of conflict that the arbitrators deem applicable. [3]In both cases the arbitrators shall take account of the terms of the contract and trade usages.
2. The arbitrators shall act as *amiables compositeurs* if the parties so decide and if they may do so under the law applicable to the arbitration.

Article VIII. Reasons for the award

The parties shall be presumed to have agreed that reasons shall be given for the award unless they
(a) either expressly declare that reasons shall not be given; or
(b) have assented to an arbitral procedure under which it is not customary to give reasons for awards, provided that in this case neither party requests before the end of the hearing, or if there has not been a hearing then before the making of the award, that reasons be given.

Article IX. Setting aside of the arbitral award

1. The setting aside in a Contracting State of an arbitral award covered by this Convention shall only constitute a ground for the refusal of recognition or enforcement in another Contracting State where such setting aside took place in a State in which, or under the law of which, the award has been made and for one of the following reasons:
   (a) the parties to the arbitration agreement were under the law applicable to them, under some incapacity or the said agreement is not valid under the law to which the parties have subjected it or, failing any indication thereon, under the law of the country where the award was made, or
   (b) the party requesting the setting aside of the award was not given proper notice of the appointment of the arbitrator or of the arbitration proceedings or was otherwise unable to present his case; or
   (c) the award deals with a difference not contemplated by or not falling within the terms of the submission to arbitration, or it contains decisions on matters beyond the scope of the submission to arbitration, provided that, if the decisions on matters submitted to arbitration can be separated from those not so submitted, that part of the award which contains decisions on matters submitted to arbitration need not be set aside;
   (d) the composition of the arbitral authority or the arbitral procedure was not in accordance with the agreement of the parties, or failing such agreement, with the provisions of Article IV of this Convention.
2. In relations between Contracting States that are also parties to the New York Convention on the Recognition and Enforcement of Foreign Arbitral Awards of 10th June 1958, paragraph 1 of this Article limits the application of Article V (1) (e) of the New York Convention solely to the cases of setting aside set out under paragraph 1 above.

Article X. Final clauses

1. This Convention is open for signature or accession by countries members of the Economic Commission for Europe and countries admitted to the Commission in a consultative capacity under paragraph 8 of the Commission's terms of reference.

2. Such countries as may participate in certain activities of the Economic Commission for Europe in accordance with paragraph 11 of the Commission's terms of reference may become Contracting Parties to this Convention by acceding thereto after its entry into force.
3. [1]The Convention shall be open for signature until 31 December 1961 inclusive. [2]Thereafter, it shall be open for accession.
4. This Convention shall be ratified.
5. Ratification or accession shall be effected by the deposit of an instrument with the Secretary-General of the United Nations.
6. When signing, ratifying or acceding to this Convention, the Contracting Parties shall communicate to the Secretary-General of the United Nations a list of the Chambers of Commerce or other institutions in their country who will exercise the functions conferred by virtue of Article IV of this Convention on Presidents of the competent Chambers of Commerce.
7. The provisions of the present Convention shall not affect the validity of multilateral or bilateral agreements concerning arbitration entered into by Contracting States.
8. [1]This Convention shall come into force on the ninetieth day after five of the countries referred to in paragraph 1 above have deposited their instruments of ratification or accession. [2]For any country ratifying or acceding to it later this Convention shall enter into force on the ninetieth day after the said country has deposited its instrument of ratification or accession.
9. [1]Any Contracting Party may denounce this Convention by so notifying the Secretary-General of the United Nations. [2]Denunciation shall take effect twelve months after the date of receipt by the Secretary-General of the notification of denunciation.
10. If, after the entry into force of this Convention, the number of Contracting Parties is reduced, as a result of denunciations, to less than five, the Convention shall cease to be in force from the date on which the last of such denunciations takes effect.
11. The Secretary-General of the United Nations shall notify the countries referred to in paragraph 1, and the countries which have become Contracting Parties under paragraph 2 above, of
    (a) declarations made under Article II, paragraph 2;
    (b) ratifications and accessions under paragraphs 1 and 2 above;
    (c) communications received in pursuance of paragraph 6 above;
    (d) the dates of entry into force of this Convention in accordance with paragraph 8 above;
    (e) denunciations under paragraph 9 above;
    (f) the termination of this Convention in accordance with paragraph 10 above.
12. After 31 December 1961, the original of this Convention shall be deposited with the Secretary-General of the United Nations, who shall transmit certified true copies to each of the countries mentioned in paragraphs 1 and 2 above.

IN WITNESS WHEREOF the undersigned, being duly authorized thereto, have signed this Convention.

DONE at Geneva, this twenty-first day of April, one thousand nine hundred and sixty-one, in a single copy in the English, French and Russian languages, each text being equally authentic.

ANNEX E

UNCITRAL Notes on Organizing Arbitral Proceedings[†]

Introduction

Purpose of the Notes

1. The purpose of the Notes is to assist arbitration practitioners by listing and briefly describing questions on which appropriately timed decisions on organizing arbitral proceedings may be useful. The text, prepared with a particular view to international arbitrations, may be used whether or not the arbitration is administered by an arbitral institution.

Non-binding character of the Notes

2. No legal requirement binding on the arbitrators or the parties is imposed by the Notes. The arbitral tribunal remains free to use the Notes as it sees fit and is not required to give reasons for disregarding them.
3. The Notes are not suitable to be used as arbitration rules, since they do not establish any obligation of the arbitral tribunal or the parties to act in a particular way. Accordingly, the use of the Notes cannot imply any modification of the arbitration rules that the parties may have agreed upon.

Discretion in conduct of proceedings and usefulness of timely decisions on organizing proceedings

4. Laws governing the arbitral procedure and arbitration rules that parties may agree upon typically allow the arbitral tribunal broad discretion and flexibility in the conduct of arbitral proceedings.[*] This is useful in that it enables the arbitral tribunal to take decisions on the organization of proceedings that take into account the circumstances of the case, the expectations of the parties and of the members of the arbitral tribunal, and the need for a just and cost-efficient resolution of the dispute.
5. Such discretion may make it desirable for the arbitral tribunal to give the parties a timely indication as to the organization of the proceedings and the manner in which the tribunal intends to proceed. This is particularly desirable in international arbitrations, where the participants may be accustomed to differing styles of conducting arbitrations. Without such guidance, a party may find aspects of the proceedings unpredictable and difficult to prepare for. That may lead to misunderstandings, delays and increased costs.

Multi-party arbitration

6. These Notes are intended for use not only in arbitrations with two parties but also in arbitrations with three or more parties. Use of the Notes in multi-party arbitration is referred to below in paragraphs 86–88 (item 18).

[†] Approved by the United Nations Commission on International Trade Law on May 28, 1996 and published in UNCITRAL Yearbook XXVII (1996), 241 *et seq.* Reprinted with kind permission of United Nations Publications.

[*] A prominent example of such rules are the UNCITRAL Arbitration Rules, which provide in article 15(1): "Subject to these Rules, the arbitral tribunal may conduct the arbitration in such manner as it considers appropriate, provided that the parties are treated with equality and that at any stage of the proceedings each party is given a full opportunity of presenting his case."

Process of making decisions on organizing arbitral proceedings

7. Decisions by the arbitral tribunal on organizing arbitral proceedings may be taken with or without previous consultations with the parties. The method chosen depends on whether, in view of the type of the question to be decided, the arbitral tribunal considers that consultations are not necessary or that hearing the views of the parties would be beneficial for increasing the predictability of the proceedings or improving the procedural atmosphere.
8. The consultations, whether they involve only the arbitrators or also the parties, can be held in one or more meetings, or can be carried out by correspondence or telecommunications such as telefax or conference telephone calls or other electronic means. Meetings may be held at the venue of arbitration or at some other appropriate location.
9. In some arbitrations a special meeting may be devoted exclusively to such procedural consultations; alternatively, the consultations may be held in conjunction with a hearing on the substance of the dispute. Practices differ as to whether such special meetings should be held and how they should be organized. Special procedural meetings of the arbitrators and the parties separate from hearings are in practice referred to by expressions such as "preliminary meeting," "pre-hearing conference," "preparatory conference," "pre-hearing review," or terms of similar meaning. The terms used partly depend on the stage of the proceedings at which the meeting is taking place.

List of matters for possible consideration in organizing arbitral proceedings

10. The Notes provide a list, followed by annotations, of matters on which the arbitral tribunal may wish to formulate decisions on organizing arbitral proceedings.
11. Given that procedural styles and practices in arbitration vary widely, that the purpose of the Notes is not to promote any practice as best practice, and that the Notes are designed for universal use, it is not attempted in the Notes to describe in detail different arbitral practices or express a preference for any of them.
12. The list, while not exhaustive, covers a broad range of situations that may arise in an arbitration. In many arbitrations, however, only a limited number of the matters mentioned in the list need to be considered. It also depends on the circumstances of the case at which stage or stages of the proceedings it would be useful to consider matters concerning the organization of the proceedings. Generally, in order not to create opportunities for unnecessary discussions and delay, it is advisable not to raise a matter prematurely, i.e. before it is clear that a decision is needed.
13. When the Notes are used, it should be borne in mind that the discretion of the arbitral tribunal in organizing the proceedings may be limited by arbitration rules, by other provisions agreed to by the parties and by the law applicable to the arbitral procedure. When an arbitration is administered by an arbitral institution, various matters discussed in the Notes may be covered by the rules and practices of that institution.

List of matters for possible consideration in organizing arbitral proceedings

ANNOTATIONS

1. Set of arbitration rules

If the parties have not agreed on a set of arbitration rules, would they wish to do so

14. Sometimes parties who have not included in their arbitration agreement a stipulation that a set of arbitration rules will govern their arbitral proceedings might wish to do so after the arbitration has begun. If that occurs, the UNCITRAL Arbitration Rules may be used either without modification or with such modifications as the parties might wish to agree upon. In the alternative, the parties might wish to adopt the rules of an arbitral institution; in that case, it may be necessary to secure the agreement of that institution and to stipulate the terms under which the arbitration could be carried out in accordance with the rules of that institution.
15. However, caution is advised as consideration of a set of arbitration rules might delay the proceedings or give rise to unnecessary controversy.
16. It should be noted that agreement on arbitration rules is not a necessity and that, if the parties do not agree on a set of arbitration rules, the arbitral tribunal has the power to continue the proceedings and determine how the case will be conducted.

2. Language of proceedings

17. Many rules and laws on arbitral procedure empower the arbitral tribunal to determine the language or languages to be used in the proceedings, if the parties have not reached an agreement thereon.

(a) Possible need for translation of documents, in full or in part

18. Some documents annexed to the statements of claim and defence or submitted later may not be in the language of the proceedings. Bearing in mind the needs of the proceedings and economy, it may be considered whether the arbitral tribunal should order that any of those documents or parts thereof should be accompanied by a translation into the language of the proceedings.

(b) Possible need for interpretation of oral presentations

19. If interpretation will be necessary during oral hearings, it is advisable to consider whether the interpretation will be simultaneous or consecutive and whether the arrangements should be the responsibility of a party or the arbitral tribunal. In an arbitration administered by an institution, interpretation as well as translation services are often arranged by the arbitral institution.

(c) Cost of translation and interpretation

20. In taking decisions about translation or interpretation, it is advisable to decide whether any or all of the costs are to be paid directly by a party or whether they will be paid out of the deposits and apportioned between the parties along with the other arbitration costs.

3. Place of arbitration

(a) Determination of the place of arbitration, if not already agreed upon by the parties

21. Arbitration rules usually allow the parties to agree on the place of arbitration, subject to the requirement of some arbitral institutions that arbitrations under their rules be conducted at a particular place, usually the location of the institution. If the place has not been so agreed upon, the rules governing the arbitration typically provide that it is in the power of the arbitral tribunal or the institution administering the arbitration to determine the place. If the arbitral tribunal is to make that determination, it may wish to hear the views of the parties before doing so.

22. Various factual and legal factors influence the choice of the place of arbitration, and their relative importance varies from case to case. Among the more prominent factors are: *(a)* suitability of the law on arbitral procedure of the place of arbitration; *(b)* whether there is a multilateral or bilateral treaty on enforcement of arbitral awards between the State where the arbitration takes place and the State or States where the award may have to be enforced; *(c)* convenience of the parties and the arbitrators, including the travel distances; *(d)* availability and cost of support services needed; and *(e)* location of the subject-matter in dispute and proximity of evidence.

(b) Possibility of meetings outside the place of arbitration

23. Many sets of arbitration rules and laws on arbitral procedure expressly allow the arbitral tribunal to hold meetings elsewhere than at the place of arbitration. For example, under the UNCITRAL Model Law on International Commercial Arbitration "the arbitral tribunal may, unless otherwise agreed by the parties, meet at any place it considers appropriate for consultation among its members, for hearing witnesses, experts or the parties, or for inspection of goods, other property or documents" (article 20(2)). The purpose of this discretion is to permit arbitral proceedings to be carried out in a manner that is most efficient and economical.

4. Administrative services that may be needed for the arbitral tribunal to carry out its functions

24. Various administrative services (e.g. hearing rooms or secretarial services) may need to be procured for the arbitral tribunal to be able to carry out its functions. When the arbitration is administered by an arbitral institution, the institution will usually provide all or a good part of the required administrative support to the arbitral tribunal. When an arbitration administered by an arbitral institution takes place away from the seat of the institution, the institution may be able to arrange for administrative services to be obtained from another source, often an arbitral institution; some arbitral institutions have entered into cooperation agreements with a view to providing mutual assistance in servicing arbitral proceedings.

25. When the case is not administered by an institution, or the involvement of the institution does not include providing administrative support, usually the administrative arrangements for the proceedings will be made by the arbitral tribunal or the presiding arbitrator; it may also be acceptable to leave some of the arrangements to the parties, or to one of the parties subject to agreement of the other party or parties. Even in such cases, a convenient source of administrative support might be found in arbitral institutions, which often offer their facilities to arbitrations not governed by the rules of the institution. Otherwise, some services could be procured from entities such as chambers of commerce, hotels or specialized firms providing secretarial or other support services.

26. Administrative services might be secured by engaging a secretary of the arbitral tribunal (also referred to as registrar, clerk, administrator or rapporteur), who carries out the tasks under the direction of the arbitral tribunal. Some arbitral institutions routinely assign such persons to the cases administered by them. In arbitrations not administered by an institution or where the arbitral institution does not appoint a secretary, some arbitrators frequently engage such persons, at least in certain types of cases, whereas many others normally conduct the proceedings without them.

27. To the extent the tasks of the secretary are purely organizational (e.g. obtaining meeting rooms and providing or coordinating secretarial services), this is usually not controversial. Differences in views, however, may arise if the tasks include legal research and other professional assistance to the arbitral tribunal (e.g. collecting case law or published commentaries on legal issues defined by the arbitral tribunal, preparing summaries from case law and publications, and sometimes also preparing drafts of procedural decisions or drafts of certain parts of the award, in particular those concerning the facts of the case). Views or expectations may differ especially where a task of the secretary is similar to professional functions of the arbitrators. Such a role of the secretary is in the view of some commentators inappropriate or is appropriate only under certain conditions, such as that the parties agree thereto. However, it is typically recognized that it is important to ensure that the secretary does not perform any decision-making function of the arbitral tribunal.

5. Deposits in respect of costs

(a) Amount to be deposited

28. In an arbitration administered by an institution, the institution often sets, on the basis of an estimate of the costs of the proceedings, the amount to be deposited as an advance for the costs of the arbitration. In other cases it is customary for the arbitral tribunal to make such an estimate and request a deposit. The estimate typically includes travel and other expenses by the arbitrators, expenditures for administrative assistance required by the arbitral tribunal, costs of any expert advice required by the arbitral tribunal, and the fees for the arbitrators. Many arbitration rules have provisions on this matter, including on whether the deposit should be made by the two parties (or all parties in a multi-party case) or only by the claimant.

(b) Management of deposits

29. When the arbitration is administered by an institution, the institution's services may include managing and accounting for the deposited money. Where that is not the case, it might be useful to clarify matters such as the type and location of the account in which the money will be kept and how the deposits will be managed.

(c) Supplementary deposits

30. If during the course of proceedings it emerges that the costs will be higher than anticipated, supplementary deposits may be required (e.g. because the arbitral tribunal decides pursuant to the arbitration rules to appoint an expert).

6. Confidentiality of information relating to the arbitration; possible agreement thereon

31. It is widely viewed that confidentiality is one of the advantageous and helpful features of arbitration. Nevertheless, there is no uniform answer in national laws as to the extent to which the participants in an arbitration are under the duty to observe the confidentiality of information relating to the case. Moreover, parties that have agreed on arbitration rules or other provisions that do not expressly address the issue of confidentiality cannot assume that all jurisdictions would recognize an implied commitment to confidentiality. Furthermore, the participants in an arbitration might not have the same understanding as regards the extent of confidentiality that is expected. Therefore, the arbitral tribunal might wish to discuss that with the parties and, if considered appropriate, record any agreed principles on the duty of confidentiality.
32. An agreement on confidentiality might cover, for example, one or more of the following matters: the material or information that is to be kept confidential (e.g. pieces of evidence, written and oral arguments, the fact that the arbitration is taking place, identity of the arbitrators, content of the award); measures for maintaining confidentiality of such information and hearings; whether any special procedures should be employed for maintaining the confidentiality of information transmitted by electronic means (e.g. because communication equipment is shared by several users, or because electronic mail over public networks is considered not sufficiently protected against unauthorized access); circumstances in which confidential

information may be disclosed in part or in whole (e.g. in the context of disclosures of information in the public domain, or if required by law or a regulatory body).

7. Routing of written communications among the parties and the arbitrators

33. To the extent the question how documents and other written communications should be routed among the parties and the arbitrators is not settled by the agreed rules, or, if an institution administers the case, by the practices of the institution, it is useful for the arbitral tribunal to clarify the question suitably early so as to avoid misunderstandings and delays.

34. Among various possible patterns of routing, one example is that a party transmits the appropriate number of copies to the arbitral tribunal, or to the arbitral institution, if one is involved, which then forwards them as appropriate. Another example is that a party is to send copies simultaneously to the arbitrators and the other party or parties. Documents and other written communications directed by the arbitral tribunal or the presiding arbitrator to one or more parties may also follow a determined pattern, such as through the arbitral institution or by direct transmission. For some communications, in particular those on organizational matters (e.g. dates for hearings), more direct routes of communication may be agreed, even if, for example, the arbitral institution acts as an intermediary for documents such as the statements of claim and defence, evidence or written arguments.

8. Telefax and other electronic means of sending documents

(a) Telefax

35. Telefax, which offers many advantages over traditional means of communication, is widely used in arbitral proceedings. Nevertheless, should it be thought that, because of the characteristics of the equipment used, it would be preferable not to rely only on a telefacsimile of a document, special arrangements may be considered, such as that a particular piece of written evidence should be mailed or otherwise physically delivered, or that certain telefax messages should be confirmed by mailing or otherwise delivering documents whose facsimile were transmitted by electronic means. When a document should not be sent by telefax, it may, however, be appropriate, in order to avoid an unnecessarily rigid procedure, for the arbitral tribunal to retain discretion to accept an advance copy of a document by telefax for the purposes of meeting a deadline, provided that the document itself is received within a reasonable time thereafter.

(b) Other electronic means (e.g. electronic mail and magnetic or optical disk)

36. It might be agreed that documents, or some of them, will be exchanged not only in paper-based form, but in addition also in an electronic form other than telefax (e.g. as electronic mail, or on a magnetic or optical disk), or only in electronic form. Since the use of electronic means depends on the aptitude of the persons involved and the availability of equipment and computer programs, agreement is necessary for such means to be used. If both paper-based and electronic means are to be used, it is advisable to decide which one is controlling and, if there is a time-limit for submitting a document, which act constitutes submission.

37. When the exchange of documents in electronic form is planned, it is useful, in order to avoid technical difficulties, to agree on matters such as: data carriers (e.g. electronic mail or computer disks) and their technical characteristics; computer programs to be used in preparing the electronic records; instructions for transforming the electronic records into human-readable form; keeping of logs and back-up records of communications sent and received; information in human-readable form that should accompany the disks (e.g. the names of the originator and recipient, computer program, titles of the electronic files and the back-up methods used); procedures when a message is lost or the communication system otherwise fails; and identification of persons who can be contacted if a problem occurs.

9. Arrangements for the exchange of written submissions

38. After the parties have initially stated their claims and defences, they may wish, or the arbitral tribunal might request them, to present further written submissions so as to prepare for the hearings or to provide the basis for a decision without hearings. In such submissions, the parties, for example, present or comment on allegations and evidence, cite or explain law, or make or react

to proposals. In practice such submissions are referred to variously as, for example, statement, memorial, counter-memorial, brief, counter-brief, reply, réplique, duplique, rebuttal or rejoinder; the terminology is a matter of linguistic usage and the scope or sequence of the submission.

(a) Scheduling of written submissions

39. It is advisable that the arbitral tribunal set time-limits for written submissions. In enforcing the time-limits, the arbitral tribunal may wish, on the one hand, to make sure that the case is not unduly protracted and, on the other hand, to reserve a degree of discretion and allow late submissions if appropriate under the circumstances. In some cases the arbitral tribunal might prefer not to plan the written submissions in advance, thus leaving such matters, including time-limits, to be decided in light of the developments in the proceedings. In other cases, the arbitral tribunal may wish to determine, when scheduling the first written submissions, the number of subsequent submissions.

40. Practices differ as to whether, after the hearings have been held, written submissions are still acceptable. While some arbitral tribunals consider post-hearing submissions unacceptable, others might request or allow them on a particular issue. Some arbitral tribunals follow the procedure according to which the parties are not requested to present written evidence and legal arguments to the arbitral tribunal before the hearings; in such a case, the arbitral tribunal may regard it as appropriate that written submissions be made after the hearings.

(b) Consecutive or simultaneous submissions

41. Written submissions on an issue may be made consecutively, i.e. the party who receives a submission is given a period of time to react with its counter-submission. Another possibility is to request each party to make the submission within the same time period to the arbitral tribunal or the institution administering the case; the received submissions are then forwarded simultaneously to the respective other party or parties. The approach used may depend on the type of issues to be commented upon and the time in which the views should be clarified. With consecutive submissions, it may take longer than with simultaneous ones to obtain views of the parties on a given issue. Consecutive submissions, however, allow the reacting party to comment on all points raised by the other party or parties, which simultaneous submissions do not; thus, simultaneous submissions might possibly necessitate further submissions.

10. Practical details concerning written submissions and evidence (e.g. method of submission, copies, numbering, references)

42. Depending on the volume and kind of documents to be handled, it might be considered whether practical arrangements on details such as the following would be helpful:
    - Whether the submissions will be made as paper documents or by electronic means, or both (see paragraphs 35–37);
    - The number of copies in which each document is to be submitted;
    - A system for numbering documents and items of evidence, and a method for marking them, including by tabs;
    - The form of references to documents (e.g. by the heading and the number assigned to the document or its date);
    - Paragraph numbering in written submissions, in order to facilitate precise references to parts of a text;
    - When translations are to be submitted as paper documents, whether the translations are to be contained in the same volume as the original texts or included in separate volumes.

11. Defining points at issue; order of deciding issues; defining relief or remedy sought

(a) Should a list of points at issue be prepared

43. In considering the parties' allegations and arguments, the arbitral tribunal may come to the conclusion that it would be useful for it or for the parties to prepare, for analytical purposes and for ease of discussion, a list of the points at issue, as opposed to those that are undisputed.

If the arbitral tribunal determines that the advantages of working on the basis of such a list outweigh the disadvantages, it chooses the appropriate stage of the proceedings for preparing a list, bearing in mind also that subsequent developments in the proceedings may require a revision of the points at issue. Such an identification of points at issue might help to concentrate on the essential matters, to reduce the number of points at issue by agreement of the parties, and to select the best and most economical process for resolving the dispute. However, possible disadvantages of preparing such a list include delay, adverse effect on the flexibility of the proceedings, or unnecessary disagreements about whether the arbitral tribunal has decided all issues submitted to it or whether the award contains decisions on matters beyond the scope of the submission to arbitration. The terms of reference required under some arbitration rules, or in agreements of parties, may serve the same purpose as the above-described list of points at issue.

(b) In which order should the points at issue be decided

44. While it is often appropriate to deal with all the points at issue collectively, the arbitral tribunal might decide to take them up during the proceedings in a particular order. The order may be due to a point being preliminary relative to another (e.g. a decision on the jurisdiction of the arbitral tribunal is preliminary to consideration of substantive issues, or the issue of responsibility for a breach of contract is preliminary to the issue of the resulting damages). A particular order may be decided also when the breach of various contracts is in dispute or when damages arising from various events are claimed.

45. If the arbitral tribunal has adopted a particular order of deciding points at issue, it might consider it appropriate to issue a decision on one of the points earlier than on the other ones. This might be done, for example, when a discrete part of a claim is ready for decision while the other parts still require extensive consideration, or when it is expected that after deciding certain issues the parties might be more inclined to settle the remaining ones. Such earlier decisions are referred to by expressions such as "partial," "interlocutory" or "interim" awards or decisions, depending on the type of issue dealt with and on whether the decision is final with respect to the issue it resolves. Questions that might be the subject of such decisions are, for example, jurisdiction of the arbitral tribunal, interim measures of protection, or the liability of a party.

(c) Is there a need to define more precisely the relief or remedy sought

46. If the arbitral tribunal considers that the relief or remedy sought is insufficiently definite, it may wish to explain to the parties the degree of definiteness with which their claims should be formulated. Such an explanation may be useful since criteria are not uniform as to how specific the claimant must be in formulating a relief or remedy.

12. Possible settlement negotiations and their effect on scheduling proceedings

47. Attitudes differ as to whether it is appropriate for the arbitral tribunal to bring up the possibility of settlement. Given the divergence of practices in this regard, the arbitral tribunal should only suggest settlement negotiations with caution. However, it may be opportune for the arbitral tribunal to schedule the proceedings in a way that might facilitate the continuation or initiation of settlement negotiations.

13. Documentary evidence

(a) Time-limits for submission of documentary evidence intended to be submitted by the parties; consequences of late submission

48. Often the written submissions of the parties contain sufficient information for the arbitral tribunal to fix the time-limit for submitting evidence. Otherwise, in order to set realistic time periods, the arbitral tribunal may wish to consult with the parties about the time that they would reasonably need.

49. The arbitral tribunal may wish to clarify that evidence submitted late will as a rule not be accepted. It may wish not to preclude itself from accepting a late submission of evidence if the party shows sufficient cause for the delay.

(b) Whether the arbitral tribunal intends to require a party to produce documentary evidence

50. Procedures and practices differ widely as to the conditions under which the arbitral tribunal may require a party to produce documents. Therefore, the arbitral tribunal might consider it useful, when the agreed arbitration rules do not provide specific conditions, to clarify to the parties the manner in which it intends to proceed.

51. The arbitral tribunal may wish to establish time-limits for the production of documents. The parties might be reminded that, if the requested party duly invited to produce documentary evidence fails to do so within the established period of time, without showing sufficient cause for such failure, the arbitral tribunal is free to draw its conclusions from the failure and may make the award on the evidence before it.

(c) Should assertions about the origin and receipt of documents and about the correctness of photocopies be assumed as accurate

52. It may be helpful for the arbitral tribunal to inform the parties that it intends to conduct the proceedings on the basis that, unless a party raises an objection to any of the following conclusions within a specified period of time: *(a)* a document is accepted as having originated from the source indicated in the document; *(b)* a copy of a dispatched communication (e.g. letter, telex, telefax or other electronic message) is accepted without further proof as having been received by the addressee; and *(c)* a copy is accepted as correct. A statement by the arbitral tribunal to that effect can simplify the introduction of documentary evidence and discourage unfounded and dilatory objections, at a late stage of the proceedings, to the probative value of documents. It is advisable to provide that the time-limit for objections will not be enforced if the arbitral tribunal considers the delay justified.

(d) Are the parties willing to submit jointly a single set of documentary evidence

53. The parties may consider submitting jointly a single set of documentary evidence whose authenticity is not disputed. The purpose would be to avoid duplicate submissions and unnecessary discussions concerning the authenticity of documents, without prejudicing the position of the parties concerning the content of the documents. Additional documents may be inserted later if the parties agree. When a single set of documents would be too voluminous to be easily manageable, it might be practical to select a number of frequently used documents and establish a set of "working" documents. A convenient arrangement of documents in the set may be according to chronological order or subject-matter. It is useful to keep a table of contents of the documents, for example, by their short headings and dates, and to provide that the parties will refer to documents by those headings and dates.

(e) Should voluminous and complicated documentary evidence be presented through summaries, tabulations, charts, extracts or samples

54. When documentary evidence is voluminous and complicated, it may save time and costs if such evidence is presented by a report of a person competent in the relevant field (e.g. public accountant or consulting engineer). The report may present the information in the form of summaries, tabulations, charts, extracts or samples. Such presentation of evidence should be combined with arrangements that give the interested party the opportunity to review the underlying data and the methodology of preparing the report.

14. Physical evidence other than documents

55. In some arbitrations the arbitral tribunal is called upon to assess physical evidence other than documents, for example, by inspecting samples of goods, viewing a video recording or observing the functioning of a machine.

(a) What arrangements should be made if physical evidence will be submitted

56. If physical evidence will be submitted, the arbitral tribunal may wish to fix the time schedule for presenting the evidence, make arrangements for the other party or parties to have a

suitable opportunity to prepare itself for the presentation of the evidence, and possibly take measures for safekeeping the items of evidence.

(b) What arrangements should be made if an on-site inspection is necessary

57. If an on-site inspection of property or goods will take place, the arbitral tribunal may consider matters such as timing, meeting places, other arrangements to provide the opportunity for all parties to be present, and the need to avoid communications between arbitrators and a party about points at issue without the presence of the other party or parties.

58. The site to be inspected is often under the control of one of the parties, which typically means that employees or representatives of that party will be present to give guidance and explanations. It should be borne in mind that statements of those representatives or employees made during an on-site inspection, as contrasted with statements those persons might make as witnesses in a hearing, should not be treated as evidence in the proceedings.

15. Witnesses

59. While laws and rules on arbitral procedure typically leave broad freedom concerning the manner of taking evidence of witnesses, practices on procedural points are varied. In order to facilitate the preparations of the parties for the hearings, the arbitral tribunal may consider it appropriate to clarify, in advance of the hearings, some or all of the following issues.

(a) Advance notice about a witness whom a party intends to present; written witnesses' statements

60. To the extent the applicable arbitration rules do not deal with the matter, the arbitral tribunal may wish to require that each party give advance notice to the arbitral tribunal and the other party or parties of any witness it intends to present. As to the content of the notice, the following is an example of what might be required, in addition to the names and addresses of the witnesses: *(a)* the subject upon which the witnesses will testify; *(b)* the language in which the witnesses will testify; and *(c)* the nature of the relationship with any of the parties, qualifications and experience of the witnesses if and to the extent these are relevant to the dispute or the testimony, and how the witnesses learned about the facts on which they will testify. However, it may not be necessary to require such a notice, in particular if the thrust of the testimony can be clearly ascertained from the party's allegations.

61. Some practitioners favour the procedure according to which the party presenting witness evidence submits a signed witness's statement containing testimony itself. It should be noted, however, that such practice, which implies interviewing the witness by the party presenting the testimony, is not known in all parts of the world and, moreover, that some practitioners disapprove of it on the ground that such contacts between the party and the witness may compromise the credibility of the testimony and are therefore improper (see paragraph 67). Notwithstanding these reservations, signed witness's testimony has advantages in that it may expedite the proceedings by making it easier for the other party or parties to prepare for the hearings or for the parties to identify uncontested matters. However, those advantages might be outweighed by the time and expense involved in obtaining the written testimony.

62. If a signed witness's statement should be made under oath or similar affirmation of truthfulness, it may be necessary to clarify by whom the oath or affirmation should be administered and whether any formal authentication will be required by the arbitral tribunal.

(b) Manner of taking oral evidence of witnesses

(i) Order in which questions will be asked and the manner in which the hearing of witnesses will be conducted

63. To the extent that the applicable rules do not provide an answer, it may be useful for the arbitral tribunal to clarify how witnesses will be heard. One of the various possibilities is that a witness is first questioned by the arbitral tribunal, whereupon questions are asked by the parties, first by the party who called the witness. Another possibility is for the witness to be questioned by the party presenting the witness and then by the other party or parties, while the arbitral tribunal might pose questions during the questioning or after the parties on points that in the tribunal's view have not been sufficiently clarified. Differences exist also as

to the degree of control the arbitral tribunal exercises over the hearing of witnesses. For example, some arbitrators prefer to permit the parties to pose questions freely and directly to the witness, but may disallow a question if a party objects; other arbitrators tend to exercise more control and may disallow a question on their initiative or even require that questions from the parties be asked through the arbitral tribunal.

(ii) Whether oral testimony will be given under oath or affirmation and, if so, in what form an oath or affirmation should be made

64. Practices and laws differ as to whether or not oral testimony is to be given under oath or affirmation. In some legal systems, the arbitrators are empowered to put witnesses on oath, but it is usually in their discretion whether they want to do so. In other systems, oral testimony under oath is either unknown or may even be considered improper as only an official such as a judge or notary may have the authority to administer oaths.

(iii) May witnesses be in the hearing room when they are not testifying

65. Some arbitrators favour the procedure that, except if the circumstances suggest otherwise, the presence of a witness in the hearing room is limited to the time the witness is testifying; the purpose is to prevent the witness from being influenced by what is said in the hearing room, or to prevent that the presence of the witness would influence another witness. Other arbitrators consider that the presence of a witness during the testimony of other witnesses may be beneficial in that possible contradictions may be readily clarified or that their presence may act as a deterrent against untrue statements. Other possible approaches may be that witnesses are not present in the hearing room before their testimony, but stay in the room after they have testified, or that the arbitral tribunal decides the question for each witness individually depending on what the arbitral tribunal considers most appropriate. The arbitral tribunal may leave the procedure to be decided during the hearings, or may give guidance on the question in advance of the hearings.

(c) The order in which the witnesses will be called

66. When several witnesses are to be heard and longer testimony is expected, it is likely to reduce costs if the order in which they will be called is known in advance and their presence can be scheduled accordingly. Each party might be invited to suggest the order in which it intends to present the witnesses, while it would be up to the arbitral tribunal to approve the scheduling and to make departures from it.

(d) Interviewing witnesses prior to their appearance at a hearing

67. In some legal systems, parties or their representatives are permitted to interview witnesses, prior to their appearance at the hearing, as to such matters as their recollection of the relevant events, their experience, qualifications or relation with a participant in the proceedings. In those legal systems such contacts are usually not permitted once the witness's oral testimony has begun. In other systems such contacts with witnesses are considered improper. In order to avoid misunderstandings, the arbitral tribunal may consider it useful to clarify what kind of contacts a party is permitted to have with a witness in the preparations for the hearings.

(e) Hearing representatives of a party

68. According to some legal systems, certain persons affiliated with a party may only be heard as representatives of the party but not as witnesses. In such a case, it may be necessary to consider ground rules for determining which persons may not testify as witnesses (e.g. certain executives, employees or agents) and for hearing statements of those persons and for questioning them.

16. Experts and expert witnesses

69. Many arbitration rules and laws on arbitral procedure address the participation of experts in arbitral proceedings. A frequent solution is that the arbitral tribunal has the power to appoint an expert to report on issues determined by the tribunal; in addition, the parties may be permitted to present expert witnesses on points at issue. In other cases, it is for the parties to present expert testimony, and it is not expected that the arbitral tribunal will appoint an expert.

(a) Expert appointed by the arbitral tribunal

70. If the arbitral tribunal is empowered to appoint an expert, one possible approach is for the tribunal to proceed directly to selecting the expert. Another possibility is to consult the parties as to who should be the expert; this may be done, for example, without mentioning a candidate, by presenting to the parties a list of candidates, soliciting proposals from the parties, or by discussing with the parties the "profile" of the expert the arbitral tribunal intends to appoint, i.e. the qualifications, experience and abilities of the expert.

(i) The expert's terms of reference

71. The purpose of the expert's terms of reference is to indicate the questions on which the expert is to provide clarification, to avoid opinions on points that are not for the expert to assess and to commit the expert to a time schedule. While the discretion to appoint an expert normally includes the determination of the expert's terms of reference, the arbitral tribunal may decide to consult the parties before finalizing the terms. It might also be useful to determine details about how the expert will receive from the parties any relevant information or have access to any relevant documents, goods or other property, so as to enable the expert to prepare the report. In order to facilitate the evaluation of the expert's report, it is advisable to require the expert to include in the report information on the method used in arriving at the conclusions and the evidence and information used in preparing the report.

(ii) The opportunity of the parties to comment on the expert's report, including by presenting expert testimony

72. Arbitration rules that contain provisions on experts usually also have provisions on the right of a party to comment on the report of the expert appointed by the arbitral tribunal. If no such provisions apply or more specific procedures than those prescribed are deemed necessary, the arbitral tribunal may, in light of those provisions, consider it opportune to determine, for example, the time period for presenting written comments of the parties, or, if hearings are to be held for the purpose of hearing the expert, the procedures for interrogating the expert by the parties or for the participation of any expert witnesses presented by the parties.

(b) Expert opinion presented by a party (expert witness)

73. If a party presents an expert opinion, the arbitral tribunal might consider requiring, for example, that the opinion be in writing, that the expert should be available to answer questions at hearings, and that, if a party will present an expert witness at a hearing, advance notice must be given or that the written opinion must be presented in advance, as in the case of other witnesses (see paragraphs 60–62).

17. Hearings

(a) Decision whether to hold hearings

74. Laws on arbitral procedure and arbitration rules often have provisions as to the cases in which oral hearings must be held and as to when the arbitral tribunal has discretion to decide whether to hold hearings.

75. If it is up to the arbitral tribunal to decide whether to hold hearings, the decision is likely to be influenced by factors such as, on the one hand, that it is usually quicker and easier to clarify points at issue pursuant to a direct confrontation of arguments than on the basis of correspondence and, on the other hand, the travel and other cost of holding hearings, and that the need of finding acceptable dates for the hearings might delay the proceedings. The arbitral tribunal may wish to consult the parties on this matter.

(b) Whether one period of hearings should be held or separate periods of hearings

76. Attitudes vary as to whether hearings should be held in a single period of hearings or in separate periods, especially when more than a few days are needed to complete the hearings. According to some arbitrators, the entire hearings should normally be held in a single period, even if the hearings are to last for more than a week. Other arbitrators in such cases tend to schedule separate periods of hearings. In some cases issues to be decided are separated, and

separate hearings set for those issues, with the aim that oral presentation on those issues will be completed within the allotted time. Among the advantages of one period of hearings are that it involves less travel costs, memory will not fade, and it is unlikely that people representing a party will change. On the other hand, the longer the hearings, the more difficult it may be to find early dates acceptable to all participants. Furthermore, separate periods of hearings may be easier to schedule, the subsequent hearings may be tailored to the development of the case, and the period between the hearings leaves time for analysing the records and negotiations between the parties aimed at narrowing the points at issue by agreement.

(c) Setting dates for hearings

77. Typically, firm dates will be fixed for hearings. Exceptionally, the arbitral tribunal may initially wish to set only "target dates" as opposed to definitive dates. This may be done at a stage of the proceedings when not all information necessary to schedule hearings is yet available, with the understanding that the target dates will either be confirmed or rescheduled within a reasonably short period. Such provisional planning can be useful to participants who are generally not available on short notice.

(d) Whether there should be a limit on the aggregate amount of time each party will have for oral arguments and questioning witnesses

78. Some arbitrators consider it useful to limit the aggregate amount of time each party has for any of the following: *(a)* making oral statements; *(b)* questioning its witnesses; and *(c)* questioning the witnesses of the other party or parties. In general, the same aggregate amount of time is considered appropriate for each party, unless the arbitral tribunal considers that a different allocation is justified. Before deciding, the arbitral tribunal may wish to consult the parties as to how much time they think they will need.

79. Such planning of time, provided it is realistic, fair and subject to judiciously firm control by the arbitral tribunal, will make it easier for the parties to plan the presentation of the various items of evidence and arguments, reduce the likelihood of running out of time towards the end of the hearings and avoid that one party would unfairly use up a disproportionate amount of time.

(e) The order in which the parties will present their arguments and evidence

80. Arbitration rules typically give broad latitude to the arbitral tribunal to determine the order of presentations at the hearings. Within that latitude, practices differ, for example, as to whether opening or closing statements are heard and their level of detail; the sequence in which the claimant and the respondent present their opening statements, arguments, witnesses and other evidence; and whether the respondent or the claimant has the last word. In view of such differences, or when no arbitration rules apply, it may foster efficiency of the proceedings if the arbitral tribunal clarifies to the parties, in advance of the hearings, the manner in which it will conduct the hearings, at least in broad lines.

(f) Length of hearings

81. The length of a hearing primarily depends on the complexity of the issues to be argued and the amount of witness evidence to be presented. The length also depends on the procedural style used in the arbitration. Some practitioners prefer to have written evidence and written arguments presented before the hearings, which thus can focus on the issues that have not been sufficiently clarified. Those practitioners generally tend to plan shorter hearings than those practitioners who prefer that most if not all evidence and arguments are presented to the arbitral tribunal orally and in full detail. In order to facilitate the parties' preparations and avoid misunderstandings, the arbitral tribunal may wish to clarify to the parties, in advance of the hearings, the intended use of time and style of work at the hearings.

(g) Arrangements for a record of the hearings

82. The arbitral tribunal should decide, possibly after consulting with the parties, on the method of preparing a record of oral statements and testimony during hearings. Among different

possibilities, one method is that the members of the arbitral tribunal take personal notes. Another is that the presiding arbitrator during the hearing dictates to a typist a summary of oral statements and testimony. A further method, possible when a secretary of the arbitral tribunal has been appointed, may be to leave to that person the preparation of a summary record. A useful, though costly, method is for professional stenographers to prepare verbatim transcripts, often within the next day or a similarly short time period. A written record may be combined with tape-recording, so as to enable reference to the tape in case of a disagreement over the written record.

83. If transcripts are to be produced, it may be considered how the persons who made the statements will be given an opportunity to check the transcripts. For example, it may be determined that the changes to the record would be approved by the parties or, failing their agreement, would be referred for decision to the arbitral tribunal.

(b) Whether and when the parties are permitted to submit notes summarizing their oral arguments

84. Some legal counsel are accustomed to giving notes summarizing their oral arguments to the arbitral tribunal and to the other party or parties. If such notes are presented, this is usually done during the hearings or shortly thereafter; in some cases, the notes are sent before the hearing. In order to avoid surprise, foster equal treatment of the parties and facilitate preparations for the hearings, advance clarification is advisable as to whether submitting such notes is acceptable and the time for doing so.

85. In closing the hearings, the arbitral tribunal will normally assume that no further proof is to be offered or submission to be made. Therefore, if notes are to be presented to be read after the closure of the hearings, the arbitral tribunal may find it worthwhile to stress that the notes should be limited to summarizing what was said orally and in particular should not refer to new evidence or new argument.

18. Multi-party arbitration

86. When a single arbitration involves more than two parties (multi-party arbitration), considerations regarding the need to organize arbitral proceedings, and matters that may be considered in that connection, are generally not different from two-party arbitrations. A possible difference may be that, because of the need to deal with more than two parties, multi-party proceedings can be more complicated to manage than bilateral proceedings. The Notes, notwithstanding a possible greater complexity of multi-party arbitration, can be used in multiparty as well as in two-party proceedings.

87. The areas of possibly increased complexity in multi-party arbitration are, for example, the flow of communications among the parties and the arbitral tribunal (see paragraphs 33, 34 and 38–41); if points at issue are to be decided at different points in time, the order of deciding them (paragraphs 44–45); the manner in which the parties will participate in hearing witnesses (paragraph 63); the appointment of experts and the participation of the parties in considering their reports (paragraphs 70–72); the scheduling of hearings (paragraph 76); the order in which the parties will present their arguments and evidence at hearings (paragraph 80).

88. The Notes, which are limited to pointing out matters that may be considered in organizing arbitral proceedings in general, do not cover the drafting of the arbitration agreement or the constitution of the arbitral tribunal, both issues that give rise to special questions in multiparty arbitration as compared to two-party arbitration.

19. Possible requirements concerning filing or delivering the award

89. Some national laws require that arbitral awards be filed or registered with a court or similar authority, or that they be delivered in a particular manner or through a particular authority. Those laws differ with respect to, for example, the type of award to which the requirement applies (e.g. to all awards or only to awards not rendered under the auspices of an arbitral institution); time periods for filing, registering or delivering the award (in some cases those time periods may be

rather short); or consequences for failing to comply with the requirement (which might be, for example, invalidity of the award or inability to enforce it in a particular manner).

Who should take steps to fulfil any requirement

90. If such a requirement exists, it is useful, some time before the award is to be issued, to plan who should take the necessary steps to meet the requirement and how the costs are to be borne.

ANNEX F

IBA Rules on the Taking of Evidence in International Arbitration*

Preamble

1. These IBA Rules on the Taking of Evidence in International Arbitration are intended to provide an efficient, economical and fair process for the taking of evidence in international arbitrations, particularly those between Parties from different legal traditions. They are designed to supplement the legal provisions and the institutional, ad hoc or other rules that apply to the conduct of the arbitration.
2. Parties and Arbitral Tribunals may adopt the IBA Rules of Evidence, in whole or in part, to govern arbitration proceedings, or they may vary them or use them as guidelines in developing their own procedures. The Rules are not intended to limit the flexibility that is inherent in, and an advantage of, international arbitration, and Parties and Arbitral Tribunals are free to adapt them to the particular circumstances of each arbitration.
3. The taking of evidence shall be conducted on the principles that each Party shall act in good faith and be entitled to know, reasonably in advance of any Evidentiary Hearing or any fact or merits determination, the evidence on which the other Parties rely.

Definitions

In the IBA Rules of Evidence:

'Arbitral Tribunal' means a sole arbitrator or a panel of arbitrators;

'Claimant' means the Party or Parties who commenced the arbitration and any Party who, through joinder or otherwise, becomes aligned with such Party or Parties;

'Document' means a writing, communication, picture, drawing, program or data of any kind, whether recorded or maintained on paper or by electronic, audio, visual or any other means;

'Evidentiary Hearing' means any hearing, whether or not held on consecutive days, at which the Arbitral Tribunal, whether in person, by teleconference, videoconference or other method, receives oral or other evidence;

'Expert Report' means a written statement by a Tribunal-Appointed Expert or a Party-Appointed Expert;

'General Rules' mean the institutional, ad hoc or other rules that apply to the conduct of the arbitration;

'IBA Rules of Evidence' or *'Rules'* means these IBA Rules on the Taking of Evidence in International Arbitration, as they may be revised or amended from time to time;

'Party' means a party to the arbitration;

'Party-Appointed Expert' means a person or organisation appointed by a Party in order to report on specific issues determined by the Party;

'Request to Produce' means a written request by a Party that another Party produce Documents;

---

* Adopted by a resolution of the IBA Council on May 29, 2010. Reproduced by kind permission of the International Bar Association, London, UK, and available at <www.ibanet.org/Publications/publications_IBA_guides_and_free_materials.aspx>. © International Bar Association.

'Respondent' means the Party or Parties against whom the Claimant made its claim, and any Party who, through joinder or otherwise, becomes aligned with such Party or Parties, and includes a Respondent making a counterclaim;

'Tribunal-Appointed Expert' means a person or organisation appointed by the Arbitral Tribunal in order to report to it on specific issues determined by the Arbitral Tribunal; and

'Witness Statement' means a written statement of testimony by a witness of fact.

Article 1 Scope of Application

1. Whenever the Parties have agreed or the Arbitral Tribunal has determined to apply the IBA Rules of Evidence, the Rules shall govern the taking of evidence, except to the extent that any specific provision of them may be found to be in conflict with any mandatory provision of law determined to be applicable to the case by the Parties or by the Arbitral Tribunal.
2. Where the Parties have agreed to apply the IBA Rules of Evidence, they shall be deemed to have agreed, in the absence of a contrary indication, to the version as current on the date of such agreement.
3. In case of conflict between any provisions of the IBA Rules of Evidence and the General Rules, the Arbitral Tribunal shall apply the IBA Rules of Evidence in the manner that it determines best in order to accomplish the purposes of both the General Rules and the IBA Rules of Evidence, unless the Parties agree to the contrary.
4. In the event of any dispute regarding the meaning of the IBA Rules of Evidence, the Arbitral Tribunal shall interpret them according to their purpose and in the manner most appropriate for the particular arbitration.
5. Insofar as the IBA Rules of Evidence and the General Rules are silent on any matter concerning the taking of evidence and the Parties have not agreed otherwise, the Arbitral Tribunal shall conduct the taking of evidence as it deems appropriate, in accordance with the general principles of the IBA Rules of Evidence.

Article 2 Consultation on Evidentiary Issues

1. The Arbitral Tribunal shall consult the Parties at the earliest appropriate time in the proceedings and invite them to consult each other with a view to agreeing on an efficient, economical and fair process for the taking of evidence.
2. The consultation on evidentiary issues may address the scope, timing and manner of the taking of evidence, including:
   (a) the preparation and submission of Witness Statements and Expert Reports;
   (b) the taking of oral testimony at any Evidentiary Hearing;
   (c) the requirements, procedure and format applicable to the production of Documents;
   (d) the level of confidentiality protection to be afforded to evidence in the arbitration; and
   (e) the promotion of efficiency, economy and conservation of resources in connection with the taking of evidence.
3. The Arbitral Tribunal is encouraged to identify to the Parties, as soon as it considers it to be appropriate, any issues:
   (a) that the Arbitral Tribunal may regard as relevant to the case and material to its outcome; and/or
   (b) for which a preliminary determination may be appropriate.

Article 3 Documents

1. Within the time ordered by the Arbitral Tribunal, each Party shall submit to the Arbitral Tribunal and to the other Parties all Documents available to it on which it relies, including public Documents and those in the public domain, except for any Documents that have already been submitted by another Party.
2. Within the time ordered by the Arbitral Tribunal, any Party may submit to the Arbitral Tribunal and to the other Parties a Request to Produce.

3. A Request to Produce shall contain:
   (a) *(i)* a description of each requested Document sufficient to identify it, or
   (ii) a description in sufficient detail (including subject matter) of a narrow and specific requested category of Documents that are reasonably believed to exist; in the case of Documents maintained in electronic form, the requesting Party may, or the Arbitral Tribunal may order that it shall be required to, identify specific files, search terms, individuals or other means of searching for such Documents in an efficient and economical manner;
   (b) a statement as to how the Documents requested are relevant to the case and material to its outcome; and
   (c) *(i)* a statement that the Documents requested are not in the possession, custody or control of the requesting Party or a statement of the reasons why it would be unreasonably burdensome for the requesting Party to produce such Documents, and
   (ii) a statement of the reasons why the requesting Party assumes the Documents requested are in the possession, custody or control of another Party.
4. Within the time ordered by the Arbitral Tribunal, the Party to whom the Request to Produce is addressed shall produce to the other Parties and, if the Arbitral Tribunal so orders, to it, all the Documents requested in its possession, custody or control as to which it makes no objection.
5. If the Party to whom the Request to Produce is addressed has an objection to some or all of the Documents requested, it shall state the objection in writing to the Arbitral Tribunal and the other Parties within the time ordered by the Arbitral Tribunal. The reasons for such objection shall be any of those set forth in Article 9.2 or a failure to satisfy any of the requirements of Article 3.3.
6. Upon receipt of any such objection, the Arbitral Tribunal may invite the relevant Parties to consult with each other with a view to resolving the objection.
7. Either Party may, within the time ordered by the Arbitral Tribunal, request the Arbitral Tribunal to rule on the objection. The Arbitral Tribunal shall then, in consultation with the Parties and in timely fashion, consider the Request to Produce and the objection. The Arbitral Tribunal may order the Party to whom such Request is addressed to produce any requested Document in its possession, custody or control as to which the Arbitral Tribunal determines that *(i)* the issues that the requesting Party wishes to prove are relevant to the case and material to its outcome; *(ii)* none of the reasons for objection set forth in Article 9.2 applies; and *(iii)* the requirements of Article 3.3 have been satisfied. Any such Document shall be produced to the other Parties and, if the Arbitral Tribunal so orders, to it.
8. In exceptional circumstances, if the propriety of an objection can be determined only by review of the Document, the Arbitral Tribunal may determine that it should not review the Document. In that event, the Arbitral Tribunal may, after consultation with the Parties, appoint an independent and impartial expert, bound to confidentiality, to review any such Document and to report on the objection. To the extent that the objection is upheld by the Arbitral Tribunal, the expert shall not disclose to the Arbitral Tribunal and to the other Parties the contents of the Document reviewed.
9. If a Party wishes to obtain the production of Documents from a person or organisation who is not a Party to the arbitration and from whom the Party cannot obtain the Documents on its own, the Party may, within the time ordered by the Arbitral Tribunal, ask it to take whatever steps are legally available to obtain the requested Documents, or seek leave from the Arbitral Tribunal to take such steps itself. The Party shall submit such request to the Arbitral Tribunal and to the other Parties in writing, and the request shall contain the particulars set forth in Article 3.3, as applicable. The Arbitral Tribunal shall decide on this request and shall take, authorize the requesting Party to take, or order any other Party to take, such steps as the Arbitral Tribunal considers appropriate if, in its discretion, it determines that *(i)* the Documents would be relevant to the case and material to its outcome, *(ii)* the requirements of Article 3.3, as applicable, have been satisfied and *(iii)* none of the reasons for objection set forth in Article 9.2 applies.
10. At any time before the arbitration is concluded, the Arbitral Tribunal may *(i)* request any Party to produce Documents, *(ii)* request any Party to use its best efforts to take or *(iii)* itself

take, any step that it considers appropriate to obtain Documents from any person or organisation. A Party to whom such a request for Documents is addressed may object to the request for any of the reasons set forth in Article 9.2. In such cases, Article 3.4 to Article 3.8 shall apply correspondingly.

11. Within the time ordered by the Arbitral Tribunal, the Parties may submit to the Arbitral Tribunal and to the other Parties any additional Documents on which they intend to rely or which they believe have become relevant to the case and material to its outcome as a consequence of the issues raised in Documents, Witness Statements or Expert Reports submitted or produced, or in other submissions of the Parties.
12. With respect to the form of submission or production of Documents:
    (a) copies of Documents shall conform to the originals and, at the request of the Arbitral Tribunal, any original shall be presented for inspection;
    (b) Documents that a Party maintains in electronic form shall be submitted or produced in the form most convenient or economical to it that is reasonably usable by the recipients, unless the Parties agree otherwise or, in the absence of such agreement, the Arbitral Tribunal decides otherwise;
    (c) a Party is not obligated to produce multiple copies of Documents which are essentially identical unless the Arbitral Tribunal decides otherwise; and
    (d) translations of Documents shall be submitted together with the originals and marked as translations with the original language identified.
13. Any Document submitted or produced by a Party or non-Party in the arbitration and not otherwise in the public domain shall be kept confidential by the Arbitral Tribunal and the other Parties, and shall be used only in connection with the arbitration. This requirement shall apply except and to the extent that disclosure may be required of a Party to fulfil a legal duty, protect or pursue a legal right, or enforce or challenge an award in bona fide legal proceedings before a state court or other judicial authority. The Arbitral Tribunal may issue orders to set forth the terms of this confidentiality. This requirement shall be without prejudice to all other obligations of confidentiality in the arbitration.
14. If the arbitration is organised into separate issues or phases (such as jurisdiction, preliminary determinations, liability or damages), the Arbitral Tribunal may, after consultation with the Parties, schedule the submission of Documents and Requests to Produce separately for each issue or phase.

Article 4 Witnesses of Fact

1. Within the time ordered by the Arbitral Tribunal, each Party shall identify the witnesses on whose testimony it intends to rely and the subject matter of that testimony.
2. Any person may present evidence as a witness, including a Party or a Party's officer, employee or other representative.
3. It shall not be improper for a Party, its officers, employees, legal advisors or other representatives to interview its witnesses or potential witnesses and to discuss their prospective testimony with them.
4. The Arbitral Tribunal may order each Party to submit within a specified time to the Arbitral Tribunal and to the other Parties Witness Statements by each witness on whose testimony it intends to rely, except for those witnesses whose testimony is sought pursuant to Articles 4.9 or 4.10. If Evidentiary Hearings are organised into separate issues or phases (such as jurisdiction, preliminary determinations, liability or damages), the Arbitral Tribunal or the Parties by agreement may schedule the submission of Witness Statements separately for each issue or phase.
5. Each Witness Statement shall contain:
    (a) the full name and address of the witness, a statement regarding his or her present and past relationship (if any) with any of the Parties, and a description of his or her background, qualifications, training and experience, if such a description may be relevant to the dispute or to the contents of the statement;

(b) a full and detailed description of the facts, and the source of the witness's information as to those facts, sufficient to serve as that witness's evidence in the matter in dispute. Documents on which the witness relies that have not already been submitted shall be provided;

(c) a statement as to the language in which the Witness Statement was originally prepared and the language in which the witness anticipates giving testimony at the Evidentiary Hearing;

(d) an affirmation of the truth of the Witness Statement; and

(e) the signature of the witness and its date and place.

6. If Witness Statements are submitted, any Party may, within the time ordered by the Arbitral Tribunal, submit to the Arbitral Tribunal and to the other Parties revised or additional Witness Statements, including statements from persons not previously named as witnesses, so long as any such revisions or additions respond only to matters contained in another Party's Witness Statements, Expert Reports or other submissions that have not been previously presented in the arbitration.

7. If a witness whose appearance has been requested pursuant to Article 8.1 fails without a valid reason to appear for testimony at an Evidentiary Hearing, the Arbitral Tribunal shall disregard any Witness Statement related to that Evidentiary Hearing by that witness unless, in exceptional circumstances, the Arbitral Tribunal decides otherwise.

8. If the appearance of a witness has not been requested pursuant to Article 8.1, none of the other Parties shall be deemed to have agreed to the correctness of the content of the Witness Statement.

9. If a Party wishes to present evidence from a person who will not appear voluntarily at its request, the Party may, within the time ordered by the Arbitral Tribunal, ask it to take whatever steps are legally available to obtain the testimony of that person, or seek leave from the Arbitral Tribunal to take such steps itself. In the case of a request to the Arbitral Tribunal, the Party shall identify the intended witness, shall describe the subjects on which the witness's testimony is sought and shall state why such subjects are relevant to the case and material to its outcome. The Arbitral Tribunal shall decide on this request and shall take, authorize the requesting Party to take or order any other Party to take, such steps as the Arbitral Tribunal considers appropriate if, in its discretion, it determines that the testimony of that witness would be relevant to the case and material to its outcome.

10. At any time before the arbitration is concluded, the Arbitral Tribunal may order any Party to provide for, or to use its best efforts to provide for, the appearance for testimony at an Evidentiary Hearing of any person, including one whose testimony has not yet been offered. A Party to whom such a request is addressed may object for any of the reasons set forth in Article 9.2.

Article 5 Party-Appointed Experts

1. A Party may rely on a Party-Appointed Expert as a means of evidence on specific issues. Within the time ordered by the Arbitral Tribunal, (i) each Party shall identify any Party-Appointed Expert on whose testimony it intends to rely and the subject-matter of such testimony; and (ii) the Party-Appointed Expert shall submit an Expert Report.

2. The Expert Report shall contain:

(a) the full name and address of the Party-Appointed Expert, a statement regarding his or her present and past relationship (if any) with any of the Parties, their legal advisors and the Arbitral Tribunal, and a description of his or her background, qualifications, training and experience;

(b) a description of the instructions pursuant to which he or she is providing his or her opinions and conclusions;

(c) a statement of his or her independence from the Parties, their legal advisors and the Arbitral Tribunal;

(d) a statement of the facts on which he or she is basing his or her expert opinions and conclusions;

(e) his or her expert opinions and conclusions, including a description of the methods, evidence and information used in arriving at the conclusions. Documents on which the Party-Appointed Expert relies that have not already been submitted shall be provided;

(f) if the Expert Report has been translated, a statement as to the language in which it was originally prepared, and the language in which the Party-Appointed Expert anticipates giving testimony at the Evidentiary Hearing;
(g) an affirmation of his or her genuine belief in the opinions expressed in the Expert Report;
(h) the signature of the Party-Appointed Expert and its date and place; and
(i) if the Expert Report has been signed by more than one person, an attribution of the entirety or specific parts of the Expert Report to each author.

3. If Expert Reports are submitted, any Party may, within the time ordered by the Arbitral Tribunal, submit to the Arbitral Tribunal and to the other Parties revised or additional Expert Reports, including reports or statements from persons not previously identified as Party-Appointed Experts, so long as any such revisions or additions respond only to matters contained in another Party's Witness Statements, Expert Reports or other submissions that have not been previously presented in the arbitration.
4. The Arbitral Tribunal in its discretion may order that any Party-Appointed Experts who will submit or who have submitted Expert Reports on the same or related issues meet and confer on such issues. At such meeting, the Party-Appointed Experts shall attempt to reach agreement on the issues within the scope of their Expert Reports, and they shall record in writing any such issues on which they reach agreement, any remaining areas of disagreement and the reasons therefore.
5. If a Party-Appointed Expert whose appearance has been requested pursuant to Article 8.1 fails without a valid reason to appear for testimony at an Evidentiary Hearing, the Arbitral Tribunal shall disregard any Expert Report by that Party-Appointed Expert related to that Evidentiary Hearing unless, in exceptional circumstances, the Arbitral Tribunal decides otherwise.
6. If the appearance of a Party-Appointed Expert has not been requested pursuant to Article 8.1, none of the other Parties shall be deemed to have agreed to the correctness of the content of the Expert Report.

Article 6 Tribunal-Appointed Experts

1. The Arbitral Tribunal, after consulting with the Parties, may appoint one or more independent Tribunal-Appointed Experts to report to it on specific issues designated by the Arbitral Tribunal. The Arbitral Tribunal shall establish the terms of reference for any Tribunal-Appointed Expert Report after consulting with the Parties. A copy of the final terms of reference shall be sent by the Arbitral Tribunal to the Parties.
2. The Tribunal-Appointed Expert shall, before accepting appointment, submit to the Arbitral Tribunal and to the Parties a description of his or her qualifications and a statement of his or her independence from the Parties, their legal advisors and the Arbitral Tribunal. Within the time ordered by the Arbitral Tribunal, the Parties shall inform the Arbitral Tribunal whether they have any objections as to the Tribunal-Appointed Expert's qualifications and independence. The Arbitral Tribunal shall decide promptly whether to accept any such objection. After the appointment of a Tribunal-Appointed Expert, a Party may object to the expert's qualifications or independence only if the objection is for reasons of which the Party becomes aware after the appointment has been made. The Arbitral Tribunal shall decide promptly what, if any, action to take.
3. Subject to the provisions of Article 9.2, the Tribunal-Appointed Expert may request a Party to provide any information or to provide access to any Documents, goods, samples, property, machinery, systems, processes or site for inspection, to the extent relevant to the case and material to its outcome. The authority of a Tribunal-Appointed Expert to request such information or access shall be the same as the authority of the Arbitral Tribunal. The Parties and their representatives shall have the right to receive any such information and to attend any such inspection. Any disagreement between a Tribunal-Appointed Expert and a Party as to the relevance, materiality or appropriateness of such a request shall be decided by the Arbitral Tribunal, in the manner provided in Articles 3.5 through 3.8. The Tribunal-Appointed Expert shall record in the Expert Report any non-compliance by a Party with an appropriate request or decision by the Arbitral Tribunal and shall describe its effects on the determination of the specific issue.

4. The Tribunal-Appointed Expert shall report in writing to the Arbitral Tribunal in an Expert Report. The Expert Report shall contain:
   (a) the full name and address of the Tribunal-Appointed Expert, and a description of his or her background, qualifications, training and experience;
   (b) a statement of the facts on which he or she is basing his or her expert opinions and conclusions;
   (c) his or her expert opinions and conclusions, including a description of the methods, evidence and information used in arriving at the conclusions. Documents on which the Tribunal-Appointed Expert relies that have not already been submitted shall be provided;
   (d) if the Expert Report has been translated, a statement as to the language in which it was originally prepared, and the language in which the Tribunal-Appointed Expert anticipates giving testimony at the Evidentiary Hearing;
   (e) an affirmation of his or her genuine belief in the opinions expressed in the Expert Report;
   (f) the signature of the Tribunal-Appointed Expert and its date and place; and
   (g) if the Expert Report has been signed by more than one person, an attribution of the entirety or specific parts of the Expert Report to each author.
5. The Arbitral Tribunal shall send a copy of such Expert Report to the Parties. The Parties may examine any information, Documents, goods, samples, property, machinery, systems, processes or site for inspection that the Tribunal-Appointed Expert has examined and any correspondence between the Arbitral Tribunal and the Tribunal-Appointed Expert. Within the time ordered by the Arbitral Tribunal, any Party shall have the opportunity to respond to the Expert Report in a submission by the Party or through a Witness Statement or an Expert Report by a Party-Appointed Expert. The Arbitral Tribunal shall send the submission, Witness Statement or Expert Report to the Tribunal-Appointed Expert and to the other Parties.
6. At the request of a Party or of the Arbitral Tribunal, the Tribunal-Appointed Expert shall be present at an Evidentiary Hearing. The Arbitral Tribunal may question the Tribunal-Appointed Expert, and he or she may be questioned by the Parties or by any Party-Appointed Expert on issues raised in his or her Expert Report, the Parties' submissions or Witness Statement or the Expert Reports made by the Party-Appointed Experts pursuant to Article 6.5.
7. Any Expert Report made by a Tribunal-Appointed Expert and its conclusions shall be assessed by the Arbitral Tribunal with due regard to all circumstances of the case.
8. The fees and expenses of a Tribunal-Appointed Expert, to be funded in a manner determined by the Arbitral Tribunal, shall form part of the costs of the arbitration.

Article 7 Inspection

Subject to the provisions of Article 9.2, the Arbitral Tribunal may, at the request of a Party or on its own motion, inspect or require the inspection by a Tribunal-Appointed Expert or a Party-Appointed Expert of any site, property, machinery or any other goods, samples, systems, processes or Documents, as it deems appropriate. The Arbitral Tribunal shall, in consultation with the Parties, determine the timing and arrangement for the inspection. The Parties and their representatives shall have the right to attend any such inspection.

Article 8 Evidentiary Hearing

1. Within the time ordered by the Arbitral Tribunal, each Party shall inform the Arbitral Tribunal and the other Parties of the witnesses whose appearance it requests. Each witness (which term includes, for the purposes of this Article, witnesses of fact and any experts) shall, subject to Article 8.2, appear for testimony at the Evidentiary Hearing if such person's appearance has been requested by any Party or by the Arbitral Tribunal. Each witness shall appear in person unless the Arbitral Tribunal allows the use of videoconference or similar technology with respect to a particular witness.
2. The Arbitral Tribunal shall at all times have complete control over the Evidentiary Hearing. The Arbitral Tribunal may limit or exclude any question to, answer by or appearance of a witness, if it considers such question, answer or appearance to be irrelevant, immaterial, unreasonably burdensome, duplicative or otherwise covered by a reason for objection set forth in Article 9.2. Questions to a witness during direct and re-direct testimony may not be unreasonably leading.

3. With respect to oral testimony at an Evidentiary Hearing:
   (a) the Claimant shall ordinarily first present the testimony of its witnesses, followed by the Respondent presenting the testimony of its witnesses;
   (b) following direct testimony, any other Party may question such witness, in an order to be determined by the Arbitral Tribunal. The Party who initially presented the witness shall subsequently have the opportunity to ask additional questions on the matters raised in the other Parties' questioning;
   (c) thereafter, the Claimant shall ordinarily first present the testimony of its Party-Appointed Experts, followed by the Respondent presenting the testimony of its Party-Appointed Experts. The Party who initially presented the Party-Appointed Expert shall subsequently have the opportunity to ask additional questions on the matters raised in the other Parties' questioning;
   (d) the Arbitral Tribunal may question a Tribunal-Appointed Expert, and he or she may be questioned by the Parties or by any Party-Appointed Expert, on issues raised in the Tribunal-Appointed Expert Report, in the Parties' submissions or in the Expert Reports made by the Party-Appointed Experts;
   (e) if the arbitration is organised into separate issues or phases (such as jurisdiction, preliminary determinations, liability and damages), the Parties may agree or the Arbitral Tribunal may order the scheduling of testimony separately for each issue or phase;
   (f) the Arbitral Tribunal, upon request of a Party or on its own motion, may vary this order of proceeding, including the arrangement of testimony by particular issues or in such a manner that witnesses be questioned at the same time and in confrontation with each other (witness conferencing);
   (g) the Arbitral Tribunal may ask questions to a witness at any time.
4. A witness of fact providing testimony shall first affirm, in a manner determined appropriate by the Arbitral Tribunal, that he or she commits to tell the truth or, in the case of an expert witness, his or her genuine belief in the opinions to be expressed at the Evidentiary Hearing. If the witness has submitted a Witness Statement or an Expert Report, the witness shall confirm it. The Parties may agree or the Arbitral Tribunal may order that the Witness Statement or Expert Report shall serve as that witness's direct testimony.
5. Subject to the provisions of Article 9.2, the Arbitral Tribunal may request any person to give oral or written evidence on any issue that the Arbitral Tribunal considers to be relevant to the case and material to its outcome. Any witness called and questioned by the Arbitral Tribunal may also be questioned by the Parties.

Article 9 Admissibility and Assessment of Evidence

1. The Arbitral Tribunal shall determine the admissibility, relevance, materiality and weight of evidence.
2. The Arbitral Tribunal shall, at the request of a Party or on its own motion, exclude from evidence or production any Document, statement, oral testimony or inspection for any of the following reasons:
   (a) lack of sufficient relevance to the case or materiality to its outcome;
   (b) legal impediment or privilege under the legal or ethical rules determined by the Arbitral Tribunal to be applicable;
   (c) unreasonable burden to produce the requested evidence;
   (d) loss or destruction of the Document that has been shown with reasonable likelihood to have occurred;
   (e) grounds of commercial or technical confidentiality that the Arbitral Tribunal determines to be compelling;
   (f) grounds of special political or institutional sensitivity (including evidence that has been classified as secret by a government or a public international institution) that the Arbitral Tribunal determines to be compelling; or
   (g) considerations of procedural economy, proportionality, fairness or equality of the Parties that the Arbitral Tribunal determines to be compelling.

3. In considering issues of legal impediment or privilege under Article 9.2(b), and insofar as permitted by any mandatory legal or ethical rules that are determined by it to be applicable, the Arbitral Tribunal may take into account:
   (a) any need to protect the confidentiality of a Document created or statement or oral communication made in connection with and for the purpose of providing or obtaining legal advice;
   (b) any need to protect the confidentiality of a Document created or statement or oral communication made in connection with and for the purpose of settlement negotiations;
   (c) the expectations of the Parties and their advisors at the time the legal impediment or privilege is said to have arisen;
   (d) any possible waiver of any applicable legal impediment or privilege by virtue of consent, earlier disclosure, affirmative use of the Document, statement, oral communication or advice contained therein, or otherwise; and
   (e) the need to maintain fairness and equality as between the Parties, particularly if they are subject to different legal or ethical rules.
4. The Arbitral Tribunal may, where appropriate, make necessary arrangements to permit evidence to be presented or considered subject to suitable confidentiality protection.
5. If a Party fails without satisfactory explanation to produce any Document requested in a Request to Produce to which it has not objected in due time or fails to produce any Document ordered to be produced by the Arbitral Tribunal, the Arbitral Tribunal may infer that such document would be adverse to the interests of that Party.
6. If a Party fails without satisfactory explanation to make available any other relevant evidence, including testimony, sought by one Party to which the Party to whom the request was addressed has not objected in due time or fails to make available any evidence, including testimony, ordered by the Arbitral Tribunal to be produced, the Arbitral Tribunal may infer that such evidence would be adverse to the interests of that Party.
7. If the Arbitral Tribunal determines that a Party has failed to conduct itself in good faith in the taking of evidence, the Arbitral Tribunal may, in addition to any other measures available under these Rules, take such failure into account in its assignment of the costs of the arbitration, including costs arising out of or in connection with the taking of evidence.

ANNEX G

IBA Guidelines on Conflicts of Interest in International Arbitration*

Since their issuance in 2004, the *IBA Guidelines on Conflicts of Interest in International Arbitration* (the 'Guidelines')[1] have gained wide acceptance within the international arbitration community. Arbitrators commonly use the Guidelines when making decisions about prospective appointments and disclosures. Likewise, parties and their counsel frequently consider the Guidelines in assessing the impartiality and independence of arbitrators, and arbitral institutions and courts also often consult the Guidelines in considering challenges to arbitrators. As contemplated when the Guidelines were first adopted, on the eve of their tenth anniversary it was considered appropriate to reflect on the accumulated experience of using them and to identify areas of possible clarification or improvement. Accordingly, in 2012, the IBA Arbitration Committee initiated a review of the Guidelines, which was conducted by an expanded Conflicts of Interest Subcommittee (the 'Subcommittee'),[2] representing diverse legal cultures and a range of perspectives, including counsel, arbitrators and arbitration users. The Subcommittee was chaired by David Arias, later co-chaired by Julie Bédard, and the review process was conducted under the leadership of Pierre Bienvenu and Bernard Hanotiau.

While the Guidelines were originally intended to apply to both commercial and investment arbitration, it was found in the course of the review process that uncertainty lingered as to their application to investment arbitration. Similarly, despite a comment in the original version of the Guidelines that their application extended to non-legal professionals serving as arbitrator, there appeared to remain uncertainty in this regard as well. A consensus emerged in favour of a general affirmation that the Guidelines apply to both commercial and investment arbitration, and to both legal and non-legal professionals serving as arbitrator.

The Subcommittee has carefully considered a number of issues that have received attention in international arbitration practice since 2004, such as the effects of so-called 'advance waivers', whether the fact of acting concurrently as counsel and arbitrator in unrelated cases raising similar legal issues warrants disclosure, 'issue' conflicts, the independence and impartiality of arbitral or administrative

* Adopted by resolution of the IBA Council on Thursday, October 23, 2014. Reproduced by kind permission of the International Bar Association, London, UK, and available at <www.ibanet.org/Publications/publications_IBA_guides_and_free_materials.aspx>. © International Bar Association.

[1] The 2004 Guidelines were drafted by a Working Group of 19 experts: Henri Alvarez, Canada; John Beechey, England; Jim Carter, United States; Emmanuel Gaillard, France; Emilio Gonzales de Castilla, Mexico; Bernard Hanotiau, Belgium; Michael Hwang, Singapore; Albert Jan van den Berg, Belgium; Doug Jones, Australia; Gabrielle Kaufmann-Kohler, Switzerland; Arthur Marriott, England; Tore Wiwen Nilsson, Sweden; Hilmar Raeschke-Kessler, Germany; David W Rivkin, United States; Klaus Sachs, Germany; Nathalie Voser, Switzerland (Rapporteur); David Williams, New Zealand; Des Williams, South Africa; and Otto de Witt Wijnen, The Netherlands (Chair).

[2] The members of the expanded Subcommittee on Conflicts of Interest were: Habib Almulla, United Arab Emirates; David Arias, Spain (Co-Chair); Julie Bédard, United States (Co-Chair); José Astigarraga, United States; Pierre Bienvenu, Canada (Review Process Co-Chair); Karl-Heinz Böckstiegel, Germany; Yves Derains, France; Teresa Giovannini, Switzerland; Eduardo Damião Gonçalves, Brazil; Bernard Hanotiau, Belgium (Review Process Co-Chair); Paula Hodges, England; Toby Landau, England; Christian Leathley, England; Carole Malinvaud, France; Ciccu Mukhopadhaya, India; Yoshimi Ohara, Japan; Tinuade Oyekunle, Nigeria; Eun Young Park, Korea; Constantine Partasides, England; Peter Rees, The Netherlands; Anke Sessler, Germany; Guido Tawil, Argentina; Jingzhou Tao, China; Gäetan Verhoosel, England (Rapporteur); Nathalie Voser, Switzerland; Nassib Ziadé, United Arab Emirates; and Alexis Mourre. Assistance was provided by: Niuscha Bassiri, Belgium; Alison Fitzgerald, Canada; Oliver Cojo, Spain; and Ricardo Dalmaso Marques, Brazil.

secretaries and third-party funding. The revised Guidelines reflect the Subcommittee's conclusions on these issues.

The Subcommittee has also considered, in view of the evolution of the global practice of international arbitration, whether the revised Guidelines should impose stricter standards in regard to arbitrator disclosure. The revised Guidelines reflect the conclusion that, while the basic approach of the 2004 Guidelines should not be altered, disclosure should be required in certain circumstances not contemplated in the 2004 Guidelines. It is also essential to reaffirm that the fact of requiring disclosure—or of an arbitrator making a disclosure—does not imply the existence of doubts as to the impartiality or independence of the arbitrator. Indeed, the standard for disclosure differs from the standard for challenge. Similarly, the revised Guidelines are not in any way intended to discourage the service as arbitrators of lawyers practising in large firms or legal associations.

The Guidelines were adopted by resolution of the IBA Council on Thursday 23 October 2014. The Guidelines are available for download at: **www.ibanet.org/Publications/publications_IBA_guides_and_free_materials.aspx**

Introduction

1. Arbitrators and party representatives are often unsure about the scope of their disclosure obligations. The growth of international business, including larger corporate groups and international law firms, has generated more disclosures and resulted in increased complexity in the analysis of disclosure and conflict of interest issues. Parties have more opportunities to use challenges of arbitrators to delay arbitrations, or to deny the opposing party the arbitrator of its choice. Disclosure of any relationship, no matter how minor or serious, may lead to unwarranted or frivolous challenges. At the same time, it is important that more information be made available to the parties, so as to protect awards against challenges based upon alleged failures to disclose, and to promote a level playing field among parties and among counsel engaged in international arbitration.
2. Parties, arbitrators, institutions and courts face complex decisions about the information that arbitrators should disclose and the standards to apply to disclosure. In addition, institutions and courts face difficult decisions when an objection or a challenge is made after a disclosure. There is a tension between, on the one hand, the parties' right to disclosure of circumstances that may call into question an arbitrator's impartiality or independence in order to protect the parties' right to a fair hearing, and, on the other hand, the need to avoid unnecessary challenges against arbitrators in order to protect the parties' ability to select arbitrators of their choosing.
3. It is in the interest of the international arbitration community that arbitration proceedings are not hindered by ill-founded challenges against arbitrators and that the legitimacy of the process is not affected by uncertainty and a lack of uniformity in the applicable standards for disclosures, objections and challenges. The 2004 Guidelines reflected the view that the standards existing at the time lacked sufficient clarity and uniformity in their application. The Guidelines, therefore, set forth some 'General Standards and Explanatory Notes on the Standards'. Moreover, in order to promote greater consistency and to avoid unnecessary challenges and arbitrator withdrawals and removals, the Guidelines list specific situations indicating whether they warrant disclosure or disqualification of an arbitrator. Such lists, designated 'Red', 'Orange' and 'Green' (the 'Application Lists'), have been updated and appear at the end of these revised Guidelines.
4. The Guidelines reflect the understanding of the IBA Arbitration Committee as to the best current international practice, firmly rooted in the principles expressed in the General Standards below. The General Standards and the Application Lists are based upon statutes and case law in a cross-section of jurisdictions, and upon the judgement and experience of practitioners involved in international arbitration. In reviewing the 2004 Guidelines, the IBA Arbitration Committee updated its analysis of the laws and practices in a number of jurisdictions. The Guidelines seek to balance the various interests of parties, representatives, arbitrators and arbitration institutions, all of whom have a responsibility for ensuring the integrity, reputation and efficiency of international arbitration. Both the 2004 Working Group and the Subcommittee

in 2012/2014 have sought and considered the views of leading arbitration institutions, corporate counsel and other persons involved in international arbitration through public consultations at IBA annual meetings, and at meetings with arbitrators and practitioners. The comments received were reviewed in detail and many were adopted. The IBA Arbitration Committee is grateful for the serious consideration given to its proposals by so many institutions and individuals.

5. The Guidelines apply to international commercial arbitration and investment arbitration, whether the representation of the parties is carried out by lawyers or non-lawyers, and irrespective of whether or not non-legal professionals serve as arbitrators.
6. These Guidelines are not legal provisions and do not override any applicable national law or arbitral rules chosen by the parties. However, it is hoped that, as was the case for the 2004 Guidelines and other sets of rules and guidelines of the IBA Arbitration Committee, the revised Guidelines will find broad acceptance within the international arbitration community, and that they will assist parties, practitioners, arbitrators, institutions and courts in dealing with these important questions of impartiality and independence. The IBA Arbitration Committee trusts that the Guidelines will be applied with robust common sense and without unduly formalistic interpretation.
7. The Application Lists cover many of the varied situations that commonly arise in practice, but they do not purport to be exhaustive, nor could they be. Nevertheless, the IBA Arbitration Committee is confident that the Application Lists provide concrete guidance that is useful in applying the General Standards. The IBA Arbitration Committee will continue to study the actual use of the Guidelines with a view to furthering their improvement.
8. In 1987, the IBA published *Rules of Ethics for International Arbitrators*. Those Rules cover more topics than these Guidelines, and they remain in effect as to subjects that are not discussed in the Guidelines. The Guidelines supersede the *Rules of Ethics* as to the matters treated here.

Part I: General Standards Regarding Impartiality, Independence and Disclosure

(1) General Principle

Every arbitrator shall be impartial and independent of the parties at the time of accepting an appointment to serve and shall remain so until the final award has been rendered or the proceedings have otherwise finally terminated.

Explanation to General Standard 1:

A fundamental principle underlying these Guidelines is that each arbitrator must be impartial and independent of the parties at the time he or she accepts an appointment to act as arbitrator, and must remain so during the entire course of the arbitration proceeding, including the time period for the correction or interpretation of a final award under the relevant rules, assuming such time period is known or readily ascertainable.

The question has arisen as to whether this obligation should extend to the period during which the award may be challenged before the relevant courts. The decision taken is that this obligation should not extend in this manner, unless the final award may be referred back to the original Arbitral Tribunal under the relevant applicable law or relevant institutional rules. Thus, the arbitrator's obligation in this regard ends when the Arbitral Tribunal has rendered the final award, and any correction or interpretation as may be permitted under the relevant rules has been issued, or the time for seeking the same has elapsed, the proceedings have been finally terminated (for example, because of a settlement), or the arbitrator otherwise no longer has jurisdiction. If, after setting aside or other proceedings, the dispute is referred back to the same Arbitral Tribunal, a fresh round of disclosure and review of potential conflicts of interests may be necessary.

(2) Conflicts of Interest

(a) An arbitrator shall decline to accept an appointment or, if the arbitration has already been commenced, refuse to continue to act as an arbitrator, if he or she has any doubt as to his or her ability to be impartial or independent.

(b) The same principle applies if facts or circumstances exist, or have arisen since the appointment, which, from the point of view of a reasonable third person having knowledge of the relevant facts and circumstances, would give rise to justifiable doubts as to the arbitrator's impartiality or independence, unless the parties have accepted the arbitrator in accordance with the requirements set out in General Standard 4.
(c) Doubts are justifiable if a reasonable third person, having knowledge of the relevant facts and circumstances, would reach the conclusion that there is a likelihood that the arbitrator may be influenced by factors other than the merits of the case as presented by the parties in reaching his or her decision.
(d) Justifiable doubts necessarily exist as to the arbitrator's impartiality or independence in any of the situations described in the Non-Waivable Red List.

Explanation to General Standard 2:

(a) If the arbitrator has doubts as to his or her ability to be impartial and independent, the arbitrator must decline the appointment. This standard should apply regardless of the stage of the proceedings. This is a basic principle that is spelled out in these Guidelines in order to avoid confusion and to foster confidence in the arbitral process.
(b) In order for standards to be applied as consistently as possible, the test for disqualification is an objective one. The wording 'impartiality or independence' derives from the widely adopted Article 12 of the United Nations Commission on International Trade Law (UNCITRAL) Model Law, and the use of an appearance test based on justifiable doubts as to the impartiality or independence of the arbitrator, as provided in Article 12(2) of the UNCITRAL Model Law, is to be applied objectively (a 'reasonable third person test'). Again, as described in the Explanation to General Standard 3(e), this standard applies regardless of the stage of the proceedings.
(c) Laws and rules that rely on the standard of justifiable doubts often do not define that standard. This General Standard is intended to provide some context for making this determination.
(d) The Non-Waivable Red List describes circumstances that necessarily raise justifiable doubts as to the arbitrator's impartiality or independence. For example, because no one is allowed to be his or her own judge, there cannot be identity between an arbitrator and a party. The parties, therefore, cannot waive the conflict of interest arising in such a situation.

(3) Disclosure by the Arbitrator

(a) If facts or circumstances exist that may, in the eyes of the parties, give rise to doubts as to the arbitrator's impartiality or independence, the arbitrator shall disclose such facts or circumstances to the parties, the arbitration institution or other appointing authority (if any, and if so required by the applicable institutional rules) and the co-arbitrators, if any, prior to accepting his or her appointment or, if thereafter, as soon as he or she learns of them.
(b) An advance declaration or waiver in relation to possible conflicts of interest arising from facts and circumstances that may arise in the future does not discharge the arbitrator's ongoing duty of disclosure under General Standard 3(a).
(c) It follows from General Standards 1 and 2(a) that an arbitrator who has made a disclosure considers himself or herself to be impartial and independent of the parties, despite the disclosed facts, and, therefore, capable of performing his or her duties as arbitrator. Otherwise, he or she would have declined the nomination or appointment at the outset, or resigned.
(d) Any doubt as to whether an arbitrator should disclose certain facts or circumstances should be resolved in favour of disclosure.
(e) When considering whether facts or circumstances exist that should be disclosed, the arbitrator shall not take into account whether the arbitration is at the beginning or at a later stage.

Explanation to General Standard 3:

(a) The arbitrator's duty to disclose under General Standard 3(a) rests on the principle that the parties have an interest in being fully informed of any facts or circumstances that may be relevant in their view. Accordingly, General Standard 3(d) provides that any doubt as to whether certain facts or circumstances should be disclosed should be resolved in favour of disclosure.

However, situations that, such as those set out in the Green List, could never lead to disqualification under the objective test set out in General Standard 2, need not be disclosed. As reflected in General Standard 3(c), a disclosure does not imply that the disclosed facts are such as to disqualify the arbitrator under General Standard 2. The duty of disclosure under General Standard 3(a) is ongoing in nature.

(b) The IBA Arbitration Committee has considered the increasing use by prospective arbitrators of declarations in respect of facts or circumstances that may arise in the future, and the possible conflicts of interest that may result, sometimes referred to as 'advance waivers'. Such declarations do not discharge the arbitrator's ongoing duty of disclosure under General Standard 3(a). The Guidelines, however, do not otherwise take a position as to the validity and effect of advance declarations or waivers, because the validity and effect of any advance declaration or waiver must be assessed in view of the specific text of the advance declaration or waiver, the particular circumstances at hand and the applicable law.

(c) A disclosure does not imply the existence of a conflict of interest. An arbitrator who has made a disclosure to the parties considers himself or herself to be impartial and independent of the parties, despite the disclosed facts, or else he or she would have declined the nomination, or resigned. An arbitrator making a disclosure thus feels capable of performing his or her duties. It is the purpose of disclosure to allow the parties to judge whether they agree with the evaluation of the arbitrator and, if they so wish, to explore the situation further. It is hoped that the promulgation of this General Standard will eliminate the misconception that disclosure itself implies doubts sufficient to disqualify the arbitrator, or even creates a presumption in favour of disqualification. Instead, any challenge should only be successful if an objective test, as set forth in General Standard 2 above, is met. Under Comment 5 of the Practical Application of the General Standards, a failure to disclose certain facts and circumstances that may, in the eyes of the parties, give rise to doubts as to the arbitrator's impartiality or independence, does not necessarily mean that a conflict of interest exists, or that a disqualification should ensue.

(d) In determining which facts should be disclosed, an arbitrator should take into account all circumstances known to him or her. If the arbitrator finds that he or she should make a disclosure, but that professional secrecy rules or other rules of practice or professional conduct prevent such disclosure, he or she should not accept the appointment, or should resign.

(e) Disclosure or disqualification (as set out in General Standards 2 and 3) should not depend on the particular stage of the arbitration. In order to determine whether the arbitrator should disclose, decline the appointment or refuse to continue to act, the facts and circumstances alone are relevant, not the current stage of the proceedings, or the consequences of the withdrawal. As a practical matter, arbitration institutions may make a distinction depending on the stage of the arbitration. Courts may likewise apply different standards. Nevertheless, no distinction is made by these Guidelines depending on the stage of the arbitral proceedings. While there are practical concerns, if an arbitrator must withdraw after the arbitration has commenced, a distinction based on the stage of the arbitration would be inconsistent with the General Standards.

(4) Waiver by the Parties

(a) If, within 30 days after the receipt of any disclosure by the arbitrator, or after a party otherwise learns of facts or circumstances that could constitute a potential conflict of interest for an arbitrator, a party does not raise an express objection with regard to that arbitrator, subject to paragraphs (b) and (c) of this General Standard, the party is deemed to have waived any potential conflict of interest in respect of the arbitrator based on such facts or circumstances and may not raise any objection based on such facts or circumstances at a later stage.

(b) However, if facts or circumstances exist as described in the Non-Waivable Red List, any waiver by a party (including any declaration or advance waiver, such as that contemplated in General Standard 3(b)), or any agreement by the parties to have such a person serve as arbitrator, shall be regarded as invalid.

(c) A person should not serve as an arbitrator when a conflict of interest, such as those exemplified in the Waivable Red List, exists. Nevertheless, such a person may accept appointment as arbitrator, or continue to act as an arbitrator, if the following conditions are met:

(i) all parties, all arbitrators and the arbitration institution, or other appointing authority (if any), have full knowledge of the conflict of interest; and
(ii) all parties expressly agree that such a person may serve as arbitrator, despite the conflict of interest.

(d) An arbitrator may assist the parties in reaching a settlement of the dispute, through conciliation, mediation or otherwise, at any stage of the proceedings. However, before doing so, the arbitrator should receive an express agreement by the parties that acting in such a manner shall not disqualify the arbitrator from continuing to serve as arbitrator. Such express agreement shall be considered to be an effective waiver of any potential conflict of interest that may arise from the arbitrator's participation in such a process, or from information that the arbitrator may learn in the process. If the assistance by the arbitrator does not lead to the final settlement of the case, the parties remain bound by their waiver. However, consistent with General Standard 2(a) and notwithstanding such agreement, the arbitrator shall resign if, as a consequence of his or her involvement in the settlement process, the arbitrator develops doubts as to his or her ability to remain impartial or independent in the future course of the arbitration.

Explanation to General Standard 4:

(a) Under General Standard 4(a), a party is deemed to have waived any potential conflict of interest, if such party has not raised an objection in respect of such conflict of interest within 30 days. This time limit should run from the date on which the party learns of the relevant facts or circumstances, including through the disclosure process.

(b) General Standard 4(b) serves to exclude from the scope of General Standard 4(a) the facts and circumstances described in the Non-Waivable Red List. Some arbitrators make declarations that seek waivers from the parties with respect to facts or circumstances that may arise in the future. Irrespective of any such waiver sought by the arbitrator, as provided in General Standard 3(b), facts and circumstances arising in the course of the arbitration should be disclosed to the parties by virtue of the arbitrator's ongoing duty of disclosure.

(c) Notwithstanding a serious conflict of interest, such as those that are described by way of example in the Waivable Red List, the parties may wish to engage such a person as an arbitrator. Here, party autonomy and the desire to have only impartial and independent arbitrators must be balanced. Persons with a serious conflict of interest, such as those that are described by way of example in the Waivable Red List, may serve as arbitrators only if the parties make fully informed, explicit waivers.

(d) The concept of the Arbitral Tribunal assisting the parties in reaching a settlement of their dispute in the course of the arbitration proceedings is well-established in some jurisdictions, but not in others. Informed consent by the parties to such a process prior to its beginning should be regarded as an effective waiver of a potential conflict of interest. Certain jurisdictions may require such consent to be in writing and signed by the parties. Subject to any requirements of applicable law, express consent may be sufficient and may be given at a hearing and reflected in the minutes or transcript of the proceeding. In addition, in order to avoid parties using an arbitrator as mediator as a means of disqualifying the arbitrator, the General Standard makes clear that the waiver should remain effective, if the mediation is unsuccessful. In giving their express consent, the parties should realise the consequences of the arbitrator assisting them in a settlement process, including the risk of the resignation of the arbitrator.

(5) Scope

(a) These Guidelines apply equally to tribunal chairs, sole arbitrators and co-arbitrators, howsoever appointed.

(b) Arbitral or administrative secretaries and assistants, to an individual arbitrator or the Arbitral Tribunal, are bound by the same duty of independence and impartiality as arbitrators, and it is the responsibility of the Arbitral Tribunal to ensure that such duty is respected at all stages of the arbitration.

Explanation to General Standard 5:

(a) Because each member of an Arbitral Tribunal has an obligation to be impartial and independent, the General Standards do not distinguish between sole arbitrators, tribunal chairs, party-appointed arbitrators or arbitrators appointed by an institution.

(b) Some arbitration institutions require arbitral or administrative secretaries and assistants to sign a declaration of independence and impartiality. Whether or not such a requirement exists, arbitral or administrative secretaries and assistants to the Arbitral Tribunal are bound by the same duty of independence and impartiality (including the duty of disclosure) as arbitrators, and it is the responsibility of the Arbitral Tribunal to ensure that such duty is respected at all stages of the arbitration. Furthermore, this duty applies to arbitral or administrative secretaries and assistants to either the Arbitral Tribunal or individual members of the Arbitral Tribunal.

(6) Relationships

(a) The arbitrator is in principle considered to bear the identity of his or her law firm, but when considering the relevance of facts or circumstances to determine whether a potential conflict of interest exists, or whether disclosure should be made, the activities of an arbitrator's law firm, if any, and the relationship of the arbitrator with the law firm, should be considered in each individual case. The fact that the activities of the arbitrator's firm involve one of the parties shall not necessarily constitute a source of such conflict, or a reason for disclosure. Similarly, if one of the parties is a member of a group with which the arbitrator's firm has a relationship, such fact should be considered in each individual case, but shall not necessarily constitute by itself a source of a conflict of interest, or a reason for disclosure.

(b) If one of the parties is a legal entity, any legal or physical person having a controlling influence on the legal entity, or a direct economic interest in, or a duty to indemnify a party for, the award to be rendered in the arbitration, may be considered to bear the identity of such party.

Explanation to General Standard 6:

(a) The growing size of law firms should be taken into account as part of today's reality in international arbitration. There is a need to balance the interests of a party to appoint the arbitrator of its choice, who may be a partner at a large law firm, and the importance of maintaining confidence in the impartiality and independence of international arbitrators. The arbitrator must, in principle, be considered to bear the identity of his or her law firm, but the activities of the arbitrator's firm should not automatically create a conflict of interest. The relevance of the activities of the arbitrator's firm, such as the nature, timing and scope of the work by the law firm, and the relationship of the arbitrator with the law firm, should be considered in each case. General Standard 6(a) uses the term 'involve' rather than 'acting for' because the relevant connections with a party may include activities other than representation on a legal matter. Although barristers' chambers should not be equated with law firms for the purposes of conflicts, and no general standard is proffered for barristers' chambers, disclosure may be warranted in view of the relationships among barristers, parties or counsel. When a party to an arbitration is a member of a group of companies, special questions regarding conflicts of interest arise. Because individual corporate structure arrangements vary widely, a catch-all rule is not appropriate. Instead, the particular circumstances of an affiliation with another entity within the same group of companies, and the relationship of that entity with the arbitrator's law firm, should be considered in each individual case.

(b) When a party in international arbitration is a legal entity, other legal and physical persons may have a controlling influence on this legal entity, or a direct economic interest in, or a duty to indemnify a party for, the award to be rendered in the arbitration. Each situation should be assessed individually, and General Standard 6(b) clarifies that such legal persons and individuals may be considered effectively to be that party. Third-party funders and insurers in relation to the dispute may have a direct economic interest in the award, and as such may be considered to be the equivalent of the party. For these purposes, the terms 'third-party funder' and 'insurer' refer to any person or entity that is contributing funds, or other material support, to the prosecution or defence of the case and that has a direct economic interest in, or a duty to indemnify a party for, the award to be rendered in the arbitration.

(7) Duty of the Parties and the Arbitrator

(a) A party shall inform an arbitrator, the Arbitral Tribunal, the other parties and the arbitration institution or other appointing authority (if any) of any relationship, direct or indirect, between the arbitrator and the party (or another company of the same group of companies, or an individual having a controlling influence on the party in the arbitration), or between the arbitrator and any person or entity with a direct economic interest in, or a duty to indemnify a party for, the award to be rendered in the arbitration. The party shall do so on its own initiative at the earliest opportunity.

(b) A party shall inform an arbitrator, the Arbitral Tribunal, the other parties and the arbitration institution or other appointing authority (if any) of the identity of its counsel appearing in the arbitration, as well as of any relationship, including membership of the same barristers' chambers, between its counsel and the arbitrator. The party shall do so on its own initiative at the earliest opportunity, and upon any change in its counsel team.

(c) In order to comply with General Standard 7(a), a party shall perform reasonable enquiries and provide any relevant information available to it.

(d) An arbitrator is under a duty to make reasonable enquiries to identify any conflict of interest, as well as any facts or circumstances that may reasonably give rise to doubts as to his or her impartiality or independence. Failure to disclose a conflict is not excused by lack of knowledge, if the arbitrator does not perform such reasonable enquiries.

Explanation to General Standard 7:

(a) The parties are required to disclose any relationship with the arbitrator. Disclosure of such relationships should reduce the risk of an unmeritorious challenge of an arbitrator's impartiality or independence based on information learned after the appointment. The parties' duty of disclosure of any relationship, direct or indirect, between the arbitrator and the party (or another company of the same group of companies, or an individual having a controlling influence on the party in the arbitration) has been extended to relationships with persons or entities having a direct economic interest in the award to be rendered in the arbitration, such as an entity providing funding for the arbitration, or having a duty to indemnify a party for the award.

(b) Counsel appearing in the arbitration, namely the persons involved in the representation of the parties in the arbitration, must be identified by the parties at the earliest opportunity. A party's duty to disclose the identity of counsel appearing in the arbitration extends to all members of that party's counsel team and arises from the outset of the proceedings.

(c) In order to satisfy their duty of disclosure, the parties are required to investigate any relevant information that is reasonably available to them. In addition, any party to an arbitration is required, at the outset and on an ongoing basis during the entirety of the proceedings, to make a reasonable effort to ascertain and to disclose available information that, applying the general standard, might affect the arbitrator's impartiality or independence.

(d) In order to satisfy their duty of disclosure under the Guidelines, arbitrators are required to investigate any relevant information that is reasonably available to them.

Part II: Practical Application of the General Standards

1. If the Guidelines are to have an important practical influence, they should address situations that are likely to occur in today's arbitration practice and should provide specific guidance to arbitrators, parties, institutions and courts as to which situations do or do not constitute conflicts of interest, or should or should not be disclosed. For this purpose, the Guidelines categorise situations that may occur in the following Application Lists. These lists cannot cover every situation. In all cases, the General Standards should control the outcome.
2. The Red List consists of two parts: 'a Non-Waivable Red List' (see General Standards 2(d) and 4(b)); and 'a Waivable Red List' (see General Standard 4(c)). These lists are non-exhaustive and detail specific situations that, depending on the facts of a given case, give rise to justifiable doubts as to the arbitrator's impartiality and independence. That is, in these circumstances, an objective conflict of interest exists from the point of view of a reasonable third person having knowledge of the relevant facts and circumstances (see General Standard 2(b)).

The Non-Waivable Red List includes situations deriving from the overriding principle that no person can be his or her own judge. Therefore, acceptance of such a situation cannot cure the conflict. The Waivable Red List covers situations that are serious but not as severe. Because of their seriousness, unlike circumstances described in the Orange List, these situations should be considered waivable, but only if and when the parties, being aware of the conflict of interest situation, expressly state their willingness to have such a person act as arbitrator, as set forth in General Standard 4(c).

3. The Orange List is a non-exhaustive list of specific situations that, depending on the facts of a given case, may, in the eyes of the parties, give rise to doubts as to the arbitrator's impartiality or independence. The Orange List thus reflects situations that would fall under General Standard 3(a), with the consequence that the arbitrator has a duty to disclose such situations. In all these situations, the parties are deemed to have accepted the arbitrator if, after disclosure, no timely objection is made, as established in General Standard 4(a).
4. Disclosure does not imply the existence of a conflict of interest; nor should it by itself result either in a disqualification of the arbitrator, or in a presumption regarding disqualification. The purpose of the disclosure is to inform the parties of a situation that they may wish to explore further in order to determine whether objectively—that is, from the point of view of a reasonable third person having knowledge of the relevant facts and circumstances—there are justifiable doubts as to the arbitrator's impartiality or independence. If the conclusion is that there are no justifiable doubts, the arbitrator can act. Apart from the situations covered by the Non-Waivable Red List, he or she can also act if there is no timely objection by the parties or, in situations covered by the Waivable Red List, if there is a specific acceptance by the parties in accordance with General Standard 4(c). If a party challenges the arbitrator, he or she can nevertheless act, if the authority that rules on the challenge decides that the challenge does not meet the objective test for disqualification.
5. A later challenge based on the fact that an arbitrator did not disclose such facts or circumstances should not result automatically in non-appointment, later disqualification or a successful challenge to any award. Nondisclosure cannot by itself make an arbitrator partial or lacking independence: only the facts or circumstances that he or she failed to disclose can do so.
6. Situations not listed in the Orange List or falling outside the time limits used in some of the Orange List situations are generally not subject to disclosure. However, an arbitrator needs to assess on a case-by-case basis whether a given situation, even though not mentioned in the Orange List, is nevertheless such as to give rise to justifiable doubts as to his or her impartiality or independence. Because the Orange List is a non-exhaustive list of examples, there may be situations not mentioned, which, depending on the circumstances, may need to be disclosed by an arbitrator. Such may be the case, for example, in the event of repeat past appointments by the same party or the same counsel beyond the three-year period provided for in the Orange List, or when an arbitrator concurrently acts as counsel in an unrelated case in which similar issues of law are raised. Likewise, an appointment made by the same party or the same counsel appearing before an arbitrator, while the case is ongoing, may also have to be disclosed, depending on the circumstances. While the Guidelines do not require disclosure of the fact that an arbitrator concurrently serves, or has in the past served, on the same Arbitral Tribunal with another member of the tribunal, or with one of the counsel in the current proceedings, an arbitrator should assess on a case-by-case basis whether the fact of having frequently served as counsel with, or as an arbitrator on, Arbitral Tribunals with another member of the tribunal may create a perceived imbalance within the tribunal. If the conclusion is 'yes', the arbitrator should consider a disclosure.
7. The Green List is a non-exhaustive list of specific situations where no appearance and no actual conflict of interest exists from an objective point of view. Thus, the arbitrator has no duty to disclose situations falling within the Green List. As stated in the Explanation to General Standard 3(a), there should be a limit to disclosure, based on reasonableness; in some situations, an objective test should prevail over the purely subjective test of 'the eyes' of the parties.
8. The borderline between the categories that comprise the Lists can be thin. It can be debated whether a certain situation should be on one List instead of another. Also, the Lists contain, for various situations, general terms such as 'significant' and 'relevant'. The Lists reflect

international principles and best practices to the extent possible. Further definition of the norms, which are to be interpreted reasonably in light of the facts and circumstances in each case, would be counterproductive.

1. Non-Waivable Red List

1.1 There is an identity between a party and the arbitrator, or the arbitrator is a legal representative or employee of an entity that is a party in the arbitration.
1.2 The arbitrator is a manager, director or member of the supervisory board, or has a controlling influence on one of the parties or an entity that has a direct economic interest in the award to be rendered in the arbitration.
1.3 The arbitrator has a significant financial or personal interest in one of the parties, or the outcome of the case.
1.4 The arbitrator or his or her firm regularly advises the party, or an affiliate of the party, and the arbitrator or his or her firm derives significant financial income therefrom.

2. Waivable Red List

2.1 Relationship of the arbitrator to the dispute
 2.1.1 The arbitrator has given legal advice, or provided an expert opinion, on the dispute to a party or an affiliate of one of the parties.
 2.1.2 The arbitrator had a prior involvement in the dispute.
2.2 Arbitrator's direct or indirect interest in the dispute
 2.2.1 The arbitrator holds shares, either directly or indirectly, in one of the parties, or an affiliate of one of the parties, this party or an affiliate being privately held.
 2.2.2 A close family member[3] of the arbitrator has a significant financial interest in the outcome of the dispute.
 2.2.3 The arbitrator, or a close family member of the arbitrator, has a close relationship with a non-party who may be liable to recourse on the part of the unsuccessful party in the dispute.
2.3 Arbitrator's relationship with the parties or counsel
 2.3.1 The arbitrator currently represents or advises one of the parties, or an affiliate of one of the parties.
 2.3.2 The arbitrator currently represents or advises the lawyer or law firm acting as counsel for one of the parties.
 2.3.3 The arbitrator is a lawyer in the same law firm as the counsel to one of the parties.
 2.3.4 The arbitrator is a manager, director or member of the supervisory board, or has a controlling influence in an affiliate[4] of one of the parties, if the affiliate is directly involved in the matters in dispute in the arbitration.
 2.3.5 The arbitrator's law firm had a previous but terminated involvement in the case without the arbitrator being involved himself or herself.
 2.3.6 The arbitrator's law firm currently has a significant commercial relationship with one of the parties, or an affiliate of one of the parties.
 2.3.7 The arbitrator regularly advises one of parties, but neither the arbitrator nor his or her firm derives a significant financial income therefrom.
 2.3.8 The arbitrator has a close family relationship with one of the parties, or with a manager, director or member of the supervisory board, or any person having a controlling influence in one of the parties, or an affiliate of one of the parties, or with a counsel representing a party.
 2.3.9 A close family member of the arbitrator has a significant financial or personal interest in one of the parties, or an affiliate of one of the parties.

[3] Throughout the Application Lists, the term 'close family member' refers to a: spouse, sibling, child, parent or life partner, in addition to any other family member with whom a close relationship exists.

[4] Throughout the Application Lists, the term 'affiliate' encompasses all companies in a group of companies, including the parent company.

3. Orange List

3.1 Previous services for one of the parties or other involvement in the case

3.1.1 The arbitrator has, within the past three years, served as counsel for one of the parties, or an affiliate of one of the parties, or has previously advised or been consulted by the party, or an affiliate of the party, making the appointment in an unrelated matter, but the arbitrator and the party, or the affiliate of the party, have no ongoing relationship.

3.1.2 The arbitrator has, within the past three years, served as counsel against one of the parties, or an affiliate of one of the parties, in an unrelated matter.

3.1.3 The arbitrator has, within the past three years, been appointed as arbitrator on two or more occasions by one of the parties, or an affiliate of one of the parties.[5]

3.1.4 The arbitrator's law firm has, within the past three years, acted for or against one of the parties, or an affiliate of one of the parties, in an unrelated matter without the involvement of the arbitrator.

3.1.5 The arbitrator currently serves, or has served within the past three years, as arbitrator in another arbitration involving one of the parties, or an affiliate of one of the parties.

3.2 Current services for one of the parties

3.2.1 The arbitrator's law firm is currently rendering services to one of the parties, or to an affiliate of one of the parties, without creating a significant commercial relationship for the law firm and without the involvement of the arbitrator.

3.2.2 A law firm or other legal organisation that shares significant fees or other revenues with the arbitrator's law firm renders services to one of the parties, or an affiliate of one of the parties, before the Arbitral Tribunal.

3.2.3 The arbitrator or his or her firm represents a party, or an affiliate of one of the parties to the arbitration, on a regular basis, but such representation does not concern the current dispute.

3.3 Relationship between an arbitrator and another arbitrator or counsel

3.3.1 The arbitrator and another arbitrator are lawyers in the same law firm.

3.3.2 The arbitrator and another arbitrator, or the counsel for one of the parties, are members of the same barristers' chambers.

3.3.3 The arbitrator was, within the past three years, a partner of, or otherwise affiliated with, another arbitrator or any of the counsel in the arbitration.

3.3.4 A lawyer in the arbitrator's law firm is an arbitrator in another dispute involving the same party or parties, or an affiliate of one of the parties.

3.3.5 A close family member of the arbitrator is a partner or employee of the law firm representing one of the parties, but is not assisting with the dispute.

3.3.6 A close personal friendship exists between an arbitrator and a counsel of a party.

3.3.7 Enmity exists between an arbitrator and counsel appearing in the arbitration.

3.3.8 The arbitrator has, within the past three years, been appointed on more than three occasions by the same counsel, or the same law firm.

3.3.9 The arbitrator and another arbitrator, or counsel for one of the parties in the arbitration, currently act or have acted together within the past three years as co-counsel.

3.4 Relationship between arbitrator and party and others involved in the arbitration

3.4.1 The arbitrator's law firm is currently acting adversely to one of the parties, or an affiliate of one of the parties.

3.4.2 The arbitrator has been associated with a party, or an affiliate of one of the parties, in a professional capacity, such as a former employee or partner.

3.4.3 A close personal friendship exists between an arbitrator and a manager or director or a member of the supervisory board of: a party; an entity that has a direct economic

[5] It may be the practice in certain types of arbitration, such as maritime, sports or commodities arbitration, to draw arbitrators from a smaller or specialised pool of individuals. If in such fields it is the custom and practice for parties to frequently appoint the same arbitrator in different cases, no disclosure of this fact is required, where all parties in the arbitration should be familiar with such custom and practice.

interest in the award to be rendered in the arbitration; or any person controlling shareholder interest, on one of the parties or an affiliate of one of the parties or a witness or expert.

3.4.4 Enmity exists between an arbitrator and a manager or director or a member of the supervisory board of: a party; an entity that has a direct economic interest in the award; or any person having a controlling influence in one of the parties or an affiliate of one of the parties or a witness or expert.

3.4.5 If the arbitrator is a former judge, he or she has, within the past three years, heard a significant case involving one of the parties, or an affiliate of one of the parties.

3.5 Other circumstances

3.5.1 The arbitrator holds shares, either directly or indirectly, that by reason of number or denomination constitute a material holding in one of the parties, or an affiliate of one of the parties, this party or affiliate being publicly listed.

3.5.2 The arbitrator has publicly advocated a position on the case, whether in a published paper, or speech, or otherwise.

3.5.3 The arbitrator holds a position with the appointing authority with respect to the dispute.

3.5.4 The arbitrator is a manager, director or member of the supervisory board, or has a controlling influence on an affiliate of one of the parties, where the affiliate is not directly involved in the matters in dispute in the arbitration.

4. Green List

4.1 Previously expressed legal opinions

4.1.1 The arbitrator has previously expressed a legal opinion (such as in a law review article or public lecture) concerning an issue that also arises in the arbitration (but this opinion is not focused on the case).

4.2 Current services for one of the parties

4.2.1 A firm, in association or in alliance with the arbitrator's law firm, but that does not share significant fees or other revenues with the arbitrator's law firm, renders services to one of the parties, or an affiliate of one of the parties, in an unrelated matter.

4.3 Contacts with another arbitrator, or with counsel for one of the parties

4.3.1 The arbitrator has a relationship with another arbitrator, or with the counsel for one of the parties, through membership in the same professional association, or social or charitable organisation, or through a social media network.

4.3.2 The arbitrator and counsel for one of the parties have previously served together as arbitrators.

4.3.3 The arbitrator teaches in the same faculty or school as another arbitrator or counsel to one of the parties, or serves as an officer of a professional association or social or charitable organisation with another arbitrator or counsel for one of the parties.

4.3.4 The arbitrator was a speaker, moderator or organiser in one or more conferences, or participated in seminars or working parties of a professional, social or charitable organisation, with another arbitrator or counsel to the parties.

4.4 Contacts between the arbitrator and one of the parties

4.4.1 The arbitrator has had an initial contact with a party, or an affiliate of a party (or their counsel) prior to appointment, if this contact is limited to the arbitrator's availability and qualifications to serve, or to the names of possible candidates for a chairperson, and did not address the merits or procedural aspects of the dispute, other than to provide the arbitrator with a basic understanding of the case.

4.4.2 The arbitrator holds an insignificant amount of shares in one of the parties, or an affiliate of one of the parties, which is publicly listed.

4.4.3 The arbitrator and a manager, director or member of the supervisory board, or any person having a controlling influence on one of the parties, or an affiliate of one of the parties, have worked together as joint experts, or in another professional capacity, including as arbitrators in the same case.

4.4.4 The arbitrator has a relationship with one of the parties or its affiliates through a social media network.

BIBLIOGRAPHY

Aden, *Internationale Handelsschiedsgerichtsbarkeit*, 2nd edn, C H Beck 2003
Aden, "Verfahrensverstoß und Ursächlichkeit für den Schiedsspruch im Aufhebungsverfahren nach § 1059 Abs. 2 Nr. 1 d ZPO," DZWIR 2013, 149
Adolphsen, Case note on LG München I, Decision of February 29, 2000, 7 O 3106/00, SpuRt 2000, 159
Adolphsen, *Internationale Dopingstrafen*, Mohr Siebeck 2003
Altenkirch, "Die Beendigung des Schiedsrichtervertrags durch den Schiedsrichter," SchiedsVZ 2014, 113
Althammer, "Verjährungshemmung durch unzulässige Klage des Rechtsnachfolgers," NJW 2011, 2172
Arbitration in Germany, see Böckstiegel/Kröll/Nacimiento (eds)
Ashford, *Handbook on International Commercial Arbitration*, Juris Publishing 2009
Bamberger/Roth (eds), *Beck'scher Online-Kommentar BGB*, 36th edn, C H Beck 2015
Bandel, *Einstweiliger Rechtsschutz im Schiedsverfahren—Zulässigkeit und Wirkungen schiedsrichterlicher und gerichtlicher einstweiliger Maßnahmen gemäß den Bestimmungen des SchiedsVfG*, C H Beck 2000
Barona Vilar, "Die neuen Reformen der UNCITRAL im Bereich des einstweiligen Rechtsschutzes in der Schiedsgerichtsbarkeit," in: Stürner/Matsumoto/Lüke/Deguchi (eds), *Festschrift für Dieter Leipold zum 70. Geburtstag*, Mohr Siebeck 2009, p 853
Bartels, "Bedeutung der Streitverkündung vor dem staatlichen Gericht für das nachfolgende schiedsrichterliche Verfahren," BB 2001, Beil. 7, p 20
Bartels, "Geheimnisverrat des Dissenters im schiedsrichterlichen Verfahren?," SchiedsVZ 2014, 133
Bauer/Arnold/Kramer, "*Schiedsvereinbarungen mit Geschäftsführern und Vorstandsmitgliedern*," AG 2014, 677
Baumbach/Hopt (eds), *Handelsgesetzbuch*, 36th edn, C H Beck 2014
Baumbach/Lauterbach/Albers/Hartmann (eds), *Zivilprozessordnung*, 74th edn, C H Beck 2016
Baumert, "Ordre public international versus ordre public interne bei inländischen Schiedssprüchen," SchiedsVZ 2014, 139
BeckOGK, see Gsell/Krüger/Lorenz/Mayer (eds)
BeckOK BGB, see Bamberger/Roth (eds)
BeckOK ZPO, see Vorwerk/Wolf (eds)
Beck'sches Rechtsanwaltshandbuch, see Büchting/Heussen (eds)
Benkard (ed), *Patentgesetz*, 11th edn, C H Beck 2015
Berger, Case note on BGH, Decision of December 3, 1993, III ZR 30/91, DZWIR 1993, 466
Berger, *The Creeping Codification of the Lex Mercatoria*, Kluwer Law International 1999
Berger, Case note on BayObLG, Decision of December 15, 1999, 4 Z Sch 23/99, EWiR 2000, 199

Berger, "Herausforderungen für die (deutsche) Schiedsgerichtsbarkeit," SchiedsVZ 2009, 289

Berger, *The Creeping Codification of the New Lex Mercatoria*, 2nd edn, Kluwer Law International 2010

Berninger/Theißen, "Das Deutsche Sportschiedsgericht in Dopingstreitigkeiten," SpuRt 2008, 185

Bernuth, "Noch einmal: Zur Erstattung von Zeithonorar in Schiedsverfahren," SchiedsVZ 2013, 212

Bertke/Schroeder, "Grenzen der Zeugenvorbereitung im staatlichen Zivilprozess und im Schiedsverfahren," SchiedsVZ 2014, 80

Bezzenberger/Bezzenberger/K Schmidt (eds), *Aktiengesetz Großkommentar, Vol 7/2: §§ 241–277*, 4th edn, 32nd suppl, De Gruyter 2013

Bilda, "Beendigung des Schiedsverfahrens durch Vergleich: Probleme des Schiedsspruchs mit vereinbartem Wortlaut," DB 2004, 171

Blackaby/Partasides/Redfern/Hunter, *Redfern and Hunter on International Arbitration*, 6th edn, Oxford University Press 2015

Böckstiegel, "Die neue Schiedsgerichtsordnung der internationalen Handelskammer," NJW 1977, 463

Böckstiegel, "Zur Vertragsgestaltung und Schiedsgerichtsbarkeit bei Infrastrukturprojekten," in: Berger/Ebke/Elsing/Großfeld/Kühne (eds), *Festschrift für Otto Sandrock zum 70. Geburtstag*, Recht und Wirtschaft 2000, p 95

Böckstiegel (ed), *Schiedsgutachten versus Schiedsgerichtsbarkeit*, Carl Heymanns 2007

Böckstiegel, "Die Schiedsgerichtsbarkeit in Deutschland—Standort und Stellenwert," SchiedsVZ 2009, 3

Böckstiegel, "Aktuelle Probleme der Investitions-Schiedsgerichtsbarkeit aus der Sicht eines Schiedsrichters," SchiedsVZ 2012, 113

Böckstiegel/Berger/Bredow (eds), *Die Beteiligung Dritter an Schiedsverfahren*, Carl Heymanns 2005

Böckstiegel/Kröll/Nacimiento (eds), *Arbitration in Germany—The Model Law in Practice*, 2nd edn, Kluwer Law International 2015

Boecker, Case note on BGH, Decision of November 2, 2000, III ZB 55/99, EWiR 2001, 345

Borges, "Die Anerkennung und Vollstreckung von Schiedssprüchen nach dem neuen Schiedsverfahrensrecht," ZZP 111 (1998), 487

Born, *International Commercial Arbitration*, 2nd edn, Kluwer Law International 2014

Borris, "Streiterledigung beim Unternehmenskauf," in: Briner/Fortier/Berger/Bredow (eds), *Law of International Business and Dispute Settlement in the 21st Century, Recht der Internationalen Wirtschaft und Streiterledigung im 21. Jahrhundert, Liber Amicorum Karl-Heinz Böckstiegel*, Carl Heymanns 2001, p 75

Borris, "Streiterledigung bei (MAC-)Klauseln in Unternehmenskaufverträgen: ein Fall für 'Fast-Track'-Schiedsverfahren," BB 2008, 294

Borris, "Die 'Ergänzenden Regeln für gesellschaftsrechtliche Streitigkeiten' der DIS ('DIS-ERGeS')," SchiedsVZ 2009, 299

Borris/L Schmidt, "Vollstreckbarkeit von Schiedssprüchen und materiellrechtliche Einwendungen des Schiedsbeklagten," SchiedsVZ 2004, 273

Borris/L Schmidt, "Nochmals: Vollstreckbarerklärung von Schiedssprüchen und materiellrechtliche Einwendungen des Schiedsbeklagten—Anmerkung zu den Beschlüssen des OLG Köln vom 23. April 2004, des OLG Düsseldorf vom 19. Januar 2005, des OLG Dresden vom 20. April 2005 und des OLG Koblenz vom 28. Juli 2005," SchiedsVZ 2005, 254

Bredow, "Schiedsspruch mit vereinbartem Wortlaut—Form und Inhalt," SchiedsVZ 2010, 295

Bretzke, "Vertrag und Vergütung des Schiedsrichters," NJW 1968, 1113

Broichmann/Matthäus, "Beurkundung von Schiedsordnungen," SchiedsVZ 2008, 274

Büchting/Heussen (eds), *Beck'sches Rechtsanwaltshandbuch*, 10th edn, C H Beck 2011

Buchwaldt, "Schiedsrichtervergütung bei vorzeitiger Verfahrensbeendigung," NJW 1994, 638

Buchwitz/Schütt, "Die Durchsetzung von Vorschussansprüchen in Schiedsverfahren," SchiedsVZ 2015, 1

Burianski/Reindl, "Truth or Dare? The Conflict Between E-discovery in International Arbitration and German Data Protection Rules," SchiedsVZ 2010, 187

Busse, "Die Bindung Dritter an Schiedsvereinbarungen," SchiedsVZ 2005, 118

Busse, "Der Schiedsvergleich als verfahrensrechtliche Falle," SchiedsVZ 2010, 57

Canaris, *Handelsrecht*, 24th edn, C H Beck 2006

Cherkeh/Schroeder, "Einstweiliger Rechtsschutz durch staatliche Gerichte im Anwendungsbereich einer Athletenvereinbarung," SpuRt 2007, 101

Christ, *Berichtigung, Auslegung und Ergänzung des Schiedsspruchs*, Peter Lang 2008

Craig/Park/Paulsson, *International Chamber of Commerce Arbitration*, 3rd edn, Oceana Publications 2000

Cremades/Lew (eds), *Parallel State and Arbitral Procedures in International Arbitration*, Kluwer Law International 2006

Dasser, "International Arbitration and Setting Aside Proceedings in Switzerland: A Statistical Analysis," 25(3) ASA Bull. 444 (2007)

Dasser, "International Arbitration and Setting Aside Proceedings in Switzerland—An Updated Statistical Analysis," 28(1) ASA Bull. 82 (2010)

Dauses (ed), *Handbuch des EU-Wirtschaftsrechts*, 36th suppl, C H Beck, Status: October 2014

Derains/Schwartz, *A Guide to the ICC Rules of Arbitration*, 2nd edn, Kluwer Law International 2005

Dütz, *Rechtsstaatlicher Gerichtsschutz im Privatrecht, Zum sachlichen Umfang der Zivilgerichtsbarkeit*, Max Gehlen 1970

Ebbing, *Private Zivilgerichte*, C H Beck 2003

Eckstein-Puhl, *Prozessbetrug im Schiedsverfahren—eine Studie zu den vom erschlichenen Schiedsspruch aufgeworfenen Fragen des Aufhebungsverfahrens gemäß § 1059 ZPO*, Peter Lang 2005

Ehricke, "Die Beschleunigung der Finalität von Schiedssprüchen nach dem neuen deutschen Schiedsverfahrensrecht," ZZP 113 (2000), 453

Eidenmüller (ed), *Alternative Streitbeilegung—Neue Entwicklungen und Strategien zur frühzeitigen Konfliktbewältigung*, C H Beck 2011

Eilmansberger, "Die Bedeutung der Art. 81 und 82 EG für Schiedsverfahren," SchiedsVZ 2006, 5

Elsing, "Streitverkündung und Schiedsverfahren," SchiedsVZ 2004, 88

Elsing, "Bemessungsgrundlagen für Honorare und Auslagen der Schiedsrichter," in: DIS (ed), *DIS-Mat. X (Kosten im Schiedsgerichtsverfahren)*, 2005, p 3

Elsing, "Zur Auslegung von Schiedsvereinbarungen," in: Genzow (ed), *Zwischen Vertragsfreiheit und Verbraucherschutz, Festschrift für Friedrich Graf von Westphalen zum 70. Geburtstag*, Otto Schmidt 2010, p 109

Elsing, "Procedural Efficiency in International Arbitration: Choosing the Best of Both Legal Worlds," SchiedsVZ 2011, 114

Engelhardt, "Aus der neueren Rechtsprechung zur Schiedsgerichtsbarkeit," JZ 1987, 227

Erman (ed), *Bürgerliches Gesetzbuch*, 14th edn, Otto Schmidt 2014

Escher/Reichert, "Die subsidiäre Zuständigkeit des Kammergerichts Berlin nach § 1062 Abs. 2 a. E. ZPO: Globale Allzuständigkeit oder minimaler Inlandsbezug?," SchiedsVZ 2007, 71

Fleischer/Goette (eds), *Münchener Kommentar zum Gesetz betreffend die Gesellschaften mit beschränkter Haftung (GmbHG), Vol 2: §§ 35–52*, 2nd edn, C H Beck 2016

Franke/Englert/Kuffer/Meyer-Postelt/Miernik/Halstenberg, *Kommentar zur Streitlösungsordnung für das Bauwesen, SL-Bau: Mediation, Schlichtung, Adjudikation, Schiedsgericht*, Werner 2010

Feldmann, *Rechtsbehelfe in der Zwangsvollstreckung aus Schiedssprüchen*, Dr Kovac 2014

Franzen, "'Parteischiedsrichter'—ein vermeidbarer Mangel der Praxis," NJW 1986, 299

Fry/Greenberg/Mazza, *The Secretariat's Guide to ICC Arbitration*, ICC 2012

Fülbier/Splittgerber, "Keine (Fernmelde-) Geheimnisse vor dem Arbeitgeber?," NJW 2012, 1995

Gaillard/Pinsolle, "Advocacy in Practice: The Use of Parallel Proceedings," in: Bishop/Kehoe (eds), *The Art of Advocacy in International Arbitration*, 2nd edn, Juris Publishing 2010, p 173

Gaillard/Savage, *Fouchard Gaillard Goldman on International Commercial Arbitration*, Kluwer Law International 1999

Gal, *Die Haftung des Schiedsrichters in der internationalen Handelsschiedsgerichtsbarkeit*, Mohr Siebeck 2009

Gaul, "Die Rechtskraft und Aufhebbarkeit des Schiedsspruchs im Verhältnis zur Verbindlichkeit des staatlichen Richterspruchs," in: Berger/Ebke/Elsing/Großfeld/Kühne (eds), *Festschrift für Otto Sandrock zum 70. Geburtstag*, Recht und Wirtschaft 2000, p 285

Gaul, "Der betrügerisch erwirkte Schiedsspruch," in: Deguchi/Lüke/Matsumoto/Stürner (eds), *Festschrift für Dieter Leipold zum 70. Geburtstag*, Mohr Siebeck 2009, p 881

Geimer, Case note on OLG Nürnberg, Decision of November 30, 2004, 12 U 2881/04, SchiedsVZ 2005, 52

Geimer, Case note on BGH, Decision of September 21, 2005, III ZB 18/05, LMK 2006, 166229

Geimer, "Zurück zum Reichsgericht: Irrelevanz der merger-Theorien—Kein Wahlrecht mehr bei der Vollstreckbarerklärung ausländischer Schiedssprüche," IPRax 2010, 346

Geis, "Unternehmen in der Flut elektronischer Kommunikation—Aktuelle Aspekte des Datenschutzes," ZD 2013, 591

Germelmann/Matthes/Prütting, *Arbeitsgerichtsgesetz*, 8th edn, C H Beck 2013

Gerstenmaier, "Beendigung des Schiedsverfahrens durch Beschluss nach § 1056 ZPO," SchiedsVZ 2010, 281

Gerstenmaier, "Zur Verzinslichkeit von Kostenerstattungsforderungen im Schiedsverfahren," SchiedsVZ 2012, 1

Goette, "Auslandsbeurkundungen im Kapitalgesellschaftsrecht," DStR 1996, 709

Goette/Habersack (eds), *Münchener Kommentar zum Aktiengesetz, Vol 4: §§ 179–277*, 3rd edn, C H Beck, Vahlen 2011

Gottwald, "Die sachliche Kontrolle internationaler Schiedssprüche durch staatliche Gerichte," in: Habscheid/Schwab (eds), *Beiträge zum Internationalen Verfahrensrecht und zur Schiedsgerichtsbarkeit, Festschrift für Heinrich Nagel zum 75. Geburtstag*, Aschendorff 1987, p 54

Gottwald/Adolphsen, "Das neue deutsche Schiedsverfahrensrecht," DStR 1998, 1017

Götz, "Der Schiedsrichter zwischen Dienstleistungserbringung und Richtertätigkeit—Zum sogenannten Spruchrichterprivileg im System der Schiedsrichterhaftung," SchiedsVZ 2012, 311

Graf von Westphalen, "Unwirksame Schiedsvereinbarungen mit Verbrauchern—notwendiger Schutz von Vorständen und Geschäftsführern," ZIP 2013, 2184
Greger/Stubbe, *Schiedsgutachten*, C H Beck 2007
Gross, "Zur Inanspruchnahme Dritter vor Schiedsgerichten in Fällen der Durchgriffshaftung," SchiedsVZ 2006, 194
Großkomm AktG, see Bezzenberger/Bezzenberger/K Schmidt (eds)
Gsell/Krüger/Lorenz/Mayer (eds), *Beck'scher Online-Großkommentar BGB*, C H Beck, Status: September 15, 2015
Gusy/Illmer, "Die ICDR Guidelines for Arbitrators Concerning Exchanges of Information—zugleich eine deutsch-U.S.-amerikanische Analyse zur Kostenreduzierung in AAA/ICDR Schiedsverfahren," SchiedsVZ 2008, 284
Haas, "Die Vorlagepflichten des Vollstreckungsgläubigers nach dem New Yorker Übereinkommen über die Anerkennung und Vollstreckung ausländischer Schiedssprüche von 1958," IPRax 2000, 432
Haas, "Aufhebungsklage und Beendigungsbeschluss nach § 1056 Abs. 2 ZPO," SchiedsVZ 2010, 286
Haas, "Das Verhältnis von schiedsgerichtlichem und staatlichem vorläufigem Rechtsschutz—Obergericht Kanton Bern, Entscheid vom 19.4.2012—ZK 12 111," ZZPInt 17 (2012), 347
Häberlein, Case note on arbitral award DIS-SV-217/02, BB 2003, Beil. 8, p 7
Habersack, Case note on BGH, Decision of April 6, 2009, II ZR 255/08—Schiedsfähigkeit II, JZ 2009, 797
Habscheid, "Die sogenannte Schiedsgerichtsbarkeit der Internationalen Handelskammer," RIW 1998, 421
Hamann/Lennarz, "Parallele Verfahren mit identischem Schiedsgericht als Lösung für Mehrparteienkonflikte?," SchiedsVZ 2006, 289
Hamann/Lennarz, "Sieben Regeln für eine schnelle, einfache und gute Schiedsklausel," BB 2007, 1009
Hanefeld/Wittinghofer, "Schiedsklauseln in Allgemeinen Geschäftsbedingungen," SchiedsVZ 2005, 217
Hantke, "Die Bildung des Schiedsgerichts," SchiedsVZ 2003, 269
Harbst, "Korruption und andere ordre public-Verstöße als Einwände im Schiedsverfahren: Inwieweit sind staatliche Gerichte an Sachverhaltsfeststellungen des Schiedsgerichts gebunden?," SchiedsVZ 2007, 22
Hausmann, "Die Aufhebung von Schiedssprüchen nach neuem deutschen Schiedsverfahrensrecht," in: Frank/Hohloch/Schlechtriem (eds), *Festschrift für Hans Stoll zum 75. Geburtstag*, Mohr Siebeck 2001, p 593
Heidel/Hüßtege/Mansel/Noack (eds), *BGB, Vol 1: Allgemeiner Teil, EGBGB*, 2nd edn, Nomos 2011
Henn, "Die Unparteilichkeit des Schiedsrichteramts," BB 1993, Beil. 17, p 13
Henn, *Schiedsverfahrensrecht*, 3rd edn, Müller Juristischer Verlag 2000
Herresthal, "Die Wirksamkeit von Schiedsabreden mit Vorständen und Geschäftsführern bei Organhaftungsstreitigkeiten," ZIP 2014, 345
Heydn, "Bindung des Insolvenzverwalters an eine Schiedsvereinbarung bei der Geltendmachung insolvenzspezifischer Rechte," SchiedsVZ 2010, 182
Hilbig, "Absoluter Verbraucherschutz bei unzulässigen AGB-Schiedsvereinbarungen?," SchiedsVZ 2010, 74
Hilger, "Zur Geltung des beschränkten Untersuchungsgrundsatzes im neuen Schiedsverfahrensrecht," BB 2000, Beil. 8, p 1

Hobeck/Weyhreter, "Anordnung von vorläufigen oder sichernden Maßnahmen durch Schiedsgerichte in ex-parte-Verfahren," SchiedsVZ 2005, 238

Hoffmann-Becking (ed), *Münchener Handbuch des Gesellschaftsrechts, Vol 4: Aktiengesellschaft*, 4th edn, C H Beck 2015

Hohmann (ed), *Arbeitsgerichtsgesetz*, 3rd edn, Nomos 2014

Holtzmann/Neuhaus, *A Guide to the UNCITRAL Model Law on International Commercial Arbitration: Legislative History and Commentary*, Kluwer Law and Taxation 1989, 1994

Horn, "Zwingendes Recht in der internationalen Schiedsgerichtsbarkeit," SchiedsVZ 2008, 209

Horvath, "Schiedsgerichtsbarkeit und Mediation—Ein glückliches Paar?," SchiedsVZ 2005, 292

ICC, ICC Commission Report Techniques for Controlling Time and Costs in Arbitration, 2nd edn, 2012

ICC, ICC Note on the Appointment, Duties and Remuneration of Administrative Secretaries of August 1, 2012

Immenga/Mestmäcker (eds), *Wettbewerbsrecht, Vol 1 EU/Part 2: Kommentar zum Europäischen Kartellrecht*, 5th edn, C H Beck 2012

International Council for Commercial Arbitration, Young ICCA Guide on Arbitral Secretaries of 2014

Jarass/Pieroth (eds), *Grundgesetz für die Bundesrepublik Deutschland, Kommentar*, 13th edn, C H Beck 2014

Jauernig (ed), *Bürgerliches Gesetzbuch*, 15th edn, C H Beck 2014

Karrer, "Naives Sparen birgt Gefahren—Kostenfragen aus Sicht der Parteien und des Schiedsgerichts," SchiedsVZ 2006, 113

Kasolowski/Schnabl, "Schiedsgutachten als Alternative zu Schiedsverfahren bei Streit über Rechtsfragen," SchiedsVZ 2012, 84

Kaufmann-Kohler/Bärtsch, "Discovery in international arbitration: How much is too much?," SchiedsVZ 2004, 13

Kersting, "Die Beendigung einer Schiedsvereinbarung durch Anrufung staatlicher Gerichte," SchiedsVZ 2013, 297

Kindler, "Beurkundungsbedürftigkeit von Schiedsgerichtsordnungen beim GmbH-Beteiligungskauf," NZG 2014, 961

Kleinschmidt, "Die Widerklage gegen einen Dritten im Schiedsverfahren," SchiedsVZ 2006, 142

Knoblach, *Sachverhaltsermittlung in der internationalen Wirtschaftsschiedsgerichtsbarkeit*, Duncker & Humblot 2003

Koch, "Schiedsgerichtsvereinbarungen und Haftpflichtversicherungsschutz," SchiedsVZ 2007, 281

Koepp, "Staatliche Diskriminierungsverbote bei der Auswahl von Schiedsrichtern?," SchiedsVZ 2011, 306

Köhne/Langner, "Geltendmachung von Gegenforderungen im internationalen Schiedsverfahren," RIW 2003, 361

König, "Zur Bestimmung des Schiedsvertragsstatuts bei fehlender Gesetzesgrundlage nach Inkrafttreten der Rom I-Verordnung," SchiedsVZ 2012, 129

Kornblum, Review of Bernd von Hoffmann, Internationale Handelsschiedsgerichtsbarkeit, die Bestimmung des maßgeblichen Rechts, Alfred Metzner 1970, KTS 1972, 59

Kornblum, "'Ordre public transnational', 'ordre public international' und 'ordre public interne' im Recht der privaten Schiedsgerichtsbarkeit," in: Habscheid/Schwab (eds), *Beiträge zum Internationalen Verfahrensrecht und zur Schiedsgerichtsbarkeit, Festschrift für Heinrich Nagel zum 75. Geburtstag*, Aschendorff 1987, p 140

Kornblum, "Das 'Gebot überparteilicher Rechtspflege' und der deutsche schiedsrechtliche ordre public," NJW 1987, 1105

Krapfl, "Zu den formellen Voraussetzungen des Antrags auf Vollstreckbarerklärung eines ausländischen Schiedsspruchs," IPRax 2001, 443

Krause, *Die geschichtliche Entwicklung des Schiedsgerichtswesens in Deutschland*, Carl Heymanns 1930

Kreindler, "Arbitral Forum Shopping," in: Cremades/Lew (eds), *Parallel State and Arbitral Procedures in International Arbitration*, Kluwer Law International 2006, p 153

Kreindler, "Die Internationale Investitionsschiedsgerichtsbarkeit und die Korruption: Eine alte Herausforderung mit neuen Antworten," SchiedsVZ 2010, 2

Kreindler, *Competence-Competence in the Face of Illegality in Contracts and Arbitration Agreements*, The Hague Academy of International Law 2013

Kreindler/Mahlich, "Das neue deutsche Schiedsverfahrensrecht aus ausländischer Sicht," NJW 1998, 563

Kreindler/Schäfer/Wolff, *Schiedsgerichtsbarkeit, Kompendium für die Praxis*, Recht und Wirtschaft 2006

Kremer/Weimann, "Die Aufhebbarkeit von Schiedssprüchen, insbesondere Zwischen- oder Teilschiedssprüchen über den Anspruchsgrund—Widerspruch zu Prinzipien der Prozessökonomie," SchiedsVZ 2007, 238

Kröll, "Das neue deutsche Schiedsrecht vor staatlichen Gerichten: Entwicklungslinien und Tendenzen 1998–2000," NJW 2001, 1173

Kröll, "Antragsvoraussetzungen und Präklusion im Verfahren zur Vollstreckbarerklärung ausländischer Schiedssprüche," IPRax 2002, 384

Kröll, "Schiedsrechtliche Rechtsprechung 2003," SchiedsVZ 2004, 113

Kröll, "Die Schiedsvereinbarung im Verfahren zur Anerkennung und Vollstreckbarerklärung ausländischer Schiedssprüche," ZZP 117 (2004), 453

Kröll, "Die internationale Zuständigkeit deutscher Gerichte für einstweiligen Rechtsschutz bei ausländischem Schiedsort," IHR 2005, 142

Kröll, "Die Entwicklung des Rechts der Schiedsgerichtsbarkeit in den Jahren 2003 und 2004," NJW 2005, 194

Kröll, "Die schiedsrechtliche Rechtsprechung 2005," SchiedsVZ 2006, 203

Kröll, "Die Entwicklung des Rechts der Schiedsgerichtsbarkeit 2005/2006," NJW 2007, 743

Kröll, "Die Entwicklung des Schiedsrechts 2007–2008," NJW 2009, 1183

Kröll, "Die schiedsrechtliche Rechtsprechung des Jahres 2010," SchiedsVZ 2011, 131 and 210

Kröll, "Die schiedsrechtliche Rechtsprechung 2012," SchiedsVZ 2013, 185

Kronke, "Internationale Schiedsverfahren nach der Reform," RIW 1998, 257

Krüger/Rauscher (eds), *Münchener Kommentar zur Zivilprozessordnung, mit Gerichtsverfassungsgesetz und Nebengesetzen, Vol 1: §§ 1–354*, 4th edn, C H Beck 2013

Krüger/Rauscher (eds), *Münchener Kommentar zur Zivilprozessordnung, mit Gerichtsverfassungsgesetz und Nebengesetzen, Vol 2: §§ 355–1024*, 4th edn, C H Beck 2012

Krüger/Rauscher (eds), *Münchener Kommentar zur Zivilprozessordnung, mit Gerichtsverfassungsgesetz und Nebengesetzen, Vol 3: §§ 1025–1109, EGZPO, GVG, EGGVG, UKlaG, Internationales und Europäisches Zivilprozessrecht*, 4th edn, C H Beck 2013

Kuhli, "Drittwirkung von Schiedsvereinbarungen im Insolvenzverfahren," SchiedsVZ 2012, 321

Kühn/Gantenberg, "Die Kostenentscheidung im Schiedsgerichtsverfahren," in: DIS (ed), *DIS-Mat. X (Kosten im Schiedsgerichtsverfahren)*, 2005, p 83

Kuhn/Löhr, "Die Urkundenvorlage nach § 142 ZPO im Spannungsfeld zwischen Sachverhaltsaufklärung und Beibringungsgrundsatz," JR 2011, 369

Lachmann, "Anmerkung zu den Entscheidungen des Bundesgerichtshofs (III ZB 43/99) und des Bayerischen Obersten Landesgerichts (4 Z Sch 5/00)," BB 2000, Beil. 12, p 8

Lachmann, "Gedanken zur Schiedsrichterablehnung aufgrund Sozietätszugehörigkeit," in: Schütze (ed), *Einheit und Vielfalt des Rechts, Festschrift für Reinhold Geimer zum 65. Geburtstag*, C H Beck 2002, p 513

Lachmann, "Klippen für die Schiedsvereinbarung," SchiedsVZ 2003, 28

Lachmann, *Handbuch für die Schiedsgerichtspraxis*, 3rd edn, Otto Schmidt 2008

Lachmann/Lachmann, "Schiedsvereinbarungen im Praxistest," BB 2000, 1633

Landbrecht, "Staatlicher Eilrechtsschutz am deutschen Schiedsort und grenzüberschreitende Vollstreckung," SchiedsVZ 2013, 241

Lappe, "Die Entwicklung des Gerichts- und Notarkostenrechts im Jahr 2005," NJW 2006, 270

Laukemann, "Effektiver einstweiliger Rechtsschutz an der Schnittstelle von Schiedsverfahren und staatlicher Justiz," ZZP 126 (2013), 175

Leisinger, *Vertraulichkeit in internationalen Schiedsverfahren*, Nomos 2012

Leitzen, *Die Anordnung vorläufiger oder sichernder Maßnahmen durch Schiedsgerichte nach § 1041 ZPO*, Carl Heymanns 2002

Lionnet/Lionnet, *Handbuch der internationalen und nationalen Schiedsgerichtsbarkeit*, 3rd edn, Boorberg 2005

Loewenheim/Meessen/Riesenkampff (eds), *Kartellrecht*, 2nd edn, C H Beck 2009

Lörcher, "Zur Stellung des Vorsitzenden im Schiedsgericht," BB 1996, Beil. 15, p 9

Lörcher/Lörcher, *Das Schiedsverfahren—national/international—nach deutschem Recht*, 2nd edn, C F Müller 2001

Lörcher/Lörcher, "Organisation eines Ad-hoc-Schiedsverfahrens," SchiedsVZ 2005, 179

Lotz, "Der Sachverständige im Schiedsverfahren," SchiedsVZ 2011, 203

Lüke/Blenske, "Die Schiedsfähigkeit von Beschlußmängelstreitigkeiten," ZGR 1998, 253

Mack, "Vollstreckungsabwehrklage und § 1053 Abs. 4 ZPO, Zur Zuständigkeit für Vollstreckungsabwehrklagen bei notarieller Vollstreckbarerklärung eines Schiedsspruchs mit vereinbartem Wortlaut," IDR 2006, 36

Magnus/Mankowski, *Brussels I Regulation*, 2nd edn, Sellier, 2012

Mallmann, "Die Bedeutung der Schiedsvereinbarung im Verfahren zur Anerkennung und Vollstreckbarerklärung ausländischer Schiedssprüche," SchiedsVZ 2004, 152

Mankowski, "Der Schiedsspruch mit vereinbartem Wortlaut," ZZP 114 (2001), 37

Mankowski, "Die Ablehnung von Schiedsrichtern," SchiedsVZ 2004, 304

Mankowski, "Rom I-Verordnung und Schiedsverfahren," RIW 2011, 30

Markert/Wilske, "Entwicklungen in der internationalen Schiedsgerichtsbarkeit im Jahr 2009 und Ausblick auf 2010," SchiedsVZ 2010, 62

Mäsch, "Schiedsvereinbarungen mit Verbrauchern," in: Bachmann/Breidenbach/Coester-Waltjen (eds), *Grenzüberschreitungen, Beiträge zum Internationalen Verfahrensrecht und zur Schiedsgerichtsbarkeit, Festschrift für Peter Schlosser zum 70. Geburtstag*, Mohr Siebeck 2005, p 529

Matsuura, "Provisions for the (re)arrangement and strengthened enforceability of Interim Measures related to Arbitral Proceedings—Proposed Revision of International Arbitration Law," in: Stürner/Matsumoto/Lüke/Deguchi (eds), *Festschrift für Dieter Leipold zum 70. Geburtstag*, Mohr Siebeck 2009, p 933

Menz, "The fourth arbitrator? Die Rolle des Administrative Secretary im Schiedsverfahren," SchiedsVZ 2015, 210

Merkt, "Zur sogenannten Präklusionsrechtsprechung des BGH bei der Anerkennung ausländischer Schiedssprüche," in: Bruns/Kern/Münch/Piekenbrock/Stadler/Tsikikas, *Festschrift für Rolf Stürner zum 70. Geburtstag*, Vol II, Mohr Siebeck 2013, p 1303

Michaels, "Anerkennung internationaler Schiedssprüche und ordre public, Anmerkung zu OGH 23.2.1998, 3 Ob 115/95, ZfRV 1999, 24," ZfRV 1999, 5

Moller, "Schiedsverfahrensnovelle und Vollstreckung ausländischer Schiedssprüche," NZG 1999, 143

Mülbert, "Der (zukünftige) Gesellschafter—stets ein Verbraucher?," in: Häuser (ed), *Festschrift für Walther Hadding zum 70. Geburtstag am 8. Mai 2004*, De Gruyter 2004, p 575

Müller/Keilmann, "Beteiligung am Schiedsverfahren wider Willen?," SchiedsVZ 2007, 113

MünchKommAktG, see Goette/Habersack (eds)

MünchKommBGB, see Säcker/Rixecker/Oetker/Limperg (eds) and Säcker/Rixecker/Oetker (eds)

MünchKommGmbHG, see Fleischer/Goette (eds)

MünchKommHGB, see K Schmidt (ed)

MünchKommZPO, see Krüger/Rauscher (eds)

Münchener Handbuch des Gesellschaftsrechts, Vol 3, see Priester/Mayer/Wicke (eds)

Münchener Handbuch des Gesellschaftsrechts, Vol 4, see Hoffmann-Becking (ed)

Musielak/Voit (eds), *Zivilprozessordnung mit Gerichtsverfassungsgesetz, Kommentar*, 12th edn, Vahlen 2015

Nagel/Gottwald, *Internationales Zivilprozessrecht*, 7th edn, Otto Schmidt 2013

Nedden/Büstgens, "Die Beratung des Schiedsgerichts—Konfliktpotential und Lösungswege," SchiedsVZ 2015, 169

Nedden/Herzberg (eds), *Praxiskommentar ICC-SchO/DIS-SchO*, Otto Schmidt 2014

Nelle, *Anspruch, Titel und Vollstreckung im internationalen Rechtsverkehr: Einwendungen gegen einen titulierten Anspruch im deutschen und europäischen Zivilprozeßrecht, mit Vergleichen zum englischen, französischen, schweizerischen und US-amerikanischen Recht*, Mohr Siebeck 2000

Oldenstam/v Pachelbel, "Confidentiality and Arbitration—a few reflections and practical notes," SchiedsVZ 2006, 31

Osterthun, *Schadensfälle im Schiedsverfahren: Vermeidung oder schiedsrichterliche Haftung*, Gregor Brand 2002

Otto, "Präklusion und Verwirkung von Vollstreckungsversagungsgründen bei der Vollstreckung ausländischer Schiedsgerichtsentscheidungen," IPRax 2012, 223

Palandt (ed), *Bürgerliches Gesetzbuch*, 75th edn, C H Beck 2016

Pantle/Kreissl, *Die Praxis des Zivilprozesses*, 4th edn, Kohlhammer 2007

Partasides, "The Fourth Arbitrator? The Role of Secretaries to Tribunals in International Arbitration," (2002) 18(2) Arb. Int'l 147

Pfeiffer, Case note on BGH, Decision of November 8, 2007, III ZB 95/06, LMK 2008, 250684

Pfeiffer, "Die Abwahl des deutschen AGB-Rechts in Inlandsfällen bei Vereinbarung eines Schiedsverfahrens," NJW 2012, 1169

Pitkowitz/Richter, "May a Neutral Third Person Serve as Arbitrator and Mediator in the same Dispute?," SchiedsVZ 2009, 225

Plaßmeier, "Ende des 'Doppelexequatur' bei ausländischen Schiedssprüchen," SchiedsVZ 2010, 82

Pörnbacher/Baur, "Die Reform der Schiedsgerichtsordnung der ICC," BB 2011, 2627

Pörnbacher/Duncker, Case note on OLG München, Decision of June 24, 2014, 34 SchH 1/2014, SchiedsVZ 2015, 207

Pörnbacher/Thiel, "Kostensicherheit in Schiedsverfahren," SchiedsVZ 2010, 14
Priester/Mayer/Wicke (eds), *Münchener Handbuch des Gesellschaftsrechts, Vol 3: Gesellschaft mit beschränkter Haftung*, 4th edn, C H Beck 2012
Prütting, "Zur Rechtsstellung des Schiedsrichters—dargestellt am richterlichen Beratungsgeheimnis," in: Gottwald/Prütting (eds), *Festschrift für Karl Heinz Schwab zum 70. Geburtstag*, C H Beck 1990, p 409
Prütting, "Vertraulichkeit in der Schiedsgerichtsbarkeit und in der Mediation," in: Berger/Bredow/Briner/Fortier (eds), *Law of International Business and Dispute Settlement in the 21st Century, Recht der Internationalen Wirtschaft und Streiterledigung im 21. Jahrhundert, Liber Amicorum Karl-Heinz-Böckstiegel*, Carl Heymanns 2001, p 629
Prütting, "Discovery im deutschen Zivilprozess?," AnwBl 2008, 153
Prütting, "Die rechtliche Stellung des Schiedsrichters," SchiedsVZ 2011, 233
Prütting/Gehrlein (eds), *ZPO, Kommentar*, 7th edn, Luchterhand 2015
Quinke, "§ 1061 ZPO und der Meistbegünstigungsgrundsatz des UNÜ—Zugleich Anmerkung zu BGH, Urt. v. 8.6.2010 (XI ZR 349/08) und BGH, Beschl. v. 30.9.2010 (III ZB 69/09)," SchiedsVZ 2011, 169
Quinke, "Säumnis im Schiedsverfahren," SchiedsVZ 2013, 129
Raeschke-Kessler/Berger, *Recht und Praxis des Schiedsverfahrens*, 3rd edn, RWS 1999
Rechberger, "Die Widersprüchlichkeit eines Schiedsspruches als Aufhebungsgrund nach österreichischem Recht," SchiedsVZ 2006, 169
Reed/Paulsson/Blackaby, *Guide to ICSID Arbitration*, 2nd edn, Kluwer Law International 2010
Reithmann/Martiny (eds), *Internationales Vertragsrecht*, 8th edn, Otto Schmidt 2015
Reul, "Effizienz im Schiedsverfahren," in: Eidenmüller (ed), *Alternative Streitbeilegung—Neue Entwicklungen und Strategien zur frühzeitigen Konfliktbewältigung*, C H Beck 2011, p 25
Rieder/Schoenemann, "Korruptionsverdacht, Zivilprozess und Schiedsverfahren," NJW 2011, 1169
Rieder/Schoenemann, "Suspicion of Corruption in Arbitration: A German Perspective," TDM 3 2013, p 8
Risse/Altenkirch, "Kostenerstattung im Schiedsverfahren: fünf Probleme aus der Praxis," SchiedsVZ 2012, 5
Risse/Frohloff, "Schadensersatzansprüche nach einstweiligen Verfügungen in Schiedsverfahren," SchiedsVZ 2011, 239
Risse/Spehl, "Zehn Ratschläge für das internationale Schiedsverfahren im Vertriebsrecht," ZVertriebsR 2012, 151
Rojahn, "Vorläufiger Rechtsschutz durch staatliche Gerichte bei Schiedsgerichtsabrede—Ist effektiver Rechtsschutz gewährleistet?," in: Harmsen/Jüngst/Rödiger (eds), *Festschrift für Wolfgang von Meibom zum 65. Geburtstag*, Carl Heymanns 2010, p 395
Rojahn/Jerger, "Richterliche Unparteilichkeit und Unabhängigkeit im Zeitalter sozialer Netzwerke," NJW 2014, 1147
Roquette/Otto (eds), *Vertragsbuch Privates Baurecht*, 2nd edn, C H Beck 2011
Roth/Altmeppen (eds), *Gesetz betreffend die Gesellschaften mit beschränkter Haftung*, 8th edn, C H Beck 2015
Säcker/Rixecker/Oetker/Limperg (eds), *Münchener Kommentar zum Bürgerlichen Gesetzbuch, Vol 1 Part 1: Allgemeiner Teil, §§ 1–240, ProstG, AGG*, 7th edn, C H Beck 2015
Säcker/Rixecker/Oetker/Limperg (eds), *Münchener Kommentar zum Bürgerlichen Gesetzbuch, Vol 2: Schuldrecht Allgemeiner Teil*, 7th edn, C H Beck 2016
Säcker/Rixecker/Oetker (eds), *Münchener Kommentar zum Bürgerlichen Gesetzbuch, Vol 4: Schuldrecht, Besonderer Teil II, §§ 611–704, EFZG, TzBfG, KSchG*, 6th edn, C H Beck 2012

Säcker/Rixecker/Oetker (eds), *Münchener Kommentar zum Bürgerlichen Gesetzbuch, Vol 6: Sachenrecht, §§ 854–1296, WEG, ErbbauRG*, 6th edn, C H Beck 2013

Säcker/Rixecker/Oetker (eds), *Münchener Kommentar zum Bürgerlichen Gesetzbuch, Vol 10: Internationales Privatrecht I, Europäisches Kollisionsrecht, Einführungsgesetz zum Bürgerlichen Gesetzbuche (Art. 1–24)*, 6th edn, C H Beck 2015

Saenger (ed), *Zivilprozessordnung: Familienverfahren, Gerichtsverfassung, Europäisches Verfahrensrecht, Handkommentar*, 6th edn, Nomos 2015

Saenger/Uphoff, "Die Geltendmachung von Zinsansprüchen für verauslagte Gerichts- und Anwaltskosten," MDR 2014, 192

Saenger/Uphoff, "Erstattungsfähigkeit anwaltlicher Zeithonorare," NJW 2014, 1412

Sandrock, "Das Gesetz zur Neuregelung des Internationalen Privatrechts und der internationalen Schiedsgerichtsbarkeit," RIW 1987, issue 5, Beil. 2, p 1

Sandrock, "'Gewöhnliche' Fehler in Schiedssprüchen: Wann können sie zur Aufhebung des Schiedsspruchs führen?," BB 2001, 2173

Sandrock, "Schiedsort in Deutschland, Gerichtskosten in den USA: Sind Letztere hier erstattungsfähig?," IDR 2004, 106

Schaaff, "Unterbricht eine Wechselklage die Verjährung der Forderung aus dem Grundgeschäft?," NJW 1986, 1029

Scheef, *Der einstweilige Rechtsschutz und die Stellung der Schiedsrichter bei dem Abschluss von Schiedsvergleichen nach dem deutschen und englischen Schiedsverfahrensrecht, eine rechtsvergleichende Untersuchung*, Peter Lang 2000

Schellhammer, *Zivilprozess*, 14th edn, Müller 2012

Schill, "Öffentlich-rechtliche Schiedsverfahren zwischen Risikobewältigung und Rechtsrisiko," DÖV 2010, 1013

von Schlabrendorff, "Geldwäsche in internationalen Schiedsverfahren," in: Bachmann/Breidenbach/Coester-Waltjen (eds), *Grenzüberschreitungen, Beiträge zum Internationalen Verfahrensrecht und zur Schiedsgerichtsbarkeit, Festschrift für Peter Schlosser zum 70. Geburtstag*, Mohr Siebeck 2005, p 851

Schlosser, "Schiedsgerichtsbarkeit und öffentlich-rechtlich beeinflußte Streitgegenstände," in: Böckstiegel/Glossner (eds), *Festschrift für Arthur Bülow zum 80. Geburtstag*, Carl Heymanns 1981, p 189

Schlosser, "Die perpetuatio litis als rechtsstaatlicher Leitgedanke des nationalen und internationalen Zivilprozeßrechts," in: Habscheid/Schwab (eds), *Beiträge zum Internationalen Verfahrensrecht und zur Schiedsgerichtsbarkeit, Festschrift für Heinrich Nagel zum 75. Geburtstag*, Aschendorff 1987, p 352

Schlosser, *Das Recht der internationalen privaten Schiedsgerichtsbarkeit*, 2nd edn, Mohr Siebeck 1989

Schlosser, "Der Grad der Unabhängigkeit einer Schiedsvereinbarung vom Hauptvertrag," in: Briner/Fortier/Berger/Bredow (eds), *Law of International Business and Dispute Settlement in the 21st Century, Recht der Internationalen Wirtschaft und Streiterledigung im 21. Jahrhundert, Liber Amicorum Karl-Heinz Böckstiegel*, Carl Heymanns 2001, p 697

Schlosser, "Befugnisse und Pflichten des Schiedsgerichtsobmanns," SchiedsVZ 2003, 1

Schlosser, "Verfahrensrechtliche und berufsrechtliche Zulässigkeit der Zeugenvorbereitung," SchiedsVZ 2004, 225

Schlosser, "Der Privatvertrag mit Zeugen und Forumsexperten," RIW 2005, 81

Schlosser, Case note on OLG Düsseldorf, Decision of February 7, 2008, I-20 W 152/07, SchiedsVZ 2008, 261

Schlosser, "EuGVVO und einstweiliger Rechtsschutz betreffend schiedsbefangene Ansprüche," IPRax 2009, 416

Schmeel, "Selbstbindung eines Schiedsgerichts in Verfahrensfragen?," Case note on OLG Frankfurt, Decision of February 17, 2011, 26 Sch 13/10, IBR 2011, 1241

F Schmidt, "Der Schiedsspruch," SchiedsVZ 2013, 32
K Schmidt, "Schiedsfähigkeit von GmbH-Beschlüssen—Eine Skizze mit Ausblicken auf das Recht der AG und der Personengesellschaften," ZGR 1988, 523
K Schmidt, "Schiedsklagen gegen Hauptversammlungsbeschlüsse? Ein Beitrag zum Innenrecht der 'kleinen AG'," AG 1995, 551
K Schmidt, "Kartellrecht im Schiedsverfahren—Neuorientierung durch VO 1/2003 und 7. GWB-Novelle?," BB 2006, 1397
K Schmidt, "Verbraucherbegriff und Verbrauchervertrag—Grundlagen des § 13 BGB," JuS 2006, 1
K Schmidt (ed), *Münchener Kommentar zum Handelsgesetzbuch, Vol 1: Erstes Buch. Handelsstand: §§ 1–104a*, 3rd edn, C H Beck 2010
Schmidt-Ahrendts/Höttler, "Anwendbares Recht bei Schiedsverfahren mit Sitz in Deutschland," SchiedsVZ 2011, 267
Schmidt-Diemnitz, "Internationale Schiedsgerichtsbarkeit—eine empirische Untersuchung," DB 1999, 369
Schneider, "Streitwert und Gebühren bei Vergleich über Hilfsaufrechnung," NJW-Spezial 2010, 475
Schorkopf, "Transparenz im Toll-Haus," NVwZ 2003, 1471
Schreuer, *The ICSID Convention: A Commentary*, 2nd edn, Cambridge University Press 2009
Schroeder, "Mareva Injunctions and Freezing Orders in International Commercial Arbitration," SchiedsVZ 2004, 26
Schroeter, "Der Schiedsspruch mit vereinbartem Wortlaut als Formäquivalent zur notariellen Beurkundung," SchiedsVZ 2006, 298
Schroth, "Einstweiliger Rechtsschutz im deutschen Schiedsverfahren," SchiedsVZ 2003, 102
Schroth, "Wem obliegt im Streitfall die verbindliche Festlegung des Gegenstandswertes/Streitwertes eines Schiedsgerichtsverfahrens?," in: DIS (ed), *DIS-Mat. X (Kosten im Schiedsgerichtsverfahren)*, 2005, p 41
Schumacher, "Das neue 10. Buch der Zivilprozeßordnung im Vergleich zum UNCITRAL-Modellgesetz über die internationale Handelsschiedsgerichtsbarkeit," BB 1998, Beil. 7, p 6
Schütze, "Dissenting Opinions im Schiedsverfahren," in: Heldrich/Uchida (eds), *Festschrift für Hideo Nakamura zum 70. Geburtstag am 2. März 1996*, Seibundo 1996, p 525
Schütze, "Einstweiliger Rechtsschutz im Schiedsverfahren," BB 1998, 1650
Schütze, "Der Schiedsspruch mit vereinbartem Wortlaut," in: Rauscher/Mansel (eds), *Festschrift für Werner Lorenz zum 80. Geburtstag*, Sellier 2001, p 275
Schütze, "Die verkannte Funktion der Schiedsvereinbarung im internationalen Zivilprozessrecht," IPRax 2006, 442
Schütze, "Das Zustandekommen des Schiedsspruchs," SchiedsVZ 2008, 10
Schütze, "No hay materia más confusa... (zu BGH, 30.10.2008—III ZB 17/08, unten S. 519, Nr. 35)," IPRax 2009, 504
Schütze, "Der Abschied vom Doppelexequatur ausländischer Schiedssprüche," RIW 2009, 817
Schütze, "Die gerichtliche Überprüfung von Entscheidungen des Schiedsgerichts," SchiedsVZ 2009, 241
Schütze (ed), *Institutionelle Schiedsgerichtsbarkeit*, 2nd edn, Carl Heymanns 2010
Schütze, "Der Abschied von der Präklusionsrechtsprechung bei der Anerkennung ausländischer Schiedssprüche," RIW 2011, 417

Schütze, *Schiedsgericht und Schiedsverfahren*, 5th edn, C H Beck 2012

Schütze/Weipert/Rieder (eds), *Münchener Vertragshandbuch, Vol 4: Wirtschaftsrecht III*, 7th edn, C H Beck 2012

Schwab, "Schiedsrichterernennung und Schiedsrichtervertrag," in: Lüke (ed), *Festschrift für Gerhard Schiedermair zum 70. Geburtstag*, C H Beck 1976, p 499

Schwab/Walter, *Schiedsgerichtsbarkeit, Systematischer Kommentar zu den Vorschriften der Zivilprozeßordnung, des Arbeitsgerichtsgesetzes, der Staatsverträge und der Kostengesetze über das privatrechtliche Schiedsgerichtsverfahren*, 7th edn, C H Beck, Helbing & Lichtenhahn 2005

Semler, "Schnelligkeit und Wirtschaftlichkeit in Schiedsverfahren," SchiedsVZ 2009, 149

Sessler, Case note on OLG München, Decision of February 13, 1997, 29 U 4891/96, BB 1998, Beil. 9, p 21

Sessler, "Schiedsgutachten in Post-M&A-Streitigkeiten," in: Böckstiegel (ed), *Schiedsgutachten versus Schiedsgerichtsbarkeit*, Carl Heymanns 2007, p 97

Seybold, *Mediation und gerichtliches Verfahren*, Dr Kovac 2009

Siegert, "Die Bedeutung der allgemeinen Grundsätze des Zivilprozeßrechts für die schiedsgerichtliche Praxis," KTS 1956, 33

Solomon, *Die Verbindlichkeit von Schiedssprüchen in der internationalen privaten Schiedsgerichtsbarkeit*, Sellier 2007

Sonnauer, *Die Kontrolle der Schiedsgerichte durch die staatlichen Gerichte*, Carl Heymanns 1992

Spetzler, Case note on KG, Decision of January 20, 2011, 20 Sch 09/09, SchiedsVZ 2011, 287

Spohnheimer, *Gestaltungsfreiheit bei antezipiertem Legalanerkenntnis des Schiedsspruchs*, Mohr Siebeck 2010

Spohnheimer, "Überlegungen zur Dogmatik des schiedsgerichtlichen Vergleichs und des Schiedsspruchs mit vereinbartem Wortlaut," in: Geimer/Schütze (eds), *Recht ohne Grenzen, Festschrift für Athanassios Kaissis zum 65. Geburtstag*, Sellier 2012, p 933

Staudinger, *BGB, Neubearbeitung, Buch 1, Allgemeiner Teil, §§ 134–138; Anh zu § 138: ProstG*, De Gruyter 2011

Staudinger, *BGB, Neubearbeitung, Buch 1, Allgemeiner Teil, §§ 164–240*, De Gruyter 2014

Stein/Jonas (eds), *Kommentar zur Zivilprozessordnung, Vol 2: §§ 41–127a*, 22nd edn, Mohr Siebeck 2004

Stein/Jonas (eds), *Kommentar zur Zivilprozessordnung, Vol 10: §§ 1025–1066*, 23rd edn, Mohr Siebeck 2014

Steinbrück, *Die Unterstützung ausländischer Schiedsverfahren durch staatliche Gerichte, Eine rechtsvergleichende Untersuchung des deutschen, österreichischen, englischen, schweizerischen, französischen und US-amerikanischen Schiedsrechts*, Mohr Siebeck 2009

Steinbrück, "Internationale Zuständigkeit deutscher Gerichte für selbstständige Beweisverfahren in Schiedssachen," IPRax 2010, 424

Stürner, "Hilfspersonen im Schiedsverfahren nach deutschem Recht," SchiedsVZ 2013, 322

Thomas/Putzo (eds), *Zivilprozessordnung, FamFG, Verfahren in Familiensachen, GVG, Einführungsgesetze, EU-Zivilverfahrensrecht, Kommentar*, 36th edn, C H Beck 2015

Thümmel, "Einstweiliger Rechtsschutz im Schiedsverfahren nach dem Entwurf zum Schiedsverfahrens-Neuregelungsgesetz," DZWIR 1997, 133

Trappe, "Richter/Schiedsrichter als Schlichter?," SchiedsVZ 2012, 79

Trappe, "Arbitration in Germany—some aspects and comparison of law," SchiedsVZ 2013, 167

Ullrich, "Außergerichtliche Kontakte zwischen Anwalt und Zeugen im Zivilprozess," NJW 2014, 1341

Voit, Case note on BGH, Decision of November 2, 2000, III ZB 55/99, ZZP 114 (2001), 355

Volze, "Der Sachverständige als Schiedsrichter," DS 2012, 379

Vorwerk/Wolf (eds), *Beck'scher Online-Kommentar ZPO*, 18th edn, C H Beck 2015

Voser, "Harmonization by Promulgating Rules of Best International Practice in International Arbitration," SchiedsVZ 2005, 113

Wagner, *Prozeßverträge: Privatautonomie im Verfahrensrecht*, Mohr Siebeck 1998

Wagner, "Der Notar als Schiedsrichter," DNotZ 2000, 421

Wagner/Bülau, "Procedural Orders by Arbitral Tribunals: In the Stays of Party Agreements?," SchiedsVZ 2013, 6

Walker, "Beseitigung und Durchbrechung der Rechtskraft," in: Canaris/Heldrich/Hopt/Roxin/Schmidt/Widmaier (eds), *50 Jahre Bundesgerichtshof, Festgabe aus der Wissenschaft*, Vol 3, C H Beck 2000, p 367

Walter, "Die Vollstreckbarerklärung als Voraussetzung bestimmter Wirkungen des Schiedsspruchs," in: Gottwald/Prütting (eds), *Festschrift für Karl Heinz Schwab zum 70. Geburtstag*, C H Beck 1990, p 539

Walther/Zimmer, "Mehr Rechtssicherheit für Compliance-Ermittlungen," BB 2013, 2933

Waßmuth, *Richtigkeitskontrolle und Rechtskraft des Schiedsspruchs mit vereinbartem Wortlaut*, Carl Heymanns 2013

Wegen/Wilske, "Die anwendbare Zeitzone für Fristen in internationalen Schiedsverfahren," SchiedsVZ 2003, 124

Weigand, "Discovery in der internationalen Schiedsgerichtsbarkeit," RIW 1992, 361

Weigand, Case note on BGH, Decision of November 2, 2000, III ZB 55/99, LM s 1053 ZPO no 1 p 4

Weigand (ed), *Practitioner's Handbook on International Arbitration*, 1st edn, C H Beck 2002

Weigand (ed), *Practitioner's Handbook on International Commercial Arbitration*, 2nd edn, Oxford University Press 2009

Weiler/Schlickum, *Praxisbuch Mediation: Falldokumentationen und Methodik zur Konfliktlösung*, 2nd edn, C H Beck 2012

Wieczorek/Schütze (eds), *Zivilprozessordnung und Nebengesetze, Vol 4: §§ 253–299a*, 4th edn, De Gruyter 2013

Wiedemann (ed), *Handbuch des Kartellrechts*, 2nd edn, C H Beck 2008

Wighardt, "Verfahrensfragen bei der Zurückverweisung der Sache an das Schiedsgericht," SchiedsVZ 2010, 252

Wilske, "Rechtsprechungsübersicht: Neuere Entscheidungen zur Schiedsgerichtsbarkeit in der US-amerikanischen Rechtsprechung," DAJV Newsletter 2011, 114

Wilske/Markert, "Entwicklungen in der internationalen Schiedsgerichtsbarkeit im Jahr 2010 und Ausblick auf 2011," SchiedsVZ 2011, 57

Wilske/Shore/Ahrens, in: "'Group of Companies Doctrine'—Where Is It Heading?," 17 Am. Rev. Int'l Arb. 73 (2006)

Wirth, Ihr Zeuge, "Herr Rechtsanwalt! Weshalb Civil-Law-Schiedsrichter Common-Law-Verfahrensrecht anwenden," SchiedsVZ 2003, 9

Witte/Hafner, "Schiedsfähigkeit von Beschlussmängelstreitigkeiten im Recht der GmbH am Maßstab der neuen BGH-Rechtsprechung und ihre Auswirkungen," DStR 2009, 2052

Wolf, "'Summarische Verfahren' im neuen Schiedsverfahrensrecht," DB 1999, 1101

Wolf/Hasenstab, "Hybride Verfahrensgestaltung internationaler Schiedsverfahren," RIW 2011, 612

Wolff, "Streitwertfestsetzung bei wertabhängiger Schiedsrichtervergütung—Schiedsrichter in eigener Sache?," SchiedsVZ 2006, 131

Wolff, "Zurückverweisung der Sache an das Schiedsgericht nach Aufhebung des Schiedsspruchs—zu den 'geeigneten Fällen' nach § 1059 Abs. 4 ZPO," SchiedsVZ 2007, 254

Wolff, Case note on BGH, Decision of March 1, 2007, III ZB 7/06, ZZP 120 (2007), 371

Wolff, "Judicial Assistance by German Courts in Aid of International Arbitration," 19 Am. Rev. Int'l Arb. 145 (2008)

Wolff, "Party Autonomy to Agree on Non-Final Arbitration?," 26(3) ASA Bull. 626 (2008)

Wolff, Case note on BGH, Decision of May 21, 2008, III ZB 14/07, LMK 2008, 265473

Wolff, Case note on BGH, Decision of December 16, 2010, III ZB 100/09, LMK 2011, 318374

Wolff (ed), *New York Convention, Convention on the Recognition and Enforcement of Foreign Arbitral Awards of 10 June 1958, Commentary*, C H Beck, Hart, Nomos 2012

Wolff, Case note on BGH, Decision of April 16, 2015, I ZB 3/14, LMK 2015, 374507

Wolff/Falk, Case note on BGH, Decision of March 30, 2006, III ZB 78/05, SchiedsVZ 2006, 280

Zekoll/Giessen, "Das ex parte-Eilverfahren und das Exequaturverfahren für schiedsgerichtliche Eilmaßnahmen im UNCITRAL Model Law—Anspruch und Wirklichkeit einer Reform," SchiedsVZ 2010, 137

Zimmermann, *Zivilprozessordnung*, 9th edn, ZAP Verlag 2011

Zöller (ed), *Zivilprozessordnung, mit FamFG (§§ 1–185, 200–270, 433–484) und Gerichtsverfassungsgesetz, den Einführungsgesetzen, mit Internationalem Zivilprozessrecht, EU-Verordnungen, Kostenanmerkungen, Kommentar*, 31st edn, Otto Schmidt 2016

Zuberbühler/Müller/Habegger (eds), *Swiss Rules of International Arbitration: Commentary*, 2nd edn, Schulthess 2013

INDEX

Introductory Note

References such as "5.95–5.100" indicate (not necessarily continuous) discussion of a topic across a range of paragraphs. In the case of topics with many references, wherever possible these have either been divided into sub-topics or only the most significant discussions of the topic have been listed. Because the entire work is about "arbitration," the use of this term as an entry point (as well as certain others that occur continually throughout the book) has been restricted. Information will be found under the corresponding detailed topics. The page numbers of Annex headings have been added here in italics.